GW00862741

Modern Risk Management
A History

Modern Risk Management
A History

Introduced by Peter Field

RISK
B O O K S

Published by Risk Books, a division of Incisive RWG Ltd

Haymarket House
28–29 Haymarket
London SW1Y 4RX
Tel: +44 (0)20 7484 9700
Fax: +44 (0)20 7484 9758
E-mail: books@riskwaters.com
Sites: www.riskbooks.com
www.riskwaters.com

Every effort has been made to secure the permission of individual copyright holders for inclusion.

© Incisive RWG Ltd 2003

ISBN 1 904 339 05 0

British Library Cataloguing in Publication Data
A catalogue record for this book is available from the British Library

Managing Editor: Sarah Jenkins
Assistant Editor: Tamsin Kennedy

Typeset by Mizpah Publishing Services, Chennai, India

Printed and bound in Spain by Espacegrafic, Pamplona Navarra

Contents

Authors

Vineer Bhansali is an executive vice president, portfolio manager, firm-wide head of analytics for portfolio management, and a senior member of PIMCO's portfolio management group. Vineer joined PIMCO in 2000, having previously been associated with Credit Suisse First Boston in proprietary fixed-income trading, and at Salomon Brothers in the New York Fixed Income Arbitrage Group. He started on Wall Street at Citibank in New York, building and managing their hybrid options trading desk. He is the author of numerous scientific and financial papers and of the book *Pricing and Managing Exotic and Hybrid Options* (McGraw Hill, 1998). He currently serves as an associate editor for the *International Journal of Theoretical and Applied Finance*. Vineer has 13 years of investment experience and holds a bachelor's degree and a master's degree in physics from the California Institute of Technology, and a PhD in theoretical particle physics from Harvard University.

Silvia Caserta graduated in mathematics from La Sapienza University in Rome, in 1996. Subsequently, she specialised in stochastic and operational research at the Mathematical Research Institute in the Netherlands. From 1997–2001, she was employed as assistant researcher at the Tinbergen Institute, Erasmus University Rotterdam, where she completed her PhD studies in economics. Her academic interests range from general economics to the mathematical theory of extreme values. Her work has been published in international journals (such as *Statistica Neerlandica*, and the *Journal of Cultural Economics*) and books. She is currently employed as risk consultant at the Financial Surveillance and Compliance department of EURONEXT stock exchanges in Amsterdam, The Netherlands.

David A. Chapman is an associate professor and the Fayez Sarofim & Co centennial fellow in the finance department at the McCombs School of Business at the University of Texas at Austin, where he has been on the faculty since 1992. He also holds an appointment as an associate professor in the economics department at Texas. David received a BA with honours from Swarthmore College, majoring in economics, an MS in applied economics, and a PhD in business administration from the University of Rochester. His research interests are primarily in the area of estimation and testing of dynamic asset pricing models. David has had articles published in *Econometrica, Journal of Finance, Review of Financial Studies, Journal of Monetary Economics, Review of Economic Dynamics, Financial Analysts*

Journal, and *Economics Letters*. He is an associate editor of the *Journal of Finance*, a faculty affiliate of the Institute for Computational Finance at The University of Texas at Austin, a member of the advisory council of the MBA Investment Fund, LLC, and the graduate advisor and head of the PhD program in the finance department at the McCombs School.

John H. Cochrane is the Thoedore O. Yntema professor of finance at the University of Chicago Graduate School of Business (GSB). He is a research associate and director of the asset program of the National Bureau of Economic Research, and an editor of the *Journal of Political Economy*. His recent publications include the book *Asset Pricing* (Princeton University Press, 2001), and articles on the term structure of interest rates, liquidity premiums in stock prices, the relation between stock prices and business cycles, option pricing when you can't perfectly hedge, and on the fiscal theory of the price level. He graduated from MIT and earned his PhD at the University of California at Berkeley, and was at the economics depart-ment of the University of Chicago before joining the GSB in 1994.

Gregory Connor is professor of finance and IAM fellow in hedge fund research at the London School of Economics. Prior to joining London School of Economics, he taught at Northwestern University, University of California Berkeley, and University College Dublin. His current research topics include factor modelling, security market pricing, and portfolio management.

Marcelo Cruz is the founder and managing director of RiskMaths in New York. He has over six years of experience in operational risk modelling and measurement and is recognised as a world-renowned expert on the subject. Prior to founding RiskMaths, Marcelo led the operational risk methodology development at UBS AG/UBS Warburg and at a large British bank, and worked as a derivatives trader for major international invest-ment banks for several years. His new book Modeling, Managing and Hedging Operational Risk (John Wiley & Sons) was published in 2002 and is a bestseller in the risk management area. Marcelo has collaborated on chapters in several risk management books, including Advances in Operational Risk (Risk Books, 2001), Extremes and Integrated Risk Management (Risk Books, 2000), Mastering Risk (Vol 2, Financial Times Prentice Hall, edited by Carol Alexander and John Hull) and Managing Hedge Fund Risk (Risk Books, 2000). He is also a member of the Board of Trustees of the Global Association of Risk Professionals (GARP), and acts as an assistant editor for several publications in the areas of finance, risk management and stochastic modelling. Marcelo has participated in the Industry Technical Working Group (ITWG) that has been helping the Basel Committee to define the standards for operational risk measurement in the new Basel Accord. He has been a sought-after speaker at first class finance congresses in more than 20 countries. Marcelo holds a PhD in mathematics, an MSC, an MBA and a BSC in economics/econometrics. He is a visiting professor of universities in the USA, Europe and Latin America.

Christopher L. Culp is an adjunct professor of finance at the Graduate School of Business of The University of Chicago, from which he also received his PhD in finance. He is also a principal at CP Risk Management LLC where he provides non-financial and financial clients with advisory consulting services on corporate financing techniques, financial strategy, and alternative methods of risk finance and risk transfer. He is co-editor (with William A. Niskanen) of *Corporate Aftershock: The Public Policy Consequences of Enron and Other Recent Disasters* (Wiley, 2003), and co-editor (with Merton H. Miller) of *Corporate Hedging in Theory and Practice: Lessons from Metallgesellschaft* (Risk Books, 1999). In addition, he is the sole author of *The ART of Risk Management: Alternative Risk Transfer, Capital Structure, and Convergences Between Insurance and Capital Markets* (Wiley, 2002), and *The Risk Management Process* (Wiley, 2001). His latest book, *Risk Transfer: Derivatives in Theory and Practice*, is forthcoming from Wiley in late 2003. Christopher is a member of the editorial advisory boards of the *Journal of Applied Corporate Finance*, the *Journal of Risk Finance*, and *Futures Industry Magazine*, and is co-editor for derivatives and risk management of *FMA Online*.

Jon Danielsson has a PhD in the economics of financial markets, and is currently a reader in finance at the London School of Economics. His research areas include financial risk, regulation of financial markets, market volatility, microstructure of foreign exchange markets, and extreme market movements. Jon has lectured at universities both in the US and Europe and has been a visiting professor at universities in the US, the Netherlands, Spain, and Germany. He has had papers published in a number of academic and trade journals, including the *Journal of Empirical Finance, Journal of Econometrics*, and *Risk*, and has consulted on several areas including market risk.

Emanuel Derman obtained a PhD in theoretical physics from Columbia University in 1973. Between 1973 and 1980 he did research in theoretical particle physics, and from 1980 to 1985 he worked at AT&T Bell Laboratories. In 1985 Emanuel joined Goldman Sachs' fixed income division where he was one of the co-developers of the Black–Derman–Toy interest rate model. From 1990 to 2000 he led the Quantitative Strategies group in the Equities division, where they pioneered the study of the volatility smile. In 2000 he become head of the firm wide Quantitative Risk Strategies group. He retired from Goldman Sachs in 2002. Emanuel was named the IAFE/Sungard

Financial Engineer of the Year 2000. He is writing a book on quantitative life, and teaching financial engineering at Columbia University.

Arnaud de Servigny is a director in Standard & Poor's Risk Solutions Group. He is responsible for quantitative research and product development. Prior to joining Standard and Poor's, Arnaud worked in the Group Risk Management Department of BNP Paribas in France, focusing on credit risk management and control. Arnaud has extensive experience in implementing quantitative credit risk mitigation techniques. Arnaud holds a PhD in financial economics, an MS in finance and a civil engineering degree. Publications include *Gestion du Risque de Credit* (Dunod Editions, 2001) and *Economie Financière* (Dunod Editions, 1999).

Casper G. de Vries is professor of economics at Erasmus University Rotterdam, The Netherlands where he teaches monetary economics and financial risk management. He is a fellow and board member of the Tinbergen Institute, he directs the financial stochastics program at the Eurandom research institute, and he serves as a member of the EMU Monitor group. His graduate training was at Purdue University; he has held positions at Texas A&M University, KU Leuven, and he has been a visiting scholar at several European and American research institutes. Casper's research interests are focused on international monetary issues, like foreign exchange rate determination and exchange rate risk, the issues surrounding the euro, financial markets risk and risk management. In his research on financial risks, he has specialised in calculating the risks on extreme events by means of statistical extreme value analysis. Other research interests are contest and auction theory, which can be applied to the theory of lobbying. He has published widely in leading internationally refereed journals.

Jin-Chuan Duan currently holds the Manulife Chair in Financial Services at Rotman School of Management, University of Toronto. He has previously taught at McGill University and Hong Kong University of Science and Technology, and held a principal investigator position at CIRANO, Montreal. Jin-Chuan has a PhD in finance from the University of Wisconsin-Madison. His research interests cover derivative securities, time-series econometrics and banking. Jin-Chuan is internationally known for his pioneering work on the GARCH option pricing model. His current research focuses on developing pricing theory and devising numerical and statistical techniques for time-series based pricing models. Jin-Chuan, who currently serves as an editor of the *International Journal of Financial Education*, is also highly interested in innovations in financial education.

Ramon Espinosa is a principal in Bank of America's Global Risk Management Advisory group. He is a specialist in the use of quantitative techniques to assess and manage foreign currency risk. Ramon consults with Bank of America clients to help them measure their exposure to foreign currency risk, identify effective strategies for managing that risk, and establish procedures to ensure the effective management of currency risk on an on-going basis. Ramon has lectured and written extensively on these topics. Prior to joining Global Risk Management Advisory, Ramon served as a senior currency strategist in Global Foreign Exchange at Bank of America, where he authored regular commentaries and reports on global economic developments, with particular focus on Latin America. Prior to joining Global Foreign Exchange, Ramon headed the Latin American Section of the Bank's Economic and Policy Research Department. Ramon has also served as a research economist at the Federal Reserve Bank of New York, and taught finance and economics at Mills College, Golden Gate University, and Boston University. Ramon holds a BA in economics from Stanford University, an MPA from the Woodrow Wilson School of Public and International Affairs at Princeton University, and a PhD in economics from Princeton University.

Peter Field is chief executive of the Risk Waters Group division of Incisive Media and of Incisive RWG Ltd. Prior to May 1, 2003, he was Chairman and Chief Executive of Risk Waters Group Ltd (RWGL). Previously an editor with Middle East Economic Digest, Financial Times Newsletters and Euromoney, he conceived the idea of *Risk* magazine and set it up for Emap plc in 1987. Peter established his own company, the precursor of RWGL, to buy the magazine from Emap in May 1988. Under Peter, the company added conferences, courses, books, directories, academic journals and web sites to develop *Risk* magazine into a brand; started new publications in other areas, notably energy and credit; and acquired the financial technology and market data titles of Waters Information Services in New York in 1999. Under Peter, RWG has promoted contemporary artists by reproducing their work on the covers of *Risk* and Risk Books, and has also sponsored over 30 concerts in London, as well as commissioning a symphony from American avant-garde composer Charles Wuorinen, premiered at London's South Bank in May 2001.

Lane Hughston holds the Professorial Chair in Financial Mathematics at King's College London. He received his DPhil in mathematics from the University of Oxford, where he was a Rhodes Scholar. Before joining King's College he was director of derivative product risk management at Merrill Lynch, where he was responsible for managing the development of pricing and hedging models for interest rate and foreign exchange derivatives. Before working at Merrill Lynch, he headed a research team at Robert Fleming Securities specialising in Japanese equity warrants and convertible bonds. Prior to that, he was Fellow and Tutor in applied mathematics at Lincoln College, Oxford. His research interests include a wide range of topics in mathematical finance and its applications in an investment-banking context, and he is the author of numerous publications in this area. He is the editor of several well-known books published by Risk Books, including *Vasicek and Beyond: Approaches to Building and Applying Interest Rate Models* (1996), *Options: Classic Approaches to Pricing and Modelling* (1999), and *The New Interest Rate Models: Recent Developments in the Theory and Application of Yield Curve Dynamics* (2000).

John Hull is the Maple Financial Group Professor of Derivatives and Risk Management in the Joseph L. Rotman School of Management at the University of Toronto and director of the Bonham Center for Finance. He has written two books *Options, Futures, and Other Derivatives* (now in its fifth edition) and *Fundamentals of Futures and Options Markets* (now in its fourth edition). Both books (published by Prentice Hall) have been translated into several languages and are widely used in trading rooms throughout the world. He has won many teaching awards, including the University of Toronto's prestigious Northrop Frye award, and was voted Financial Engineer of the Year in 1999 by the International Association of Financial Engineers.

Robert Jarrow is a professor at the Johnson Graduate School of Management Cornell University and managing director of Kamakura Corporation. He was the 1997 IAFE Financial Engineer of the year. His publications include four books as well as over 85 publications in finance and economic journals. He is renowned for his work on the Heath–Jarrow–Morton model and the Jarrow–Turnbull reduced form credit risk model. He is also the originator of the forward price measure, and characterising forward and futures prices under stochastic interest rates. He is the managing editor of *Mathematical Finance* and an associate editor of various other journals. His interests are in the area of term structure models, credit risk, liquidity risk, and capital allocation theory.

Philippe Jorion is professor of finance at the Graduate School of Management at the University of California at Irvine. He holds an MBA and a PhD from the University of Chicago, and a degree in engineering from the University of Brussels. Philippe has authored more than seventy publications directed at academics and practitioners on the topics of risk management and international finance. He has written a number of books, including *Value at Risk: The New Benchmark for Managing Financial Risk*, and the *Financial Risk Manager Handbook*. Philippe is a frequent speaker at academic and professional conferences. He is on the editorial board of a number of finance journals and is editor-in-chief of the *Journal of Risk*.

Geoff Kates is managing director of Lepus, a management consultancy specialising in research, consulting and marketing. Lepus defines and implements business/technical strategy in a number of areas including risk management (market, credit, operational and regulatory), client information management, STP, and cost optimisation. Before starting Lepus, he was head of computer development at Tokai Bank Europe. Prior to this, he was IT director for fixed income, derivatives and futures broking at BZW and head of IT for Abbey National Baring Derivatives.

Barbara Kavanagh is a principal in the risk management consulting firm of CP Risk Management LLC, Chicago, Illinois, and also teaches at IIT's Graduate School of Trading Markets. Prior to her current position, she was the senior credit officer in ABN AMRO's North American investment bank, and also spent several years with KPMG and Ernst & Young engaged in risk management consulting globally. Her career began inside the Federal Reserve Board (the Fed), where she largely focused on international banking and trading markets. While there, she ultimately rose to the executive level and, among other things, acted as liaison between the Fed and Chicago's derivative exchanges and assisted the Fed governors in policy matters related to OTC trading markets, asset backed securities, and structured finance transactions.

Robert A. Korajczyk is Harry G. Guthmann Distinguished Professor of Finance at the Kellogg School of Management, Northwestern University. Robert received AB, MBA and PhD degrees from the University of Chicago. He has been a member of the Kellogg School faculty since 1982 and has held visiting faculty positions at the University of Chicago, the Hong Kong University of Science and Technology, and the University of Vienna. Robert's research interests are in the areas of investments, corporate finance, and international finance. He is a recipient of the New York Stock Exchange Award for Best Paper on Equity Trading presented at the 1993 Western Finance Association annual meetings, and the *Review of Financial Studies* Best Paper Award, 1991. His editorial positions include Editor: *Review of Financial Studies* (1993–1996) and Associate Editor: *Review of Financial Studies* (1989–1993, 1997–1999), *Journal of Business & Economic Statistics* (1988–1993), *Journal of Financial and Quantitative Analysis* (1992–present), *Emerging Markets Quarterly* (1996–2001), *Journal of Empirical Finance* (1991–present), and *Review of Quantitative Finance and Accounting* (1990–1993).

Edward N. Krapels is an expert on a wide variety of energy markets and the author of many studies and reports on natural gas and electricity market dynamics. Most recently, he has been a key participant in the development of several major North American transmission projects and an advisor on evolving electricity policy. He has written about gas, power, and petroleum risk management, including a series of monographs for *Risk* entitled "Guide to Electricity Trading and Hedging" (2000), "Guide to Natural Gas Hedging" (1999), and "Crude Oil Hedging: Benchmarking Price Protection Strategies" (1998). Edward received his PhD at the Paul H. Nitze School of Advanced International Studies, John Hopkins University, his MA at the University of Chicago, and his BA at the University of North Carolina, Chapel Hill.

James Lam serves as a senior risk advisor to a group of select clients. Prior to working with his own clientele, he was founder and president of ERisk, and a partner at Oliver, Wyman & Company. Previously, James was chief risk officer at Fidelity Investments and GE Capital Markets Services. He has authored over 50 book chapters and articles, and recently completed a new book entitled *Enterprise Risk Management* (John Wiley & Sons, 2003). In 1997, the Global Association of Risk Professionals (GARP) named James the first-ever Financial Risk Manager of the Year. He is a frequent speaker at industry conferences. He is an adjunct professor of finance at Babson College, where he teaches MBA classes in enterprise risk management and advanced derivatives.

William Margrabe is president of The William Margrabe Group, Inc, that develops, documents, evaluates, and fine-tunes pricing and risk-management models for consulting clients for all purposes – accounting, lawsuits, regulatory compliance, risk management, and trading. William earned his PhD and studied risk management and option pricing at the University of Chicago. He taught those topics at Wharton and applied them while working for Freddie Mac, Bankers Trust, Morgan Stanley, and Salomon Brothers. Recently, he co-authored an article about estimating volatility for Asian option pricing and a paper about the notorious P&G–Bankers Trust "5/30" swap. Financial professionals know him best for his pioneering papers on exchange options ("Margrabe options"), forward and futures prices, and multivariate derivative products.

David Mengle is head of research for the International Swaps and Derivatives Association (ISDA), with responsibility for ISDA's education and survey activities. He also teaches courses in economics and risk management at the Fordham University Graduate School of Business in New York. Prior to joining ISDA in November 2001, David worked in the Derivatives Strategies Group at JP Morgan in New York. Before that, he was a research economist with the Federal Reserve Bank of Richmond, specialising in bank regulation, payment system risk, and market value accounting. David holds a BA from The Citadel and a PhD in economics from the University of California, Los Angeles.

Robert C. Merton is currently the John and Natty McArthur University Professor at the Harvard Business School. Prior to joining the faculty of Harvard in 1988, he served on the finance faculty of MIT's Sloan School of Management for eighteen years. He is a co-founder and chief science officer of Integrated Finance Limited, a specialised investment bank. Robert is past president of the American Finance Association and a member of the National Academy of Sciences. From 1988 to 1992, Robert served as a senior advisor to Office of the Chairman, Salomon Inc. In 1993, he co-founded Long-Term Capital Management and served as a principal until 1999. From 1999–2001, Robert was a senior advisor to JP Morgan & Co Incorporated. In 1997 he received the Alfred Nobel Memorial Prize in Economic Sciences for his contributions to finance theory. Robert has also been recognised for his achievements in translating theory into practice. In 1993, he received the inaugural Financial Engineer of the Year Award from the International Association of Financial Engineers. In 1998 he was named in *Derivatives Strategy* magazine's Hall of Fame. In 2002, he was named in the *Risk* magazine Hall of Fame and in 2003, *Risk* magazine also gave him its Lifetime Achievement Award for contributions to the field of risk management. A distinguished fellow of the Institute for Quantitative Research in Finance ("Q Group"), Robert received the Nicholas Molodovsky Award from the Association of Investment Management and Research in 2003. Robert obtained a BS in engineering mathematics from Columbia University in 1966, an MS in applied mathematics from California Institute of Technology in 1967 and a PhD in economics from Massachusetts Institute of Technology in 1970.

Richard Metcalfe is co-head of the European Office of the International Swaps and Derivatives Association (ISDA), London, where he has worked since 1999. He is working on a range of policy issues, including equity derivatives, operational risk (Basel Accord/CAD Review), operations, and trading practice. Richard's previous career, from 1987–1999, involved derivatives/risk management journalism, working for *Risk*, The Economist, IFR newsletters and Futures & OTC World (editor). He also worked in corporate communications for SWIFT in Brussels. He has an MA in modern languages (Russian and Spanish) from Oxford University.

Arnold Miyamoto is managing director and global head of research, for Global Foreign Exchange and Emerging Markets. Arnold's teams perform fixed income and foreign exchange strategy, relative value analysis and risk management advisory. He is the lead author of over sixty research articles relating to foreign currency risk and portfolio management. Prior to joining Bank of America, Arnold directed foreign currency research and product development at TSA Capital Management, an institutional money management firm specialising in asset allocation and managed futures strategies. Arnold also worked at Leland O'Brien Rubinstein (LOR), a pioneer in the application of derivatives in asset management. Arnold holds a BS degree in Chemical Engineering from the University of California, Santa Barbara. He also holds an MBA from UCLA where he was a fellow in finance.

John Nash has been a member of the World Bank staff since 1986, working in Latin America and Caribbean agricultural operations (1986–88); the International Trade Research Group in Development Economics vice-presidency (1988–1996); and Europe and Central Asia agricultural operations (1996–December, 2001). Since January 2002, he has been advisor for commodities and trade in the Agriculture and Rural Development department of the Environmentally and Socially Sustainable Development vice-presidency. John was previously with the US Federal Trade Commission (1983–88), holding positions that included assistant director for Trade Regulation Rules and economic advisor to the chairman. Prior to that, he was assistant professor of economics at Texas A&M University (1980–83). John holds an MSc and PhD in economics, from the University of Chicago (1982) and a BS in economics from Texas A&M University (1975). He has published material on topics such as trade policy in Latin America, Africa and South Asia, transition economies, agricultural policy adjustment; agricultural price policy, commodity price stabilisation and capital mobility.

Yana O'Sullivan is a consultant at Lepus, a management consultancy in investment banking and technology providing research and consulting services to the leading financial institutions in the UK and North America. Yana's main area of specialisation is risk management with specific interest in the new Basel Accord and operational risk. Prior to joining Lepus, Yana obtained a PhD in English linguistics from the University of Exeter. She also holds an MA in Modern Languages from St Petersburg State University, Russia.

Funke Oyewole is the program coordinator for the Commodity Risk Management Group in the World Bank. Prior to joining the World Bank, Funke practiced as an attorney in Washington DC. Her main area of expertise was foreign policy and international trade law. Since joining the World Bank, she has also served as the external affairs officer for the Bank's work in Health and Education. As the program coordinator for the Commodities Risk Management group, Funke has assisted in the development and implementation of the overall strategic communications for the International Task Force (ITF) on Commodity Risk Management and also plays a key role in implementing the work and business plan of the unit. Funke has a Bachelors of Law degree from the University of Kent, Canterbury, UK.

Neil D. Pearson is a professor of finance at the University of Illinois at Urbana-Champaign. He previously held a faculty position at the University of Rochester, and spent a year as a visiting academic at the SEC. His research includes work on the development, estimation, and evaluation of models for pricing and hedging various derivatives and other financial instruments. Neil has published papers in a number of academic journals, is an associate editor of the *Journal of Financial Economics*, the *Journal of Financial and Quantitative Analysis*, and *Economics Bulletin*, and has written a book *Risk Budgeting: Portfolio Problem Solving with Value-at-Risk* published by John Wiley & Sons. He has consulted for a number of US and international banks, working on term structure models, the evaluation of derivatives pricing models, and some issues that arise in the computation of "value-at-risk" measures. He received his PhD from the Massachusetts Institute of Technology.

Jeff Porter is business leader of the Weather Derivatives Trading Group at Hess Energy Trading Company (HETCO). He joined HETCO in May 2000. Prior to HETCO he was co-business leader of the Weather Derivatives Group at Koch Industries Inc from 1998–2000. Jeff is a founding and current board member of the Weather Risk Management Association. He is a frequent speaker and presenter at various weather risk management conferences. Jeff received his MBA from Brigham Young University in 1995.

Riccardo Rebonato is head of group market risk for the RBS Group, and head of the RBS Group Quantitative Research Centre (QUARC). He is also a visiting lecturer at Oxford University (mathematical finance) and diploma and visiting fellow at the applied mathematical department. He is a member of the board of directors of ISDA and of the board of trustees for GARP. He holds doctorates in nuclear engineering and science of materials/solid state physics. Prior to joining the RBS, he was head of the complex derivatives trading desk and of the complex derivatives research group at Barclays Capital, where he worked for nine years. Before that he was research fellow in physics at Corpus Christi College, Oxford, UK. He is the author of the books *Modern Pricing of Interest-Rate Derivatives* (2002), *Interest-Rate Option Models* (1996, 1998), *Volatility and Correlation in Option Pricing* (1999). He has published papers on finance in academic journals, and is on the editorial board of several journals. He is a regular speaker at conferences worldwide.

Olivier Renault is an associate in Standard & Poor's Risk Solutions Group. He is responsible for research into portfolio modelling. He holds a PhD in financial economics from the University of Louvain, Belgium. Prior to joining Standard and Poor's, Olivier was lecturer in finance at the London School of Economics where he taught derivatives and risk. He was also a consultant for several fund management and financial services companies. His main areas of research are derivatives and credit risk, with a particular interest in empirical issues.

Virginia Reynolds Parker has expertise in both traditional and alternative investment strategies, combined with a strong background in currency risk and returns, independent risk measurement and management of multi-manager hedge fund portfolios and principal protection guarantees. She is well known for developing industry-recognised performance benchmarks for foreign exchange. Her research is well known, including a book, *Managing Hedge Fund Risk*, published in 2000 (Risk Books) and translated into Japanese in 2001. She is a frequent speaker at industry conferences sharing her research on hedge funds, foreign exchange, and risk management. From 1988 until 1995, Virginia was managing director and director of research and risk management at Ferrell Capital Management, where she guided the firm's portfolio structuring, asset allocation strategies, new product development and risk management. She has served as a trustee and managed assets for a family office since 1984. Virginia earned an AB in economics and political science from Duke University in 1980. She is currently enrolled in the OPM program at Harvard Business School. She is a chartered financial analyst, a member of the New York Society of Security Analysts, the AIMR, the International Association of Financial Engineers (IAFE), the Steering Committee for the IAFE's Investor Risk Committee, and board member of the Foundation for Managed Derivative Research.

Dan Rosen is vice president of strategy at Algorithmics. In this role, he oversees the company's long-term growth and the sustainability of Algorithmics' business. Dan is also an associate faculty member of the University of Toronto's Program in mathematical finance, and one of the founders of Algorithmics' RiskLab. Prior to joining Algorithmics in 1995, he was a research associate at the University of Toronto's Centre for Management of Technology. Dan holds several degrees, including an MASc and a PhD in applied sciences from the University of Toronto.

David M. Rowe is group executive vice president for risk management at SunGard Trading and Risk Systems, having joined SunGard in July of 1999. In this role he advises operating units on risk management functionality and development priorities in their software applications. He also appears frequently at industry conferences and seminars and writes a monthly column for *Risk* magazine. Previous to joining SunGard, David was senior vice president in charge of the Risk Management Information group at Bank of America in San Francisco. In that role, he was responsible for the design, deployment, maintenance and operation of market and credit risk systems for the bank's global FX, derivative and securities trading activities. David's earlier positions include: chief financial officer of Security Pacific Securities, Inc (the broker-dealer subsidiary of the former Security Pacific Corp), executive vice president and director of research for Townsend-Greenspan & Co (Alan Greenspan's economic consulting company prior to becoming Chairman of the Federal Reserve) and president of Wharton Econometric Forecasting Associates in Philadelphia. David holds a PhD in econometrics and finance from the University of Pennsylvania, an MBA in finance with a concentration in money and banking from the Wharton Graduate School of Business Administration, and a BA in economics with distinction from Carleton College.

Mark Rubinstein is the Paul Stephens Professor of Applied Investment Analysis at the Haas School of Business at the University of California at Berkeley. He is a graduate of Harvard University, Stanford University and the University of California at Los Angeles. Mark is renowned for his work on the binomial options pricing model (also known as the Cox–Ross–Rubinstein model) as well as his early work on asset pricing in the 1970s. His publications include the books *Options Markets* and *Rubinstein on Derivatives*, as well as more than 50 publications in leading finance and economic journals. He is currently an associate editor of eight journals in these areas. In 1993, he served as President of the American Finance Association. He has won numerous prizes and awards for his research and writing on derivatives including International Financial Engineer of the Year for 1995. Most recently, he won the Graham and Dodd award for 2002 for the best article published during the year 2001 in the *Financial Analysts Journal*. His current research concerns the history of the financial theory of investments.

Paul A. Samuelson is institute professor emeritus at the Massachusetts Institute of Technology, and Sendai Bank visiting professor of political economy at New York University's Stern School of Management. He studied at the University of Chicago and Harvard and received the Nobel Prize in Economics in 1970. Paul was an economic advisor to presidents Kennedy and Johnson, and has been a consultant to the Federal Reserve, US Treasury, and the Congressional Budget Office. He was an early contributor to the new modern theory of finance, and has served as a trustee of the Teachers Insurance and Annuity Association College Retirement Equities Fund (TIAA-CREF). He now serves on the Finance Committee of the National Academy of Sciences. As well as having authored a bestselling introductory economics textbook, *Economics* (1948, 2001), translated into more than 40 languages, he also wrote *Foundations of Economic Analysis* (1947; enlarged edition 1983). Five volumes of *The Collected Scientific Papers* *of Paul A. Samuelson* (1966–1986) have appeared and the sixth and seventh volumes are in preparation. With Robert Solow and other joint authors he has contributed to several dozen books on economic theory and policy.

Olivier Scaillet is professor of probability and statistics at HEC Genève and FAME. He holds both a masters and PhD from University Paris IX Dauphine in applied mathematics. Professor Scaillet's research expertise is in the area of asset pricing, econometric theory and econometrics applied to finance and insurance. He has published several papers in leading journals in econometrics and finance, and co-authored a book on financial econometrics. He has been one of the winners of the bi-annual award for the best paper published in the Journal of Empirical Finance. He is also a long-term advisor for the research teams of BNP Paribas located in Paris and London.

Carola von Schenk was born in Hamburg in Germany, but spent her early childhood in Peru and most of her childhood and teenage years in Vienna. Carola moved to Paris in 1988 to read political science at the Institute d'Etudes Politiques and then on to London, where she studied political science and history at the London School of Economics. She graduated from the LSE with a Masters degree in Russian politics in 1993. After stints as a commissioning editor and market research analyst, Carola decided to pursue a career in journalism and has been working in this field for the past five years, covering financial risk management, asset management and pension reform issues for various specialist publications, including *Risk* magazine and some *FT Business* publications.

Emmanuelle Sebton is co-head of the European Office of the International Swaps and Derivatives Association (ISDA), London. Previously, Emmanuelle worked in the policy department of the UK Financial Services Authority, where she was responsible for reviewing the treatment of credit risk mitigation and the possibility for regulators to rely on internal ratings, as part of the 1988 Capital Accord review. She also held positions at the French Tresor and Caisse des Depots et Consignations, where she developed an Asset Liability Management unit. Emmanuelle holds a masters in economics and finance, a law degree, and is an ENA graduate.

Alan C. Shapiro is the Ivadelle and Theodore Johnson Professor of Banking, Marshall School of Business, University of Southern California. Prior to joining USC, he was an assistant professor at the Wharton School of the University of Pennsylvania. His specialties are corporate and international financial management and strategy. His best-selling textbook *Multinational Financial Management* (John Wiley & Sons, seventh edition, 2003) is used in most of the leading MBA programs around the world. He has also written *Modern Corporate Finance* (Macmillan, 1990), *Foundations of*

Multinational Financial Management (John Wiley & Sons, fourth edition, 2001), *International Corporate Finance* (Ballinger, 1989), and (with Sheldon Balbirer) *Modern Corporate Finance: An Interdisciplinary Approach to Value Creation* (Prentice-Hall, 2000).

Hyun Song Shin is professor of finance at the London School of Economics and senior research fellow of Nuffield College, Oxford. His main research interests are in information economics and game theory, with applications to asset pricing, risk, disclosures and financial regulation. He is co-director of the regulation and financial stability programme of the Financial Markets Group (FMG) at LSE, and has served as managing editor of the Review of Economic Studies. He has served as academic consultant for the Bank of England and the Bank for International Settlements. His first degree was in philosophy, politics and economics (at Oxford University), and his doctorate was in economics (also from Oxford). He has held previous academic posts at the Universities of Oxford and Southampton.

Panos Varangis joined the World Bank in 1987. He is currently a lead economist at the World Bank's Agriculture and Rural Development Department. In his current position, he is leading the Commodity Risk Management Group (CRMG) that looks into issues related to commodity price and weather risk management. He joined from the Development Research Group where he was involved in research areas related to commodity markets, and in particular risk management and finance, weather index insurance, and commodity market liberalisation. Prior to that, he was with the Commodities Policy and Analysis Unit. Panos has worked extensively in the areas of agricultural policies, risk management, and commodity marketing and trade finance systems. He has initiated a project to examine the application of weather risk management products to agriculture in developing countries. Panos holds an MA degree in economics from Georgetown University and a PhD degree in economics from Columbia University, New York.

Rohan G. Williamson is an assistant professor of finance at Georgetown University. He specialises in international finance, corporate finance and corporate risk management/hedging. He is currently conducting research in the areas of corporate investment decisions, foreign currency exposure, corporate liquidity, and international corporate governance. He has taught various courses in international and corporate finance to executives, undergraduate, and graduate students. He has contributed to both academic and practitioner publications in various areas. He is a former financial analyst with the Chrysler Corporation. Rohan received his PhD from the Ohio State University.

Introduction

Peter Field

Risk Waters Group

The astonishing fact about the risk management business is how fast it's grown and how widely it's spread through all aspects of corporate life. Not for nothing was the subtitle *The Tools that Changed Finance* chosen for the book, *Derivatives*, by Phelim and Feidhlim Boyle that was published by Risk Books in 2001.

This book seeks to highlight the key elements in this amazing growth (of both risk management and the derivatives products that largely underpin that business) but it's worth putting into perspective at the outset how radically the world has changed since the early days.

As we'll see later in the book, the early 1970s was the period when some key theoretical bases for the development of risk management were nailed down, particularly the Black–Scholes model, but it was the early 1980s before the markets started to take off with the first public cross-currency and interest-rate swaps and the rapid growth of over-the-counter (OTC) options. And it's mostly developments in these markets, and in their time frame, that this book covers, as opposed to the exchange markets.

Even in the early 1980s, the language of risk management was still inchoate. "Risk" was a relatively new word in the vocabulary of those outside the insurance industry and outside a small part of the investing market. "Derivative" was known more as a pejorative term in the popular music industry. Even in 1987, when I launched *Risk* magazine, the products we talked of were swaps on the one hand – capital market products, offered through the OTC market, mostly in London and New York – and futures and options on the other – largely exchange products and mostly in Chicago. Risk was even of such little interest to Americans that the word was available as a trademark in the US in 1988. Now, it would be impossible to register such a generic name as a trademark, while every possible combination of words starting with "risk" has been used in registering web names and addresses.

I remember gatecrashing the Citicorp party during the Berlin annual meetings of the World Bank and IMF in 1988. On the receiving line, the chairman, John Reed, said to me, looking at my name badge, "*Risk*? I shouldn't be letting you in." To which I replied, "But surely you know all about it." (I was able to remind Reed of this conversation six years later at a party at the Bank of England to celebrate its 300th anniversary. Robert Merton collared Reed, introduced him to me again in front of Eddie George, the Governor, and told him, "You should be reading *Risk*. It's one of the best financial magazines in the world.")

Reed's predecessor Walter Wriston had in 1986 published a collection of essays with the great title *Risk and Other Four-Letter Words*, but almost none of the pages dealt with risk in the sense that major banks understand it today. Indeed, when I had met Wriston in 1983, he was very eloquent about the new players and technology that would compete with banks in the future, but even though he was aware of the swaps market he failed to predict any sweeping changes to be wrought by derivatives. Also, the bank's asset/liability management policy seemed to be very simple by today's standards, judging by his comment, "We basically run a flat book."

This is no criticism of Wriston who was one of the more prescient and successful bank chairmen of the last half of the 20th century, and who built Citicorp into the biggest bank in the world. But his comments and writings reflected the way the world was then. Many other examples of such basic approaches to risk management spring to mind. In 1987, Eugene Rotberg, the man in charge of Merrill Lynch's new risk management function and a former World Bank treasurer, described to *Risk* the main tool he used to analyse risk; it was a Bloomberg terminal, then a fledgling system barely known outside the US.

As in all upheavals, there was a multitude of pressures leading to the risk management revolution, but it took time for them to coalesce. The theorists like Black, Scholes and Merton had spoken; their work continued to be amplified and extended, by themselves and other researchers. World markets were feeling the effects of trade expansion and market-influenced interest rates and currency rates. Technology – in particular hand-held calculators capable of dealing with advanced mathematics, and later the personal computer – came along to make the number crunching easier and faster, and therefore the emergence of more complex products easier.

Chicago, the home of agricultural markets since 1848, had foreseen the potential for expanding into the financial markets as early as 1972, when the Chicago Mercantile Exchange launched futures contracts on seven currencies. The following year, the Chicago Board of Trade (CBOT) introduced options on individual stocks, launching what became the Chicago Board Options Exchange, and in 1977 the CBOT brought in its US Treasury bond futures; not only one of the most successful exchange products ever but the one most used by firms in the OTC market for laying off their interest-rate risk. These developments in Chicago took the application of risk management techniques a stage further by allowing proper markets to develop. Before 1973, options were written on a one-off, customised basis; so, according to Clifford Smith, Jr, Charles Smithson and Lee Wakeman, writing in the *Handbook of Currency and Interest Rate Risk Management* (1990), "there was little volume, little liquidity and virtually no secondary market. The growth of the options market occurred after the Chicago Board Options Exchange standardised the contracts and developed an active secondary market." The exchange markets led the way into the early 1980s, unaware that a new and much bigger market, the OTC market, was about to overtake them.

In New York at the beginning of 1987, I knew something major was in the air. There were warning signs that market exuberance was leading to excesses. Merrill Lynch had good reason to establish a fledgling risk management function because in April that year it took a US$377 million hit on mortgage-backed securities. In the same month, First Boston lost US$100 million, mostly on US Treasury bond options. And the worst events of that year were yet to come.

At the same time, end-users desperately needed help with problems they hadn't faced before. I talked to corporate treasurers who worried about the cost of borrowing because there was no longer any certainty in the trend or range of movement in interest rates – it hadn't been that long ago that US prime had gone to 21.5%. Exporters worried about their exposure to European currencies in the aftermath of the delinking of the US dollar from gold in 1981. Commodity prices, especially energy prices in the wake of the huge oil price rises of 1973 and 1978, were now being subjected to the same market pressures. Increasing numbers of household names in corporate America were tapping the Swiss franc and Deutschmark markets, where rates were lower, and then swapping the proceeds back to US dollars. Everywhere you looked was volatility – great for traders, not so great for firms and individuals on fixed budgets.

No wonder they were happy over at the swaps desks of the major commercial and investment banks in New York, where young traders talked with almost religious fervour about the potential of the swaps markets and of even newer products like caps, collars and floors. And there was no doubt a lot of these made sense. As early as 1988, *Risk* was able to write of the corporate use of a cap in an acquisition – the take-over by the British food and drink major, Grand Metropolitan (now Diageo), of Pillsbury, owner of Burger King and Häagen-Dazs ice cream. (It was gratifying to find out that Adrian Coats, who in March 2003 accepted *Risk*'s Corporate Risk Manager of the Year award on behalf of Scottish Power, had been involved with that early deal when he was at Grand Met). What didn't make sense for non-financial corporations, as the book later shows, was to try and beat banks at their own game. Hence another British food and drink company, Allied Lyons (now Allied Domecq), lost £147 million in 1991 because it wrote options for the premium income.[1]

If the swaps and options desks of OTC dealers were abuzz in 1987, they were nowhere near as frenetic as the floors of the Chicago exchanges. The mayhem that I observed on my first visits to the Chicago Mercantile Exchange and the Chicago Board of Trade in the early 1980s made me wonder about the efficiency of the open-outcry system, while remembering that a huge amount of genuine business was being done, given how massive the Treasury and equity markets were in the US.

In those early days, there was rivalry between New York and Chicago. It was a regional issue but overlaid also by tension between the exchanges, which were transparent, regulated and standardised, and the OTC markets, which were privately negotiated, customised and, according to many critics, unregulated. The OTC markets, which soon developed elements of standardisation as volume grew, needed the exchanges but looked down on them as poor cousins, partly because of various past scandals in Chicago, one bizarre result of which is that to this day, onion futures cannot be traded on a board of trade in the US. Of course, Wall Street's record is hardly unblemished, as the events leading up to the 1929 crash and much more recent breaches of corporate governance have shown.

Early annual meetings of the International Swap Dealers Association (ISDA) in the 1980s and early 1990s paid only lip service to the role of exchanges, while annual meetings of the Futures Industry Association (FIA) in Boca Raton, Florida, were often conducted as if the OTC markets had never emerged or had anything to do with the exchange markets. The only notable exception was the complaint by speakers year after year that the costs of regulation by the Commodity Futures Trading Commission (CFTC) put them at a disadvantage compared with "unregulated" dealers on Wall Street. Floor traders usually seemed more concerned about their golf handicaps than the vast new business being built up by banks in the OTC market, which in a sense represented a lost opportunity for the exchanges.

Fortunes were legitimately made and lost on the exchanges, as speculators or "locals" fulfilled their role, assuming risk that others wanted to lay off. "See that building over there?," one hoarse and sweaty trader in a garish jacket said to me on the floor of the CBOT in about 1989, pointing to a skyscraper that did its best to compete with the Sears Tower, then the tallest in the world, "That guy there in that pit used to own it," he explained pointing to a man who looked no different to all the other traders milling around, "But he lost everything last year and had to sell it. Now he's on his way to buying it back again."

Another factor that propelled derivatives into mainstream finance was also apparent before 1987. That was the tendency for Wall Street houses to hire rocket scientists – many it is said were refugees from a downsized NASA – or at least physicists or mathematicians – to handle the increasingly quantitative problems that were confronting the firms and their clients. It was this interaction between academia (or at least those with heavy academic credentials) and the real world of the markets that did more than anything to speed up the pace of innovation. *Risk* magazine itself played a role in this interaction, providing a conduit for the transmission of the latest theories on products and pricing from the quants to traders, salesmen and clients.

The most famous "rocket scientist", Fischer Black, though a physicist and mathematician, wasn't in fact typical of that breed, since he quite often forsook complex mathematical expositions in favour of simple, practical explanations.[2] When I first met him early in 1987 in his cramped office at Goldman Sachs, his keyboard on his knees as he completed whatever he was writing before giving a generous amount of time to myself and a colleague, I was struck not only by his humility but also by the number of ideas he managed to throw out in such a short space of time. His humility shone through in his 1990 *Risk* (Vol. 3, No. 3, pp. 11–13) article: "I continue to be amazed at the success of option products," Black began, and continued: "I sometimes wonder why people still use the Black– Scholes formula, since it is based on such simple assumptions – unrealistically simple assumptions." But, he added, "that weakness is also its greatest strength".

Black's collaborator, Myron Scholes, moved to Wall Street later, working for Salomon Brothers in 1990–93 and helping the firm set up its special purpose derivatives products subsidiary, Salomon Swapco.

Black and Scholes and their work with Robert Merton are of course at the heart of this book, which is why the model adorns the cover. But it's worth noting that their model wasn't so well known even in 1987. Black is famous now, partly because of the award of the Nobel Prize to Scholes and Merton in 1997, and although it's sad that he didn't live long enough to receive the award himself, he must have known before he died in August 1995 of the industry efforts to lobby the Nobel Prize Committee to speed up their deliberations.

In 1987, however, it was still a relatively narrow circle that was interested in what Black did. After all, "The Holes in Black–Scholes" had actually been written ten or more years earlier and circulated privately. But no publisher had seen it as useful follow-up to the original paper. This lack of interest was somewhat ironic in view of the problems Black and Scholes had in getting their original, seminal paper published.

What changed everything and brought all these disparate strands together was the October 1987 equity market crash – in percentage terms worse even than the 1929 crash. That made Wall Street houses and banks sit up and seriously assess both the nature and the extent of their risk for the first time, as they went through months of cutbacks, restricted spending and changes of strategy.

Once the initial shock had eased, there was the typical over-reaction on the bounce-back: a wave of innovation that sometimes went too far, as every house on the street vied with each other to appear as the leader in risk management. In the process, the needs of the customer were often overlooked and many products were never actually used. One British bank even advertised a list of products in *Risk*, which included several joke fictional products, such as "flying hedge" and "moon rocket" options. A major American bank listed an option-type product in one of *Risk*'s early directories but no one at their London office or US headquarters was able to explain what it was. At a bank in Tokyo in 1991, three young Japanese employees, all with PhDs from New York University, spent 45 minutes explaining to me a new option product for which they had identified no customers.

While there was clearly no dearth of ideas at that time, there were shortages of skilled people, so banks tried to jump-start their derivatives activities by hiring whole teams from other firms, or acquiring smaller firms. Citibank staff were picked off heavily by other banks in 1983/84 and for a long time ex-Citibankers dom-inated the swaps desks at other houses, helping create the close-knit nature of the community. Credit Suisse Financial Products was established overnight when Allen Wheat and 18 others defected from Bankers Trust in 1990. Swiss Bank Corporation (now UBS) acquired the Chicago options boutique O'Connor Associates in 1992 and several O'Connor partners rose to high positions within the Swiss bank. (In a neat twist, one of these, Jim McNulty, later left the OTC market to become chief executive of the Chicago Mercantile Exchange in February 2000).

What came out of all this activity was an incredible amount of new thinking and creativity. It created the type of environ-ment where anything seemed possible. Thus, Bankers Trust, a bank debarred from the US equity markets and strong in fixed-income, used its fixed-income expertise and personnel to lead the pack in equity derivatives when that market started to burgeon in 1988. Many of the new ideas are now standard products or techniques in the markets, as the pages of *Risk* over the years attest.

There was a lot written in the late 1980s and early 1990s about exotic options, swaptions and various equity derivatives, as well as binomial, trinomial and bushy trees, and smiles. Then came the shift away from products and valuation to risk management, as the first corporate losses from derivatives came to light. Value-at-risk, then enterprise-wide risk management became the focus for a time. As credit risk came to the fore after the Asian, Russian and Long-Term Capital Management crises, that subject and credit derivatives began to dominate the risk management debate. At the beginning of the new millennium, the focus had shifted again, this time to capital, because of the proposed Basel II accord, and to operational risk, partly because of the terrorist outrages of September 11, 2001, but also because of the inclusion in the Basel proposal of a charge against capital for operational risk for the first time. It was around this time too that new areas were brought into the risk management framework – weather, emissions, the environment generally, freight, lumber and — for a short but tempestuous period until the demise of Enron in December 2001 – bandwidth.

Now, in contrast to the early 1980s, awareness of risk permeates the lives of almost everyone on the planet. At the business level, no firm, however small, can afford to ignore it. Risk management products are now used by a vast array of institutions, corporations, governments, public bodies and others, not only in the major financial centres but also in many smaller ones. Companies outside the financial sector have had to move risk management to the core of their decision-making. No longer is it enough to have a risk manager taking a liability-insurance viewpoint. Risk management has become a board-level concern, if not a direct concern of the chief executive. The post of "chief risk officer" is becoming quite common on both sides of the Atlantic. In the UK, major public companies are required to vest one board director with responsibility for risk management.

And at the personal level, there is a far greater awareness of risk because of terrorism, the loss of job security, higher levels of indebtedness and greater stock market volatility. Many people unwittingly use or benefit directly from risk management products through fixed-rate mortgages or guaranteed savings products, or indirectly through the management of their pension fund (if they have one left).

Risk, instead of being a footnote to business, is the pivot around which all else revolves. I was struck by how far we have come when I saw a report of speeches in May 2003 by the US Federal Reserve Board (Fed) Chairman, Alan Greenspan, and another governor of the Fed, Susan Schmidt Bies. Greenspan put derivatives at the centre of the current corporate governance debate. The OTC market, he said on May 7, 2003, "has played an important and successful role in the management of risk at financial institutions, a major element of their corporate governance." He also pointed out later, sounding like an ISDA spokesman from the early 1990s: "Credit losses on derivatives have occurred at a rate that it is a small fraction, for example, of the loss rate on commercial and industrial loans."

Bies in a speech a day later told internal auditors: "Although directors are not expected to understand every nuance of every line of business or to oversee every transaction, they do have the responsibility for setting the tone regarding their corporations' risk-taking and establishing an effective monitoring program." She was clearly surprised by a 2002 survey of 178 corporate directors that she quoted, which revealed that 45% admitted that their organisation did not have a formal enterprise-risk management process – or any other formal method of identifying risk.

Greenspan's public endorsements of the value of derivatives highlight one of the other quite remarkable conclusions about the past 15 years in the risk management industry: how successful it has been in deflecting all attempts to regulate it directly (it is of course regulated in the sense that all the major players are subject to oversight by one or more banking or securities supervisory body).

It's easy to forget this if you go back to the dark days of the early to mid-1990s when it seemed for a time that regulation of the dirty "D" word was close to inevitable (and I had to consider if there would be a future for *Risk* magazine). It sounds a little dramatic now but if the CFTC had got its hands on swaps – and there were several powerful attempts to facilitate this in the late 1980s and 1990s – the market would be nowhere near where it is today. Only in December 2000 did the Commodity Futures Modernization Act provide legal certainty for "non-retail" swaps – and then only if they are not traded "on a futures-style trading exchange". As Chairman Greenspan said in his May 7, 2003 speech cited earlier, "The success to date [of the OTC derivatives market] clearly could not have been achieved were it not for counterparties' substantial freedom from regulatory constraints on the terms of OTC contracts. This freedom allows derivatives counterparties to craft contracts that transfer risks in the most effective way to those most willing and financially capable of absorbing them."

A decade ago, official attitudes were very different. The President of the Federal Reserve Bank of New York, Gerald Corrigan, in a speech in January 1992 fired up the opposition to derivatives by sharply questioning the suitability for clients of many off-balance-sheet products and telling bankers to take a "very, very hard look at off-balance-sheet activities". To make his message clear, he added: "I hope this sounds like a warning because it is."

Corrigan's successor at the New York Fed when Corrigan moved into the private sector in 1993 was William McDonough. He also didn't tolerate lightly what he thought was the industry's complacency in the face of criticism, and he gave a respected academic speaker at a conference I attended in Miami in about 1995 a hard time for making light of the issue. The speaker's crime was to parody the slogan from the National Rifle Association, "Guns don't kill people – people kill people," by substituting "Derivatives" for "Guns".

The industry played into the critics' hands in 1994 and 1995, when a whole series of disasters such as Procter & Gamble, Orange County and Barings seemed to substantiate what Corrigan and others had said. You could argue until you were blue in the face that most of these so-called derivatives disasters weren't about the mis-selling or mishandling of products, more about basic faults in management, whether at the bank selling the product or the company buying it, but you couldn't deny the outlook for derivatives was bleak then. If you had read some of the articles in the American press or listened to some of the politicians, you would have seen derivatives as instruments devised by the Devil himself – or "weapons of mass destruction", as Warren Buffet said as recently as March 2003.

The hysteria about derivatives generated endless official and private sector reports, mostly unflattering. *Risk* published a booklet in 1994, *Fighting Fire with Facts*, which Stephen Greene, then chief general counsel of Credit Suisse Financial Products, compiled from his reading of more than a dozen reports on the OTC derivatives markets and other reliable sources. He built a compelling case for not interfering with the markets. He claimed a "solid empirical foundation" to the case "that the OTC derivatives markets pose no special or unique risks requiring an immediate legislative response".

Gradually, as the Barings saga faded away and nothing further eclipsed it, the furore died down. The industry itself addressed some of the more obvious problems, using the Group of Thirty report in July 1993 as a guide. ISDA (now the International Swaps and Derivatives Association) stepped up its lobbying and its educational activities. There have been further major losses, such as those resulting from LTCM in 1998 (in particular UBS's US$693 million write-off), those in the sterling swaptions market in August 1999 and the hits from Argentina's debt moratorium in December 2001, as well as further scandals, such as those surrounding the collapse of Enron, also in that month, but the markets have absorbed these shocks remarkably well. And nobody now realistically expects legislation to provide a solution. The US Financial Accounting Standards Board introduced Statement no. 133 on accounting for derivative instruments and hedging activities in June 2000 and in January 2001 the leading central banks proposed the Basel II Accord, which probably won't be implemented until 2007, but neither of these threatened the very existence of the derivatives markets in the way the proposals being bandied around in 1994–95 would have done. In fact, at the centre of the Basel process is the idea that the larger banks are best left to a system of self-regulation, within some broadly defined parameters.

On top of this, there has been the change of heart of some former critics. Corrigan softened his line soon after his broadside against derivatives, perhaps because he joined the industry as an adviser to Goldman Sachs in 1993. And at the top of the world's most important central bank, officers wax positively lyrical about derivatives. In November 2002, Greenspan told the Council on Foreign Relations, in Washington, DC: "Conceptual advances in pricing options and other complex financial products, along with improvements in computer and telecommunications technologies, have significantly lowered the costs of, and expanded the opportunities for, hedging risks that were not readily deflected in earlier decades. These increasingly complex financial instruments have especially contributed, particularly over the past couple of stressful years, to the development of a far more flexible, efficient and resilient financial system than existed just a quarter-century ago."

Whereas 10 years ago a commonly expressed fear was that derivatives would cause a major disaster, now Greenspan praises derivatives for averting one. Because of derivatives, he said in his May 7, 2003 speech, "not only have individual financial institutions become less vulnerable to shocks from underlying risk factors, but also the financial system as a whole has become more resilient." His evidence? "Even the largest corporate defaults in history (WorldCom and Enron) and the largest sovereign default in history (Argentina) have not significantly impaired the capital of any major financial intermediary."

I think it would be hard to find a better way to summarise why this book covers an exceptionally important part of recent economic history.

---

1 For a useful listing of all such events, see URL: http://bodurtha.georgetown.edu/enron/derivatives_events.htm.

2 See his famous "Holes in Black–Scholes" article in *Risk* in 1988 (volume 3, number 3, pp. 11–13) or "Living up to the Model" in *Risk* (volume 1, number 4, pp. 30–33) in 1990.

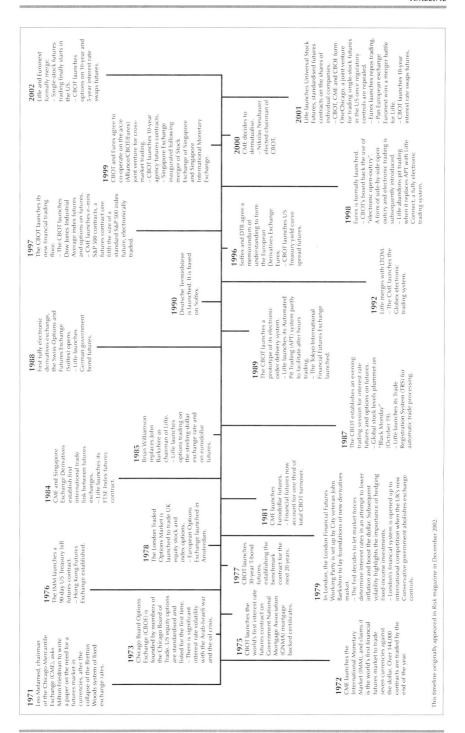

1971
Leo Melamed, chairman of the Chicago Mercantile Exchange (CME), asks Milton Friedman to write a paper on the need for a futures market in currencies, after the collapse of the Bretton Woods system of fixed exchange rates.

1972
CME launches the International Monetary Market (IMM), and claims it is the world's first financial futures market to trade seven currencies against the dollar. Over 144,000 contracts are traded by the end of the year.

1973
Chicago Board Options Exchange (CBOE) is founded by members of the Chicago Board of Trade. US equity options are standardised and listed for the first time.
– There is significant interest rate volatility with the Arab-Israeli war and the oil crisis.

1975
CBOT launches the world's first interest rate futures contract on Government National Mortgage Association (GNMA) mortgage backed certificates.

1976
The IMM launches a 90-day US Treasury bill futures contract.
– Hong Kong Futures Exchange established.

1977
CBOT launches 30-year T-bond futures, establishing the benchmark contract for the next 20 years.

1978
The London Traded Options Market is launched to trade UK equity stock and index options.
– European Options Exchange launched in Amsterdam.

1979
In London, the London Financial Futures Working Party is set up by City veteran John Barkshire to lay foundations of new derivatives market.
– The Fed decides to let market forces determine interest rates in an attempt to lower inflation and boost the dollar. Subsequent volatility highlights the importance of hedging fixed-income investments.
– London's financial system is opened up to international competition when the UK's new Conservative government abolishes exchange controls.

1981
CME launches Eurodollar futures.
– Financial futures now account for one third of total CBOT turnover.

1984
CME and Singapore Exchange Derivatives establish first international trade link between futures exchanges.
– Liffe launches its FTSE Index futures contract.

1985
Brian Williamson replaces John Barkshire as chairman of Liffe.
– Liffe launches options trading on the sterling-dollar exchange rate and on eurodollar futures.

1987
The CBOT establishes an evening trading session for interest rate futures and options on futures.
– Global stock levels plummet on "Black Monday" (October 19).
– Liffe launches its Trade Registration System (TRS) for automatic trade processing.

1988
First fully electronic derivatives exchange, the Swiss Options and Futures Exchange (Soffex) opens.
– Liffe launches German government bond futures.

1989
The CBOT launches a prototype of its electronic order delivery system.
– Liffe launches its Automated Pit Trading (APT) system partly to facilitate after hours trading.
– The Tokyo International Financial Futures Exchange launched.

1990
Deutsche Terminbörse is launched. It is based on Soffex.

1992
Liffe merges with LTOM.
– The CME launches the Globex electronic trading system.

1996
Soffex and DTB agree a memorandum of understanding to form the European Derivatives Exchange Eurex.
– CBOT launches US Treasury yield curve spread futures.

1997
The CBOT launches its new financial trading floor.
– The CBOT launches the Dow Jones Industrial Average index futures and options on futures.
– CME launches e-mini S&P 500 contracts, a futures contract one fifth the size of a standard S&P 500 index future, electronically traded.

1998
Eurex is formally launched.
– CBOT's board back the use of "electronic open-outcry". A form of side-by-side open outcry and electronic trading is subsequently introduced.
– Liffe abandons pit trading when it replaces APT with Liffe Connect, a fully electronic trading system.

1999
CBOT and Eurex agree to co-operate on the a/c/e (Alliance/CBOT/Eurex) joint venture for cross-market trading.
– CBOT launches 10-year agency futures contracts.
– Singapore Exchange inaugurated following merger of Stock Exchange of Singapore and Singapore International Monetary Exchange.

2000
CME decides to demutualise.
– Nikolas Neubauer elected chairman of CBOT.

2001
Liffe launches Universal Stock Futures, standardised futures contracts on the shares of individual companies.
– CBOT, CME and CBOE form OneChicago, a joint venture for trading single-stock futures in the US once regulatory controls are repealed.
– Eurex launches repos trading.
– Pan European exchange Euronext wins a merger battle for Liffe.
– CBOT launches 10-year interest rate swaps futures.

2002
Liffe and Euronext formally merge.
– Single-stock futures trading finally starts in the US.
– CBOT launches options on 10-year and 5-year interest rate swaps futures.

This timeline originally appeared in *Risk* magazine in December 2002.

Part I

The Rationale of Risk Management

1

Risk Management as a Process

David Mengle

International Swaps and Derivatives Association

Most of the chapters in this book describe in detail the development of the theories, methodologies and products used by institutions to manage risks. Others discuss risk management strategies used by institutions to control or alter the risks that arise as part of their core businesses. The purpose of this chapter, in contrast, is to outline the general characteristics of risk management processes that are in place today at major market participants.

Risk management processes exist to carry out the following general functions:

❏ to designate responsibility and establish accountability for risk management;
❏ to collect, analyse and report to management quantitative information on risks taken by businesses;
❏ to develop and enforce risk standards, limits and controls; and
❏ to identify and help resolve problems associated with risks taken by business units.

The form of the processes used by institutions to perform the above functions can vary greatly across firms according to corporate culture, management philosophy, regulatory environment and other factors.

Some institutions, for example, might make business units responsible for carrying out many elements of the risk management process, while others assign authority and responsibility to a centralised risk management unit. Alternatively, some institutions might give the risk management function the authority to challenge and possibly alter decisions of the business units, while others might confine the risk management group to an informational function with the responsibility of bringing violations or disagreements to the attention of senior management for resolution. Any of the above alternatives might be justifiable in the context of one corporate environment but would be totally inappropriate in the context of another.

Despite the differences among institutions, it is possible to describe some general characteristics of current risk management processes. The characteristics allow for a high degree of diversity but they are uniform in that they are heavily influenced by and make extensive use of the theories and practices described in this book. The remainder of this chapter describes six characteristics of risk management processes as they are found in today's financial institutions. The characteristics are derived primarily from experience with market risk management processes, although it is reasonable to expect a convergence over time of market risk and credit risk management practices.

INTERNAL CONTROLS AND INDEPENDENCE OF FUNCTIONS

The economic theory of organisations distinguishes between two functions; principal and agent. Principals are the owners (usually the shareholders) of a firm, and are entitled to the net income (whether positive or negative) of the firm's activities. The principals in turn engage agents to perform some service on the principals' behalf. This relationship – known as agency relationship – exists at many levels: between shareholders and boards of directors, between boards and senior management, between senior and subordinate levels of management, and so on.

There is an inherent potential for conflicts within a firm because the economic incentives faced by the agents are often different from those faced by the principals. In order to control such conflicts and avoid the problems they might cause, firms have instituted measures such as monitoring procedures, direct controls on the actions of agents and the separation of risk taking functions from control functions. Monitoring, internal controls and independence are not recent inventions: they have long been the basis for the financial control and audit functions within a firm.

But a market risk management function that is independent from risk taking functions is a recent innovation. The need for independence of risk management arose during the 1980s, when firms expanded their range of risk-taking activities while also discovering the risks inherent in their traditional activities. Nominally independent business activities could lead to unintended concentrations of risks, which could only be uncovered by analysing the risk profile at the firm level. Further, the dynamic nature of derivatives credit exposures increased the need for market risk information across functions. The result is that the major financial firms had established independent risk management functions by the early 1990s. Indeed, the Group of Thirty included in its study, *Derivatives: Practices and Principals* (Group of Thirty, 1993), a recommendation that firms establish independent market risk management units. The Group noted that at the time of the report about 60% of firms already had independent market risk units; the proportion had grown to 90% a year later. Regulators subsequently added further impetus by making independence of market risk management a precondition for the use of internal models under the Basel capital standards for market risk.

Several episodes have served to remind market participants of the importance of controls and independence, and in the process provided valuable lessons to the industry. The most notable was the 1995 failure of Barings, which demonstrated the importance of strong lines of control and accountability, of senior management's understanding of its business activities and of the importance of segregation of duties.

QUANTIFICATION OF RISKS

Institutions attempt to quantify risks because doing so makes risk management more precise and it also makes risk more transparent. That is, expressing risks in numerical rather than qualitative terms provides a "common language" for risk management throughout the organisation. Market risk management units have consequently been one of the primary users of the theories and methodologies described elsewhere in this book.

The volatile economic environment of the 1980s created increased potential for losses. First, firms faced more volatile exchange and interest rates following the breakdown of the Bretton Woods fixed exchange rate system as well as the sustained inflation of the 1970s. By the 1980s, energy prices provided an additional source of volatility. Second, disintermediation and deregulation in the 1980s led to new pressures on funding costs and therefore to pressures on margins. Finally, the savings and loan crisis in the United States, in which an entire class of institutions was caught between long-term fixed rate loans and rising costs of funding, demonstrated the need to monitor and control interest income and expense. Given the possibility of sudden, unanticipated losses, institutions had increased incentives to measure more closely the risks they faced.

Risk quantification at financial institutions progressed through three recognisable stages. The first stage was repricing gap analysis, which projected the effects of interest rate changes on net interest income. Gap analysis was oriented primarily toward institutions that did not mark-to-market, and was primarily used by the asset liability management businesses of banks. It has the advantage of simplicity and ease of communication, but quickly runs into limitations as managers seek more precision in risk measurement.

The second stage was duration analysis, which had the advantage of taking into account the effect of rate changes on market values. Duration analysis effectively converts financial instruments into zero coupon equivalents, and in so doing has the advantage of creating a common unit of measure for market risks. Although an improvement in many ways on gap analysis, duration analysis was difficult to apply to changing yield curve environments and could not incorporate correlation effects. Duration analysis nonetheless is commonly used in analysis of bonds and forms the basis for sensitivity measures used in value-at-risk (VAR) measurements.

The third stage was VAR, which measures potential change in the mark-to-market value of trading portfolios. VAR has the advantage of incorporating correlations effects, and also goes further than duration analysis in creating a common unit of measure for risks. The use of VAR became so widespread by the mid-1990s that it formed the basis of the Basel capital standards for market risk. As a measure of potential loss, VAR concepts are now being extended to credit risk in the form of economic capital measures.

MANAGEMENT OF RISKS, NOT PRODUCTS

The growth of financial innovation during the 1980s presented a challenge for those attempting to track the risks faced by an institution: as the number of products grew, so did the necessity to track the risks presented by the product. Fortunately, another development, namely, of derivatives contracts, provided a means of meeting the challenge.

Prior to the introduction of derivatives, each type of financial contract was treated as a bundle of discrete, inseparable risks. It was generally either costly or infeasible to attempt to alter the risk profile of a given contract. Derivatives contracts, however, changed all this by making it possible to break down contracts into component risks and then to manage the risks separately. For example, dealers do not manage dollar–yen cross-currency swaps in a separate book, but instead break the risks down into dollar interest rate risk, yen interest rate risk, and yen–dollar currency risk. The advantage of the ability to decompose contracts into fundamental risks is that the variety and complexity of products can continue to grow as client needs and market conditions dictate, while retaining two advantages: first, the development of a new product does not necessarily require the development of a new risk management methodology unique to that product; and second, the ability to disaggregate risks into standard risk types makes it possible to hedge seemingly illiquid contracts in highly liquid markets for the component risks.

DIVERSIFICATION

The financial benefits of diversification are well known: if the returns on securities in a portfolio are less than perfectly correlated with each other, the risk of the portfolio will be less than the sum of the risks of the individual components. Widespread adoption of VAR measures has facilitated the diversification of risks and the ability to measure the degree of diversification. Further, capital standards are moving toward recognition of diversification benefits. One of the tasks of the risk management process is to ensure that businesses managed on a decentralised basis are diversified as a group and do not unwittingly cause risk concentrations.

But diversification in practice presents challenges beyond the simple statistical benefits. First, there is a trade-off between diversification and specialisation. Diversification seeks to reduce volatility of returns by reducing correlation, but does not affect the return itself; specialisation, in contrast, seeks to increase returns but normally involves increasing correlation. The result is that the pursuit of diversification by firms is far from a simple mechanical process. Second, diversification of credit risks has proven to be more challenging than that of market risks, at least in part because relationship considerations limit the feasibility of rebalancing credit portfolios. Finally, correlations are not necessarily stable over time, and in fact tend to increase during market crisis situations. Risk managers therefore face the twin challenge of seeking diversification while developing ways – stress testing, for example – of protecting their firms during periods when markets move together.

MARK-TO-MARKET

The 1993 Group of Thirty report recommended that firms mark their portfolios to market daily for risk management purposes, regardless of the method used for financial reporting. A survey conducted as an annex to the report found that 83% of dealers marked to market; by the following year the number had grown to 95%. Mark-to-market valuation gained rapid acceptance for at least four reasons. First, historical cost-based numbers do not provide information relevant to evaluating the effects of market changes; this is especially true when measuring the counterparty credit exposure of a derivatives contract. Second, only marking-to-market provides the means to assess the effectiveness of a hedge, especially for option positions. Third, the experience of the effects of market risk during the banking crisis of the 1980s impressed on market participants the importance of measuring the effects on portfolios of changes in market conditions. Finally, the development of liquid markets for previously untraded contracts, such as loans, has both increased the availability of market information and increased the incentive to track changes in current values.

Still controversial, however, is the question of whether to extend market valuation to financial reporting. On the one hand, current values would by their nature be more relevant to current conditions than those based on historical cost numbers. On the other hand, the lack of liquid markets for all types of contract introduces more subjectivity and more difficulties of verification in numbers based on market values than in those based on historical costs. In addition, market valuation implicitly assumes that a portfolio could be liquidated at the reported numbers, when in fact that might not be the case during periods of market illiquidity. In order to choose between the two methods, it will first be necessary to define the purpose of accounting and financial reporting. When the primary purpose was control and verification, historical cost numbers were probably sufficient. But if investors and regulators decide that the primary purpose of accounting is now to portray the economic condition of a corporate entity, then a great deal of work remains in developing new measures that might usefully attain this goal.

EMPHASIS ON THE EFFICIENT USE OF ECONOMIC CAPITAL

At the beginning of the 1980s, capital was one of several measures used by supervisors to evaluate the condition of a bank; by the end of the decade, it had displaced any other criteria as the primary subject of regulatory attention. The new emphasis was embodied in the 1988 Basel Capital Accord, which was primarily concerned with avoiding problems caused by undercapitalised banks. Since the implementation of the Accord, banks have developed an increased appreciation of the importance of capital. But they also came to appreciate the cost of capital as well.

The result has been that banks are increasingly treating economic capital as an important but costly resource that must be optimised. This has led to the development of performance measures such as risk-adjusted return on capital and economic value added, which are closely related to VAR measures. The risk management function plays a role in the capital optimisation process because it is the source of measurements of the amount of capital used by the firm's risk taking activities.

The foregoing characteristics describe the less glamorous side of risk management, yet the side that most directly affects the various employees of an institution. If a risk management process has not been articulated, put in place and maintained, then all the theories, strategies and methodologies described elsewhere in this book will have little practical consequence. Evidence continues to accumulate – Procter & Gamble in 1994, Barings in 1995, Long-Term Capital Management in 1998, Enron in 2002, and whatever educational experience lies in ambush – in support of the importance of process and as sources of experience to improve further the processes that are in place today.

BIBLIOGRAPHY

Group of Thirty, 1993, "Derivatives: Practices and Principles" (Washington, DC).

Group of Thirty, 1994, "Derivatives: Practices and Principles – Follow-up surveys of industry practices" (Washington, DC).

2

An Overview of the Evolution of the Over-the-counter Derivatives Market

Carola von Schenk*

Freelance Journalist

The earliest examples of derivative transactions are found far back in history. The Code of Hammurabi, a set of written laws carved onto stone plates in ancient Babylonian script some 3,800 years ago, has been cited as embedding the world's first recorded option contract.[1] More recently, in the 17th Century, options on tulip bulbs and equity were traded on the Amsterdam stock exchange.[2] Two centuries later, exchange-traded commodity futures emerged in Chicago and equity options were traded over-the-counter (OTC), ie, privately negotiated – in New York and Paris.[3,4]

However, it is only over the past 25–30 years that exchange-traded and OTC derivatives contracts – on commodities and financial underlyings – have grown into a massive, highly liquid global market. According to the most recent data published by the Bank for International Settlements in Basel (see Table 1), today, a staggering notional US$142 trillion is outstanding globally in OTC contracts and the trading value of exchange-traded derivatives stands at US$197 trillion.[5]

Originally, the OTC derivatives market burgeoned partly on the back of the financial futures exchanges that emerged in the United States in the early and mid-1970s (see the timeline at the front of this volume). Since then, however, it has taken the undisputed lead in the risk management arena.

*I sincerely thank all those who helped me with my research for this chapter by sharing their insight, experiences and time.

Table 1 Growth in notional outstanding amounts in OTC derivatives (Data are year-end figures in US$. Sources: pre-1998 – ISDA*; 1998–2002 – BIS)

2002	141.7 trillion
2001	111 trillion
2000	95.2 trillion
1999	88.2 trillion
1998	80 trillion
1997	29 trillion
1996	25.5 trillion
1995	17.7 trillion
1994	11.3 trillion
1993	8.5 trillion
1992	5.3 trillion
1991	4.4 trillion
1990	3.5 trillion
1989	2.5 trillion
1988	1.7 trillion
1987	866 billion

*The ISDA data records only notional amounts outstanding in interest-rate and currency derivatives.

By allowing the unbundling and dissemination of risk, the self-regulated OTC market has helped change the risk profile of the world's financial systems and economies – for the better. "Derivatives have permitted financial risks to be unbundled in ways that have facilitated both their measurement and their management," Alan Greenspan, chairman of the US Federal Reserve Board (Fed), said in a speech in May 2003.[6] "As a result," he added, "not only have individual financial institutions become less vulnerable to shocks from underlying risk factors, but also the financial system as a whole has become more resilient."

OTC derivatives have opened up unprecedented opportunities for risk mitigation, taking and management – and thereby also for funding and investing. Borrowers can tap into different capital markets through tailor-made instruments, devised with the help of these OTC tools, that suit their own needs and investors' preferences. The choice of mortgage terms has increased manifold, while structured capital-protected equity products provide retail investors with easy access to what for many is a new asset class. OTC derivatives are also increasingly important tools for institutional investors, such as pension funds and life insurers, in their quest to up returns in the current low interest-rate environment.

Such advances in risk management and the choice of financial products could not have been brought about by the exchange-traded derivatives market with its tight regulations. Today, this fact is broadly recognised by authorities around the globe. Commenting on the topic in 2003, US Fed chairman Alan Greenspan said, "[The] success to date could not have been achieved were it not for counterparties' substantial freedom from regulatory constraints on the terms of OTC contracts. This freedom allows the derivatives counterparties to craft contracts that transfer risks in the most effective way to those most willing and financially capable of absorbing them."[7]

But the modern OTC derivatives market has changed its face beyond recognition over the roughly two decades of its existence. It took several years, and the commitment and creativity of pioneering individuals, for the market to develop the liquidity, depth and standardisation that have been and are its essential features. The market's evolution has been, and continues to be, multidimensional. Each of these dimensions has fed the growth in volume and, most importantly, liquidity.

The number of different contract types has increased dramatically. The market rapidly evolved to encompass not only swaps – the first type of OTC derivative – but also options, hybrids and other highly structured, exotic contracts. Albeit with some delay, OTC derivatives technology was applied to risk categories other than the currency and interest rate exposures these tools were first invented to deal with. Today, an OTC market on equity, commodity, credit and weather risk, to name but the major risk categories, exists. More are being added continuously.[8] These segments nurture one another's depth and liquidity, as newcomers to one arena will often move to use these types of tools on other risk categories as well.

The number – and diversity – of market participants has soared and continues to grow. At its inception in the late 1970s/early 1980s, the OTC derivatives arena was the prerogative of a handful of US banks and other major bond market players, mainly large US firms and the World Bank. In 2003, most commercial and investment banks, asset management houses, insurance companies, and many pension funds, non-financial firms, governments and non-governmental institutions around the globe use OTC derivatives.[9]

The global trade association representing OTC derivatives market participants – the International Swaps and Derivatives Association (ISDA) – has a membership of more than 600 dealers, end-users and associated services across 46 countries on six continents.[10] It was founded in 1985, albeit under a different name.

The market has also benefited from the expansion of the uses of these financial products. Initially employed solely for risk management and hedging purposes, today's OTC derivatives are also the bread and butter of a huge community of speculators and arbitrageurs – not least the massive hedge fund industry that has sprung up over the past decade. Overall, these players add depth and liquidity to the market.

But the need for risk mitigation and management remains at the core of the OTC derivatives business. Products that do not meet these requirements will not be successful. The very reason this market came into existence was that its products addressed pressing real needs for non-financial and financial institutions. Few of the early-day pioneers in this industry would have predicted the market's exponential growth. But they were aware that their inventions were breaking new and promising grounds.

ORIGINS

The first OTC derivative transactions – cross-currency and interest-rate swaps – emerged in the late 1970s and early 1980s. These deals catered to the needs of financial institutions and corporations to hedge their exposure to what was, for many of these market participants, an unprecedented volatility in currency and interest rates.

This volatility characterised those years. The demise in 1972 of the 1944 Bretton Woods system of fixed exchange rates, and its replacement with floating rate mechanisms, led to levels of currency volatility unknown in the post-World War Two era. Then, in 1973, the first Organization of Petroleum Exporting Countries (OPEC) oil embargo and the resulting period of rising oil prices hit economies around the globe. Partly as a result, the US and Europe were haunted by rampant inflation throughout the 1970s.

Moves in the US and elsewhere to relax the tight fiscal and monetary policies introduced new levels of interest rate volatility. In 1979, the US Fed, under its new chairman Paul Volcker, abandoned its policy of controlling interest rates. Dramatic rises and falls in US interest rates in the immediate aftermath and during the 1980s were the outcome. In the UK, the Conservative government that came to power in 1979 took a similarly liberalising stance.

Such currency and interest rate volatility was causing severe distress to corporates and financial institutions, catapulting the need for financial risk management onto their agenda. Firms were becoming increasingly global in their trade, investment and funding activities, but those that were listed, in particular, also faced punishment by their stockholders for losses on risks they were not paid to manage. Commercial banks started to encounter severe asset-liability mismatches.

But the changing structure of the world's financial system also contained some of the preconditions for the OTC derivatives markets. Europe's and Japan's growing economies were beginning to yield alternative pools of corporate capital to the US economy and capital market that had by far dominated the post-war era. These asset pools provided the seeds for the eurodollar markets that emerged at the time. The globalisation of financial markets and economies entailed that increasingly, parties with offsetting needs and risks could now be found on both sides of the Atlantic – and beyond.

But how was such risk transfer to take place? And how could the currency and interest rate risks be managed?

In 1972, the world's first foreign-exchange futures started trading on the new International Money Market of the Chicago Mercantile Exchange. In 1975, interest-rate futures staged their debut on the Chicago Board of Trade. These early exchange-traded financial derivatives – as well as the stock options that started to trade on the new Chicago Board Options Exchange in 1973 – were highly successful, and the exchanges rolled out several more such derivative contracts in the 1970s.

These exchange-traded instruments prospered on the advances in financial theory and risk management of the preceding decades and the early 1970s. In the 1950s, Harry Markowitz's portfolio theory had moulded the concept of risk as volatility, and Franco Modigliani and Merton Miller's work had led corporates to focus on the asset side of their balance sheet for creating value.[11] Most importantly, in 1973, Fischer Black and Myron Scholes published their seminal options pricing formula, which paved the way for valuations of stock options and the other new types of financial derivatives that would soon emerge.

The burgeoning exchange-traded derivatives industry also benefited from advances in technology that were surfacing at the time. In 1975, for example, Texas Instruments launched a hand-held calculator that computerised option value and hedge ratios based on the Black–Scholes formula – making it substantially easier to apply the formula's complex methodology. In the late 1970s, the advent of personal computers (PCs) and the binomial options pricing model developed by Stephen Ross, John Cox and Mark Rubinstein, using simple numerical techniques that could be run on PCs, opened up options pricing and thus options trading to a much larger community.[12]

Options and futures trading on the Chicago exchanges in the 1970s certainly put portfolio and option theory to the test and introduced the concept of higher finance to a broader range of players. But what these new financial instruments failed to do was to earnestly address the hedging needs faced by corporates and financial institutions at the time. Exchange-traded derivative contracts had very limited fixed terms and typically short maturities. Firms' exposures tended to be longer term and complex.

It was left to banks to come up with risk management solutions for themselves and their clients. In the latter half of the 1970s, their corporate finance departments started arranging back-to-back loans between clients with opposing currency requirements. They were the precursors of the cross-currency swap – dubbed the first financial OTC derivative contract of the modern risk management era. These loans, typically between a US and a European company, were huge successes, as they tended to cut currency exposure and funding costs.

The first currency and interest rate swaps were probably negotiated as early as the late 1970s. Players in this market had realised that instead of exchanging the principal of parallel loans, they could simply swap the rate payments. But these early deals tended to be small and one-offs. In 1981 and 1982, two transactions would create publicity for and establish more firmly the credibility and legitimacy of such OTC contracts.

In August 1981, the World Bank and IBM entered into a cross-currency swap with five- and seven-year maturities (see Panel 1). This transaction, worth US$290 million, was widely publicised at the time. It was one of the largest deals in those days and involved two of the most sophisticated and high-profile borrowers. Then, in 1982, the US Student Loan Marketing Agency – dubbed Sallie Mae – began entering into large interest-rate swaps, mainly with US savings and loans banks that had opposing risk management needs (see Panel 2).

Over the next few years, a growing number of currency and interest-rate swaps were done. Some pioneering firms, such as Salomon Brothers, Citibank, Bankers Trust and JP Morgan, which arranged these deals, saw the potential of this new financial technology. They started to take positions and warehousing deals,

---

PANEL 1 THE IBM/WORLD BANK CROSS-CURRENCY SWAP

Back in 1981, the World Bank was keen to borrow as many Swiss francs and Deutschmarks as it could. US interest rates were very high and the comparative rates in Germany and Switzerland quite low. However, Swiss and German authorities feared the institution would crowd out other borrowers. Meanwhile, IBM had borrowed in Deutschmark and Swiss francs, which were by far the broadest and deepest credit markets at the time. The firm was now looking to hedge its long-term liability in those foreign currencies. Salomon Brothers came up with a solution. The World Bank would issue notes at 16% for US$210 million due on 1 April, 1986, and similar seven-year notes for US$80 million. It would then enter into a cross-currency swap with IBM. The transaction – executed in August 1981 – allowed the World Bank to borrow Swiss francs and Deutschmark at a lower cost than if it had tapped those markets directly. IBM obtained the currency hedges it required, which were not otherwise available at the time.

PANEL 2 SALLIE MAE'S INTEREST-RATE SWAP PROGRAMME

In 1982, the Student Loan Marketing Agency (SLMA), dubbed Sallie Mae, for the first time had to fund itself in the capital markets. Sallie Mae is a publicly held company that functions as the national secondary market for student loans in the US. These loans are floating-rate products, with yields equal to the average rate of all three-month US T-Bill auctions held during the quarter. Back in the early 1980s, there was no T-Bill floating-rate market. However, with its AAA-credit rating, Sallie Mae had access to cheap funding. Its solution was to enter into interest-rate swap contracts, mainly with US savings and loan banks that had floating rate liabilities – the saving deposits, and fixed rate assets – the mortgages.

thereby providing vital liquidity to the market. By the mid-1980s, most of these players had set up specialised swap desks. They also started devising new, more complex and highly customised types of structures. For example, caps were invented, soon to be followed by collars, which were created to overcome many corporates' aversion to paying option premium.[13]

In 1982, the commercial launch of the Lotus 1-2-3 spreadsheet by Mitch Kapor delivered a vital and desperately needed risk management tool to the burgeoning OTC derivatives industry. The concept of capital adequacy for financial institutions was burgeoning and beginning to change the way banks thought about their business – and their risks.[14] Computer power was at hand, but the risk management software still had to be developed from scratch by each house. Most banks' early risk management systems were spreadsheet-based. Spreadsheet technology had been around for several years. Lotus 1-2-3, which was run on PCs, provided banks with price systems for interest rate and currency swaps. It was an immediate success.[15]

MATURING

However, one key stumbling block was preventing the market in these early OTC contracts from taking off big time and from developing into a trading market: documentation. The fact was that there were no standard documents or terms for these deals. Each transaction required lengthy negotiations on the terms of the deal and the contract, and the associated costs were immense.

In 1984, a small group of swaps pioneers – including Denise Boutross-McGlone, who had been working on swaps at Sallie Mae back in the early 1980s, and Tom Jasper, who in the early 1980s had built and ran Salomon Brother's swaps trading desk – realised that the industry as a whole would benefit if they could agree on a set of standardised terms. They came together and the following year founded ISDA – at the time called the International Swap Dealers Association.[16] These visionaries immediately set about standardising documentation. ISDA's successes at standardising documentation, as well as dealing practices and risk mitigation, allowed the OTC derivatives market to evolve into a trading market.

In 1985, the association published its standard terms and definitions for swaps. In 1987, it came out with its first standardised documentation – the Master Agreement. This would be revised in 1992 and 2002. The Master Agreement enabled market participants to deal with a variety of products by using a single document. This not only cut transaction costs, but reduced legal uncertainty and credit risk, lowering capital costs by allowing for the closeout netting of contractual obligations.

Once standardised documentation was at hand, it became easier, faster and cheaper to execute these OTC deals. Trading volumes soared – albeit still to low levels compared to today's volumes. The earliest publicly available data are for 1987, when ISDA started compiling OTC derivatives volumes. According to the ISDA data, the notional amount outstanding in these contracts stood at US$866 billion in 1987. By 1988, it had doubled to US$1.7 trillion. It has continued to rise sharply since (see Table 1).

A liquid trading market for OTC derivatives emerged rapidly, and a new breed of market participant – the inter-dealer broker – jumped onto its bandwagon. Money brokers launched swap desks alongside their traditional business. And in 1986, the first independent swap broker, Michael Spencer's Intercapital, set up shop. Today, operating as Icap, it is the world's largest swaps broker. These firms added liquidity and price transparency to the OTC market. They were also a welcome source of information for the new end-users and dealers, which were entering this arena at the time.

Banks' OTC derivatives businesses were growing – not just in volume but also in complexity. More and more risk management needs were being identified and products tailored to meet demands of the market. In 1985, the first swaptions emerged. At about the same time, asset swaps and collar swaps were invented, followed by dual-currency swaps in 1986/7 and callable swaps in 1987/8.[17] These are just a few examples. The innovation in swap and other OTC derivatives products on interest rate and currency risk has continued since.

By 1987, banks had also started applying OTC derivative concepts to other risk categories. One of the first OTC equity derivative deals was the quanto transaction devised by Bankers Trust in 1986. Then in 1987 the October stock market crash severely hit investors, who suffered substantial losses on their portfolios. In the aftermath of the crisis, they were keen to hedge such exposure, a demand that triggered the emergence of capital-protected or guaranteed products. Today, these are a major segment of the OTC equity derivatives market and one that would boom in the 1990s. OTC equity derivatives volumes were also boosted as liquid stock market indices emerged. For example, in the late 1980s, a huge market in put options on the Nikkei-225 index developed. It prospered on fears, particularly amongst foreign investors with benchmarks that required exposure to the market, that the bubble in the Japanese economy would burst. Other OTC derivative technology applications on equity risk followed. A few years later, for example, privatisation programmes across Europe often involved employee shareholder deals with embedded stock options. For much of the 1990s, equity investors were also keen to lock in their profits in the bull markets. The OTC derivatives industry delivered the products that would meet this demand.

Equity risk was not the only underlying that OTC derivative concepts were being applied to. The first OTC commodity derivative contracts, too, surfaced in around 1987. But again, this new segment would really take off only several years later. The catalyst was the 1990 Gulf war that led to a sharp rise in oil price and thus, for example, in jet fuel price. These events triggered the development of an OTC market in jet fuel, initially as a hedging tool for airlines. Since then, OTC derivatives have emerged on a myriad of commodities, including petrochemicals, gas, precious metals, electricity and weather.

Additionally, in the late 1980s, credit derivatives were being devised, mainly on country risk. For example, put options on asset swaps emerged catering to investors seeking to hedge their exposure to southern Europe, Italy in particular, when the European exchange rate mechanism ran into difficulties. But when the credit derivatives market really took off in the 1990s, it was on corporate rather than sovereign risk. Its most liquid segment today, the corporate credit default swap (CDS) market, began to take shape in 1993/4. Again, a catalyst was needed to boost volumes. It came in the late 1990s in the form of deteriorating credit quality, a fragmented corporate bond market and fears that the government bond market would dry up as Europe, in particular, cut its deficits. At about the same time, a new application for CDSs surfaced, when JP Morgan devised what is said to be the first synthetic collateralised loan obligation. This tool allowed the transfer of credit risk via a CDS on a pool of reference assets rather than selling these themselves, and opened up an entirely new risk management arena to banks, which many have since keenly tapped.

Back in the 1980s, the quest to apply the OTC derivatives structuring and modelling expertise to new types of risk was also closely linked to the massive investments that banks were making in the construction of pricing models and trading systems for their growing interest rate and currency derivatives businesses. They wanted to maximise the profits on these investments by using them for as much of their business as possible. They were also searching for new and (initially, at least) high-margin products, as margins on their existing OTC business dropped rapidly with the advances in pricing and hedging and technology. Swap margins, for example, collapsed after Lotus 1-2-3 was rolled out to the market.[18]

In those early days, pricing, trading and risk management programmes and systems had to be devised in-house. A third-party software vendor industry would only spring up in earnest in the latter half of the 1980s, partly drawing on tools that had been developed inside the banks. The banks hired physicists, mathematicians and other scientists, who built analytical models and the related technology. Many of these individuals soon started to trade and structure derivatives. Nowadays, Wall Street has become an established employer of such highly analytical academics. Back in the 1980s, this was a novel symbiosis.

As of around 1986, pricing tools and systems started to appear on the market, boosting volumes while driving down margins. SwapWare, the interest-rate and currency swap pricing system, was launched. Peter Cyrus started selling Fenics, the foreign-exchange options pricing programme he had devised a few years earlier while trading currency options at Bank of America; this has since become an industry standard. Joe Patrina founded Wall Street Systems and came out with one of the first integrated front-to-back office systems available commercially.

As their derivatives business boomed in the second half of the 1980s, banks started to think more seriously about beefing up their risk management systems and models. Progress on this front again paved the way for larger derivatives volumes. These had been somewhat capped by the lack of up-to-date information on overall exposures. Many trading houses were already marking to market their positions for accounting purposes, and a precursor of the 1989 value-at-risk (VAR) concept had emerged – probable overnight profit and loss. The idea was to present senior management of a firm with a single figure on the institution's daily market risk. In around 1990, another important risk management tool – Monte Carlo simulations – was invented, paving the way for the simultaneous pricing of various derivative products.[19] The first enterprise-wide risk management systems also emerged in the 1980s. They included the system rolled out by Cristóbal Conde's Devon Systems and RiskWatch, the tool of Ron Dembo's Algorithmics. These pioneering products found little resonance in the financial world at the time, although this would change abruptly in the mid-1990s.

In 1993, a Washington-based think tank, the Group of Thirty (G-30), published a document entitled *Derivatives: Principles and Practices* that called for the establishment of independent risk oversight, and market and credit risk management functions with clear authority, independent of the dealing function. The G-30 recommendations were adopted by many institutions and set risk management standards. The 1995 Baring Brothers bankruptcy, somewhat resulting from lack of such supervision, successfully focused many firms on the risks associated with failing to do so.

Cross-asset class trading and risk systems started to be rolled out. In 1994, JP Morgan launched its ground-breaking RiskMetrics system, a market risk measurement tool that was available free of charge over the Internet. This sparked widespread adoption of VAR as a risk management standard.[20]

This period saw a major breakthrough for the OTC derivatives industry on another front, too. International banking supervisors in Basel accepted closeout netting under the ISDA Master Agreement as enforceable and as a capital reduction tool. Banks could now get the full benefits of netting, and the full advantages of OTC derivative transactions came to the fore. Consequently, OTC derivative trading volumes, and the number of market participants (as evidenced not least in the sharp rise in ISDA members post-1994) soared.

The past eight years or so have been a period of unabated growth for the OTC derivatives industry. The market matured and weathered major crises, plus siren calls from prominent participants such as Warren Buffet. Derivative debacles of UK local authorities in the late 1980s, Germany's Metallgesellschaft, Proctor & Gamble and Orange County in the US, and Barings and Long-Term Capital Management in the 1990s, also served as warnings to the industry. They challenged and yet reinforced the OTC derivatives market's self-regulatory nature, and its solidity as the industry overcame these crises and learnt its lessons. These crises and the associated lessons are well illustrated in Part IX of this volume.

OTC derivatives volumes, the depth and liquidity of the market's segments, and the number of players have continued to rise, due to continued advances on all those fronts that were vital to its birth: documentation, product development, pricing and hedging strategies, and risk management.

LOOKING AHEAD

The OTC derivatives market will continue to grow. Growth in its mature segments – notably currency and interest rates – may somewhat level off, simply because it comes from a high base. But even these domains will see new players coming in and new regional markets opening up. China is one such example, the European countries that will join the European Union in 2004 are another. Online trading of a growing number of OTC derivative contracts is also opening up the market to new players and levelling the playing field.

The new international bank capital accord, Basel II, that will take effect in late 2006/early 2007, has focused institutions' attention on credit and operational risk, and is triggering major advances in these arenas. Such progress is already feeding the OTC derivatives market. Banks are off-loading some of their credit exposures ahead of Basel II. The development of internal credit ratings should further boost the market for trading credit exposure.

Whether or not operational risk derivatives ever become a reality, Basel II's stipulation of an operational risk capital charge has put this type of risk higher up on institutions' agenda. Related efforts at improving operational efficiency will benefit the OTC derivatives industry as a whole. Some of the largest losses in this field – such as the Barings bankruptcy – have been incurred by what may be termed operational shortcomings.

Instead of having been buried – as at times of crises was often feared – the OTC derivatives market has in recent years gained much acceptance as an invaluable risk management and mitigation arena. This has been evidenced by the recent comments of US Fed chairman Alan Greenspan on the OTC derivatives market, cited above.

1 Nicholas Dunbar, *Inventing Money*, John Wiley & Sons Ltd, 2001, p. 25.
2 Chapter 3 in this volume.
3 Dunbar, pp. 27–8.
4 Chapter 3 in this volume.
5 See BIS Quarterly Review June 2003.
6 Remarks at the 2003 Conference on Bank Structure and Competition, Chicago, Illinois, on 8 May 2003.
7 Remarks at the 2003 Conference on Bank Structure and Competition, Chicago, Illinois, on 8 May 2003.
8 Recently, for example, several banks launched economic derivatives, as reported by *Risk's* November 2002 edition (p. 18). In Chapter 18 of this volume, Marcelo Cruz talks about the prospective emergence in coming years of operational risk derivatives.
9 A recent survey by the International Swaps and Derivatives Association found that more than 90% of the world's 500 largest corporates use derivatives to hedge their risks.
10 This community includes representatives of the software, systems and consultancy industries catering to the OTC derivatives market that have emerged alongside it.
11 Alfred Steinherr, 2000, *Derivatives: The Wild Beasts of Finance* (John Wiley & Sons Ltd), p. 110.
12 *Risk*, December 2002, p. 66.
13 *Risk*, December 1997, p. 98.
14 Capital adequacy would be incorporated into international banking regulations in 1988 (Basel I).
15 Dunbar, p. 83.
16 ISDA changed its name to the current one in 1993.
17 *Risk*, December 1997, p. 97.
18 *Risk*, December 1997, p. 120.
19 Dunbar, p. 108.
20 *Risk*, December 1997, p. 107.

Part II

The Roots and Development of Modern Financial Modelling Techniques

3

Option Pricing Models and Stochastic Methods in Finance, 1900–1990

William Margrabe[*,1]

The William Margrabe Group, Inc

This chapter describes how Fischer Black, Myron S. Scholes, and Robert C. Merton discovered "a new method to determine the value of derivative products," for which Merton and Scholes won the Nobel Prize in Economics in 1997, and which laid the foundation for the derivatives industries. Also, we discuss earlier research that may have influenced their work, and subsequent key research that they influenced.

INTRODUCTION

> To study history means submitting to chaos and nevertheless retaining faith in order and meaning. It is a very serious task …
> Father Jacobus, in *The Glass Bead Game* (Hesse, 1969).

Our story of option pricing models and stochastic methods in finance begins with Bachelier's (1900) breakthroughs, which

* Personal communications: The author acknowledges helpful comments and other assistance from Yaacov Bergman, Peter Carr, Don Chance, Tom Copeland, John Cox, Darrell Duffie, Michael Gamze, Michael Harrison, Espen Haug, David Kreps, Bill Lane, Paul Mason, Larry McMillan, Perry Mehrling, Robert Merton, Stephen Ross, Mark Rubinstein, Myron Scholes, William Sharpe, Hans Stoll, Edward Stringham, Domingo Tavella, Zvi Wiener, and Paul Wilmott, but claims all responsibility for remaining weaknesses of this chapter. Please bring errors and omissions to the author's attention via www.Margrabe.com, where he will also publish errata and additional bibliographical information.

influenced only a few mathematicians over the next half-century; a dark age for stochastic finance. Around 1955 the rate of discovery accelerated, leading to the results of Samuelson (1965) and Samuelson–Merton (1969). However, at the heart of our story is the seminal work of Fischer Black and Myron S. Scholes (Black–Scholes, 1973), and Robert C. Merton (1973a), for which Merton and Scholes won the Bank of Sweden Prize in Economic Sciences in Memory of Alfred Nobel for 1997. Theoreticians relaxed the Black, Scholes, and Merton assumptions and applied their methods to additional problems. The result has been a revolution in the theory and practice of option pricing and risk management.

A SHORT HISTORY OF OPTIONS[2]

The earliest "options" were apparently instalment purchases that the sellers could not enforce. About 15 to 18 centuries BC, Jacob's installment purchase of the right to marry Laban's younger daughter, Rachel, was a compound option, in effect (*Bible*, Genesis 29). Around 550 BC, Thales of Miletus, "having a little money, … gave "deposits"– which authorities consider to be option premia – for the use of all the olive-presses in Chios and Miletus" (Aristotle, 350 BC). Cochrane (2000) argues that:

❏ the futures contracts that tulip speculators used during the "Tulip Bubble" of 1634–1637 were unenforceable; and so
❏ the "futures contracts" were options and the quoted "futures prices" were strike prices.

In the 17th Century, forward contracts and explicit equity call and put option contracts traded on the Amsterdam stock exchange (Stringham, 2001). In the 1870s equity options traded over-the-counter (OTC) in New York (Kairys and Valerio, 1997). Options and forward contracts on French government bonds traded around 1900 in Paris (Bachelier, 1900). From the 1930s equity options traded on the Chicago Board of Trade (Scholes, 1998, p. 351). After April 26, 1973, when the Chicago Board Options Exchange (CBOE) started trading listed American equity call options, trading volume grew rapidly. Soon, exchanges around the world offered trading also in options on bonds, futures contracts, and currencies.

BACHELIER (1900)

Bachelier (1900) invented the mathematics of Brownian motion to analyse the options on French government bonds that traded in Paris. His theory – despite assuming that the underlying futures price was normal, not lognormal, diffusion – was so far ahead of the field that it was largely a monument to the futility of being right before the right people could appreciate it. Contemporary mathematicians nitpicked his details and contemporary finance professionals ignored him. Bachelier's greatest impact was via his influence on Itô, whose work on stochastic processes was the foundation for Merton's continuous-time financial modelling.

THE 1920s–1960s

In 1955 or 1956, while Samuelson was supervising Kruizenga's (1956) dissertation, he found Bachelier's (1900) dissertation in the MIT library (Merton, 1990, p. 330; Taqqu, 2001, p. 28). Unfortunately, this discovery had no appreciable impact on Kruizenga's dissertation, which assumed that the underlying price was normally distributed and re-derived Bachelier's pricing equation, and little direct impact on the development of stochastic finance.

Sprenkle (1961) assumed that stock prices are lognormal, and assumed that the warrant price equals the expected payoff, adjusted arbitrarily for risk. Sprenkle's pricing equation includes the unknown, expected rate of return on the stock (Smith, 1976, pp. 16–17).

Boness (1964) assumed lognormal diffusion and risk neutrality, and discounted the expected return on the call by the stock's unknown, constant expected rate of return. Smith (1976) showed that Boness's pricing equation would have been identical to that of Black–Scholes (1973), if the expected rate of return on stock were the risk-free rate of interest.

Samuelson (1965) discussed the merits of the "geometric" ("exponential") random walk and described "no-arbitrage" bounds on warrant prices. He assumed that a warrant's present value is its expected value at expiration, discounted at the constant rate, β, whereas a stock's present value is its expected value, discounted at the constant rate, α. Samuelson (1972) showed that if one assumes a lognormal distribution for stock price, and if

$\alpha = \beta = r$ (the risk-free rate), then Samuelson's pricing equation is essentially the Black–Scholes (1973) equation.

Thorp and Kassouf (1967) empirically estimated warrant value as a function of underlying stock price. They used this estimate to create a hedged portfolio of warrant and underlying stock.

Stoll (1969) developed put-call parity theory and tested it with data from the put-call dealers' association. Merton (1973b) pointed out that put-call parity applies exactly only to options for which early exercise is impossible or irrational.

Samuelson–Merton (1969) assumed that an investor maximises expected utility, and derived the "reservation price" at which the investor is indifferent between being a buyer or a seller of an option. They illustrated their "util-prob" model in the context of a geometric binomial random walk.

THE BLACK–SCHOLES–MERTON BREAKTHROUGH[3]
Black–Scholes (1973)

Before 1968, Black, then at a consulting firm in Cambridge, Massachusetts, had been applying the capital asset pricing model (CAPM) to warrants and underlying shares, assuming that the excess expected rate of return on each was proportional to its systematic risk. Black tried many ways to analyse this issue, but they weren't working (Bernstein, 1992, p. 210).

However, Black, applying an idea that he got from Jack Treynor, did a Taylor series expansion of warrant value as a function of stock price and calendar time, keeping only the first order term in time and first and second order terms in stock price. At this point "it became obvious ... how to create a zero-beta portfolio that would have an expected rate of return equal to the rate of interest," (Scholes, 1998, p. 354). Black (1976b, p. 4) recalls having "notes containing the differential equation that are dated June, 1969".

Before 1969, Scholes, then on the MIT faculty, had been trying to use the CAPM to figure out the zero-beta portfolio of warrant and shares, with the number of shares changing each period. Scholes wasn't able to solve analytically for the number of shares to sell to create the zero-beta portfolio.

In 1969 Black and Scholes started talking about warrant pricing and exchanged notes (Scholes, 1998, pp. 353–354). Neither Black, nor Scholes was familiar with the Itô stochastic calculus that

Merton had used to develop continuous-time optimal consumption and investment rules (Merton and Scholes).

Black, even with his PhD in applied mathematics from Harvard, did not know the standard methods for solving partial differential equations (PDEs). Nor did he recognise their PDE as the heat equation (Black, 1976b, p. 5). Black and Scholes tried a number of approaches to gain an understanding of the pricing equation and its derivatives, including using numerical methods and graphs (Scholes*).

Since the expected rate of return on shares didn't appear in the PDE, Black and Scholes concluded that it was arbitrary, so they set it equal to the known and constant rate of interest. With constant drift rate and variance rate the stock price at expiration would have a lognormal distribution. That suggested using a variation of Sprenkle's (1961) solution. They took all the appropriate derivatives and substituted them into their PDE, finding no contradictions. Thus, by the winter of 1970 (January–March) Black and Scholes had their Black–Scholes (1973) pricing equation. (Scholes*).

In July 1970 Black and Scholes presented their model at a conference that Wells Fargo Bank sponsored at MIT's Sloan School. Merton overslept their presentation (Bernstein, 1992, p. 223). Around August 1970 Scholes told a sceptical Merton about the Black–Scholes PDE and pricing model (Scholes*). Merton confirmed that their result was correct, and supplied them with a derivation that used the Itô calculus and involved a perfect hedge of all risk. They published that derivation as the main derivation of their PDE, giving Merton credit for it in a footnote, and published their original, zero-beta derivation as an alternative derivation.

The *Journal of Political Economy* (*JPE*) and *Review of Economics and Statistics* (*RES*) rejected the Black–Scholes theoretical paper without peer review (Bernstein, 1992, p. 220–221; Scholes, 1998, pp. 356–357).

While Black and Scholes sought a journal that would publish their theoretical paper, they tested their theory with data from the OTC market (Black–Scholes, 1972, p. 399). Although the market did not seem to be efficient if they ignored transaction costs, they saw no way for a trader to take advantage of the apparent mispricing, given transactions costs. They presented their results at the December 27–29, 1971 American Finance Association meeting, and the *Journal of Finance* published their pricing equation and test results in its May 1972 issue of papers and proceedings.

As a version of Black–Scholes (1973) twisted slowly, slowly in the wind, Merton Miller and Eugene Fama intermediated with the *JPE*'s editors, who reconsidered the Black–Scholes paper, accepting the revised version they received on May 9, 1972 (Bernstein, 1992, p. 220–221). Black–Scholes (1973) appeared in the *JPE*'s May/June 1973 issue.

Black–Scholes (1973) is significant, mainly for showing how to use hedging to obtain the PDE, deriving the pricing equation, and providing applications to corporate finance, such as showing that common stock is a call option on the firm's assets.

Merton (1973a)

At the end of 1969, Merton was on the faculty at MIT and poised to make discoveries about option pricing. After Samuelson–Merton (1969), he was familiar with many important issues in option pricing. He had mastered and applied the continuous-time mathematics that would be the foundation for nearly all subsequent option pricing theory. Merton (1971) discusses the mathematics of Itô processes and the crucial, but far from obvious, definition of the budget constraint in that context. However, he was focusing his attention on continuous-time models not related to options.

By 1970, no later than his discussion with Scholes, Merton was thinking about option pricing again. After Merton verified the Black–Scholes (1973) PDE by using the Itô calculus and constructing a *perfect* hedge portfolio that eliminated all risk, not just systematic risk, he coined the phrase, "Black–Scholes model", in his 1970 working paper (Merton*).

Merton soon wrote a classic paper that became Merton (1973a), which makes two major contributions.

❏ It shows how to dynamically replicate an option with a changing portfolio of stock and cash. (Merton*). Merton's method assumes only the existence of non-satiated potential arbitrageurs, not the stronger assumption of capital market equilibrium.

❏ It extends Black–Scholes (1973) in several directions, allowing the rate of interest to move stochastically, dividends to be non-zero, the exercise price to change, and exercise to be American-style.

It also shows how to value a down-and-out call option (Merton, 1998, p. 326).

Paul MacAvoy, editor of the *Bell Journal of Economics and Management Science* and one of Merton's colleagues, accepted Merton's paper before the *JPE* agreed to publish Black–Scholes (1973). Merton asked MacAvoy to hold up publication of Merton's paper, until a journal accepted and published the Black–Scholes paper (Merton*). Thus, the nearly simultaneous publication of the Black–Scholes (1973) and Merton (1973a) papers is no mere coincidence.

REACTION

Many practitioners and academics embraced the Black–Scholes (1973) and Merton (1973a) results, immediately. The residual level of scepticism has diminished over time.

Practitioners

The rapid growth in the derivatives industries after 1973 was no mere coincidence.[4] The Chicago Board Options Exchange (CBOE) opened for business in April 1973, a month before the *JPE* published the Black–Scholes article (Bernstein, 1992, p. 225). Younger practitioners, particularly, tended to embrace the Black–Scholes model, because it proved useful for marking books and managing risk, even though CBOE options were American and the Black–Scholes (1973) model was for European options. Texas Instruments soon sold a hand-held calculator that computed option values and hedge ratios.

By the early 1980s Wall Street firms were hiring economics and finance professors, who could help with pricing and managing the risk of portfolios of financial products. By the late 1980s Wall Street was hiring "financial engineers" with physics and applied mathematics backgrounds.

Academics

For years after May 1973 careful scholars raised thoughtful and serious questions about the Black–Scholes–Merton derivations of results that practitioners were using daily around the world. However, after years of controversy, the scholarly consensus is that the Black–Scholes–Merton pricing equation follows from some set of acceptable assumptions, even if they include such currently non-intuitive expressions as "square-integrability".

The Bank of Sweden prize in economic sciences in memory of Alfred Nobel for 1997
The press release about the Bank of Sweden Prize in Economic Sciences in memory of Alfred Nobel for 1997 states that the award is "for a new method to determine the value of derivatives." It reads, in part:

> "Robert C. Merton and Myron S. Scholes have, in collaboration with the late Fischer Black, developed a pioneering formula for the valuation of stock options. Their methodology has paved the way for economic valuations in many areas. It has also generated new types of financial instruments and facilitated more efficient risk management in society."

RELAXED ASSUMPTIONS AND ADDITIONAL APPLICATIONS
The results in Black–Scholes (1973, p. 640) depend on seven assumptions, which were stronger than necessary (see Table 1). Merton (1973a) was the first to relax an assumption, allowing a stochastic yield for a default-free zero coupon bond maturing at option expiration. Merton (1976) assumes a combined diffusion plus jump process. Cox–Ross (1976b) assumes a compound jump process. Wiggins (1985) and Hull–White (1987) allow stochastic volatility. Relaxing the perfect market assumptions has proved most problematic.

Many authors have used Black–Scholes–Merton methods to value products other than European calls and puts. These applications are both univariate and multivariate. We distinguish between multivariate applications with multiple risk factors and multiple observation times for a single risk factor.

Table 1 Black–Scholes (1973, p. 640) assumptions

1.	Known and constant rate of interest
2.	Lognormal diffusion, constant variance
3.	No dividends or other distributions
4.	Call or put option, European exercise
5–7.	Perfect markets[5]

Univariate applications

A univariate application of the Black–Scholes–Merton method has a single underlying risk factor, and is the Black–Scholes–Merton PDE plus initial and boundary conditions peculiar to the application. The most significant univariate option applications, from 1973–1990, were extracting the Arrow–Debreu prices from the option pricing formula (Black, 1974) and valuing the following products: an arbitrary "European" payoff (Black, 1974); corporate debt with the "option to default" (Merton, 1974); a European call or a put on a futures contract (Black, 1976a); and currency options (Garman–Kohlhagen, 1983; Grabbe, 1983).[6]

Multiple risk factors

Applications of the Black–Scholes–Merton approach, but with multiple risk factors, consist of solutions to a multivariate extension of the Black–Scholes–Merton PDE plus multivariate initial and boundary conditions. The most significant multivariate applications in the period 1973–1990, were for valuing the following products: an option to exchange one asset for another (Margrabe, 1978); an arbitrary European payoff function of an arbitrary number of underlying risky assets (Margrabe, 1982); an option on the maximum or minimum of two assets (Stulz, 1982); an option on the maximum or minimum of several assets (Johnson, 1987).

Multiple observation times for a single price

The most significant applications of the Black–Scholes–Merton method to path-dependent options, which have a payoff that depends on a single underlying price, observed at different times, are to the following: European down-and-out call option (Merton, 1973a); American option on dividend-paying stock (Black, 1974; Schwartz, 1977; Parkinson, 1978; Cox–Ross–Rubinstein, 1979); corporate debt with multiple coupons (Geske, 1977); compound options (Geske, 1979b); lookback option (Goldman–Sosin–Gatto, 1979); and European option on observed average over time of one underlying price (Kemna–Vorst, 1990).[7] Carr (1988) shows how to value a compound exchange option, which involves both a pair of underlying prices and observations at different dates.

NUMERICAL METHODS

Numerical methods have gone hand-in-hand with option pricing models since 1973. Black–Scholes (1973) expressed option value in terms of the cumulative normal distribution function, $N(x)$, which one ordinarily computes by using a polynomial or rational approximation, except for special cases, such as $N(0) = \frac{1}{2}$.

Numerical methods allow us to apply the Black–Scholes–Merton methodology to infinitely many problems, whose solutions we can express only as integrals or boundary value problems. Many methods are available to numerically solve such problems, and a good numerical methods textbook or reference book – such as Press, *et al* (1988, 1992) – will explain some of them.

Binomial, trinomial, multinomial

Binomial models of price movement go back to Bachelier (1900), Sprenkle (1961; 1964) and Samuelson–Merton (1969). However, Cox–Ross (1976a) shows that arbitrage-free pricing implies probabilities that figure in the pricing of the arbitrary claim, and they compute them.[8] Sharpe (1978) uses arbitrage-free one and two-period, exponential binomial models. Cox–Ross–Rubinstein (1979) and Rendleman–Bartter (1979) extend Sharpe's (1978) idea to develop binomial pricing models of the sort that have allowed many practitioners to avoid heavy mathematics yet understand the ideas of hedging and replication and build commercial pricing models. The binomial model approaches the Black–Scholes–Merton model in the limit as the time step approaches zero.

Trinomial models have applications for pricing claims with one and two risk factors. Parkinson's (1978) trinomial model is an ingenious numerical solution to the free-boundary problem inherent in valuing an American option. Tanenbaum (1985) presents a trinomial model for two correlated risk factors. Boyle (1988) develops a lattice framework (quadrinomial model) for the same purpose.

Binomial, trinomial, and other multinomial models proved practical for pricing American options, but closed-form solutions are more computationally efficient for pricing European call and put options.

Option pricing as a boundary value problem

A key element of the Black–Scholes–Merton approach is to derive a parabolic partial differential equation (PDE) that describes how the underlying price moves, and terminal and boundary conditions to model the product. The PDE and conditions define a boundary value problem.

One could price a typical "European" ("American") product – ie, one with determinate, contingent, or optional cashflows at (or before) expiration – by solving a boundary value problem, using standard numerical methods, such as finite difference, finite element, and Monte Carlo algorithms. The finance literature has developed multinomial pricing models to the same effect.

Numerically solving the PDE

Bachelier (1900), Black–Scholes (1973), and Merton (1973a) point out that their partial differential equations are forms of the heat equation. Explicit, implicit, and combined explicit-implicit finite difference methods for solving the heat equation had been around for decades before 1973. Explicit methods figure out the value at a "parent" node (earlier date), based on values at corresponding "child" nodes (later date), and resemble a binomial or trinomial algorithm. Implicit methods require solving many simultaneous equations to find the values at a set of "parent" nodes as functions of the values at a set of "child" nodes.

Schwartz (1977) shows how to use an explicit finite difference algorithm to value an American call option.

Monte Carlo simulation

In 1899 Lord Rayleigh showed that he could approximately solve a parabolic partial differential equation by using a one-dimensional random walk with no absorbing barriers. After World War II nuclear scientists used Monte Carlo methods to study neutron diffusion (Fishman, 1995, p. 2). By 1973, Monte Carlo methods for approximately evaluating an integral were standard enough to appear in Schaum's outline of numerical methods (Scheid, 1968, pp. 401–406).

Boyle (1977) was the first published application of a Monte Carlo approach to European option pricing. Efforts to price American options with Monte Carlo methods began with Bossaerts (1989). Progress since then has been substantial and includes implementation of Merton's (1973a) idea, involving choosing the optimal high-contact boundary for an American call.

Integral solutions for European products

Given Black–Scholes–Merton assumptions, one can ordinarily express the value of an arbitrary "European" product – ie, one with no possible cashflow until expiration – as an integral. The justifications for this fall under a variety of headings, such as: Green's function, Feynman–Kaç functional, Arrow–Debreu pricing, risk-neutral pricing, and Martingale representation.[9]

Black (1974) specifies the integral for the general univariate case, and Margrabe (1982) extends Black's result to N underlying prices. Geske (1977) shows coupon-paying corporate debt as a compound option and expresses its value as an n-dimensional integral for a single underlying price.

The idea of evaluating an integral by numerical quadrature to value an option goes back to at least Samuelson (1965).

FURTHER EXTENSIONS

New extensions and applications of the basic Black–Scholes–Merton methodology have appeared at a dizzying rate, but the newer papers tend to explore portions of niches that earlier papers exposed. Given that, and the fact that paper, ink, and the reader's time are scarce resources, we have ended our discussion in 1990 – with one exception.

Namely, some of the more interesting, recent applications grow out of the need to value "real options", including refineries, oil fields, and other risky investment opportunities. Copeland says that real options modelling is gradually replacing the net present value modelling. Carr (1988) points out that researchers modelled many early real options as options to exchange one asset for another (Margrabe, 1978), or compound options (Geske, 1979b). Carr's (1988) model generalises those models. Today, many real options are much more complex than that (see Copeland–Antikarov, 2001).

CONCLUSION

Our history of option pricing and stochastic methods in finance began with Bachelier (1900), which contains a new mathematical model for Brownian motion and an option-pricing model that was state of the art for 55 years. Unfortunately, financial economists and practitioners ignored Bachelier, who had little direct impact on financial modelling. However, in the 1940s Bachelier's new mathematics influenced Itô's work, which in the 1970s Merton applied with distinction.

The discoveries of Black–Scholes (1973) and Merton (1973a) are at the heart of our story. Black–Scholes (1973) shows that both the CAPM and Merton's arbitrage argument imply a PDE, which they solve, producing their option pricing equation. Also, they point out that shares are call options on a corporation's assets, which indicates the value of their model for corporate finance. Merton (1973) derives a more general PDE by using Itô's lemma and assuming that the option value moves to avoid arbitrage – without assuming capital market equilibrium. He also extends the Black–Scholes results in several important ways.

Black–Scholes–Merton results and methods provide a roadmap for others to follow to value many new and old financial products and manage their risk. Through the 1990s the underlying risk factors were mainly interest rates and prices of bonds, commodities, and equities. The demand for front, middle, and back-office systems to value and manage the risk associated with these products resulted in a derived demand for software applications and talented and trained personnel to build the software and operate the systems. One could almost hear a loud sucking sound, as the derivatives industries pulled "quants" out of physics and other quantitative disciplines. Gradually, developers learned that they could choose from a wide variety of numerical methods to solve problems mechanically, when relatively simple pricing equations were not readily available.

Why did it take some 70 years from Bachelier's brilliant dissertation to the prize-winning Black–Scholes–Merton development of the option pricing model and methods? It was a communications problem. Bachelier transmitted a potentially fascinating message, but neither it, nor its significance was clear. His unconventional mathematical training led to notation and style that put off most French mathematicians, even though he was French. His greatest impact was in the 1920s and 1930s on Khinchine and Kolmogorov, and in the 1940s on Itô (Taqqu, 2001). Their need for his information gave them the incentive to read his noisy message. The businesspersons and economists of Bachelier's day didn't speak advanced mathematics of any sort, so his message didn't reach them. Circa 1970 Merton was motivated and able to receive Itô's message, and the result was outstanding.

Why did it take some four years from Black–Scholes–Merton's 1973 breakthrough until articles applying finite difference and Monte Carlo techniques appeared in the literature? Again, it was most likely a problem with communications. Certain applied mathematicians knew how to solve boundary value problems numerically, and certain businesspersons had a need to price American options. Unfortunately, at first, they were not communicating effectively.

We are optimistic that they will communicate better in the future. Derivative products and risk management issues are growing more important in the financial sector, and stochastic methods are appropriate for analysing many of them. Management is increasingly aware of the contributions that quants can make, and quants are eager to help.

1 We are not the first to attempt write a history of derivatives or pricing models. Smith (1976) thoroughly reviews the technical literature from Bachelier (1900) to about 1976. Black (1989) discusses "How We Came Up with the Option Formula". General readers and professionals can benefit from reading Bernstein (1992, ch. 11) story about the development of option pricing models. The Merton–Scholes (1995) eulogy to Fischer Black gives us a perspective on the man that goes beyond the Black–Scholes (1973) model. Chance (1995) tabulates key developments in the history of derivative products and their pricing models and Chance (1998) elaborates on some of the more important of these. Smithson and Song (1998) update Smithson's (1991) "family tree" and taxonomy of pricing models that appear in articles published through 1993. The practitioner who wants to see a plethora of pricing equations and VisualBasic code will find it in Haug (1998). The 1997 Nobel Prize lectures of Merton (1998) and Scholes (1998) are exceedingly well-informed discussions the development of the Black–Scholes–Merton results, applications through 1997, and prospects for the future. Duffie (1998) focuses on the contributions of Fischer Black, Robert C. Merton, and Myron Scholes to economics, while Marsh–Kobayashi (2000) focuses on their contributions to the financial services industry.
2 Gastineau (1988), Kairys–Valerio (1997), and Chance (1998) contain brief histories of derivative products.
3 Black (1989), Bernstein (1992, chapter 11), Merton–Scholes (1995), Merton (1998), and Scholes (1998) have already discussed the development of the Black–Scholes–Merton option valuation results and methodology, at length, so we can be brief.
4 Scholes (1998, p. 350) mentions the exchange, OTC, and academic derivatives industries.
5 Black–Scholes (1973) mentions specifically three assumptions that we summarise by "perfect capital markets"; zero transaction costs; unlimited leverage at the riskless rate; and no penalties for selling short.
6 However, we discuss American and barrier options, later.
7 The more general methods of Parkinson (1978), CRR (1979), and finite difference approaches have reduced the significance of specific methods to value call options on dividend-paying shares.
8 That is, now the price is here, but an instant it can go to either point A or point B.
9 See Cox–Ross (1976b).

BIBLIOGRAPHY

Aristotle, 350 BC, *Politics*, Book I, Part XI. URL: http://classics.mit.edu/Aristotle/politics. 1.one.html.

Bachelier, L., 1900, "Théorie de la Spéculation"; translation in Cootner (1964), pp. 17–79.

Banz, R. W., and M. H. Miller, 1977, "Prices for State-Contingent Claims: Some Estimates and Applications", *Journal of Business* 51, pp. 653–72.

Bernstein, P. L., 1992, *Capital Ideas: The Improbable Origins of Modern Wall Street* (New York: Free Press).

The Bible, Genesis 29, URL: http://www.bible.com.

Black, F., 1974, "The Pricing of Complex Options and Corporate Liabilities", University of Chicago.

Black, F., 1976a, "The Pricing of Commodity Contracts", *Journal of Financial Economics* 3, pp. 167–79; reprinted in L. Hughston (ed), 1999, *Options: Classic Approaches to Pricing and Modelling*, Chapter 8 (London: Risk Books).

Black, F., 1976b, "Fischer Black on Options 1".

Black, F., 1989, "How We Came Up with the Option Formula", *Journal of Portfolio Management* 15(2) , pp. 4–8.

Black, F., and M. Scholes, 1972, "The Valuation of Options Contracts and a Test of Market Efficiency", *Journal of Finance* 27, pp. 399–417.

Black, F., and M. Scholes, 1973, "The Pricing of Options and Corporate Liabilities", *Journal of Political Economy* 81, pp. 637–54, reprinted in L. Hughston (ed), 1999, *Options: Classic Approaches to Pricing and Modelling*, Chapter 3 (London: Risk Books).

Boness, A. J., 1964, "Some evidence on the profitability of trading in put and call options", in Cootner, 1964, pp. 475–96.

Bossaerts, P., 1989, "Simulation Estimators of Optimal Early Exercise", Carnegie Mellon University.

Boyle, P., 1977, "Options: A Monte Carlo Approach", *Journal of Financial Economics* 4, pp. 323–38, reprinted in L. Hughston (ed), 1999, *Options: Classic Approaches to Pricing and Modelling*, Chapter 10 (London: Risk Books).

Boyle, P., 1988, "A Lattice Framework for Option Pricing with Two State Variables", *Journal of Financial and Quantitative Analysis* 23, pp. 1–12.

Breeden, D. T., and R. H. Litzenberger, 1977, "Prices of State-Contingent Claims Implicit in Option Prices", *Journal of Business* 51, pp. 621–51, reprinted in L. Hughston (ed), 1999, *Options: Classic Approaches to Pricing and Modelling*, Chapter 11 (London: Risk Books).

Carr, P., 1988, "The Value of Sequential Exchange Opportunities", *Journal of Finance* 43, pp. 1235–56.

Chance, D. M., 1995, "A Chronology of Derivatives", *Derivatives Quarterly* 2, pp. 53–60.

Chance, D. M., 1998, "A Brief History of Derivatives", essay 5 of *Essays in Derivatives* (New Hope, PA: Fabozzi), pp. 16–20.

Cochrane, J. H., 2000, "Review of *Famous First Bubbles* by Peter M. Garber", University of Chicago. URL: http://gsbwww.uchicago.edu/fac/john.cochrane/research/Papers/ garber.doc.

Cootner, P., (ed), 1964, *The Random Character of Stock Market Prices* (Cambridge, MA: MIT Press.)

Copeland, T., and V. Antikarov, 2001, *Real Options; a practitioner's guide* (New York: Texere).

Cox, J. C., and S. A. Ross, 1976a, "A Survey of Some New Results in Financial Option Pricing Theory", *Journal of Finance* 31, pp. 383–402, reprinted in G. Constantinedes and A. G. Malliaris (eds), 2000, *Options Markets* (Northampton, MA: Edward Elgar).

Cox, J. C., and S. A. Ross, 1976b, "The Valuation of Options for Alternative Stochastic Processes", *Journal of Financial Economics* 3, pp. 145–66; reprinted in L. Hughston (ed), 1999, *Options: Classic Approaches to Pricing and Modelling*, Chapter 7 (London: Risk Books).

Cox, J. C., S. A. Ross, and M. Rubinstein, 1979, "Option Pricing: A Simplified Approach", *Journal of Financial Economics* 7, pp. 229–63.

Duffie, D., 1998, "Black, Merton and Scholes – Their Central Contributions to Economics", *Scandinavian Journal of Economics* 100, pp. 411–424.

Fishman, G. S., 1995, *Monte Carlo; Concepts, Algorithms, and Applications* (New York: Springer).

Garman, M. B., and S. W. Kohlhagen, 1983, "Foreign Currency Option Values", *Journal of International Money and Finance* 2, pp. 231–37; reprinted in L. Hughston (ed), 1999, *Options: Classic Approaches to Pricing and Modelling*, Chapter 14 (London: Risk Books).

Gastineau, G. L., 1988, *The Options Manual*, Third edition (New York: McGraw-Hill).

Geske, R., 1977, "The valuation of corporate liabilities as compound option", *Journal of Financial and Quantitative Analysis* 12, pp. 541–52.

Geske, R., 1979b, "The Valuation of Compound Options", *Journal of Financial Economics* 7, pp. 63–81; reprinted in L. Hughston, (ed), 1999, *Options: Classic Approaches to Pricing and Modelling*, Chapter 13 (London: Risk Books).

Goldman, B. M., H. B. Sosin, and M. A. Gatto, 1979. "Path Dependent Options: Buy at the Low, Sell at the High", *Journal of Finance* 34, pp. 1111–27.

Grabbe, J. O., 1983, "The Pricing of Call and Put Options on Foreign Exchange", *Journal of International Money and Finance* 2, pp. 239–53.

Haug, E. G., 1998, *Option Pricing Formulas* (New York: McGraw-Hill).

Hull, J. C., and A. White, 1987, "The Pricing of Options on Assets with Stochastic Volatilities", *Journal of Finance* 42, pp. 281–300; reprinted in L. Hughston (ed), 1999, *Options: Classic Approaches to Pricing and Modelling*, Chapter 15 (London: Risk Books).

Johnson, H., 1987, "Options on the Maximum or the Minimum of Several Assets", *Journal of Financial and Quantitative Analysis* 22, pp. 277–83.

Kairys, Jr., J. P. and N. Valerio, 1997, "Market for Equity Options in the 1870's", *Journal of Finance* 52, pp. 1707–23.

Kemna, A., and A. Vorst, 1990, "A Pricing Method for Options Based on Average Asset Values", *Journal of Banking and Finance* 23, pp. 113–29; reprinted in L. Hughston (ed), 1999, *Options: Classic Approaches to Pricing and Modelling*, Chapter 16 (London: Risk Books).

Kruizenga, R. J., 1956, "Put and Call Options: A Theoretical and Market Analysis", PhD thesis, MIT.

Margrabe, W., 1978, "The Value of an Option to Exchange One Asset for Another", *Journal of Finance* 33, pp. 177–86; reprinted in L. Hughston (ed), 1999, *Options: Classic Approaches to Pricing and Modelling*, Chapter 12 (London: Risk Books).

Margrabe, W., 1982, "A Theory of the Price of a Claim Contingent on N Asset-Prices", Working Paper 8201, George Washington University.

Marsh, T., and T. Kobayashi, 2000, "The Contributions of Professors Fischer Black, Robert Merton and Myron Scholes to the Financial Services Industry", *International Review of Finance* 1, pp. 295–315.

Merton, R. C., 1970, "A Dynamic General Equilibrium Model of the Asset Market and Its Application to the Pricing of the Capital Structure of the Firm", Working Paper No. 497–70 (Cambridge, MA: A. P. Sloan School of Management, MIT), reprinted in R. Merton 1990, *Continuous-Time Finance*, Chapter 11, pp. 357–87 (Cambridge, MA, Basil Blackwell.).

Merton, R. C., 1971, "Optimum Consumption and Portfolio Rules in a Continuous-Time Model", *Journal of Economic Theory* 3, pp. 373–413; reprinted in R. Merton, 1990, *Continuous-Time Finance*, Chapter 5, pp. 120–65 (Cambridge, MA, Basil Blackwell).

Merton, R. C., 1973a, "Theory of Rational Option Pricing", *Bell Journal Economics and Management Science* 4, pp. 141–83; reprinted in R. Merton, 1990, *Continuous-Time Finance*, Chapter 8, pp. 255–308 (Cambridge, MA, Basil Blackwell).

Merton, R. C., 1973b, "The Relationship Between Put and Call Option Prices: Comment", *Journal of Finance* 28, pp. 183–84.

Merton, R. C., 1974, "On the Pricing of Corporate Debt", *Journal of Finance* 29, pp. 449–70; reprinted in R. Merton 1990, *Continuous-Time Finance*, Chapter 12, pp. 388–412 (Cambridge, MA, Basil Blackwell).

Merton, R. C., 1976, "Option Pricing When Underlying Stock Returns are Discontinuous", *Journal of Financial Economics* 3, pp. 125–44; reprinted in R. Merton, 1990, *Continuous-Time Finance*, Chapter 9, pp. 309–29.

Merton, R. C., 1990, *Continuous-Time Finance* (Cambridge, MA: Basil Blackwell).

Merton, R. C., 1998, "Applications of Option-Pricing Theory: Twenty-Five Years Later", *American Economic Review* 88 (June 1998), pp. 323–49. URL: http://dor.hbs.edu/fi_redirect.jhtml?facInfo=bio&facEmId=rmerton.

Merton, R. C., and M. Scholes, 1995, "Fischer Black", *Journal of Finance* 50 (December), pp. 1359–70.

Parkinson, M., 1977, "Option Pricing: The American Put", *Journal of Business* 50, pp. 21–36.

Press, W. H., S. A. Teukolsky, W. T. Vetterling, and B. P. Flannery, 1993, *Numerical Recipes in C*, Second Edition (Cambridge University Press).

Rendleman, R., and B. Bartter, 1979, "Two-State Option Pricing", *Journal of Finance* 34, pp. 1093–110.

The Royal Swedish Academy of Sciences, 1997, Press Release: "The Sveriges Riksbank (Bank of Sweden) Prize in Economic Sciences in Memory of Alfred Nobel for 1997", 14 October 1997. URL: http://www.nobel.se/economics/laureates/1997/press.html.

Samuelson, P. A., 1965, "Rational Theory of Warrant Pricing", *Industrial Management Review* 6, pp. 13–31; reprinted in L. Hughston (ed), 1999, *Options: Classic Approaches to Pricing and Modelling*, Chapter 1 (London: Risk Books).

Samuelson, P. A., 1972, "Mathematics of speculative price", in R. H. Day and S. M. Robinson (eds), *Mathematical Topics in Economic Theory and Computation* (Philadelphia: SIAM), reprinted in Volume 4 of The Collected Scientific Papers of P. A. Samuelson, article 240.

Samuelson, P. A., and R. C. Merton, 1969, "A Complete Model of Warrant Pricing that Maximises Utility", *Sloan Management Review*, pp. 17–46. reprinted in R. Merton, 1990, Chapter 7, pp. 215–54.

Scheid, F., 1968, *Theory and Problems of Numerical Analysis* (New York: McGraw-Hill).

Scholes, M., 1998, "Derivatives in a Dynamic Environment", *American Economic Review* 88 (June 1998), pp. 350–70.

Schwartz, E. S., 1977, "The Valuation of Warrants: Implementing a New Approach", *Journal of Financial Economics* 4, pp. 79–93; reprinted in L. Hughston (ed), 1999, *Options: Classic Approaches to Pricing and Modelling*, Chapter 9 (London: Risk Books).

Sharpe, W. F., 1978, *Investments* (Englewood Cliffs, New Jersy: Prentice-Hall).

Smith, C. W., Jr., 1976, "Option Pricing; a Review", *Journal of Financial Economics* 3, pp. 3–51.

Smithson, C., 1991, "Wonderful life", *Risk*, pp. 37–44; reprinted at URL: http://www.rutterassociates.com/Articles/_Family%20Tree%20of%20Options%20(Risk,%20Oct91).htm.

Smithson, C., and S. Song, 1998, "Extended family", *A Nobel model; A Risk supplement: 25 years of Black-Scholes-Merton*, pp. 14–18. (London: Risk Publications), links to reprints of parts 1 and 2 of an earlier version are available at URL: http://www.rutterassociates.com/G.html.

Sprenkle, C. M., 1961, "Warrant Prices as Indicators of Expectations and Preferences", *Yale Economic Essays* 1, reprinted in P. Cootner (ed), 1964, *The Random Character of Stock Market Prices*, pp. 412–74. (Cambridge, MA: MIT Press).

Stoll, H., 1969, "The Relationship between Put and Call Option Prices", *Journal of Finance* 24, pp. 801–24; reprinted in L. Hughston (ed), 1999, *Options: Classic Approaches to Pricing and Modelling*, Chapter 2 (London: Risk Books).

Stringham, E., 2002, "The Extralegal Development of Securities Trading in Seventeenth-Century Amsterdam", *Quarterly Review of Economics and Finance*, forthcoming.

Stulz, R., 1982, "Options on the Minimum or Maximum of Two Risky Assets, Analysis and Applications", *Journal of Financial Economics* 10, pp. 161–85.

Tanenbaum, R., 1985, "Beyond Portfolio Insurance, or, The Poor Person's Portfolio Protective Put Pricing Paradigm", presented to the Investment Technology Association, New York.

Taqqu, M., 2001, "Bachelier and his Times: A Conversation with Bernard Bru", URL: http://neyman.mathematik.uni-freiburg.de/bfsweb/LBachelier/bachelier_kap1.pdf.

Thorp, E. O., and S. Kassouf, 1967, *Beat the Market* (New York: Random House).

Wiggins, J. B., 1985, "Stochastic Variance Option Pricing", Sloan School of Management, MIT.

4

Markowitz Mean-Variance Portfolio Theory

Neil D. Pearson

University of Illinois at Urbana-Champaign

INTRODUCTION

In its own right, the mean-variance theory, originally due to Markowitz (Markowitz, 1952; 1959; 1987), is an important theory of how investors optimally should select portfolios, ie, it is an important normative theory of portfolio choice. Beyond that, the Markowitz mean-variance framework provides the foundation for the capital asset pricing model (CAPM), and related theories of asset pricing that purport to describe expected returns. In addition, these ideas have played an influential role in risk measurement; factor models used to model portfolio returns are elaborations of the "single-factor" model often associated with the CAPM, and simple (ie, delta-normal) versions of value-at-risk (VAR) are based on calculations of the mean and variance of portfolio returns. These areas – normative portfolio choice, equilibrium theories of risk and return, and techniques of risk measurement – comprise the intellectual underpinnings of much of modern finance. Despite their central role in modern finance, the importance of these ideas was not initially recognised. Markowitz's ideas about mean-variance portfolio choice were originally developed in his PhD dissertation in the economics department of the University of Chicago. Markowitz (1990) recounts that at his dissertation defense Milton Friedman argued that the dissertation was "not economics", and that Markowitz could therefore not be awarded a degree in economics. Fortunately, Professor Friedman's argument did not carry the day, and the young Markowitz successfully defended his dissertation.

This chapter briefly describes the mean-variance theory and discusses some traditional criticisms of it. It then describes implementations of mean-variance optimisation, and summarises the key difficulty. The chapter concludes by briefly indicating some further developments and applications of the theory.

THE MEAN-VARIANCE THEORY

Diversification is the focus of the mean-variance theory. In retrospect, the role of diversification seems so obvious that it might be difficult to believe that presenting a theory of optimal portfolio choice based on diversification could eventually lead to the 1990 Prize in Economic Sciences in Memory of Alfred Nobel. But that we take for granted diversification and the mean-variance framework is a measure of how influential Markowitz has been. When he began his work, the literature did not contain a correct analysis of diversification. Markowitz (1990) says that the principles of portfolio theory came to him while he was reading arguments in the then standard work by Williams (1938) that implied that investors should invest only in the security which gives the maximum expected return.

The insight that led to the theory is the recognition that diversification can be modelled using the covariance matrix of portfolio returns. The value of a portfolio is the weighted (by size of positions) sum of the values of the securities in the portfolio, and the portfolio return is the weighted (by proportion of portfolio value) sum of the returns on the constituent securities. Thus, the portfolio return is a linear combination of random variables; the returns of the securities that comprise the portfolio. This immediately leads to the following expressions for the mean and variance of the portfolio return:

$$E[r] = \sum_{i=1}^{N} w_i E[r_i] \tag{1}$$

$$\text{var}[r] = \sum_{i=1}^{N} \sum_{j=1}^{N} w_i w_j \sigma_i \sigma_j \rho_{ij} \tag{2}$$

where r is the portfolio return, r_i is the return on the ith of the N securities in the portfolio, w_i is the fraction of the portfolio value invested in the i-th security, σ_i is the standard deviation of the returns on the ith security, and ρ_{ij} is the correlation between the returns of the ith and jth securities. Recognising that when $i = j$ the correlation $\rho_{ij} = 1$ and the covariance $\sigma_i\sigma_j\rho_{ij} = \sigma_i^2$, the variance of the returns of the ith security, Equation (1) becomes

$$\text{var}[r] = \sum_{i=1}^{N}\sum_{j=1}^{N} w_i w_j \sigma_i \sigma_j \rho_{ij} = \sum_{i=1}^{N} w_i^2 \, \text{var}[r_i] + \sum_{i=1}^{N}\sum_{j \neq i}^{N} w_i w_j \, \text{cov}[r_i, r_j] \quad (3)$$

The right-hand side of Equation (3) includes N variance terms and $N(N-1)$ covariance terms, so that, except in the cases of uncorrelated returns or portfolios with very few securities, the covariance terms dominate the calculation.

The mean-variance theory says that investors should select from the set of what are now called mean-variance efficient portfolios. A mean-variance efficient portfolio is one that has the maximum expected return (mean) for a given level of variance. These efficient portfolios can be obtained by first finding the minimum variance portfolio for each possible mean return; a minimum variance portfolio solves the problem

$$\min_{\{w_i\}} \sum_{i=1}^{N}\sum_{j=1}^{N} w_i w_j \sigma_i \sigma_j \rho_{ij} \quad (4)$$

subject to the constraints

$$\sum_{i=1}^{N} w_i E[r_i] = \mu \quad (5)$$

$$\sum_{i=1}^{N} w_i = 1 \quad (6)$$

The second constraint, given in Equation (6), simply requires that the portfolio be fully invested. Letting the portfolio mean return μ vary from negative to positive infinity traces out the set of minimum variance portfolios. The parabola shown in Figure 1 is an

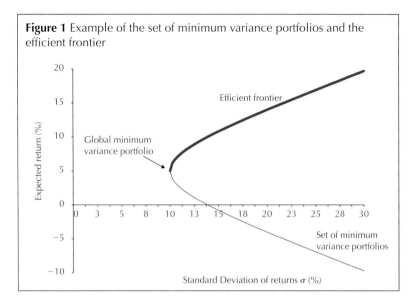

Figure 1 Example of the set of minimum variance portfolios and the efficient frontier

example of this set. Following the standard convention, it shows the minimum variance portfolios in terms of the portfolio standard deviation $\sigma = \sqrt{\text{var}(r)}$ and mean μ instead of the mean and variance. In particular, for each level of the expected return μ on the left-hand axis, it shows the minimum portfolio standard deviation σ that can be achieved from portfolios of the N securities. Each point corresponds to a particular portfolio that achieves that combination of standard deviation and expected return.

The efficient frontier is the upper portion to the right of the point labelled "global minimum variance portfolio", and is shown in a slightly heavier line. The global minimum variance portfolio itself is the portfolio with the minimum variance or standard deviation that can be achieved, subject to the constraint, given in Equation (6), that the portfolio be fully invested. The global minimum variance is not zero because:

1. we have not yet allowed for a risk-free asset, such as US Treasury bills; and
2. it is assumed that no two securities or combinations of securities have perfectly correlated returns, so it is impossible to create a risk-free position.

The mean-variance theory states that investors should select from among those portfolios on the efficient frontier; for every other choice, there exists a portfolio on the efficient frontier with the same variance or standard deviation but higher expected return.

If we introduce a risk-free asset with return r_0 and let w_0 denote the fraction of the portfolio invested in it, the set of minimum variance portfolios is given by

$$\min_{\{w_i\}} \sum_{i=1}^{N} \sum_{j=1}^{N} w_i w_j \sigma_i \sigma_j \rho_{ij} \tag{7}$$

subject to the constraints

$$\sum_{i=1}^{N} w_i E[r_i] + w_0 r_0 = \mu \tag{8}$$

$$\sum_{i=0}^{N} w_i = 1 \tag{9}$$

Using the last constraint to eliminate w_0, Equation (8) becomes

$$\sum_{i=1}^{N} w_i (E[r_i] - r_0) + r_0 = \mu \tag{10}$$

By investing all of her wealth in the risk-free security (that is, setting $w_0 = 1$ and $w_i = 0$ for $i \neq 0$) the investor can now achieve a portfolio standard deviation of zero and a return equal to the risk-free rate of 2%; this point is shown on the left-hand side of Figure 2. Of course, the investor can still obtain the (σ, μ) combination shown by the point labelled (20%, 14%). By taking convex combinations of these two points, the investor can obtain any combination on the line segment connecting them. For example, by investing one-half of her portfolio in the risk-free asset and one-half in the portfolio with $\sigma = 20\%$, $\mu = 14\%$, the investor can achieve a (σ, μ) combination of (0%, 2%)/2 + (20%, 14%)/2 = (10%, 7%), which is also shown in Figure 2. Further, by taking a negative position in the risk-free asset (borrowing), the investor can obtain points on the red line to the right of the point (20%, 14%). Because the investor can achieve all of

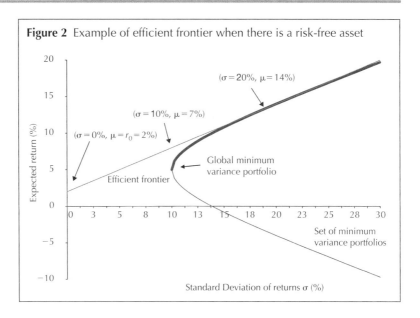

Figure 2 Example of efficient frontier when there is a risk-free asset

the (σ, μ) combinations on the line, when there is a risk-free asset it is the efficient frontier.

The analysis so far has ignored short-sale constraints of the form $w_i \geq 0$ and restrictions on the maximum possible positions in various securities or asset classes, perhaps of the form $w_i \leq k_i$ or $\sum_{i \text{ in industry } Z} w_i \leq k$. In actual implementations of the mean-variance portfolio theory it is common to have such constraints in addition to Equations (3) and (4). Such constraints affect the efficient frontier, as some efficient portfolios will no longer be feasible. For example, if borrowing is forbidden (ie, if there is a constraint $w_0 \geq 0$), it will not be possible to achieve the (σ, μ) combinations on the line to the right of the point (20%, 14%). Instead, to the right of (20%, 14%) the efficient frontier will consist of the segment of the parabola to the right of (20%, 14%).

TRADITIONAL CONCERNS: DOES THE MEAN-VARIANCE THEORY MAKE SENSE?

The issue of whether a portfolio theory based on mean and variance makes any sense cannot be avoided. For investors to care only about mean and variance, it must be that either:

1. investors have quadratic utility functions; or

2. the joint distribution of the returns on securities is such that portfolio returns (that is, linear combinations of securities returns) can be completely characterised by mean and variance.

Both of these conditions are manifestly false. If utility functions are quadratic and concave (ie, investors are risk averse) then for sufficiently high wealth levels utility will be decreasing in wealth. The distributional assumptions required are equally unsupportable, as it is impossible for the returns on both a risky security and options on that security to satisfy them. In addition, there are issues of skewness and excess kurtosis of returns that have received a great deal of attention in recent years.

Further, it is unlikely that investors care only about end-of-period wealth, as assumed in the theory. For example, having low wealth when capital market investment opportunities are good, allowing for a future recovery in wealth and consumption, will be less painful than low wealth when investment opportunities are poor. It seems better to assume that investors care about lifetime consumption and perhaps the value of any bequest that they leave, as in the intertemporal consumption-portfolio problem and capital asset pricing model studied by Merton (1971, 1973). If investors care about lifetime consumption they will want to hold portfolios that hedge changes in investment opportunities, eg they will want to hold portfolios that tend to have positive returns when investment opportunities are poor. In Merton's analysis, investors fail to hold such hedge portfolios only if they have log utility (which makes them myopic) or when securities returns are uncorrelated with changes in investment opportunities, eliminating the ability to hedge such changes.

Markowitz recognised that the mean-variance criterion is only an approximation to investors' expected utility, and he (Markowitz, 1959) and others (Levy and Markowitz, 1979; Kroll, Levy, and Markowitz, 1984; Ederington, 1986; and Simaan, 1987) have devoted a great deal of effort to showing that the mean-variance criterion is an adequate approximation to reasonable utility functions for the diversified portfolios that investors typically hold. Markowitz also recognised that end-of-period wealth is not an investor's only concern, but he devoted less attention to this. The real proof of the reasonableness of the mean-variance framework lies not in Markowitz's calculations, but rather in the extent to which market participants use it.

USING THE MEAN-VARIANCE THEORY

On one level, the mean-variance theory has been wildly successful. Despite its limitations it is the starting point for thinking about risk and return, and its influence is so pervasive that we often are unaware of it.

In addition to providing the standard framework for thinking about risk and return, the mean-variance theory is directly implemented by some investors who use "mean-variance optimisation" to select their portfolios. The two most popular applications are asset allocation and equity portfolio optimisation. In both cases, the optimisation is used to find those portfolios with maximum expected return for a given level of risk, ie, to identify those portfolios on the efficient frontier. There are, however, some differences between the two approaches.

In an asset allocation study, the number of risky assets is typically in the range of five to 20, and there are often few optimisation constraints. The assets generally include broad asset classes such as US and international equities, US and international bonds, emerging markets, real estate, and venture capital. The inputs (means, standard deviations, and correlations) are often based on estimates computed from historical returns, and the results are used as a guide to allocations among the asset classes.

An equity portfolio optimisation generally involves many more securities, typically hundreds for a domestic portfolio, and perhaps thousands for an international portfolio. Equity portfolio optimisations also typically include constraints on the maximum investments in individual securities, industry and sector concentrations, and perhaps others. In addition, it is common to do the analysis in terms of benchmark-relative returns and portfolio weights. That is, the returns r_i above are replaced by benchmark-relative returns $r_i - r_b$, where r_b is the return on a benchmark (eg, the S&P 500 index), the variances and covariances above are replaced by the variances and covariances of the relative returns, and the weights w_i are interpreted as deviations from the weights in the benchmark portfolio. Because these weights need not sum to one (it is usually feasible simply to invest in the benchmark portfolio, in which case the deviations from the benchmark are zero), there is typically no constraint analogous to Equation (6). Finally, the inputs are typically not based on historical data, but on some combination of proprietary forecasts, judgement, and asset pricing models, eg, some version or generalisation of the CAPM.

Yet another use of mean-variance optimisation is to create a tracking or index fund from a subset of the securities in the index. In this case the expected relative returns $r_i - r_b$ are assumed to be zero, and the optimiser is used to find the portfolio with the minimum tracking error subject to constraints on portfolio composition.

WHY DOESN'T EVERYONE USE MEAN-VARIANCE OPTIMISATION?

There are reasons to think that the mean-variance framework is a reasonable approximation, and it is taken for granted in much thinking about risk and return. Further, mean-variance optimisation is clearly feasible: some market participants do it, and consultants and software vendors sell optimisers. But despite the ubiquity of the framework, only a small fraction of market participants use optimisers. Why is this?

The short answer is that the "optimised" portfolios are often not optimal (see, eg, Michaud, 1989; 1998). To implement the mean-variance theory, one needs estimates of expected returns, variances, and covariances. If one had the right inputs, the optimised portfolio would be optimal. But one never has exactly the right inputs, and sometimes has quite poor estimates of them.

The estimation of expected returns is particularly problematic, for two reasons:

1. statistical estimates of mean returns based on past data are imprecise; and
2. the results of mean-variance optimisation can be very sensitive to the estimates of the expected returns (eg, Jobson and Korkie, 1980; 1981).

To get a sense of this, suppose that we want to use 120 months (10 years) of past returns to estimate the mean monthly return of a security for which the standard deviation of monthly returns is 8%. In this case the standard error of the estimate will be $\frac{8}{\sqrt{120}} = 0.73\%$, and with probability 5% the estimate will be more than

1.96(0.73) = 1.43 percentage points from the true mean of 8%. An error of 1.43 percentage points might not seem excessive. But if we repeat the exercise for a dozen or more asset classes it is likely that the error will be large for at least one or two asset classes; if we carry out the exercise for hundreds of securities it is almost certain that the error will be large for a few. The mean-variance optimiser will then tell us to take extremely large positions in the asset classes or securities for which we have badly overestimated the expected return, and short positions (or no investment, if short positions are not permitted) in the asset classes or securities for which we have badly underestimated the expected return. Thus, even though the historical average return is an unbiased estimator of the expected return, the estimate of the expected return on the "optimised" portfolio will be a badly biased estimate of the expected return on that portfolio. If we graph the efficient frontier in the (σ, μ) space in the usual way, the estimated efficient frontier will be shifted upward and to the left relative, and the mean-variance trade-off will appear to be more favourable than it actually is.

This problem is not unique to estimates of expected returns computed using historical data. Any estimate of expected returns, however obtained, will contain some errors, and the optimiser will tell the user to establish large positions in the asset classes or securities for which the user has overestimated the expected return, and to take short positions in the asset classes or securities for which he or she has underestimated the expected return.

Estimation errors in the covariance matrix can also be problematic. To see the issue, consider a simple example where one uses five years of monthly returns to estimate the covariance matrix of the returns of 100 securities. An unfortunate mathematical fact is that the covariance matrix estimated from 60 months of data will have rank of at most 60, ie, it will be singular. The financial interpretation of a singular estimated covariance matrix is that it will be possible to form portfolios that have (according to the estimated covariance matrix) no risk. This problem can be addressed by imposing some structure on the covariance matrix, perhaps using factor models. A cost of this, however, is that one runs the risk of assuming an incorrect form of the covariance matrix.

Recognising that the problem is that the optimiser tends to "plunge" in certain asset classes or securities, a simple *ad hoc* solution is to impose upper bounds on the weights and short-sale constraints. While this yields reasonable portfolio weights, they are not necessarily mean-variance efficient – the portfolios are to a large extent determined by the constraints. A more recent approach addresses the problem by improvements in estimation approaches, both by imposing restrictions implied by asset pricing theory and by using Bayesian and related techniques (Frost and Savorino, 1986; Ledoit, 1994; 1997). These approaches are appealing in that they comprise a coherent, logically consistent attack on the underlying estimation problem rather than an *ad hoc* patch affixed at the end, but they are not yet well accepted. Michaud (1998) provides a full discussion of these estimation issues and their implications.

CONCLUSION

As discussed above, the Markowitz mean-variance theory has been enormously influential – almost all of our thinking about risk and return begins with mean and variance. Moreover, many of the techniques of modern risk measurement such as VAR, Sharpe ratios, risk-adjusted return on capital (RAROC), return on risk-adjusted capital (RORAC), and risk-adjusted return on risk-adjusted capital (RARORAC) (see Chapters 4 and 8 of the current volume), are based on the mean-variance framework. Even modelling techniques such as extreme value theory and copulas, which explicitly reject the mean-variance framework, are symptoms of its success, because they are motivated by a desire to address its limitations. Despite this influence, the mean-variance theory has not been wholly successful as a method of picking optimal portfolios – it is too difficult to estimate the inputs with the required accuracy. Recent techniques to address this issue seem promising, but have not yet achieved acceptance.

BIBLIOGRAPHY

Ederington, L.H., 1986, "Mean-Variance as an Approximation to Expected Utility Maximization", Working Paper 86-5, Washington University.

Frost, P., and J. Savarino, 1986, "An Empirical Bayes Approach to Efficient Portfolio Selection", *Journal of Financial and Quantitative Analysis* 21(3), pp. 293–305.

Jobson, J.D., and B. Korkie, 1980, "Estimation for Markowitz Efficient Portfolios", *Journal of the American Statistical Association* 75(371), pp. 544–54.

Jobson, J.D., and B. Korkie, 1981, "Putting Markowitz Theory to Work", *Journal of Portfolio Management* 7(4), pp. 70–4.

Kroll, Y., H. Levy, and H.M. Markowitz, 1984, "Mean Variance versus Direct Utility Maximization", *Journal of Finance* 33(1), pp. 47–61.

Ledoit, O., 1994, "Portfolio Selection: Improved Covariance Matrix Estimation", Working Paper, MIT Sloan School of Management.

Ledoit, O., 1997, "Improved Estimation of the Covariance Matrix of Stock Returns with an Application to Portfolio Selection", Working Paper, Anderson School of Management at UCLA.

Levy, H., and H. M. Markowitz, 1979, "Approximating Expected Utility by a Function of Mean and Variance", *American Economic Review* 69(3), pp. 308–17.

Markowitz, H.M., 1952. "Portfolio Selection", *Journal of Finance* 7(1), pp. 77–91.

Markowitz, H.M., 1959, *Portfolio Selection: Efficient Diversification of Investments* (New York: John Wiley & Sons).

Markowitz, H.M., 1987, *Mean-Variance Analysis in Portfolio Choice and Capital Markets* (Cambridge, MA: Blackwell).

Markowitz, H.M., 1990, "Foundations of Portfolio Theory", Nobel Lecture; reprinted in *The Founders of Modern Finance: Their Prize-winning Concepts and 1990 Nobel Lectures* (Charlottesville, VA: The Institute of Chartered Financial Analysts).

Merton, R.C., 1971, "Optimum Consumption and Portfolio Rules in a Continuous-time Model", *Journal of Economic Theory* 3(4), pp. 373–413.

Merton, R.C., 1973, "An Intertemporal Capital Asset Pricing Model", *Econometrica* 41(5), pp. 867–87.

Michaud, R.O., 1989, "The Markowitz Optimisation Enigma: Is Optimised Optimal?", *Financial Analysts Journal* 45(1), pp. 31–42.

Michaud, R.O., 1998, *Efficient Asset Management: A Practical Guide to Stock Portfolio Optimisation and Asset Allocation* (Boston: Harvard Business School Press).

Simaan, Y., 1987, "Portfolio Selection and Capital Asset Pricing for a Class of Non-Spherical Distributions of Assets Returns", PhD dissertation, Baruch College, The City University of New York.

Williams, J.B., 1938, *The Theory of Investment Value* (Cambridge, MA: Harvard University Press).

5

Equilibrium Asset Pricing and Discount Factors: Overview and Implications for Derivatives Valuation and Risk Management

John H. Cochrane and Christopher L. Culp

Graduate School of Business, The University of Chicago

Price is expected discounted payoff. This fundamental relation underlies all asset pricing. The discount factor is an index of "bad times". Because investors are willing to pay more for assets that do well in bad times, the risk premium on any asset is determined by how it co-varies with the discount factor. All of asset pricing comes down to techniques for measuring a discount factor in a way that is useful for specific applications. We first survey the theoretically pure consumption-based discount factor model and some of its practical counterparts, including the capital asset pricing model (CAPM) and intertemporal CAPM. We also survey recent literature that points to recession and distress-related components of a discount factor to supplement the traditional market portfolio/ beta component. As an important practical implication, we show how asset pricing concepts can help investors and hedgers distinguish properly between "systematic" and "idiosyncratic" risk. We also explain how a little bit of thinking about the fundamental determinants of discount factors can go a long way towards evaluating market price of risks that bedevil practical application of derivative pricing theories. Finally, we emphasise where the pure theory requires various stages of equilibrium and market completeness, and where the theory can still be used out of such equilibrium or in the presence of incomplete markets.

INTRODUCTION

All of asset pricing comes down to one central idea: the value of an asset is equal to its expected discounted payoff. The rest is elaboration, special cases, a closet full of clever tricks, and, above all, a set of specifications for the discount factor that make this central idea useful for one or another application.

There are two fundamental and polar approaches to applying the central idea: *absolute* and *relative* asset pricing. In *absolute* pricing, we value a bundle of cashflows (dividends, coupons and principle, option payoffs, firm profits, etc) based on its exposure to fundamental sources of macroeconomic risk. Equivalently, we find a discount factor by thinking about what macroeconomic states are of particular concern to investors. The CAPM is a paradigm example of this approach. Virtually all such models are based on some notion of general equilibrium in order to use aggregate rather than individual risks, or to substitute an easily measured index such as the market return (CAPM) for poorly measured consumption. They are therefore often called equilibrium asset pricing models.

In *relative* pricing, by contrast, we ask what we can learn about one asset's value *given* the prices of some other assets. We do not ask from where the prices of the other assets came, and we use as little information about macroeconomic risk factors as possible. Modigliani and Miller (1958) pioneered this approach in valuing a firm *given* prices for its equity and debt, and Black and Scholes (1976) famously used this approach to value options and corporate liabilities *given* stock and bond prices.

Absolute pricing offers generality – it can be applied to anything – at the cost of precision in many applications. Relative pricing offers simplicity and tractability – it can be done easily, at least to a first approximation – at the cost of often-limited practical applicability.[1] Most good applications do not use one extreme or the other, but rather a blend of absolute and relative approaches appropriate for the problem at hand. Even the most die-hard applications of the CAPM, for example, usually take the market risk premium as given. Conversely, most realistic option pricing exercises implicitly use some absolute pricing model to characterise pesky "market prices of risk" that cannot be perfectly hedged.

Why should you care? Study of the "assumptions" behind theoretical models is often viewed as about the driest subject in finance.

But understanding these models and the assumptions under which they hold is vital before modern ideas can be correctly and creatively applied to actual financial problems. To value a potential investment, for example, you have to know what discount rate to use. Does the famed CAPM "beta" give the right discount rate? Even if the investor holds a portfolio different than the market portfolio, such as owning a small business? Even if other investors do not hold the market portfolio as the CAPM assumes? Or, suppose you want to set up a hedging program, but a perfect hedge is impossible. How should you value the residual risks or tracking errors? How do you know when you should take *more* of those residual risks in order to profit from their premia? Only by really understanding where absolute equilibrium asset pricing models come from can you begin to confidently answer these sorts of questions.

The theory we survey here is at the foundation of everything in asset pricing. It may look simple in hindsight, but this theory led directly to five Nobel Prize presentations in economic sciences, and to at least another five indirectly.[2] This chapter is longer than the others in this book, but it is so because our contribution is unifying: rather than devoting a separate chapter in this section to each application of the single fundamental value equation, we survey them all and show how they are each applications of the same simple idea.

THE ECONOMIC INTUITION FOR VALUING
UNCERTAIN CASHFLOW STREAMS

The basic objective of asset pricing is to determine the value of any stream of uncertain cashflows. Consider an asset with a single cashflow or payoff x_{t+1} at time $t + 1$. (This payoff can be the price at $t + 1$ plus any dividend, so we have not abandoned the real world.) We find the value of this payoff by asking what the stream is worth to an investor.[3] The answer is:

$$p_t = E_t \left[\beta \frac{u_c(c_{t+1})}{u_c(c_t)} x_{t+1} \right] \tag{1}$$

where β is the investor's discount rate, $E_t[\cdot]$ denotes an expected value conditional on information available at time t, and $u_c(c_t)$ is the benefit to the investor of a small additional unit of consumption received at time period t (ie, the "marginal utility" of time t consumption).

This is the basic equation underlying all of asset pricing, so it is worth understanding carefully. (The appendix presents a mathematical derivation.) Investors do not value money directly. The theory adopts a more sophisticated approach and recognises that the pleasure or "utility" of the consumption that money can buy is what really matters. That is why u_c and β enter Equation (1). Specifically, people value money more if it comes sooner, and if it comes in bad times when they really need it rather than good times when they are already doing well. A β slightly less than one and a marginal utility function u_c that declines as c increases capture these important considerations. If the economist's "utility function" sounds strange, just think of $u_c(c_t)$ as an index of "bad times", or a measure of how painful it is to give up a dollar at date t.

Equation (1) then describes the investor's optimal portfolio decision as marginal cost of investment equals marginal benefit. The true cost of an extra dollar invested is the price of the asset p_t (how many dollars the investor had to give up) times the value of a dollar (utility cost to the investor) $u_c(c_t)$ at time t. The true benefit is the expectation E_t of the dollar payoff x_{t+1} times the value of a dollar $u_c(c_{t+1})$ at time $t + 1$, times β which discounts future value (utility) back to time t.

The logic of Equation (1) is often confused. Equation (1) is usually used to describe a market "in equilibrium", *after* the investor has reached his or her optimum portfolio. But to get to that optimum, the investor had to know the price p_t. What's going on? In watching a market "in equilibrium", we are like scientists, watching over the market in white lab coats and trying to under-stand what it does. Equation (1) holds once the investor has found the optimal portfolio, but it does not describe causes on the right and effects on the left. If we observe consumption and payoff, we can use this equation to determine what the price must be. If we observe consumption and prices (a common case), we can use the equation to learn what the expected payoff (eg, expected return in the case of stocks) must be. If we observe price, consumption, and payoff (the entire distribution of payoffs, mind you, not just how it happened to come out a few times), then we can use Equation (1) to decide that the world really does make sense after all.

We can also use Equation (1) to think of the value of payoff x_{t+1} to an investor who has *not* yet bought any of that asset – ie, who has not found the optimum portfolio or when the market is "out of equilibrium". This interpretation is especially important in thinking about the potential value of securities that have not been created or are not traded or in giving portfolio advice. Now the value p_t need not correspond to the market price (there might not be one), and the investor need not know what the price is. Still, we can compute the value of a *small incremental investment* in this uncertain cashflow to *this particular investor* by Equation (1). If there is a market price, and the value to the investor is greater than that price, we can recommend a buy. Similarly, we can compare our private valuation with market prices of derivatives to evaluate the desirability and cost of various hedging opportunities.[4]

THE FUNDAMENTAL VALUE EQUATION

We commonly split the fundamental value Equation (1) into two parts, one that expresses price as an expected discounted payoff

$$p_t = E_t[m_{t+1}\, x_{t+1}] \qquad (2)$$

and one that relates the *stochastic discount factor* m_{t+1} to the *intertemporal marginal rate of substitution*, the rate at which the investor is willing to substitute one unit of consumption now for one unit of consumption later:

$$m_{t+1} = \beta \frac{u_c(c_{t+1})}{u_c(c_t)} \qquad (3)$$

The term m_{t+1} is called a *stochastic discount factor* by analogy with simple present value rules. We are used to discounting a payoff by some discount factor or required rate of return R – if x_{t+1} is known:

$$p_t = \frac{1}{R}\, x_{t+1}$$

The term m_{t+1} acts exactly as such a discount factor in Equation (2). The discount factor term m_{t+1} is *stochastic* because nobody at time t knows what consumption will be at time $t+1$ (whether $t+1$ will be a good or bad time), and hence nobody knows what $u_c(c_{t+1})$ will turn out to be. It is random, in the same way stock returns are random.

This randomness of the discount factor is crucial. As the index of good and bad times, the stochastic discount factor is high if time $t+1$ turns out to be a bad time (ie, consumption is low). Assets that pay off well in bad times are particularly valuable, and Equation (2) will give them an appropriately high price.

In finance, we commonly do not think too much about consumption and utility functions. The stochastic discount factor remains an index of bad times (strictly speaking, *growth* in bad times). Finance theorists tend to think directly about discount factor models in which data such as the market return are used as indicators of bad vs good times.

The fundamental valuation equation in different guises

The stochastic discount factor representation of the fundamental value equation, Equation (2), can be expressed in a number of different and equivalent ways depending on the nature of the particular financial problem being solved, and the history and traditions of different fields. (As usual, unification came after the fact.)

If we use required returns to value a project or compute a capital budget, we typically use a different, risk-adjusted required return for each project. The beauty of Equations (1) or (2) is that the *same* discount factor can be used for *all* assets, simply by putting it inside the expectation – m is a *universal* discount factor. Capital budgeting thus can be undertaken using Equation (2) directly. For a project that costs I_t in initial investment and generates X_{t+1} in revenue at time $t+1$, the usual net present value criterion tells us to undertake the investment if its value is greater than its cost,

$$E_t[m_{t+1} \, X_{t+1}] \geq I_t$$

In applications to stocks and portfolios, it is often convenient to think about rates of return rather than prices. To do so, we divide both sides of Equation (2) by p_t (or recognise that a return is a payoff with price equal to one):

$$1 = E_t[m_{t+1} R_{t+1}] \qquad (4)$$

where R_{t+1} is the gross return on the asset (x_{t+1} divided by p_t). Thus, simply use "return" for the payoff x and one for price to apply the equation to stocks and portfolio problems. Similarly, if we want to work with returns in excess of the risk-free rate $r_{t+1} \equiv R_{t+1} - R^f$ then Equation (4) becomes[5]

$$0 = E_t[m_{t+1} r_{t+1}] \qquad (5)$$

In equity analysis, we are used to a slight transformation of Equation (5). Using a superscript i to remind us that there are many assets, writing out the definition of covariance $E(mr^i) = E(m)E(r^i) + \text{cov}(m, r^i)$ and the definition of a regression coefficient $\beta_i = \text{cov}(m, r^i)/\text{var}(m)$ and then defining $\lambda = -\text{var}(m)/E(m)$, we can write Equation (5) in classic form as

$$E_t(r^i) = \beta_i \lambda \qquad (6)$$

The expected excess return of each asset should be proportional to its beta.

This is not the CAPM – it is *perfectly general*. The beta here is calculated relative to the discount factor, not the market return. All the assumptions of the CAPM (or other models) come in substituting the market portfolio return or some other index for the discount factor.

To determine the fixed price in a forward purchase contract or swap, we look for the fixed price or rate K that equates the *initial* discounted expected value of the transaction to zero. Otherwise, one of the two parties would walk away from the deal. If a forward purchase contract calls for the future delivery of one unit of an asset at time $t + 1$ whose value on that date is P_{t+1}, then the fixed price in the forward is found as[6]

$$E_t[m_{t+1} (P_{t+1} - K)] = 0 \Rightarrow K = E_t[P_{t+1}] + \text{cov}_t(m_{t+1}, P_{t+1})R^f$$

In other words, the forward price K is the expected future spot price of the asset to be purchased at time $t+1$ plus a term that reflects how the discount factor co-varies with the underlying spot price – as we shall see later, a "risk premium". The second term is grossed up by the risk-free rate to reflect the fact that the terms of the contract are set at time t but the contract is settled at time $t+1$.

In option pricing and fixed income applications, the discount factor m_{t+1} is often used to define a set of "risk-neutral probabilities". Equation (2) is written simply as

$$p_t = \frac{1}{R^f} E_t^* \left[x_{t+1} \right]$$

where the $*$ reminds us to take the expectation with an artificial set of probabilities that are scaled by m_{t+1}. We can either use the discount factor to make good payments in bad states more important in determining the price, or we can boost up the probabilities of those states to the same effect. Risk aversion is the same thing as overestimating the probability of bad events.

All these formulations are just different ways of writing the same thing. Continuous-time asset pricing models also all reduce to the analogue to Equation (2) in continuous time.[7]

UNDERSTANDING "SYSTEMATIC" RISK

Asset pricing is about risk and reward. Identifying risks and assessing the premium one earns for bearing risks are the central questions for asset pricing, and the point of theory is to provide necessary quantitative tools to answer these questions. Risk managers tend to classify risk as market, credit, liquidity, operational, or legal. Portfolio managers tend to think of market risk, and the risks associated with certain styles such as size, value, and growth, as well as risks associated with industry and country portfolios.

Financial economists tend instead to distinguish between "systematic" and "idiosyncratic" risk. And of course, not all risk is bad – you only earn a premium over risk-free interest rates by taking on some risk! What risks should we pay attention to? And how are these concepts related?

"Systematic" vs "Idiosyncratic" risk

A central and classic idea in asset pricing is that only systematic risk generates a premium. Idiosyncratic risks are "not priced", meaning that you earn no more than the interest rate for holding them. That is why we employ risk managers to get rid of idiosyncratic risks.[8] Plausible, but a theory proves its worth by helping us to understand what "systematic" and "idiosyncratic" mean in this context.

By using the definition of covariance $E(mx) = E(m)E(x) + \text{cov}(m, x)$ we can re-write the fundamental value Equation (2) as

$$p_t = \frac{E_t\left[x_{t+1}\right]}{R^f} + \text{cov}\left(m_{t+1}, x_{t+1}\right) \qquad (7)$$

This equation says that asset prices are equal to the expected cashflow discounted at the risk-free rate, plus a risk premium. The risk premium depends on the *covariance* of the payoff with the discount factor. This covariance is typically a negative number, so most assets have a lower price than otherwise (or a higher average return) as compensation for risk.

Here's why. Recall that the discount factor is an indicator of *bad* times. Most assets pay off well in *good* times. Thus, most asset returns and payoffs co-vary negatively with the discount factor. The converse case drives home the intuition. Insurance is a terrible investment. The average return is negative – you pay more in premiums than you receive, on average, in settlements. Yet people willingly buy insurance. Why? Because insurance pays off well in bad times – just as the house stops smouldering, a cheque arrives in the post. The value of insurance is *higher* than predicted by the standard present value formula, because the covariance term is *positive*. Financial assets are "anti-insurance", and it is this feature, and *only* this feature, that generates a risk premium and allows risky assets to pay more than the interest rate.

Equation (7) has a dramatic implication: a risk may be very large in the sense of having a high *variance*, but if it is uncorrelated with the discount factor, its *covariance* is zero, and it generates no premium. Its price is just the expected payoff discounted at the risk-free rate. *The volatility of the asset's cashflow per se is completely irrelevant to its risk premium.*

To see why in more detail, consider an investor who adds a small fraction Ψ of the asset to their portfolio. Her consumption at time $t + 1$ is now $c_{t+1} + \Psi x_{t+1}$. As always, the investor cares about the variance of *consumption* and the variance of the utility that consumption generates, not any characteristics of single assets that, in a portfolio, determine the wealth from which they draw consumption. For a small asset purchase, the variance of the investor's new time $t + 1$ consumption is

$$\text{Var}(c_{t+1}) + 2\Psi\text{Cov}(c_{t+1}, x_{t+1}) + \Psi^2 \text{Var}(x_{t+1})$$

The covariance with consumption, and hence with marginal utility m, enters with a coefficient Ψ, while the variance is a second-order effect. For a small (marginal) investment Ψ, the covariance of the cashflows on the asset with consumption is much more important to how buying the asset affects consumption – what investors care about in the end – than the volatility of the asset's cashflows.

Now we can really understand and precisely define "systematic" vs "idiosyncratic" risk. *The systematic part of any risk is that part that is perfectly correlated with the discount factor.* It is the part that generates a risk premium. The idiosyncratic part of any risk is that part that is uncorrelated with the discount factor; it generates no premium.

We can divide any payoff into systematic and idiosyncratic components by simply running a regression of the payoff on the discount factor:

$$x_{t+1} = \beta m_{t+1} + \varepsilon_{t+1} \tag{8}$$

payoff = systematic part + idiosyncratic part

Regression residuals ε_{t+1} are, by construction, uncorrelated with the right hand variable.

Once again, this modern version of the theory is perfectly general. Systematic means correlated with the investor's marginal utility – *full stop*. This is true no matter what "asset pricing model" – no matter what specification of the discount factor – is correct. The CAPM, for example is one special case of the general theory. It specifies that the discount factor is linearly related to the market return $m_{t+1} = a - bR_{t+1}$ (more on this below). Hence, it defines systematic risk for every asset by regressions of returns on to the market portfolio return.

In many portfolio management applications, "systematic" and "diversifiable" components are defined with multiple regressions on style portfolios, including size, book to market value, and industry groupings as well as the market portfolio. Implicitly, these definitions correspond to models that the discount factor is a function of these portfolio groupings. These specifications are fine, but they are special cases and they reflect lots of hidden assumptions. Other specifications may be useful.

When variance does matter

The proposition that variance does not matter for risk premia does not mean "ignore variance in setting up your portfolio". Again, Equations (2) and (7) refer only to *marginal* valuations. That is appropriate *after* the investor has already set up an optimal portfolio, or for deciding which asset to *start* buying. For very little portfolio changes, covariance matters more than variance.

For big asset purchases and sales of the sort one considers while setting up the optimal portfolio to begin with, however, variance can matter a lot. If an investor buys a big part of a payoff, the variance *will* start to affect the properties of consumption, marginal utility, and hence the investor's discount factor. So, by all means *do* consider variance in making the big changes required to set up a portfolio!

Diversification, hedging, and special investors

We often think of "idiosyncratic" risks as those risks that affect a particular security only, leaving all others untouched. Such idiosyncratic risks include firm-specific risks like operational and liquidity risk, as well as those components of market and credit risk that are unique to the firm in question. This is a good approximation in many cases, but understanding the correct definition we can quickly see how it is only an approximation.

A risk that moves many securities, but is uncorrelated with the discount factor, is also "idiosyncratic". The market as a whole is built of individual securities, so each "idiosyncratic" risk is in fact a small part of the "total" risk. Many apparently "firm-specific" risks – a drop in sales, an accounting fiasco, etc – also hit many other firms in the market, and thus *become* "market risks". We often call "idiosyncratic" risks "diversifiable" because they largely disappear in well-diversified portfolios. This too is a good approximation, but specific to the CAPM world that the market portfolio return captures the discount factor and thus defines "systematic" risk.

A good counterexample for all these cases is to think of an investor who must hold a large part of some risk. Consider, for example, the owner of a business who must hold a large amount of one company's stock. Risks correlated with the business or company stock will be "systematic" for this investor, albeit not necessarily for the market as a whole. The investor thus must require a premium to hold such risks, even though the market as a whole would not require such a premium. The CAPM is only an appropriate cost of capital for investment decisions if the investor holds the market portfolio, and thus his or her discount factor depends only on the market portfolio. For the vast majority of investors, this is not the case.

Although idiosyncratic risk does not matter for pricing, it is not necessarily easy to avoid it. Much of the art of risk management and corporate finance consists of just how to shed oneself of idiosyncratic or residual, non-priced, risk. The fact that risk managers focus on market, credit, liquidity, operational, or legal risk rather than systematic vs unsystematic risk reflects the different techniques needed to hedge different varieties of idiosyncratic risk. Risk managers, however, need to understand the real distinction between systematic and idiosyncratic risk so that they do not hedge good risks, ones that bring rewards, as well.

THE CAPITAL ASSET PRICING MODEL AND THE CONSUMPTION CAPITAL ASSET PRICING MODEL

A critical question for practical application remains: what data do we use for the discount factor m? The search to populate m with actual data has led to the many "named" asset pricing models. All of these models are just special cases of the fundamental value equation. They add additional structure, usually from simple general equilibrium modelling, to substitute some other variable for consumption in the discount factor.

The consumption CAPM

Armed with our presentation of the theory so far, the simple, obvious approach is to assume some reasonable utility function (power or quadratic forms are popular), use the easily available aggregate consumption data, and apply pricing Equations (2) or (7) directly. This is the famous approach of Lucas (1978) and Hansen and Singleton (1982).

A little less directly, but more popular in finance, we can linearly approximate the discount factor as a function of consumption:

$$m_{t+1} \approx a - \gamma \Delta c_{t+1}$$

where Δc_{t+1} denotes consumption growth and γ is a constant of proportionality.[9] This specification for the discount factor together with our fundamental value equation, Equation (2), is equivalent to the statement more popular in finance in terms of average returns and betas:

$$E(R^i) = R^f + \beta_{i,\Delta c} \lambda_{\Delta c} \qquad (9)$$

where $E(R^i)$ denotes the average return on the ith asset, $\beta_{i,\Delta c}$ is the regression beta of the asset return on consumption growth, and $\lambda_{\Delta c}$ is a market risk premium. Equation (9) predicts that assets with higher consumption betas will have higher average returns, with the market risk premium as constant of proportionality. This is the form of Breeden's (1979) famous statement of the consumption capital asset pricing model (CCAPM).

The basic idea is really natural. We need an indicator of bad and good times. If you really want to know how people feel, don't listen to them whine, watch where they go out to dinner. Consumption reveals everything we need to know about current wealth, future wealth, investment opportunities, and so on. Compared to many of the models discussed later, the CCAPM in all its simplicity avoids the theoretical problems associated with restrictive and unrealistic assumptions. (Historically, the CCAPM came last, in order to repair those problems.)

Although a complete answer to most absolute asset pricing questions in principle, this consumption-based approach does not (yet) work well in practice. As one might imagine from even a rudimentary experience with the data, running regressions of returns on the Government's consumption growth numbers does not reveal much. Instead, financial economists use a wide variety of tricks of the trade that, while requiring heroic "assumptions" to derive them as perfect truth, nonetheless have great intuitive appeal and have performed well in a variety of applications. At heart, they all involve substituting or proxying some other variables for hard-to-measures consumption.

The CAPM

The simplest and probably still the most popular model is the single-factor CAPM developed by Sharpe (1964) and Lintner (1965), and later extended by Black (1972). In the usual statement of the CAPM, the expected return of asset j is higher as its beta is higher, with the expected return on the market portfolio as a constant of proportionality:

$$E(R^j) = R^f + \beta_j\left[E(R^m) - R^f\right] \tag{10}$$

where R^j and R^m denote one-period arithmetic returns on asset j and the market, R^f denotes the risk-free interest rate, and where β_j is the regression coefficient of the return on the market, or

$$\beta_j = \frac{\text{Cov}(R^j, R^m)}{\text{Var}(R^m)}$$

The CAPM is *mathematically identical* to a specification of the discount factor that is linear in the market return, rather than linear in consumption growth

$$m_{t+1} = a - bR^m_{t+1} \tag{11}$$

a and b are free parameters that can be determined by the risk-free rate and market premium which are taken as given values in Equation (10). (See Equation (6) to make the connection between Equation (10) and a discount factor.)

The CAPM was a huge empirical success for a generation. Categories of assets have now been identified, however, whose average returns bear no relation to betas calculated against traditional proxy indices for the market portfolio. (Efforts to find theoretically purer proxies for the market portfolio of world invested wealth (Roll, 1977) do not help.) In addition, the betas calculated against several new risk factors apart from the market have been empirically shown to help explain why some average returns are higher than others. Prominent examples include the "small firm" and "value" effects (Banz, 1981, and Fama and French, 1993).

The CAPM discount factor model is a sensible approximation. When the market tanks, most people are unhappy! But it is clearly only an approximation. To *derive* the CAPM formally, you need to state assumptions under which a linear function of the market return is a *completely sufficient* indicator of good and bad times. The essence of the various formal derivations of the CAPM is to get every investor's consumption growth to depend only on the market return.[10]

The CAPM (and all following models) is not an *alternative* to the consumption-based model, it is a *special case*. Now, consumption surely goes down when the market return goes down, but, in the real world, other things matter as well. For the CAPM to hold, people cannot think that market fluctuations are temporary, and hence ignore a bad day and go out to dinner anyway. Instead, we must have returns that are independent over time. People cannot have jobs, houses, cars, businesses, or other sources of income that sustain them through market crashes, or these other things will start to matter to consumption and the discount factor. In addition, all investors in a CAPM world must hold the same portfolio of assets – the market portfolio.

Having seen how the sausage is made, we should be surprised, if anything, that the CAPM lasted as long as it did. We should not be surprised that it ultimately proved a first approximation.

MULTI-FACTOR MODELS

Linear factor models dominate empirical asset pricing in the post-CAPM world. Linear factor pricing models measure the discount factor – ie, specify indices of bad times – with a model of the form

$$m_{t+1} = \beta \frac{u_c\left(c_{t+1}\right)}{u_c\left(c_t\right)} = a + b_1 f_{t+1}^1 + b_2 f_{t+1}^2 + L + b_N f_{t+1}^N \tag{12}$$

where a, b_1, ..., b_N are free parameters and where f^j is the jth "risk factor".

What exactly does one use for factors f_{t+1}? In general, factor models look for variables that are plausible proxies for aggregate consumption or marginal utility growth (measures of whether times are getting better or worse). This is just like the CAPM, with additional indicators of good and bad times.

Intertemporal capital asset pricing model
Merton's (1973) multi-factor intertemporal CAPM (ICAPM) model was the first theoretical implementation of this idea. The ICAPM recognises that investors care about the market return, so that is the first risk factor. The extra factors are innovations to "state variables" that describe an investor's consumption-portfolio decision. Other things being equal, investors prefer assets that pay off well when there is news that *future* returns will be bad. Such assets provide insurance; they help to reduce the risk of long-term investments. Covariance with this kind of news thus will drive risk premia as well as the market return.

In the traditional statement of the model, corresponding to the expected-return statement of the CAPM in Equation (10),

$$E(R^j) - R^f = \gamma \, \text{Cov}(R^j, R^m) + \lambda_z \text{Cov}(R^j, \Delta z)$$

where γ and λ_z are constants (the same for all assets), R^m denotes the market (wealth) return and Δz indicates the news or the return on a "factor-mimicking portfolio" of returns correlated with that news.[11] Technically, this model generalises the CAPM assumption that the market return is independent over time.

Equivalently, for a given value of the market return, investors will feel poorer and will lower consumption if there is bad news about subsequent investment opportunities.[12] News about subsequent returns thus should drive our discount factor, as well as current market returns.

The ICAPM does not tell us the precise *identity* of the state variables, and, as a result, it is only after 30 years of theoretical fame that the ICAPM has received its first serious tests – tests that do not just cite it as inspiration for ad-hoc multifactor models, but actually check whether the factors do forecast returns as the theory says they should (see Ferson and Harvey, 1999). It is not yet common in applications.

One of the most popular current multi-factor models is the Fama-French three-factor model (Fama and French, 1993, 1996). The Fama-French model includes the market portfolio, a portfolio of small minus big stocks (SMB), and a portfolio of high book/market minus low book/market stocks (HML). In expected return language, average returns on all assets are linearly related to their regression betas on these three portfolios. In discount factor language, the discount factor is a linear function of these three portfolios, as the CAPM discount factor is a linear function of the market return.

This model is popular because the betas on the additional factors *do* explain the variation of average returns across the size and book-to-market portfolios, and market betas do not. The model is not a tautology. Size and book-to-market sorted portfolios do not have to move together, and move more as their average returns rise. Size and book to market betas also explain the variation of average returns across additional portfolio sorts, beyond those that they were constructed to explain (Fama and French, 1996). This kind of more general good performance is the hallmark of an empirically useful model.

The open question for the Fama-French model is: "what are the additional sources of risk about which investors are *economically* concerned?" It is well and good to say that investors fear "value" risk uncorrelated with the market, but why? Put another way, the sales talk for "value" portfolios is that, since other investors are so afraid of this risk, you, the remaining mean-variance investor, should load up on the "value" portfolio that provides high reward for small market beta. Fine, but if the *average* investor is really scared of this value risk, maybe you should be, too. If value risk turns out to be risk of poor performance during a financial crisis, for example, are you sure you want to take that risk? To answer this question, we really need to understand what fundamental macroeconomic risks are behind the value effect, not just understand a set of mimicking portfolios that capture them for empirical work.

An empirical counterpart to this worry is that the Fama-French model found its limitations as well. Namely, average returns on "momentum" portfolios go in the *opposite* direction predicted by Fama-French betas (see Fama and French, 1996). This can be cured by adding a fourth "momentum" factor, the return on a portfolio long recent winners and short recent losers. For all purposes except performance attribution (where it is exactly the right thing to do), however, this fix smells of such *ad-hockery* that nobody wants to take it seriously. We do not want to add a new factor for every anomaly. On the other hand, multifactor models used in many industry applications suffer no such compunction and proudly use 50 or 60 portfolios as factors, picked purely on the basis of in-sample empirical performance.

Macroeconomic multifactor models

The alternative to finding essentially ad-hoc portfolio factors that perform well for a given sample is to sit back and think about risk factors that make sense given the fundamental economic intuition. What variables are good indicators of bad vs good times for a large number of investors? The market return obviously still belongs. Following ICAPM intuition, variables that forecast future investment opportunities such as price/earnings ratios, the level of interest rates, etc, make sense. Indicators of recessions may belong as well, such as proprietary and labour income, the value of housing or other non-marketed assets, business investment, and so forth. The CAPM and ICAPM exclude these variables (ie, they derive relations in which the discount factor is *only* a function of the market return and state variables) by presuming that investors have no jobs or other assets; they simply live off their portfolios of financial assets. Because investors *do* have jobs and other assets, bad times for these will spill over into market premia.

With this intuition, a wide variety of asset pricing models have been used that tie average returns to macroeconomic risks. The grandfather of all of these is the Chen, Roll, and Ross (1986) multifactor model. They used interest rates, industrial production, inflation, and bond spreads to measure "bad times" in the discount factor. More recently, multi-factor models have used macroeconomic risk factors such as labour income (Jagannathan and Wang, 1996) and investment growth (Cochrane, 1991a, 1996) to explain expected stock returns.

Conditional factor models in which factors at time $t + 1$ are scaled by information variables at time t are also increasingly popular ways to allow betas and factor risk premia to vary over time (see Cochrane, 1996 and Lettau and Ludvigson, 2001).

All the special cases of the fundamental value equation that we have discussed so far impose the simplifying but very unrealistic assumption that markets are "complete", ie, investors have insured or hedged away all personal risks, and the only risks that affect their inter-temporal marginal rates of substitution (IMRS) are aggregate, market-wide or economy-wide risks. This too is obviously an extreme simplification, so it is worth seeing if removing the simplification works. Duffie and Constantinides (1996), for example, investigate a model in which the *cross-sectional* dispersion of labour income growth matters. Given that the *overall* income is what it is, it is a "bad time" if there is a lot of cross-sectional risk; you might become very rich, but you might also become very poor.

In addition, researchers such as Pastor and Stambaugh (2001) are finally documenting the importance of liquidity. Once dismissed as an institutional friction that is "assumed away" in complete markets, it seems that assets paying off poorly in times of poor market liquidity must pay higher average returns, *viz*, the discount factor is affected by liquidity. The marginal utility of a US dollar, delivered in the middle of a market meltdown such as after the Russian bond default and LTCM collapse, may well have been very high.

The current state of affairs – better than it looks

Unfortunately, no single empirical representation "wins", and the quest for a simple, reliable and commonly accepted implementation of the fundamental value equation continues. Models that are theoretically purer or that work over a wider range of applications tend to do worse in any given application and sample than models which are motivated by a specific application and sample. The "right" model, even if we had it, would take a long time to emerge relative to the large number of spurious fish in each pond.

This survey looks maddeningly tangled, with a long (and yet woefully incomplete!) list of approaches. But this appearance hides an exciting common theoretical and empirical consensus that has emerged from all this work: in addition to the market return specified by the CAPM, there are a few additional important dimensions of risk that drive premia in asset markets. If you take on assets with high betas on these risks, you will get higher returns on average, but these assets will all collapse together at times that many investors find very inconvenient. Those "times" are sometimes related to recessions – when peoples' job prospects are risky, wages are doing poorly, investment and new business formation are at a standstill – and at other times related to financial distress, poor market liquidity, and the like – when a US dollar in your pocket or an easily-liquidatable investment with a high price would be particularly convenient. The long list of empirical approaches mentioned above really only disagree about which particular data series to use to construct the best indicators of these two kinds of "bad times" unrelated to overall market returns.

FIXED INCOME AND COMMODITIES

The models used to price fixed income assets, commodities, and derivatives often simply amount to fairly *ad hoc* discount factor models. Consider first the factor models or affine models that dominate bond pricing, following Vasicek (1977), Brennan and Schwartz (1979), and Cox, Ingersoll and Ross (1985). In principle, valuing a bond is easier than valuing other securities, because the payoff is fixed. A one-year discount bond that will definitely pay one US dollar in one year's time has a value today of simply

$$p_t^{(1)} = E_t[m_{t+1}] \qquad (13)$$

where the superscript denotes maturity. To generate a bond-pricing model, you write down some model for the discount factor and then take expectations.

What makes bond pricing interesting and technically challenging is the presence of many maturities. For example, you can think of a two-period bond as a security whose payoff is a one-period bond, or as a two-period security directly. Its price is

$$p_t^{(2)} = E_t\left[m_{t+1}\, p_{t+1}^{(1)} \right] = E_t\left[m_{t+1}\, m_{t+2} \right] \qquad (14)$$

Pursuing the first equality in Equation (14), you can see an interesting recursion developing, leading to differential equations for prices (across maturity). Pursuing the second equality, you can see interesting expectations or integrals to take.

Still, we need a discount factor model to value bonds; so bond-pricing models all come down to discount factor models. The simplest example with which to show this point concretely is the discrete-time Vasicek model.[13] We write the following time series model for the discount factor:

$$\ln(m_{t+1}) = -x_t + \varepsilon_{t+1}$$
$$x_{t+1} = (1 - \phi)\mu + \phi x_t + \delta_{t+1}$$

where ϕ and μ are parameters and ε and δ are shock/error terms. We then find the prices and yields of one and two period bonds from the fundamental value equation, Equation (13), and Equation (14).[14] The result is a "one-factor model" for yields:

$$y_t^{(1)} = (1-\phi)\mu_y + y_{t-1}^{(1)} + \delta_{t+1}$$
$$y_t^{(2)} = const + \tfrac{1}{2}(1+\phi)y_t^{(1)} + \tfrac{1}{2}\text{cov}(\delta, \varepsilon)$$

The short rate $y_t^{(1)}$ evolves on its own as an autoregressive order one process (AR(1)). The two-period bond yield, and all other yields, are then linear functions of the one-year yield. All yields move in lockstep. "Two-factor" and "multi-factor" models work in the same way. For example, the Brennan and Schwartz (1979) two factor model has a long rate as well as a short rate moving autonomously and then all other yields following as functions of these two.

This model is *not* composed of an AR (1) for the short rate plus "arbitrage." The fly in the ointment is the third term in the last equation cov(δ, ε); this is the "market price of interest rate risk". It is the covariance of interest rate shocks with the discount factor. From Equation (7), we recognise it as the risk premium that an asset must pay whose payoff goes up and down with the interest rate. As this term varies, the two-year bond yield can take on any value. Term structure models typically just estimate this term as a free parameter – ie, the models pick this term to fit bond yields as well as possible.

That's fine as far as it goes, but it does not obviate what we are doing here. Just as before, cov(δ, ε) specifies the "systematic" part of interest rate risk. It specifies whether the marginal utility of consumption is higher or lower when interest rates rise unexpectedly. It specifies whether higher interest rates correspond to "good times" or "bad times", and how much so. Term structure models are no more immune from assumptions about consumption, macroeconomic risks, and so forth than anywhere else. Current term structure models are much like financial multi-factor models, discussed in the last section. The discount factor depends on rather arbitrary portfolio returns, selected for empirical fit (in sample) rather than even armchair theorising about good and bad states.

Often the discount factor modelling is implicit in a transformation to "risk-neutral probabilities". Recall that we can write the fundamental value equation as

$$p_t = E_t\left[m_{t+1}x_{t+1}\right] = \frac{1}{R^f}E_t^*\left[x_{t+1}\right]$$

where the $*$ indicates a expectation under altered "risk-neutral" probabilities. The transformation from E_t to E_t^* is called a "change of measure", and m_{t+1} is the transformation function. Algebraic manipulations can be much easier after the change of measure, but the economic content and implicit discount factor modelling are not changed. Exactly the same information must go in to forming the change of measure that goes into specifying the discount factor or market price of risk. In the same way, bond price authors often do not present the discount factor, but go directly to assumptions about the market price of risk, which we have labelled cov(δ, ε).

Similarly, the Gibson and Schwartz (1990) model for valuing long-term oil derivatives is based on oil price movements and changes in the convenience yield. Their model requires a "market price of oil price risk" and the "market price of convenience yield risk". These parameters are usually estimated to make the model fit well. Again, they are equivalent to specifying a discount factor.

The Keynesian risk premium on forward contracts is a third example of a commonly discussed "risk premium" equivalent to a statement about discount factors. In his *Treastise on Money* (Keynes, 1930), Keynes argued that speculators demand a risk premium from hedgers in order to accept a risk that hedgers want to "insure away". Keynes further argued that because hedgers tend to be long the underlying asset on average, they tend to be short forwards on average. The risk premium thus indicates a systematic bias of forward prices to be *above* expected future spot prices, so that for a forward purchase contract with fixed price K requiring the future delivery on an asset worth P_{t+1},

$$K = E_t[P_{t+1}] + \Theta$$

where Θ is the Keynesian risk premium, such that $\Theta > 0$.

Surprisingly, many people still adopt the Keynesian view that futures and forwards are biased predictors of future spot prices because speculators require a risk premium from hedgers. Yet, we saw earlier that the fixed price in a forward should just be

$$K = E_t[P_{t+1}] + \text{cov}_t(m_{t+1}, P_{t+1})R^f$$

The Keynesian risk premium amounts to an assumption about discount factors just like any other risk premium. The idea that *hedgers'* specific exposure drives the risk premium is an interesting one. It implies that both hedgers and investors at large are not perfectly diversified – that hedger's marginal utility drives risk premia in this market, even though aggregate marginal utility might produce no risk premium at all.

ARBITRAGE AND NEAR-ARBITRAGE PRICING

So far, we have only discussed "absolute" pricing methods. These methods specify a discount factor that can in principle price any asset, using only fundamental information (ie, the source of aggregate risks). In many applications, that is a far more powerful tool than is called for. Usually, we do not need to value every asset, we only want to value one asset, and we are happy to use the information about the prices of similar assets in order to do so. In this case a *relative* pricing approach is useful. To find the value of a McDonald's hamburger, absolute pricing starts thinking about how much it costs to feed a cow. Relative pricing looks at the price of a hamburger at Burger King. For many purposes, such as deciding where to eat, this is good enough. In finance, option valuation and corporate finance (the use of comparable investments to determine required rates of return) are the prime applications of relative pricing methods.

The central question is, as always, how to construct a discount factor. The relative pricing approach uses information from *other* asset prices in order to construct a discount factor useful for pricing a *given* asset.

Arbitrage pricing

Arbitrage pricing is the purest case of relative pricing, as it makes the least assumptions about investors, utility functions, and so forth in specifying the discount factor. When it works, this approach neatly cuts short the endless discussion over what are the true risk factors, market price of risk, and so on. Black–Scholes option pricing is the canonical example. The Black–Scholes formula expresses the option price *given* the stock and bond prices.

The only assumption we need to derive an arbitrage pricing relation such as the Black–Scholes formula is that there is *some* discount factor that generates the price of the focus asset (option) and the basis assets (stock, bond). As long as there is some discount factor, then the "Law of One Price" must hold: two ways of generating the same payoff must have the same value.[15] If payoffs x, y, z are related by $z = x + y$, then their prices prices must obey $p(z) = p(x) + p(y)$.[16] The key insight in the Black–Scholes formula is that you can dynamically hedge an option with a stock and a bond. The payoff of the option is the same as the payoff of the hedge portfolio. Hence, the price of the option must be the same as the value of the hedge portfolio. (Arbitrage pricing should really be called "Law of One Price pricing", and probably would be if the latter were not such an ugly a name.)

Another way to look at the same thing paves the way for more complex relative pricing. Because the existence of *any* discount factor implies the Law of One Price, *any* discount factor that prices the basis assets (stock and bond) must give the same result for the focus asset (option). Following this insight, we can price options by simply constructing any discount factor that prices the stock and bond. This task is easy. For example, once you know p_t, the choice

$$m^*_{t+1} = x'_{t+1} E_t (x_{t+1} \, x'_{t+1})^{-1} pt$$

does a pretty good job of satisfying $p_t = E_t(x_{t+1}\, m^*_{t+1})$! (The primes denote transpose and allow for vectors of prices and payoffs in the formula.) Then we can simply use the discount factor m^* to value the option.[17]

The discount factor m^* is not unique. There are many discount factors that price the stock and bond. For example, a new discount factor $m_{t+1} = m^*_{t+1} + \varepsilon_{t+1}$ where ε_{t+1} is any random variable uncorrelated with payoffs $E_t(\varepsilon_{t+1}\, x_{t+1}) = 0$ will do. But with arbitrage pricing it does not matter which one you use. They all give the same option value.

Arbitrage pricing is still technically challenging, because these trivial-sounding statements hold at every point in time, and you have to chain it all back from expiration to find the actual option price. This means solving a differential equation or an integral. But technical challenges are a lot easier to solve than economic challenges – ie, finding the right absolute asset pricing model.

You can see the attraction of arbitrage pricing. Rather than learn about discount factors from macroeconomics, introspection, philosophy, or oversimplified economic theories, we can simply construct useful discount factors from available assets and use them to price derivatives. Put another way, every asset pricing model posits that there is *some* discount factor, so implications that derive from the mere existence of a discount factor are common to every asset pricing model; we do not have to choose which asset pricing model to use if all discount factors give the same answer. Arbitrage pricing seems so pure that option pricing theorists, financial engineers, and risk managers often sneer at the models we have presented above.

Arbitrage pricing, however, is not completely assumption-free. It assumes that there is *some* discount factor. In turn, this assumption requires that there is at least one unconstrained investor out there forming an optimal portfolio. We need to know nothing about the utility function and consumption stream (ie, what states of nature the investor fears) – we will learn all we need to know about that from stock and bond prices – but we do need something. The Law of One Price is routinely violated in retail stores – the price of a 907.2 gram bottle of ketchup is *not* twice the price of a 453.6 gram bottle – so it does reflect some assumptions. It is not a law of nature.

Much more seriously, application of relative pricing techniques to real-world problems is not nearly as straightforward as the Black–Scholes example suggests. The lost car keys are usually not right under the streetlight. In practically every interesting application, even a textbook-perfect hedge is exposed to *some* risk arising from institutional frictions, transactions costs, illiquidity, and so forth. More often, there is no textbook-perfect hedge, due to non-marketed risks such as changing volatility, shifting interest rates, asset specific liquidity premia, non-marketed fundamental securities, etc. And when there is no way to *perfectly* replicate the payoff of the focus asset with some portfolio of other assets, there is no way to perfectly "arbitrage price" the focus asset. The premia for market prices of the unavoidable basis risks will matter. Different, and apparently arbitrary, choices among the many discount factors that price hedge assets (different choices of ε in $m = m^* + \varepsilon$) produce different valuations for the derivatives. We cannot avoid the questions: "how big are the extra risks" and "what is the premium for those extra risks?"

At this point, we could simply return to the beginning and try to answer these questions using some implementation of the fundamental value equation. But we usually want to avoid an extended discussion of CAPM versus ICAPM and consumption in every little application. Many option-pricing exercises leave "market price of risk" assumptions as free parameters, as we discussed above for term structure and commodity models. But in many cases, the market price of risk assumptions matter a lot, and pulling them out of thin air is very unsatisfactory. Instead, we can add a little "absolute" information to winnow down the range of possible discount factors, while still using the information in hedge assets (stock and bond) as much as possible. This works because in most options pricing applications, the residual or tracking error risks are *small*. It only takes a little discount factor economics to make sure that small residuals have small effects on values.

Arbitrage bounds

What can we say about discount factors? The weakest thing we can say in general (beyond existence) is that investors always like more over less.[18] Marginal utility is positive, and this implies that the discount factor is positive. Keep in mind that the discount factor is random, so "positive" means "positive in every state of the world at time $t + 1$, no matter what happens".

As the existence of a discount factor implies the Law of One Price, a positive discount factor has a nice portfolio interpretation: the "principle of no arbitrage". If a payoff x cannot be negative and might be positive, then it gets a positive price. (Multiplying two positive things in $E_t(m_{t+1} x_{t+1})$ and taking the average, we must get a positive result. In finance terminology, this stronger property is called "arbitrage". Colloquial use of "arbitrage" usually refers to the Law of One Price).

Positive discount factors lead to "arbitrage bounds" on option prices when we cannot completely hedge the option payoff. We solve the problem: "what are the largest and smallest option prices we can generate, searching over all positive discount factors that price stock and bond?" More formally, we solve

$$\max_{\{m_{t+1}\}} E_t\left(m_{t+1} \, x_{t+1}^{\text{option}}\right)$$
$$s.t. \quad p_t^{\text{stock}} = E_t\left(m_{t+1} \, x_{t+1}^{\text{stock}}\right)$$
$$s.t. \quad p_t^{\text{bond}} = E_t\left(m_{t+1} \, x_{t+1}^{\text{bond}}\right) \tag{15}$$
$$s.t. \quad m_{t+1} > 0$$

Most textbooks solve this problem more simply for a simple European call option. For example, we note that the call option payoff is always positive, so its price must always be positive. In more complex situations, this discount factor search (a linear program) is the only way to make sure you have not forgotten some clever dominating portfolio, and it can provide useful arbitrage bounds even in dynamic applications (see Ritchken, 1985).

BEYOND ARBITRAGE: A LITTLE BIT OF ABSOLUTE PRICING GOES A LONG WAY

Alas, arbitrage bounds are too wide for many applications. They still allow us to generate weird option prices, because there are weird positive discount factors that nonetheless price the stock and bond. For example, we generate the lower arbitrage bound on a European call option $C(t) > 0$ by imagining a discount factor arbitrarily close to zero any time the option finishes in-the-money. Now we are all happy when the stock market goes up, but so wildly happy that more money has become *worthless?* Surely we can sensibly restrict the discount factor more than that without getting back into the messy model business.

Following this insight, a number of approaches suggest how to use *a little* absolute pricing even in traditional relative pricing situations in order to at least bound the effects of un-hedgeable residual risks. Equivalently, we can combine information about the discount factor from basis assets (stock, bond) whose prices we do not want to question with relatively weak but hence robust information about the discount factor available from economic theory and practical experience in many markets.

The arbitrage pricing theory

Ross's (1976b) arbitrage pricing theory (APT) is the first such mixture of a little absolute pricing into a fundamentally relative-pricing problem. His APT is also a second source of inspiration for the factors in multi-factor models.

Ross pointed out that many *portfolios* of stocks can be reasonably approximated as linear combinations of the return on a few basic or "factor" portfolios. In equations, we can run a regression of the focus portfolio on factor portfolios,

$$R_{t+1}^i = a + \beta_1^i f_{t+1}^1 + \beta_2^i f_{t+1}^2 + \cdots + \varepsilon_{t+1}^i$$

and the error term will be small. For example, most of the thousands of mutual funds' returns can be quite well approximated once we know the funds' style in terms of market, size, value, and a few industry groupings. If the actual, ex-post, returns on these portfolios can be approximated in this way, it stands to reason that the expected returns can also be so approximated. If not, one could buy the focus portfolio, short the right hand side combination of the factor portfolio returns, and earn a high return with little risk. As a result we derive a multi-factor representation in which average returns depend on the betas on the factor portfolios.

$$E(R_{t+1}^i) = R^f + \beta_1^i \lambda_1 + \beta_2^i \lambda_2 + \cdots \tag{16}$$

Equivalently, a discount factor that is a linear function of the factor returns will do a good job of pricing the focus portfolios. Of course, like any relative pricing approach, the APT's applicability is limited. You cannot apply it to assets whose returns are poorly approximated by the returns of the few basic portfolios – assets with large residuals ε^i_{t+1}.

Unfortunately, if you are willing to say nothing at all about absolute pricing – utility functions, risk aversion, macroeconomic states, etc, – then *any* residual risk ε^i_{t+1} can have an *arbitrarily* large price or risk premium, and the hoped for APT approximation can be arbitrarily wrong. With any error, the Law of One Price alone says nothing about the focus portfolio. For stock portfolios, arbitrage (positive discount factors) does not help, as no portfolio of stocks does better than another portfolio *always*.

Ross realised a way out of this dilemma. If the risk premium associated with a residual ε^i_{t+1} were very large, it would be a very attractive investment in terms of its Sharpe ratio (ratio of mean return to standard deviation). A high Sharpe ratio is not an arbitrage opportunity or a violation of the Law of One Price, but extremely high Sharpe ratios are nonetheless unlikely to persist. If we rule out very high Sharpe ratios *in addition to* the Law of One Price and principle of no arbitrage, we do obtain a well-behaved approximate APT. Small errors ε^i_{t+1} now must mean small risk premia, so Equation (16) will hold as a good approximation.

Ruling out high Sharpe ratios is another little bit of absolute pricing. It is equivalent to the assumption that discount factors are not too *volatile*. Precisely, Hansen and Jagannathan (1991) show that the maximum possible Sharpe ratio attained by all assets priced by a particular discount factor is given by [19]

$$\sigma(m) = \frac{1}{R^f} \max_{\{R:s.t.1=E(mR)\}} \left\{ \frac{E(R) - R^f}{\sigma(R)} \right\}$$

Limiting volatility is an additional but plausible and mild restriction on marginal utility. Does marginal utility growth – growth in the pleasure we get from an extra US dollar's consumption – really vary by more than, say, 50% per year? The historical market Sharpe ratio is 0.5 (8% mean, 16% standard deviation), so even such a high bound on discount factor volatility is enough to restrict market prices of risk to CAPM values.

In more economic terms, the volatility of the discount factor is given by the volatility of consumption growth times the risk aversion coefficient. If we know that at least one marginal investors' consumption growth varies less than, say, 5% per year, and risk aversion is sensible – say, less than 10 – then we know that the discount factor varies by less than 0.5 per year, and the maximum Sharpe ratio should be less than 0.5. Equivalently, we might be willing to assume that "traders will take any Sharpe ratio more than twice the Sharpe ratio of the market as a whole" and impose that maximum Sharpe ratio in evaluating the premium for residual risks.

Derivatives valuation bounds

Cochrane and Saá-Requejo (2001) apply Ross's idea to option pricing, when either market frictions (eg, you cannot trade continuously) or non-marketed risks (eg, stochastic volatility or interest rates) break simple arbitrage pricing and require us to evaluate market prices of risks. Cochrane and Saá-Requejo find that the upper and lower bounds on option prices (searching over all discount factors that price stock and bond) are positive *and* have limited volatility. This amounts to adding an additional restriction to arbitrage bound Equation (15):

$$
\begin{aligned}
&\max_{\{m_{t+1}\}} E_t\left(m_{t+1}\, x_{t+1}^{\text{option}}\right) \\
&s.t. \ \ p_t^{\text{stock}} = E_t\left(m_{t+1}\, x_{t+1}^{\text{stock}}\right) \\
&s.t. \ \ p_t^{\text{bond}} = E_t\left(m_{t+1}\, x_{t+1}^{\text{bond}}\right) \\
&s.t. \ \ m_{t+1} > 0 \\
&s.t. \ \ \sigma(m) \le R^f\, h
\end{aligned}
\tag{17}
$$

The last restriction is the novelty over arbitrage bounds. h is the upper limit on discount factor volatility; the extra assumption is that investors would want to take any bet with a Sharpe ratio greater than h. Cochrane and Saá-Requejo (2001) find that the resulting bounds on option prices are much tighter than the arbitrage bounds that result from ignoring the last term – ie, the bounds that result from arbitrary assignment of the market price of residual risk.

For option pricing, both positive discount factors and a limit on discount factor volatility are important. So far, the discount factor interpretation has been a matter of aesthetics. You could solve problems (for example) imposing a positive discount factor or by checking that all positive payoffs had positive prices. The restrictions in Equation (17) have no pure portfolio interpretation. The only way to put all these ideas together is to add restrictions on the discount factor, tightening the bounds on option pricing. They have to be posed and solved with discount factor methods.

This is only the beginning. Bernardo and Ledoit (2000) add the restriction that discount factors cannot be too small or too large, $a \leq m \leq b$. This is a sensible tightening of the arbitrage restriction $m \geq 0$. It also produces usefully tight option pricing bounds. Constantinides and Zariphopoulou (1999) consider the sensible restriction that higher index values must make investors happier. The discount factor m thus must be a monotonically decreasing function of the stock index. The beauty of a discount factor framework is that it is easy to add all these restrictions and more together.

CONCLUSION

All of asset pricing comes down to one simple idea: price equals expected discounted payoff. The art is in what one should use for a discount factor.

We surveyed "absolute" approaches such as the CAPM and consumption CAPM that infer the discount factor from measures of macroeconomic or financial "bad times". We emphasised that a sound grasp of asset pricing theory is required to define systematic risk and thus to identify those remaining risks on which investors and firms should focus their risk management efforts, and to define "good risks" which give high returns to investors who take them. We surveyed term structure and derivatives models that specify much simpler and more ad hoc discount factor models, resulting in free parameters for market prices of risk. We surveyed "relative pricing" approaches that learn about the discount factor for pricing one asset from information in other assets. We argued that a little bit of economics, a little bit of absolute pricing (such as a limit on discount factor volatility) can help to plug the market price of risk holes in much applied option pricing and resulting risk management.

The fundamental value equation has significant implications for finance in general and for portfolio selection, capital budgeting, hedge evaluation, and derivatives valuation applications in particular. Far from being distantly related to risk management, the consumption model and all its special cases and empirical representations are, in fact, as central to risk management as they are to all finance.

APPENDIX: DERIVATION OF THE FUNDAMENTAL VALUE EQUATION

To describe what an investor likes and dislikes, and hence to think about how the investor values an asset, we employ the standard economist's model that investors want to find the highest value of a "utility function":[20]

$$U(c_t, c_{t+1}) = u(c_t) + \beta E_t[u(c_{t+1})]$$

$u(c_t)$ describes how more consumption at time t makes the investor happier. We typically assume that investors always prefer more to less ($u_c(c) > 0$), and each incremental unit of consumption brings slightly less happiness than the unit before it ($u_{cc}(c) < 0$).

Now think of a financial asset whose price at time t is p_t and whose payoff (total value) at time $t+1$ is x_{t+1}. The investor can freely buy or sell as much of this asset as they like at time t. How much will they buy or sell? To find the answer, denote $e(t)$ as their consumption level before they buy any of the asset, and denote by ξ the amount of the asset they choose to buy. Then, their problem is to choose the ξ that solves

$$\max_{\xi} u(c_t) + E_t\left[\beta u(c_{t+1})\right]$$
$$s.t.\ c_t = e_t - \xi p_t$$
$$s.t.\ c_{t+1} = e_{t+1} + \xi x_{t+1}$$

Substitute the two constraints into the objective, and take a derivative with respect to the ξ. Set the derivative equal to zero to characterise the maximum. The result is that the investor's optimal consumption-investment choice satisfies

$$p_t u'(c_t) = E_t[\beta u'(c_{t+1})x_{t+1}]$$

or, rearranging with price on the left and the rest on the right,

$$p_t = E_t \left[\beta \frac{u_c(c_{t+1})}{u_c(c_t)} x_{t+1} \right]$$

1 Culp (2003) explores the relative-pricing approach in the subsequent chapter of this volume.
2 Winners of the Nobel Prize in Economic Sciences for their specific contributions to the theory of finance are Harry M. Markowitz (1990), Merton H. Miller (1990), William F. Sharpe (1990), Robert C. Merton (1997), and Myron S. Scholes (1997). Other Nobel laureates whose work had a critical impact on finance include John R. Hicks (1972), Kenneth J. Arrow (1972), Gerard Debreu (1983), Franco Modigliani (1985), and Robert E. Lucas, Jr. (1995).
3 The discussion here and in the next two sections is adapted from Cochrane (2001).
4 As a matter of theory, this only really works for investors. Corporations do not have utility functions and thus engage in a different type of analysis of hedging opportunities – see Culp (2001, 2002a).
5 Derivation: For any two returns R^j and R^k, $E_t[m_{t+1}(R^j - R^k)] = E_t[m_{t+1}R^j] - E_t[m_{t+1}R^k] = 0$, where $R^k = R^f$ is a special case.
6 Derivation: Note that $R^f = 1/E(m)$ and $E(mP) = E(m)E(P) + cov(m, P)$ and solve.
7 See, for example, Ross (1976b) and Cox, Ross, and Rubinstein (1979). Cochrane (2001) discusses the relations between discrete-time and continuous-time formulations of the problem and how to implement discount factors in continuous time.
8 Alternatively, that is why investors diversify their holdings to get rid of these risks on their own. See Culp (2003).
9 The parameter γ can be interpreted as the degree of risk aversion.
10 Cochrane (2001) shows different derivations of the CAPM under alternative assumptions and provides a comparison of the multiple approaches.
11 z is usually a vector of multiple state variables and factor-mimicking portfolios.
12 Technically, this statement requires a risk aversion coefficient greater than one, but that is the usual case.
13 This treatment is adapted from Campell, Lo, and MacKinlay (1997).
14 Derivation: The price and yield of a one-period bond are

$$p_t^{(1)} = E_t[m_{t+1}] = E_t\left[e^{\ln(m_{t+1})}\right] = E_t\left[e^{-x_t+\varepsilon_{t+1}}\right] = e^{-x_t+\frac{1}{2}\sigma_\varepsilon^2}$$

$$y_t^{(1)} = -\ln(p_t) = x_t - \frac{1}{2}\sigma_\varepsilon^2$$

With an adjustment to the constant μ, the state variable x thus is the short rate $y_t^{(1)}$. Things get more interesting with a two-year bond:

$$y_t^{(2)} = -\frac{1}{2}\ln E_t[m_{t+1}\, m_{t+2}] = -\frac{1}{2}\ln E_t\left[e^{-x_t-x_{t+1}+\varepsilon_{t+1}+\varepsilon_{t+2}}\right] = -\frac{1}{2}\ln E_t\left[e^{-(1+\phi)x_t-(1-\phi)\mu-\delta_{t+1}+\varepsilon_{t+1}+\varepsilon_{t+2}}\right]$$

$$y_t^{(2)} = \frac{1}{2}(1+\phi)x_t + \frac{1}{2}(1-\phi)\mu + \frac{1}{2}cov(\delta,\varepsilon) - \frac{1}{4}\sigma_\delta^2 - \frac{1}{2}\sigma_\varepsilon^2$$

$$y_t^{(2)} = \frac{1}{2}(1-\phi)\mu + \frac{1}{2}(1+\phi)\,y_t^{(1)} + \frac{1}{2}cov(\delta,\varepsilon) - \frac{1}{4}\left\{\sigma_\delta^2 + (1-\phi)\left(\sigma_\varepsilon^2\right)\right\}$$

15 The converse statement is one of the most famous founding theorems of finance. If the Law of One Price holds, then there exists a discount factor. See Ross (1976), Harrison and Kreps (1979), and Hansen and Richard (1987).

16 Proof: $E[m(x + y)] = E(mx) + E(my)$.

17 See Cochrane (2001) for the algebra.

18 You can always burn or give away what you do not want, so less is never preferred to more.

19 Proof: $0 = E(m(R - R^f)) = E(m)E(R - R^f) + \sigma(m)\sigma(R)\rho(m, R)$

$$E(m)\frac{E(R - R^f)}{\sigma(R)\rho(m, R)} = \sigma(m)$$

Correlations are less than one.

20 This simple formulation treats all consumers as alike and presumes that utility is "additively separable" across time. Numerous alternatives to this simple set-up have been proposed. See, for example, Constantinides (1990). Many alternatives are reviewed in Cochrane (1997, 1999a, 1999b).

BIBLIOGRAPHY

Banz, R. W., 1981, "The Relationship Between Return and Market Value of Common Stocks", *Journal of Financial Economics* 9, pp. 3–18.

Black, F., 1972, "Capital Market Equilibrium with Restricted Borrowing", *Journal of Business* 45, pp. 444–55.

Black, F., and M. Scholes, 1973, "The Pricing of Options and Corporate Liabilities", *Journal of Political Economy* 81, pp. 637–54.

Bernardo, A. E., and O. Ledoit, 2000, "Gain, Loss, and Asset Pricing", *Journal of Political Economy* 108, pp. 144–72.

Billingsley, P., 1995, *Probability and Measure* (New York: Wiley Interscience).

Breeden, D., 1979, "An Intertemporal Asset Pricing Model with Stochastic Consumption and Investment Opportunities", *Journal of Financial Economics* 7, pp. 265–96.

Brennan, M. J., and E. S. Schwartz, 1979, "A Continuous-Time Approach to the Pricing of Bonds", *Journal of Banking and Finance* 3, pp. 133–55.

Campbell, J., A. Lo, and C. MacKinlay, 1996, *The Econometrics of Financial Markets* (Princeton University Press).

Chen, N.-F., R. Roll, and S. A. Ross, 1986, "Economic Forces and the Stock Market", *Journal of Business* 59, pp. 383–403.

Cochrane, J. H., 1991a, "Production-Based Asset Pricing and the Link Between Stock Returns and Economic Fluctuations", *Journal of Finance* 46, pp. 207–34.

Cochrane, J. H., 1991b, "Volatility Tests and Efficient Markets: A Review Essay", *Journal of Monetary Economics* 27, pp. 463–85.

Cochrane, J. H., 1996, "A Cross-Sectional Test of an Investment-Based Asset Pricing Model", *Journal of Political Economy* 104, pp. 572–621.

Cochrane, J. H., 1997, "Where is the Market Going? Uncertain Facts and Novel Theories", *Federal Reserve Bank of Chicago Economic Perspectives* 21, pp. 3–37.

Cochrane, J. H., 1999a, "New Facts in Finance", *Federal Reserve Bank of Chicago Economic Perspectives* 23, pp. 36–58.

Cochrane, J. H., 1999b, "Portfolio Advice for a Multi-factor World", *Federal Reserve Bank of Chicago Economic Perspectives*, 23, pp. 59–78.

Cochrane, J. H., 2001, *Asset Pricing* (Princeton University Press).

Cochrane, J. H., and J. Saá-Requejo, 2000, "Beyond Arbitrage: Good Deal Asset Price Bounds in Incomplete Markets", *Journal of Political Economy* 108, pp. 79–119.

Constantinides, G. M., 1990, "Habit Formation: A Resolution of the Equity Premium Puzzle", *Journal of Political Economy* 98, pp. 519–43.

Constantinides, G. M., and D. Duffie, 1996, "Asset Pricing with Heterogeneous Consumers", *Journal of Political Economy* 104, pp. 219–40.

Constantinides, G. M., and T. Zariphopoulou, 1999, "Bounds on Prices of Contingent Claims in an Intertemporal Economy with Proportional Transaction Costs and General Preferences", *Finance and Stochastics* 3, pp. 345–69.

Cox, J. C., S. A. Ross, and M. Rubinstein, 1979, "Option Pricing: A Simplified Approach", *Journal of Financial Economics* 7, pp. 229–63.

Cox, J. C., J. E. Ingersoll, and S. A. Ross, 1985, "A Theory of the Term Structure of Interest Rates", *Econometrica* 53, pp. 385–408.

Culp, C. L., 2001, *The Risk Management Process: Business Strategy and Tactics* (New York: John Wiley and Sons).

Culp, C. L., 2002a, *The ART of Risk Management: Alternative Risk Transfer, Capital Structure, and the Convergence of Insurance and Capital Markets* (New York: John Wiley and Sons).

Culp, C. L., 2002b, "Normal Backwardation (Theory of)", in *Encyclopedia of Financial Engineering and Risk Management* (London: Fitzroy-Dearborn Publishers, forthcoming).

Culp, C. L., 2003, "Modigliani-Miller Propositions", in *Modern Risk Management: A History* (London: Risk Books, forthcoming), in this volume.

Fama, E. F., 1991, "Efficient Markets II", *Journal of Finance* 46, pp. 1575–1618.

Fama, E. F., and K. R. French, 1993, "Common Risk Factors in the Returns on Stocks and Bonds", *Journal of Financial Economics* 33, pp. 3–56.

Fama, E. F., and K. R. French, 1996, "Multi-factor Explanations of Asset-Pricing Anomalies", *Journal of Finance* 47, pp. 426–65.

Ferson, W., and C. R. Harvey, 1999, "Conditioning Variables and the Cross-Section of Stock Returns", *Journal of Finance* 54, pp. 1325–60.

Gibson, R., and E. S. Schwartz, 1990, "Stochastic Convenience Yield and the Pricing of Oil Contingent Claims", *Journal of Finance* 45, pp. 959–76.

Hansen, L. P., and R. Jagannathan, 1991, "Implications of Security Market Data for Models of Dynamic Economies", *Journal of Political Economy* 99, pp. 225–62.

Hansen, L. P., and S. F. Richard, 1987, "The Role of Conditioning Information in Deducing Testable Restrictions Implied by Dynamic Asset Pricing Models", *Econometrica* 55, pp. 557–90.

Hansen, L. P., and K. J. Singleton, 1982, "Generalised Instrumental Variables Estimation of Nonlinear Rational Expectations Models", *Econometrica* 50, pp. 1269–86.

Harrison, J. M., and D. M. Kreps, 1979, "Martingales and Arbitrage in Multiperiod Securities Markets", *Journal of Economic Theory* 20, pp. 381–408.

Ho, T. S. Y., and S.-B. Lee, 1983, "Term Structure Movements and Pricing Interest Rate Contingent Claims", *Journal of Finance* 41, pp. 1011–29.

Jagannathan, R., and Z. Wang, 1996, "The Conditional CAPM and the Cross-Section of Expected Returns", *Journal of Finance* 51, pp. 3–53.

Keynes, J. M., 1930, "A Treatise on Money", (Macmillan).

Lettau, M., and S. C. Ludvigson, 2001, "Consumption, Aggregate Wealth, and Expected Stock Returns", *Journal of Finance* 56, pp. 815–49.

Lintner, J., 1965, "The Valuation of Risky Assets and the Selection of Risky Investments in Stock Portfolios and Capital Budgets", *Review of Economics and Statistics* 47, pp. 13–37.

Lucas, R. E., 1978, "Asset Prices in an Exchange Economy", *Econometrica* 46, pp. 1429–46.

Merton, R. W., 1973, "An Intertemporal Capital Asset Pricing Model", *Econometrica* 41, pp. 867–87.

Modigliani, F., and M. H. Miller, 1958, "The Cost of Capital, Corporation Finance, and the Theory of Investment", *American Economic Review* 48(2), pp. 261–97.

Pastor, L., and R. F. Stambaugh, 2001, "Liquidity Risk and Expected Stock Returns", NBER Working Paper No. w8462 (September). Forthcoming *Journal of Political Economy*.

Ritchken, P. H., 1985, "On Option Pricing Bounds", *Journal of Finance* 40, pp. 1219–33.

Roll, R., 1977, "A Critique of the Asset Pricing Theory's Tests' Part I: On Past and Potential Testability of the Theory", *Journal of Financial Economics* 4, pp. 129–76.

Ross, S. A., 1976a, "The Arbitrage Theory of Capital Asset Pricing", *Journal of Economic Theory* 13, pp. 341–60.

Ross. S. A., 1976b, "Risk, Return and Arbitrage", in I. Friend and J. Bicksler (eds), *Risk and Return in Finance: Volume I*, pp. 189–218 (Cambridge: Ballinger).

Rubinstein, M., 1976, "The Valuation of Uncertain Income Streams and the Price of Options", *Bell Journal of Economics* 7, pp. 407–25.

Sharpe, W., 1964, "Capital Asset Prices: A Theory of Market Equilibrium Under Conditions of Risk", *Journal of Finance* 19, pp. 425–42.

Vasicek, O., 1977, "An Equilibrium Characterization of the Term Structure", *Journal of Financial Economics* 5, pp. 177–88.

6

The Modigliani–Miller Propositions

Christopher L. Culp

The University of Chicago and CP Risk Management LLC

The celebrated Modigliani–Miller propositions are the cornerstones of modern corporation finance. The propositions imply that, under certain assumptions, a firm's value and cost of capital are based on the expected cashflows and risks of its real net assets, not on the company's financial structure and policies. A thorough understanding of the M&M propositions – when they hold, when they do not, and why – can help risk managers understand when a value-maximising firm can increase its value through hedging, how the construction of a hedge should be related to the firm's reasons for hedging, and how risk management and financing decisions can sometimes be integrated to reduce the firm's weighted average cost of capital.

INTRODUCTION

The 1958 paper by Franco Modigliani and Merton Miller (M&M), "The Cost of Capital, Corporation Finance, and the Theory of Investment," is almost universally regarded as having created the modern theory of corporate finance. As Ross says, "If the view of the progress of science that interprets it as one of changing paradigms has merit, then surely the work of Miller and Modigliani provides a laboratory example of a violently shifted paradigm" (Ross, 1988, p. 127).

The basic import of the M&M propositions is that under certain assumptions, the financial structure and decisions of a firm have no impact on its value, cost of capital, or investment criteria. That the importance of these irrelevance propositions in both the theory and practice of finance has not waned over the last nearly 50 years strikes some as odd, given that propositions reveal when financial decisions do *not* matter to a firm. But understanding when financial policy *doesn't* matter is requisite to understanding *when it does*. Accordingly, this article begins first by explaining the M&M irrelevance propositions, and then provides a brief analysis of how the M&M irrelevancies give rise to *relevancies* for corporate risk management decisions.

THE MOST RELEVANT "IRRELEVANCIES" IN FINANCE

Prior to M&M, the conventional belief was that because debt was cheaper than equity, a firm's value should rise with increases in leverage, at least up to some threshold level of debt beyond which a company would have difficulty servicing.[1] Consequently, the average cost of capital for a firm was thought to *fall* for increases in debt, as long as the firm avoided truly excessive leverage.

M&M showed that this conventional wisdom was wrong, at least under certain assumptions. The assumptions under which the M&M irrelevance propositions hold are as follows.[2]

❏ *Perfect Capital Markets.* Capital markets are perfect in the sense of no taxes, no transaction costs, no institutional frictions (eg, short selling restrictions on securities), and no costs of bankruptcy or financial distress.

❏ *Symmetric Information.* All investors and managers have the same information about the quality of a firm's investments *and* have identical (as well as correct) perceptions concerning the impact of new information on the prices of securities.

❏ *Given Investment Strategies.* Investment decisions by firms are presumed to be given exogenously.

❏ *Rational Behaviour.* Investors prefer more to less and do not leave any risk-free arbitrage opportunities unexploited.

❏ *Equal Access.* Firms and individuals can issue the same securities in the capital markets on exactly the same terms.[3]

The fundamental implication of these assumptions is that the value of a firm and its cost of capital depend entirely on the *real assets* that the firm owns, not on the firm's financial structure. More specifically,

M&M showed that under the above assumptions, four specific types of "irrelevancies" emerge.

Proposition I: the irrelevance of capital structure to firm value

M&M Proposition I states that "the market value of any firm is independent of its capital structure and is given by capitalising its expected return at the rate ρ_k appropriate to its [risk] class" (M&M, 1958, p. 268). Equivalently, "the average cost of capital to any firm is completely independent of its capital structure..." (*Id.*). So, the value of an unlevered firm should be the same as the value of a levered firm holding the same assets. Using M&M's notation, Proposition I can be stated mathematically as

$$V_j \equiv S_j + D_j = \frac{\overline{X}_j}{\rho_k} \tag{1}$$

where V_j is the market value of firm j, S_j and D_j are the market values of the firm's outstanding equity and debt, respectively, $\overline{X}_j$ is the expected profit on the firm's assets, and ρ_k is the expected return on assets of risk type k. Alternatively, the firm's average cost of capital depends only on the capitalisation rate associated with the firm's assets, ρ_k, and not on the relative proportions of debt and equity it issues:

$$\frac{\overline{X}_j}{V_j} = \rho_k \tag{2}$$

Saying that the value of a firm is independent of its capital structure is not quite equivalent, of course, to saying that the security holders of a firm are completely indifferent to the firm's financing choices. For that, you need the additional assumption that the bonds issued by the firm contain covenants that preserve "me-first rules" (see Fama and Miller, 1972; Fama, 1978). Such rules protect debt holders by requiring the firm to assign seniority to *existing* debt holders so that any *newly issued* debt is junior in priority. Equity holders are in turn protected by me-first rules that require any early retirements of debt to begin with the most junior issues.

To prove Proposition I, M&M argued that investors need not invest in levered firms to take whatever advantage leverage itself might have. Instead, investors could invest in unlevered firms and borrow on their own account to manufacture "homemade leverage". If the assets held by the levered and unlevered firm are identical, both strategies will yield the same payoff under the M&M assumptions. To preclude the existence of risk-free arbitrage opportunities, the costs of the strategies thus must be the same, and, hence, the values of the levered and unlevered firms must be equal.

Grundy (2002) describes "three paths" used by M&M at various points to prove this irrelevance. Specifically, arbitrage can be carried out by individual investors, intermediaries acting on behalf of investors (eg, investment banks), or by supply adjustments within the corporate sector as a whole.[4] If, say, taxes or transaction costs interfere with arbitrage by one of these groups, either of the other two could take its place and the same irrelevance result would be obtained.[5]

Note that the proof of M&M Proposition I has probably had as big an impact on finance as the proposition itself. Importantly, M&M were the first to use a "no arbitrage" approach to characterising asset prices. The alternative approach would have required M&M to derive the values of a levered and unlevered in terms of some equilibrium asset pricing model, including those surveyed by Cochrane and Culp (2003) in the present volume. Alas, such models remain as difficult to implement empirically today as they did in 1958 (Cochrane, 2001). M&M thus avoided this problem by characterising the values of the levered and unlevered firms in *relative* terms, or terms that would hold for *any* absolute market values and irrespective of the "true" equilibrium asset pricing model. This no arbitrage approach, later popularised by Black and Scholes (1973) to price equity options, is now a staple of derivatives valuation and financial engineering.

Proposition II: the irrelevance of leverage to weighted-average cost of capital

M&M argued that "[a] number of writers have stated close equivalents to our Proposition I although by appealing to intuition rather than by attempting a proof … Proposition II, however, so far as we have been able to discover is new" (M&M, 1958, p. 271).

Proposition II holds that "the expected yield of a share of stock is equal to the appropriate capitalisation rate ρ_k for a pure equity stream in that [risk] class, plus a premium related to financial risk equal to the debt-to-equity ratio times the spread between ρ_k and r ... " where ρ_k is defined as earlier as the risk-adjusted return on assets and r is the interest rate on the firm's debt. Formally, Proposition II can be written as

$$i_j = \rho_k + \left(\rho_k - r\right)\frac{D_j}{S_j} \tag{3}$$

where i_j is the expected return on the equity of levered firm j.

Stated differently, Proposition I showed that if leverage has any benefit, firms and investors are equally capable of manufacturing it, so leverage does not impact the value of the firm. Proposition II then shows that leverage itself has no benefit for a firm's cost of capital. The gains from using cheap borrowed funds are exactly offset by the higher expected return stockholders will require to compensate them for the risk of higher leverage.

Proposition II requires little to prove it, apart from Proposition I. The expected return on the stock issued by levered firm j is *by definition*

$$i_j = \frac{\overline{X}_j - rD_j}{S_j} \tag{4}$$

If Proposition I holds, then Equation (1) holds. Substituting Equation (1) into Equation (4) yields Equation (3). So, the expected return on equity for a leveraged firm is equal to the expected return on equity for an otherwise identical unlevered firm plus a penalty for debt. Conversely, under the M&M assumptions, the weighted-average cost of capital (WACC) is thus not affected by leverage.

Proposition III: the irrelevance of financing methods to investment decisions

Less widely known but nevertheless equally insightful, M&M's Proposition III states that "the cut-off point for investment ... will be completely unaffected by the type of security used to finance the investment" (M&M, 1958, p. 288). If the return on investment is greater than the firm's WACC, then the investment makes sense for that firm. Because the firm's WACC does not change with its capital structure, the desirability of an investment thus is based purely on a comparison of the expected return on that investment to the expected return on the firm's assets, both adjusted for risk.

To derive Proposition III, M&M assume that management is acting in the best interests of the stockholders. But M&M admit this might not be the case. Indeed, Fama and Miller (1972) extend the M&M analysis and show that the unique investment objective implied by the M&M assumptions is the "market value rule". When managers follow the market value rule, they pursue only those investment opportunities that maximise the market value of the firm. This is *not* equivalent to the popular criteria of "shareholder" or "stakeholder" value maximisation, but rather to maximising the *combined* wealth of *all* security holders.[6] And M&M Proposition III still holds under the assumption that managers follow the market value rule.

Additional proposition: the irrelevance of dividends to firm value

Dividend irrelevance was not an explicit "proposition" in M&M's original 1958 paper, but rather emerged in M&M's 1959 reply to David Durand's criticisms of the original paper. And as Grundy (2002, p. xix) aptly puts it, "the meat came after the gruel of the reply, however, and might have been lost had the dividend implications of the capital structure propositions not been published separately [as M&M (1961)]". M&M (1961, p. 414) conclude "given a firm's investment policy, the dividend payout policy it chooses to follow will affect neither the current price of its shares nor the total return to its shareholders".

The basic proof of dividend irrelevance is similar to the proof of capital structure irrelevance. Ignoring all announcement effects from dividends, a higher dividend payout implies a lower capital gain.[7] But all investors care about is their *total return*. If dividends are themselves value-enhancing, an investor need not invest in a dividend-paying firm to reap those benefits, but can instead create homemade dividends on a personal account. Alternatively, intermediaries could buy up the shares of firms following "sub-optimal" dividend policies and repackage them into "optimal" mixtures of capital gains and dividends. Or firms could accomplish the same result themselves through share repurchases or acquisitions. As in the proof of Proposition I, any of the three paths provide an arbitrage mechanism that ultimately guarantees the irrelevance of a firm's dividend policy under the M&M assumptions.

THE M&M PROPOSITIONS, THE "REAL WORLD", AND IMPLICATIONS FOR RISK MANAGEMENT

Many critics of the M&M propositions focused on the seeming implausibility of the assumptions under which the propositions hold.[8] But Miller (1988) addressed this point particularly well in his usual insightful and adept style:

> … the view that capital structure is literally irrelevant or that "nothing matters" in corporate finance … is far from what we ever actually said about the real world applications of our theoretical propositions. Looking back now, perhaps we should have put more emphasis on the other, upbeat side of the "nothing matters" coin: showing what *doesn't* matter can also show, by implication, what *does* (Miller, 1988, p. 100).

In that connection, a substantial academic literature exists that attempts to explore the question of "optimal capital structure" in the M&M framework. Far too deep and wide to survey here, interested readers are referred to Harris and Raviv (1990), still a remarkably complete survey even given its age.[9] The focus for the remainder of this chapter is *solely* on the implications of M&M for risk management.[10]

Because risk management decisions are in effect types of capital structure or financing decisions, not surprising is that the same assumptions guaranteeing capital structure irrelevance *also* guarantee the irrelevance of risk management. Under the M&M assumptions, the value of a firm and its WACC thus are independent of any deliberate actions taken by the firm's management to change the firm's risk profile. The reason is simple: shareholders can engage in homemade risk management. An investor worried about rising jet fuel prices who owns stock in an airline that does not hedge, for example, can buy stock in a refinery. Similarly, the owner of stock in an airline that *does* hedge can short the stock of a refinery if she desires a greater jet fuel price exposure. Either way, the M&M assumptions and method of proof guarantee that investors are essentially indifferent to whether or not hedging is done by the firm, by investors on their own account, or by intermediaries acting on behalf of investors.[11]

Armed with this risk management irrelevance proposition, three particularly useful questions about risk management now can be answered. When *can* risk management increase the value of a firm? How is a firm's hedging strategy affected by the underlying reason that risk management adds to its value? When and how can alternative risk management methods affect a firm's WACC differently?

Why value-maximising firms hedge

In order for risk management to increase the value of the firm, it either must increase the firm's expected cashflows or lower its WACC. Two decades of theoretical and empirical work suggests that risk management can help companies increase (or protect) their expected net cashflows mainly in the following ways:[12]

❑ reducing expected tax liabilities when the firm faces a convex tax schedule;

❑ reducing the expected costs of financial distress;

❑ reducing potential conflicts between a company's creditors and stockholders, including the possibility that "debt overhang" results in the sacrifice of valuable strategic investments;

❑ mitigating managerial risk aversion that (in the absence of hedging) could lead managers to over invest in excessively conservative projects;

❑ reducing under investment that arises from unexpected depletions of internal cash when the firm faces higher and rising external financing costs that exceed the benefits of the new investment at the margin; and

❑ exploiting perceived comparative information advantages by engaging in "selective hedging".

As this list suggests, value-increasing risk management has little to do with dampening swings in reported earnings or even, as many academics have suggested, minimising the "variance" of cashflows.[13] For most companies, the main contribution of risk management is likely to be its role in minimising the probability of *costly* financial distress.[14] In this sense, the optimal risk management policy may be one that provides a kind of insurance against "worst-case" scenarios. And even when the company has relatively little debt, management may choose to purchase such catastrophic insurance to protect the company's ability to carry out the major investments that are part of its strategic plan.[15]

In the process of insuring against catastrophic outcomes and preserving a minimal level of cashflow, companies will generally discover that they can operate with less capital (or at least less equity capital) than if they left their exposures unmanaged. And to the extent that hedging proves to be a cheap substitute for capital, risk management is a value-adding proposition.[16]

How value-maximising firms should hedge

Apart from merely explaining *why* firms can increase their value from hedging, understanding the role played by each of the M&M assumptions can also help explain the critical relation between *why* firms hedge and *how* they should hedge. The value of a firm is linked directly to its cashflows, and a firm's earnings are basically just its operating cashflow with the appropriate accounting rules overlaid. But despite the close relations of these three measures, they can be quite different when viewed through a risk manager's eyes.

To take a simple example, the popular model of Froot, Scharfstein, and Stein (1993) shows how a firm can increase its value by taking steps to reduce its cashflow volatility, and, hence, to reduce its dependencies on costly external finance. A firm faced with that situation, however, would find little benefit to hedging, say, a physical purchase agreement with futures contracts. Because futures are marked to market and resettled at least daily, even a "perfect hedge" in a *value* sense can increase *cashflow volatility*. A firm that benefits from cashflow hedging thus should adopt a *cashflow hedge* – and similarly for other specific risk management objectives. Culp and Miller (1995, 1999) and Culp (2001) provide further discussion and examples of this point.

Relations between corporate financing and risk management decisions

Financial executives of companies that face sharp increases in business or financial risk have two basic ways of protecting the solvency and strategic viability of their organisations: they can transfer those risks to investors or other firms through insurance and derivatives; or they can raise additional capital, typically by issuing new equity, in anticipation of the need to cover potential losses. Fundamentally, corporate financing and risk management decisions are two sides of the same coin.

In that context, understanding in an M&M framework why a firm might benefit from a particular capital structure may have equally strong implications for how the firm should manage its risks. When the M&M assumption of perfect and symmetric information is relaxed, for example, and managers are better informed than investors about the quality of the firm's investments, adverse selection costs can increase a firm's cost of capital. More specifically, investors are likely to assume that firms will issue securities only when they are overpriced, and this expectation depresses the price investors are willing to pay for the securities. This more or less predictable chain of events in turn has the potential to create a self-fulfilling prophecy wherein firms *do* indeed prefer to issue new securities only when they are overpriced. The result is a "pecking order" in which companies prefer to use internal funds rather than issuing external securities – and, when outside capital is necessary, to issue less risky securities like debt rather than riskier equity instruments (Myers, 1984; Myers and Majluf, 1984).

The nature of the information asymmetry strongly influences the size of the discount attributable to adverse selection. Any source of external finance (except risk-free debt) will change in value when more accurate information is revealed about the quality of the firm's investments. The more a security changes in value for a given information release (ie, the riskier the security), the larger is the adverse selection discount. Similarly, firms with a significant proportion of intangible investments or real options will be harder for investors to evaluate and will hence suffer larger discounts arising from larger informational asymmetries.

One way to reduce the costs stemming from this information-based discount is to issue securities to a small group of investors who have both significant incentives to verify the true quality of a firm's investments and the capabilities to make such an evaluation. Similarly, firms can use "contingent capital" products, such as Swiss Re's Committed Long Term Capital Solutions (CLOCS), to *integrate* the firm's risk management and corporate financing decisions, while simultaneously reducing adverse selection costs. Culp (2002b) provides a more detailed discussion of such integrated risk management and corporate financing products, and Culp (2002a) analyses such products in the context of competing theories of optimal capital structure.

CONCLUSION

Understanding when and why the M&M propositions *do* hold is central to understanding when and why *they don't*. The M&M propositions thus provide the starting point for many theoretical and empirical explorations in finance, including issues such as optimal capital structure, dividend policy, security design, performance evaluation, and the like. And as briefly shown here, no corporate risk manager can afford to ignore the M&M propositions either, as they include the foundational logic behind when, why, and how value-maximising firms should hedge.

1   M&M characterise what happens (according to the conventional view) when a firm reaches its threshold leverage ratio as follows: "Beyond [the threshold], the [expected stock return] will presumably rise sharply as the market discounts 'excessive' trading on the equity" (M&M, 1958, p. 277). Today, proponents of a leverage threshold argue that this threshold kicks in when the increased probability of financial distress created by high leverage levels offset the other benefits of debt. See, for example, Myers (1984) and Culp (2002a) for an explanation of this "trade-off" theory of optimal capital structure.

2   These actually are not the original assumptions as presented by M&M, but rather are based on the slightly simpler version presented in Fama (1978). Nothing is lost by working with this version of the assumptions.

3   Fama (1978) shows that this assumption can be relaxed if it is replaced with the assumptions that no firm is a monopolistic supplier of any security *and* firms all maximise their total market value at whatever prices are given from a perfectly competitive securities market.

4   See also M&M (1959), Fama and Miller (1972), and Fama (1978).

5   How taxes affect the M&M propositions has received considerable attention, including by M&M themselves in their famous 1963 "correction" paper. See also Miller (1977, 1988) and Modigliani (1982, 1988).

6   See also Fama (1978) and Jensen (2001).

7   The informational content of dividend announcements was later explored by Miller and Rock (1985) and many others.

8   See, for example, the recent paper by Fama and French (2002).

9   See also Culp (2002a).

10 Much of the remainder of this section draws heavily on Culp (2001, 2002a,c).

11 As with the proof of the M&M propositions, moreover, any of the standard three channels are available to help ensure that risk management in and of itself cannot change the value of the firm. Note also from the example that this line of reasoning applies *regardless* of investors' risk preferences.

12 See Part I of Culp (2001) for a reasonably thorough summary of the different major theories, including some not explicitly mentioned here.

13 The unsubstantiated role of "variance" played in many early theories of corporate hedging is criticised in Culp and Miller (1995, 1999).

14 As the italics are meant to suggest, the possibility of financial distress is not necessarily value-reducing for all firms. In fact, for mature companies with large and stable operating cashflow and limited investment opportunities, high leverage, which of course raises the probability of financial distress, may be a value-increasing strategy by reducing managers' natural tendency to spend (and thereby waste) excess cashflow. See Jensen and Meckling (1976) and Jensen (1986).

15 See, for example, Smith and Stulz (1985) and Froot, Scharfstein, and Stein (1993).

16 For discussions of how risk management has the potential to reduce a company's cost of capital, see Shimpi (2002) and Culp (2002a).

BIBLIOGRAPHY

Black, F., and M. Scholes, 1973, "The Pricing of Options and Corporate Liabilities", *Journal of Political Economy*, 81(3), pp. 637–54.

Cochrane, J. H., 2001, *Asset Pricing* (Princeton University Press).

Cochrane, J. H., and C. L. Culp, 2003, "Equilibrium Asset Pricing Models", *Modern Risk Management: A History* (London: Risk Books).

Culp, C. L., 2001, *The Risk Management Process: Business Strategy and Tactics* (New York: John Wiley & Sons).

Culp, C. L., 2002a, *The ART of Risk Management: Alternative Risk Transfer, Capital Structure, and the Convergence of Insurance and Capital Markets* (New York: John Wiley & Sons).

Culp, C. L., 2002b, "Contingent Capital: Integrating Corporate Financing and Risk Management Decisions", *Journal of Applied Corporate Finance*, 15(1), pp. 9–18.

Culp, C. L., 2002c, "The Revolution in Corporate Risk Management: A Decade of Innovations in Process and Products", *Journal of Applied Corporate Finance*, 14(4), pp. 8–26.

Culp, C. L., and M. H. Miller, 1995, "Hedging in the Theory of Corporate Finance: A Reply to Our Critics", *Journal of Applied Corporate Finance*, 8(1), pp. 121–7.

Culp, C. L., and M. H. Miller, 1999, "Introduction: *Why* a Firm Hedges Affects *How* a Firm Hedges", in C. L. Culp and M. H. Miller (eds), *Corporate Hedging in Theory and Practice: Lessons from Metallgesellschaft*, pp. xix–xxiii (London: Risk Books).

Fama, E. F., 1978, "The Effects of a Firm's Investment and Financing Decisions on the Welfare of Its Security Holders", *American Economic Review*, 68(3), pp. 272–84.

Fama, E. F., and K. R. French, 2002, "Testing Trade-Off and Pecking Order Predictions About Dividends and Debt", *Review of Financial Studies*, 15(1), pp. 1–33.

Fama, E. F., and M. H. Miller, 1972, *The Theory of Finance* (New York: Holt, Rinehart, and Winston).

Froot, K. A., D. S. Scharfstein, and J. C. Stein, 1993, "Risk Management: Coordinating Investment and Financing Policies", *Journal of Finance*, 48(5), pp. 1629–58.

Grundy, B. D., 2002, "Preface" in B. D. Grundy (ed), *Selected Works of Merton H. Miller, A Celebration of Markets – Volume 1: Finance*, pp. xv–xxviii (The University of Chicago Press).

Harris, M., and A. Raviv, 1991, "The Theory of Capital Structure", *Journal of Finance*, 46(1), pp. 297–355.

Jensen, M. C., 1986, "Agency Costs of Free Cash Flows, Corporate Finance and Takeovers", *American Economic Review*, 76(2), pp. 323–29.

Jensen, M. C., 2001, "Value Maximisation, Stakeholder Theory, and the Corporate Objective Function", *Journal of Applied Corporate Finance*, 14(3).

Jensen, M. C., and W. H. Meckling, 1976, "Theory of the Firm: Managerial Behavior, Agency Costs and Ownership Structure", *Journal of Financial Economics*, 3(4), pp. 305–60.

Miller, M. H., 1977, "Debt and Taxes", *Journal of Finance*, 32(2), pp. 261–75.

Miller, M. H., 1988, "The Modigliani–Miller Propositions After Thirty Years", *Journal of Economic Perspectives*, 2(4), pp. 99–120.

Miller, M. H., 1991, "Leverage", *Journal of Finance*, 46(2), pp. 479–88.

Miller, M. H., and K. Rock, 1985, "Dividend Policy Under Asymmetric Information", *Journal of Finance*, 40(4), pp. 1031–51.

Modigliani, F., 1982, "Debt, Dividend Policy, Taxes, Inflation and Market Valuation", *Journal of Finance*, 37(2), pp. 255–73.

Modigliani, F., 1988, "MM – Past, Present, Future", *Journal of Economic Perspectives*, 2(4), pp. 149–58.

Modigliani, F., and M. H. Miller, 1958, "The Cost of Capital, Corporation Finance, and the Theory of Investment", *American Economic Review*, 48(3), pp. 261–97.

Modigliani, F., and M. H. Miller, 1959, "The Cost of Capital, Corporation Finance, and the Theory of Investment: Reply", *American Economic Review*, 49(4), pp. 655–69.

Modigliani, F., and M. H. Miller, 1961, "Dividend Policy, Growth, and the Valuation of Shares", *Journal of Business*, 34(4), pp. 411–33.

Modigliani, F., and M. H. Miller, 1963, "Corporate Income Taxes and the Cost of Capital: A Correction", *American Economic Review*, 53(3), pp. 433–43.

Myers, S. C., 1977, "Determinants of Corporate Borrowing", *Journal of Financial Economics*, 5, pp. 147–75.

Myers, S. C., 1984, "The Capital Structure Puzzle", *Journal of Finance*, 39(3), pp. 575–92.

Myers, S. C., and N. S. Majluf, 1984, "Corporate Financing and Investment Decisions When Firms Have Information That Investors Do Not Have", *Journal of Financial Economics*, 13, pp. 187–221.

Ross, S. A., 1988, "Comment on the Modigliani–Miller Propositions", *Journal of Economic Perspectives*, 2(4), pp. 127–33.

Shimpi, P. A., 2002, "Integrating Risk Management and Capital Management", *Journal of Applied Corporate Finance*, 14(4), pp. 27–40.

Smith, C. W., Jr., and R. M. Stulz, 1985, "The Determinants of Firms' Hedging Policies", *Journal of Financial and Quantitative Analysis*, 20(4), pp. 391–405.

7

The Past, Present and Future of Term Structure Modelling

Lane Hughston

King's College London

"You ask what is the use of classification, arrangement, systematisation? – I answer you: order and simplification are the first steps toward the mastery of a subject – the actual enemy is the unknown."

Thomas Mann, *The Magic Mountain* (1924)

INTRODUCTION

One of the most significant developments of the last fifteen years in the culture of risk management has been the general rise in importance of "mathematical finance" as a self-contained discipline. In the 1970s and well into the 1980s, most of the work on interest rate term structure, and indeed on the theory of asset pricing and derivatives in general, was carried out in economics departments, or in the finance departments of business schools. This was and continues to be a somewhat uncomfortable arrangement on account of the conflicting demands of the coexisting "mathematical" and "non-mathematical" cultures typically found in such departments. One is reminded of C. P. Snow's "two cultures". Even now, in some otherwise distinguished business schools, the level of mathematics required for an MBA degree scarcely exceeds that of basic algebra and routine spreadsheet calculations, and woe be to the ambitious university lecturer who would assume a knowledge of calculus or probability. This paradoxical state of affairs is exacerbated by the counterproductive practice applied at some universities of using anonymous student reviews to determine salary rises and other conditions for the professors who learn quickly enough that it pays to go with the flow and water the mathematics down to the level deemed to be acceptable by the majority.

Fortunately, the trend appears to be shifting. This is due in part no doubt to the continued absorption and acceptance of substantial mathematical concepts and innovations in finance by what might be called a "trickle down" process. It is an interesting exercise to glance through the five successive editions of J. C. Hull's successful text-book *Options, Futures, and Other Derivatives* (Hull, 2002), for example, to get a feeling for the steady advance in the level of mathematical argument recognised as being appropriate for MBA students in some of the more progressive management schools. What is particularly encouraging, however, is the way in which *mathematics* departments at universities have picked up the subject: by shrugging off the burden of trying to educate the mathematically illiterate, and avoiding the temptation to offer watered down management courses, the result is a more solidly grounded education in the "hard core" aspects of finance, required both for theoretical advances as well as for serious applications in an industrial context.

The rise of the role of the regulator in the derivatives markets has also had a beneficial effect, and one hopes that the regulatory bodies will continue to concentrate their resources on ensuring that high standards of quantitative finance are being applied in those circumstances where they are needed. This means in particular that the requisite manpower of personnel adequately and properly trained in the rigours of mathematical finance should be deployed in investment banks and other financial entities and institutions, including fund management organisations of all types, insurance companies, corporate and sovereign treasuries, and of course the regulating bodies themselves. To be more specific, one should add that the employment of computer programmers, physicists, economists, and the like, for this purpose, however well trained they may be as such, will not necessarily be adequate: we live in a world of increasing specialisation, and it does make sense to insist in this connection on an MSc or PhD in quantitative or mathematical finance, or some other tangible evidence of serious academic qualifications in the area (for example, relevant publications).

In this chapter I will review some of the advances made in interest rate theory over the last fifteen years, a period that by coincidence more or less spans the interval of my own involvement with the subject so far. There will also be some scope for the discussion of recent and new lines of research, and some speculations about the future. The presentation will be by necessity somewhat uneven and desultory, with some anecdotes and occasional digressions. This is not the style in which I would normally write for, say, a technical article, but on the other hand I hope the reader will not find my historical musings and occasionally biased opinions out of place in the present context. It is impossible to do justice to the subject as a whole in a short chapter such as this, so I have stuck to those areas with which I am most familiar. Thus, for example, I will have very little of a direct nature to say about numerical methods or the use of econometric techniques for the "estimation" of interest rate models, but this is not to be construed as suggesting that these areas are unimportant or without significant recent developments (and a glance at a list of recent publications by Y. Ait-Sahalia, D. Chapman, N. Pearson, or K. Singleton, for instance, would quickly dispel any doubts on that issue). Indeed, as J. M. Keynes and subsequent generations of economists have long recognised, the theory of interest lies at the heart of the whole of finance, and as a consequence any advance in this area needs to be scrutinised both for its potential applications as well as its possible implications for our understanding of asset price dynamics in general.

OVERVIEW OF THE "STANDARD" MODEL FOR ASSET PRICE DYNAMICS

Let me briefly review what might be regarded as the "standard model" for asset price dynamics. Interest rate theory is then best seen as an integral part of such a scheme. We model the economy by a probability space $\Pi = (\Omega, F, P)$, together with the augmented filtration F_t generated by a multi-dimensional Brownian motion $W_t^\alpha (\alpha = 1, \ldots, n)$ over some fixed time horizon $0 \leq t \leq T$, where T may be infinite. Asset prices are then assumed to be continuous and modelled by Ito processes on Π, subject collectively to a condition of no arbitrage.

Before we elaborate on the significance and limitations of the continuity requirement implicit in the standard model, a brief digression will be appropriate on the origins of the "no-arbitrage" idea, and its role in modern finance. Those of you who have had occasion to read it will agree, I think, that Samuelson's 1965 article "Rational Theory of Warrant Pricing" has a visionary quality to it. One is fascinated by how close the paper comes to achieving the Black–Scholes formula – without quite getting there! There are hints of many of the ingredients needed: geometric Brownian motion as a basic model for asset dynamics, the martingale idea, the significance of arbitrage relations, and the basic shape of the price curves for calls and puts. "It is only as people act to take advantage of transient bargain opportunities that the bargains disappear." What more succinct formulation of the "no-arbitrage" principle could we ask for?

Today, as then, of course, we like wherever possible to embellish such maxims with the elements of mathematical precision. It is not surprising that one of the most important areas of research on the rise over the last fifteen years has been the attempt to systematically generalise the admissible categories of price processes to more general classes of semimartingales, and also to characterise in precise terms the relations that must hold between the movements of various assets in order to ensure no arbitrage. This line of research, which goes well beyond the consideration of elementary "jump diffusion" models, has been actively and successfully pursued by a host of financial mathematicians. The theory of Levy processes, in particular, plays an important role in some of these investigations, as do the issues associated with semi-parametric modelling and extreme value theory. The applications of general semimartingale theory in a banking or risk management context have, thus far, been relatively limited, and it remains to be seen how this promising and in many respects natural "extension" of the standard theory will pan out in terms of practical utility. Some eminent researchers, including B. Mandelbrot, for example, have maintained, in effect, that the Brownian paradigm is fundamentally flawed as a basis for asset price dynamics. I am not so sure that the majority of practitioners would agree with this point of view (does that mean that the better part of derivatives risk management as it is currently practiced by major financial institutions is similarly flawed?), but one should not ignore the fact that such words are being uttered in some quarters. Equally, it is a useful and important exercise to see just how far the Brownian paradigm can be taken, and where it leads. But the fact that I stick to the Wiener space Π as the underlying model for the economy here does not mean I am opposed to its extension, or perhaps even its abandonment altogether at some point, should that prove necessary.

That being said, let us now examine in more detail the basics of asset pricing in the standard model. Assume for a start that we have a system of m risky assets with prices S_t^i at time t, where $i = 1,\ldots,m$. The asset price processes are determined by a stochastic system of the form

$$\frac{\mathrm{d}S_t^i}{S_t^i} = \mu_t^i\mathrm{d}t + \sum_{\alpha=1}^{n} \sigma_t^{i\alpha}\mathrm{d}W_t^\alpha \qquad (1)$$

The drift process μ_t^i and the vectorial volatility process $\sigma_t^{i\alpha}$ appearing here are taken to be progressively measurable with respect to the filtration F_t, and to satisfy technical conditions sufficient to ensure that Equation (1) is well defined.

Intuitively speaking, progressive measurability means that these processes depend on the path of the Brownian motion only up to time t, thus on the one hand ensuring an element of causality in the theory (no information being transmitted back from the future), but also ensuring that there are no extraneous sources of uncertainty in the economy other than those already posited. It may seem extreme to assume that all randomness in the economy can be modelled in this way, but the point here is that the Wiener space Π is fantastically large, and is richly and beautifully structured. Indeed, most of the familiar asset pricing models based on Π barely scratch the surface of the intricate geometry of this probability space. I shall argue later, however, that the geometry of Π is intimately tied with the foundations of interest rate theory, and can be exploited to effect a promising "classification, arrangement, and simplification" of the subject.

In Equation (1) we have for each asset a set of n distinct volatility processes comprising the vector process labelled $\sigma_t^{i\alpha}$. Thus at time t the magnitude in the price fluctuation of asset number i due to the Brownian factor number α is given by $\sigma_t^{i\alpha}$, which we call the volatility matrix associated with the given set of assets. This is an m-by-n

rectangular matrix process, the exogenous specification of which, along with the drift rate processes μ_t^i, determines the asset price processes, once initial prices have been given. In fact, the solution of Equation (1) can be expressed in the form

$$S_t^i = S_0^i \exp\left[\int_{s=0}^{t} \mu_s^i ds + \int_{s=0}^{t} \sigma_s^i dW_s - \frac{1}{2}\int_{s=0}^{t} \sigma_s^{i2} ds\right] \qquad (2)$$

Here, and elsewhere in what follows, for convenience, we suppress the Wiener process indices, and there is an implied summation.

The idea that an exogenously specified drift and volatility can be used to establish an expression of the form given in Equation (2) for the asset price was the starting point for the illuminating treatment of the options pricing problem in the case of multiple assets given by Bensoussan (1984). Up to that time most investigations had tended to assume some "special form" for these processes, eg, that they could be expressed as functions of the current levels of the asset prices, thus rendering the system Markovian. One might say that there have been several significant "entry points" for mathematics along the way in the development of finance theory. One was the introduction of Ito calculus by Merton as the leading modelling methodology for asset dynamics. Another was the introduction of martingale methods by Harrison and Kreps (1979) and Harrison and Pliska (1981) as the basis for understanding the relation between the no-arbitrage condition and the "risk-neutral valuation" technique. It was the paper by Bensoussan alluded to above that tied these ideas together into a form now more or less universally used as a point of embarkation for modern applications.

Bensoussan also clarified the nature of the *market completeness assumption* required for a consistent endogenous treatment of the derivatives pricing problem. This assumption is, so to speak, the Achilles heel of the risk-neutral valuation theory. That this is the case has been long recognised; one wonders nevertheless to what extent an element of "wishful completeness" continues to be smuggled into the risk management systems and mark-to-market methodologies employed by financial institutions.

The naive use of the Black–Scholes formula in inappropriate contexts is only the most transparent example of the phenomenon. In practice, it may very well be the case that savvy traders and risk managers recognise the risks associated with incompleteness, and simply accept these as part of the business plan, with appropriate adjustments to pricing and hedging formulae, based largely on experience and intuitive judgment, to allow for unhedgeable risks. But to what extent is this being quantified at the level of the firm, or recognised by the regulators?

Equally worrying is the situation where a young "quant" at an investment bank, with the intention of being "practical", and pressured by traders and marketers to get on with things, will go ahead and apply a risk-neutral valuation methodology in an incomplete market setting, thinking that the result will be adequate as an "approximation". One of the most important challenges for today's risk managers and regulators is to ensure that such approximations are genuine when they are applied. It is for this reason, I think, that the senior management of financial institutions should include representatives well versed in the culture of modern mathematical finance; for only then can one be confident that the pressured quants will be "backed up" at a sufficiently high level when conflict arises, as will and does happen from time to time in any such organisation – and I am not merely speaking of highly placed and independent "risk management" officers (an essential feature already in place at most investment banks). In any event, continued advances are being made in the understanding of derivative pricing in incomplete markets, a problem that is intimately related to another thorny topic, that of stochastic volatility and its relation to the implied volatility smile skew.

It is important to remember, in this connection, that the issues of derivatives pricing and derivatives hedging are to some extent distinguishable. To be sure, if we know how to hedge a derivative, then we can work out its price. That is the gift that was given to us by Black, Scholes, and Merton. For pricing alone, however, we can get by with less – the specification of the state price density will suffice, and it is indeed the view now of many finance theorists that the "pricing kernel" should be regarded as the more fundamental object of financial analysis, and that hedging arguments constitute a kind of luxury that should only be partaken of when they are in season.

ARBITRAGE-FREE DYNAMICS FOR RISKY ASSET SYSTEMS

The condition of no arbitrage among the given assets in the economy, and hence the existence of the pricing kernel, is usually understood as arising as follows. We assume that a risk-free investment over a short period of time, offering a definite rate of return over that interval, pays a rate of return given by an exogenously specified non-negative interest rate process r_t that is progressively measurable with respect to the filtration F_t generated by the multi-dimensional Brownian motion. Then for no arbitrage we require that if any portfolio of the given assets with price S_t^i and portfolio position θ^i offers, instantaneously, at time t, a definite rate of return, then that rate of return must in fact be the interest rate r_t. By a "definite" rate of return at time t we mean that the portfolio volatility should vanish at that time, in other words $\sum_i \theta^i S_t^i \sigma_t^{i\alpha} = 0$. For any admissible choice of θ^i satisfying this condition at time t we therefore require $\sum_i \theta^i S_t^i (\mu_t^i + \delta_t^i) = r_t \sum_i \theta^i S_t^i$. This is the condition that the total rate of return on the portfolio at that time is given by the interest rate. We note that the total return is composed of two terms consisting of (a) the gain on the actual value of the portfolio position, and (b) the value of the dividends paid during the given small interval of time, where δ_t^i is the proportional dividend rate for the asset S_t^i. Thus δ_t^i denotes the dividend paid, per share, as a fraction of the value of the share at that time. As a consequence we deduce the well-known *instantaneous no-arbitrage condition* on the structure of the drift rate, namely, that it should be of the form

$$\mu_t^i = r_t - \delta_t^i + \lambda_t \sigma_t^i \tag{3}$$

for some progressively measurable vector process λ_t^α independent of the value of i. This is the so-called risk premium vector, which has the economic interpretation of being the "extra" rate of return, above the interest rate, per unit of volatility in the factor α.

Once we deduce the existence of a market risk premium process we can insert Equation (3) into Equation (1) to obtain the following stochastic differential system for the arbitrage-free asset price dynamics:

$$\frac{\mathrm{d}S_t^i}{S_t^i} = (r_t - \delta_t^i)\mathrm{d}t + \sigma_t^i(\mathrm{d}W_t + \lambda_t \mathrm{d}t) \qquad (4)$$

All the above is applicable in the situation where the assets are assumed to have a "limited liability" property – that is to say, come what may, their value is positive. But the no-arbitrage idea applies, more generally, to the wider category of assets that might more correctly be called "positions", which can in principle swing into the red as well as the black – for example, swap products in their numerous modern manifestations. In that case if S_t^i denotes the value (positive or negative) of asset (or position) number i at time t, then the relevant stochastic system is given by

$$\mathrm{d}S_t^i = (r_t S_t^i - D_t^i)\mathrm{d}t + \psi_t^i(\mathrm{d}W_t + \lambda_t \mathrm{d}t) \qquad (5)$$

Here D_t^i and ψ_t^i denote, respectively, the "absolute" dividend flow and the absolute volatility associated with the given asset.

The principle of no arbitrage comes into play in derivatives pricing with the observation going back to Black and Scholes (1973) that derivatives need not be viewed as fundamentally different from the assets already under consideration, and should therefore be regarded as part of the same system. In other words, we should regard derivatives as being included among the enumerated assets or positions belonging to the stochastic systems in Equations (4) and (5). The pricing of derivatives can then be achieved by observing that the processes M_t^i defined by

$$M_t^i = V_t S_t^i + \int_{s=0}^{t} V_s D_s^i \mathrm{d}s \qquad (6)$$

are martingales with respect to the given Wiener measure and filtration. Here the state price density V_t first makes its appearance, like a captain coming above board and taking command only after the ship is well at sea, and is defined by

$$V_t = \exp\left[-\int_{s=0}^{t} r_s \mathrm{d}s - \int_{s=0}^{t} \lambda_s \mathrm{d}W_s - \frac{1}{2}\int_{s=0}^{t} \lambda_s^2 \mathrm{d}s \right] \qquad (7)$$

REMARKS ON THE EXIGENCY OF EXOGENEITY

Despite its attractions, there are a few conceptual problems with the point of view on the nature of asset pricing espoused in the remarks above. One problem is the implicit assumption that there is a single "price" for a given asset at any instant in time. Thus we ignore bid-ask spreads, transaction costs, and the like. I do not regard this as a "fundamental" problem, but rather something more in the spirit of a simplifying assumption. In reality, the market consists of a large number of agents with heterogeneous preferences. If the price at which I am willing to buy is not less than the price at which you are willing to sell, after all attendant supernumerary cashflows are taken into account (fees, taxes, etc), and if we make contact, then there is a possibility that a transaction will take place. I see no problem in principle with the idea of a fully-fledged stochastic theory of market microstructure in continuous time, and on that basis it is probably acceptable to regard the current version of the standard model as simply an approximation of what is yet to come. In fact, there may be more mileage to be gained in generalisations of the standard model (based on Brownian motion) to multi-agent scenarios, than there is generalising the single agent theory to the general semi-martingale situation. Then according to the line of argument put forward in Flesaker and Hughston (1997), for each agent there is an "exchange rate" process, which for each pair of assets i and j specifies the number of assets of type j that the agent is willing to exchange for one unit of asset i. It seems likely that the idea of multiple filtrations on the probability space is a key notion in this connection, a concept already being advanced in theories of insider trading and imperfect accounting, eg, as in the work of K. Back, D. Duffie, and D. Lando.

On the other hand, even in the single agent case with the standard filtration, I am left uncomfortable with the idea of a purely exogenous specification of the various processes for the interest rate, the risk premium, the dividend rate (whether proportional or absolute), and the volatility (whether proportional or absolute). There is too much freedom. "Exogenous specification" sounds like a nice idea, but how is this meant to work in practice? Just where are all these processes meant to come from? Does the modeller expect the specs for these processes to be handed over on a platter (or its modern day equivalent, a compact disk) by some superior modeller higher up in the ranks of the firm, or, perhaps, by a regulator? Clearly not. But, in a sense, this is just the way that a good deal of interest rate modelling has been pursued over the last decade. The essence of the framework of Heath, Jarrow and Morton (1992) (HJM) is that the volatility structure of the instantaneous forward rates can be "freely specified", and it is this that leads to a variation of the "exogeneity" problem, the curse that comes to us, one might say, as a consequence of our abandonment of the concept of stationary equilibrium.

ARBITRAGE-FREE DYNAMICS OF INTEREST RATE SYSTEMS

Let us look at the matter a little more closely as it applies in particular to the case of interest rate systems. The assets in this case include a money market account B_t, satisfying $dB_t = r_t B_t dt$ and an arbitrage-free system of discount bond processes P_{tT} satisfying

$$\frac{dP_{tT}}{P_{tT}} = r_t dt + \Omega_{tT}(dW_t + \lambda_t dt) \tag{8}$$

Here P_{tT} denotes the price at time t of a discount bond that pays unity at the maturity date T, and the discount bond proportional volatility is denoted Ω_{tT}. In the HJM framework it is implicitly assumed, reasonably enough, that the discount bond system is differentiable (in an appropriate sense) in the maturity date, thus allowing us to define the so-called instantaneous forward rates (or forward short rates) by the relation $f_{tT} = -\partial_T \ln P_{tT}$ where ∂_T denotes differentiation with respect to T. Then the bond prices can be recovered by integrating this equation and writing

$$P_{tT} = \exp\left(-\int_t^T f_{tu} du\right) \tag{9}$$

a relation that also incorporates the bond maturity condition. The stochastic system for the instantaneous forward rates implied by Equation (8) is the well-known HJM equation, which in integral form reads

$$f_{tT} = -\partial_T \ln P_{0T} - \int_{s=0}^{t} \sigma_{sT} \Omega_{sT} ds + \int_{s=0}^{t} \sigma_{sT}(dW_s + \lambda_s ds) \tag{10}$$

where $\sigma_{tT} = -\partial_T \Omega_{tT}$. Clearly then, the exogenous specification of the instantaneous forward rate volatilities, together with the risk premium and the initial discount curve, is sufficient to determine f_{tT}, and hence P_{tT}. We also recover B_t since $r_t = f_{tt}$. The seductive idea of the HJM theory that made it so compelling was that "if we work in the risk-neutral measure, then all we have to do is model the instantaneous forward rate volatilities, and that's that". An extraordinary amount of effort was thus made in the late 1980s and the 1990s, both in academia and in the banks, to explore the consequences of this singular observation.

REMARKS ON THE HEATH–JARROW–MORTON REVOLUTION AND ITS CONSEQUENCES

To put matters in perspective, it should be stated categorically that the "HJM revolution", which took place roughly over the period 1987–1992, has probably been the most singularly important development in the recent history of term structure modelling. One should also mention the contributions of Babbs (1996) who independently arrived at more or less the same results. During this period, dating from the initial circulation of the HJM working paper to its eventual publication, there was evidently a kind of struggle taking place between two schools of thought on interest rate theory. The first school promoted first and foremost the ideas of equilibrium economics. The second school of thought proposed a dynamical theory of interest rates according to which the current value of the yield curve would be regarded as input data (see eg, Carverhill, 1995; Baxter, 1997). The first point of view is maintained, for instance, in the influential paper of Cox, Ingersoll, and Ross (1985) (CIR), even though the "extended" version of the CIR model (with time dependent "parameters", see, eg, Jamshidian, 1995; Maghsoodi, 1996) falls into the second category. The second school of thought, that of "evolutionary" models, which was initiated in the well known paper of Ho and Lee (1986), was just what was needed at the time by the investment banks as a basis for their interest rate risk management, and this is perhaps why the ideas in the HJM working paper were accepted more quickly by the practitioners than by the academic community. I remember Farshid Jamshidian once recalling the tremendous impact that HJM results made at the investment bank where he was working at the time when the first draft of the paper arrived, and how its practical implications were appreciated almost immediately by the community of modellers and traders.

One should understand, incidentally, that the HJM development took place even while extensive modelling work continued to be carried out using more "classical" methods, with considerable success – some notable examples of this period include the Hull–White–Jamshidian model, the Black–Derman–Toy model, and the Black–Karazinski model. See Duffie (1996) for an excellent survey of short-rate Markovian models, many of which have been implemented and used in practice. The succinct review of term structure models by Smithson and Song (1995) also captures very well a sense of the state of play in the subject at that time. For a nice example of work within the HJM framework we mention the Ritchken–Sankarasubramanian model (1995).

It seems to me that the "continuous updating approach", according to which one inputs fresh interest rate market data as it becomes available, which has been criticised by some economists as being methodologically inconsistent, but is widely used in financial institutions as an essential part of the "mark-to-market philosophy", can be understood rationally by use of the ideas of stochastic filtering theory. According to this view, the "correct" interest rate model is, at any time, simply the most parsimonious consistent with the given market data, in some appropriate sense. This point of view is consistent, broadly speaking, with the idea of the multi-agent market alluded to earlier. The problem then is to define more precisely what might be meant by "most parsimonious".

Although the HJM framework was originally based on the stochastic dynamics of the instantaneous forward rates, it suffices (and is in some respects more natural) to work directly with the associated discount bond system. In fact, we can integrate the stochastic system for the bond prices directly, to obtain the formula

$$P_{tT} = P_{0tT} \exp\left[\int_{s=0}^{t} (\Omega_{sT} - \Omega_{st})(dW_s + \lambda_s ds) - \frac{1}{2} \int_{s=0}^{t} (\Omega_{sT}^2 - \Omega_{st}^2)ds \right] \quad (11)$$

where $P_{0tT} = P_{0T}/P_{0t}$ denotes the t-forward price, made at time 0, for the discount bond maturing at time T. The corresponding expression for the money market account is then given by

$$B_t = (P_{0t})^{-1} \exp\left[\int_{s=0}^{t} \Omega_{st}(dW_s + \lambda_s ds) - \frac{1}{2} \int_{s=0}^{t} \Omega_{st}^2 ds \right] \qquad (12)$$

It is evident that if the discount bond volatility process, the market risk premium, and the initial discount curve are specified, then the interest rate system is determined completely. In particular, the short rate can be recovered by differentiating the money market account.

THE ADVENT OF THE MARKET MODEL METHOD

A good example of an important spin-off of the HJM approach, which has enjoyed considerable popularity in its own right as a basis for applications, is the so-called "market model" methodology. There are a number of different variations on this approach – too many to attempt to survey here – according to which the forward Libor rates and/or swap rates associated with the discount bond system are regarded as the "fundamental" dynamical entities. In its simplest form, the idea of a market model is as follows. The forward Libor rates L_{tab} are defined in a standard way by the relation

$$P_{tab} = \frac{1}{1 + (b-a)L_{tab}} \qquad (13)$$

where $P_{tab} = P_{tb}/P_{ta}$ denotes the forward price made at time t for purchase of a b-maturity discount bond at time a. For convenience we introduce a "tenor" parameter $\delta = b - a$, and write $L_{ta}^{\delta} = L_{tab}$. It is then a straightforward exercise in Ito calculus to work out the dynamics of L_{ta}^{δ}, starting from the bond price dynamics given by Equation (8). The result is a relation of the following form:

$$\frac{dL_{ta}^{\delta}}{L_{ta}^{\delta}} = \frac{(1 + \delta L_{ta}^{\delta})}{\delta L_{ta}^{\delta}} (\Omega_{t,a} - \Omega_{t,a+\delta})(dW_t + \lambda_t dt - \Omega_{t,a+\delta} dt) \qquad (14)$$

The key observation that follows on from this is that if $\omega_{t,a}$ is a prescribed deterministic volatility process for a given fixed tenor then we can solve the equation

$$\frac{(1+\delta L_{ta}^{\delta})}{\delta L_{ta}^{\delta}}(\Omega_{t,a}-\Omega_{t,a+\delta})=\omega_{t,a} \tag{15}$$

for the bond volatility in terms of the forward Libor rates and $\omega_{t,a}$. This demonstrates the crucial fact that there exists an HJM model with the prescribed deterministic volatility for the given forward Libor rate. The next step is to change measure so as to eliminate the drift, which can clearly be carried out since now we know the bond volatility process. As a consequence, we are left with a lognormal process for the forward Libor rate in the new measure.

It is generally recognised that the market model framework has probably been the most influential development in interest rate theory in the post-1992 years following the advent of the HJM approach. Many authors have contributed, in one way or another, and to varying degrees, to its origination and promulgation, and it would be impossible here to attempt with any success an objective account of the development of the market models and their various extensions, with all the relevant attributions. The list would undoubtedly include names such as P. Balland, A. Brace, D. Gatarek, B. Goldys, P. Hunt, F. Jamshidian, J. Kennedy, K. R. Miltersen, M. Musiela, A. Pelsser, R. Rebonato, M. Rutkowski, K. Sandmann, and D. Sondermann, to mention but a few, but there are of course others as well. Some of the early work in this area was circulated in working papers and the like, or spread by word of mouth at seminars and conferences. It is widely said, I think, that it was one particular such piece – a working paper of Brace, Gatarek and Musiela (BGM) – that had the effect of first putting market models squarely "on the map" as far as banking applications were concerned. This would therefore be an appropriate moment, in connection with the publication of the present anniversary volume, to recall that the celebrated BGM paper first appeared in print as an invited contribution to the book *Vasicek and Beyond, Approaches to Building and Applying Interest Rate Models* (Hughston, 1996). I count it a piece of good fortune to have been asked by Conrad Gardner, then at Risk Books, to be the editor of that book, and it was at the urging of Nicolas Rabeau and other colleagues at Merrill Lynch at the time that we sought the inclusion of the BGM article, which was then in circulation as a draft paper and being studied avidly by the practitioner community. Meanwhile, the subject continues to develop. Comprehensive surveys of the theory and application of market models and their extensions can be found in Musiela and Rutkowski (1997), Pelsser (2001), and Rebonato (2002), and there are many other good references too. It remains to be seen how well the market model methodology will stand the test of time and cope with more general asset classes, eg, systems involving foreign exchange and credit.

POSITIVE INTEREST, POTENTIALS, AND PRICING KERNELS

It would be a mistake, however, to presume that during the period of the explosive growth of interest in the market model methodology, all was quiet elsewhere in the development of interest rate theory. If the market models were "practical", it could hardly be argued that they were "fundamental". Nevertheless, substantial work was being carried out throughout the 1990s, and indeed into the present, on what might be referred to as the foundations of interest rate dynamics. It goes without saying, I hope, that simply because a piece of work is "foundational" does not mean it is without application. Indeed, to some extent the measure of success of such work is the degree to which applications can eventually be developed, and with what readiness.

One example in this line is the so-called "positive interest" approach that I developed in collaboration with Bjorn Flesaker in the mid 1990s (Flesaker and Hughston 1996; 1997; 1998). The idea for this arose in discussions in March 1995 when we were both attending a conference in Zurich organised by the Olsen Associates group on high frequency financial data, and the resulting working paper was first presented at the Derivatives Securities conference organised by Robert Jarrow and Stuart Turnbull in late April that year. We had been motivated at the time in part by a short paper by L. C. G. Rogers, which was published in *Risk*, that made a compelling attack on the viability of Gaussian interest rate models on the grounds that under certain circumstances large negative interest rates can arise, consequently distorting the pricing and hedging of derivative positions (see Rogers, 1996). The problem thus suggested was to find a nice formulation of the HJM theory that would also ensure interest rate positivity.

The upshot of all this was the somewhat surprising result that for any positive interest HJM model, the discount bond price process can be written in the form of the following quotient:

$$P_{tT} = \frac{\int_T^\infty (-\partial_s P_{0s})M_{ts}\,ds}{\int_t^\infty (-\partial_s P_{0s})M_{ts}\,ds} \qquad (16)$$

This is what became known as the "positive interest" representation for the general admissible interest rate model. Indeed, one can verify by inspection that if initial interest rates satisfy the positivity conditions $0 < P_{0t} \leq 1$ and $\partial_t P_{0t} < 0$, and if the martingale family M_{ts} is positive definite and initially equal to unity, then the positive interest conditions $0 < P_{tT} \leq 1$ and $\partial_T P_{tT} < 0$ are satisfied for future valuation dates and for bonds of all maturities. A representation in the form of Equation (16) exists for any martingale measure equivalent to the natural measure. That is to say, in the absence of arbitrage, and with the provision of some mild technical conditions, given any probability measure $\hat{P}$ equivalent to the natural measure P, there exists a corresponding martingale family $\hat{M}_{ts}$ such that the discount bond system is given by an integral representation of the form of Equation (16), and in the case of a complete market the representation thus obtained is unique.

One of the virtues of the integral representation was that it allowed one to generate new classes of interest rate models, some of which were very simple and yet had hitherto gone unnoticed up to that time. A notable example was the so-called rational model, for which P_{iT} has the simple form

$$P_{tT} = \frac{A_T M_t + B_T}{A_t M_t + B_t} \qquad (17)$$

where A_t and B_t are positive decreasing functions such that the initial term structure is given by $A_t + B_t = P_{0t}$, and M_t is any positive martingale normalised to unity at time 0. In the special case where

M_t is a lognormally distributed process of the form

$$M_t = \exp\left[\int_{s=0}^{t} \sigma_s dW_s \; -\frac{1}{2}\int_{s=0}^{t}\sigma_s^2 ds\right] \qquad (18)$$

where σ_s is deterministic, we obtain the so-called rational lognormal model.

Another nice example thus emerging is the quasi-lognormal model introduced in Brody and Hughston (2002). Further discussion of the "positive interest" approach and various important extensions and generalisations thereof can be found in Rogers (1997); Rutkowski (1997); Musiela and Rutkowski (1997); Hunt and Kennedy (2000); and Jin and Glasserman (2001).

From the present perspective it seems that the unifying feature of much of this line of development is the fact that the positive interest property can be embodied in the requirement that *the state price density should be a supermartingale*. Writing V_t for the state price density, the discount bond system is then given by

$$P_{tT} = \frac{E_t[V_T]}{V_t} \qquad (19)$$

and the supermartingale property $E_t[V_T] \leq V_t$ is sufficient to ensure that interest rates remain non-negative. The idea that the state price density should be modelled directly in this connection figures significantly in the work of Constantinides (1992), and also that of Rogers (1997) who observed that if one insists on the additional reasonable condition that the value of a discount bond should vanish in the limit of infinite maturity then the associated super-martingale is a potential. By the term "potential" we mean a positive supermartingale with the property that its expectation vanishes in the limit of large time. The point here is that since the theory of potentials is a fairly well-developed subject (see, eg, Meyer, 1966) one can take advantage of the fact to build new explicit families of interest rate models satisfying various nice properties, a line of research that has been pursued actively by Rogers and his co-authors, tapping rich veins in the theory of Markov processes.

One regular feature of much research in stochastic finance has been the tendency to confine the time horizon of the economy to a finite span. This artifice is often introduced for technical reasons, and indeed the familiar results associated with the Black–Scholes formula, arising from the geometric Brownian motion model, require an assumption of this nature on account of the bad behaviour of the change of measure at infinity in that case. So much the worse for Black–Scholes. It is not at all clear that the "generality" gained by truncation of the future is mathematically natural, and a more interesting question is: just what are the restrictions that arise when one imposes the condition of good behaviour over an infinite time horizon. This condition is relevant in the theory of interest rates, since it is implicit in the idea of a potential. By that argument, given the fundamental status of interest rate theory in relation to other aspects of financial thinking, it is natural to consider imposing a similar condition on other asset classes.

Indeed, in interest rate theory there is much to be said for the idea that the whole yield curve (including all maturities out to infinity) should be regarded as the appropriate dynamical object. This has led to a number of investigations in recent years concerning the "space" of yield curves, with a view to interpreting the HJM theory as a kind of dynamics on this space. In this connection it is appropriate to note particularly the work of T. Bjork and his colleagues (see, eg, Bjork and Christensen, 1999; Bjork 2001, and references cited therein). These investigations tie in closely also with attempts to construct a theory of "infinite dimensional" HJM models, that is to say, models driven by infinite dimensional Brownian motion. The first example of an infinite dimensional interest rate model is in Kennedy (1995). Since then much more has been achieved, and one could refer, for example, to the work of R. Goldstein, P. Santa-Clara, D. Sornette, and M. Chu in this line, and the contribution by Bouchaud, Sagna, Cont, El Karoui, and Potters (1998). More recently the Vienna, ETH Zurich, and Princeton groups have been particularly active in this area: see eg, Filipovic (2001), Filipovic and Teichmann (2002), and references cited therein. Given that the mathematical theory of stochastic processes on Hilbert space is now on a sound footing (Da Prato and Zabczyk, 1992), the time may indeed be ripe for the further consideration of such models. The nervous model implementor may wonder if this approach is, perhaps, a shade imparsimonious; but to think as such is to miss the point, for with Hilbert space come new "economies" of thought that more than compensate for the superficial "extravagance" of its infinite dimensionality. Perhaps we should bear in mind that the inventor of "Hilbert" space was von Neumann, also the creator of our utility functions and our game theory, and if he was happy with it, well then perhaps we should be too. In any case, it is a topic certainly worthy of further serious investigation in the context of interest rate theory.

If the positive interest property is imposed on the space of all yield curves, along with the correct asymptotic condition for large matur-ity, then there is in fact a natural Hilbert space structure associated directly with this space. In particular, suppose $x \mapsto P_{0x}$ for $x \geq 0$ denotes the discount function, and assume that the derivative of P_{0x} exists and is continuous. Then the following propositions are equivalent: (a) the discount bond system has positive interest and vanishes in the limit of large x; and (b) the derivative $\rho(x) = -\partial_x P_{0x}$ has the properties of a density function with total mass unity. As a consequence, the corresponding square-root density function $\xi(x) = (\rho(x))^{1/2}$ can be interpreted as an element of the Hilbert space of square-integrable functions on the positive part of the real line. More specifically, $\xi(x)$ belongs to the positive orthant of the unit sphere in the Hilbert space $L^2(\mathbb{R}^+)$. This means that the space of "admissible" yield curves (as defined above) has a natural realisation as a submanifold of $L^2(\mathbb{R}^+)$ and inherits a number of features from the geometry of that space. This construction gives rise to a "natural" geometry for the space of yield curves, and in particular to a natural distance measure on this space and a link with the theory of information geometry. See Brody and Hughston (2001; 2002) for further details of this line of investigation.

THE CHAOTIC APPROACH TO INTEREST RATE MODELLING

In conclusion, let me mention a newer approach to interest rate theory which I think has a good deal of promise, that combines a number of features of the positive interest models, the potential models, and the theory of square-root densities. This is the so-called "chaotic" approach, which gives a construction for the general positive interest HJM model quite parsimoniously by means of the specification of a single random variable, labelled X_∞, which we shall call the generator of the model.

The idea is as follows. Let us assume as a consequence of the absence of arbitrage the existence of a state price density V_t for the economy, in terms of which any derivative with a European-style payout H_T at time T can be valued by the martingale relation

$$H_t = \frac{1}{V_t} E_t \left[V_T H_T \right] \qquad (20)$$

We note that the quotient V_T / V_t appearing here can be interpreted as the "pricing kernel" for the economy, and the discount bond formula in Equation (19) arises in particular as a special case. A similar relation is valid for any asset that pays a continuous random cashflow D_t in perpetuity, and the value H_t at time t of such an asset is of the form

$$H_t = \frac{1}{V_t} E_t \left[\int_t^\infty V_s D_s ds \right] \qquad (21)$$

In particular, suppose that the asset under consideration is a perpetual floating rate note, paying the short rate on a continuous basis. One can think of this as a money market account based on a unit principal, the proceeds of which are being siphoned off on a daily basis to generate the required dividend flow. It should be evident in this case that the note itself retains a constant value (ie, the unit principal). Setting $H_t = 1$ and $D_t = r_t$ in Equation (21) we immediately deduce that

$$V_t = E_t \left[\int_t^\infty V_s r_s ds \right] \qquad (22)$$

We shall make it an *axiom* that a perpetual floating rate note on a unit principal has value unity, thus ensuring the existence of the expectation and integration involved here. Equation (22), which incorporates the potential condition, can also be obtained by integrating the stochastic differential equation satisfied by the state price density, and taking a conditional expectation, making use of the potential condition. Now let η_t denote any vectorial process with the property that $\eta_t^2 = V_t r_t$. Then a short calculation making use of the Ito isometry shows that V_t is given by the conditional variance

$$V_t = E_t \left[(X_\infty - E_t(X_\infty))^2 \right] \tag{23}$$

where the random variable X_∞ is defined to be

$$X_\infty = \int_0^\infty \eta_s dW_s \tag{24}$$

Thus, given X_∞, we compute the state price density by use of Equation (23), and the corresponding interest rate model by Equation (19). We note that by construction the random variable X_∞ is square integrable, ie, its variance exists, and thus we write $X_\infty \in L^2(\Pi)$, where $\Pi = (\Omega, F, P)$. It follows therefore that *every interest rate model corresponds to an element of $L^2(\Pi)$*.

Next we make use of the fact that any square integrable function on the Wiener space Π has a unique chaos expansion. In the case of a one dimensional Brownian motion this means we can write:

$$X_\infty = \phi + \int_{s_1=0}^\infty \phi_{s_1} dW_{s_1} + \int_{s_1=0}^\infty \int_{s_2=0}^{s_1} \phi_{s_1 s_2} dW_{s_1} dW_{s_2} + \cdots \tag{25}$$

Here ϕ is a constant (which we can set to zero without loss of generality), ϕ_{s_1} is a deterministic function of one variable, $\phi_{s_1 s_2}$ is a deterministic function of two variables, and so on. The existence of such an expansion was shown by Wiener (1938) in a landmark paper entitled "The Homogeneous Chaos". The version of the theory generally known today, as embodied in Equation (25), is due to Ito (1951). The important point in the present context is that once we specify the "chaos coefficients" ϕ_{s_1}, $\phi_{s_1 s_2}$, etc, then the interest rate model is completely determined.

It turns out that the pure first chaos models, for which ϕ_{s_1} is the only non-vanishing chaos coefficient, are completely deterministic, and in fact all deterministic interest rate models can be seen as arising in this way. Thus the space of first chaos models is isomorphic to the space of admissible yield curves. The simplest non-deterministic interest rate models are those for which the second chaos is non-vanishing. In particular, if ϕ_{s_1} is non-vanishing and if $\phi_{s_1 s_2}$ factorises into a product of two functions, then the resulting "factorisable second chaos model" is completely tractable, in the sense that it admits exact formulae for bond options and swaptions of all maturities, as well as an analytical formula for the discount bond system.

The space of square integrable Wiener functionals has a very rich structure that can be used to classify, arrange, and systematise the entire family of admissible interest rate models. In particular, there is a special submanifold of $L^2(\Pi)$ which consists of random variables such that each chaos coefficient factorises all the way down the line into products of the same function of one variable. Such elements of $L^2(\Pi)$ are called "coherent" (the term comes from laser physics), and together they comprise the "coherent submanifold". The coherent models have the property that although the state price density is random, the interest rate system is deterministic. They form a "basis" in the space of interest rate models in the sense that the generator of any interest rate model can be expressed as a superposition of coherent generators. In particular, by taking finite superpositions of coherent generators, we are led again to models that possess a high degree of tractability.

For further details of the "chaotic approach" see Hughston and Rafailidis (2002), and Brody and Hughston (2003). An additional interesting feature of this line of investigation is the scheme according to which other classes can be incorporated. One might refer to this as a chaotic version of the theory of Amin and Jarrow (1992). In particular, for each risky asset offering a continuous dividend stream there is an associated element of $L^2(\Pi)$ that generates the interest rate system for discount bonds denominated in that asset and paying one unit of the given asset at maturity. The exchange rate between two such assets (eg, the US dollar and the euro, or the yen and an ounce of gold) is then given by the ratio of the conditional variances of the associated generators. This raises the interesting question of to what extent the smile curves arising in connection with options on these price processes can be parametrised in terms of the associated chaos coefficients. If this is indeed possible, then one will have achieved in effect a unified theory of interest rate dynamics and stochastic volatility.

BIBLIOGRAPHY

Amin, K. I., and R. Jarrow, 1992, "Pricing Options and Risky Assets in a Stochastic Interest Rate Economy", *Mathematical Finance* 2(4), pp. 217–37.

Babbs, S., 1996, "A Family of Ito Process Models for the Term Structure of Interest Rates", in L. P. Hughston (ed), *Vasicek and Beyond: Approaches to Building and Applying Interest Rate Models*, pp. 253–71 (London: Risk Books).

Balland, P., and L. P. Hughston, 2000, "Markov Market Model Consistent with Cap Smile", *International Journal of Theoretical and Applied Finance* 5(2), pp. 161–81.

Baxter, M. W., 1997, "General Interest Rate Models and the Universality of HJM", in M. A. H. Dempster and S. R. Pliska (eds), *Mathematics of Derivative Securities*, pp. 315–35. (Cambridge University Press).

Bensoussan, A., 1984, "On the Theory of Option Pricing", *Acta Applicandae mathematicae* 2, 139–58.

Bjork, T., and B. J. Christensen, 1999, "Interest Rate Dynamics and Consistent Forward Rate Curves", *Mathematical Finance* 9(4), pp. 323–48.

Bjork, T., 2001, "A Geometric View of Interest Rate Theory", in E. Jouini, J. Cvitanic and M. Musiela (eds), *Handbook in Mathematical Finance* (Cambridge University Press).

Black, F., E. Derman, and W. Toy, 1990, "A One-Factor Model of Interest Rates and Its Application to Treasury Bond Options", *Financial Analysts Journal*, January–February 1990, pp. 33–9.

Black, F., and P. Karasinski, 1991, "Bond and Option pricing when Short Rates are Lognormal", *Financial Analysts Journal*, July–August 1991, pp. 52–9.

Black, F., and M. Scholes, 1973, "The Pricing of Options and Corporate Liabilities", *Journal of Political Economy* 81, pp. 637–54.

Bouchaud, J-P., N. Sagna., R. Cont, N. El-Karoui, and M. Potters, 1998, "Strings Attached", *Risk* 11(7), pp. 56–9.

Brace, A., D. Gatarek, and M. Musiela, 1996, "The Market Model of Interest Rate Dynamics", in L. Hughston (ed), *Vasicek and Beyond: Approaches to Building and Applying Interest Rate Models*, pp. 305–26 (London: Risk Books), and Math Finance 7, pp. 125–55 (1997).

Brody, D. C., and L. P. Hughston, 2001, "Interest Rates and Information Geometry", *Proceedings of the Royal Society A*, 457, pp. 1343–63.

Brody, D. C., and L. P. Hughston, 2002, "Entropy and Information in the Interest Rate Term Structure", *Quantitative Finance* 2, pp. 70–80.

Brody, D. C., and L. P. Hughston, 2003, "Chaos and Coherence: a New Framework for Interest Rate Modelling", Proceedings of the Royal Society.

Carverhill, A., 1995, "A Simplified Exposition of the Heath, Jarrow, and Morton Model" *Stochastics and Stochastics Reports* 53, pp. 227–40.

Constantinides, G. M., 1992, "A Theory of the Nominal Term Structure of Interest Rates", *Review of Financial Studies* 5, pp. 531–52.

Cox, J. C., J. E. Ingersoll, and S. A. Ross, 1985, "A Theory of the Term Structure of Interest Rates", *Econometrica* 53(2), pp. 385–407.

Da Prato, G., and J. Zabczyk, 1992, "Stochastic Equations in Infinite Dimensions" (Cambridge University Press).

Davis, M., 1997, "Option Pricing in Incomplete Markets with an Application to Transaction Cost Models", in M. A. H. Dempster and S. R. Pliska (eds), *Mathematics of Derivative Securities* (Cambridge University Press).

Delbaen, F., and W. Schachermayer, 1994, "The Fundamental Theorem of Asset Pricing", *Mathematische Annalen* 300. pp. 463–520.

Duffie, D., 1996, "State-Space Models of the Term Structure of Interest Rates", in L. Hughston (ed), *Vasicek and Beyond: Approaches to Building and Applying Interest Rate Models*, pp. 273–90 (London: Risk Books).

Filipovic, D., 2001, "Consistency Problem for HJM Interest Rate Models", Lecture Notes in Mathematics 1760, (Berlin: Springer Verlag).

Filipovic, D., and J. Teichmann, 2002, "Existence of Invariant Manifolds for Stochastic Equations in Infinite Dimension", forthcoming in *Journal of Functional Analysis*.

Flesaker, B., and L. P. Hughston, 1996, "Positive Interest", *Risk Magazine*, 9(1), pp. 46–9. Reprinted in L. P. Hughston (ed), *Vasicek and Beyond: Approaches to Building and Applying Interest Rate Models*, pp. 343–51 (London: Risk Books), and M. Broadie and P. Glasserman (eds), *Hedging with Trees: Advances in Pricing and Risk Managing Derivatives*, pp. 115–24 (London: Risk Books).

Flesaker, B., and L. P. Hughston, 1997, "International Models for Interest Rates and Foreign Exchange", *NetExposure* 1(3), pp. 55–79; reprinted in the L. P. Hughston (ed), 2000, *The New Interest Rate Models*, Risk Books.

Flesaker, B., and L. P. Hughston, 1998, "Positive Interest: An Afterword", in M. Broadie and P. Glasserman (eds), *Hedging with Trees: Advances in Pricing and Risk Managing Derivatives* pp. 115–24 (London: Risk Books).

Harrison, J. M., and D. Kreps, 1979, "Martingales and Arbitrage in Multiperiod Securities Markets", *Journal of Economic theory* 20, pp. 381–408.

Harrison, J. M., and S. R. Pliska, 1981, "Martingales and Stochastic Integrals in the Theory of Continuous Trading", *Stochastic Processes and their Applications*, 11, pp. 215–60.

Heath, D., R. Jarrow, and A. Morton, 1992, "Bond pricing and the term structure of interest rates: a new methodology for contingent claims valuation", *Econometrica* 60(1), 77–105.

Ho, T. S. Y., and S. B. Lee, 1986, "Term Structure Movements and Pricing Interest Rate Contingent Claims", *Journal of Finance* 41(5), pp. 1011–29.

Hughston, L. P., (ed), 1996, *Vasicek and Beyond: Approaches to Building and Applying Interest Rate Models* (London: Risk Books).

Hughston, L. P., (ed), 2000, *The New Interest Rate Models: Recent Developments in the Theory and Application of Yield Curve Dynamics* (London: Risk Books).

Hughston, L. P., and A. Rafailidis, 2002, "A Chaotic Approach to Interest Rate Modelling", Working Paper, King's College London.

Hull, J. C., 2002, *Options, Futures, and Other Derivatives*, Fifth Edition (Upper Saddle River, NJ: Prentice Hall).

Hull, J. C., and A. White, 1990, "Pricing Interest Rate Derivative Securities", *Review of Financial Studies* 3(4), pp. 573–92.

Hunt, P., J. Kennedy and A. Pelsser, 2000, "Markov-Functional Interest Rate Models", *Finance and Stochastics* 4(4), 391–408.

Hunt, P., and J. Kennedy, 2000, *Financial Derivatives in Thoery and Practice* (New York: John Wiley & Sons).

Jamshidian, F., 1991, "Bond and Option Evaluation in the Gaussian Interest Rate Model", *Research in Finance* 9, pp. 131–70.

Jamshidian, F., 1995, "A Simple Class of Square-Root Interest Rate Models", *Applied Mathematical Finance* 2, pp. 61–72.

Jamshidian, F., 1997, "Libor and Swap Market Models and Measures", *Finance and Stochastics* 1, pp. 293–330.

Jin, Y., and P. Glasserman, 2001, "Equilibrium Positive Interest Rates: A Unified View", *Review of Financial Studies,* 14, pp. 187–214.

Kennedy, D. P., 1996, "Characterising Gaussian Models of the Term Structure", *Mathematical Finance* 7(2), pp. 107–18.

Maghsoodi, Y., 1996, "Solution of the Extended CIR Term Structure and Bond Option Valuation", *Mathematical Finance* 6(1), pp. 89–109.

Meyer, P., 1966, *Probability and Potentials* (Waltham, MA: Blaisdell Publishing Company).

Musiela, M., and M. Rutkowski, 1997, *Martingale Models in Financial Modelling* (Berlin: Springer Verlag).

Pelsser, A., 2001, *Efficient Methods for Valuing Interest Rate Derivatives* (Berlin: Springer Verlag).

Rebonato, R., 2002, *Modern Theory of Interest Rate Models* (Princeton University Press).

Ritchken, P., and L. Sankarasubramanian, 1995, "Volatility Structure of Forward Rates and the Dynamics of the Term Structure", *Mathematical Finance* 5, pp. 55–72.

Rogers, L. C. G., 1996 "Gaussian errors", *Risk* 9(1), pp. 42–5.

Rogers, L. C. G., 1997, "The Potential Approach to the Term Structure of Interest Rates and Foreign Exchange Rates", *Mathematical Finance* 7, pp. 157–76.

Rutkowski, M., 1997, "A Note on the Flesaker–Hughston Model of the Term Structure of Interest Rates", *Applied Mathematical Finance* 4, pp. 151–63.

Samuelson, P. A., 1965, "Rational Theory of Warrant Pricing", *Industrial Management Review* 6, pp. 13–31.

Smithson, C., and S. Song, 1995, "Extended Family (2)", *Risk* 8(11), pp. 52–3.

Part III

The Development of Risk Management Software

8

The Development of Risk Management Software

Dan Rosen

Algorithmics Incorporated

Due to the sheer volume and complexity of business in today's financial institutions, modern risk management requires sophisticated technology to collect and analyse relevant data and to calculate exposures. This technology has co-evolved with risk management practice, and has facilitated a number of innovations in exposure measurement and control. Risk systems have made use of evolving state-of-the-art computing, and built on emerging methodological and technological standards. Although the technology started out in market risk within trading books, it now covers credit, liquidity and other risks, stretches across into the banking book, and is also applicable to asset management, insurance, and other sectors. The technology has progressed from simply measuring exposures, to providing institutions with real-time risk-adjusted information for their strategic decisions. Enterprise risk management has evolved rapidly over the last ten years from a small group doing calculations outside of a bank's operations to being an integral part of a bank's architecture.

Risk management practice and computer technology first converged in the emerging options markets of the 1970s. As the derivatives markets grew, so did awareness of their dangers and the demand for more sophisticated ways of managing risk. Since then, the methodology and technology for measuring and monitoring exposures developed hand-in-hand. When regulators called for a new function in banks of independent oversight of risk, the seeds of the technology to support it were already there. Since then, risk systems have made enormous progress, with a new third-party industry springing up to provide a range of applications, from independent solutions to truly enterprise-wide systems. The development of scenario-based approaches has enabled the integration of market, credit, liquidity and other risk analyses. Today frameworks and the first published risk management standard help solve the enormous computational challenges presented by today's institutions, including banks, asset managers, insurance companies and others, while supporting the convergence of risk management with asset and liability management and strategic financial decision-making.

COMPUTER-AIDED RISK MANAGEMENT: IN THE BEGINNING...

Risk management as an independent function with oversight of an institution's market and credit exposures did not emerge until well into the 1990s. As it did so, technology was on hand for the newly appointed risk controllers to start to accurately measure and aggregate their exposures in order to get an enterprise-wide view of their risk.

But the technology did not just spring up overnight – it gradually evolved alongside the development of the theory and practice of risk management. In fact, the two are so closely intertwined it is often hard to distinguish where practice has driven technology and vice versa. Certainly in the case of regulation, the advance in the technical ability to measure risks has been a major factor prompting the Basel II proposals for a new Capital Accord (Basel Committee, 2001). And without doubt, the task of enterprise risk management at financial institutions is now so enormous and involves so much data and computation that it would be inconceivable without modern hardware and specialised enterprise-wide software systems.

The origins of today's risk management practice can be traced back to the probability theories of 17th Century French mathematicians Pascal and Fermat, while the model for modern computers can be found in the Analytic Engine created by Englishman Charles Babbage in the 19th Century. But their significant point of convergence took place in the new option trading pits of Chicago in the early 1970s. It was there that traders desperately needed a tool to help them quickly do the complex mathematics of the recently invented Black–Scholes model to price the risk of their trades. It so happens that just at that time, Texas Instruments was looking for applications that would show off the capabilities of its new electronic calculator, and advertised its abilities to work out "Black–Scholes values" in *The Wall Street Journal* in 1973 (Bernstein, 1996). Traders seized on the machine and ever since then risk practice and technology have evolved hand in hand.

The success of Black–Scholes helped launch the derivatives markets which grew steadily through the 1970s and 1980s and then exponentially in the 1990s. Volumes were matched by an explosion in the diversity of products, as traders and quantitative analysts (quants) discovered ever more creative ways of isolating and pricing a whole range of risks, from equity prices to interest and exchange rates movements. And at each step along the way, traders and quants were making use of evolving digital technology.

In 1975, the Altair 8800, the first "personal computer" (PC), appeared, quickly followed by machines from Apple, Commodore and Tandy. But the relevance of these machines to finance, and to business in general, only really became clear with the invention of VisiCalc, the original electronic spreadsheet, by Dan Bricklin and Bob Frankston. Now traders and quants had a tool that would not only carry out calculations, but also allowed them to perform "what-ifs" and a myriad of other functions that could help them explore risk, although it would be sometime before a PC sat on every desktop and the spreadsheet was as ubiquitous as it is today.

It was through the application of these tools to the new financial markets that the seeds of the third-party risk technology industry were sown. In 1983, Chris Conde, who would later become head of US financial software company SunGard, used the just-launched IBM PC to develop Devon, the first commercially available options pricing application (*Risk*, 1997). About the same time, Oklahoma-based banker Rod Beckström began exploring swaps pricing with an Apple II and VisiCalc, eventually launching the first interest rate and currency swaps pricing program, called Swapware, in 1986.

But although technology gave users the ability to create more diverse products, this led to its own problems, especially with the growth in the over-the-counter (OTC) markets. As complexity increased, so did the risks – especially when the products were in naive or inexperienced hands. Several organisations found themselves on the wrong end of highly leveraged deals that turned sour, while others used the new markets to speculate, only to crash and burn in spectacular fashion. The London Borough Council of Hammersmith and Fulham in the UK, Gibson Greetings, Procter and Gamble in the US, and Metalgesellschaft in Germany were among the big losers and their experience alerted markets to the potential dangers that lurked in derivatives deals – but it was not only market risk that was the problem. OTC deals did not have the safeguards of exchange-traded products, and users found themselves exposed to enormous credit, legal and settlement risk.

GROUP OF THIRTY RECOMMENDATIONS OF 1993

The authorities became increasingly concerned at the systemic implications of risks in the markets and began to threaten action. In July 1993, the Group of Thirty (G30), a Washington-based body representing the major industrialised nations, issued a seminal report, *Derivatives – Practices and Principles*, in which it argued for self-regulation and set out guidelines of best practice. These specifically included technology, and it recommended that dealers and end-users "establish management information systems sophisticated enough to measure, manage, and report the risks of derivatives activities in a timely and precise manner" (Group of Thirty, 1993).

Furthermore, the G30 report identified that one of the key obstacles to achieving comprehensive risk management was the difficulty of integrating the various component systems that support the full lifecycle of the derivatives trading process.

But most significantly, the report introduced the concept of "independent risk oversight", and recommended that organisations should "establish market and credit risk management functions with clear authority, independent of the dealing function." Although some banks were already moving in this direction, and software was already available to support them, this was the first authoritative statement backing the introduction of a separate risk function.

By the time of the report, many banks had developed their own computer-based trading systems for their various derivatives and cash instruments, or were taking advantage of the whole range of third-party systems that had become available. Wall Street Systems in New York, Lombard Risk Systems in London, and Murex in France were among the first to offer specialised software for derivatives pricing, trading and back office functions. At the same time, a group of software suppliers emerged that exploited the way in which spreadsheets had by this time proliferated in dealing rooms and they created a new breed of add-in programs for pricing and risk analytics. Among the pioneers were Tech Hackers in New York, Monis and Mamdouh Barakat Risk Management in London, and Financial Engineering Associates (FEA) in California.

But while these applications gave traders some market risk tools on their desktops, they could not give a comprehensive and consolidated view of risk across their business. Banks and other trading organisations tended to operate their trading activities in silos, with separate desks and computer systems for interest rates, foreign exchange, equities and so on, creating a major obstacle to an integrated view of risk incorporating all financial functions within the bank. The new function of independent risk oversight that the report called for – and which later became known as "enterprise risk management" – required a completely new type of technology.

THE RISE OF ENTERPRISE-WIDE RISK MANAGEMENT SOFTWARE

It was exactly these issues that Ron Dembo set out to address when he established Algorithmics in 1989. As an operations research expert on consultancy projects at banks and corporates, he saw first hand how the separation of trading desks into silos prevented management from gaining an overview on the organisation's operations and from taking advantage of economies of scale, such as netting risks across desks. His answer was to develop RiskWatch, the first enterprise-wide risk management application (*Risk*, 1997). RiskWatch was designed to sit apart from the various trading systems, and to gather in their position data, mark it to market, and aggregate it into a single portfolio on which a variety of risk analytics could be performed. RiskWatch also implicitly supported the concept of independent risk oversight that the G30 was to articulate four years later. It would also anticipate the requirements of the 1998 amendment to the Basel Capital Accord (the regulatory document which established risk management as an imperative in the banking community (Basel Committee, 1998)) for banks to have an integrated system if they wanted to use internal models to measure their market risks.

Other software houses appeared fairly soon afterwards with similar aims, such as Hawaii-based Kamakura, New York-based Sailfish Systems (since acquired by Reuters) and Zurich-based Iris Integrated Risk Management, and helped establish enterprise risk management systems as a category of software distinct from trading and back office systems.

The new risk systems took advantage of the quantitative approaches to measuring risk that were emerging in the 1990s, such as value-at-risk (VAR) and risk-adjusted-return-on-capital (RAROC), that for the first time allowed the comparison of risk on very different things. Before VAR, it was almost impossible to aggregate, say, the duration of a bond with the delta of an equity. The new methodologies made it possible to consolidate risk across trading desks and to estimate total market exposures. Again, there was an intimate link between practice and technology. When JP Morgan published its RiskMetrics VAR methodology in 1994, validating the concept and providing a standardised approach, it listed nine technology and data vendors, including Algorithmics, FEA, and Wall Street Systems, that could help banks implement the methodology (JP Morgan, 1994).

Defining the components of enterprise risk management systems
As experience in implementing the new technology grew, Massachusetts-based Meridien Research distinguished four elements of an enterprise risk management system (Meridien, 1997). First, there was an integration element that connects to all the relevant source systems; trading, market data, back office, etc, and transports the data either to a data warehouse or direct to the analytics element. This technology, often called "middleware", could have various degrees of intelligence, such as the ability to map the data into a common format for aggregation and manipulation. Next, there was the database element, both for gathering the input data and for storing the output of the analysis. Then there was the analysis element to "calculate exposures and compare them with the risk appetite of the institution". (The new risk

management systems vendors usually included at least some of their own pricing and analytical models, although to various degrees they allowed their clients to incorporate their own proprietary models or those of the add-in specialists.) And finally, there was the reporting element, which formatted the output of the analysis and presented it to the user, with perhaps some ability for further ad-hoc analysis.

Although risk management technology is much more sophisticated now than it was at the time of Meridien's report in 1997, data integration and storage, analytics and reporting remain the fundamental elements of a risk system today.

Banks obtained the elements of their risk systems from a variety of sources; sometimes from general middleware, database or reporting technology vendors, or they built them in-house along with spreadsheet-based analytical components. Initially, the risk management systems vendors concentrated on the analytics component, sometimes with only rudimentary offerings in the other areas. However, experience has taught that all components are critical, and since then the vendors have developed their capabilities in data and reporting as well, sometimes in alliance with other specialists, and now offer stronger products across the board.

TEARING DOWN THE SILOS

As the Meridien report highlighted, data integration was a major task for institutions, because of the silos in which the various source systems operated and the limited flexibility and incompatibility of their legacy systems. Likewise, data storage presented a number of challenges in terms of volumes and the performance of the database, and raised issues about whether the storage should be centralised or distributed, what level of granularity the data should be gathered in, and so on. At first glance, it would appear that these should be transitional problems that would disappear once an integrated data infrastructure was in place. Certainly, the problems are easier to deal with in smaller organisations with fewer specialised business units, but in larger organisations they have proved a tremendous challenge. Organisations have been slow to change their internal structures. And although the initial focus of risk management practice and technology was on market risk, it soon became apparent that the new methodologies could also be applied to credit and other risks, and that given the scale of credit risk in particular, emphasised by the Asia and Russian debt crises of the late 1990s, it was essential to extend the technology to cover as many risk factors as possible. So the integration task has been ongoing, with more source systems needing to be linked into the data infrastructure as more elements of the business are brought into the enterprise risk management process. Therefore, a unified data management infrastructure has become an even more essential component of a risk system.

Methods for tackling credit risk were in fact developing in parallel with those of market risk management all through the 1980s and 1990s. As well as rating the creditworthiness of corporates and other organisations, companies such as Moody's KMV and Standard & Poor's, both based in New York, were collecting databases of defaults and losses, and devising models to estimate probabilities of default and loss for organisations using the data.

Meanwhile, others were working on the management of interest rate risk on company balance sheets and implementing their methods in asset and liability management systems, or trying to get a grip on the panoply of other risks that banks and other organisations face, such as legal, reputational, and technological, that are now generally collected under the banner of operational risk. But while it was inevitable that these threads should at some point converge and intertwine in an all-embracing enterprise risk management system, in practice their integration is challenging.

Asset management approaches built on the work in the 1950s and 1960s of US economists Harry Markowitz, William Sharpe, and others, were being developed to support portfolio diversification and the need to take into account the variance and covariance of investment holdings in managing risk.

For example, leading credit risk analytical models, such as Credit Suisse First Boston's CreditRisk+, JP Morgans' Credit-Metrics and Tom Wilson's CreditPortfolioView, tend to assume the independence of market and credit risk factors. However, in practice, market and credit events are often highly correlated. Fortunately, the power of today's technology offers another approach whereby scenarios of events can be simulated that take into account macroeconomic and other factors, such as changes in interest and foreign exchange rates, and how these affect market and credit risk exposures and the way in which these can be correlated. Furthermore, by running the scenarios over a number of time steps, it is possible to capture the dynamics of portfolios and how their risks evolve over time, and to take into account things like liquidity risk, which brought down Long-Term Capital Management in 1998, threatening the stability of the international markets and increasing the demand for sophisticated risk tools.

Credit risk does not just reside in the trading book of course, and is an even more critical consideration with loan portfolios and the banking book. The advantage of the scenario simulation approach is that it can incorporate multiple risk factors across both the trading and banking books. But to do so, it requires a framework that encompasses the underlying strategies and activities of the bank, and which provides a technological infrastructure for gathering and computing the relevant data. However, because risk management is still an evolving science, it has proved essential that this framework should also remain open and adaptable to change and innovation. In 1999, US Federal Reserve Board chairman Alan Greenspan warned of the dangers of "mechanical or formulaic approaches [to the assessment of risk] that, whether intentionally or not, effectively lock us into particular technologies long after they become outmoded" (Greenspan, 1999). What the industry was striving for, he suggested, was "a framework whose underlying strategies may remain relatively fixed, but within which changes in application can be made as both bankers and supervisors learn more" (Greenspan, 1999).

MARK-TO-FUTURE

Ron Dembo's design for enterprise risk systems software was based on such a framework (Dembo, 1998). In May 2000, Algorithmics placed it in the public domain under the name *Mark-to-Future* (MtF) (Algorithmics, 2000), revealing an advanced framework based on scenarios. Not only does MtF provide a scenario-based methodology for looking at how portfolio value evolves over time, it also offers a solution to the performance challenge of enterprise risk systems. By decomposing risk by instrument, MtF makes the computational task more tractable and enables calculations to be done once but used many times for various portfolios and for various measures such as VAR, credit limits, and so on. It also enables the calculations to be distributed over many processors and makes the goal of real-time risk measurement, at least for incremental risks, achievable. MtF solved one of the main issues in risk management software design – the integration of all financial risk found throughout an institution, encompassing market, credit, liquidity, and operational risk as well as asset and liability management. MtF is at the heart of Algo Suite, Algorithmics advanced, market proven, enterprise-wide risk management solution.

Distributed computing is one of a number of technological advances that risk management systems have taken on board over the years. Following their use of PCs or mainframes on which they developed their early risk system prototypes, banks and vendors adopted client server and n-tier (where n is two or more) technology architectures that emerged from the computer industry during the 1990s. These divide applications into the user interface (client) element, which can run on a desktop PC, and the data and analytical calculation elements, which run on one or more powerful server computers because of their computational demands.

Applications have been broken down even further using so-called component-based technology. This subdivides and encapsulates elements of applications, from pricing models to scenario generators to reporting programs, into self-contained units that can be optimised independently and reused and configured in various ways to improve flexibility and reliability, and to reduce development and implementation costs. One of the most important consequences of this approach is that it gives institutions far more flexibility about where they get their risk technology from and how they put it together. Now they can move more easily from custom-built internal components that can be expensive to upgrade and maintain, to standard external components from the third-party vendors.

As with methodologies, technology standards have also played an important role in the advance of risk management systems. From computer operating systems (Unix and Microsoft Windows), to databases (relational database standards), to programming languages and development tools (C++, Java, Visual Basic, etc), technology standards have made it easier to develop and integrate components and applications both within the risk management function and into the organisation's overall technology environment. More recently, the adoption of the eXtended Markup Language (XML) for data formatting is making it simpler to exchange information between systems, and to achieve straight-through processing (STP) of transactions. On the communications front, the Internet and its associated standards have enabled a sea change in the way in which institutions can access and distribute information and applications. This applies not only in terms of making applications and data available internally, or perhaps to customers via web sites, but it also enables risk technology vendors to set up as online application service providers (ASPs) and to offer institutions their analytics and reporting on an outsourced basis. Similarly, it has enabled a number of custodian banks, prime brokers and data and analytics vendors, such as State Street, Morgan Stanley and Bloomberg, to incorporate risk management into their portfolio of services. Bloomberg's approach marks an important milestone in the field of risk management – true, real time risk management on demand for both buy and sell-side institutions. An alliance between Bloomberg and Algorithmics Incorporated has produced the Algo Risk application – the first real time, truly scalable risk management application that delivers powerful risk analytics through user friendly reports to Bloomberg subscribers.

THE RISK TECHNOLOGY SPREAD

Most of the innovations in risk technology have taken place in banking, but it is not the only sector that requires systems to measure and monitor exposures. Corporates, asset managers, insurance companies and energy companies all need enterprise risk systems, and have been adopting and adapting the technologies that grew up in banking. Vendors specialising in these sectors have appeared, such as Askari and Barra for buy-side firms, and KWI and OpenLink for energy, while some vendors that originally started out in banking have taken advantage of the expertise and technology infrastructures they had already built up and have developed modules for the asset management and energy industries. Many of the fundamental requirements of the systems, such as a comprehensive data architecture and a central risk engine, are the same across the different sectors, although there are different instruments that must be supported, as well as different analytics (such as tracking error in asset management), and functions (such as scheduling in energy).

Meanwhile, within banking itself, the convergence of the threads of risk management has been moving apace, not only in terms of integrated market and credit risk, but also with asset and liability management (ALM) and strategic financial decision-making. Furthermore, Basel II has put banks on notice that they will have to start applying the techniques of market and credit risk to operational risk, and banks and their vendors are now exploring how technology can be part of this process.

Risk systems have developed enormously since the days of calculators running Black–Scholes pricing models. Nowadays, they take advantage of the most advanced hardware, software and communications technology to create highly sophisticated applications that are becoming central to the way that organisations plan and do business. Risk management is no longer simply a reactive or compliance reporting function, but is becoming proactive and providing critical information for decision-making at all levels of the business.

THE FUTURE

Developments aren't finished. The business environment continues to evolve, with new markets such as weather derivatives and bandwidth, and new mechanisms such as e-commerce platforms appearing all the time. And financial institutions themselves are constantly transforming themselves, often through mergers and acquisitions. As we move into the 21st Century, the pace of change is only likely to increase. Therefore, it is critical that banks and other organisations have a technology infrastructure that can embrace change and integrate risk management with capital allocation and business decision-making.

By using third-party components based on open industry standards, the bank of the future will be able to build a unified data and analytical architecture that connects its business silos and rationalises its existing array of applications. The result will be one-time data and deal input, with straight through processing across all products and markets, and a unified position-keeping core.

A single analytical engine will allow for scenario-based investigations of all key business decisions and their risks. Total exposure will be known and distributed in real time.

This simplified yet robust technology infrastructure will do away with the need for separate specialised systems for each of the bank's different entities and functions, with their separate maintenance and support teams, and will result in significant cost savings in IT. Already there are examples of future-focused banks employing this approach and reaping the rewards both strategically and through quick returns on their investments.

Within this unified architecture, all transaction and credit information, rates, and other data will be extracted in real time and mapped into a consistent format based on the XML standard and stored in a single logical database. This will be the sole source for the analytical engine, and any other applications that need the data. Traders, risk managers, back office staff and senior management will all access this same source for consistent and timely information.

By implementing this technology it will be possible to examine in real time the incremental risk and return of every proposed investment or trade in the context of all the institution's portfolios before any decision is taken. The technology will enable the bank of the future to effectively allocate its economic and regulatory capital on a risk-adjusted basis. Traders and others will be remunerated on their risk-adjusted earnings and not on earnings alone, orienting them in line with the bank's goals.

The bank that masters this technology will have a tremendous competitive advantage. Such a bank will be ready for the future, with an open and flexible framework that can embrace innovation and change.

Of the future, Ron Dembo of Algorithmics wrote: "Arguably for the first time, risk is undergoing a comprehensive dissection, a process that simultaneously informs us in new detail and allows us to adopt and invent new techniques for risk sharing. Both in our ability to map and understand risk, and in our ability to build mechanisms that will allow us to manipulate risk, far from being at a dead end, we are in an era of rich, astonishing, and (thanks to technology) possible unprecedented progress" (Dembo and Freeman, 1997).

CONCLUSION

The story of risk management cannot be disentangled from the story of its supporting technology. From its origins in the options markets of the 1970s, the technology embraced emerging methodologies and practices while offering solutions to the enormous problems posed by increasingly complex and volatile markets. Risk systems have built on computing standards to create flexible frameworks and powerful applications that can encompass market, credit, liquidity and other risks, and can be applied equally to banking, asset management, insurance and other sectors. In doing so, risk management has evolved from a reactive and compliance reporting function to a proactive function that supports the business at all levels of decision-making.

BIBLIOGRAPHY

Alexander, C., (ed) 1998, "Mark-to-Future: a consistent firm-wide paradigm for measuring risk and return". (New York: John Wiley & Sons).

Basel Committee on Banking Supervision, 1998, Amendment to the Capital Accord to incorporate market risks, Bank for International Settlements.

Bernstein, P., 1996, *Against the Gods: The Remarkable Story of Risk*, p. 302 (New York: John Wiley & Sons).

BIS, Secretariat of the Basel Committee on Banking Supervision, 2001, "The New Basel Capital Accord: an explanatory note".

Dembo, R., 1998, "Mark-to-Future" *Morgan Stanley Dean Witter Global Equity and Derivatives Markets*, March 11, pp. 6–16 and Dembo, R., 1998, *Risk Management and Analysis*, Volume I: *Measuring and Modeling Financial Risk* (New York: John Wiley & Sons).

Dembo, R., A. Aziz, D. Rosen, and M. Zerbs, 2000, "Mark-to-Future: A Framework for Measuring Risk and Reward" (Toronto: Algorithmics).

Dembo, R., and A. Freeman, 1997, "Silicon Valley Seduces Wall Street", *Risk*, December, p. 118, also in Dembo, R., 1998, *Seeing Tomorrow*, p. 17, (Toronto: McClelland & Stewart).

Global Derivatives Study Group, 1993, "Derivatives: Practices and Principles" (Washington: Group of Thirty).

Greenspan, A., 1999, "The evolution of bank supervision", speech to the American Bankers Association, Phoenix, Arizona.

JP Morgan, 1994, "Introduction to RiskMetrics" (New York: JP Morgan).

Meridien Research, Inc, 1997, "Vendor-Provided Enterprise Risk Technology Solutions" (Massachusetts: Meridien Research, Inc).

Part IV

The Development of Risk Measures and Methodologies

9

The Origin and Development of Value-at-Risk

Olivier Scaillet*

HEC Geneva and International Center for Financial Asset
Management and Engineering (FAME)

This chapter briefly retraces the origin and development of value-at-risk (VAR) and is meant to be a concise introduction to this risk measure. It includes a short description of the two benchmark methodologies to compute VAR, namely the variance-covariance approach and the historical approach.

INTRODUCTION

Risk management is inherent to human activity, and financial activity is surely not an exception. The past decade has witnessed numerous developments in financial risk management. One of them has attracted most of the attention, namely the concept of VAR. Our objective here is to overview the factors underlying its origin and development, and to describe in a nutshell the two benchmark methodologies for its computation.[1]

WHAT IS VALUE-AT-RISK?

VAR can be defined as a percentile of a profit and loss distribution over a specified horizon. To be specific, suppose we are in charge of measuring the risk of a portfolio allocated in bonds, equities and options. A cautious mind might wonder what the amount

*The author would like to thank the Swiss National Science Foundation for its financial support through the National Center of Competence in Research "Financial Valuation and Risk Management". He is also grateful to M. Franscini and R. Gencay for helpful comments.

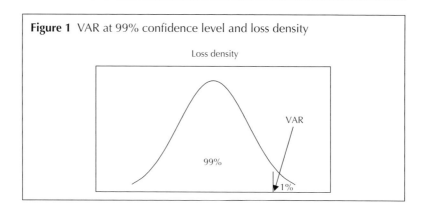

Figure 1 VAR at 99% confidence level and loss density

Loss density

VAR

99%

1%

(in euros, say) is such that we can be 99% sure that losses will not exceed that amount over a ten-day horizon. The VAR for a 99% confidence level and a ten-day holding period will answer that particular question. It is the amount that we do not dare to loose in 99% of the cases over the next ten days.[2,3] In statistical terms it is the 99th percentile of the loss distribution (see Figure 1) computed over a ten-day horizon, namely the loss level such that a 0.99 proportion of the losses lie below it and a 0.01 proportion of the losses lie above it.[4] From a computational point of view this VAR or *absolute VAR* can also be obtained by taking minus the first percentile of the distribution of the portfolio returns over a ten-day horizon and multiplying this value, known as *percentage VAR*, by the current level of the portfolio.[5]

Comparison with standard deviation
Students of modern portfolio theory (see Chapter 4 in this volume) are familiar with another statistical concept for measuring risk, namely the standard deviation. The standard deviation is the square root of the variance, which itself is the average of the squared deviations of the data from their mean. If deviations are large (and hence so is the standard deviation), returns are widely spread, and therefore risk is important. Standard deviation is a symmetric measure of risk, and its use implicitly assumes that we believe that profits and losses are mirror images of each other: a one million loss has the same chance to occur as a one million gain, and the same applies to any other loss. This symmetry characteristic appears to be the main difference between the two risk measures.

While the claim of symmetry may be approximately true for a loss distribution relating to simple assets as a long equity position, it is far from being so when considering options. To be long a call option gives unlimited upside potential with limited downside risk, more precisely limited to the premium paid upfront. Conversely, to be short a call option can produce unlimited losses with no chance of profit beyond the cashed premium. The profit and loss distribution is asymmetric in both cases and opting for standard deviation to assess the risk of derivatives can be very misleading. In contrast VAR captures this asymmetry by focusing only on potential large losses.

THE ORIGIN AND DEVELOPMENT OF VALUE-AT-RISK

The development of VAR over the past decade has been driven by joint efforts coming from regulators and banks to design efficient risk management procedures.

Banking regulatory initiatives

On the regulatory side the landmark Basle accord of 1988 provided the first step (see Chapter 27 in this volume for further elaboration) toward tighter risk management and international risk-based capital adequacy standards. This accord was initially developed by the Basle Committee on Banking Supervision, and later endorsed by the central bank governors of the G-10 countries.[6] It defines two minimum standards for meeting acceptable capital adequacy requirements: an assets-to-capital multiple and a risk-based ratio. The first standard is an overall measure of the bank's capital adequacy. The second measure focuses on credit risk associated with specific on- and off-balance-sheet asset categories. It takes the form of a solvency ratio, the famous Cooke ratio, and is defined as the ratio of capital to risk weighted on-balance-sheet plus off-balance-sheet exposures, where the weights are assigned on the basis of counterparty credit risk. Hence the Basle Accord essentially stipulates that a minimum capital requirement should be held as a safety cushion against credit risk. This first step, even if crucial, fails nevertheless to recognise the importance of diversification effects and netting, as well as the need to guard against market risk alongside credit risk.

A crucial second step was made in April 1995 to incorporate rules about market risk associated with debt and equity positions. The Basle Committee issued at that time a consultative proposal to amend the initial Accord, which was formally adopted in 1996, "the 1996 amendment", and implemented in 1998, "BIS98". Furthermore the authorities recognise in BIS98 the complexity of correctly assessing market risk exposure, especially for derivative products, such as options. Flexibility in the modelling of the multiple components of market risk is now allowed. This means that sophisticated institutions, namely institutions with an independent risk management function in place and sound risk management practice in vigour, are permitted to choose between their own "internal VAR model", referred to as the "internal model approach", and the standard model, proposed by the Committee, referred to as the "standardised approach". Hence VAR is being officially promoted as sound risk practice and a helpful device to determine the capital financial institutions need to set aside to cover market risk. As a matter of fact, the regulatory capital charge for banks using internal models for market risk is set according to a given multiple of the VAR, computed on a ten-day horizon for a 99% confidence level. This creates incentives to design efficient proprietary VAR measurement systems in order to capture diversification effects by realistically modelling the dependence between trading positions.

Banking industry initiatives

In the late 1970s and 1980s a number of financial institutions already started work on internal models to measure and aggregate risks across the institution as a whole. Indeed, banks have long recognised that managing financial risks is their core business. Better risk management systems allow them to allocate their capital more efficiently when facing the usual trade-off between reward and risk, and are therefore a nice source of comparative advantages. These systems also support their management consultancy business. In some cases they are sold to clients such as other financial institutions and large corporates who could not afford to develop them internally.

A major breakthrough in that field was the RiskMetrics system developed by JP Morgan and shared freely on the World Wide Web since 1994. This downloadable system provides financial data sets fed by the financial information group Reuters, and a methodology to calculate the VAR of an entire portfolio.[7] VAR software systems tapping into RiskMetrics were quickly proposed by party vendors and this made the methodology an instant benchmark. The RiskMetrics system is said to have been created on impulse by a request from the chairman of JP Morgan, Dennis Weatherstone. He asked his staff to deliver to him a daily one-page report indicating risk and potential losses over the next 24 hours across the bank's entire trading portfolio. This report, the famous "4.15 report", was to be given to him at 4.15 pm each day, after the close of trading. In order to meet this demand the JP Morgan staff had to design a neat methodology to measure risks across different trading positions across the whole institution, and then aggregate these risks into a single number. This number was derived from standard portfolio theory using estimated standard deviations and correlations of financial asset returns. While this theory based on a normality assumption was fairly straightforward, putting the system into practice required a tremendous amount of work, such as the choice of measurement conventions, data sets and statistical techniques.

Since then, other VAR systems have been built using approaches other than portfolio theory. For instance, the historical approach directly relies on the distribution of past returns to estimate the VAR. More sophisticated systems have also been developed exploiting Monte Carlo and other simulation techniques based on stress scenarios (see Chapter 10 in this volume) to refine the measurement of risk. More advanced statistical techniques are implemented and they certainly have their advantages (see Chapters 11, 12 and 13 in this volume). These systems are powerful and, in principle, give better results than systems only based on portfolio theory or historical approaches. However they are more costly to develop, and more difficult to operate and maintain.

Impact on corporate reporting

In 1997 the US Securities and Exchange Commission issued disclosure rules related to the use of derivative securities. This was essentially dictated by their concern about undisclosed risks lurking in off-balance-sheet instruments and their influence on the healthiness of corporates (see Part 9 in this volume). The rules allow corporates to choose one of three possible ways of disclosing risks from derivatives use: a tabulation of the fair market value, a sensitivity measure, or VAR. The availability (free or not) of VAR systems has without doubt helped corporates to match these new reporting rules. Consequently VAR practice is now widely embraced by the non-financial sector and one can read about VAR calculations in the annual reports of many large companies.

COMPUTATIONS OF VALUE-AT-RISK

Before describing the two main methodologies leading to VAR estimates, namely the variance-covariance approach and the historical approach, we first outline the framework, define formally the VAR and discuss briefly incremental VAR.

Framework and definition

Let us consider n financial assets with prices $p_{i,t}$, $i = 1,\ldots, n$, at date t. The set of prices $p_{i,0}, p_{i,1}, p_{i,2},\ldots, p_{i,T}$ forms a sample of price data for the asset i. The one-day returns of asset i are computed from $y_{i,t} = (p_{i,t} - p_{i,t-1})/(p_{i,t-1})$ or $y_{i,t} = \ln[(p_{i,t})/(p_{i,t-1})]$.[8] Let us further take a portfolio made of these n assets with allocations $a_1,\ldots, a_i,\ldots, a_n$ in values (percentage allocation). The portfolio return at date t is given by $r_t = \sum_{i=1}^{n} a_i y_{i,t} = a_1 y_{1,t} + a_2 y_{2,t} +\cdots+ a_n y_{n,t}$ ie, the sum of each allocation multiplied by the corresponding asset return. The percentage VAR for a one-day horizon and a confidence level α associated to that portfolio then solves:

$$P[r_t + VAR(a_1,\ldots, a_n, \alpha) < 0] = 1 - \alpha$$
$$\Leftrightarrow \quad P[-r_t > VAR(a_1,\ldots, a_n, \alpha)] = 1 - \alpha$$

The percentage VAR is thus the return so that, when added to the portfolio return, the probability that the global return is negative is equal to $1-\alpha$, say 1% if $\alpha = 99\%$. It is a quantile of the loss return distribution and is a function of the portfolio allocations $a_1,\ldots, a_i,\ldots, a_n$ and the loss probability level α.

Incremental value-at-risk

The sensitivity of the VAR with respect to modifications in the allocation associated to asset i is given by the first derivative $\partial VAR(a_1,\ldots, a_n, \alpha)/\partial a_i$ of the VAR with respect to the allocation a_i.

Since the decomposition $VAR(a_1,\ldots, a_n, \alpha) = \sum_{i=1}^{n} a_i[\partial VAR(a_1,\ldots, a_n, \alpha)/\partial a_i]$ holds by Euler's theorem, the quantity $a_i[\partial VAR(a_1,\ldots, a_n, \alpha)/\partial a_i]$ corresponds to the contribution of asset i to the global risk of the portfolio measured by the VAR (see Garman, 1996 and 1997; Gouriéroux, Laurent and Scaillet, 2000). These quantities are called incremental VAR, and allow the ranking of assets by their risk contributions and the determination of the (locally) most risky ones.

The variance-covariance approach

The variance-covariance approach relies on a normality assumption concerning the statistical behaviour of returns. It underlies the approach developed in Riskmetrics based on portfolio theory and is widely adopted in banks as a reference because of its computational simplicity. Let us denote by m_i and σ_{ij}, $i,j = 1, \ldots, n$, the means of, and covariances between, returns. Then the explicit VAR expression is

$$VAR(a_1,\ldots, a_n, \alpha) = -\mu + z_\alpha \sigma$$

with z_α denoting the α-quantile of a standard normal variable, and where $\mu = \sum_{i=1}^{n} a_i m_i$ and $\sigma^2 = \sum_{i=1}^{n} \sum_{j=1}^{n} a_i a_j \sigma_{ij}$ correspond to the mean and variance of the portfolio returns, respectively.[9] To get an estimate one has simply to replace the unknown means and covariances in the above expression by the associated (weighted or not) empirical means and covariances.

The historical approach

The aforementioned computational method relies on a normality assumption. This assumption may lead to the underestimation of the VAR, especially in the case of negatively skewed and leptokurtic return distributions (fat long left tail). The historical approach is based on the empirical distribution (histogram) of the data and does not rely on any parametric assumption to describe the behaviour of the returns. The idea is to use historical return data of individual stocks, compute the corresponding portfolio returns and estimate the VAR using empirical estimates. The portfolio return r_t at date t is given by $r_t = \sum_{i=1}^{n} a_i y_{i,t}$, and this leads to a "history" of portfolio returns $r_1, r_2, \ldots, r_T$ or a "history" of loss returns $-r_1, -r_2, \ldots, -r_T$ based on the allocations $a_1, \ldots, a_n$. Since the percentage VAR corresponds to a quantile of the loss distribution, we may estimate it from the empirical quantile computed from the history of loss returns. The estimated percentage VAR at loss probability level $\alpha = 99\%$ will be the ninety-ninth percentile of the empirical loss distribution.

CONCLUSION

In light of the previous sections, the evolution of financial risk management over the past decade may look, in an oversimplified picture, like a quest to synthesise risk in a single and easy-to-compute number, the VAR. Even if this quest is successful in most aspects, further advances in risk management techniques are still needed since risk is far from being ultimately tamed.

1 For more extensive treatment and detail on our topic we refer the reader to the books by Jorion (1997), Dowd (1998), and Crouhy, Galai and Mark (2001).

2 The word risk has roots in the Italian word "rischiare" which means to dare.

3 Usual loss probability levels and time horizons are either 99% or 95% and one day or ten days, respectively.

4 Losses correspond here to lost amounts and are thus taken with a positive sign (the usual agreement in force in actuarial sciences). If we consider a profit distribution (mirror image of the loss distribution where losses are assigned a negative value) the computed VAR will be minus the 1st percentile of the profit distribution computed over a ten-day horizon.

5 The term "relative VAR" refers to a VAR relative to the average loss, ie, the average loss (with positive sign) is subtracted from the absolute VAR.

6 On the Basle Committee sit senior officials of the central banks and supervisory authorities from the G-10 countries as well as officials from Switzerland and Luxembourg. The Accord was fully implemented in 1993 in the 12 ratifying countries. This accord is also known as "the BIS requirements" since the Basle Committee meets four times a year, usually in Basle, Switzerland, under the patronage of the Bank for International Settlements (BIS).

7 Technical documents, software and data sets are downloadable from http://www.riskmetrics.com.

8 A ten-day horizon would require $y_{i,t} = (p_{i,t} - p_{i,t-10})/(p_{i,t-10})$ or $y_{i,t} = \ln[(p_{i,t})/(p_{i,t-10})]$.

9 Recall that for a given random variable X, the α-quantile z_α is the level z such that $P[X \le z] = \alpha$. If X is distributed as a standard normal random variable, we get $z_{0.95} = 1.645$ and $z_{0.99} = 2.326$ when $\alpha = 95\%$ and $\alpha = 99\%$, respectively.

BIBLIOGRAPHY

Crouhy, M., D. Galai and R. Mark, 2001, *Risk Management* (New York: McGraw Hill).

Dowd, K., 1998, *Beyond Value at Risk: The New Science of Risk Management* (New York: John Wiley & Sons).

Garman, M., 1996, "Improving on VaR", *Risk*, 9, pp. 61–3.

Garman, M., 1997, "Taking VaR to Pieces", *Risk*, 10, pp. 70–1.

Gouriéroux, C., J.-P. Laurent and O. Scaillet, 2000, "Sensitivity Analysis of Value at Risk", *Journal of Empirical Finance*, 7, pp. 225–45.

Jorion, P., 1997, *Value at Risk: The New Benchmark for Controlling Market Risk* (Chicago: Irwin).

10

Stress Testing in Risk Management

Vineer Bhansali

PIMCO

In this chapter we discuss stress testing of portfolio risk. We review the fundamental features that any competing stress testing algorithms should share, and then discuss some of the recent advances that make stress testing algorithms mathematically sound and economical to implement.

INTRODUCTION

Portfolio risk measurement begins with the identification of a set of fundamental market variables that drive the prices of securities that constitute the portfolio. The values taken by fundamental market variables are determined by demand and supply, perceptions of security specific return and risk, liquidity, and the overall level of risk-aversion of investors. Stress testing is the measurement of the sensitivity of an aggregate portfolio to certain pre-defined scenarios of the market variables. Reasonable shock magnitudes, and the probability of occurence can be determined either by doing a distributional analysis of past history of the market factors, or by overlaying the forecast of economic conditions to forecast factor realisations. End-users of the scenario analysis determine whether the factor shocks should be defined by reference to orthogonal factors, or with respect to correlated factors. End-users are also usually responsible for estimating the relative likelihood of different stress events happening, ie, for the estimation or forecast of the risk factor distribution, since stress tests intrinsically carry no probability information. In principle, knowledge of all the moments of the full distribution of factors, including the factor covariances, is required to determine the total risk of the portfolio, either with correlated factors that are intuitive to the end-user, or orthogonal factors that are usually non-intuitive but economical. In practice, however, the risk of sufficiently well diversified portfolios can be replicated by just retaining the leading moments of the full portfolio distribution. Finally, the time horizon relevant to the stress test has to be identified.

This chapter will systematically discuss the elements of stress testing described above from the point of view of a market participant and risk management "practioner". Since the author's experience is in fixed income markets, all examples are drawn from the same. Mathematical details have been left out to give the reader a general and complete overview of relevant issues. A good discussion of various approaches to stress testing, including the mathematical details may be found in the literature (Jorion, 2001). The interested reader is also referred to the survey of practice performed by the Bank of International Settlements, and to the extensive bibliography provided there (BIS, 2000; 2001).

IDENTIFICATION OF MARKET VARIABLES

To ensure that the chosen stress shock algorithm is dynamical and leads to real-time risk management, the first step is to identify the variables that are the drivers of security prices. For instance, the price of a treasury bond is determined by the level of all rates along the yield curve. One can choose these market rates to be par yields, spot yields, or forward yields of the treasury curve, or if one chooses, a different rate benchmark can be used. Increasingly, the London Interbank Offered Rate (Libor) swap curve is being used as the benchmark. This is not a fundamental change in the paradigm, but simply a change of measurement reference. If one uses the swap curve as the benchmark, then the risk of the treasury bond needs to be measured with reference to two variables, the swap yield curve, and the swap spread between the treasury curve and the swap curve at each forward point. Choosing a good benchmark simply makes interpretation of the output of the stress-testing system more useful and efficient.

As the portfolio becomes more complex, holding, for instance, corporate bonds, mortgage backed securities, inflation linked bonds, tax-exempt bonds, equity linked structures, the market variable set has to be appropriately generalised to include credit spreads, implied volatility, prepayments, implied inflation rates, equity prices and implied volatility, etc. Representative traded securities can be selected whose linear combinations give measurements of each of these factor exposures. In short, this is nothing but the extension of the classic option pricing approach of creating a dynamical portfolio of idealised systematic risks that can be replicated by holding positions in certain complete sets of benchmark securities to keep a hypothetical portfolio locally hedged. This point is key to any stress testing analysis – unless all possible dominant stress factors are included in the risk management, and representative securities that are "carriers" of those securities are found, the approach will not capture portfolio risk.

TRANSLATING MARKET VARIABLES TO SYSTEMATIC RISK FACTORS

To translate market variables to risk factors, a model is required. The model can be very simple or very complex, and the degree of complexity really depends on the needs of the end-user. For instance, for a treasury bond, the sensitivity of the price of the bond to parallel shifts in the yield can be computed in closed form by a formula for duration, or duration plus convexity (Tuckman, 2002). On the other hand, the sensitivity of the bond can also be computed to all orders by simply shifting the underlying yield curve in parallel by a predetermined amount. The impact of actual shifts of the yield curve depends on how the dynamical evolution of the yield curve itself is specified and calibrated. There are again numerous choices for yield curve construction – one can use a simple single factor model calibrated to points on the yield curve, or more complex multi-factor models that are calibrated to the benchmark yield curve, volatilities and correlations of instruments, and allow for more sophisticated yield curve dynamics. There are two key points to remember. First, if there are not enough securities with liquid traded prices, then a complex model can fail in the calibration step, and it can actually be worse as a tool than a simple approximation. Second, going to a complex model drastically increases the number of computations that need to be done, and is really only justified if the portfolio consists of complex securities with embedded options that cannot be priced using simple approximations. So, whereas the stress testing of a portfolio heavy in mortgage backed securities will benefit from a complex model for yield curves, prepayments and volatilities, a portfolio that consists simply of non-callable treasury bonds will not benefit appreciably.

Once models for the classes of securities are available, to obtain the stress risk, one simply moves the underlying factors in a self-consistent (arbitrage-free) way, reads the change in prices, and computes the risk-factor exposures. For a complex fixed income portfolio, the risk-factors that span the portfolio might consist of impact due to level shifts (in many different countries if the portfolio holds global bonds), curve steepening or flattening shocks, shocks to spreads via changes of option adjusted spreads, etc. At any given point in time, the risk-manager will look at this zoo of factor exposures and decide which ones are of concern and which ones are not of concern, given his beliefs about the possible impact of market movements. Then, the partial sensitivity of the portfolio to a given factor shock is simply the product of the factor loading and the expected magnitude of the factor shock.

The factor shocks are like the equity beta concept that anyone who has studied the capital asset pricing model (CAPM) knows. The expected return of the portfolio is proportional to the beta loading to each different factor. This is the primary reason behind doing scenario analysis – unless one knows the source of returns due to factor shocks, one does not know whether the performance is due to luck or to investor skill. A greater return generally comes with greater risk, unless there are arbitrage opportunities (more on this later in the chapter).

NON-SYSTEMATIC RISK

Two different portfolios, or for that matter, any number of investors, may be ranked for their skill by first benchmarking them to the same index, and then by limiting them in terms of the maximum relative exposures they can take for each systematic factor shock. Given a set of such portfolios, the residual dispersion in performance is by definition due to non-systematic factor exposures. The immediate question then is – how does one do scenario analysis for non-systematic, or security specific, risk? For example, in the world of fixed income arbitrage, a common trade is to short the on-the-run bond (the most current issue), and buy the off-the-run bond (an older issue). The difference in yields between the two issues is commonly thought to be a free gain, and most stress testing systems will capture no risk due to the spread trade (especially if the two bonds are close in maturity and coupon). But this ignores possibly one of the biggest systematic risks of all – that of liquidity risk. The reason behind the spread between the on-the-run and off-the-run bonds is due to the differential performance of the two securities in periods of crisis. During periods of crisis, holders of the new issue find it easier to raise cash against the security as collateral in the repurchase (repo) market. In periods of crisis, such as 1998, the value of the liquidity premium can become enormous, almost a 15 standard deviation event! This example points to two principles. First, the underlying distributions of security pairs may frequently be non-Gaussian, and the apparent normal behaviour is due to the fact that the liquidity risk factor is being ignored due to its relative infrequency. Second, and more importantly, it points to the completeness problem in its naked glory, ie, if any factor is ignored, the risk system can be fooled to think that there is no risk while there is in fact an enormous amount of risk (especially when the assumption of no-risk leads to leveraging the opportunity). It is a good idea to remember that what seems to be a non-systematic or security specific factor will in time get arbitraged away and will become a systematic risk factor that needs to be stress shocked.

Two questions also immediately arise:

1. how does one measure the liquidity risk factor; and
2. how does one shock the liquidity risk factor?

Clearly, one cannot just use the history of the bond vs old bond spread to measure the distribution of the liquidity factor, since it is very fat-tailed, and there might not be enough data for calibration. However, the lack of probability information does not mean that one cannot shock the liquidity risk factor to measure its impact on the portfolio. A simple approach is to assume that as liquidity gets spotty the cost of funding rises by a large amount, ie, the repo-reverse differential blows out, and to measure the impact of this assumption on the portfolio. Another, more sophisticated approach is to think of liquidity shock as equivalent to taking correlations to extreme values. Explicit models for such regime switching behaviour may be built (Kim, 2002).

CHOOSING THE SHOCK MAGNITUDES

The magnitude of each factor shock has to serve three important purposes. First, the shock magnitude has to be large enough to capture a large portion of the factor risk. For example, a one basis point shock will not really serve the scenario analysis well for mortgage-backed securities since it does not capture much of the negative convexity, especially when the embedded optionality is more complex. The shock magnitude has to be chosen larger. Second, the shock magnitude has to be realistic in the context of historical and anticipated future outcomes. For instance, shocking interest rates by five hundred basis points would certainly capture the negative convexity of a mortgage security, but would probably be useless as a tool to illuminate risk management on a daily basis, and thus useless for risk-taking as well. Arbitrage bounds on possible outcomes correspond to the final and most important constraint on stress testing. In many realistic cases it may simply be mathematically inconsistent to simultaneously shock a number of correlated shock factors by independent large amounts. There are numerous practitioners who advertise stress shocks across various correlated factors that are large and are designed to make investors psychologically comfortable, but unfortunately many of those stress shocks cannot occur simultaneously. To take an extreme example, assume that there are two independent stress shocks of the currently low yielding Japanese yield curve; the first one is a parallel shift up or down by 50 basis points, and the second one is a steepening or flattening of 50 basis points. Given the low yields in Japan at the time of writing, you cannot reasonably have a 50 basis point steepening and a 50 basis point downward parallel shock simultaneously since that would drive some yields below zero. On the other hand, you can have a shock of the level upwards of 50 basis points with a 50 basis point flattening. The point is that the correlation matrix of stress shocks is highly constrained, and it is simply not possible to imagine any and all scenario shocks as equally likely. In a recent paper we discuss the constraints on the correlation matrix using a simple geometrical rule (Bhansali and Wise, 2001).

Of course, the analysis can also be turned on its head. Given a portfolio with factor exposures and a covariance matrix of the factors (and higher moments if a tail analysis is of interest), one can solve for the combination of factor shocks that would lead to maximal loss, or to a given threshold loss.

HISTORICAL VS FORWARD LOOKING

Of course, if one were to use historical periods to estimate the shock magnitudes and shock correlations, or particular crisis days, one is assured that there would be no mathematical inconsistencies. However, history based stress testing assumes that the future will repeat particular days or combination of days from the past. Obviously, this rarely holds true in real markets. Every crisis is different in its microscopic details. Future probabilities, especially in stressed situations are not similar to past probabilities. Stress tests are tools to gauge potential vulnerability to exceptional but plausible events (BIS, 2001). The risk manager who is really interested in assuring portfolio safety for the *future* instead of the past needs to forecast what elements of the portfolio stand to negatively impact the portfolio, and stress test them simultaneously and consistently. This is necessarily subjective, but very flexible, because the risk manager has the ability to visualise outcomes that have never been realised and create them consistently. Weighing the likely outcomes higher than the unlikely ones, the risk manager then has the ability to apply the relevant controls to the portfolio according to the risks that make sense.

Details of this approach are presented in Bhansali and Wise (2001). First, the risk manager identifies which factor exposures have the most loading, ie, which factors can impact the portfolio the most independently, and in conjunction. Then the risk manager chooses magnitudes for the factor shocks and the level of correlation between the factor shocks, ie, how likely is it that the shocks happen simultaneously. Of course, changing the correlations for some factor shocks cannot be done by freely changing many other factor correlations at the same time (otherwise the correlation matrix can become mathematically inconsistent). But since the risk manager usually has different degrees of confidence in certain correlation forecasts, the approach gives the risk manager the ability to weigh how the correlation matrix adjusts itself to be mathematically consistent, while at the same time creating a shocked environment that is complete.

CHOICE OF TIME HORIZON

The choice of stress test time horizon becomes very important for portfolios that run a mismatch between assets and liabilities. For leveraged portfolios, the impact of stress tests has special relevance for the time interval for which securities are lent out or borrowed, not only because an adverse market movement can result in margin calls and forced liquidation, but also because defaults of counterparties can lead to significant loss of mark-to-market. Most stress test algorithms assume that the scenarios are realised over an instantaneous period. While this is simple to implement, it has the significant shortcoming that for portfolios that derive significant income from options or "carry" trades, the overall risk of the portfolio is overstated. In principle, we find that it is better to shock the arbitrage-free market realisation for a forward horizon date, where the horizon date is chosen to be the average time to which the portfolio is expected to perform.

CONCLUSION

We have discussed the elements that a consistent and useful stress-testing or scenario analysis algorithm must possess. The author's opinion is that creating the stress test analysis is only as good as the inputs that go into the selection of possible outcomes, and hence is necessarily subjective. There is no mechanical way to create a fit-all stress testing process, and risk-takers and investors have to rely on their experience to consciously decide what elements of the algorithm are "art" and what elements are "science".

BIBLIOGRAPHY

Bank of International Settlements (BIS), 2000, "Stress testing by large financial institutions: Current practice and aggregation issues", URL: http://www.bis.org/publ/cgfs14.pdf.

Bank of International Settlements (BIS), 2001, "A survey of stress tests and current practice at major financial institutions", Bank of International Settlements, URL: http://www.bis.org/publ/cgfs18.htm.

Bhansali, V., and M. B. Wise, 2001, "Forecasting portfolio risk in normal and stressed markets", *Journal of Risk* 4(1), pp. 91–106.

Jorion, P., 2001, "Value at Risk", Second Edition (New York: McGraw Hill).

Kim, J., and C. C. Finger, 2002, "A stress test to incorporate correlation breakdown", forthcoming, *Journal of Risk*.

Tuckman, B., 2002, "Fixed Income Securities", Second Edition (New York: John Wiley & Sons).

11

Extreme Value Theory and Statistics for Heavy Tail Data

Silvia Caserta* and Casper G. de Vries[†]

EURONEXT NV; Erasmus University Rotterdam and Tinbergen Institute

In extreme value theory (EVT) one studies the distribution of the maximum and minimum values of random variables as the sample size increases. EVT is widely used in engineering problems like the determination of dyke height as a function of the highest flood levels and their frequency. Paralleling the growth of risk management, there is a recent interest in EVT for finance. EVT has proven to be a useful theoretical and statistical tool to calculate risk measures like VAR (ie, from the optimist's point of view, the portfolio value that will be exceeded with a high probability).

This chapter presents in a simple way the basic concepts of EVT, and the statistical techniques used to analyse extreme market movements. We start with a visual analysis of market index returns, to emphasise the frequent occurrence of large market swings. This shows that the return distribution has heavier tails than the normal distribution. If the distribution has heavy tails, EVT shows that the probability on the most extreme loss returns is governed by a particular function. This function has the nice property of being first order self-additive. This property can be exploited to reduce the computational burden to the risk manager. We introduce the

*The views expressed are those of the authors and do not necessarily represent those of Euronext.
[†]Corresponding author.

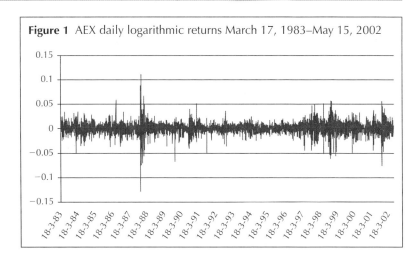

Figure 1 AEX daily logarithmic returns March 17, 1983–May 15, 2002

statistical techniques, which are used to estimate this function, and provide a short case study.

EXTREMES IN FINANCIAL RETURNS

Even though it is often expedient and fruitful to assume that asset returns are normally distributed, it is also well known that empirical return distributions contain an excessive amount of extremes relative to the normal model; see Campbell, Lo and MacKinlay (1997). To show this data feature we plotted in Figure 1 the log-returns from the daily closing prices of the AEX stock market index over the period March 17, 1983–May 15, 2002. One can easily recognise the various crashes and market rallies at the end of 1987, the Asian Crisis in 1997, the Russian Crisis in 1998 and the recent market turmoil.

In Figure 2 we generated an equal amount of pseudo random numbers by drawing from a normal distribution with the same mean and standard deviation as in the AEX return data (the y-axis is the same scale as in Figure 1). Relative to the normal data, the true returns do exhibit many larger and smaller spikes, which sometimes appear in clusters. For risk management with its focus on outliers this deviation from normality is crucial and cannot be ignored. This data feature is the so-called heavy tail feature, referring to the power shape of the tails of the density (the normal has a light tail as the tails of the density fall towards zero at an exponential rate). A Student-t distribution, for example, would fit the picture much better.

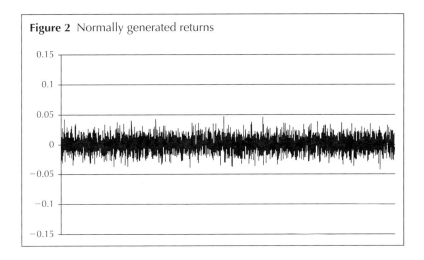

Figure 2 Normally generated returns

EXTREME VALUE THEORY

The EVT gives an approximation to the distribution of the maximum and minimum values of random variables as the sample size increases. The advantage is that the limit laws provided by EVT do not require a detailed knowledge of the distribution, which generates the returns (this is in analogy with the advantage of the central limit law for averages). Moreover, EVT implies that the probability on very large losses is governed by a simple function, again regardless of the specific distribution that underlies the return process.[1] This limit result is exploited in risk management to construct semi-parametric portfolio value-at-risk (VAR) estimates around and beyond the largest loss.

Let $X_1, X_2,...,X_n$ be a sample of random variables of size n. We can think of $X_1, X_2,...,X_n$ as the returns on the AEX index. The maximum M_n and the minimum m_n of the returns are defined as

$$M_n = \max\{X_1, X_2,...,X_n\} \quad \text{and} \quad m_n = \min\{X_1, X_2,...,X_n\}.$$

The worst case VAR might thus be calculated as $-m_n$ times the portfolio value. Examples of maximum and minimum values of the AEX are reported in Table 1.

When one increases the sample size by moving down in the table, the maximum increases or is unchanged and the minimum decreases or is unchanged. In the following we study the (limit)

Table 1 AEX max-min returns

Period	Maximum (%)	Minimum (%)
15-12-2001/15-05-2002	2.7	−2.2
15-11-2001/15-05-2002	2.7	−2.2
15-10-2001/15-05-2002	4.1	−4.8
15-09-2001/15-05-2002	5.6	−7.5

distribution of the maximum and the minimum as the sample size grows (unboundedly).

From now on we concentrate on positive random variables only, since by changing the sign on X_i one can reduce the study of minima to the study of maxima. Assume that the random variables are independent and identically distributed with (cumulative) distribution function $F(x)$. The probability that the maximum is less or equal to a pre-specified value is given by

$$\Pr\{M_n \leq x\} = \Pr\{X_1 \leq x,\dots,X_n \leq x\}$$
$$= \Pr\{X_1 \leq x\}\cdots\Pr\{X_n \leq x\} = [F(x)]^n \qquad (1)$$

Unfortunately, $[F(x)]^n$ is mostly impractical to calculate even for moderate values of n.[2] Still worse, in most cases we do not even know $F(x)$. Fortunately, the approximation to $[F(x)]^n$ offered by EVT is very helpful.

Albeit $F(x)$ is not known, the efficiency of EVT is increased if we capitalise on the fact that the return series exhibits the spikes observed in Figure 1. To this end we need a precise definition of heavy tail distributions; see Feller (1971).

Definition 1
We say that the distribution of the returns F(x) *has a heavy upper tail for the positive returns* X_i, *if (for large x)*

$$1 - F(x) = x^{-\alpha} L(x) \qquad \text{as } x \to \infty,\, \alpha > 0, \qquad (2)$$

and the function L(x) *is such that for any x > 0*

$$\lim_{t \to \infty} L(tx) / L(t) = 1. \qquad (3)$$

The tail of the distribution factors into two parts, the $L(x)$ function and the power part. The $L(x)$ function is asymptotically unimportant since $L(tx) \approx L(t)$ for large t (one says $L(\cdot)$ varies slowly at infinity). The tail of the distribution is dominated by the power part $x^{-\alpha}$. If $L(x)$ is constant then $F(x)$ in Equation (2) is the Pareto distribution, while in case of eg, the Student-t distribution $L(x)$ is not constant (for the Student-t α equals the degrees of freedom). The coefficient α is called the tail index and indicates the number of bounded moments. Note that the larger is the tail index α, the less extreme is the behaviour of the returns. Due to the power part, the tail of $F(x)$ in the end always falls off more slowly than the tails of distributions such as the normal and lognormal, which have exponential like tails. Most financial data appear to be heavy tailed in this sense.

We can now state the main result from EVT. If the distribution $F(x)$ satisfies Equation (2), then EVT shows that if the sample size n becomes large

$$\lim_{n \to \infty} \Pr\{M_n / a_n \leq x\} = \lim_{n \to \infty}[F(a_n x)]^n = e^{-x^{-\alpha}}, \quad \alpha > 0 \qquad (4)$$

where a_n is a sequence of positive scaling numbers (needed to obtain a non-trivial limit law, cf the central limit law).

Equation (4) tells us that when we use a large but finite sample of returns, the distribution of the maximum can be approximated by

$$\Pr\{M_n \leq x\} \approx G(x) = e^{-a_n^{\alpha} x^{-\alpha}} \qquad (5)$$

This implies an approximate density $g(x) = \alpha a_n^{\alpha} x^{-\alpha-1} e^{-a_n^{\alpha} x^{-\alpha}}$, which for large values of x reads (since $\exp(-a_n^{\alpha} x^{-\alpha}) \to 1$ as $x \to \infty$)

$$g(x) \approx h(x) = \alpha a_n^{\alpha} x^{-\alpha-1} \qquad (6)$$

Note that $h(x)$ in Equation (6) is the density of a Pareto distribution $H(x) = 1 - a_n^{\alpha} x$ on $[a_n, \infty)$. Thus the heavy tail feature of $F(x)$ is transferred to the limit distribution for the maximum.

The converse is also true. That is to say, if Equation (4) holds for a distribution $F(x)$, then Equation (2) is implied. To give a heuristic explanation for this, consider Equation (5) which holds that $F^n \approx G$ or $F \approx G^{1/n}$. Upon differentiation we get an expression for the density

$$f(x) \approx \frac{1}{n} G(x)^{1/n-1} g(x) = \frac{1}{n} G(x)^{1/n} \alpha a_n^\alpha x^{-\alpha-1}$$

One shows that the $n^{-1} G(x)^{1/n} \alpha a_n^\alpha$ part is in fact a slowly varying function, ie, respects the limit in Equation (3). Thus the density $f(x)$ factors into a power part $x^{-\alpha-1}$ and a slowly varying part, just like the density $g(x)$ for the maximum. Hence, the tail of the return density $f(x)$ necessarily has a Pareto like tail shape.

Thus whether we focus on the distribution of the maximum M_n in large samples, or on the distribution of very large x (extreme VAR levels), are two sides of the same coin. The two-way street relation between Equations (2) and (4) is important when we discuss estimation. To summarise, the above shows that if we are only interested in the tail behaviour and the occurrence of extreme values, we do not need to model a specific distribution $F(x)$ of the returns. Instead we can proceed by estimating the "Pareto factor" $ax^{-\alpha}$ for large values of x.

In case the distribution does not exhibit the heavy tail feature, the EVT implies that one of two other limit distributions may apply. Which case applies depends on whether the distribution has finite endpoints, or has exponential like tails. See Reiss and Thomas (2001) or Embrechts, Klueppelberg and Mikosch (1997) for further details.

In risk management applications one usually calculates the VAR for several time horizons (eg, for internal use and regulatory purposes). This would in principle require re-estimation of the Pareto factor at the different frequencies. However, due to an important additivity property of distributions that satisfy Equation (2), such repeated estimation is unnecessary. Recall that the sum of two consecutive daily log-returns is equal to the two-day log-return. Fortunately, if two random variables are heavy tailed, then the distribution of their sum is also heavy tailed. Specifically, Feller (1971) showed that if X_1, X_2 are independent and satisfy Equation (2), we have that

$$\Pr\{X_1 + X_2 > x\} \approx 2ax^{-\alpha} \qquad x > 0, \quad \alpha > 0 \qquad (7)$$

where $X_1 + X_2$ is the two-day logarithmic return. Hence, once the scale factor a and the tail index α have been estimated, one can rescale linearly the probabilities for the desired time horizon.

Conversely, if the probability level is kept constant, one can adjust the VAR level for the time horizon by inverting Equation (7). This yields the alpha-root of time rule.

Proposition (The α-root rule)
The extreme returns estimates over *T*-days are equal to the one-day extreme returns estimates multiplied by the alpha root of the considered time horizon *T*.

Compare the above result $T^{1/\alpha}$ to the case of the normal distribution when the scaling has to be done by the square root $T^{1/2}$ of the time horizon *T*. For many financial data one finds that $\alpha > 2$ so that the scaling factor is smaller than in case of normality, ie, using the normal scaling factor induces overly conservative capital levels at longer horizons (while using the normal model to calculate VAR levels at short horizons may be imprudent).

STATISTICS OF EXTREMES
For applications the norming constant and the tail index need to be estimated to obtain the Pareto factor. One possible estimation procedure is to create sub-sample maxima, and apply maximum likelihood to Equation (5); see eg, Longin (2000). Since there can be multiple extreme realisations in a single subsample, an efficient use of the data is to exploit the tight connection between Equations (4) and (2), and use all realisations above a certain high threshold *s*, say, to estimate the tail part of the unknown density $f(x)$; see eg, Hols and De Vries (1991) or Danielsson and De Vries (2000) for this approach. In this semi-parametric set-up the tail index α is commonly estimated by means of Hill's procedure; see Panel 1.

PANEL 1 THE HILL ESTIMATOR
The Hill estimator is motivated by the maximum likelihood estimator for the power coefficient of the Pareto density $h(x)$ in Equation (6). First note that the conditional Pareto density reads $h(x|x > s) = \alpha(x/s)^{-\alpha-1} s^{-1}$. Taking logarithms and differentiating with respect to α yields

$$\partial \log h(x|x > s)/\partial\alpha = 1/\alpha - \log(x/s)$$

The Hill estimator is found by equating this first order condition to zero, replacing x with realisations $X_i > s$, and summing over these elements.

Solving for $1/\alpha$ gives

$$\frac{1}{\hat{\alpha}} = \frac{1}{k}\sum_{i=1}^{k}\log\frac{X_{(i)}}{s}$$

where the $X_{(i)}$ are the largest descending order statistics $X_{(1)} \geq X_{(2)} \geq \dots \geq X_{(k)} \geq s \geq X_{(k+1)} \geq \dots \geq X_{(n)}$, pertaining to the sample $X_1, X_2, \dots, X_n$, and where n is the number of observations. The number k is the number of extreme returns above s, where s is the point from where the Pareto approximation applies.

Once the tail index has been estimated, we can directly estimate large quantiles (returns x), ie, there is no need to first estimate the scaling constant a in the Pareto factor. This is explained further in Panel 2.

PANEL 2 THE QUANTILE ESTIMATOR

Large quantile estimates can be obtained as follows. Consider two tail probabilities $p = 1-F(x_p)$ and $t = 1-F(x_t)$. For example, take $p < 1/n < t \leq k/n$, where n is the number of observations and k is the number of extreme returns we use. Let x_p and x_t denote the quantiles corresponding to the probability levels p and t. Then, by the Pareto approximation we deduce that $p \approx ax_p^{-\alpha}$ and $t \approx ax_t^{-\alpha}$. Combining these two expressions yields $x_p \approx x_t(t/p)^{1/\alpha}$. Let $t \approx m/n$, m integer, be the empirical distribution function at t. Replace x_t by X_{m+1}, which is the $m + 1$ largest positive return. This provides the following quantile estimator

$$\hat{x}_p = X_{m+1}\left(\frac{m}{np}\right)^{1/\hat{\alpha}}$$

where $\hat{\alpha}$ is the Hill estimator of the tail index α; see de Haan *et al.* (1994).

We now illustrate these techniques on the daily AEX returns as described in the first section of this chapter. Using the Hill estimator we find that for the positive returns $\alpha = 3.0$ ($k = 119$, $n = 4{,}849$), and for the negative returns $\alpha = 2.6$ ($k = 153$). These values confirm the typical results from academic research that the tail index is so low that only

Table 2 AEX index estimated returns

Positive return level (Years)	Positive (%)	Negative (%)
Daily extreme returns estimates		
25	12.0	12.5
20	11.0	11.5
15	10.5	10.5
Two-day extreme returns estimates		
25	15.1	15.7
20	13.9	14.5
15	13.0	13.2

the first few moments are bounded, and that the tail index for the positive returns is larger than the index for the negative returns.

Extreme return estimates are presented in Table 2, using $\alpha = 3$. The risks of loss (or gain) are expressed as events that occur once every few years, and are given in the first column. The associated return estimates appear in columns two (gains) and three (losses). For example, the 25-year positive return level means that on average once every 25 years there is a one-day positive return higher than 12%. The estimates for the two-day returns are obtained by using the alpha-root of time rule, ie, by multiplication of the one-day return estimates with the factor $2^{1/3}$. Other methods typically underestimate the loss (and gain) levels reported in this table and hence their relevance for risk management.

CONCLUSIONS

In this chapter we have presented the basic concepts of extreme value theory and the statistics of extremes. Particularly, we have shown how this theory is beneficial to the investigation of the occurrence of large and as of yet unseen market movements.

The way in which we have presented the theory relied on the assumption that the returns are independently distributed. Empirical research has shown that even though autocorrelation in the returns is very low, there are clusters of volatility (dependence in the second moment). Fortunately, the theory of extremes also holds for dependent variables, see McNeil and Frey (2000) who study conditional VAR. Nevertheless, the alpha-root of time rule has to be adapted when the data are dependent. Apart from time dependency, the cross sectional dependency is also of interest for the co-dependence between different asset markets in view of possible systemic risk. The multivariate dependency can be captured via a copula function, (see Chapter 12 of this volume).

The long and short of all this is that it is essential for risk managers to peek beyond the sample, for which EVT offers a reliable and coherent method.

1 An introductory textbook to EVT with many applications is Reiss and Thomas (2001). A rigorous treatise is Embrechts, Klueppelberg and Mikosch (1997).

2 As a simple example, suppose that $F(x)$ is the normal distribution with mean zero and variance one: $F(x) = \Pr\{X \le x\} = \frac{1}{\sqrt{2\pi}} \int_{-\infty}^{x} e^{-x^2/2} dx$. Then $[F(x)]^n$ can not be directly solved already for n larger than three.

BIBLIOGRAPHY

Cambell, J. Y., A. W. Lo, and A. C. MacKinlay, 1997, *The Econometrics of Financial Markets*, (Princeton University Press).

Danielsson, J., and C. G. de Vries, 2000, "Value-at-Risk and Extreme Returns", *Annales D'Economie et de Statistique*, 60, pp. 239–70.

Embrechts, P., C. Klueppelberg, and T. Mikosch, 1997, *Modelling Extremal Events for Insurance and Finance* (Berlin: Springer-Verlag).

Feller, W., 1971, *An Introduction to Probability Theory and its Applications*, Second Edition, Volume II (John Wiley & Sons).

Haan, de L., D. W. Jansen., K. Koedijk, and C. G. de Vries, 1994, "Safety First Portfolio Selection, Extreme Value Theory and Long Run Asset Risks", in J. Galambos, J. Lechner, E. Simiu and N. Macri (eds), *Extreme Value Theory and Applications*, pp. 471–87.

Hols, M., and C. G. de Vries, 1991, "The Limiting Distribution of Extremal Exchange Rate Yields", *Journal of Applied Econometrics*, 6, pp. 287–302.

Longin, F. M., 2000, "From VaR to Stress Testing: The Extreme Value Approach", *Journal of Banking and Finance*, 24, pp. 1097–130.

McNeill, A., and R. Frey, 2000, "Estimation of Tail-Related Risk Measures for Heteroscedastic Financial Time Series: An Extreme Value Approach", *Journal of Empirical Finance*, 7, pp. 271–300.

Reiss, R. D., and M. Thomas, 2001, *Statistical Analysis of Extreme Values*, Second Edition (Birkhauser).

12

The Copula

David A. Chapman

McCombs School of Business, University of Texas at Austin

The copula – or dependence function – is a flexible way of constructing multivariate distributions from general univariate distributions. As such, it offers the opportunity to generalise the concept of dependence between financial time series. This flexibility has already been applied to describing the dynamics of exchange rates, stock returns, and metals returns, and to the modelling of credit risk dynamics.

INTRODUCTION

The key to solving most practical problems in portfolio theory and risk management is a clear understanding of the joint dynamics of asset returns, interest rates, and/or exchange rates. It is a straightforward, although by no means simple, process to model the individual dynamics of any single component to one of these problems. However, how do these individual pieces fit together in a common, tractable multivariate distribution?

If the multivariate normal distribution was a sufficient description for asset returns, then the answer to the question just posed would be simple: the correlation coefficient would provide a complete description of the connection between the univariate components. However, what is a reasonable joint distribution for interest rates, whose marginal distribution might be non-central chi-square, and exchange rates, whose marginal distribution might be Student-t? As further motivation, there is ample evidence that conditional correlations among financial time series may not be the same as unconditional correlations.[1]

One approach to answering all these questions lies in the theory of the copula (or dependence function), which provides a general method for constructing consistent and tractable joint distributions from a pair (set) of given marginal distributions. In particular, Sklar's theorem (see Sklar, 1959 and Nelsen, 1999), the fundamental result in copula theory, justifies decomposing a multivariate distribution into the information in the marginal distributions and the copula, which captures all of the joint dynamics in a set of random variables. The fundamental work in Patton (2002a, b) extends the theory of copulas to allow for the conditional dynamics that are necessary to characterise financial data.

The generality of the decomposition in Sklar's theorem suggests that copulas can be useful in analysing a wide variety of financial decision problems. For example, they can provide important information in hedging either firm value or the value of derivative security contracts when there are multiple sources of risk. This theory is also well suited to providing parsimonious descriptions of stylised facts for the returns to a wide variety of marketed assets. The applications of copulas to problems in finance is still in its infancy; nonetheless, they are rapidly growing and include both data description and understanding the problem of managing credit risk.

THE COPULA

Let us begin with the simplest case. Suppose that the estimation problem involves data that has no time series aspect to it. In particular, let X be a random variable with a cumulative distribution function F. The probability of an independent sample drawn from this distribution – or of test statistics calculated from these data – are determined by this cumulative distribution function. The probability integral transform of X, a concept developed in Fisher (1936), states that as long as F is continuous, then $U \equiv F(X)$ has a uniform $(0, 1)$ distribution. This result holds regardless of the original distribution of X. Let Y denote a second random variable, with a cumulative distribution function G and a probability integral transform of $V \equiv G(Y)$.

The unconditional copula of (X, Y) is defined as the joint distribution of the integral transforms U and V. Formally, the unconditional two-dimensional copula is a function that has the following properties.[2]

❏ It is a function $C: [0, 1] \times [0, 1] \rightarrow [0, 1]$.
❏ $C(u, 0) = C(0, v) = 0$ for all $u, v \in [0, 1]$.
❏ $C(u, 1) = u$ and $C(1, v) = v$ for all $u, \in [0, 1]$.
❏ Finally,

$$V_C([u_1, u_2] \times [v_1, v_2]) \equiv C(u_2, v_2) - C(u_1, v_2) - C(u_2, v_1) + C(u_1, v_1) \geq 0$$

for all $u_1, u_2, v_1, v_2 \in [0, 1]$ such that $u_1 \leq u_2$ and $v_1 \leq v_2$

From a modelling perspective, the copula is an extremely attractive concept precisely because it partitions the information in a joint distribution into the information from the individual marginal distributions (F and G) and the copula which uses no information about the marginal distributions but summarises all of the joint behaviour of X and Y.

This statement is fomalised in *Sklar's Theorem*, the primary theoretical result in the copula literature. Sklar's theorem states: let H be a bivariate distribution function with marginal distribution functions F and G. Then there exists a copula C such that

$$H(x, y) = C(F(x), G(x))$$

for all $(x, y) \in (\mathbb{R} \cup \{\pm\infty\}) \times (\mathbb{R} \cup \{\pm\infty\})$, where $\mathbb{R}$ is the real line. Conversely, for any univariate distribution functions F and G and any copula C, the function H is a bivariate distribution function with marginal distributions F and G. Furthermore, if F and G are continuous, then C is unique.

It is the converse in the theorem that gives the copula value in an empirical setting: given marginal distributions F and G and some valid C, it explains how to construct a valid joint distribution that is consistent with the pre-specified marginal distributions. Examples of common parametric choices for C are shown in Panel 1. Conceptually, it is straightforward to extend these results from the bivariate case to the case of an arbitrary k dimensional distribution.

PANEL 1 PARAMETRIC COPULAS

The specific choice of copula function, C, determines the "recipe" for building $H(\bullet, \bullet)$ from $F(\bullet)$ and $G(\bullet)$. Examples of common bivariate copulas include:

1. The normal copula:

$$C(u,v;\rho) = \int_{-\infty}^{\Phi^{-1}(u)} \int_{-\infty}^{\Phi^{-1}(v)} \frac{1}{2\pi\sqrt{1-\rho^2}} \exp\left\{-\frac{r^2+s^2-2\rho rs}{2(1-\rho^2)}\right\} dr\,ds$$

where Φ^{-1} is the inverse of the univariate standard normal cumulative density function and $\rho \in (-1, 1)$.

2. Plackett's copula:

$$C(u,v;\psi) = \begin{cases} \dfrac{1+(\psi-1)(u+v)-\sqrt{(1+(\psi-1)(u+v))^2-4\psi(\psi-1)uv}}{2(\psi-1)} & \text{if } \psi \geq 0, \psi \neq 1 \\ u \cdot v & \text{if } \psi = 1 \end{cases}$$

3. Clayton's copula:

$$C(u,v;\delta) = \begin{cases} (u^{-\delta}+v^{-\delta}-1)^{-\frac{1}{\delta}} & \text{if } \delta > 0 \\ u \cdot v & \text{if } \delta = 1 \end{cases}$$

Note that the copula can be defined in terms of the probability density functions instead of the cumulative distribution functions.

When considering an application to financial data, the unconditional copula has the considerable disadvantage of defining the unconditional joint distribution of, say, stock returns and exchange rates. This, by construction, abstracts from the temporal nature of the data, and the time series dynamics are critically important for most of the interesting applications to financial decision-making. This implies that the true objects of interest are the joint and marginal conditional distributions. For example, the mean and volatility of short-term US Treasury rates – conditional on the most recent realised values of these data – varies dramatically from their unconditional (or "long-run") counterparts.[3] Patton (2002a) extends the notion of the copula to include distributions whose moments vary with conditioning information (see Panel 2).

The decomposition of joint conditional distributions into components that are related to individual time series and a component that describes their joint variation is important both theoretically and for the estimation of alternative time series models. Patton (2002b) describes a two-step maximum likelihood-based approach to the estimation of copula-based models of financial time series dynamics (see Panel 3). Applications of the theory of copulas to a variety of financial decision problems are described, briefly, in the following section.

PANEL 2 THE CONDITIONAL COPULA

Patton (2002a) defines the conditional copula (conditional on some random variable W) as:

The conditional copula of $(X, Y) \mid W$, where $X \mid W$ has the distribution function F and $Y \mid W$ has the distribution function G, is the conditional joint distribution of $U \equiv F(X \mid W)$ and $V \equiv G(Y \mid W)$.

The conditional version of Sklar's theorem is:

Let F be the conditional distribution of $X \mid W$, G be the conditional distribution of $Y \mid W$, and H be the joint conditional distribution of $(X, Y) \mid W$. Assume that F and G are continuous in x and y. Then there exists a unique conditional copula C such that:

$$H(x, y \mid w) = C(F(x \mid w), G(x \mid w))$$

for all $(x, y) \in (\mathbb{R} \cup \{\pm\infty\}) \times (\mathbb{R} \cup \{\pm\infty\})$ and $w \in W$, where $\mathbb{R}$ is the real line. Conversely, if we let F be the conditional distribution of $X \mid W$, G be the conditional distribution of $Y \mid W$, and C be a conditional copula, then the function H (defined above) is a conditional bivariate distribution function with conditional marginal distributions F and G.

PANEL 3 ESTIMATING A CONDITIONAL COPULA MODEL

Patton (2002a) describes how to construct a two-stage maximum likelihood estimator of the parameters of a multivariate density function modelled using a copula. The heart of the intuition of the estimator is that the copula separates the density into individual densities and the copula that connects the individual densities, and the two stages of the estimator mirror this decomposition.

The following estimator can be applied to situations where the joint log-likelihood of the (bivariate) data, $L_{XY}(\theta_0)$ can be written as:

$$L_{XY}(\theta_0) = L_X(\varphi_0) + L_Y(\gamma_0) + L_C(\varphi_0, \gamma_0, \kappa_0)$$

where L_X, L_Y, and L_C are the log-likelihoods of X, Y, and the copula, respectively, and $\theta_0 = (\varphi_0, \gamma_0, \kappa_0)'$ is the true parameter vector.[4] Central to the estimation is the notion that φ_0 and γ_0 can be estimated from data on X and Y alone and that, given $\hat{\varphi}$ and $\hat{\gamma}$, it is possible to construct an efficient estimate of κ_0. Patton (2002a) proves the consistency and asymptotic normality of the two-stage estimator, as well as deriving the form of the covariance matrix of the parameter estimates.

APPLICATIONS

Application 1: modelling asset price dynamics

One obvious application of the theory of the copula is to allow for flexible modelling of the joint dynamics of financial time series. Patton (2002b) looks at daily observations of the log-difference of the Deutschmark/US dollar exchange rate and the US dollar/yen exchange rate for the eleven-year period from January 2, 1991– December 31, 2001. These series have the advantages of being both liquid (meaning that recorded prices likely reflect actual trades) and commonly modelled in the literature on financial econometrics. Patton (2002b) specifies the Deutschmark/US dollar log exchange rate differences as following a first-order autoregression for the conditional mean and a GARCH(1,1) model (with Student-t distributed shocks) for the conditional variance (see Panel 4), and the US dollar/yen log exchange rate difference follows a more complicated autoregressive model for the conditional mean and a GARCH(1,1) model with different degrees of freedom for the conditional variance.

Patton (2002b) concludes the following.

1. It is important to allow for different tail thicknesses in the marginal distributions of the different exchange rates. This is impossible to do within conventional multivariate generalisations of GARCH models.
2. There is evidence of significant asymmetry in the correlations of the two exchange rates, with correlations between the rates being stronger when the US dollar appreciated relative to the Deutschmark and the yen.
3. There was strong evidence of a structural break in the exchange rate conditional dependence functions following the introduction

---

PANEL 4 THE GARCH(1,1) MODEL

The generalised autoregressive conditional heteroskedasticity (GARCH) model, introduced in Bollerslev (1986), is a workhorse in the financial econometrics literature. The AR(1)-GARCH(1,1) specification for a time series x_t says that x_t evolves according to the following rule:

$$x_t = \mu + \rho x_{t-1} + \varepsilon_t$$

and

$$\sqrt{\frac{v_x}{\sigma_{x,t}^2(v_x - 2)}}\, \varepsilon_t \sim iid\, t_{vx} \tag{4}$$

where

$$\sigma_{x,t}^2 = \omega + \beta \sigma_{x,t-1}^2 + \alpha \varepsilon_{t-1}^2 \tag{5}$$

and t_{vx} is the univariate Student-t distribution with v_x degrees of freedom. Note that the GARCH model can be driven by (normalised) errors with different marginal distributions, including the normal distribution.

---

of the euro in January 1999. All of these fundamental features of the data are more readily apparent when the joint dynamics are decomposed into distinct marginal and joint effects.

Malevergne and Sornette (2001) use the copula to model the dependence between a variety of different assets. In particular, they use ten years of daily returns to six different exchange rates between the US dollar and major and developing market currencies, eight years of daily data on six different metals prices from the London Metal Exchange, and daily returns to twenty two large stocks listed on the New York Stock Exchange (NYSE), measured for the six years between 1991 and 1996. Malevergne and Sornette (2001) ask whether or not the pairwise dependence between the assets within (but not across) each of these three groups can be adequately characterised using a normal copula. Using a variety of different test statistics, they conclude that:

1. exchange rates, over both the full period and two five-year sub periods, are generally consistent with the normal copula,

although (consistent with Patton, 2002b) this specification does have trouble fitting the tail properties of the data;

2. the joint behaviour of metals returns are generally inconsistent with a normal copula; and

3. most of the pairs of stocks are consistent with a normal copula.

Application 2: managing credit risk

Conventional credit risk models, including those commonly employed in practice, assume that market interest rates are constant. Therefore, by construction, they cannot accommodate the joint dynamics of market risk and credit risk; ie, the extra return required by the market as compensation for the possibility of default, and the amount of recovery in the event of default. Jarrow and Turnbull (2000) construct a reduced-form model of credit risk in which the probability of default (over any instant) depends on both the spot interest rate and on unexpected changes in the market return. The dynamics of the correlation between these common factors is critical to the performance of the credit risk model, and it can be state-dependent in potentially complicated ways. Up to this point, the literature has measured these correlations using simple linear regressions.

Schönbucher and Schubert (2001) consider the problem of correlated default using a variety of different copula functions to connect the default probabilities of individual issuers. Individual default occurs when a "default countdown process" reaches some trigger level that is unobservable to the market.[5] In a series of numerical examples, Schönbucher and Schubert (2001) demonstrate that different copulas can accommodate a variety of dynamics, ranging from symmetric default probabilities across issuers to arbitrary constant default probability changes across issuers. Finally, Schönbucher and Schubert (2001) suggest how normal copulas for joint default events could be estimated or calibrated to actual default events.

CONCLUSIONS

The application of copulas to analysing financial data is still in its infancy. Already, however, it has been applied to returns from a variety of different financial markets and to a variety of different decision problems. Given the flexibility that it offers for character-ising higher order dependence among different series, the use of this technique is almost certain going to become more widespread in a variety of applications ranging from value-at-risk (VAR) and dynamic hedging of firm value and options positions, to the estab-lishment of important stylised facts about the joint dynamics of returns from different market settings.

1   See Ang and Chen (2002) for evidence on asymmetric correlation in US stock returns, and see Hund (2000) for evidence of asymmetric correlation in the returns to dollar-denominated debt from developing countries.
2   See Patton (2002b) for a proof of this result. It follows directly from Fisher's result on the dis-tribution of the univariate probability transform and the fact that the copula is a bivariate distribution function.
3   See Chapman and Pearson (2001) for a recent summary of the stylised facts about interest rate dynamics.
4   See Patton (2002a) for a discussion of estimation situations where this decomposition is not possible.
5   This approach is in the spirit of Lando (1998).

BIBLIOGRAPHY

Ang, A., and J. Chen, 2002, "Asymmetric Correlations of Equity Portfolios", *Journal of Financial Economics*, 63, pp. 443–94.

Bollerslev, T., 1986, "Generalised Autoregressive Conditional Heteroskedasticity", *Journal of Econometrics*, 31, pp. 307–57.

Chapman, D. A., and N. D. Pearson, 2001, "Recent Advances in Estimating Term Structure Models", *Financial Analysts Journal* 57(4), pp. 77–95.

Fisher, R. A., 1936, *Statistical Methods for Research Workers*, Sixth Edition (London: Oliver & Boyd).

Hund, J., 2002, "Correlation Dynamics of Sovereign Spreads", Working Paper, A. B. Freeman School, Tulane University.

Jarrow, R. A., and S. M. Turnbull, 2000, "The Intersection of Market and Credit Risk", Journal of Banking and Finance, 24, pp. 271–99.

Lando, D., 1998, "On Cox Processes and Credit Risky Securities", Review of Derivatives Research, 2, pp. 99–120.

Malevergne, Y., and D. Sornette, 2001, "Testing the Gaussian Copula Hypothesis for Financial Assets Dependences", Working Paper, Université de Nice-Sophia Antipolis and UCLA.

Nelson, R. B., 1999, *An Introduction to Copulas* (New York: Springer-Verlag).

Patton, A. J., 2002a, "Estimating Copula Models for Times Series of Possibly Different Lengths", Working Paper, University of California at San Diego.

Patton, A. J., 2002b, "Modelling Time-Varying Exchange Rate Dependence Using the Conditional Copula", Working Paper, University of California at San Diego.

Schönbucher, P. J., and D. Schubert, 2001, "Copula-Dependent Default Risk in Intensity Models", Working Paper, Bonn University.

Sklar, A., 1959, "Fonctions de repartition a n dimensions et leurs marges," Publ. Inst. Statistics, Univ. Paris, 8, pp. 229–31.

13

Modelling Volatility

Jin-Chuan Duan

Rotman School of Management, University of Toronto

Volatility is an attractive concept but without using a model, it is an intangible entity. This article formalises key concepts about volatility and illustrates the differences and similarities between the continuous and discrete-time modelling approaches. The critical concepts of conditional vs unconditional volatility, as well as local vs cumulative volatility, are discussed. This chapter also touches upon option pricing and volatility forecasting.

INTRODUCTION

Financial data such as stock prices, exchange rates and interest rates change over time. Regardless of the reasons for the changes, it is clear from a cursory observation of these markets that the price changes are rapid and their magnitudes are often quite large measured over a short time span. We commonly refer to this price change phenomenon as volatility. When price swings are big for a given financial asset, it is said that this asset is volatile. If during a particular period of time most assets are volatile, the market is also said to be volatile. Volatility as such is easily understood and seems unambiguous until we try to take a step further towards quantifying it. Can we say something intelligent above and beyond a gut feeling about volatility? In other words, can we sensibly model volatility and make a good use of a formal quantification?

There are different ways to measure the amplitude of price swings. For the purpose of this chapter, we use standard deviation to represent volatility because it is the most commonly used volatility yardstick in the literature. Modelling volatility is not a trivial task mainly because, unlike price, volatility cannot be directly observed. In order to model volatility, we must first come up with a conceptual device and use it to indirectly infer from the observed data sample. As a result, volatility inevitably becomes a model-specific quantity. Beyond casual discussions, it is more helpful to think of volatility in terms of a given model.

With different data sets, one is bound to have different volatility estimates. Different data sets could be due to different time periods, sampling frequencies or contract specifications. For example, the implied volatility, a commonly encountered term in the options literature, refers to using the Black–Scholes (1973) option pricing model to compute a volatility figure from an option price of given exercise price, maturity and type (call or put). Since the Black–Scholes model assumes that volatility for the underlying asset is constant and price is lognormally distributed, the implied volatility concept is only meaningful under these assumptions. In other words, it is highly model-specific. Furthermore, this volatility is inferred from a particular option contract (exercise price, maturity and type) at some point in time; it may be a different value when one considers an option that is different in type, exercise price, maturity, or point in time.

It is common for investors to view their investments in terms of returns (a percentage above the price paid). Quite often, and more conveniently in fact, one can think of volatility in terms of return variability. This brings forward an important consideration of volatility in the dimension of duration. A financial return is always measured over a period of some duration. Daily return is, for example, different from monthly return in terms of duration, and hence their volatilities are expected to be different. In some contexts, ignoring duration, due to the simplicity of the problem, does not lead to confusion. As a general rule, one should always be mindful of duration and its implications on return volatility.

Last but not least is the concept of conditional vs unconditional volatility. An example can help us appreciate the distinction. The volatility of a monthly return occurring one year from now, assessed one year later, is expected to be smaller than the volatility of the same return assessed right now, because we will presumably acquire additional information over the forthcoming one-year period. The information accumulated over this period should help us better ascertain the return. Conditional volatility refers to the situation where we assess volatility at the starting point of the period of interest. In terms of this example, it refers to the volatility one year later, at which time the monthly return is assessed. Unconditional volatility is, on the other hand, the volatility assessed at the time going back into the infinite past; like having observed nothing. Our example of the monthly volatility being assessed now is neither conditional nor unconditional. We may view it as partially conditional because the information up to the current time has been incorporated, but not the information that could have been accumulated in the year to come. In the case of independent asset returns, the information accumulated over one year will not help reduce return uncertainty because the monthly return over the period of interest is independent of any previous return by assumption. If returns are related over time, it is fairly obvious that the information accumulated could be useful in reducing return uncertainty.

In this chapter, we will formalise to whatever extent possible all of the above-mentioned issues. The constant volatility model and a popular class of time-varying volatility models, known as the GARCH model, are introduced to highlight the conceptual differences. We then turn to option pricing and volatility forecasting.

CONTINUOUS VS DISCRETE-TIME APPROACHES

A time series of financial data $\{x_1, x_2, ..., x_T\}$ is given. This data series spans over a period of time from 0 to T and is sampled at some frequency, eg, daily. We intend to formalise the volatility concept using this time series. If the data points are recorded interest rates, then x_t is the interest rate at time t. If a price series of some financial asset is given instead, then x_t should be regarded as the asset return measured from $t-1$ to t. Typically in the literature, continuously compounded returns are used.

There are two ways of viewing this observed time series. One can contemplate a continuous-time stochastic process underlying this time series. The data series is simply a partial recording of what has happened. Alternatively, one can directly postulate a discrete-time stochastic process describing only the evolution over the discrete time points on which data is available. Although these two approaches face the same data series, the resulting volatility concepts are different. For the continuous-time model, the shortest duration over which a return can be defined is an instant, although such returns are not observed, whereas for the discrete-time model, the minimum duration is one period. For ease of exposition, I will refer to the return defined over the shortest possible period for a model as a local return. Any return over more than one minimum period is referred to as a cumulative return. The volatilities corresponding to these returns are referred to as local and cumulative volatilities, respectively. A one-period return (or volatility) in the discrete-time model is thus a local return (local volatility), but the same one-period return is a cumulative return (or cumulative volatility) under the continuous-time model.

The geometric Brownian motion model is a good example of a continuous-time model that can help our understanding. Assume the asset price follows the stochastic differential equation:

$$d\ln S_t = \mu dt + \sigma dW_t$$

where W_t is a Wiener process, $d\ln S_t$ is the local return (continuously compounded), μdt is the expected local return and $\sigma\sqrt{dt}$ is the local volatility. This continuous-time model is special for there is a simple analytical solution to the stochastic differential equation as follows:

$$\ln \frac{S_t}{S_{t-\tau}} = \mu\tau + \sigma(W_t - W_{t-\tau})$$

This solution allows us to easily consider a cumulative return and volatility over any duration. Specifically, $\ln(S_t/S_{t-\tau})$ is a τ-period return, which is normally distributed with the expected cumulative return $\mu\tau$ and the cumulative volatility $\sigma\sqrt{\tau}$. The data point x_t is for $\tau = 1$. Implied by the geometric Brownian motion model, the discrete-time equivalent model for the return data series has independent, identically distributed (i.i.d.) normal random variables with mean μ and volatility σ. For this discrete-time model, each of the data points is a local return with local volatility σ.

An n-period cumulative return starting from time t can be written as

$$\ln \frac{S_{t+n}}{S_t} = \ln \frac{S_{t+1}}{S_t} + \ln \frac{S_{t+2}}{S_{t+1}} + \cdots + \ln \frac{S_{t+n}}{S_{t+n-1}}$$

$$= x_{t+1} + x_{t+2} + \cdots + x_{t+n}$$

The n-period cumulative return is thus a sum of n i.i.d. one-period returns, which clearly has the mean of $n\mu$ and the volatility of $\sqrt{n}\sigma$. Not surprisingly, this result is in agreement with using the continuous-time model directly by setting $\tau = n$.

Equivalence between continuous and discrete-time models for the observed data sample can be established in this case, mainly because aggregating the continuous-time model derives the discrete-time model. Time aggregation is generally difficult for more complex models. If one starts by a discrete-time model, it is even harder to come up with a continuous-time model that gives rise to the particular discrete-time model after time aggregation.

Time aggregation is an important practical issue regardless of whether a particular model permits analytical aggregation. Applications often require us to go from local returns to a cumulative return. For example, one may want to use a data sample of daily returns to estimate the monthly volatility. Scaling daily volatility by the square root of the length of a month, which is a seemingly innocent practice, is actually only valid under the assumption of i.i.d. returns.

CONDITIONAL VS UNCONDITIONAL VOLATILITY

For the i.i.d. model discussed in the preceding section, information available at, say, time t has no bearing on how the next local return or any future cumulative return will behave. The concept of conditioning on information is clearly not a meaningful one in such a context. Before we introduce the concept of conditioning, we want to take a look of financial data to see whether it is worthwhile to commit efforts to this issue. Figure 1 is a plot of the daily S&P 500 index returns from January 3, 1992 to December 29, 2000. It is

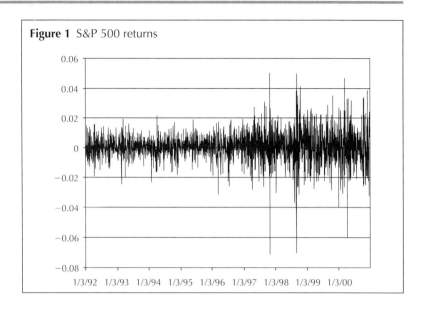

Figure 1 S&P 500 returns

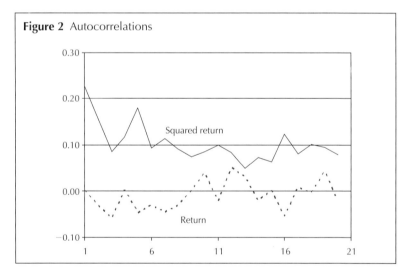

Figure 2 Autocorrelations

evident from this plot that returns over time are not independent because return volatilities are clustered together, meaning a large (small) volatility is likely to be followed by a period of large (small) volatilities.

Autocorrelations of the return and the squared return for various lags are plotted in Figure 2. Very low return autocorrelation shown in this figure suggests that a return is not really correlated with its preceding returns. The result for squared returns shows a different pattern, however. The correlation between the two consecutive squared returns is greater than 0.2. Together, an interesting return characteristic emerges. Consecutive returns are not correlated but their magnitudes are. In other words, given a high return at time t, one has no idea whether the next return will be positive or negative, but one can expect the next return to be large in magnitude. This suggests to us that volatilities (specifically local volatilities) are correlated. In short, returns are dependent over time via volatility dependence. A common belief about asset returns being a random walk reflects the illusion of finding no autocorrelation in returns, but overlooks the dependence through autocorrelated volatilities.[1]

Since the current and past return realisations affect the volatility of future returns, it is imperative for us to consider volatility in light of the information available. Adopting the concept of conditioning is not only natural but also indispensable for having a meaningful discussion of volatility. A concrete model can be used to facilitate our understanding of conditional volatility. We will now take a popular time series model for asset volatility, generalised autoregressive conditional heteroskedastic (GARCH), to formally describe the concept.

Assume that the one-period return is governed by the following non-linear asymmetric GARCH system (see Engle and Ng, 1993):

$$x_t = \mu + \sigma_t \varepsilon_t$$
$$\sigma_t^2 = \beta_0 + \beta_1 \sigma_{t-1}^2 + \beta_2 \sigma_{t-1}^2 (\varepsilon_{t-1} - \theta)^2$$
$$\varepsilon_t \big| F_{t-1} \sim N(0, 1)$$

where $\beta_0 > 0$, $\beta_1 \geq 0$ and $\beta_2 \geq 0$. Recall that x_t is the return from time $t-1$ to t. The system implies that mean return and standard deviation at time $t-1$ are μ and σ_t. Volatility σ_t depends on its previous volatility and an earlier random shock to the system. By this model, volatility evolves randomly over time and could have a volatility reverting behaviour under some suitable restriction on parameters. In other words, the volatility of the system has a tendency to revert back to some fixed value even though it is subject to shocks regularly. Parameter θ in the volatility equation allows for asymmetric volatility responses to positive and negative return shocks. The return innovation $\sigma_t \varepsilon_t$ is assumed to be normally distributed with mean 0 and standard deviation σ_t.

Volatility is known at the beginning point of a period, although it is random overall. This is true because the elements on the right hand side of the equation for σ_t are known at time $t-1$. It is somewhat like the one-period interest rate because it is deterministic locally but random over time. By conditioning on the information available at time $t-1$, the next period return, viewed locally, is normally distributed with mean μ and standard deviation σ_t. We will refer to σ_t as local volatility or conditional one-period volatility. Because our focus is on volatility, we have for convenience assumed constant μ. Similarly, we have used the assumption of normally distributed returns to simplify the discussion. It is by no means a necessity. Even with the conditional normality assumption, the one-period return viewed from a distance will not be normally distributed due to the random effect of volatility.

In contrast to the local or conditional concept, we can think about the problem as if all information has been removed. That is to think about the mean and standard deviation of x_t from a time point in the infinite past. We will refer to them as unconditional mean return and volatility. Since μ is a constant, it will continue to be the unconditional mean return regardless of whether information is used or not. For volatility viewed from the infinite past, we need to first form an expectation of σ_t^2 and then use the square root of the resulting value as the unconditional volatility. For the above GARCH system, the unconditional volatility can be easily derived, which is given in the next section. The unconditional volatility is often referred to as the stationary volatility because the randomly evolved volatility tends to revert to this level.

If one mistakes the dependent return system as having constant volatility, it amounts to viewing the one-period return subject to the stationary volatility. This mistaken belief will lead us to overlook the contribution of the accumulated information right up to the time point, which should help us ascertain the upcoming asset return. Going back to Figure 1, it amounts to ignoring the valuable information implicit in a particular return's location in the time sequence. It can also be likened to randomly rearranging the sequence of returns so that the pattern related to the time sequence is destroyed. Different beliefs about the "correct" model yield different volatility estimates. Using different lengths of data samples also leads to different volatility estimates under the same model. For example, using the entire S&P 500 daily returns to estimate the constant volatility model on December 29, 2000 for the next day return volatility, we have 0.945% per day (or 15% per annum using 252 trading days). If only the returns in year 2000 are used, the volatility estimate becomes 1.4% (or 22.23% per annum). Using the GARCH model and the whole data sample, the next day return volatility assessed on December 29, 2000 will be 0.1457% (23.13% per annum). Strictly under the constant volatility model, 15% per annum should be superior to 22.23% because the data sample for the former is larger. But 22.23% volatility obviously better reflects the nature of the market on December 29, 2000, which the time-varying volatility model like GARCH attempts to capture.

VOLATILITY TERM STRUCTURE

In applications, we are often interested in a return over several basic periods; for example, we may want to determine a portfolio's performance on a monthly basis while working with the daily data. The cumulative return is related to its duration, and its volatility (ie, cumulative volatility) is a function of duration. Cumulative volatility as a function of duration is the volatility term structure. Obviously, cumulative volatility is likely to increase simply due to measuring return over a longer horizon. It is thus customary to standardise it by the square root of duration. The rationale for this standardisation is the constant volatility i.i.d. model discussed earlier.

The volatility term structure can be unconditional or conditional. This distinction is meaningful only when information plays a role in determining the volatility term structure. Under the constant volatility i.i.d. model, the volatility term structure is always flat, and thus there is no need to differentiate between them. However, we have shown that information is important in characterising the return behaviour. The volatility term structure should thus reflect the accumulated information. For this, we must rely on a model.

The GARCH model is again used to demonstrate the concept. Let $E_t(\sigma^2_{t+k})$ denote the expected value of the local variance (for the period from time $t+k-1$ to $t+k$) conditional on the time t information. This amounts to forming an expectation at some time point about the local volatility for a future period. The GARCH model described earlier leads to the following result:

$$E_t(\sigma_{t+k}^2) = \bar{\sigma}^2 + \left[\beta_1 + \beta_2(1+\theta^2)\right]^{k-1}(\sigma_{t+1}^2 - \bar{\sigma}^2)$$

where $\bar{\sigma}$ is the stationary volatility equal to $\sqrt{\beta_0/[1-\beta_1-\beta_2(1+\theta^2)]}$ if the value of the persistence parameter $\beta_1 + \beta_2(1+\theta^2)$ is less than 1. The persistence parameter governs how fast the conditional expected local volatility (k periods ahead) converges to the stationary volatility. The closer its value is to one; the slower the convergence speed (or the more pronounced the volatility clustering).

The standardised cumulative volatility of duration n, conditional on the time t information, follows from the uncorrelated feature of consecutive returns. It can be written as $\sqrt{(1/n)(\sum_{i=1}^{n} E_t(\sigma_{t+i}^2))}$. Clearly, the standardised cumulative volatility at time t is a function of the local volatility σ_{t+1} and duration n. The information available at time t is summarised in σ_{t+1} and the relevant term is n. To illustrate the volatility term structure numerically, we estimate the GARCH model using the S&P 500 return data described earlier. The parameter estimates are $\mu = 4.15 \times 10^{-4}$, $\beta_0 = 1.1834 \times 10^{-6}$, $\beta_1 = 0.875$, $\beta_2 = 0.07345$ and $\theta = 0.74272$. These parameter values reflect a high volatility persistence because the calculated persistence parameter value is close to one.

The three curves in Figure 3 are obtained using the estimated parameter values. The volatilities are reported by multiplying the square root of 252. The horizontal axis represents the number of trading days over which the cumulative return is measured. The stationary volatility term structure is a horizontal line because it does not reflect the prevailing market condition. The conditional volatility term structure reflects the market condition, however. On December 21, 2000, the market is deemed volatile, the next one-day return volatility is high and a cumulative volatility measured over a longer horizon decreases with its duration. It slowly approaches the stationary level because the standardised cumulative volatility is essentially an average figure. The slow rate of convergence

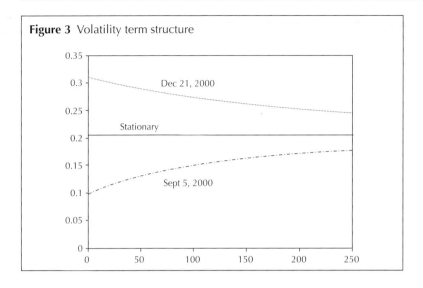

Figure 3 Volatility term structure

results from high volatility persistence of the data. The conditional volatility term structure for September 5, 2000 is similar except it reflects a tranquil market.

OPTION PRICING AND THE IMPLIED VOLATILITY SURFACE

One of the key motivations for modelling volatility has been to deal with derivative contracts. It is often said that trading options is really about trading on volatility. The celebrated Black–Scholes option pricing formula started an era of rigorously examining the issue of option pricing or volatility modelling. Among all inputs required for this formula, volatility is the only one that cannot be observed directly. One of the premises for the Black–Scholes model is an asset price with constant volatility that is lognormally distributed. If this model is sound, one should be able to just plug in the sample standard deviation of asset returns to adequately price the options. Alternatively, if one uses the formula to back out the implied volatilities corresponding to different option contracts on the same underlying asset, one should find them to be roughly equal with no discernible pattern in relation to their contract specifications. The empirical evidence reported in the literature turns out to be against the Black–Scholes model, however.

Option prices for a given maturity essentially reflect how the market views the cumulative return distribution weighted by some subjective tradeoffs among returns in different states of the world. Such a weighted distribution is often referred to as the risk-neutral distribution. Different exercise prices simply restrict the payouts to different parts of the cumulative risk-neutral distribution. In a way, we can say option pricing is about obtaining a good risk-neutral cumulative distribution, and the cumulative volatility is naturally of interest.

Empirically, it is typical to observe a downward sloping curve of volatilities, implied by the Black–Scholes models, for equity call option contracts over a range of increasing exercise prices. Such a curve is known as a volatility smile/skew. The curve of implied volatilities for different maturities while fixing the exercise price is, on the other hand, referred to as the implied volatility term structure. Such a curve may slope upwards or downwards and sometimes even exhibits a hump. When different exercise prices and maturities are considered jointly, we have the implied volatility surface. The implied volatility surface for all major stock index options has been shown in empirical studies to have the same basic shape, which is clear evidence against the constant volatility lognormality assumption of the Black–Scholes model. One may say that the implied volatility is really not volatility at all; rather it is some sort of transformation of an option price.

The observed implied volatility surface is informative neverthe-less. Its regularity, for example, can help trading because one can anticipate, say, how much an in-the-money call option should be priced at relative to an at-the-money call. Many attempts to model the evolution of the implied volatility surface do so directly without trying to tie it back to the actual system governing the underlying asset price.[2] Such an approach has limited potentials, however, because it misses the critical linkage between the deriva-tive securities and the underlying asset on which the derivatives are written.

The observed implied volatility surface can be viewed as an additional piece of information above and beyond which is conveyed by the sample of returns for the underlying asset. It is suggestive as to which model for the underlying asset return process is more suitable. Take the GARCH model discussed earlier as an example. Figure 3 shows that the volatility term structure, without considering the complexity associated with the option pricing theory, already slopes in a direction depending on the market condition. Such a feature seems consistent with the observed implied volatility surface. With the option pricing theory under GARCH (Duan, 1995), one can actually go beyond the properties of the underlying asset and show that the observed implied volatility surface is predicted by such a time-varying volatility model.[3]

VOLATILITY FORECASTING

Volatility forecasting is an often-heard term and is commonly used to motivate volatility modelling. It is, however, not clear how meaningful it is above and beyond providing a number with which one may gauge how volatile an asset return is likely to be in the future. If volatility evolves randomly over time, isn't it a necessity for us to have a whole volatility dynamic so that we can completely characterise the cumulative return distribution? A random volatility should not be mixed up with parameter uncertainty associated with estimation error. In principle, the estimation error diminishes when the sample becomes larger. A random volatility is inherently stochastic and will not become more certain when the sample size becomes larger. A volatility forecast obtains an average value, conditional on the information available. It is only one aspect of volatility and clearly misses out many of the distributional features of volatility.

If volatility is random, we cannot simply plug the volatility forecast into the Black–Scholes formula, because it is inconsistent with the modelling assumption of that formula. If it is an unknown constant, there is nothing to forecast and the only issue is the estimation error. It is thus clear that volatility forecasting has little value in option pricing. This being said, one can still form a volatility forecast under many random volatility models if needed. The GARCH model described in this chapter, for example, has an easy solution. The volatility term structure given earlier is, in fact, such a forecast for various cumulative volatilities.

Realised volatility is sometimes used to study whether a given volatility model is a good description of data. As the name suggests, the realised volatility measures how volatile the return realisations are over a target period; for example, the daily realised volatility over a three-month period is calculated as the standard deviation of the daily returns over the three-month period. But what is this realised volatility supposed to match? For the GARCH model, one can show that the expected value for the square of realised volatility equals the square of the cumulative volatility obtained earlier. In other words, they should be equal on average if one repeatedly compares the realised and forecasted volatilities. Although one should be mindful of some technical issues involved in this type of statistical analysis, it is an idea that is conceptually sound and may lend some support to volatility forecasting.[4]

CONCLUSION

Volatility is a common vocabulary in the world of finance. In this chapter, we set out to turn the concept of volatility into a more concrete object. First, this chapter makes the attempt to bridge the continuous and discrete-time modelling approaches. It becomes clear that the standard constant volatility model is at odds with the data. Since such a model is also incapable of differentiating the conditional vs unconditional volatility, the GARCH system is introduced as a way of better understanding the return dynamics. Aggregating local volatilities into a cumulative volatility then allows us to have a more meaningfully discussion on the volatility term structure and on its implications for option pricing and volatility forecasting.

Although a particular GARCH model is used to show key concepts about volatility, it is by no means a necessity for introducing these concepts. In fact, any serially dependent random volatility model will serve the purpose although it may not have the analytical convenience and/or empirical performance comparable to that of the GARCH model. In the option pricing literature, a class of models known as stochastic volatility has long been considered. These models are actually the limiting cases of the GARCH model that let the length of the basic time period shrink to zero.[5] The GARCH model is, however, considerably easier to estimate and work with. To date, the GARCH model is arguably the only family of volatility models that perform well and are reasonably parsimonious.

1 For an extensive discussion on modelling financial time series, estimating models and diagnostic analyses, readers are referred to Pagan (1996).

2 See, for example, Rubinstein (1994), Derman and Kani (1994) and Dupire (1994).

3 See, for example, Duan (1996), Heston and Nandi (2000) and Duan and Zhang (2001).

4   See Andersen and Bollerslev (1998) for discussions on the technical issues related to volatility forecasting.

5   See, for example, Nelson (1990) and Duan (1997) for the limiting cases of the GARCH model.

BIBLIOGRAPHY

Andersen, T., and T. Bollerslev, 1998, "Answering the Skeptics: Yes, Standard Volatility Models Do Provide Good Volatility Forecasts", *International Economic Review,* 39, pp. 885–905.

Black, F., and M. Scholes, 1973, "The Pricing of Options and Corporate Liabilities", *Journal of Political Economy,* 81, pp. 637–59.

Derman, E., and I. Kani, 1994, "Riding on a Smile", *Risk,* (February), pp. 32–9.

Duan, J.-C., 1995, "The GARCH Option Pricing Model", *Mathematical Finance,* 5, pp. 13–32.

Duan, J.-C., 1996, "Cracking the Smile", *Risk,* (December), pp. 55–9.

Duan, J.-C., 1997, "Augmented GARCH(p,q) Process and its Diffusion Limit", *Journal of Econometrics,* 79, pp. 197–127.

Duan, J.-C., and H. Zhang, 2001, "Pricing Hang Seng Index Options around the Asian Financial Crisis", *Journal of Banking and Finance,* 25, pp. 1989–2014.

Dupire, B., 1994, "Pricing with a Smile", *Risk,* (Jan 1994), pp. 18–20.

Engle, R., and V. Ng, 1993, "Measuring and Testing the Impact of News on Volatility", *Journal of Finance,* 48, pp. 1749–78.

Heston, S., and S. Nandi, 2000, "A Closed-Form GARCH Option Valuation Model", *Review of Financial Studies,* 13, pp. 585–625.

Nelson, D., 1990, "ARCH Models as Diffusion Approximations", *Journal of Econometrics,* 45, pp. 7–38.

Pagan, A., 1996, "The Econometrics of Financial Markets", *Journal of Empirical Finance,* 3, pp. 15–102.

Rubinstein, M., 1994, "Implied Binomial Tree", *Journal of Finance,* 49, pp. 771–818.

14

The Evolution of Counterparty Credit Risk Management

David M. Rowe

SunGard Trading and Risk Systems

Pre-settlement counterparty credit exposure came to the fore shortly before *Risk* magazine was launched in 1987. It gained additional visibility when the Bank for International Settlements (BIS) insisted that such credit exposure be recognised in the first Basel Capital Accord. In the past 15 years there has been much progress in measuring and managing the associated risks, but the author argues that much remains to be done.

IGNORANCE IS BLISS – PRE-1985

It is said that success has many parents but failure is an orphan. Surely the massive expansion and pervasive influence of derivatives during the last two decades of the twentieth century stands as one of the great success stories of that period. True to form, there are many claimants to the title of first swap arranger. By now the truth is probably lost in the mist of time, but the date of the first swap appears to have been sometime in 1981. At that stage, these were truly arranged contracts. I have even heard of deal parties to celebrate each swap like those often held after the closing of large syndicated loans.

The primary form of credit risk associated with trading in those days was settlement risk. Recognition of this had been driven home painfully by the failure of Bankhaus Herstatt during the trading day on June 26, 1974.[1] Even in the early 1980s, daily turnover in the foreign exchange (FX) spot and forward markets was in the hundreds of billions of dollars. Such volumes gave rise to serious concern about the credit risk of such contracts from the time payment instructions became irrevocable to the time the agreed exchange amount was received. As the new swap dealers were quick to point out, however, settlement on most of their transactions was on a net basis, which meant there was no settlement risk.

Looking beyond the settlement risk issue, there was only limited understanding of the pre-settlement credit implications of term derivative transactions. Some people thought that since there was no exchange of principal on an interest rate swap there was no credit risk. After all, one cannot claim loss of future interest payments on a loan when a borrower defaults. The fact that most credit officers were thoroughly steeped in the historical cost accounting framework was an additional obstacle to a clear understanding of these mark-to-market instruments. Furthermore, derivative volumes were small and counterparties were virtually all investment grade names. These factors combined to make pre-settlement credit exposure a latent and largely ignored risk aspect of derivative trading in the early 1980s.

INCREASED MATERIALITY AND VISIBILITY

By 1986, swap market volumes had grown significantly and so had current mark-to-market exposures. Gradually the realisation spread that these positive market values represented material credit risky balance sheet assets similar to corporate and industrial bank loans. As such, counterparties to such trades clearly should be subjected to credit review and transactions should only be done within an approved credit exposure limit.[2] But there was one nagging problem. When making a traditional loan it doesn't require complex mathematical analysis to answer the question "how big is the loan?" The answer to that question is clearly stated in the proposed term sheet. While some would point out that the fair value of a loan fluctuates just as the price of a bond does, historical cost accounting treats the principal amount as fixed.

For swaps, there are two problems. First, they are usually done near par. Initial market values only reflect the slightly off-market impact of a dealer's bid/offer spread. This initial value, however, is only a small fraction of the potential future exposure that may materialise as a deal ages and market conditions change. Thus current exposure, especially current exposure on newly executed deals, is not a realistic measure of the true potential loss from a downgrade or default on the part of the counterparty. Second, market fluctuations lead to constant revisions in the exposure, however measured. Such unstable exposure presented an entirely new dimension of uncertainty that many traditional credit control personnel found difficult to incorporate into their thinking.

THE FIRST BASEL CAPITAL ACCORD

The derivative credit exposure issue received added attention when the Basel Committee on Banking Supervision began to develop its initial rules for minimum regulatory capital requirements in 1986 and 1987. The committee realised that the current market values of a bank's derivative contracts did not capture their full potential credit exposure. As a result, they set out to derive reasonably simple rules to calibrate potential increases in such credit exposure, based on volatility in the underlying market data and the resulting impact on fair values of broad categories of trades. The result was the now well-known add-on approach to measuring potential future exposure.

Several comments are in order regarding the structure and parameters of the initial Basel add-on calculation.

❏ The approach was intended to be simple to implement so that even small banks with a few hedge contracts could perform the calculation without difficulty.
❏ It was only intended to capture the increase in *aggregate* exposure. It was neither proposed nor intended as a satisfactory approach to measuring individual counterparty exposures.
❏ It provided only very limited recognition of the tenor of exposure by offering different parameters for contracts with more than or less than one year to maturity.
❏ The same add-ons were applied to both at-the-money and away-from-the-money contracts, despite the amortisation toward zero in the value of many contracts as they approach maturity.
❏ It treated each transaction in isolation. While this greatly simplified the mechanics of the calculation, it completely ignored the degree of co-variation in value among multiple deals.

❑ Recognising that portfolio effects had been ignored, the parameters of the method were calibrated to reflect an assumed average degree of portfolio diversification.

❑ While the potential increase in *aggregate* exposure was probably not unreasonable, the *marginal change* in potential exposure from adding or deleting a single deal was highly unreliable and could even be directionally incorrect.

A negative consequence of Basel's add-on method was to provide apparent regulatory sanction for this approach. While adequate for estimating aggregate potential exposure, it was, and is, quite unsuitable when applied at the individual counterparty level or to evaluating the marginal exposure of a new deal. The essential problem is the implicit assumption of an average degree of diversification. In fact, individual counterparty portfolios exhibit widely differing diversification characteristics. The most obvious and striking example is an offsetting transaction where the market value moves in a precisely opposite direction to that of an existing trade in response to changing market conditions. If the two trades are not legally nettable, the second trade has almost zero impact on potential exposure. If they are legally nettable, then the second trade significantly reduces potential exposure. The add-on approach, however, will produce an unrealistic increase in measured exposure in both cases.

Despite these widely recognised shortcomings, most institutions adopted some variation in the add-on method for tracking and setting limits for counterparty credit exposure. This was driven by the comparative simplicity and modest cost of deploying such a system. Given the huge trading losses experienced in the mid-1980s, market risk was viewed as the most serious issue requiring attention and resources. Building a more sophisticated system for controlling trading credit risk simply was not a serious consideration at most institutions.

While adopting the add-on approach, bank credit departments invariably insisted on more conservative parameters internally than those employed in regulatory capital calculations. Partly this was driven by a recognition of the fact that the purposes for the two calculations were different. Primarily, however, it reflected an inherent distrust among traditional credit officers of these fancy new instruments. By making the numbers larger, it was felt the volumes could be limited and the associated risks constrained. The result tended to be greatly inflated potential exposure estimates that often had only an infinitesimal chance of materialising as actual exposure-at-default in the future.

NETTING COMES INTO ITS OWN

Another trend in the late 1980s and early 1990s was the legal battle to make netting enforceable under the bankruptcy laws in various countries. The International Swaps and Derivatives Association (then known as the International Swap Dealers Association) (ISDA) lead the way in most countries around the world. ISDA formulated standard contract language and waged multiple campaigns to gain legislative recognition of the enforceability of netting under the terms of such contracts when one party declared bankruptcy.

While we think of netting as the accepted norm today, it is still far from universal. Indeed, even in the US netting is of questionable enforceability when dealing with certain types of institutions. Examples are insurance companies and public utilities where bankruptcy claims are adjudicated in some type of state administrative process rather than under the US bankruptcy code or laws governing federally insured financial institutions.

The most frequent circumstance today is for netting to be partially enforceable across relevant sets of transactions. Certain deals are entered into under terms of an enforceable netting agreement. These are nettable against each other but their combined net market value, if negative, cannot be offset against exposure in other nettable pools or against transactions done outside any enforceable netting agreement. This introduces an added layer of complexity to the analysis. It also means that legal contract information must be captured and properly reflected in the calculations if they are to be robust in reflecting the impact of enforceable netting.

ORGANISATIONAL OBSTACLES TO IMPROVEMENT

A number of organisational obstacles stood in the way of better credit exposure measurement systems. As already mentioned, cost was an important issue, especially when market risk was viewed as the really serious hazard. Most credit officers just wanted to limit an activity they viewed as fraught with risks they didn't understand, and that they weren't sure the traders understood either.

Perhaps equally serious, there was little support from the business side for the cost of improved credit exposure estimation systems. On reflection, this is not too surprising. Traders live and die on the basis of three things:

1. accurate pricing;
2. clear and reliable understanding of their open positions (usually expressed in terms of Greek letter sensitivities); and
3. realistic assessments of their potential losses (either in the form of a formal value-at-risk (VAR) estimate or, more likely, in terms of their own intuitive understanding of market volatility relative to their open positions).

These three factors are part of their daily lives, of the very air they breathe. Credit risk, on the other hand, seems like a remote contingency with little relevance. Traders usually regard credit risk oversight as a distasteful nuisance, a series of hurdles to be overcome. The point is to get the deals done. If a counterparty's limit is full, the usual attitude is "just raise the limit and let me get on with my job!"

Unfortunately, unsophisticated credit exposure measurement systems tended to intensify the inherent cultural conflict between traders and credit officers. Traders realised that add-on based exposure estimates, at least at the counterparty level, were inconsistent and inflated. They particularly recognised that marginal exposure implications were unreliable. This became painfully obvious when counterparties did offsetting trades to neutralise future changes in their net positions, and the system indicated that these increased credit exposure! All this reinforced traders' cynicism about credit oversight in general. They insisted that they were being constrained by a system that was inconsistent and arbitrary while credit staff were left to defend the indefensible.

Another obstacle to improved systems was limited analytical talent in the risk management side of the organisation. The big financial opportunities were in trading and it was difficult to attract the best quants and system engineers to the risk management side of an institution. As a result, while the business had little interest in more sophisticated credit exposure measurement, risk management staff often lacked the analytical vision to formulate a better approach. The prevailing attitude on the credit risk side often tended to be, "make the numbers bigger and that will make us safer." Unfortunately, this tended to undermine the credibility of the exposure estimates even among credit approvers. The result was an unhealthy behavioural feedback loop. In effect, outstanding loan balances and potential trading credit exposures were two different currencies with an uncertain exchange rate between them. Each limit approver was required by circumstances to decide how to translate the one to the other. In such a situation, it was impossible to generate consistent credit decisions across the organisation.

THE IMPETUS FOR CHANGE

With all these obstacles, one might ask how did any improvement occur? In some cases there was a fortunate convergence of technical expertise, management vision and institutional emphasis on deploying best practice risk methods. More often than not, however, the impetus for change came at the point when credit availability began to constrain the ability to do business. As long as volume was modest and counterparties were solid investment grade names this was not a serious problem. Credit limits were generally available to cover even the inflated exposure estimates produced by a conservative add-on approach.

Moving into the 1990s, however, volumes continued to grow while smaller and less creditworthy counterparties entered the market. Gradually the old arguments about the exposures "not being real" and the estimates "being inflated" became less compelling. Credit approvers grew more reluctant to approve increased trading credit limits in the face of already large measured exposures for good names and for new exposure to lower quality names. Eventually situations arose where credit officers would say, in effect: "I don't care how inflated the numbers are, I'm not putting my name on an approval bigger than the current limit, full stop. Justify more realistic estimates and then maybe we can talk." This resulted in a real business incentive for more realistic exposure measurement and a willingness to spend some money to make it happen.

ESSENTIAL FEATURES FOR CONSISTENT EXPOSURE ESTIMATION

Given the incentives and resources to build an improved exposure estimation system, it was useful to consider what features were essential and what features, though not essential, were desirable in such a system. This discussion generally came down to the following essential features.

❏ *A foundation in historical behaviour.* Generally it was agreed that historical market behaviour should be the foundation on which such a system was built. While some argued for a more conservative "worst case" approach, most recognised the dangers of inflated estimates losing their credibility. This inevitably leads to varied and highly subjective approval standards across the organisation and to an ultimate loss of control over the process.

❏ *Proper recognition of offsets and diversification.* Failure to treat the dynamic interaction among trades in a counterparty's portfolio was recognised as the most obvious shortcoming of the add-on approach. This was particularly obvious relative to marginal exposure calculations. An add-on based system would show exposure increasing when a new trade was added even when it actually reduced exposure by offsetting pre-existing imbalances in the counterparty's portfolio. Few things do more to undermine the credibility of a credit risk system than getting the sign of marginal exposure wrong!

❏ *Incorporation of market data correlations.* Clearly correlations between pairs of rates and/or prices are among the less stable parameters of market dynamics. Nevertheless, most analysts agreed that incorporating reasonable estimates of such correlations was an important aspect of realistic exposure estimation.[3]

❏ *Exposure profiles rather than single loan equivalent amounts.* Another major flaw of the add-on approach was that it gave no insight into the timing of potential future exposure. Sometimes the potential exposures by deal would be "stacked" in the order of their maturity, but this ignores the fact that swap exposures peak in the middle of a contract's life, not at the end. Any credit analyst will say that the timing of when exposure occurs is often central to whether the risk is acceptable. Whatever else it did, a revised trading credit methodology needed to produce insights into the timing of exposure.

❏ *Rigorous treatment of netting.* By the 1990s, netting was becoming more widely accepted in law around the world. This made a reliable treatment of netting increasingly important for accurate exposure estimates. Capturing the impact of enforceable netting in the current exposure is easy. The difficult issue is reflecting it in potential future exposure. A minor revision to the Basel capital rules in April of 1995 introduced a very crude way of reflecting the growth in the enforceability of netting. This was based on the portfolio ratio of current net exposure, to the extent netting is deemed enforceable, vs current gross exposure. Again, while arguably appropriate for an aggregate exposure adjustment, this approach is much too crude to be reliable when applied to individual counterparty portfolios. A more rigorous approach was clearly necessary.

The common thread running through these essential features was an attempt to incorporate all significant structural factors into the exposure estimation process. The goal was to produce results that were conceptually consistent across counterparties and throughout the projection period. Specifically, the probability of the projected potential exposure actually materialising on any relevant future date should be as consistent as is practically possible. It should not matter whether a portfolio contains one deal, a small number of similar deals, or a large and varied range of deals with two-way sensitivities and multiple market drivers. Likewise, the statistical properties of the exposure estimates should not change over the course of a projection as some deals mature and the complexity of the portfolio changes.

DESIRABLE FEATURES FOR EFFECTIVE RISK MANAGEMENT

The initial goal for improved exposure estimation was simply to get more realistic results on a periodic basis. Daily or even weekly runs were the normal target frequency. This provided a sound basis for setting and managing credit exposure limits. There was an issue of how to provide availability information to traders in order to hold them accountable for complying with the limits. This usually was done by one of two methods.

❑ A parallel set of limits might be set up on the basis of a much simpler measurement scheme. For example, the old add-on calculations might be used.

❑ Alternatively, the sophisticated exposure profiles could be imported into the trading limit system. These would be augmented by conservative exposure increases for new deals between updates from batch runs of the more sophisticated exposure estimation system.

In both cases, incremental exposure of new deals would be added to the existing exposure based on fairly simple additive rules and tracked against limits. Such systems would also provide traders with availability reports or what-if capabilities. It was usually the job of a credit limits administration unit to assure that authorised trades between full exposure simulations would only rarely result in excesses when the batch update was run.

Even in the early 1990s, however, a set of more ambitious goals began to emerge. Progress has been made on some of them, but many remain future aspirations even today. Among these longer-term goals were the following.

❑ *Real-time updates on a global basis.* The lag between deals being committed and their credit implications being reflected in the limit system has long been recognised as a source of additional risk. It has generally been necessary to settle for one of two compromises in this area. Global real-time exposure capture can be accomplished if the metrics used are quite simple. Such an approach is used for some products by at least a couple of dozen banks today, usually for foreign exchange trading. Alternatively, a sophisticated measurement method can be combined with real-time deal capture at the local trading room level if the exposure calculations are integrated with the front-office dealing system. This is more common in the fixed income derivative area. Combining global real-time deal capture with sophisticated measurement techniques to answer availability queries remains a future aspiration.

❑ *What-if capabilities linked to the front-office booking systems.* Ideally the limits system should be closely integrated with the front office trading environment. Traders should not have to do double entry to determine availability. Often a counterparty will have sufficient availability that a full what-if check is unnecessary. Visual inspection will assure that a proposed deal can be accommodated within the limit. If a full what-if simulation is needed, however, it should be possible for the exposure engine to pick up the necessary details from the front office trading system.

❏ *"Trading floor response times" using sophisticated measurement methods.* Anyone who has been there knows that "trading floor response times" usually means almost instantaneous. Especially in the foreign exchange trading arena, response time requirements are extremely short, usually two to three seconds. The computational complexity traditionally required to produce acceptably robust exposure measures has, to date, been impossible to reconcile with these demanding response times on a commercially acceptable basis.

❏ *Exposure decomposition and "wrong-way exposure" reporting.* As described above, measuring exposure consistently and reliably is an important goal. It also is important, however, to be able to dissect the portfolio imbalances that give rise to such exposure. This can be done by recording the impact on exposure of controlled deviations in individual market variables from their expected paths. This reveals the type of market events that would drive exposure higher and is an important guide to what types of trades would be risk reducing for a given counterparty. Proper organisation of such results also allows risk managers to determine which counterparties will exhibit rising exposure in response to an unfolding market event such as a big currency devaluation or a commodity price shift.

Combining such sensitivities with user-specified wrong-way exposures also can be very useful. This allows reporting that highlights those counterparties who are likely to exhibit weakened credit status in response to the very same market events that result in increased exposure.

❏ *Optimal professional counterparty selection.* Market makers in derivatives are deal takers when it comes to their end-users. Clients have a fundamental risk to hedge and come to a dealer to take an offsetting position. When professional market makers need to hedge their own open market positions, however, they are deal givers. They will need to pay away the bid or offer spread to the other professional market maker with whom they place the trade. At that moment, there is almost free credit risk reduction available to the market risk hedger. By choosing one professional counterparty, potential credit exposure may be reduced, whereas choosing another counterparty will result in a potential credit exposure increase. Careful risk source sensitivity analysis and exposition can provide the necessary information to make the appropriate risk reducing choices as these opportunities arises.

❏ *Marginal credit cost implications of a new transaction.* This can reasonably be called the Holy Grail of desired functionality. Today exposure is estimated only as a measure to compare to approved limits. As long as a trader is within limit, there is no other impact on incentives or behaviour. In effect, traders are compensated for maximising gross trading profits subject to constraints in the form of market risk and credit risk limits. If marginal exposure could be calculated accurately in a few seconds, it would be possible to present traders with the incremental credit charge associated with a proposed trade. This would mean the spread on the trade would have to cover this charge before the trader realised a net profit. In effect, it would allow market makers to compensate traders on the basis of maximising risk-adjusted profits. In the process, it would bring traders' incentives into much closer alignment with the goals of the institution.

ALTERNATE APPROACHES TO ACHIEVING ESSENTIAL MEASUREMENT OBJECTIVES

There are three potential approaches to achieving the essential objectives needed for consistent exposure estimation.

1. *Monte Carlo simulation with full revaluation.* This involves revaluing all uncompleted terms and conditions for every deal at multiple future dates under several thousand hypothetical sets of market conditions. Needless to say, this is very computationally intensive. Depending on the complexity and volume of the deals in the portfolio, it typically takes several hours to process all the desired exposure profiles. In some cases, the processing time exceeds the available daily window and can only be run on

weekends. While this is analytically the most robust approach, the computing power and processing time required often make it impractical for day-to-day use. This has given rise to a search for alternatives that offer almost the same reliability with considerably less computational burden.

2. *Monte Carlo with grid-based pricing.* The most obvious alternative to full-valuation Monte Carlo is one that simplifies the generation of hypothetical future values of the transactions. An attractive approach is to use grid-based pricing. In this method, a small number of full valuations are performed for every deal at every future simulation date based on controlled deviations from the status quo evolution of market variables. These results are saved and reused in the subsequent Monte Carlo step. Instead of performing full revaluations for each of several thousand hypothetical market scenarios, prices are derived by interpolation off the price grid. The interpolations are based on where the market variables in a given scenario fall relative to the controlled changes used to construct the grid. The grid may be more or less complex, incorporating different numbers of market drivers for a given deal. Likewise the interpolation methods may vary in complexity from linear to quadratic or higher order approximations to the value surface.

Obviously the more complex the interpolation the smaller the gain in computational efficiency. How complex to make the calculation is a matter of time and budget resources and is also affected by the complexity of the trades involved. In general, however, grid-based pricing can make the update process several times faster than full valuation Monte Carlo. The scenario specific transaction values are not as precise in the grid-based pricing approach as they are using full revaluation. It is important to realise, however, that the characteristics of the hypothetical future market conditions are themselves subject to considerable uncertainty. As a former associate of mine once said, it is easy to refine within the margin of error. Doing so gains little in the way of actual precision (although it may create a false sense of security) and often creates serious operational and maintenance issues.

3. *Advanced analytic approximation.* Within the past two years, advanced analytic methods have been developed that provide

remarkably robust approximations to the results of full-blown Monte Carlo simulations. While not foolproof, these methods usually give results that fall within the range produced by Monte Carlo simulations with small vs large numbers of draws. Certain ill conditioned combinations of a small number of trades can lead to non-trivial errors. As a result, periodic Monte Carlo runs are important to catch such situations in those rare instances where they arise. Nevertheless, these methods are generally quite reliable and can reduce the time to evaluate the exposure of a large counterparty portfolio from minutes to seconds.

ALTERNATE ASPIRATIONS FOR USE OF SIMULATION-BASED EXPOSURE ESTIMATION

Given the advances of the past ten years, there is little excuse for any institution with significant derivative activity to operate with nothing but add-on style credit exposure estimates for internal measurement and control. Saying that, there are three distinct levels of sophistication in the application of simulation-based exposure estimates.

1. *As an overnight supplement to less sophisticated measures.* This is where most institutions are today. Daily trading activity is controlled by fairly unsophisticated measures, at least relative to newly booked transactions. Even if sophisticated exposure profiles are calculated periodically and fed back into the trading limit system, deals done between updates are typically assessed in a much simpler fashion. This inevitably leads to overstated exposure and may result in turning away deals that could be done within limit if more sophisticated exposure estimates were available on a timelier basis. Such a system also cannot offer meaningful insight into the marginal impact of a proposed trade. Nevertheless, it is a giant step beyond having nothing but add-on based exposure estimates. Properly configured, such batch systems also can provide valuable portfolio concentration and risk source sensitivity information. A key success factor is making such information conveniently available to relevant decision-makers in multiple locations.

2. *Intra-day simulated exposure updates for new trades.* This approach requires capturing new trades as they are made and transferring them to a central exposure evaluation system. Once received centrally, the counterparty exposure profile or profiles affected by a new deal are updated in the background. Depending on the size of the portfolios affected, and the volume of trades being processed in this way, the latency is likely to be from a few minutes to an hour or longer. The advantage of this approach is that portfolio effects are reflected faster than with nothing but batch updates of the simulations. Also, if a counterparty's exposure is close to the limit, it is possible to configure such a system to allow a small number of what-if simulations based on proposed new deals. While not able to support a large volume of what-if inquiries, this limited capability can provide support for booking risk-reducing deals that would otherwise be denied based on limit excesses.

While this may seem like a small departure from the first configuration, there is a major difference. To achieve intra-day updates requires moving from a batch to an event driven system architecture. Sufficient trade details need to be captured to allow the simulations to run and exposure updates need to be made while new limit inquiries and transactions are taking place. This requires a significant revamping of the entire process when starting from a batch mode approach. Given the rather modest improvement in business functionality, the cost of such a change is often viewed as excessive.

3. *Use of simulation-based exposure for what-if limit checking and pricing implications.* This is the last "desirable feature" described previously. If accurate simulation-based exposure could be performed on a what-if basis in a matter of seconds, it would offer significant advantages. By providing an accurate estimate of the amount and timing of incremental exposure, reflecting all major effects of offsets and diversification, this would be the basis for reasonable estimates of the cost of the associated incremental credit risk. In addition to creating a minimum spread for exposure increasing deals, such a system would encourage aggressive pricing for exposure reducing deals. Traders' performance could be measured on the basis of risk-adjusted returns not gross trading profit. Until the development of the advanced analytical approximation methods described above, this aspiration was

commercially impractical. While such a system could have been built technically using Monte Carlo techniques, the cost in hardware and support has heretofore made it commercially impractical. With such methods, such a system becomes far more commercially justifiable.[4]

THE NEXT 15 YEARS

Looking back on the last 15 years, it is clear that there has been a massive improvement in our understanding, measurement and management of trading counterparty credit exposure and credit risk. I fully expect that looking back to today on the 30th anniversary of *Risk*, current methods will look just as outdated as those of 1987 appear to us currently. Nevertheless, I think the broad outlines of that world can be discerned in unexploited capabilities already available.

A general trend I expect to see over the next 15 years is increasing use of risk information for tactical as well as strategic decisions. Today most risk information is used to make high-level resource allocation decisions using some variation of risk-adjusted return on capital (RAROC), or to enforce risk limit controls. Most tactical decisions are still made on the basis of limited local information. Loans and other traditional credit facilities are evaluated on the basis of the financial strength of the obligor with only limited attention paid to portfolio implications. Derivative trades are priced based on how the contract fits the current market risk imbalances and, to a lesser extent, the credit worthiness and sophistication of the counterparty. In neither case are facilities available to assess broader portfolio risk implications. A number of capabilities already available, however, support an expectation of considerable progress along these lines in coming years.

❑ *Massive expansion in communication capacity.* The current sad financial state of the telecommunications industry is a reflection of significant excess capacity. This is largely a reflection of massive expansion combined with slower than expected penetration of broadband access among consumers in industrial countries. Such penetration eventually will occur, however, driven in significant measure by access to on-demand streaming video. In that setting, voice, text and numerical data will be minor portions of the total information flow. This will facilitate the much greater communication volume required to provide real-time updates and what-if inquiries to support thousands of daily decisions.

❑ *Evolving semantic standards based on extensible mark-up language.* Extensible mark-up language (XML) has rapidly been accepted as the syntax for self-describing messages. To be practical, however, XML must be supplemented with a series of semantic conventions relevant to specific types of information. Financial products mark-up language (FpML) is one such effort in the financial derivatives arena and there are several others in related fields. Development of these semantic standards is a slow and laborious process. The task is magnified by the need to build a critical core of institutional support through consensus. Progress is being made, however, and such protocols can be expected to be an important tool supporting, real-time, event-driven data exchange in coming years.

❑ *Browser-based information access capabilities.* An essential feature of an effective risk information system is not just reliable source data and sound analytics, but effective delivery of the resulting information. To realise the potential of risk information to improve tactical decisions requires that such results be delivered to many thousands of staff members. Furthermore, it must be tailored to their particular job needs and responsibilities as well as their personally preferred means of absorbing information. Finally, it must be possible to upgrade the system with added or modified functionality on a continuing basis without excessive coordination problems between the central server and the remote users' desktops. Fortunately, the rise of the Internet offers technology that is ideally suited to address this problem. Browser-based technology still cannot deliver the full richness and performance of client server applications, but the gap is narrowing. In addition, continued improvements in communication and computing speeds may well make the differences perceptually insignificant in a few years. It may be that a few key "power users" will continue to be supported by client-server configurations, but the vast majority of users will be fully and effectively served by web-based information access and display tools.

❏ *Robust approximations to Monte Carlo results.* As noted earlier, recently developed techniques offer the prospect for robust approximations to the results of computationally intense Monte Carlo runs for a small fraction of the processing resources. Deployment of such methods would avoid the need for two measurement systems, one robust but slow and the other crude but fast. Such capabilities would also support risk-adjusted pricing by supplying traders with the marginal cost of risk *before* a quote is given to the client. This carries the potential for a major overhaul in how traders' performance is evaluated and their compensation is determined.

CONCLUSION

It is said that forecasting is difficult, especially if it's about the future. I am sure, when the reality arrives, that there will be much to criticise in the vision I have articulated for the year 2017. Nevertheless, systems to capture and present the "macro" implications of "micro" business decisions are becoming progressively more feasible and less expensive. Regardless of the details, I feel confident that in 15 years time risk management will be far less separated from the business and be far less of an after-the-fact function than it is today. Rather it will be a pervasive influence on day-to-day decisions at all levels.

1   See http://newrisk.ifci.ch/134710.htm for an interesting summary.
2   In current terminology, this is a limit on the maximum loss given default.
3   A less commonly recognised point was that correlations appropriate for market risk may not be appropriate for credit exposure estimation. Credit exposure should be based on estimates of longer-term trend correlations rather than daily change correlations, since credit exposure must be simulated many months and even years into the future.
4   Recently, at least one or two bulge bracket firms have deployed systems that save deal level results from an overnight Monte Carlo run with a modest number of draws, usually no more than 1000. New deals are then simulated and the results added to those from the overnight run, after which a new aggregation is performed. This reportedly allows simulation-based what-if results in a matter of seconds, albeit based on a resonably small Monte Carlo sample.

BIBLIOGRAPHY

Derivative Credit Risk, 2nd Edition – Further Advances in Measurement and Management, (London: Risk Books), 1999.

Rowe, D., 1993, "Curves of Confidence" *Risk*, November.

15

Theory and Practice of Model Risk Management

Riccardo Rebonato

Royal Bank of Scotland and Oxford University

Model risk is a topic of great, and growing, interest in the risk management arena. Financial institutions are obviously concerned about the possibility of direct losses arising from mis-marked complex instruments. They are becoming even more concerned, however, about the implications that evidence of model risk mis-management can have on their reputation, and on their perceived ability to control their business.

WHY MODEL RISK MATTERS

Model risk inhabits, by definition, the opaque area where the value of instruments cannot be fully and directly ascertained in the market. The valuation of these products must be arrived at by means of marking-to-model, and therefore always contain a subjective component. In these days of heightened sensitivity to aggressive or opaque accounting, the ability to rely on sound practices to control model risk can have share-price implications well beyond the monetary value of the mis-marked positions. It is also for this reason that financial institutions place increasing importance on the effective management of model risk. Unfortunately, there is a widespread lack of clarity as to what model risk management should achieve, and about which tools should be used for the purpose. In this chapter I intend to answer these questions, to provide theoretical justification for my views and to suggest some practical ways to tackle the problem.

THEORY
What is model risk?

There are several distinct possible meanings for the expression "model risk". The most common one refers to the risk that, after observing a set of prices for the underlying and hedging instruments, different but identically calibrated models might produce different prices for the same exotic product. Since, presumably, at most only one model can be "true", this would expose the trader to the risk of using a mis-specified model. This is the angle explored, for instance, by Sidenius (2000) in the interest rate area: in his study of model risk, significantly different prices were obtained for exotic instruments after the underlying bonds and (a subset of) the underlying plain vanilla options were correctly priced. The question has intrinsic interest, but it is not clear what use can be made of this information for risk management purposes, unless additional assumptions are made about the behaviour of the trader after the transaction. Shall we assume that she will hedge her position on the basis of the model recommendations? Should we assume that the trader will hedge at all? What constraints and limits (value-at-risk ((VAR)), vega, etc) is the trader subject to? Will the trader recalibrate their model using historical or market data? Under what accountancy regime will the value of the position be recorded?[1]

Another common interpretation of the term "model risk" is the following. Let's assume that the trader, after making a price using a given model in a derivative product (complex or plain vanilla), follows the dynamic hedging strategy prescribed by the model. How well will the trader fare by the expiry of the derivative? Green and Figlewski (1999), answer this question assuming that the trader recalibrates their model based on historical data. Hull and Suo (2001) and Longstaff, Santa-Clara and Schwartz (2002) address the same topic assuming daily re-calibration of the model to market prices. What all these approaches have in common is the implicit or explicit identification of model risk with the risk that a complex product might be bought or sold for the "wrong" price, or that losses will be incurred because of an "incorrect" hedging strategy.

These are certainly interesting questions, and they are probably the most relevant ones from the trader's perspective. For a single exotic desk, in fact, selling optionality too cheaply is likely to cause an uneven but steady haemorrhaging of money out of the book, and can ultimately cause the demise of the trader. From the perspective of the financial institution, however, losses incurred in this fashion are unlikely to be of such magnitude to have a major bottom-line or reputational impact. In this respect the exotic trader is, from the bank's perspective, little different than a proprietary trader in, say, spot foreign exchange (FX). *As long as the exotic trader's positions can be accurately marked to market*, the risk for a financial institution arising from trading in complex options using a mis-specified model can be controlled with the same non-VAR risk management measures applied to other traders (eg, stop losses). What differentiates trading in opaque instruments from other trading activities is the possibility that the bank might accumulate a large volume of aggressively-marked opaque products. When, eventually, the true market prices are discovered, the book value re-adjustment is sudden, and can be very large. Stop-loss limits are ineffective to deal with this situation, since the gates can only be shut once the horse has well and truly bolted.[2]

In this chapter I will therefore argue that, from the perspective *not of the trader*, but of a financial institution the most relevant question is the following: if the price of a product cannot be frequently and reliably observed in the market, how can we ascribe a price to it in between observation times in such a way as to minimise the risk that its book-and-records value might be proven to be wrong? This question directly leads to the following definition (adapted from Rebonato 2001b):

> Model risk is the risk of occurrence of a significant difference between the mark-to-model value of a complex and/or illiquid instrument, and the price at which the same instrument is revealed to have traded in the market.

This is the meaning of "model risk" that I intend to cover in this chapter.

There are several points worth noticing. First of all, from the definition it follows that, if reliable prices for all instruments were observable at all times, model risk would not exist. The market prices might be unreasonable, counterintuitive, perhaps even arbitrageable, but they constitute the only basis for a robust mark-to-market.

Another important observation is that the instrument in question may, but need not, be complex or held off-balance sheet: model risk has often been associated with complex derivatives products, but a deeply out-of-the money call (the plain-vanilla option *par excellence*) and an illiquid corporate bond (a prototypical on-balance-sheet instrument) can both present substantial model risk. What both these instruments have in common is that the value at which they would trade in the market cannot be readily ascertained via screen quotes, intelligence of market transactions or broker quotes. A model must therefore be used in order to associate on a daily basis a value to these instruments for books-and-records purposes.

The last proviso is essential, and brings me to the last important observation about the definition above: in my discussion, model risk arises not because of a discrepancy between the model value and the "true" value of an instrument (whatever that might mean), but because of a discrepancy between the model value and the value that must be recorded for accounting purposes. From the perspective I have chosen, model risk is therefore intimately linked to trading-book products (that must be marked to market on a daily basis). I shall argue below that this need of marking to market daily, together with institutional and regulatory constraints, have profound implications for the price of these opaque instruments. This does not mean that the value of instruments held on the banking book cannot be arrived at using (sometimes very complex) models. The dynamics between "fundamental value', price adjustment and modelling practice is however so different, that, in the present context, it is counterproductive to analyse trading-book and banking-book products from the same perspective.

Isn't there just one value? Efficient markets revisited

In the previous section I have repeatedly referred to "true" and "fundamental" value on the one hand, and to mark-to-market value on the other as two potentially different concepts. I have also hinted that the value of an instrument might have to be looked at differently depending on whether it resides on the trading or the banking book. Doesn't this fly in the face of financial theory (that equates price and value), and of the efficient-market hypothesis in particular? The whiff of sulphur associated with these claims is so strong, that it can't be ignored. I maintain that understanding why "value" can have different meanings in different contexts is crucial to model risk, and well worth the effort. Let's rehearse the standard argument first.

The efficient market hypothesis (EMH) can be formulated in forms of wider and wider applicability (see, eg, Shleifer, 2000). The most radical form requires that all economic agents are fully informed and perfectly rational. If they can all observe the same price history they will all arrive at prices by discounting the expected future cashflows from a security at a discount rate dependent on the uncertainty of the security and their risk aversion. In this sense the value of the security is said to embed all the information available in the market, its value to be linked to "fundamentals", and markets to be informationally efficient. All securities are fairly priced, excess returns simply reflect excess risk, and five-dollar notes cannot be found lying on the pavement.

A weaker form of market efficiency (but one which arrives at the same conclusions) does not require all economic agents to be rational, but allows for a set of investors who price securities on sentiment or with imperfect information. Will this affect the market price? Actually, one can show that as long as the actions of the uninformed, irrational investors are random ("uncorrelated"), their actions will cancel out and the market will clear at the same prices that would be obtained if all the agents were perfectly rational.

Surely, however, the zero-correlation assumption is far too strong to be swallowed by anybody who has witnessed the recent dot.com mania. The very essence of bubbles, after all, is that the actions of uninformed, or sentiment-driven, investors are just the opposite of uncorrelated. If this is the case, supply and demand, rather than fundamentals, will determine the price of a security. Is this the end of the efficient market hypothesis? Not quite. Let there be irrational *and* co-ordinated investors. As long as there also exist rational, well-informed agents who can value securities on the basis of fundamentals, price anomalies will not persist. These pseudo-arbitrageurs will in fact buy the irrationally cheap securities and sell the sentimentally expensive ones, and by so doing will drive the price back to the fundamentals.[3] Whether it is due to irrationality and sentiment or to any other cause, in this framework, excess demand automatically creates extra supply, and vice versa. Therefore, as long as these pseudo-arbitrageurs can freely take their positions, supply and demand will not affect equilibrium prices, these will again be based on the suitably discounted expectation of their future cashflows (the "fundamentals") and the efficient-market hypothesis still rules.[4]

It is important to stress that the EMH is not only intellectually pleasing, but has also been extensively tested and has emerged, by and large, vindicated. The "by-and-large" qualifier, however, is crucial for my argument. In the multi-trillion market of all the traded securities, a theory that accounts for the prices of 99.9% of observed instruments can at the same time be splendidly successful, and yet leave up for grabs on the pavement enough five-dollar notes to make a meaningful difference to the end-of-year accounts and the share prices of many a financial institution. This is more likely to be true if the instruments in question are particularly opaque and if the reputational amplifying effect mentioned in the introductory section is at play. The possibility that the pseudo-arbitrageurs might not be able always to bring prices in line with fundamentals should therefore be given serious consideration.

Pseudo-arbitrageurs in trouble

What can prevent pseudo-arbitrageurs from carrying out their task of bringing prices in line with fundamentals? To begin with, these pseudo-arbitrageurs (hedge funds, relative-value traders, etc) often take positions not with their own money, but as agents of investors or shareholders. If the product is complex, and so is the model necessary to arrive at its price, the ultimate owners of the funds at risk might lack the knowledge, expertise or inclination to asses the fair value, and will have to rely on their agent's judgement. This trust, however, will not be extended for too long a period of time, and certainly not for many years.[5] Therefore, the time span over which securities are to revert to their fundamental value must be relatively short (and almost certainly will not extend beyond the next bonus date). If the supply-and-demand dynamics were such that the mispriced instrument might move even more violently out of line with fundamentals, the position of the pseudo-arbitrageur will swing into the red, and the "trust-me-I-am-a-pseudo-arbitrageur" line might rapidly loose its appeal with the investors and shareholders.

Another source of danger for relative-value traders is the existence of institutional and regulatory constraints that might force the liquidation of positions before they can be shown to be "right": the

EMH does not know about the existence of stop-loss limits, VAR limits, concentration limits etc.

Poor liquidity, often compounded with the ability of the market to guess the position of a large relative-value player, also contributes to the difficulties of pseudo-arbitrageurs. Consider for instance the case of a pseudo-arbitrageur who, on the basis of a perfectly sound model, concluded that traded equity implied volatilities are implausibly high, and entered large short-volatility trades to exploit this anomaly. If the market became aware of these positions, and if, perhaps because of the institutional constraints mentioned above, the pseudo-arbitrageur had to try to unwind these short positions before they had come into the money, the latter could experience a very painful short squeeze.[6]

Finally, very high information costs might act as a barrier to entry, or limit the number, of pseudo-arbitrageurs. Reliable models require teams of quantitative analysts to devise them, scores of programmers to implement them, powerful computers to run them and expensive data sources to validate them.[7] The perceived market inefficiency must therefore be sufficiently large not only to allow risk-adjusted exceptional profits after bid-offer spreads, but also to justify the initial investment.

In short, because of all of the above, the life of the pseudo-arbitrageur can be, if not nasty, brutish and short, at least unpleasant, difficult, and fraught with danger. As a result, even in the presence of a severe imbalance of supply or demand, relative-value traders might be more reluctant to step in and bring prices in line with fundamentals than the EMH assumes.

Why does it matter for model risk?

Let us look more closely at the features of the trades that, on the basis of the above discussion, one might most plausibly expect to be priced out of line with their "true" value. One feature was their complexity (with its double repercussions on the agency relationship and on the information costs); another was their poor liquidity and transparency; a third was the existence of limit structures that might cause the unwinding of trades before they can be shown to be right. All of these features perfectly apply to those products for which model risk is most acute. If this analysis is correct, however, it has profound implications as to how to control model risk, and, ultimately, as to what the source of model risk is.

If you belong to the EMH school, "things can only get better", and do so quickly: markets will always become more efficient and liquid, models truer to life, and their truth will always be swiftly recognised.[8] Therefore model risk is simply the risk that the model currently used to mark positions might not be sophisticated and realistic enough. For an EMH believer, finding a "better" model is the surest way to ensure that the marks of a financial institution will be in line with the (efficient) market prices. An important corollary of this view is that there should be no distinction between the model a front office trader would want to use to price a given instrument, and the model to be used for recognising its value for books-and-record purposes.

Much of the existing literature on model risk tends to implicitly endorse the view of the world underpinned by the EMH hypothesis, placing the emphasis as it does on the possibility that the model used might not be "accurate" or "sophisticated" enough. In this strand of works, creating a "better" model is seen as the best defence against model risk. The model validation department of an institution that subscribes to such a view typically has enshrined in its "mission statement" the requirement that the hypothesis underlying the model used for mark-to-model should be tested for "soundness and validity". If asked to choose between models to be used for books-and-records valuation, the same model validation unit will generally go for the theoretically more appealing and sophisticated one. If one keeps in mind that the ultimate goal of marking to model is to guess the price where the same product would actually trade in the market, the corollary of this policy is that the "better model" and the "market-chosen model" (ie, value and price) must coincide.

If, on the other hand, one believes that the EMH, while generally valid, might not apply to many of the products for which model risk is relevant, the situation is very different. Over the time scales relevant for model risk, the market might stray even further away from the righteous path. The model that will prevail tomorrow (or, rather, the model that will reproduce tomorrow's prices) need not necessarily be more realistic than today's model. Anecdotal evidence suggests that, for instance, after the liquidity crunch associated with the Russia crisis, traders reverted to pricing Bermudan swaptions with cruder and more conservative models, such as the Black–Derman–Toy, rather than with the indubitably more sophisticated and realistic LIBOR market models.

This state of affairs creates a fundamental tension between front-office traders and risk mangers insofar as model risk is concerned.

Traders and risk managers part ways

Within the EMH framework the goals of traders and risk managers are aligned: a superior model will bring the trader a competitive advantage, and will be recognised as such by the market with very little time lag. From this point of view, an accurate mark-to-market is purely a reflection of the best information available, and "true" (fundamental) value, market price and model price all coincide. It therefore makes perfect sense to have a single research centre, devoted to the study and implementation of the best model, which will serve the needs of the front-office trader and of the risk manager just as well. Looked at from this angle, model risk is simply the risk that our current model might not be good enough, and can be reduced by creating better and better models that will track the monotonic, if not linear, improvement of the markets' informational efficiency.

If we believe, however, that pseudo-arbitrageurs might in practice be seriously hindered in bringing all prices in line with fundamentals, model risk looks very different. Across both sides of the EMH divide there is little doubt that what should be recorded for books-and-records purposes should be the best guess for the price that a given product would fetch in the market. For the EMH sceptic, however, there is no guarantee that the "best" available model (ie, the model that most closely prices the instrument in line with fundamentals) should produce this price. Furthermore, there is no guarantee that the market, instead of swiftly recognising the error of its ways, might not stray even more seriously away from fundamentals.

Ultimately, whenever a trader enters a position, she must believe that, in some sense, the market is "wrong". For the risk manager concerned about model risk, on the other hand, the market must be right by definition. For the EMH believer the market can only be wrong for a short period of time (if at all), so there is no real disconnect between the risk-manager's price, and the trader's best price. For the EMH-sceptical risk managers, on the other hand, there is an irreconcilable tension between front-office pricing, and the risk management model price.

The parable of the two volatility traders

To illustrate further the origin of this tension, let's analyse a stylised but instructive example. Two plain vanilla option traders (one working for Efficient Bank, and the second for Sceptical Bank) have carefully analysed the volatility behaviour of a certain stock, and both concluded that its level should be centred around 20%. The stock is not particularly liquid, and the brokers' quotes, obtained with irregular frequency, do not deviate sufficiently from their estimate to warrant entering a trade. One day, without any-thing noticeable having happened in the market, the volatility quote appeared at 10%. Two huge five-dollar notes are now lying on the floor, and both traders swiftly pick them up. Both traders intend to crystallise the value of the mis-priced option by engaging in gamma trading, ie they are both long gamma and will dynami-cally hold a delta-neutralising amount of stock, as dictated by their model *calibrated to 20% volatility*.

Life is easy for the Efficient Bank trader. She will go to her risk manager, convince her that the model used to estimate volatility is correct and argue that the informationally efficient market will soon adjust the implied volatility quote back to 20%. This has important implications. First of all, the profit from the trade can be booked immediately: the front office and risk management share the same state-of-the-art model, and both concur that the price for the option in line with fundamentals should be obtained with a 20% volatility. Furthermore, should another five-dollar note appear on the pavement the trader of Efficient Bank will have every reason and incentive to pick it up again.

The coincidence of the front office and middle office models has yet another consequence. The trader works on a "volatility arbi-trage" desk, and his managers are happy for him to take a view on volatility, but not to take a substantial position in the underlying. They have therefore granted him very tight delta limits. This, how-ever, creates no problem, because his strategy is to be delta-neutral at every point in time and in order to enjoy the fact that she has bought (at 10%) "cheap convexity". Crucially, in order to crystallise the model profits from trade, she will engage in a dynamic hedging strategy based on the superior model (calibrated with a 20% volatility), not on the temporarily erroneous market model. Since middle-office again shares the same model, the risk manager calculates the delta of the position exactly in the same way as the trader, and therefore sees the whole portfolio perfectly within the desk's delta limits (actually, fully delta neutral).

Life is much harder for the trader at Sceptical Bank. She also works on a volatility arbitrage desk with tight delta limits, and her middle office function also recognises that the model she uses is sound and plausible and concurs that the market must be going through a phase of summer madness. The similarities, however, virtually end here. Her risk management function does not believe that a superior model must be endorsed by the market with effectively no delay, and therefore is not prepared to recognise the model value implied by the 10% trade as an immediate profit. A model provision will be set aside. Since the trader will not be able to book (all) the model profit upfront, she will have to rely on the profit dripping into the position over the life of the option as a result of trading the gamma. This process will be relatively slow, the more so the longer the maturity of the option. During this period the trader is exposed to the risk that another "rogue" volatility quote, say at 5%, might even create a negative mark-to-market for her position. Her reaction to a second five-dollar note will therefore be considerably different from that of her colleague at Efficient Bank. Furthermore, in order to carry out her gamma-trading programme she will have to buy and sell delta amounts of stock based on her best estimate of the "true" volatility (20%). Middle office, however, who have observed the 10% trade, uses the model calibrated with the lower volatility to calculate the delta exposure of the trade, and therefore does not regard her position as delta-neutral at all. She utilises more VAR than her colleague, might soon hit against her delta limit, and, if her trading performance is measured on the basis of VAR utilisation, she will be deemed to be doing, on a risk-adjusted basis, more poorly than her colleague.

This parable could be expanded further, but the central message is clear: different approaches to model risk management can generate very different behaviours and incentives for otherwise identical traders. The natural question is: which approach better serves the interests of a bank? In the long run, which bank will be more successful, Efficient Bank or Sceptical Bank?

The role of liquidity and of risk aversion

In order to answer this question at least two important elements, absent in the hyper-stylised example above, must be brought into the discussion: the role of liquidity and of risk aversion in the formation of prices. In the following discussion the two concepts are linked, but, for simplicity, it is simpler to analyse them in turn. Let us start with liquidity. The analysis underpinning EMH, which automatically equates the market price with the informationally most efficient price, pays little attention to the role of liquidity. Yet model risk is, by definition, most acute for illiquid products (that trade, and whose prices are therefore observed, relatively infrequently). In situations of market distress investors are happy to pay a premium to hold securities that can be sold easily at a readily ascertainable price. The trading dynamics in the months that followed the Russian default and the LTCM crisis of 1998 have often been described as a flight to quality, but a careful observation of the instruments that were sought after or disposed of would make the name "flight to liquidity" more appropriate: US Treasuries, of course, were very popular, but, since they enjoy both safety and liquidity, it is difficult to tell which features the investors were after. The unprecedented yield discrepancies that occurred at the time between on-the-runs and off-the-runs treasuries (both backed by the full faith of the US Treasury) gives a first indication that it was liquidity that loomed large in the investors' mind. Another popular product in those days was Danish mortgage-backed securities. These are bonds of the highest credit quality, (no default has been recorded in over 300 years) but with an outstanding stock that cannot compare with their US cousins (and therefore with more limited liquidity). In some of most the troubled days of the late summer of 1998 they traded for as little as 60 cents in the US$ on an option-adjusted basis. These, and similar, observations suggest that investors not only pay a premium for liquidity, but that this liquidity premium can be strongly state- and time-dependent.

This poses some crucial questions for model risk management. Looking closely again at Danish mortgage-backed-securities, the typical trade of the day, that many hedge funds and several banks were engaged in, was simple: they would buy a mortgage-backed security, purchase a Bermudan swaption on the amortising principal to protect themselves against pre-payment risk, fund themselves at LIBOR and still lock in a small but almost risk-free profit. Sound as the strategy might have been, it took into no account that, in order to put it in place, the pseudo-arbitrageurs had to take a long position in an instrument (the Danish mortgage bond) with adequate liquidity in normal market conditions, but prone to trade at a liquidity discount in stress situations. Arguably, the "fundamentals" (the suitably discounted expected cashflows from Danish mortgagors) had not changed because of the Russia/LTCM turmoil; yet, because of the high value placed on liquidity, the market price of the securities did. Those market players who were subject to daily marking-to-market of their trades were quickly hitting against stop loss or other limits, or were facing margin calls, and were forced to liquidate the self-same positions, further contributing to the negative price dynamics. The traders at Sceptical Bank had to cut their positions first, those at Efficient Bank held on to their "sound" positions longer, but ultimately found themselves no better able than King Canut to stem the tide, and liquidated at larger losses.

The second, and related, element missing form the previous discussion is the stochastic nature of risk aversion. It is well known that, when a pricing model is calibrated to market prices, the resulting "implied values" (reversion levels, jump frequencies, reversion speeds, etc) are not the econometrically observed ones, but the ones that would prevail under the pricing measure (ie, they are risk-adjusted). This is readily handled within the EMH framework, because the expected cashflows are discounted at a rate that takes risk aversion into account. If this risk aversion, however, can vary stochastically over time, the knowledge that "some" future degree of risk aversion (unknown today) will prevail tomorrow, such that the future prices will be accurately accounted for, is of little comfort. Typically, for the sake of tractability, financial models tend to make the market price of risk either a constant (Vasicek, 1977), or a deterministic function of time (as implicitly happens in the Hull–White (1993) model), or a simple function of the state variable (Cox, Ingersoll and Ross, 1985). The very notation typically used to denote the market price of risk, $\lambda(t)$, tends to suggest that it should be a deterministic function of time. Unfortunately, there is ample evidence that risk aversion changes in an unpredictable way (stochastically) over time: equity smiles, which can be plausibly linked to the risk-adjusted jump frequency, suddenly made their appearance after the 1987 stock market crash: sellers of equity put options became more "afraid" of jumps after October 1987 than they were before. Similarly, non-monotonic smiles in the caplet and swaption volatility surfaces appeared after the turmoil that followed the Russia events. During the same period, swap spreads widened beyond what any risk-neutral estimation of bank default risk might suggest plausible.

The consequences of this for model risk are far-reaching, and we do not need to invoke any shortcomings of the EMH to understand them. Let us assume that a trader has a perfectly correct model (ie, a model that, *on a risk-adjusted basis*, prices perfectly in line with fundamentals), and that supply and demand does not appreciably influence prices. Still, if the compensation the market requires for the various sources of risk (jump risk, volatility risk, swap spread risk, etc) varies stochastically over time, the same trader cannot be confident that today's calibration to the market prices (which embeds *today's* risk aversion) will be valid tomorrow. As we have said, if the relevant market prices were always readily observable, model risk would not exist. But, in the absence of frequent reliable quotes, a model's ability to recover *today's* prices would be no guarantee that next months' prices will also be correctly recovered. Of course, leaving aside again the possible shortcomings of the EMH, if we had a "correct model" and we included in the state variables available for its calibration also the future (stochastic) risk aversion, we could hope to obtain at least a conditional distribution for the future market prices. Unfortunately, daily time series of risk aversion to jumps, volatility, spread risk, etc, from which future joint probability distributions of these variables and of the "traditional" observable risk factors could be obtained, do not belong to the world of the here-and-now.

The technology of option pricing
There is yet another reason why the way the model price of a given product is calculated might change in the future. The idea that the

price of a financial instrument might be arrived at using a complex mathematical formula is relatively new, and can be traced back to the Black–Scholes (1973) formula. Of course, formulae were used before that for pricing purposes, for instance in order to convert the price of a bond into its gross redemption yield. Even when no closed-form solutions existed, as is indeed the case for the gross redemption yield, these pre-Black–Scholes early formulae generally provided totally transparent transformations from one set of variables to another, and did not carry along a heavy baggage of model assumptions.

Bona fide model-based pricing, on the other hand, can be characterised by the fact that the reliability of a pricing formula hinges on the applicability and realism of a complex set of assumptions about the market (eg, its completeness, the ability to enter short positions, the absence of taxes or transaction costs, etc) and about the process for the underlying state variables (eg, continuous or discontinuous paths, etc). Given the relatively short history of model-based approach to pricing, it is therefore not surprising that the models used by the trader community have evolved rapidly and radically. (See Rebonato, 2002 for a survey of the evolution of interest-rate modelling). Very often, however, the adoption of new models has been driven not by their superior explanatory power, but by concomitant, and difficult-to-predict, technological and numerical advances. Trading houses did not, for instance, suddenly "see the light" and begin adopting in the mid 1990s the Heath–Jarrow–Morton/LIBOR-market-model paradigm simply because they realised it was "a better model". I have argued elsewhere (see again Rebonato, 2002) that its generalised adoption (at least for path-dependent securities) would not have been possible had important and independent advances not simultaneously been made in the Monte Carlo area. It is also interesting that for a few years compound options were deemed to be too difficult to handle with the same approach, and trading houses were therefore using different models for different products on their interest-rate books. The provocatively-titled article "Throwing Away a Billion Dollars" (Longstaff, Santa-Clara and Schwartz, 2002), which has created great controversy in both the academic and trading communities, indeed argued that those institutions using single-factor models of the old school were, by so doing, leaving on the table a significant portion of the theoretically available profits (the billion dollars in the title). It is easy to see how an article of this type might change the pricing consensus for a product over a very short period of time.

More generally, there is a spectrum of continuously evolving opinions regarding the criteria on the basis of which the quality of a model should be assessed. The ability to recover the prices of the underlying plain vanilla options is an obvious desideratum. It has soon been realised, however, that it is not too difficult to achieve this goal in isolation if no control is imposed on other financial features, such as the time-homogeneity of the evolution of the smile surface or of the term structure of volatilities. The consensus as to which of these features are important also evolves over time, and does so at a strongly non-constant pace: non-monotonic interest-rate smiles "suddenly" appeared after the turmoil triggered by the Russia events, and stochastic-volatility or jump-diffusion extensions of the LIBOR market model were just as suddenly deemed to be desirable.

Theoretical conclusions

Recall that we defined model risk as the risk that our mark-to-model might not reflect the price an instrument would fetch in the market. If the EMH held exactly true, the price of all products would always coincide with their value. Guessing the level of a future transaction (its future market price) would therefore be tantamount to estimating its fundamental value. In an informationally efficient market, the better the model, the greater the likelihood that this identification of future price and value will be realised. Simply put, model risk would simply be the risk that our model is not good enough.

I have argued however that the way prices of complex and/or illiquid instruments are arrived at in the market can be influenced by a variety of factors that in the EMH analysis either should be irrelevant (ultimately, supply and demand), or are poorly accounted for (stochastically varying risk aversion), or are generally altogether neglected (say, liquidity). Whether markets "ultimately" do always move towards greater efficiency is a fundamentally important question, but one of a more metaphysical than empirical flavour. In the short run, I believe that the deviations from greater efficiency can be significant, and I have argued that this affects the concept of model risk, and the practice of its management. In my view, the task faced by the model risk manager can therefore be summarised as follows: guessing how future ways of arriving at prices might differ from the accepted wisdom of today, without assuming that the direction of model evolution is fully pre-ordained.

If we accept these conclusions we can derive some indications as to how the task can be carried out in practice. This is tackled in the next section.

PRACTICE

The theoretical treatment presented above can provide some useful guidelines as to how model risk management can be carried out in practice. The first casualty of the way to look at model risk I have advocated is the traditional concept of model validation.

Inadequacy of traditional model validation

Model validation is usually meant to be the review of the assumptions and of the implementation of the model used by the front office for pricing deals, and by finance to mark their value. Absence of computational mistakes is clearly a requirement for a valid valuation methodology. The idea, however, that a review of the model assumptions per se can give reassurance as to the correct mark-to-market is much more difficult to justify. Rejecting a model because "it allows for negative rates", because "it does not allow for stochastic volatility" or because "it neglects the stochastic nature of discounting" can be totally inappropriate, from the risk manager's perspective, if the market is happy to live with these blemishes, at least for particular products. Similarly, requiring that a product should be marked-to-market using a more sophisticated model (ie, a model which makes more realistic assumptions) can be equally misguided if, for any of the reasons discussed earlier, the market has not embraced the "superior" approach.

From the perspective of the risk manager, the first and foremost task in model risk management is the identification of the model ("right" or "wrong" as it may be) currently used by the market in order to arrive at the observed traded prices. In order to carry out this task the risk manager will require a variety of sources: in particular, market intelligence and contacts with members of the trader community at other institutions are invaluable. In addition, also very important is the ability to reverse-engineer observed prices using a variety of models in order to "guess" which model is currently most likely to be used in order to arrive at the observed traded prices. In order to carry out this task the risk manager will need a variety of properly calibrated valuation models, and information about as many traded prices as possible.

The next important task of the risk manager is to surmise how today's accepted pricing methodology might change in the future. Notice that the expression "pricing methodology" makes reference not just to the model per se, but also to the valuation of the underlying instruments, to its calibration, and possibly, to its numerical implementation. In the light of the earlier discussion, the risk manager should not assume that this dynamic process of change should necessarily take place in an evolutionary sense towards better and more realistic models and more liquid and efficient markets. An interesting question for a model risk manager, for instance, could be: "How would the price of a complex instrument change if a particular hedging instrument (say, a very-long-dated FX option) were no longer available tomorrow?" The next sections will describe in some detail how these tasks (gathering market intelligence, reverse engineering of prices, and guessing what the market-chosen future model might be) can be carried out in practice.

Gathering market intelligence

In the context of model risk, market intelligence is first and foremost the ability to "see" the largest possible number of transactions, and the levels where they trade. When a trade has been lost in a competitive-tender situation, the sales force can often provide information as to where the trade "went in the market", how many other players submitted a more aggressive bid, etc. No matter how good or convincing a theoretical model might be, few states of affairs should worry a risk manger more than the trader who, using this model, consistently beats all competing banks in a competitive-tender situation. In this respect, contacts with brokers, traders or risk managers at other institutions can provide what is possibly the most effective "early-alert system".

Being aware of the latest market developments, and of academic papers can be very useful in guessing which direction the market might evolve tomorrow (the caveat of a non-linear evolution towards ever greater "perfection" should, of course, always be kept in mind). Professional conferences are useful in this context in order to gauge the market's reception of new ideas, and the likelihood of their becoming the next market standard.

Another possible cause for concern is the sudden occurrence of large-notional trades for which it is difficult to establish a clear rationale on the basis of customer-driven demand. The motivation behind these trades could be the very actions of pseudo-arbitrageurs who were discussed earlier. These players might have identified particular types of transaction for which common market assumptions or practices cannot be justified. Historically, examples of such trades have been, for instance, LIBOR-in-arrears swaps, forward-starting swaptions, CMS caps, etc. In these cases, the risk manager should not feel automatically reassured by discovering a *bona fide* "customer" name on the trade tickets, since the trusted client could be in a back-to-back transaction with a market professional.

In summary, it should be stressed that, without at least some anchor points of solid knowledge about the levels and the nature of actual market transactions, the task of the model risk manager is utterly hopeless. To a large extent, the model risk management task can be described as an interpolation and extrapolation exercise that simply cannot be carried out in an informational vacuum.

Reverse engineering – plain vanilla instruments

Let us assume that adequate market intelligence has been gathered. The next task is to reverse engineer these prices, ie, to try and find the set of pricing methodologies that can best account for them. The exercise should be carried out starting from the simplest building blocks. For instance, in the interest rate arena a LIBOR yield curve generator should be tested first, with special attention devoted to slightly off-market deals: a small number of forward-starting or off-coupon swaps, swaps with "stubs" at the beginning or the end, odd-maturity/reset/frequency transactions, etc, can often provide more useful information than thousands of totally standard trades.[9]

The next stage in the reverse-engineering process would be the recovery of the prices of plain vanilla options. Typically, market quotes are readily available for a relatively small range of maturities and for strikes that are not too far from the at-the-money level. The creation of a full smile surface that extends well into the wings is essential in model risk management both for the direct risk of mis-marked out-of-the-money options, and because large portions of the smile surface typically constitute the inputs to models used for more complex products.

Much as it would be desirable, it is not always necessary, or indeed possible, for a "model" in the traditional sense (ie, for a description of the process of the underlying) to account for the observed market prices of plain vanilla options. A number of surface-fitting methodologies that do not assume particular dynamics for the underlying state variables have been proposed for the task, and the criteria for choosing among them are not always clear-cut. Apart from the fact that quality of fit, robustness of the estimation procedure and stability of the optimised param-eters for small variations in the inputs are often desirable features. More fundamentally, producing a smooth and well-behaved *inter*-polation between observed prices (implied volatlities) is not too arduous a task.[10] Where most of the model risk often resides, how-ever, is for the opaque out-of-the-money strikes and/or long matur-ities where few reliable quotes are observed (the *extra*polation part of the exercise). It is therefore important to check that the chosen smile-surface-generator behaves well not so much in the centre of the smile surface, but also in the wings.

Reverse engineering – complex products

At this point we can assume that the model risk manager has a satisfactory understanding of the market dynamics behind the largest trades (trading levels, competition with other players, nature of the demand for the product, etc); that she has confidence in the congruence between the methodology used in-house to price the fundamental building blocks (eg, the yield curves) and the corres-ponding market practice; and that she can trust the approach used to account for the prices of plain vanilla options not just for close-to-at-the-money liquid calls and puts, but also for the far out corners of the smile surface. The next task she must face is the valuation of complex products.

Moving from plain vanilla to complex instruments, the number of opaque variables that can affect their prices sharply increases.

For plain vanilla options, the description of how the model-independent implied volatility changes with maturity and strike gives the full information about the associated prices.[11] Therefore, a relatively simple, model-independent parametrisation of the smile surface as a function of strike or maturity is not too arduous to achieve. Unfortunately, the price of complex products may depend on a much larger number of variables: for instance, on full yield curves and term structure of volatilities, on correlation matrices, on credit transition matrices, etc. As a consequence, finding a clever model-independent algorithm that can account for observed market prices over a large range of this multi-dimensional space is almost impossible, and an appropriately calibrated model (ie, a specification of the processes for the underlying stochastic variables) must almost always be used.

For practical applications and for illustration purposes the discussion can be profitably split between interest-rate products and equity of FX-based instruments. For the former, it is often claimed that the LIBOR market model approach has "won the day" and that a wide industry consensus has crystallised around this pricing methodology (see Chapter 1 of Rebonato, 2002 for a history of the developments that led to the LIBOR market model). While this can be true, it is often forgotten that the LIBOR market model approach ultimately describes conditions of no-arbitrage among forward rates, and that it only becomes a "model" once specific choices are made for the instantaneous volatility and correlation functions. Significant pricing differences can therefore arise between traders who use the same pricing approach, but who choose different functional forms for the input functions. The likelihood of encountering in the market different choices for volatility and correlations is increased by the fact that there exists an infinity of volatility functions that can perfectly reproduce the observed market prices of caplets or European swaptions. Furthermore, no consensus exists as to which market prices the model should be calibrated to (caplets or swaptions, or to both simultaneously). Finally, the number of factors that should be used for pricing certain products (notably, Bermudan swaptions) is still open for debate (the more-than-academic importance of this issue is demonstrated by the very title of the controversial Longstaff, Santa-Clara and Schwartz, 2002 paper that dealt with the pricing impact of the number of factors: "Throwing Away a Billion Dollars"). Therefore, even if a general consensus has emerged regarding the pricing approach, substantial differences still exist, even in the standard version of the model, as to its actual implementation (and hence to the prices it can produce).[12] In my opinion, certain strategies for choosing the volatility functions are financially much more satisfactory than others, and should be employed by a trader. From the risk management perspective, however, the possibility should be entertained that the market might disagree with the "optimal" choice, and that prices substantially at variance might be produced by different calibrations (to caplets only, to swaptions only, to both markets) and/or by different functional choices ("flat" volatilities, time-homogeneous volatilities, forward-rate and time-dependent volatilities, etc).

The state of affairs is significantly different for complex equity or FX-based products. A similar broad consensus about the most desirable pricing approach has not been reached yet, and several major pricing philosophies uneasily coexist: jump-diffusions, stochastic-volatility, local-volatility and gamma variance, to name just a few. Matters are not simplified by the fact that combinations of these approaches (eg, of local-volatility with either jump-diffusion or with stochastic volatility, or of jump-diffusions with stochastic volatilities) have been proposed. The number of "fitting parameters" is sometimes staggering (more than twenty for the combined stochastic-volatility/jump-diffusion approach), and the calibration methodologies, often based on chi-square minimisation techniques, tend to produce solutions of similar numerical quality, but with completely different parameters.

The shift in market consensus as to the best "model of the month" has been more rapid and fitful in equities and FX than in the interest-rate arena, perhaps indicating that each competing approach is perceived as a partial solution, whose blemishes and advantages must be weighed and reassessed on a continuous basis. The local-volatility approach, for instance, has been amply criticised for its poor hedging performance and for implausible evolution of the smile surface that it implies. Nonetheless, many traders and risk managers like to use it for the "comfort factor" provided by its ability to recover by construction the prices of the underlying plain vanilla options.

In the light of the discussion above, my recommendation for the prudent model risk manager is not difficult to guess: several models, with fits of similar (good) quality to the plain vanilla market prices should be used to identify a range of possible future market prices. In the same spirit, different calibration methodologies, that produce similar prices for calls and puts but possibly very different prices for complex products, should also be used in parallel. And, finally, the risk manager should not unquestioningly assume that an intellectually more satisfactory model or calibration strategy will necessarily be chosen by the market.

1   The accountancy regime can make a substantial difference to the timing of the recorded profits. Assume that, perhaps because of poor information, an agent sells short-dated equity options of a wide range of strikes and maturities a bit too cheaply (ie a bit below where professional traders would manage to sell the same options). On a mark-to-market basis the trades will immediately show a loss. Options are priced in the market, however, as discounted expectations in the risk-neutral measure, not in the objective (econometric) measure. Therefore it is possible that the liabilities generated by the same options, left unhedged, might be more than covered, on an actuarial basis, by the premia received. The strategy of continuously selling options at a loss on a mark-to-market basis, but at actuarially advantageous prices might therefore be profitable on an accrual-accounting basis.

2   Unfortunately, the neat distinction between the "haemorrhaging" of the trader's profitability that can be controlled by exercising the stop-loss discipline and the sudden realisation of a loss due to mis-marking of position can sometimes become rather blurred: this can occur when the frequent, but relatively small, losses due to wrong model choice induce the unscrupulous trader to influence the marking of his book in a flattering fashion. The trader's ability, and temptation, to do so will be greater, the more opaque the products in which she trades.

3   "Pseudo-arbitrage" is defined in this context as the "simultaneous purchase and sale of the same, or essentially similar, security [...] for advantageously different prices" (Sharpe and Alexander, 1998)

4   Criticisms of the EMH simply based on the observation that not all investors are rational are therefore irrelevant: the EMH can still hold even if there are irrational investors, and if their actions are co-ordinated. As long as unfettered pseudo-arbitrageurs exist we can simply *pretend* that all agents are rational, and we would get exactly the same results. The situation can be compared with game theory, which has also been criticised on the basis of requiring hyper-rational players. Yet, as long as suitable reward and punishment mechanisms are in place, we can successfully analyse evolutionary problems (Maynard Smith, 1982) as *if* we were dealing with purely rational agents (even if, in the evolutionary context, the "players" might actually be amoebas). Showing that amoebas are not fully rational is neither very difficult, nor very productive in a discussion of the usefulness of game theory to tackle evolutionary problems.

5   Indeed, in order to limit the risk of investors suddenly pulling their money out, many hedge funds impose restrictions on their investors' ability to withdraw funds at will.

6   As far as can be ascertained from public information (see, eg, Dunbar, 1999) this is indeed part of what happened to the hedge fund LTCM in the autumn of 1998.

7   When, in the late 1990s, I used to trade complex interest-rate derivatives the farm of computers needed to price and hedge the trades on our books made my group rank immediately after Los Alamos National Laboratories in terms of computing power.

8   Not *too* swiftly, though, if the pseudo-arbitrageurs want to be able to pick up their five-dollar bills. The EMH needs the pseudo-arbitrageurs, but, after all, their efforts can only be worth the trouble if markets adjust to fundamentals with a finite speed.

9   The idea behind LIBOR-in-arrears swaps, for instance, that caught quite a few naïve banks off guard in 1994, is based on a simple variation on the standard-swap theme (the pay-off time in the arrears swap coincide with the reset time, instead of occurring an accrual period later).

10 Quoting an implied volatility does not imply an endorsement of the Black (or of any other) model. It is simply the "wrong number to plug into the wrong formula to get the right price" (Rebonato, 1999).

11 In the case of swaptions the situation is somewhat more complex, because the implied volatility is a function of maturity, expiry of the option and length of the underlying.

12 The "standard" version of the LIBOR market model does not allow for smiles, which have become more and more pronounced, and complex in shape, after the market turmoil of summer/autumn 1998. Several modifications that can be "grafted" on top of the LIBOR-market-model approach have been proposed (see, eg, Rebonato, 2001, Rebonato and Joshi, 2002, Andersen and Andreasen, 2002, Glasserman and Kou, 1998).

BIBLIOGRAPHY

Andersen, L., and J. Andreasen, 1997, "Volatility Skews and Extension of the LIBOR Market Model", forthcoming, *Risk.*

Cox, J., J. E. Ingersoll and S. A. Ross, 1985, "A Theory of the Term Structure of Interest Rates" Econometrica, 53, pp. 385–407.

Dunbar, N., *Inventing Money,* 1999 (John Wiley & Sons).

Glasserman, P., and S. G. Kou, 2000, "The Term Structure of Simple Forward Rates with Jump Risk", Working Paper, Columbia University.

Green, T. C., and S. Figlewski, 1999, "Market Risk and Model Risk for a Financial Institution Writing Options", *Journal of Finance,* 34, pp. 1111–27.

Hull, J., and W. Suo, 2001, "A Methodology for Assessing Model Risk and its Application to the Implied Volatility Function Model", Working Paper, University of Toronto.

Hull, J., and A. White, 1993, "Bond Option Pricing Based on a Model for the Evolution of Bond Prices", *Advances in Futures and Option Research,* 6.

Longstaff, F. A., P. Santa-Clara, and E. Schwartz, 2002, "Throwing Away a Billion Dollars: The Case of Sub-Optimal Exercise Strategies in the Swaptions Market", forthcoming, *Journal of Financial Economics.*

Maynard Smith, J., 1982, *Evolution and the Theory of Games* (Cambridge University Press).

Rebonato, R., 1999, *Volatility and Correlation* (John Wiley & Sons).

Rebonato, R., 2001a, "The Stochastic Volatility LIBOR Market Model", *Risk,* October 2001, pp. 105–10.

Rebonato, R., 2001b, "Managing Model Risk" in C. Alexander (ed), *Handbook of Risk Management,* (FT-Prentice Hall).

Rebonato, R., 2002, *Modern Pricing of Interest-Rate Derivatives: the LIBOR Market Model and Beyond,* (New Jersey: Princeton University Press).

Rebonato, R., and M. Joshi, 2002, "A Joint Empirical/Theoretical Investigation of the Modes of Deformation of Swaption Matrices: Implications for the Stochastic-Volatility LIBOR Market Model", forthcoming *International Journal of Theoretical and Applied Finance*, and Working Paper, QUARC, (Quantitative Research Centre), URL: www.rebonato.com.

Sharpe, W., and G. Alexander, 1998, *Investments*, Sixth Edition (Prentice Hall).

Shleifer, A., 2000, Inefficient Markets: an Introduction to Behavioural Finance (Oxford University Press).

Sidenius, J., 2000, "Evaluating new research exploring practical aspects of multi-factor Libor market models" Presented at the 7th annual forum – Global Derivatives 2000 – ParisPress, Oxford.

Vasicek, O., 1977, "An Equilibrium Characterization of the Term Structure" *Journal of Financial Economics*, 5(1), pp. 77–188.

Part V

The Development
of Financial Risk
Identification

16

A Retrospective Look at Market Risk*

Barbara Kavanagh

CP Risk Management LLC

INTRODUCTION

A comprehensive review of the history of market risk, its measurement and management would require that this book expand into numerous volumes. Indeed, Sargent and Velde's publication, *The Big Problem of Small Change*, (Sargent and Velde, 2003) devotes 432 pages to meaningful consideration of one small but longstanding dimension of market risk – the recurring scarcity and relative depreciation of small currency tokens in money regimes vis-à-vis larger coins, a dilemma as old as 400 BC. This risk dimension continues to be relevant today, particularly with the recent introduction of the euro in currency and coin form.

We similarly know that commodity price risk and efforts to manage it can be traced back to at least the 12th Century, with trade merchants even then entering into forward contracts that were economic equivalents and precursors to the grain futures contracts currently trading on Chicago's futures exchanges. For the purpose of this text, then, we must take as a given that market risk has in fact existed for centuries, as well as efforts to manage it. We can only consider here the most important mechanisms firms have developed to deal with age-old market risk within the last 25 years. And in the interest of brevity, we can only do so at a very general level.

*The author wishes to thank Christopher Culp, managing director of CP Risk Management LLC, and Till Guldimann, vice chairman of Sungard, for their discussions with the author of events in the evolution of market risk. In the end, however, I am solely responsible for the text of this piece and any errors contained herein.

One can divide the tools available today for measuring and managing market risk into two populations – those *ex ante* in nature and those available for use *ex post*. This text is divided in a similar fashion. The *"ex ante"* tool kit has three very important components to it:

1. risk limits;
2. risk policies; and
3. capital allocation methodologies such as value-at-risk (VAR) and risk-adjusted return on capital (RAROC).

Once an industry participant has taken on market risk (inevitable, should one wish to earn returns for shareholders), a separate population of tools is available with which to manage those risks. Many have evolved or emerged in the last 25 years. These include:

❏ derivatives, both exchange traded and privately negotiated or over-the-counter (OTC) in nature;
❏ securitisation and/or asset/liability divestitures, and
❏ insurance products and the world of "alternative risk transfer", (ART).

Each of these tools and their recent evolution are briefly discussed in the following sections.

THE EVOLUTION OF VALUE-AT-RISK

The early 1980s brought a period of unprecedented interest rate movements and levels, which inevitably affected currency markets and relative currency values. In the US, the consequences were most obviously manifest by a record number of failures of financial institutions, with anaemic earnings performance and capital erosion often characterising those other firms that were able to survive. The importance of asset/liability management suddenly came into its own, with financial institutions suddenly aware that the repricing characteristics of non-trading assets and liabilities were dramatically askew and related risk measurement techniques woefully inadequate. Existing market risk measurement and limit techniques were not appropriately dealing with the leakage in companies' profits and losses (P&Ls), nor were they forecasting prospective earnings effects should this disparity continue.

For multinational trading institutions like JP Morgan that also ran large trading rooms with large multi-currency positions across the entire length of term structures, the effects of interest rate gyrations – relative and absolute – were further felt in this aspect of their business. Most trading firms at the time had simply set notional limits per currency across the time horizon. It suddenly became transparent that those limits did not meaningfully act to constrain risk. Daily reports of trading positions vis-à-vis notional limits were suddenly revealed as giving no meaningful representation of a firm's vulnerability to changes in interest rates or currencies. Further, we importantly lacked a way to calculate risk as we moved across business lines within diversified firms. Apples could not be compared to oranges or pears; what we now call "the banking book" contained inherent interest rate risk exposure measured and managed by a separate team using a separate language and measurement technique from those dealing with the trading room. Management lacked a common denominator allowing it to sum the amount of earnings or capital at risk throughout the entire organisation.

These were the very events leading to the birth of probability-based VAR measurement techniques that would ultimately be available for application across all enterprise business lines, financial or non-financial in nature. While the VAR concept was simultaneously engineered in several major Wall Street firms, Till Guldimann beautifully recounts, in "The Story of Risk Metrics" (Guldimann, 2000), the historic, ten-year long evolution of VAR measurement techniques within JP Morgan and the public launch of RiskMetrics. In retrospect, it would prove extraordinarily important in modern market risk history – JP Morgan released RiskMetrics nearly simultaneous with the Bank for International Settlements (BIS) adopting a VAR-based approach to regulatory capital measurements for market risk at major trading banks globally. The confluence of these two events, as well as the industry's release of the pivotal G30 Report, lead to a global adoption of VAR as *the* market risk measurement technique standard. Those VAR measurement techniques are discussed in greater detail in Chapters 4 and 9 of this volume.

Value-at-risk limits and policies

The advent of VAR and subsequent proliferation of methodologies by which to measure and apply it within a firm held tremendous importance for firm management. One could now analytically and deliberately suballocate risk limits across currencies, equities, commodities and interest rate risks, as well as their subcategories, and determine *ex ante* – at a specified confidence interval – how much market risk one wished to take in the banking vs trading books. Senior management could now set more meaningful limits, based on data sets and probability rather than anecdotal decision-making. In short, notional limits were abandoned and replaced with a simpler, yet more meaningful and concise, limit structure. Technological developments during the same time frame likewise allowed one to measure and report to senior management end of day position risks vs prescribed limits on a daily basis, from the individual business line, product or trading desk level to aggregation at the firm-wide level. Correlations and covariances could be measured and tracked. Harry Markowitz's portfolio theory, an academic concept developed in the late 1950s, now had real business application in more than an investment portfolio context.

Risk-adjusted return on capital and capital allocation methodologies

We now know, of course, that the seminal question is relative risk-adjusted returns on capital. While JP Morgan engineered its own VAR approach and the RiskMetrics market risk toolkit, Bankers' Trust Company developed its VAR concept and was pioneering methodologies by which one could measure *relative* risk-adjusted returns across varying business lines and within an entire enterprise. Its analytics group chose to tackle what was then a major management question with no analytic framework for the answer: given that capital is a scarce commodity, how much should go to one trading book vs another, or trading in the aggregate vs commercial lending? Whereas corporate executives had long had certain measures for calculating returns from various business lines after the fact, they did not systematically or analytically factor in the amount of risk taken to generate those returns. Perhaps more importantly, they were relevant measurements only *after* business ventures were undertaken – no market risk measurement tool existed to provide meaningful comparative data to a senior executive facing the dilemma of where next to take on risk.

Should newly raised capital or internally generated earnings be allocated to fund penetration of a new market or undertake lending of a new type, or instead be re-deployed in trading G7 currencies or bonds? And of all the global fixed income bond markets within which one could take positions, was the firm better off putting capital at risk in the US or Europe, Asia or South America? The advent of RAROC and analogous analytical capital allocation methodologies would allow firm management to address age-old market risk within a meaningful analytical framework consistent with shareholder interests. One could compare earnings from trading US treasuries with those from trading junk bonds, now adjusting for the varied risk attributes of each of those markets. Perhaps more importantly, RAROC would allow us to decide *before hand* whether, on a risk-adjusted basis, the company was better off in one venture or another. Management now had an analytical platform on which to make better capital allocation decisions.

It is undoubtedly one of the most important recent evolutionary events in risk management. While Bankers' Trust initially developed the concept within the context of trading market risk, it ultimately extended it internally across all business lines – banking or trading in nature. The current constructs in the marketplace attempt to take into consideration all risk dimensions – market, credit, operational, and liquidity. We will undoubtedly see further refinements in this frontier over the next 10 years as measurement conventions and methodological approaches improve, particularly with respect to the last three named risk dimensions.

A REVOLUTION IN *EX POST* MARKET RISK MANAGEMENT TECHNIQUES

While the last 20 years have brought landmark developments in methods of measuring and limiting market risk, they have also brought an explosion of new mechanisms for firms to manage market risk ex post, or after being taken on by a firm. These market risk management tools can be classified into the following categories: first, the evolution of OTC derivative products to compete and complement those offered by exchanges; next, securitisation and subsequent related evolutionary vehicles for asset or liability divesture, such as collateralised debt obligations (CDOs), collateralised loan obligations (CLOs), and special purpose vehicles (SPVs); and finally, the advent of products offered by the insurance sector – ART and protection for "tail" events.

Exchanges and over-the-counter products

As mentioned previously, merchants were engaged in forward contracts for the sale or purchase of commodities as long ago as the 12th Century. By the 1600s, the Dutch had devised a futures contract on tulips to accommodate growing price speculation in that market. By the mid-1800s, the Chicago Board of Trade (CBOT) was formed, and in 1865 it began offering its first futures contracts – forwards with an element of standardisation. The Chicago Mercantile Exchange (CME) as we know it today was essentially organised in 1919, a successor to Chicago's Butter and Egg Board of 1898. Yet we tend to think of the CME today in terms of its tremendously successful Eurodollar and currency futures contracts introduced in the 1970s and 1980s. The latter afforded the extraordinarily large currency spot and forward markets with an important standardised mechanism for hedging. In 1973, the Chicago Board of Options Exchange (CBOE) was formed, the first organised exchange trading standardised options on equity stocks. Shortly after it opened its doors, Fisher Black and Myron Scholes released their seminal work, forming the foundation of options pricing theory as we know it today. Within a few short years, CBOE traders had hand held calculators pre-programmed with the Black–Scholes formula.

In 1981, IBM and The World Bank entered into what is generally regarded as the first modern interest rate swap, a landmark contract in that it is often thought of as marking the birth of the OTC derivatives market as we know it today. It seems doubtful that the engineers behind that deal could possibly foresee the proliferation of other contracts that would follow in the subsequent 20 years, in many ways each an extension of that first innovation. Cross currency swaps were first to follow, in no small part attributable to the tremendous increase in foreign exchange (FX) volatility following the Bretton Woods act. And about the same time, swap contracts on commodities were engineered. The spectrum of OTC products that followed was extraordinary, generally born out of the hedging needs of some end-user. The diversified product spectrum now available to market participants – both on or off exchange – represents an extraordinary array of instruments with which companies could modify their market risk profiles. It would also lead to the parallel development of a wide array of pricing models and systems technology innovations necessary to handle these products from an operational and accounting perspective; these aspects are discussed in greater length in Chapters 5 and 8 of this volume.

Securitisation and sales/divestures

In just over 20 years, we have created a global market known as structured finance, affording corporations a wide means of managing risks endemic to their business.

The initial vision of Louis Ranieri of Solomon Brothers, long regarded as the father of securitisation, seems simplistic now in hindsight, but at the time it was a revolutionary concept – bundle home mortgages and issue securities representing sequential claims on their cashflows. The markets have since extended the concept to creating special purpose subsidiaries or vehicles housing everything from OTC derivative contracts to utility stranded costs, film rights, earthquake and hurricane reinsurance obligations, or nearly any form of receivable a corporation could possibly originate. We now have CDOs and CLOs, and, most recently, credit linked notes issued by SPVs and synthetically replicating Enron credit exposure. Corporations now have the option of not just divesting of entire assets or liabilities; they can instead sell the risk dimensions of any one of them they are uncomfortable retaining.

Alternative risk transfer products

While Europeans seem to have accepted the commonality between some insurance and banking products, Americans have tended historically to view the two worlds as separate. This may be a function of two things – US regulation that historically separated the two worlds (recently abandoned), and terminological differences making the two worlds seem distinctly different. But in fact, the insurance sector is increasingly offering products that compete with customary capital market products emanating from the banking sector. They are designed to meet the same end – capital optimisation and risk transfer. The economic substance of these insurance

ART products and the other products mentioned above are the same. The toolkit now available to manage market risk *ex post* has expanded yet again – a Fortune 500 company should now be approaching Swiss Re as well as Goldman Sachs or Merrill Lynch to structure solutions to their risk transfer concerns. The end-user has multiple competing methodologies with which to manage its risk profile in a customised fashion.

CONCLUSIONS: FUTURE PROSPECTS

Necessity is so often attributed with being the mother of invention. Hence we see the Dutch innovation of a futures contract to hedge Tulipmania in the 1600s (Smithson, 1998). As many of the chapters in this book show, however, the innovations in market risk management and measurement techniques over the last 25 years were not only a function of economic necessity, but also possible because of technologic innovation – the computer – and academic theories available for application. Statistics and probability theory have existed for hundreds of years, but option pricing theory and computational speed in data analysis are recent innovations. Our current state of market risk management is also attributable in no small part to academic research in applied finance, operations research, and other related fields.

Importantly, the conceptual underpinnings of measuring market risk are now being extended as a framework for analysing credit and operations risk. At the same time, certain dimensions of market risk – like liquidity and the term structure of volatility – will continue to be the focus of market practitioners as we collectively attempt to improve market risk measurement. We will undoubtedly see significant improvements and greater market consensus in measuring these risk dimensions, and likely more product innovation and volume as pricing and liquidity issues are resolved. To some extent, the global regulatory framework will affect developments in this area, both favourably and unfavourably. Further, we should expect to see insurance products increasingly competing with those currently offered by capital markets, offering end-users an even wider spectrum of vehicles for managing risk. That competition will likely yield even more product innovation, benefiting market makers and end-users alike.

BIBLIOGRAPHY

Global Derivatives Study Group, 1993, "Derivatives: Practices and Principles" (Group of Thirty).

Guldimann, T., 2000, "The Story of Risk Metrics", *Risk*, 13(1), pp. 56–8.

Sargent, T.J. and F.R. Velde, 2003, *The Big Problem of Small Change* (Princeton University Press).

Smithson, C.W. and C.W. Smith, 1998, Managing Financial Risk: A Guide to Derivative Products, Financial Engineering, and Value Maximization, Third Edition (New York: McGraw-Hill).

17

Credit Risk from a Bank's Perspective

Arnaud de Servigny and Olivier Renault

Standard and Poor's Risk Solutions

There has never been a better time to study credit risk: 2001 and 2002 have been record years for the number of defaults, spreads are at all time highs, and the supervisors are busy changing the treatment of credit risk in prudential regulation. This buoyant environment has lead to a wealth of new research being carried out and implemented in the industry over the past five to ten years.

This chapter surveys the development of credit risk management from a bank's perspective. The specificity of credit risk has only been recognised recently and its quantitative treatment has lagged that of market risk by several years. Progress in its understanding and its pricing have induced the creation of a plethora of new products designed to hedge or to take positions in credit risk.

We first review the main driving forces behind the development of credit risk management and summarise the current approaches to credit risk in a portfolio. We then look at what the implications of the possibility of trading credit are for banks and finally provide some views about the likely future directions for this market.

CHANGING CREDIT MARKETS

The banking industry has changed considerably over the last few decades. Almost everywhere in the world it is operating in a financial market environment. Originally, lending money was a bilateral transaction involving a lending bank and its customer for the whole term of the operation. A close scrutiny of the customer's quality, a monitoring of its evolution and the negotiation of collateral for the loan represented the gist of banking. With financial markets and external investors, the lending business has significantly changed in several directions.

The development of secondary markets for credit risk products has enabled a rationalisation of delegated monitoring done by banks or by external independent providers such as rating agencies. Secondary dealing and risk transfer vehicles such as collateralised debt obligations (CDOs) and derivatives have also provided enhanced liquidity and a better quantification of risk through spreads. As a result, credit is no longer limited to loans but a wide range of products such as bonds, credit derivatives, CDOs, etc, has become widely available.

The second very important change is linked with the introduction of portfolio theory "Markowitz-style" to credit.[1] Ten years ago, not many banks would have had a very clear idea of the composition of their loan portfolio – at that time, the focus was on the size of the balance sheet. The real estate crisis at the beginning of the 1990s has lead banks to reassess their approach to risk and counterparty diversification. Banks try to avoid over-concentration on a limited number of customers or on a single industry. The current challenge is to measure the benefits of diversification and to share them between credit lines in a portfolio.

The third driving force behind the development of credit markets is the varying degrees of risk aversion of credit stakeholders. It is clear that a bank, an insurance company, a hedge fund and a personal investor do not share the same risk appetite. This diversity is a strong rationale for the transfer of risk through hedging and protection buying and selling. Defining what is suitable for an agent, given its risk aversion, implies being able to quantify risk precisely. This explains the strong growth in the development of quantitative approaches to credit risk.

Finally, one needs to acknowledge that credit risk quantification requires a degree of technical sophistication which until recently was not available to banks. The reason for this is the non-normality of credit losses (see Figure 1), which makes it impossible to stay in the standard Gaussian paradigm of the standard portfolio theory. New theoretical advances as well as enhanced computing

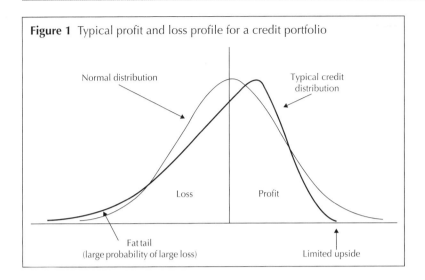

Figure 1 Typical profit and loss profile for a credit portfolio

power has enabled the development of specific models for credit pricing and hedging.

IDENTIFYING AND MANAGING CREDIT RISK FROM A BANK'S PERSPECTIVE

What is credit risk? This seemingly simple question does not have a simple answer: does it correspond to the risk of default of a company or of a credit line, or to a risk of loss? Credit risk is broader than default risk as it includes both the risk of a loss induced by a default event, but also the losses caused by rating downgrades or the widening of credit spreads, for example.

Within the financial industry some consensus has emerged about the main building blocks of the *default* risk of an individual credit instrument:

❑ *definition of a default event*: several definitions exist, all linked with some delay or absence of payment, but also sometimes with major changes in the status of the issuer or with transaction restructuring.[2]
❑ *exposure at default:* the amount of exposure that a lender has at the moment of default.[3]
❑ *probabilities of default at horizon t*: the probability of a company (or of a specific credit instrument) defaulting at a given horizon t.

❏ *recovery rate*: the proportion of money lent that is recovered in the event of a default.

❏ *expected loss*: this average anticipated loss is the product of the exposure at default, times the probability of default, times the loss rate (one minus the recovery rate).

Several techniques have been proposed to estimate these parameters. We now briefly summarise them:

Probabilities of default at horizon t: the main question is how to take into account past and current information to evaluate credit quality with a good predictive power. There are currently three main types of approaches:

❏ *Scoring models* – qualitative and quantitative variables known to impact on default probability are identified and combined into a weighting function that produces a score. The analyst then interprets the value of this output as an indicator of the borrower's default likelihood. Discriminant analysis and logit/probit models fall into this category. These are quite powerful tools; however, they tend to be sensitive to the choice of time horizon and many of them require frequent recalibration. This is the most popular approach used for retail credit and loans to smaller companies.

❏ *Ratings* – based on expert judgement by internal or external analysts and on a limited set of variables, borrowers are classified into buckets reflecting their credit riskiness. This approach differs from scoring models in that it is much less mechanical and relies crucially on the analyst's experience and overall opinion. An ex post analysis enables us to evaluate the link between ratings and the frequency of observed defaults on the rated universe. Figure 2 is a plot of cumulated default frequencies of bonds in Standard and Poor's rating categories. Given the stability of observed default rates per class of ratings and the stability of rating criteria, credit ratings can be used as default predictors. The main advantage of ratings is that they incorporate a large quantity of both public and private information into a synthetic output. The mapping of ratings to default frequencies can be made conditional on the macroeconomic cycle. The main limitation of ratings is that the rated universe tends to be restricted to large entities.

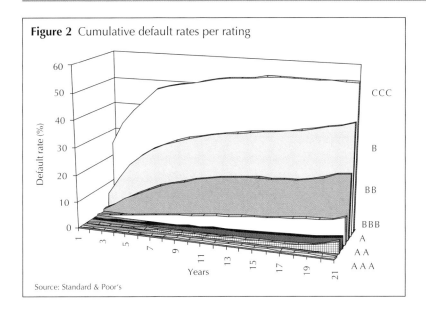

Figure 2 Cumulative default rates per rating

Source: Standard & Poor's

❑ *Market-based models* – several techniques exist which extract credit quality information from market data such as equity prices or spreads. This approach, pioneered by Merton (1974), treats equity and bonds as options on the value of the issuing firm. An assessment of the volatility of the firm's assets and of the level of liability provides a marked-to-market indicator of credit quality. This indicator can be influenced by noise, bubbles and liquidity issues in the equity markets, but can serve as early warning of credit quality changes.

Another technique is to extract information from credit spreads to identify the credit quality of a company. This potentially promising field has not yet come to maturity because spreads come as a blend of default probability, expected recovery and liquidity premium which are not easy to disentangle.

Recovery rates: much less diversity is available in the estimation of recovery rates than for probabilities of default. Two main techniques exist:

❑ *Specifying a recovery function* – it has been common practice to define recovery not as a constant but as a random variable following some (beta) distribution calibrated to the empirical mean and variance. There is little empirical support for the choice of

265

one functional form vs another. In our view, it mainly reflects the lack of information in this area. A more advanced specification consists of extracting an empirical distribution from default data through nonparametric estimation techniques.

❏ *Building a recovery model* – an alternative approach is to try and understand the drivers of recovery on a sample of defaulted credit instruments and to build a recovery model (often using a scoring approach) based on this population.

Once the bank has made its modelling choices for individual positions, it still needs to devise a method to aggregate them into a portfolio model, taking into account diversification benefits. The latter are crucial in the comparative advantage banks can extract from the size of their portfolio and in their prospects in a market environment.

The industry practice has very much been driven by approaches developed for equity portfolios. Credit risk is broken down into *idiosyncratic* risk, assumed not to require any of the bank's economic capital, and *systematic* risk for which economic capital must be put aside. Systematic risk is the risk shared by many different credit instruments and which is therefore impossible to diversify away. This is typically linked to countries, industries or the macroeconomic cycle. It is the main source of portfolio losses and can impact significantly on the robustness and the solvability of the bank. The objective for a bank is therefore to assess quantitatively how systematic changes should be covered in order to avoid bankruptcy or depositors confidence crisis.

Most of the banking business has up to now followed a convergent path based on three characteristics.

❏ An understanding of individual instruments' credit quality behaviour (univariate dimension). The tool often used is a transition matrix that defines the probabilities of migration from and to various risk classes.[4]

❏ An attempt to account for multivariate dependence structure, often through correlation matrices. Newer approaches based on copulas have also been introduced (see for example, McNeil and Nyfeler, 2001).

❏ The recourse to scenarios or Monte Carlo simulations to calculate loss measures such as expected tail loss or credit value-at-risk (VAR).[5]

This portfolio measurement approach should not be seen as set in stone, but as an ongoing process to try and obtain robust results. A lot of research still needs to be carried out in order to address several weaknesses. For example, the stability (Markovian behaviour) of transition matrices is questionable as is the validity of correlation to account for non-Gaussian dependences, etc. Furthermore, the interaction between credit risk and market risk as well as the treatment of liquidity risk are still relatively unexplored topics.

TRADING CREDIT RISK

The substantial effort banks have made in terms of quantifying credit risk is helping to find a common language with financial markets. The fact that ratings, equity and spread-based information are used by banks is a good example of this convergence. We are still nonetheless far from a marked-to-market approach to loan portfolios within banks and the question of the validity of such a transition is not obtaining a clear consensus.

New opportunities for credit trading have emerged, driven by potential "arbitrages".[6] There are many sources of arbitrage: trading price differentials between loans and bonds, arbitrage between internal pricing, given the bank's risk aversion and market pricing, arbitrage between regulatory requirements and shareholders requirements, etc. To take advantage of these opportunities, new credit derivative products seem to be invented every month, ranging from options on credit spreads, default or total return swaps, to synthetic CDOs. Figure 3 illustrates the cashflows of a simple credit swap contract. This product is similar to an insurance contract where risk is transferred against the payment of a fee.

From a bank's standpoint, it is clear that the prospect of selling off parts of its loan portfolio in the markets should not be a reason to be less selective at the origination stage. We have seen recently that liquidity in the market for credit transactions can dry out and spreads widen dramatically, leaving banks with large amounts of unwanted credit instruments on their books. Furthermore one of the major roles of banks is to perform delegated monitoring and to maximise its knowledge on counterparties. As a result, a sound credit approval process, appropriate hedging of the banks credit position through collateral, covenants etc, are more important than ever.

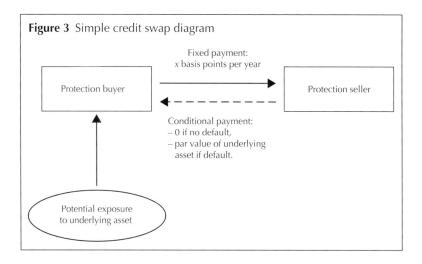

Figure 3 Simple credit swap diagram

Fixed payment:
x basis points per year

Protection buyer

Protection seller

Conditional payment:
– 0 if no default,
– par value of underlying
  asset if default.

Potential exposure
to underlying asset

What is changing however is the way to set credit limits, *a priori*, based on qualitative judgement only. Banks now have a better picture of their global exposure at a portfolio level, but they are just beginning on the way of active portfolio management. Their ability to follow such a portfolio management path will have a strong impact on the liquidity of credit risk markets.

PROSPECTS FOR CREDIT MARKETS

Two trends can be observed from a market standpoint. First of all a strong standardisation of many derivative transactions through standardised contracts (thanks to an ISDA initiative) is underway. It will ensure greater liquidity and a more widespread use of these products.

At the same time, a greater choice of protections, underlying credit assets etc, is becoming available over-the-counter, largely based on synthetic transactions. They will provide tailor-made solutions to banks requirements.

In the future, as research advances, one avenue of development could be for hedging products covering both market and credit risk or, possibly, liquidity features.

CONCLUSION

Progress in finance theory, advances in computer power, the combination of internal (shareholders) and external (regulators) pressures on banks have led to a spectacular growth in the diversity of credit instruments and in the size of credit markets. The aim of this chapter was to give an overview of the motivation behind the development of credit risk management, and an assessment of the current market practice and of the impact on banks of the existence of new products for credit trading.

1 See Chapter 4 about portfolio theory in this volume.
2 Uncertainty about the precise definition of a default event has led to several litigations between counterparties of credit derivatives.
3 Calculating the exposure at default can prove quite difficult. A bank, for example, can have granted lines of credit which are usually not drawn but can be drawn by a company facing a liquidity crisis just prior to default.
4 Some models consider transitions to default only (eg, CreditRisk +), others include migration to other ratings (eg, CreditMetrics).
5 In rare cases, such as CreditRisk +, the loss distribution can be derived analytically.
6 Most of these trading strategies are actually not risk-free.

BIBLIOGRAPHY

Merton, R., 1974, "On the Pricing of Corporate Debt: The Risk Structure of Interest Rates", *Journal of Finance*, 29, pp. 449–70.

McNeil, A., and M. Nyfeler, 2001, "Copulas and Credit Models", *Risk*, 14(10), pp. 111–14.

18

Operational Risk: Past, Present and Future

Marcelo Cruz

RiskMaths

This chapter describes how operational risk has evolved since 1995, when this new branch of risk management was first mentioned in the financial industry. As the push for a formal definition of operational risk came under the turmoil of large operational loss events, a careful description of one of the largest events that ever happened, the one at Nomura Securities in Japan, is provided below. A brief discussion of early measurement methodologies attempted by large institutions in the 1990s, with a special emphasis on articles published by *Risk* magazine, is provided as well as a few questions that delineate the future of operational risk in the next few years.

Operational risk (OR), a recently delineated branch of risk management, has evolved considerably in the last five years. The term "operational risk" probably first received widespread recognition in 1995 following the notorious bankruptcy of Barings Bank in which a trader brought the bank, one of the oldest in the UK, down by hiding loss-making positions in futures and derivatives instruments in the Asian markets. This single event caused the financial markets to recognise this separate risk category, comprising risks that could not be classified as either credit or market risk, and which could significantly effect the bottom-line results of a financial institution. Several other large losses arising from the manifestation of operational risk soon followed, such as those involving

Daiwa Bank and Nomura Securities in Japan, the latter being particularly illustrative of this newly categorised risk type that is embedded in banking operations but which had not been given appropriate recognition, let alone fully understood or measured previously.

CASE STUDY

Following the collapse of Barings in March 1997, Nomura Securities Co, the world's largest brokerage in the 1990s, released information to the market that two of its directors had made unauthorised stock trades and channelled the resulting profits to a real estate company which was, in this case, linked to "sokaiya" criminals.[1] The trades in question had started as early as the spring of 1993 and may have continued through to the summer of 1996 at which point the Securities and Exchange Surveillance Commission in Japan initiated investigations into the irregularities.

This was not an isolated incident, however, as Nomura had previously been affected by similar activities. In 1991, it was embroiled in a national scandal for compensating large clients for losses on investments, these payments being made at the expense of foreign clients and smaller domestic customers. Nomura eventually named favoured customers who had received about US$1 billion in payments after the stock market fell dramatically in 1990. This event also revealed links between Nomura and the high-profile leader of one of the largest criminal gangs of Japan. The police investigated allegations that this gang leader made millions after Nomura lent him shares of hotel operator Tokyo Corp and then recommended the stock to other customers, driving up prices.

Nomura was also accused in March 1997 by Australian regulators that its London-based subsidiary, Nomura International plc, had manipulated futures prices in the Australian Futures Exchange. The direct operational losses for the company arising from the investigation were tremendous, but in addition to these losses, the more intangible loss in terms of standing was concretely reflected in the performance of Nomura shares at the stock exchanges where it was listed. At the start of the investigation in March 1997, the share price plunged by 10%, and following the report of the Securities Commission, it dropped another 6%, directly impacting on shareholders. A less immediate, but no less significant consequence was the damage these events caused to future business for Nomura, mainly in its relationships with governments and large corporations, which are extremely conservative in terms of probity. Four days after the scandal was revealed, America's largest pension fund, the California Public Employees' Retirement System (Calpers), said it would stop trading with Nomura and it joined a long list of Japanese pension-fund managers, local government and other customers. This customer flight could have a cost to Nomura of US$413 million in lost revenue from trading commissions and underwriting new securities just in the month after the scandal was exposed (let alone considering any losses arising from fines by market authorities). After this event, closely following the Barings and Daiwa incidents, the industry started to realise in 1997 that this newly recognised type of risk could tremendously impact their bottom-line and, consequently, use of the term "operational risk" started to become more common and formalised.

The consequences of this series of unfortunate events for Nomura are typical of these exceptional operational situations. On one hand there is the direct, relatively immediate impact of the operational loss and, on the other hand, there is the longer-term "reputational" risk caused by flight of customers, precipitated strategic decisions, etc. Operational risk, in the view of the industry and the regulators, is related to the first type of loss, ie, those that cause direct impact on the cost basis, rather than the longer-term revenue implications. (The impact on future revenue streams does not form a part of the current modelling framework.)

A recent survey sponsored by the British Bankers Association showed that banks currently estimate that their major risks are split into credit (60%), market/liquidity (15%) and operational (25%). These figures are rough estimates because no bank currently has a reliable measure for losses arising from operational risks, the difficulty being primarily in splitting out losses arising from credit risk and those from operational risk. When banks start measuring their operational losses more they will probably conclude that the operational risk share represents a larger proportion of overall losses. Probably the share would be more along the lines of 50% attributable to credit risk and 35% to operational risk as represented in Figure 1. Nevertheless, the most important conclusion from the

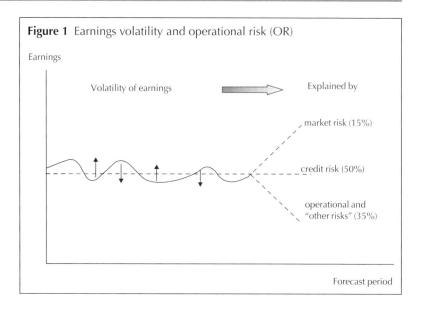

Figure 1 Earnings volatility and operational risk (OR)

survey is that the industry is rapidly realising the importance of operational risk within risk management as a whole.[2]

The concept of operational risk as a separate risk category was generated as a result of the turmoil resulting from large, never before seen operational loss events, ensuring that a formal definition was hard to come across at the outset. The initial definition of operational risk was a "negative" one, ie, it encompassed those risks not related to credit and/or market risks. This was a very hard definition to work with as pretty much every aspect of the organisation could be deemed to be subject to operational risk, even bad management decisions – although it was not the objective of the industry to include these in the framework at that time. More recently, the Basel Committee on Banking Supervision (BCBS) has defined operational risk as "the risk of direct or indirect loss resulting from inadequate or failed internal processes, people and systems or from external events".[3] Therefore, operational risk is deemed to manifest itself as losses originating from operational errors of any sort that affect the net earnings of the bank.

Ultimately, a financial institution will want to measure the impact of events arising from operational risk upon its profit and loss (P&L) (as is done for credit and market risks), where these losses give rise to any extra volatility in earnings. Although this volatility has been present as long as banks have existed, only recently have banks started to worry about measuring it in isolation from the volatility arising from credit and market risks. Additionally, banks are now becoming concerned with the volatility of the cost side of the P&L account, where previously attention had been focused exclusively upon the revenue side. Figure 1 depicts the idea of explaining the volatility of earnings by credit, market and operational risk.

In general, the situation faced by an analyst is that the problems related to developing a framework for classifying the causes of (and ultimately quantifying the effects of) operational risk may seem abstract on first inspection. The usual classification of the causes of operational risk is either "system problems" or "poor controls". This kind of classification, however, may lead to misclassification and/or double counting. A more appropriate way of defining the events which are to be included in the classification is to recognise that not all "system problems", for example, will generate an impact on the P&L (whilst appreciating the converse of this, ie, it is possible that a "system problem" may generate several different impacts upon the results, eg, in the areas of "interest expenses", "stock exchange penalties", and so on). A more meaningful/appropriate schema, therefore, is the classification of losses by the area of impact on the results, as the ultimate objective is to explain the volatility of the earnings arising from the direct impact of the losses on the results. Therefore, classification of the losses into items that directly affect the P&L, like "legal suits", "interest expenses", and the like is needed. Figure 2 depicts the situation.

Another decision to be made is in relation to the modelling design, which may be done either by process or by seeing the system as a whole. Modelling by processing can be quite frustrating as large financial institutions would have several thousand processes and modelling each and every process can be almost impossible. A more tractable approach is to choose a few types of operational errors and see how they apply to the processes and not the opposite: if a process is liable to failure, but brings no direct adverse monetary consequence, it may be left for a second or later round of the modelling process.

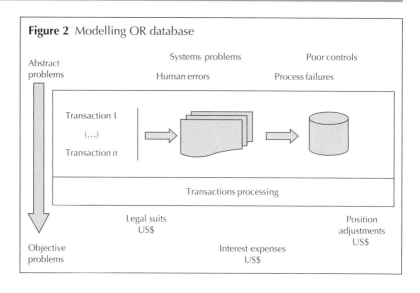

Figure 2 Modelling OR database

The causes and effects of the operational events are still very commonly confused. For example, it is still very common to see operational risk types as "human/people risk" or even "system risk", although these types of events are merely the causes of the risk not the outcome, the latter being the monetary consequence. A classification based on causes is prone to errors/misunderstandings especially when a large number of loss events are being considered, such as transaction processing risk. Where there are a significant number of loss events, it is very difficult to distinguish those errors caused by system or human errors, or even classify a human error as "inexperience" or "lack of supervision". Every classification that depends on subjectivity should be avoided at this stage.

Given the above, it should be noted that identifying both cause and effect are important in the operational risk measurement framework. In relation to market risk, when calculating value-at-risk (VAR), an analyst will know that the volatility of a certain asset changed and it is certainly important to understand the reasons for it, but the qualitative reason is not incorporated into the VAR measure, except as a technical note; the same might be said about cause and effect in relation to operational risk. The analyst might detect, for example, an increase in interest expenses, and will investigate and deduce that the problem might be the lack of understanding of a new settlement system or just a capacity problem.

This brings us to the basics of measurement of operational risk, which in my view is a function of the control environment of the organisation, rather than an exclusive link to past internal or external losses. In this respect, an organisation with a good control environment is less risky in operational risk terms than an organisation with a poor control environment, and keeping this in mind makes it easier to understand the operational risk process. For example, the event at Barings happened because a trader was responsible for performing the trades and, at the same time, acting as a nominally independent control function in relation to them. There was a clear lack of oversight and misrepresentation of responsibilities inside the control infrastructure of the organisation in question.[4]

A BRIEF REVIEW OF THE INITIAL APPROACHES FOR TACKLING OPERATIONAL RISK

Finding a methodology to measure and manage OR is challenging. On the input side, there are few objective metrics in the financial market and certainly no generally available template, such as Riskmetrics (1995) in the field of market risk, since OR is a relatively new and undeveloped subject. However, due to regulatory and even shareholders demands, the pressure to develop a measurement methodology was (is!) very high. Many institutions have had some initial thoughts on OR but just few of them have released or discussed with the industry their findings in the 1990s. The models and insights presented in this section were openly presented at an early stage of discussions, either at seminars or published in magazines such as *Risk* and *Euromoney* in the 1990s. All of the institutions that published deserve praise for publishing or presenting their thoughts at such an early stage. It is important to highlight that the methodologies shown in this section were presented and developed 5–7 years ago. If the understanding of what OR might encompass came relatively recently in the middle of the 1990s, towards the end of the decade the first tentative models and approaches were presented. A few of the most prominent are described below.

Bankers Trust

Bankers Trust (today part of the Deutsche Bank group) was one of the few banks to have shown publicly some sections of its own

277

model for measuring and managing operational risk. In reality the model brought together several qualitative methods and very few quantitative ones. They started their model by defining operational risk as "encompassing all dimensions of the firm's decentralised resources – client relationship, personnel, the physical plant, property and assets" for which Bankers Trust is responsible, as well as technology resources. Certain areas such as regulatory risk and fraud risk were classified as "external areas".

Bearing in mind their definition of operational risk, the Bankers Trust approach measures the level of economic capital to support OR on three fronts, namely portfolio, business-specific and product. The model relied heavily on historical data. As they did not have a broad and trustworthy database, they made an effort to construct one from external sources. For some risks that were more difficult to quantify and measure, such as the cost of a technology failure, Bankers Trust developed estimates. These estimates were arrived at through sending questionnaires to the heads of the business units. Bankers Trust then started to compile their own database, mainly because their system uses simulations based on historical data. Despite their best efforts, they reported problems in gathering a complete database of all operational risk factors.

Barclays

For comparison, Barclays did not have a comprehensive model for operational risk management (once again in the 1990s), but defined operational risk at the time as "fraud, failures in controls and the like", while they also separately defined business risk as any other change in costs, leading to earnings volatility or margin changes. They estimated that around 70% of the bank's earnings volatility was due to provisions; the remaining 30% was put down to business and operational risk. Barclays considered operational risk to represent a smaller proportion of this figure than business risk because, in their judgment at the time, OR was made up of a large number of very specific risks that are not correlated and so tend to "cancel each other out". Barclays' model relied strongly on controls and insurance for OR management. Nevertheless, they were one of the first financial institutions to establish an operational risk team with a reach across all of their global operations (an approach also adopted by the Royal Bank of Scotland) that used some quite sophisticated methods to evaluate the likelihood of future OR events. Their model used a statistical tool, generally applied in reliability theory, known as mean time between failures (MTBF) that is also used in the aviation industry to assess the likelihood of failure for the parts in an aircraft engine. Barclays applied this technique to human behaviour, but the rationale for this was unclear as there are problems in extending the techniques to human processing systems even narrowly defined ones such as settlements, simply because it is hard to draw parallels between subjectively evaluated human behaviour to the objective performance of an engine part. It also presented problems when trying to allocate capital based on "time differences". In this case, the monetary impact is not being measured and, ultimately, this figure is what we need for financial risk management. Barclays also collated a database on external operational risk events in corporations across business sectors. They appeared to be trying to find correlation between operational risks in retail banking and a supermarket, for example.

Touche Ross

Another approach was developed by Touche Ross in 1995 (today Deloitte Touche Ross). The approach was almost absolutely qualitative and used a risk assessment "matrix", which categorised the institution's operational risk across all activities. It ranked the risk in five ordinal levels, ranging from 5 (high) to 1 (low), representing "relative VAR" or "a subjective judgment of the relative risk". Touche Ross' methods used historical data as well as subjective opinion to define the matrices. It used a cost index that is a measure of the amount of money spent on managing those risks. The quotient "risk management/cost index" was the risk index divided by the cost index. According to the model's framework, this quantified the VAR. The variables of the model were not "objectively" measured, however, the article insists that "it is essential that a more objective approach is found to the identification of operational risk…". In order to build an "objective approach" as proposed by Touche Ross, one should have a complete database of events with associated monetary impact (costs), infer correlations between events, and calculate volatilities, leading to a VAR.

Bank of America

Bank of America originally considered what they call "business risk ... or non-portfolio risk, the kind of risk you would find in any type of business". Their approach was initially to consider businesses outside the bank, and on a sectoral basis, and look at the capital structures employed in each business type but, apparently, it was not a successful approach as they could not find appropriate analogues. Their next step was to focus instead on a set of eight or so key ratios (such as operating expenses to fixed costs) as a way of comparing businesses and as a way of comparing individual business units with the bank. They also used internal surveys on the riskiness of their business. However, without benchmarks most respondents stated that their business units carried a "medium" risk, suggesting that the questionnaires were not properly designed. Their methodology was finally characterised by considering the "level of fixed costs and non-interest expenses, and set aside a percentage against operational risk". They take 25% of fixed costs and 50% of non-interest expenses, and multiply by a correlation factor that takes into account the fact that all three major risks (credit, market and operational) are connected. Bank of America strived to refine this correlation factor and decided to create a database on business risk events by sector in the same way as Barclays had done.

Chase Manhattan Bank

Chase Manhattan Bank (today part of the JP Morgan Chase financial group) classified OR as arising from activities associated with their fiduciary dealings, execution, fraud, business interruption, settlement, legal/regulatory, and the composition of their fixed costs. Nevertheless, for model purposes they proposed that incurring OR gave rise to its own return and defined this as the difference between the firm's overall return and the total return from investment activities (ie, taking credit and/or market risk). Chase attempted to measure OR using the capital asset pricing model (CAPM). Using the CAPM, they assumed they could determine the total return for the bank and the investment return. The difference between them, they reckoned, is the return arising from incurring OR. (An explanation was not provided as to what would happen if the overall risk of the firm remains the same, but the credit and/or market risk were to increase, leading to OR tending to zero.) Chase's model, at that time, missed a clear definition of OR. They simply defined OR "negatively", ie, the difference of total risk minus the market and credit risk. This makes it impossible to identify the activities that give rise to OR, and consequently manage it. They also did not describe how to measure OR by business unit or area, with attendant problems in allocating capital by business unit. In addition to the subjective definition of OR, many parameters used to evaluate OR were based simply on a market consensus. The capital is allocated to OR based on the formula:

$$r \text{ (operational risk)} = r \text{ (firm)} - r \text{ (investment risk)}$$
$$\text{required earnings (OR)} = r \text{ (OR)} \times \text{book value (firm)}$$
$$\text{Capital for OR} = \text{required earnings (OR)} / r \text{ (firm)}$$

Commonwealth Bank of Australia

The Commonwealth Bank of Australia (CBA) developed an earnings volatility approach, which proposed a hybrid calculation methodology, involving both a quantitative statistical volatility analysis and a qualitative risk estimation process. CBA's method also involved a workshop process between the business units and a central risk function. CBA measures the earnings volatilities of each business unit by attempting to identify the drivers of these volatilities (mostly subjectively). The drivers not related to credit or market risk are deemed to be due to operational risk (ie, operational risk = residual risk). By using this method, they claim to have found the extent to which OR influenced the business unit's results. A standard VAR-statistical treatment based on confidence levels was then applied to the "OR factor". However, once again there was a clear lack of OR definition as they applied the "negative" definition in their modelling.

In 1998, Cruz *et al* (1998) presented the first fully quantitative approach to measure operational risk in the *Journal of Risk*.

More recently a software vendor has developed a product based on Bayesian networks (a type of neural network) but this type of modelling has not been widely accepted due to a lack of transparency and difficulty in validating the methodology and the model results (non-linear models are "black boxes" – ie, more difficult to validate and analyse).

OPERATIONAL RISK IN THE NEXT 15 YEARS: WHAT TO EXPECT AND WHAT OBSTACLES NEED TO BE OVERCOME

In my view, there are a few areas in which we are going to see great progress in the next few years: management, measurement and hedging. These important issues are discussed below:

Measurement: would that be a benchmark for measuring OR?

In my opinion we are very close to answering that question as many institutions are moving ahead with their model-building projects and realising that a VAR-like, statistical based approach is showing excellent results and the outcomes can be fully validated and back tested (several techniques and even a structured model were presented in Cruz, 2002). The figures generated by these models might be eventually supplemented by structured scenario analysis and stress tests, in much the same way as in credit or market risk VAR models.

Management: can banks improve control and operate like most industries and in the way reducing OR?

In the process of collecting internal loss data and key risk indicators, the banking industry will learn a great deal about their internal control environment(s), which is operational risk's main driver. More sophisticated structured techniques based on linear multifactor models will be developed (several banks are already in the process of developing these). Such models, integrated with the operational VAR system, provide a very powerful tool to manage OR and allow management to reduce the risk to acceptable levels.

Hedging: is insurance an effective hedge for OR?

The discussions about the appropriateness of insurance to protect against operational risks have been dominating the topic of operational risk hedging. The main issue is that the definition and classification of operational risk varies significantly. Therefore, insurers fear being held liable for losses that have not been factored into their premium calculations. As a result, insurers generally word policies very carefully in order to exclude risks that are not definite in amount, time, place or cause. Consequently, this may lead to gaps in the available cover, preventing the insurance of all sub-risks comprising OR (although some "business risk types", which are not included in regulatory capital, might be included). In addition, there is the possibility of lengthy disputes over whether a loss really is covered or not depending on whether policies have been appropriately worded. This can frequently lead to long delays in the payment of claims. Specific policies offered by insurance companies to financial institutions include bankers blanket bond, professional indemnity, directors and officers liability, employment practices liability, non-financial property, general and other liabilities. In addition to these products, insurers have recently started to offer coverage for unauthorised trading and organisational liability.

Discussions arising from the revision of the Basel Accord on capital adequacy discussions resulted in the Basel Committee pointing out a number of potential pitfalls with insurance for operational risk and other forms of outsourcing. Some of these points are as follows.

❏ The insurance industry is not sufficiently well capitalised vis-à-vis the banking industry. A bank that is transferring risk may be better capitalised than the accepting insurance company.
❏ Blanket cover is not available. There are many different contracts for different elements, which do not fit together sufficiently well, possibly leading to gaps where there is no insurance cover or inefficient over-laps.
❏ Limiting conditions and exclusion clauses lead to doubt regarding payment in the event of failure.
❏ Delays in payment could result in serious damage to the claimant.
❏ It is difficult to determine the true economic value of insurance purchased in the absence of sufficient and appropriate data.[5]

Therefore, although it appears that the Basel Committee may be prepared to consider insurance as a mitigant for operational risk, there are a number of issues that need to be addressed by the financial services industry before it is finally accepted. An industry forum has recently been established in London and several new ideas are being formulated including, for example, the development of global master agreements, similar to those for credit derivatives.

These would pre-define the risks embedded in a policy thereby avoiding the problem of lengthy wording in insurance policies and reducing costs.

In addition to straightforward insurance, a new market for operational risk derivatives will probably develop in the next few years. Such products overcome many of the problems presented by insurance.

CONCLUSION

Operational risk has recently come to the fore as a new area of risk management and developments, in terms of recognition and categorisation of risks in this area and model development, appears to be more rapid than ever seen before in the field of risk management. We should praise the contribution of Risk Waters Group as a forum of discussion for the new ideas in the area. Operational risk will probably show many more advances in the next few years.

1   "Sokaiya" refers to groups that blackmail companies by threatening to harass company executives at annual shareholders' meetings.
2   On a personal note, I have been lecturing on the subject since 1996. At that time operational risk merited just a small and isolated slot in risk management seminars and the attendance was limited to no more than five or six people. As a sign of the growing appreciation of this topic, currently there are two-day seminars devoted exclusively to the subject and the attendance in most cases has to be limited due to auditorium limitations. Despite all the interest, challenges in the area are still considerable and growing as little has been done so far, especially on the measurement side. Most lectures and publications in the subject are still very qualitative and few in the industry have addressed the challenge of attempting to quantify OR in a rigorous and objective way.
3   The inclusion of the word "indirect" caused some misunderstandings in the industry. Direct losses are those that impact directly the results, eg, a fine or levy paid to a regulator for some irregularity or an interest expense paid to a counterparty for late settlement. Indirect losses are those that arise from another cause and do not have a direct impact on the bottom line. For example, a computer system crashes during the afternoon and for this reason a number of transactions are not properly settled, resulting in indirect consequences such as reputational risk, interest claims etc, which have an indirect impact upon the costs (and also revenues in some cases). In a paper issued in January 2001, the BCBS stated that it would require capital to be held for both direct and *certain* indirect losses (without stating those that fall into this category): however, it is also explicitly stated that the costs of improvement in controls, preventative action and quality assurance as well as investment in new systems will not be included.
4   Coming back to the example of Nomura, the series of operational losses was also probably due to an extremely poor control environment that gave rise, ultimately, to such extreme losses.
5   The last of these points highlights a more general issue in the area of operational risk, namely the availability and quality of relevant data.

BIBLIOGRAPHY

Cruz, M., 2002, "Modeling, Measuring and Hedging Operational Risk", John Wiley & Sons.

Cruz, M., R. Coleman and G. Salkin, 1998, "Modeling and Measuring Operational Risk", *Journal of Risk*, no. 1, pp. 63–72.

Euromoney, no. 74, September 1996, "Operational Risk: Risk Management's Final Frontier", pp. 74–9.

Hoffman, D. and M. Johnson, 1996, "Operating Procedures", *Risk*, 9, no. 10, pp. 25–9.

Wilson, D. 1995, "VaR in Operation", Risk Magazine, 8, no. 12, pp. 44–5.

19

Enterprise-wide Risk Management

James Lam

James Lam & Associates

Enterprise-wide risk management (ERM) is widely recognised as the best-practice approach to measuring and managing all aspects of risk within a company. Companies successful in ERM have reported dramatic improvements in shareholder value, early risk detection, loss experience, and regulatory capital relief. While most risk managers recognise the value of ERM, they face key obstacles such as lack of management buy-in, insufficient data, and failure to clearly demonstrate tangible benefits. In this chapter, we will discuss:

❏ history and rationale for ERM;
❏ key forces driving ERM today;
❏ an ERM framework and current best practices;
❏ overcoming common obstacles for successful implementation; and
❏ the future for ERM.

HISTORY AND RATIONALE

As an early advocate of ERM, I would point to the early 1990s and the development of triple-A rated derivative products companies (DPCs) as one of the first applications of ERM in the financial services industry. Merrill Lynch established the first DPC (Merrill Lynch Derivative Products) in order to offer a triple-A rating to the company's derivative clients, many of whom would only deal with triple-A or double-A counterparties. Other financial institutions followed with similar structures. These DPCs provided the perfect setting for ERM. They were separately capitalised legal entities that had exposures to credit risk, market risk, and operational risk.[1] They were required to measure and manage all of their risks on an integrated basis, and report their risk exposures to the rating agencies regularly so that their independent triple-A ratings could be confirmed. The DPCs were also involved in a business where risks are highly interdependent. For example, a counterparty downgrade (credit risk) can trigger collateral or closeout events (liquidity risk). The credit exposure (credit risk) at the time of a downgrade is dependent on market price movements (market risk). Finally, downgrade triggers require appropriate legal documentation (operational risk) to provide the intended protection, and the unwinding of one position will likely lead to new hedging requirements (market risk).

In fact, one of the key reasons for ERM is the interdependencies among the risk exposures faced by companies. Let's consider some of the common risks faced by financial institutions and how they are interrelated.

❑ Inadequate loan documentation (an operational/process risk) would increase the severity of losses in the event of loan defaults (a credit risk).

❑ An unexpected decline in real estate prices (a market risk) would increase the default rate of real estate loans and securities (a credit risk).

❑ A general decline in equity prices (a market risk) would decrease asset management, mergers and acquisitions (M&A) and investment banking fees (business risk).

❑ A sharp increase in energy prices (market risk) would impact the credit exposures of energy trades (counterparty risk) as well as the credit conditions of energy-dependent borrowers (credit risk).

❑ A large earthquake or hurricane (an event risk) would affect not only the facilities of a bank (an operational risk) but also the loss experience of impacted real estate loans and securities (a credit risk).

Beyond financial institutions, energy firms also face highly interdependent risks given their integrated supply-chain relationships. Besides the need to manage interrelated risks, there are at least five other important reasons why a company should establish an ERM program. The first of these reasons is the need to manage aggregate risk exposures on an enterprise-wide basis. While a risk exposure, say the credit exposure to XYZ Corporation, is acceptable for a given business unit, the aggregate exposure to XYZ across business units may be excessive. A second and related issue is that risk aggregation will result in more efficient risk transfer strategies (eg, hedging, insurance) because natural offsets will be first considered. Third, a company needs to manage the interdependencies among the business and operating units. For example, if the IT department does not manage its contingency planning effectively, it may hinder the business activities of line units. Or if the bank's treasury unit does not secure funds at attractive rates, the lending units will not be able to originate loans at acceptable margins. Fourth, most companies have various risk and oversight functions (eg, risk management, audit, legal, compliance, quality, etc) and an ERM approach will facilitate better communication and teamwork among these functions. Last but not least, the fifth reason is that ERM supports more effective corporate governance because the board and senior management will be able to make risk-return tradeoff decisions on a consistent basis. Given the rationale discussed above, the need to measure and manage all of a company's risks and their interdependencies is why many leading companies have taken a more integrated ERM approach.

KEY FORCES DRIVING ERM TODAY

There are key forces driving the growth in, and acceptance of, ERM. These forces include corporate disasters that have raised the level of awareness of board members and senior executives, regulatory and industry initiatives that have advocated an ERM approach, and ERM programs that have experienced tangible and significant benefits. Let's briefly examine these key forces.

❏ *Corporate disasters*. Recent headline stories such as Enron and WorldCom represent dramatic examples of corporate governance failures. Sadly, these events are only the recent entries to a long roster of corporate failures resulting from various risks. Other notable disasters include Long-Term Capital Management (market risk compounded by leverage and liquidity risk), Power Company of America (default resulting from market risk and supplier default), and Barings Bank (operational risk in the form of a rogue trader). Collectively, these disasters represent a series of wake-up calls with respect to the consequences of ineffective risk management.

❏ *Regulatory actions.* In response to the corporate disasters, regulators including the Securities and Exchange Commission (SEC) and the Federal Reserve have increased their examination, regulatory capital, and enforcement standards. In the forefront of these initiatives, the SEC began a few years ago a crackdown on "earnings management" (or the use of reserves and other accounting methods to artificially smooth out earnings). More recently, the SEC has been responding to a growing list of cases of outright corporate and accounting fraud. Beyond examination and enforcement actions, a financial institution's risk profile has implications for required capital. In international banking, the new Basle initiative (BIS II) has established a direct linkage between minimum regulatory capital and a bank's underlying credit risk, market risk, and operational risk.

❏ *Industry initiatives.* A number of industry initiatives have been organised around the world to establish frameworks and standards for corporate governance and risk management. In response to major losses and lawsuits resulting from the misuse of derivatives in the early 1990s, the Group of 30 Report (1993) provided risk standards for derivatives dealers and end-users. In response to corporate fraud and corporate governance concerns, auditing and accounting groups in different countries organised other studies. The Treadway Report (United States, 1992) produced the Committe of Sponsoring Organizations (COSO) framework of internal control, while the Turnbull report (United Kingdom, 1999) and the Dey Report (Canada, 1994) developed similar guidelines. It is noteworthy that the Turnbull and Dey reports were supported by the stock exchanges in London and Toronto, respectively. Moreover, the Toronto Stock Exchange requires listed companies to report on their ERM programs annually.

❏ *Corporate programs.* Corporations have reported significant benefits from their risk management programs, including stock price improvement, debt-rating upgrades, early warning of risks, loss reduction, and regulatory capital relief. Financial institutions are clear leaders in implementing advanced risk management programs because of financial deregulation and the fact that risk management represents a core competency. A financial institution's profitability and survival is heavily dependent on its ability to manage credit losses and price volatilities. Energy firms have in recent years increased their investments in sophisticated risk management programs. Deregulation has also played a role here – increasing energy price volatility for both suppliers and buyers. Even manufacturers have increasingly taken an ERM approach to risk management.

ERM FRAMEWORK AND BEST PRACTICES

Current best practices in ERM can be the subject of an entire book. In this section I will only highlight best practices using an ERM framework that I developed in 1999.[2] The process of measuring and managing enterprise-wide risks is too complex to do without a systematic framework. There are a variety of ERM frameworks developed by industry groups, regulatory agencies, and consulting firms.

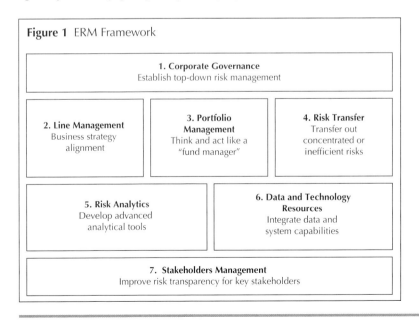

Figure 1 ERM Framework

1. Corporate Governance
Establish top-down risk management

2. Line Management
Business strategy alignment

3. Portfolio Management
Think and act like a "fund manager"

4. Risk Transfer
Transfer out concentrated or inefficient risks

5. Risk Analytics
Develop advanced analytical tools

6. Data and Technology Resources
Integrate data and system capabilities

7. Stakeholders Management
Improve risk transparency for key stakeholders

Management should either adopt one of these frameworks or develop a customised approach based on the company's risk profile. Regardless, an ERM framework should address seven key components of internal control and risk management. Each of these components must be developed and linked to work as an integrated whole. The seven components (see Figure 1), and related best practices, are discussed below:

❏ *Corporate governance* – to ensure that the board of directors and management have established the appropriate organisational processes and corporate controls to measure and manage risk across the company. Best practices include recruiting independent board members with solid finance and risk management skills; establishing an independent ERM function headed by a powerful chief risk officer (CRO); and paying sufficient attention to the "soft side" of risk management (ie, culture, values, incentives).

❏ *Line management* – to integrate risk management into the revenue generating activities of the company, including business development, product and relationship management, pricing, and so on. Best practices include alignment between business and risk strategies, risk-based pricing models, pre-transaction risk analysis, and integrated business and risk reviews. A current challenge for financial institutions is to draw a fine line between relationship management (which is a best practice for cross-selling products to ensure overall relationship profitability) and tying (which is illegal).

❏ *Portfolio management* – to aggregate risk exposures, incorporate diversification effects and monitor risk concentrations against established risk limits. Best practices include explicit risk limits (eg, credit exposure limits by obligor and industry, market risk limits by product or exposure, and operational risk limits such as maximum error rates), liquidity management and contingency plans, and the definition of an optimal target risk portfolio based on the underlying risk-return tradeoffs.

❏ *Risk transfer* – to mitigate risk exposures that are deemed too high, or are more cost-effective to transfer out to a third party than to hold in the company's risk portfolio. Best practices include the ability to execute risk transfer strategies at the portfolio (vs transaction) level, making consistent economic trade-off decisions between risk retention and various hedging or insurance strategies, and establishing a monitoring process to ensure that the risk transfer strategies are in fact achieving their objectives.

❑ *Risk analytics* – to provide the risk measurement, analysis, and reporting tools to quantify the company's risk exposures as well as track external variables. Best practices include volatility-based models (eg, value-at-risk, earnings-at-risk, economic capital), risk-adjusted profitability models (eg, risk-adjusted return on capital or RAROC, shareholder value contribution), and simulation and scenario-based models that stress test the portfolio under pre-determined or computer-generated scenarios. Moreover, an integrated risk report should be developed for senior management and the board that clearly identify key risks, and facilitate critical business and policy decisions.

❑ *Data and technology resources* – to provide the data management and processing capabilities. Best practices include a detailed loss and incident database that captures all credit, market, and operational events; a mapping algorithm that supports the aggregation of same or similar risk exposures; and real-time tracking of risk exposures that are highly volatile and/or that have severe consequences.

❑ *Stakeholder management* – to communicate and report the company's risk information to its key stakeholders, such as investors, rating agencies, and regulators. Beyond meeting the increasing demand for risk transparency from these key stakeholders, it is in the company's best interests to more effectively communicate its risk profile. After all, the losses that cause the most damage to stakeholder confidence, and the company's stock price, are the unexpected ones. Best-practice companies leverage their ERM programs to improve internal control as well as external communication.

OVERCOMING COMMON OBSTACLES

While most risk professionals recognise the value of ERM, they are faced with some key issues and obstacles. These obstacles, and strategies to overcome them, are discussed below:

❑ *Lack of buy-in from the board, senior executives, or line managers.* There is clear resistance against most corporate-wide programs,

especially in dealing with something as sensitive as risk management. To gain buy-in, it is important that a compelling vision is
established for ERM. This vision is not just a "motherhood/apple
pie" mission statement, but rather a clear articulation of how
ERM will be practiced – the reports, processes, systems, and
management decisions and actions. A business case and
roadmap should also be established that lay out the initiatives
that will be undertaken and the expected benefits that would be
achieved.

❏ *Ineffective and inconsistent risk measurement and reporting.* Many
companies produce literally hundreds of pages of risk reports
each month that are generated by various oversight functions.
These reports don't meet the needs of senior management and
the board because there is too much data and too few insights.
A concise, meaningful, and decision-oriented ERM report
should be developed. This report should clearly communicate
the key risk exposures for the company, the important trends
and uncertainties, as well as the recommended actions or alternatives for senior management.

❏ *Redundancies and gaps across different risk and oversight functions.*
Without appropriate coordination and teamwork, the various
risk management and oversight functions may miss some critical emerging issues while paying too much attention to less
important matters. For example, the US homeland security initiative is meant to coordinate the activities of the FBI, CIA, and
other security agencies. Similarly, an ERM function should coordinate the activities of risk management, audit, compliance, and
other oversight units. The definition of roles and responsibilities
is always an integral part of an ERM program.

❏ *Insufficient human, systems, and data resources.* ERM is usually
a multi-year effort that requires significant resources.
Establishing an ERM framework is not a part-time job.
Numerous ERM initiatives with good intentions have failed
because the company did not allocate the right level and/or mix
of resources. For example, a bank may appoint a full-time or
part-time project manager, and organise a task force or committee to meet every week or month. Issues are discussed but soon
everyone gets frustrated because nothing ever gets done and
the issues remain unresolved. The lesson from these failed

initiatives is to get the best resources in the first place. A company should establish an appropriate budget for ERM based on their development needs.

❑ *Failure to clearly demonstrate "early wins" and sustainable benefits.* Management wants to see results from any major investment, including ERM. Without evidence of tangible benefits, an ERM program may lose momentum, supporters, and eventually resources that are critical to its success. Therefore, it is often wise to use pilots to test various aspects of the ERM program in order to demonstrate "early wins", such as a reduction in losses or a business application (eg, risk-based pricing) that will support growth and profitability. It is also important that the ERM program is achieving quarterly milestones and other measures of success.

THE FUTURE FOR ERM

The future is bright for ERM and the risk professionals who are involved. The underlying rationale for ERM is sound given the interdependent nature of risks. Clearly, the corporate disasters and regulatory initiatives will continue to assert significant pressure on corporate boards and senior management to improve enterprise-wide risk management. However, ERM is more than a regulatory compliance issue. ERM is fundamentally changing the way companies think about, measure, and manage risk. In the future, ERM will go beyond the integration of credit risk, market risk, and operational risk. Best-practice companies will fully integrate their ERM programs into their business management processes, including product and relationship management, M&A, and business strategies. In short, ERM will not only be a better mousetrap for managing downside risks, but a means to optimise upside potential by supporting better business and growth strategies.

ERM is also an unprecedented opportunity for risk professionals to think more broadly about their businesses, add maximum value to their companies, and enhance their professional development. Witness the increasing demand for, and escalating salaries of, chief risk officers (CROs) and others skilled in ERM. Just as the technology revolution has moved programmers from computer rooms to chief information officer positions and then business leaders, ERM will empower risk professionals to become CROs, and someday chief executive officers (CEOs).

1 The initial DPCs were structured with mirrored transactions with the parent companies in order to remove market risk from the DPCs. However, later structures had market risk exposures embedded in them.

2 For a full discussion of this framework, see "Enterprise-Wide Risk Management: Staying Ahead of the Convergence Curve", *The Journal of Lending and Credit Risk Management*, June 1999.

BIBLIOGRAPHY

Committee of Sponsoring Organizations (COSO), 1992, "Internal Control-Integrated Framework" (New York: The American Institute of Certified Public Accountants).

Group of 30, 1993, "Derivatives: Practices and Principles".

The Institute of Chartered Accountants, 1999, "Internal Control" (The Turnbull Report).

The Toronto Stock Exchange Committee on Corporate Governance (The Dey Committee), 1994, "Guidelines for Improved Corporate Governance".

20

Endogenous Risk

Jon Danielsson and Hyun Song Shin*

London School of Economics

Endogenous risk refers to the risk from shocks that are generated and amplified *within* the system. It stands in contrast to exogenous risk, which refers to shocks that arrive from *outside* the system. Financial markets are subject to both types of risk. However, the greatest damage is done from risk of the endogenous kind. This is our central thesis. We will substantiate our claim by reference to three episodes – the stock market crash of 1987, the LTCM Crisis of 1998, and the collapse of the US dollar against the yen in October 1998.

Our main concern is with financial markets. However, endogenous risk is important in other contexts, and it is illuminating to begin with an example drawn from engineering – that of the wobbly Millennium Bridge over the River Thames. This was a classic case where neglect of endogenous risk led to a serious and highly publicised blunder in bridge design and construction.

AN ANALOGY: THE MILLENNIUM BRIDGE

On June 10, 2000, the Queen opened the Millennium Bridge – the first new Thames crossing for over a hundred years, constructed at a cost of £18 million. The 325 metre-long structure used an innovative "lateral suspension" design, built without the tall supporting

*The authors thank Sverrir Sigudrsson for valuable comments.

columns that are more familiar with other suspension bridges. The vision was of a "blade of light" across the River Thames, connecting St Paul's Cathedral with the new Tate Modern gallery. Many thousands of people turned up on the opening day – a sunny but slightly windy English summer's day – and crowded on to the bridge. The structure was designed to cope easily with this kind of weight. However, within moments of the bridge's opening, it began to wobble violently. The wobble (or "lateral excitation") was so violent that some pedestrians had to cling on to the side-rails of the bridge, and others suffered from nausea. News videos of the day can be obtained from several websites that show some of the drama.[1] The wobble was so bad that the bridge had to be closed down – and it was to remain closed for over 18 months. What went wrong? How could such a prestigious project suffer from such a highly publicised debacle? The answer is revealing. It goes to the heart of the nature of endogenous risk, and how we should neglect it at our peril.

When engineers used shaking machines to send vibrations through the bridge, they found that horizontal vibrations at 1 hertz (one complete cycle per second) set off the S-shaped wobble seen on the opening day. This was an important clue. Normal walking pace is around two strides per second, which produces a vertical force of around 250 Newtons (55 pounds) at 2 hertz. However, there is also a small sideways force caused by the sway of our body mass due to the fact that our legs are slightly apart.[2] This force (around 25 Newtons or 5.5 pounds) is directed to the left when we are on our left foot, and to the right when we are on our right foot. This force occurs at half the frequency (or at 1 hertz). This was the frequency that was causing the problems. But should this matter? The sideways movement when we walk need not matter if one person's sway to the left is cancelled out by another person's sway to the right. It is only when many people walked in step that the sideways force would be a problem. It is well known that soldiers should break step before they cross a bridge. But with thousands of individuals each walking at random, could this be a problem?

Or to put it another way, what is the probability that a thousand people walking at random will end up walking exactly in step? It is tempting to say "close to zero", or "negligible". After all, if each person's step were an independent event, then the probability of everyone walking in step would be the product of many small numbers – giving us a probability close to zero. Presumably, this is the reason why Arup – the bridge engineers – did not take this into account. However, this is exactly where endogenous risk comes in. What we must take into account is the way that people react to their environment. Pedestrians on the bridge react to how the bridge is moving. When the bridge moves under your feet, it is a natural reaction for people to adjust their stance to regain balance. But here is the catch. When the bridge moves, everyone adjusts his or her stance at the same time. This synchronised movement pushes the bridge that the people are standing on, and makes the bridge move even more. This, in turn, makes the people adjust their stance more drastically, and so on. In other words, the wobble of the bridge feeds on itself. When the bridge wobbles, everyone adjusts their stance, which sets off an even worse wobble, which makes the people adjust even more, and so on. So, the wobble will continue and get stronger even though the initial shock (say, a gust of wind) has long passed. It is an example of a force that is generated and amplified *within* the system. It is an *endogenous* response. It is very different from a shock that comes from a storm or an earthquake, which are *exogenous* to the system.

So, let us reconsider the question. On a blustery day, what is the probability that a thousand people walking at random on the Millennium Bridge will end up walking exactly in step? Far from the probability being close to zero, the probability is close to one! Sooner or later, a gust of wind will set off a movement in the bridge, and when there are enough people on the bridge, they will end up walking in step for sure.[3]

FINANCIAL RISK MANAGEMENT

What lessons can we draw from the Millennium Bridge for the practice of financial risk management? Financial markets are the supreme example of an environment where individuals react to what's happening around them, but where individuals' actions drive the realised outcomes themselves. The feedback loop of actions to outcomes, back to actions has a fertile environment in which to develop. Endogenous risk appears whenever there is the conjunction of:

1. individuals reacting to their environment; and
2. where the individual actions affect their environment.

The idea that market distress can feed on itself is not new. The idea is quite intuitive, and the theme is familiar among front-line market traders and the financial press. When asset prices fall and traders get closer to their trading limits, they are forced to sell. But this selling pressure sets off further downward pressure on asset prices, which induces a further round of selling, and so on. Here, the downward spiral in asset prices is endogenous. It is a response that is generated *within* the financial system. Just as a gust of wind can set in motion the wobble in the Millennium Bridge, an outside shock has the potential to send the market into a tailspin if the conditions are right. The following passage from the *Economist* magazine is typical.[4]

> "So-called value-at-risk models (VAR) blend science and art. They estimate how much a portfolio could lose in a single bad day. If that amount gets too large, the VAR model signals that the bank should sell. The trouble is that lots of banks have similar investments and similar VAR models. In periods when markets everywhere decline, the models can tell everybody to sell the same things at the same time, making market conditions much worse. In effect, they can, and often do, create a vicious feedback loop."

To their credit, many regulators have recognised the potentially destabilising effects of market sensitive risk regulation. More thoughtful central bankers have recognised and highlighted the dangers of endogenously generated risk (see, for instance, Crockett, 2000). This concern has also been reflected in practice. In the days following the terrorist attacks on New York and Washington on September 11, 2001, financial markets around the world were buffeted by unprecedented turbulence. In response to the short-term disruption to the smooth functioning of markets, the authorities responded by suspending various solvency tests applied to large financial institutions such as life insurance firms. In the UK, for instance, the usual "resilience test" applied to life insurance companies (in which the firm has to demonstrate solvency in the face of a further 25% market decline) was suspended for several weeks. More recently, following the renewed decline in stocks markets in the summer of 2002, the Financial Services Authority (FSA) – the UK regulator – has diluted the resilience test so as to pre-empt the destabilising forced sales of stocks by the major market players.[5]

Nevertheless, the fact remains that the overall framework for risk regulation relies on a prudential perspective that views each financial institution on its own. The framework tends to neglect the system-wide perspective. Hence, the blind spot in conventional risk management techniques, and especially the supervisory approach to the regulation of risk, is the presumption that risk management is a single-person decision problem – ie, a *game against nature*. That is, uncertainty governing price movements is assumed to be exogenous, and assumed not to depend on the actions of other decision makers. The analogy is with a meteorologist trying to predict the weather. The weather is unaffected by the predictions issued by weather forecasters and the consequent actions that these forecasts generate. Financial markets are different. When short run price changes are influenced by the trading decisions of market participants (as surely they must be), then shifts in the beliefs of market participants will lead to actions that precipitate certain outcomes. There is, in other words, a feedback effect from the beliefs of market participants to the actual outcome in the market. Indeed, there are strong reasons to believe that this feedback effect will reinforce any exogenous pressures on prices arising from the fundamentals.

A gambling analogy is useful. If the underlying uncertainty facing a trader were exogenous, modelling risk is akin to a gambler facing a spin of a roulette wheel, where the bets placed by him and other gamblers do not affect the outcome of the spin. However, when the outcome depends on the actions of other traders, risk modelling resembles poker more than roulette. Current risk management practices rest on the roulette view of uncertainty. The roulette wheel may have an unknown number of outcomes with differing probabilities, but as long as the outcome is unaffected by the actions of other gamblers, it is simply a matter of applying standard statistical techniques to past outcomes to enumerate what these outcomes are, and to estimate their respective probabilities. Many of the sophisticated techniques in the current state of the art can be seen as alternative ways of refining such estimation procedures, as well as tracking the non-linear payoff structures arising from derivative securities. To the extent that the stochastic process governing asset prices depends on what traders do, this view of the world is invalid. The uncertainty facing traders is endogenous, and depends on the actions of market participants. To neglect this is to commit the same error as the engineers of the Millennium Bridge.

In normal market conditions, when trading is orderly and markets function well, there is little harm in treating uncertainty as being exogenous. However, during a crisis, such a naive worldview is likely to throw up nasty surprises. Since risk management systems are in place precisely to deal with such exceptional episodes, what happens during tranquil market conditions is largely irrelevant. When short run changes in prices depend on the actions of other traders, the "roulette wheel" view of uncertainty is no longer adequate.

Major disruptions to financial markets almost always arise from the whiplash effect of endogenous risk. Let us flesh out our argument by reference to three episodes, which must rank as the most dramatic episodes in financial markets in recent memory – the 1987 crash, the LTCM crisis, and the collapse of the US dollar/yen in October 1998.

Crash of 1987

The Brady Commission's report (1988) attributed the magnitude and swiftness of the price decline in the 1987 stock market crash to practices such as portfolio insurance and dynamic hedging techniques. Such trading techniques have the property that they dictate selling an asset when its price falls and buying it when the price rises. In other words, it dictates a "sell cheap, buy dear" strategy. It generates precisely the kind of vicious feedback loop that destabilises markets. Best estimates then suggested that around US$100 billion in funds were following formal portfolio insurance programs, representing around 3% of the pre-crash market value. However, this is almost certainly an underestimate of total selling pressure arising from informal hedging techniques such as stop-loss orders (see the survey evidence presented in Shiller, 1987).

To understand why portfolio insurance dictates a "sell cheap, buy dear strategy", it is worth recounting how the payoff from holding a put option on an underlying asset can be approximated by a dynamic trading strategy on the underlying asset. In its simplest form, the strategy relies on the *delta* of the put option. The delta of a put option is the rate of change of its price with respect to the change in the underlying fundamental asset. Thus, if Π is the price of the put option and p is the price of the underlying asset, the delta Δ is given by

$$\Delta = \frac{d\Pi}{dp} < 0$$

Black and Scholes (1973) in their celebrated paper on option pricing noted that the portfolio consisting of:

$$\begin{cases} \Delta & \text{underlying asset} \\ -1 & \text{put option} \end{cases}$$

is locally risk-free with respect to changes in p. This is because when the price changes slightly, the gain or loss from the holding of the underlying asset (given by Δ) is matched by an exactly offsetting loss or gain from the change in the price of the put option $(-\Delta)$. This insight is used in the derivation of the Black–Scholes formula by arguing that the above portfolio must earn the same return as the risk-free asset.

An analogous argument can be used to show that the payoff from the put option can be replicated by holding a suitable portfolio of the underlying asset and cash. Suppose a trader starts with a cash balance of Π, which also happens to be the price of the put option that the trader wishes to replicate. With this wealth, the trader can either purchase the put option itself, or purchase the portfolio:

$$\begin{cases} \Delta & \text{underlying asset} \\ -p\Delta + \Pi & \text{cash} \end{cases} \tag{1}$$

Since the trader wishes to replicate a put option, Δ is negative. This portfolio is financed by selling short $|\Delta|$ units of the underlying asset at price p, and adding the proceeds to the cash balance.

Now, suppose the price changes to p'. The value of the portfolio at the new price is

$$\overbrace{\Delta p'}^{\text{short asset}} + \overbrace{\Pi - p\Delta}^{\text{cash holding}} = \Pi + \Delta(p' - p)$$
$$\simeq \Pi'$$

where Π' is the price of the put option given p'. Thus, the trader manages to approximate the wealth of a trader who starts out by holding the put option itself. Since the approximation is linear, the accuracy of the approximation is greater the smaller the price change. The trader then forms the new portfolio:

$$\simeq \begin{cases} \Delta' & \text{underlying asset} \\ -p'\Delta' + \Pi' & \text{cash} \end{cases} \qquad (2)$$

which is affordable given his wealth of Π'. Proceeding in this way, the trader reaches the date of maturity of the option. If the option expires in-the-money, Equation (2) is

$$\begin{cases} -1 & \text{underlying asset} \\ p+(x-p) & \text{cash} \end{cases}$$

while if the option expires out-of-the-money, Equation (2) is

$$\begin{cases} 0 & \text{underlying asset} \\ 0 & \text{cash} \end{cases}$$

Either way, the final value of the trader's portfolio is

$$\max\{x-p, 0\}$$

which is the payoff to buying and holding one put at the beginning.

Traded options exist only for well-established markets, and only for relatively short maturities. For very long-dated options, or for specific assets, dynamic replication is the only avenue open to traders if they wish to hedge an implicit short put position. For instance, a fund manager who has sold long-term retail funds that guarantee the capital, the implicit put must be replicated in some way. If an investment bank has sold the fund manager an over-the-counter put, then the burden of replication is placed on the investment bank that sold the option.

More directly relevant for our purposes is the practice of portfolio insurance that was quite common until the 1987 stock market crash, and identified in the Brady Commission report as being an important contributory factor in the crash. The dynamic hedging strategy sketched above has the property that it dictates selling of the underlying asset when its price *falls*, and dictates buying the underlying asset when its price *rises*. This is because the delta of a put option becomes more negative as the price of the underlying asset falls. In other words, the dynamic replication entails a "sell cheap, buy dear" strategy.

When the trader is small relative to the market as a whole, or when the active traders in the market hold diverse positions, one would expect little or no feedback of the traders' decisions on the market dynamics itself. However, when a large segment of the market is engaged in such trading strategies, the market dynamics may be affected by the trading strategy itself, and hence lead to potentially destabilising price paths. The stock market crash of 1987 is a classic example of endogenous risk, and the potentially destabilising feedback effect on market dynamics of concerted selling pressure arising from mechanical trading rules.

The Brady Commission report (1988) notes that whereas some portfolio insurers rebalanced several times per day, many others followed the strategy of rebalancing their portfolios once a day – at the open, based on the prior day's close. The sparse trading ensured that transaction costs would be low, but this was achieved at the cost of the accuracy of the approximation, especially if the price moved in one direction only over several days. More seriously, the implicit selling pressure arising from the mechanical trading rules of the traders had the potential of influencing the price of the underlying asset itself, thereby introducing further rounds of selling. During the days leading up to the crash of October 19, 1987 the stock market had experienced sharp falls. In the period from Wednesday October 14 to Friday October 16, the market declined by around 10%. The sales dictated by dynamic hedging models amounted to around US$12 billion (either in cash or futures), but the actual sales had only been around US$4 billion. This meant that by the time of the open on Monday morning, there was a substantial amount of pent-up selling pressure. The imbalance between purchases and sales meant that much of the underlying market for stocks did not function. Instead, traders attempted to use the index futures market to hedge their exposures. The S&P index futures sold at large discounts to the cash market on Monday 19 and Tuesday 20 for this reason.

The important lesson to emerge from the 1987 stock market crash is that the dynamic replication of put options by portfolio rebalancing may not be possible in times of market distress. When a large segment of the market attempts to follow identical trading strategies, the liquidity of the market is impaired to such an extent that the market ceases to function in the way necessary for the dynamic trading strategy. In situations such as this, the uncertainty governing stock returns is better described as being *endogenous* rather than *exogenous*. The returns are generated partly by the increased selling pressure from the traders.

The LTCM crisis of 1998

The summer of 1998 was a particularly turbulent episode for the mature financial markets of the United States and Europe. The events are well summarised in two official reports into the events by the Bank for International Settlements (BIS) and the International Monetary Fund (IMF).[6] The origins and the personalities behind Long-Term Capital Management have been well aired through books such as that by Lowenstein (2000). The mainstay of LTCM's trading strategy were convergence or relative value trades in which a long position in one asset would be hedged by having a matching short position in another asset whose returns were highly correlated with the first. The motivation was to reap the rewards of higher returns of the long position, while hedging away the risks by means of the matching short position. Usually, the long position would be in a relatively illiquid or riskier asset whose expected returns were higher than the hedging asset. For instance, a trader would hold a long position in off-the-run treasuries, which traded at a higher yield, but then hedge the interest rate risk by holding a short position in on-the-run treasuries. Other examples include mortgage backed securities, swaps, and corporate bonds, all hedged with short positions in on-the-run treasuries. Another favourite trade of LTCM was the European convergence trade of Italian government bonds against German bunds as the launch date of the Euro approached.

For several years, the convergence trades of LTCM produced rich rewards, and spawned many copycat funds. More importantly, LTCM's very success bred many imitators in the proprietary trading desks of the major investment banks. As more and more players with similar trading strategies crowded into the market, the spreads narrowed on the favoured convergence trades, eroding the profit margin for all the players. The relative tranquillity of the markets also lulled the players into a false sense of security and spurred them on to increase their leverage, which reduced the spreads further. By the spring of 1998, the convergence funds had to venture into new and uncharted markets in order to find profitable trades. The scene was set for a reversal of some kind.

The exact date of the reversal is difficult to pinpoint, but the disbanding of the Salomon Brothers bond arbitrage desk on July 6, 1998 was a clear milestone.[7] As the convergence trades were unwound, the long positions were sold, and the short positions were bought back. This entailed adverse price shocks for all other traders that started out with similar positions. For some traders whose leverage was high relative to capital, this would entail losses on their positions sufficient to trigger margin calls on their losing positions. They would be forced to unwind their trades, which tended to reinforce the adverse price moves. Given the huge levels of leverage and the widespread nature of the trades, the vicious feedback loop was gradually set in motion in which adverse price moves led to liquidations, which further fed the adverse price moves. Schematically, we would have the following feedback loop where market distress would feed on itself.

$$\text{Margin Calls} \Rightarrow \text{Unwind Leveraged Trades}$$
$$\Uparrow \qquad\qquad\qquad\qquad \Downarrow$$
$$\text{Distress} \quad \Leftarrow \quad \text{Adverse Price Move}$$

This is a classic example of endogenous risk. The unprecedented price movements were not simply a freak of nature, much like a "perfect storm" that would hit perhaps only once in the lifetime of the Universe. To believe this would be to make the same mistake as the engineers of the Millennium Bridge. The probability of a thousand people (walking at random) all ending up walking in perfect step is not close to zero. Given the right conditions, it is a near certainty. Similarly, the unprecedented price moves in the summer of 1998 were not simply the result of extremely bad luck. Given the extensive copycat behaviour of other traders and the large implicit leverage involved, it was only a matter of time before the system would be hit by a small external shock that would send it into reverse. Once the system began to go into reverse, the internal dynamics of the feedback loop would take hold with a vengeance, and send it into a tailspin. The probability of this collapse is far from zero. Under the right conditions, it is a near certainty. Again, it is the *endogenous* risk that is doing the harm.

US dollar/yen in october 1998

The same perspective is useful in understanding the behaviour of the US dollar against the yen over two memorable days in October 1998 – 7th and 8th – when the US dollar fell from 131 yen to 112 yen by lunchtime in London on Thursday 8, bouncing back sharply to end New York trading at 119 yen. October 7 and 8, 1998 were two of the most turbulent days of trading in financial markets in recent memory, which also saw sharp falls in longer dated government bonds and the virtual seizing up of markets for corporate debt, and for less liquid government debt instruments.

The fall in the US dollar was especially dramatic given its strength throughout the spring and summer of 1998, reaching its high of 147.26 yen on August 11. Many commentators were predicting that US dollar/yen would reach 150 or perhaps 200 by the end of the year, especially in the light of the apparent failure of the joint intervention by the US and Japan on June 17 to support the yen more than temporarily. The conventional wisdom among academics, commentators and traders alike was that the yen was bound to fall, and that it was a matter of the speed and the magnitude of its fall rather than the direction. Indeed, by the summer of 1998, this conventional wisdom had almost acquired the status of an immutable truth. Although such arrogance seems misplaced with the benefit of hindsight, it is easy to see how such a confident view arose. Since the spring of 1995, the US dollar had continued to appreciate against the yen (with a brief respite in mid-1997), and the contrasting macroeconomic fortunes of the US and Japan, with strong growth in the former and weakness in the latter – seemed to presage more of the same in the months ahead.

The combination of an appreciating US dollar and the large interest rate differential between Japan and the US gave rise to the singularly profitable trading opportunity of borrowing yen, buying

US dollar assets, and gaining both on the appreciation of the US dollar and the interest rate differential. This "yen carry" trade was widespread among hedge funds, the proprietary trading desks of investment banks, and even some corporations. Funds were raised in the interbank market through term repurchase agreements, or by issuing money market paper. Then these funds would be swapped for foreign currency or exchanged in the spot market to fund purchases of higher-yielding assets, including US corporate bonds, mortgage-backed securities and also even riskier instruments such as the Russian government's short-term bonds (GKOs). Japanese banks also resorted to the yen-carry trade by accumulating foreign assets. In the first three quarters of 1998, the net holdings of assets denominated in foreign currencies increased by about US$44 billion, while the holdings of yen-denominated assets abroad declined by US$103 billion (International Monetary Fund, 1998, p. 127). Thus, the conventional wisdom concerning the relentless rise in US dollar/yen was also apparently shared by the Japanese institutions.

The initial weakening of the US dollar was relatively orderly, falling by less than 10% against both the yen and the Deutschmark between mid-August and early October. However, in the week beginning October 5, 1998, the decline of the US dollar against the yen accelerated sharply – closing down roughly 15% over the week. Significantly, the fall in the US dollar against the Deutschmark was much less pronounced, falling less than 2% during the week. It was also noteworthy how this fall in US dollar/yen coincided with an unprecedented steepening of the yield curve for mature markets outside Japan, as bond yields bounced back from their historical lows. During the same week, the yield gap between three month rates and 10-year rates widened by 85 basis points in the US, 60 basis points in the UK, and 50 basis points in Germany. The coincidence of:

1. the rapid fall in US dollar/yen;
2. the less precipitous fall in US dollar/Deutschmark; and
3. the rapid steepening of the yield curve in markets outside Japan;

are consistent with the rapid unwinding (or attempted unwinding) of the yen carry trades in place at the time.

One of the implications of a highly leveraged market going into reversal is that a *moderate* fall in asset value is highly unlikely. Either the asset does not fall in value at all, or the value falls by a large amount. The logic of the mutually reinforcing effects of selling into a falling market dictates this conclusion. The fall in US dollar/yen is also likely to have been exaggerated by stop-loss orders, and by the cancellation of barrier options and the unwinding of associated hedging positions by dealers. One estimate of the volume of outstanding yen foreign currency contracts at the end of June was in excess of US$3.3 trillion (Bank of Japan, 1998). Just as in the stock market crash of 1987, the effect of such trading techniques is to exaggerate price movements, by selling into a falling market. In retrospect, the distribution of asset prices referred to above is exactly what one should expect in a market which is marked by such high levels of leverage, undertaken by many diverse institutions. The unwinding of yen carry trades proceeded at such a pace that press reports referred to market rumours of the imminent collapse of one or more hedge funds. The Bank of Japan reported large buying of yen by at least one large hedge fund (Financial Times, 1998).

The poignant irony could not have been lost on observers of the Asian financial crisis. Just a year earlier, the hedge funds and assorted proprietary trading desks of investment banks had profited handsomely from the stampede by Asian borrowers with unhedged dollar liabilities to cover their positions in a desperate attempt to keep afloat. In October 1998, these same "sharks" had become their own bait. It was now they who were scrambling to cover their positions. The logic of mutually reinforcing sales meant that the harder they tried to swim away, the more they provoked the feeding frenzy. The sense of fear was palpable during the turbulent trading of October 8. With sentiment already fragile after the forced rescue of LTCM, rumours of the imminent collapse of a major hedge fund further reinforced the disengagement from risk. Yet again, it was endogenous risk that drove the most dramatic market movements.

CONCLUSION

What lessons should we draw from all this? The first general lesson is that an effective risk manager should be able to make an intelligent distinction between those cases where the standard "roulette wheel" view of uncertainty is sufficient, and to distinguish those cases from instances where the endogeneity of risk is important. Common sense and a feel for the underlying pressures lying dormant in the market are essential complements to any quantitative risk management tool that merely looks back at the recent past.

When there are diverse opinions in the market, and where these diverse opinions are reflected in the diversity of trading strategies and positions, treating risk as being exogenous would be appropriate. When risk is exogenous, the trader is playing a game against nature – that is, the statistical relationships are determined *outside* the system. Hence the roulette wheel view of the world suffices, and efforts can be directed towards the refinements of statistical or engineering tools of measurement and perturbation, such as identifying the correct probability densities from past data, estimating the co-movements in returns, and dealing with the non-linear payoffs from derivatives. Stress testing in such a context is simple, since the shocks that arrive are correctly modelled as being something that hits the market from the outside.

Endogenous uncertainty matters whenever there is the conjunction of: traders reacting to market outcomes; and where the traders' actions *affect* market outcomes. These conditions are most likely to be in effect when there is a prevailing orthodoxy concerning the direction of market outcomes, and where such unanimity leads to similar positions or trading strategies. In such an environment, the uncertainty in the market is generated and modified by the response of individual traders to the unfolding events. Recognising these features is essential to intelligent risk management that takes account of endogenous risk.

What of the implications for quantitative risk management and of stress testing? What are the alternatives to the current suite of techniques that draw from engineering analogies? First, the margin of error in the stress test must be chosen intelligently. When a bank's portfolio is subject to a simulated shock, the margin of error should not be based on the assumption that all other market conditions remain unchanged. If the shock is likely to affect the actions of *other* market participants, the system-wide impact of the shock may be much larger in practice than the initial shock that one is simulating. For the engineers of the Millennium Bridge, it was not enough simply to subject the model of the bridge to strong storms or other outside shocks assuming that other things would remain unchanged. The system has the potential for its own dynamic response, and this potential should be explicitly modelled.

So, what is to be done? For financial markets, tracking the potential for the dynamic response of the market entails explicitly solving the equilibrium of the system and tracking its evolution over time. This is not the place to embark on a full description of the kinds of methods that can be employed, suffice to say that models drawn from financial economics – both of the competitive equilibrium variety and game-theoretic variety – are promising future directions for research. The reader is referred to Danielsson, Shin and Zigrand (2002), Danielsson and Zigrand (2002), and Morris and Shin (2000) for examples.

1   See, for example, the realplayer videos of the opening day on the BBC news site at URL: http://news.bbc.co.uk/hi/english/static/in_depth/uk/2000/millennium_bridge/default.stm.

2   See "Bad Vibrations" *New Scientist*, vol. 167, issue 2246, July 8, 2000, page 14. See also the webpage set up by Arup – the contruction engineers of the bridge at URL: http://www.arup.com/millenniumbridge/challenge/oscillation.html.

3   In the tests that followed the closure of the bridge, Arup found that the wobble was a highly non-linear function of the number of pedestrians. The critical number of people that started the wobble was 156. Up to that number, the movement increased only slightly as more people came on the bridge. However, with ten more people, the wobble increased at a sharply higher rate. See http://www.arup.com/millenniumbridge/challenge/results.html.

4   The Economist Magazine, Oct 12, 2000.

5   *Financial Times, Weekend Money*, June 28, 2002, "Insolvency rules are eased for life offices" by Jason Corcoran.

6   The BIS report *A Review of Financial Market Events in Autumn 1998* can be obtained from: www.bis.org/publ/cgfs12.htm. See also chapter III of the IMF's *World Economic Outlook and International Capital Markets: Interim Assessment*, www.imf.org/external/pubs/ft/weo/weo1298/index.htm.

7   The added irony being that the main protagonists at LTCM began their careers at Salomons.

BIBLIOGRAPHY

Bank for International Settlements, 1999, "A Review of Financial Market Events in Autumn 1998", CGFS Publication Number 12, Bank for International Settlements, URL: http://www.bis.org/publ/cgfs12.htm.

Bank of Japan, 1998, *Regular Derivatives Market Statistics in Japan* (Tokyo: Bank of Japan).

Black, F., and M. Scholes, 1973, "The Pricing of Options and Corporate Liabilities", *Journal of Political Economy*, 81, pp. 637–59.

Brady, N., 1988, *Report of the Presidential Task Force on Market Mechanisms* (Washington DC: Government Printing Office).

Crockett, A., 2000, "Marrying the Micro- and Macro-Prudential Dimensions of Financial Stability" (Basel: Bank for International Settlements), URL: http://www.bis.org/review/rr000921b.pdf.

Danielsson, J., H. S. Shin, and J-P. Zigrand, 2002, "The Impact of Risk Regulation on Price Dynamics", URL: http://www.riskresearch.org.

Danielsson, J., and J-P. Zigrand, 2002, "What Happens when you Regulate Risk? Evidence from a Simple Equilibrium Model", URL: http://www.riskresearch.org.

Financial Times, 1998, "Market stunned by volatile US dollar", October 9, p. 19.

International Monetary Fund, 1998, *World Economic Outlook and International Capital Markets: Interim Assessment*, URL: http://www.imf.org/external/pubs/ft/weo/weo1298/index.htm.

Lowenstein, R., 2000, *When Genius Failed – The Rise and Fall of Long-Term Capital Management* (New York: Random House).

Morris, S., and H. S. Shin, 2000, "Market Risk with Interdependent Choice", URL: http://www.nuff.ox.ac.uk/users/shin/working.htm.

Shiller, R., 1987, "Investor Behavior in the October 1987 Stock Market Crash: Survey Evidence" NBER discussion paper 2446, reprinted in *Market Volatility*, 1990 (MIT Press).

Part VI

The Use of Risk Management

21

Multi-National Corporate Risk Management Practice*

Arnold Miyamoto and Ramon Espinosa

Risk Management Advisory

Firms face a variety of market risks, ranging from foreign currency and interest rate risk, to commodity price risk. Over the past decade, as sales and operations have become increasingly global and competition in markets has intensified, foreign currency risk management has grown in importance as a determinant of a firm's ability to compete effectively and return value to shareholders. Fortunately, however, the past decade has also seen a broadening and deepening of the markets for instruments that may be used to manage currency risk. In this chapter, the authors review the practice of foreign currency risk management in multi-national corporations.

Effective management of market risk should allow companies to grow and increase shareholder value, while selectively avoiding the damaging effects of adverse market developments. In theory, therefore, risk managers should identify and implement policies and strategies that maximise shareholder value. In practice, however,

*This material is not intended as an offer or solicitation for the purchase or sale of any currency or financial instrument. Opinions expressed are our present opinions only and are subject to change without notice. This material is based upon information, which we consider reliable, but we do not represent that it is accurate or complete, and it should not be relied upon as such. We may, from time to time, have long or short positions in, and buy and sell, currencies and other financial instruments identical to those mentioned in this material. © 2002, Bank of America.

for many publicly held companies, risk management is a balancing act between shareholder economics and accounting presentation. Indeed, risk managers must be mindful of the accounting treatment of hedges, as quarterly and annual earnings announcements become critical determinants of projected corporate welfare.

WHY HEDGE CURRENCY RISK?

In general, multinational corporations appear to attach a relatively low priority to the management of foreign currency risk. Only infrequently, for instance, is a high corporate officer such as the chief financial officer or treasurer involved in foreign currency hedging; rather, the responsibility for currency hedging typically resides with an assistant treasurer or below and is but one of several activities for which they are responsible. And while we often hear clients state their intention to review foreign exchange (FX) risk management policies and update hedging strategies, more often than not they fail to complete these tasks.

Why is FX risk management accorded such low priority? Most likely, several *assumptions* have contributed to this state of affairs. First, firm managers may presume that the *costs* of currency risk are small because direct exposures seem small, currency moves are perceived to be transitory and temporary ("currencies go up and go down, but over time they are a zero-sum game"), and in any event, "equity analysts" tend to overlook earnings shortfalls due to currency fluctuations. Second, managers may presume that the *benefits* of managing currency risk are likely to be small because the ability of shareholders to manage currency risk means that firms will not be compensated for currency risk management that they themselves undertake. Finally, given the perception of limited risks and minimal benefits, firms may believe that it is simpler and cheaper to self-insure rather than use currency derivatives to manage exposures.

While the points above may appear to establish a case against managing currency risk, close inspection of each suggests that the case is not as strong as it appears. Indeed, we would argue that the evidence presents a compelling case for strengthening and attaching greater priority to currency risk management efforts.

To begin, consider the argument that currency exposures are "small". Quite likely, this perception reflects the tendency of many firms to focus on only transaction exposures, and in particular the exposure of *recorded*, foreign-currency-denominated monetary assets and liabilities to currency fluctuations. However, by focusing on only recorded items, firms ignore the risks associated with future foreign currency transactions. In the aggregate, such transactions likely dwarf those currently recognised on the balance sheet. In addition, by focusing on recognised foreign-currency denominated transactions, firms may miss important indirect exposures, such as the sensitivity of prices and volumes to currency fluctuations and what this implies for future earnings. Regardless of what management elects to focus on, foreign exchange is an enterprise level risk.

The tendency to focus on the currency exposure of near-term, recorded transactions may also reflect the presumption that currency moves are transitory, making currencies are a "zero-sum game" – ie, because currencies are likely to go up and then down again, any near-term loss is likely to be reversed by gains in the future. If this were true, then it might be logical for firms with perpetual lives to view FX hedging as an unnecessary and even wasteful exercise. As appealing as this argument might seem, however, it would be more compelling if supported by empirical evidence. Even casual study of Figure 1, which shows long-term cumulative movements of the euro, sterling, and yen against the US dollar, suggests that currencies tend to trend over extended periods of time, rather than display a "zero-sum" tendency. More rigorous statistical analysis of currency movements also supports the conclusion that the zero sum theory is not valid.[1]

The zero-sum argument is further undermined if we recognise that notional exposures are unlikely to remain constant over time, so the effects of currency fluctuations are unlikely to cancel. Moreover, the argument is weakened further by recognition of the fact that the effects of currency moves may well be asymmetric (ie, the "benefits" from favourable currency moves may not match the "pain" resulting from adverse moves because the latter may put debt covenants in jeopardy, limit key research and investment spending, or otherwise impose non-recoverable costs on the firm).

Finally, while "analysts" in the past may have been inclined to discount earnings shortfalls due to adverse currency moves, such

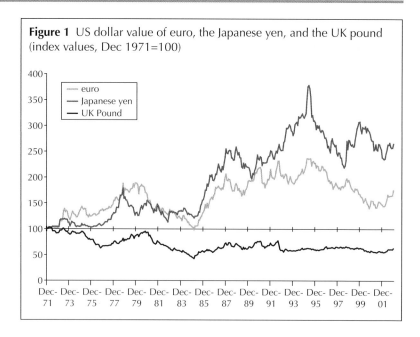

Figure 1 US dollar value of euro, the Japanese yen, and the UK pound (index values, Dec 1971=100)

an attitude seems less likely now. Indeed, in the current environment of heightened scrutiny and weak performance, any unanticipated earnings shortfall may bring significant adverse consequences for shareholders. For example, Figure 2 shows the change in value of a portfolio of companies experiencing earnings shortfalls attributable to adverse currency moves (data from the fall of 2000). In aggregate, the average equity decline was 15% in the day following the earnings announcement.

The second presumption – that the benefits of managing currency risk are likely to be small because shareholders can manage currency risk themselves and, therefore, will not compensate firms for managing that risk – is a variant of the Miller–Modigliani theory on the invariance of firm value with respect to financial decisions.[1] As others have demonstrated, however, their theoretical result tends to vanish in the presence of informational asymmetries, transaction and bankruptcy costs, and taxes. Even more compelling, perhaps, is the complication that many investors may not be free to manage currency risk themselves and, therefore, may reward firms that undertake that effort. Consider, for instance, a typical institutional investor holding a portfolio of "domestic"

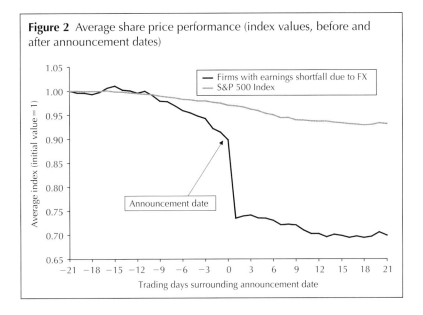

Figure 2 Average share price performance (index values, before and after announcement dates)

equities. Even though the portfolio includes only "domestic" equities, many of the firms represented in the portfolio will be multi-national firms with currency exposure. It is most likely, however, that an investor will operate under investment guidelines prohibiting the introduction of currency overlay positions into the "domestic" equity portfolio. Because a majority of investors may not be able to manage the currency risk inherent in individual equities, firms are likely to be rewarded for managing such risks.

Finally, even if firms perceive currency exposures to be small and the benefits of hedging limited, they must recognise that not hedging amounts to self-insuring. As such, the firm should allocate capital to protect against shortfalls due to currency fluctuations. If the shareholders are the source of this insurance, then the cost of the self-protection is the cost of equity. If existing operations are the source of capital, then the cost becomes the opportunity cost of foregone investment. In either case, while self-insuring may seem a reasonable solution, the pertinent question is whether self-insuring foreign currency exposures is cost efficient? If the alternative is hedging an exposure with a forward contract, then the firm can protect itself fully from exchange rate moves at a "cost" equal to the percentage difference between the spot and forward exchange rates at the time of hedge execution. As described below, this "cost" will reflect the interest rate differential between the two currencies, and, depending on the relative levels of interest rates, may in fact prove to be a gain rather than a cost. Thus, self-insuring may be an expensive alternative, if hedging with forwards is less costly than self-insurance. Blindly opting for self-insurance without regard to the market cost of hedging, therefore, may result in an inefficient use of corporate capital.

WHAT CURRENCY RISKS DO COMPANIES FACE?

Foreign exchange exposure takes several forms. Some currency exposures, such as sales, expenses, investments, or borrowings denominated in a currency other than a firm's base (or, more precisely, functional) currency, are easily identified. Other exposures may be indirect and less easily identified. For instance, a firm whose activities fall entirely within a single country and involve a single currency may nevertheless have exposure to currency fluctuations if its principal competitor is foreign, with a foreign-currency cost basis. In the latter case, currency fluctuations will affect the firm's competitiveness and economic performance.

To help in the design and execution of effective risk management strategies, both from an accounting and an economic perspective, currency exposures tend to be grouped into several categories: transaction, translation, anticipatory, contingent, and other economic.

❏ *Transaction exposure* considers the effects of currency fluctuations on the base (functional) currency values of an entity's foreign currency denominated transactions (eg, components sourced offshore and paid for in foreign currency). Fundamentally, transaction exposure is the re-measurement risk associated with recognised monetary assets and liabilities denominated in a currency other than the entity's functional currency. Under US Generally Accepted Accounting Principles (GAAP), changes in the functional currency values of such items due to currency fluctuations must pass to income each period. This is the currency exposure that companies hedge most commonly.

❏ *Translation exposure* occurs when a single enterprise is comprised of several smaller entities having different functional currencies; the need to prepare a single set of consolidated financial statements leaves risk of translation exposure. Balance sheet translation gives rise to gains and losses that, under US GAAP, accrue to the cumulative translation adjustment (CTA) account, an equity item. Income translation leaves consolidated net earnings exposed to currency risk.

❏ *Anticipatory exposures* are an "economic cousin" of transaction exposure. These are *forecast* transactions denominated in a currency other than the entity's functional currency.

❏ *Contingent exposures*, another cousin of transaction exposure, are exposures that may or may not come into existence, depending on the nature of a non-financial-market event. A typical example would involve a company bidding on a business contract involving cashflows in foreign currency.

❏ *Other economic exposure* – covers all other effects of currency moves on cashflows (functional currency and non-functional currency) and, thereby, the value of the firm. For instance, this category would include the effects of currency moves on the sales volumes of products priced in a firm's functional currency.

HEDGING INSTRUMENTS

Surveys of FX market activity and FX risk management practices suggest that corporations tend to rely on three instruments for the majority of their foreign currency hedging: forward contracts (including FX swaps), vanilla currency options, and option combinations such as collars (known as range forwards in the language of FX). Forward contracts, the most common and simplest foreign currency hedge instrument, exist in two forms: deliverable and non-deliverable forwards. Both instruments are over-the-counter contracts, and as such they afford risk managers considerable flexibility in terms of tenor, currency pair, and notional amount.

In a deliverable forward contract, the two parties agree to exchange an amount of one currency for a specific amount of a second, with the actual delivery (ie, settlement) of the currencies occurring on a date beyond the standard spot settlement date. Since only the settlement date distinguishes a forward transaction from a spot transaction, the rate of exchange in a deliverable forward contract is simply the spot rate adjusted by the time values of the two currencies involved (over the tenor of the forward).

Figure 3 Forward hedge protecting UK pound value of euro 100 mm sales in 6-months

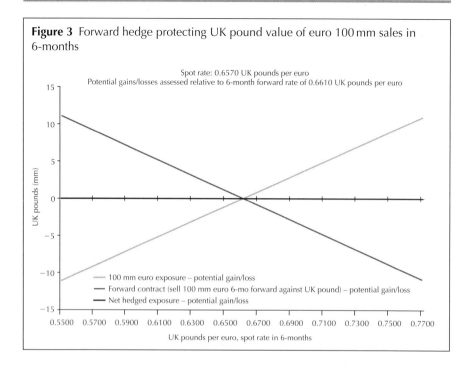

Spot rate: 0.6570 UK pounds per euro
Potential gains/losses assessed relative to 6-month forward rate of 0.6610 UK pounds per euro

- 100 mm euro exposure – potential gain/loss
- Forward contract (sell 100 mm euro 6-mo forward against UK pound) – potential gain/loss
- Net hedged exposure – potential gain/loss

UK pounds (mm)

UK pounds per euro, spot rate in 6-months

The forward rate is derived to eliminate any arbitrage opportunities that may exist between the spot exchange and interest rate markets. Since the value of the fixed-price forward contract varies with movements in the spot rate, an appropriately sized forward contract can serve as an effective hedge of a foreign currency exposure, whose functional currency value varies with movements in the spot rate (see Figure 3). Ample liquidity in deliverable forwards for the major currency pairs, such as euro/US dollar, euro/sterling, and US dollar/yen, extends out several years.

Non-deliverable forwards (NDFs) operate very much like forward contracts with the exception that there is no physical delivery of the two currencies involved. Instead, the contract is cash-settled at expiration in US dollars or in another major currency. In practice, one party compensates the other an amount equal to the value of the deviation between the NDF contract rate and the spot rate on the settlement date (taken from a source specified in the contract), applied to the notional value of the contract.[2] NDFs represent an innovation developed to deal with situations in which exchange controls (actual or feared) might impede the delivery of the two currencies. As such, they tend to be the most liquid forwards available for exotic currencies, such as the Brazilian real and the Korean won, whose markets are subject to controls.[3]

The presence of capital controls prevents incipient arbitrage flows, which determine the pricing of deliverable forwards, from providing a complete basis for the pricing of NDFs. Accordingly, the pricing of NDFs tends to reflect additional factors, such as market sentiment about the future level of the spot rate. And because market sentiment, especially regarding the levels of exotic currencies, can be volatile, the differential between NDF and spot rates (ie, the forward points) for an exotic currency may be more volatile than the comparable differential between the deliverable forward and spot rates for a major currency.[3]

Because appropriately sized forward contracts generate gains/losses that offset adverse/favourable currency moves, they are useful hedges when the underlying exposure is certain, the currency risk is perceived to be symmetric, and the risk management objective is to eliminate all "surprises" (both good and bad). However, if one of these conditions fails to hold – ie, the exposure is uncertain, or the risk is perceived to be asymmetric (because the currency is viewed as more likely to move in one direction rather than the other, or because currency moves in one direction affect the firm differently than moves in the opposite direction), or the firm seeks to protect itself only from bad surprises rather than all surprises – then forwards may not be the most appropriate hedge instrument. In these circumstances, a foreign currency option may be a more appropriate hedge instrument.

A currency option conveys to the owner (holder) the right, but not the obligation, to buy or sell a predetermined amount of one currency for a pre-determined amount of another currency, for a set period of time.[4] The relationship between the two currency amounts defines the strike of the option; the worst-case rate at which the holder may exchange one currency against the other. Because a purchased option is similar to insurance – it provides protection should the currency move adversely, but it may be ignored if the currency moves favourably – an option may be a useful hedge for uncertain exposures, asymmetric exposures, and asymmetric goals.[5]

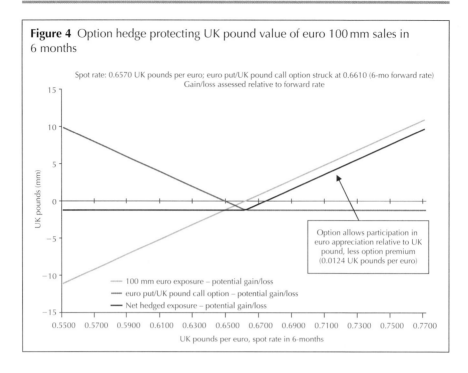

Figure 4 Option hedge protecting UK pound value of euro 100 mm sales in 6 months

Spot rate: 0.6570 UK pounds per euro; euro put/UK pound call option struck at 0.6610 (6-mo forward rate)
Gain/loss assessed relative to forward rate

Option allows participation in euro appreciation relative to UK pound, less option premium (0.0124 UK pounds per euro)

——— 100 mm euro exposure – potential gain/loss
—— euro put/UK pound call option – potential gain/loss
—— Net hedged exposure – potential gain/loss

UK pounds (mm)

UK pounds per euro, spot rate in 6-months

Because the holder of an option realises positive value or zero value, an option has an *expected* value greater than zero. Accordingly, to acquire an option, one must pay for it; this cost is referred to as the option premium. In general, the option premium depends on the tenor of the option (the longer the tenor, the greater the premium), the level of the strike rate relative to market rates (the more favourable the strike, the higher the premium), and the market's perception of the currency pair's movement potential over the life of the option (the greater the perceived movement potential, the greater the premium).

Because companies are often reluctant to pay the option premium, they often rely on one of several alternatives to reduce the amount of premium paid.[6] They might consider moving the strike on the option to a less favourable level. Alternatively, they might employ an option combination – in which one option is purchased and another sold – to reduce the net premium paid. Option combinations can be attractive because hedging with a simple purchased option protects the hedger fully from adverse currency moves but enables them to participate *fully* in favourable moves (see Figure 4).

If the hedger is willing to forego the benefit from some part of the favourable move, however, it can sell (to a bank) an option corresponding to the value of the currency move they are willing to forego. The premium received from the sold option finances the purchase of the option protecting against adverse currency moves.

A collar, also known as a range forward, is a very common combination hedge. To put in place a range forward to manage the risk associated with a long euro and short sterling exposure, for instance, a hedger would purchase a euro put/sterling call struck at a level somewhat less favourable than the current forward rate, and sell a euro call/sterling put (for the same notional amount) struck at a similarly less favourable level than the forward rate. The purchased euro put/sterling call would yield protection against euro depreciation relative to the strike on that option, while the sale of the euro call/sterling would mean that the hedger would forego any benefit from euro appreciation beyond the strike on that option. However, with the premium received from the sale of the euro call/sterling financing the purchase of the euro put/sterling call, the hedger will pay little, or zero, net premium.

HEDGING IN PRACTICE

Our own surveys, and those of third-parties, suggest that virtually all firms that manage foreign currency risk endeavour to identify and manage the transaction exposures associated with recognised balance sheet items (payables and receivables) and firm commitments. As such, exposures send to be certain (ie, subject to little forecast uncertainty); firms tend to hedge close to 100% of such exposures.[7] By a wide margin, foreign currency forward contracts tend to be the instrument of choice for hedging such "certain" transaction exposures.

Our experience and surveys also suggest that a smaller percentage (though still a majority), of firms hedge the exposures associated with forecast transactions, and hedging such exposures out to a tenor of 12-months is not uncommon. As with transaction exposures, forward contracts tend to be the instrument of choice; however, options are also used, because they deal effectively with the uncertainty of the exposures. To the extent that firms rely on forwards to hedge forecast exposures, they typically phase-in hedges (ie, begin by hedging only a fraction of the forecast amount, and then increase the hedge coverage as time passes and the forecast becomes more certain).

Our experience also suggests that only about one-in-three firms hedges translation risk – the exposure that derives from the translation of foreign balance sheets and earnings. Since the effects of balance sheet translation accrue to firm equity (the cumulative translation adjustment account), many firms choose to live with such currency induced fluctuations in equity.[8] At times, however, firms may choose to hedge this risk, to protect the economic value of an investment in a foreign entity, or to protect debt-to-equity or other financial statement ratios. While the translation of future earnings constitutes a real economic exposure, firms often choose not to hedge this variant of translation exposure because stand-alone hedges of earnings do not qualify for special accounting under US GAAP. Such hedges have to be marked-to-market, with changes in value taken to earnings each period; as such, their use, although justifiable on economic grounds, might increase volatility in interim earnings.

Finally, although other economic exposures may in fact prove to be a firm's most important currency exposures, only a handful of firms attempt to quantify this exposure and manage it using forwards or currency options.[9] Firms eschew hedging economic exposure because quantifying it is difficult and costly. Moreover, derivatives used to hedge such exposures would not qualify for any special accounting, creating the possibility of mismatches between the timing of the "real" exposures and timing at which hedge gain/losses affect reported earnings.

1   Miller, M. H., and F. Modigliani, 1961, "Dividend Policy, Growth and the Valuation of Shares", *Journal of Business*, 34, 411–433.
2   As an example, assume a company enters into a three-month NDF contract to sell 100 mm Brazilian reais against US dollars at a rate of 3.80 reais per USD. In three months, if the exchange rate is trading below (above) 3.80 reais per US dollar, then the company (bank) will compensate the bank (company) the US dollar value of the differential, applied to BRL 100 mm notional. The NDF enables the company to protect the US dollar value of the BRL 100 mm at 3.80 reais per US dollar.
3   In addition to pricing, the risk management consequences of NDFs differ (slightly) from those for deliverable forwards because NDFs leave the hedger with the underlying foreign currency. As such, the hedger is left with basis risk between the spot rate referenced in the NDF contract and the actual rate at which they are able to transact in the spot market, as well as broader transfer risk should controls be imposed on the local market.

4 While foreign currency options are similar to equity and interest rate options, they differ in that a given currency option is both a put option and a call option. This somewhat surprising result follows from the fact that every currency exchange involves the purchase of one currency and the sale of another. Hence, a currency option conveys the right to purchase (or "call") one currency and to sell (put) another. Note, therefore, that the holder of a euro call/sterling put option has a very different right than the holder of a euro put/sterling call option. The former will benefit from appreciation of the euro, while the latter will benefit from depreciation of the euro.

5 As with other types of insurance, a firm that purchases an option as a hedge will be best off if it never exercises it. Of course, had the firm known "before the fact" that it would never exercise the option, it would never have purchased it in the first place. Unfortunately, however, risk management decisions must be made before the future is known. As such, options offer value as risk management tools.

6 One reason firms may have difficulty purchasing options and paying the premium is that, after purchasing an option, they should logically "root" for the option to expire worthless and unexercised. In that case, they will have had no need for the insurance provided by the option, and they will be free to transact at the more favourable market rate.

7 See Bank of America Monograph # 158, "Corporate America: FX risk Management 2000/01."

8 Firms may choose to hedge currency gains and losses accruing to equity if they anticipate liquidating their investment in the foreign entity in the near term and want to protect the economic value of the investment, or if potential CTA-induced equity fluctuations might place debt covenants (balance sheet ratios) at risk.

9 In our surveys, only one in six firms attempts to quantify or manage these exposures.

BIBLIOGRAPHY

Alexander, C., 1998, *Risk Management and Analysis*, Volume I, *Measuring and Modeling Financial Risk*, (New York: John Wiley & Sons).

Bird, J., and V. Yee, 2001, "Corporate America: FX Risk Management 2000", Bank of America Risk Research Monograph, No. 158.

Bird, J., and V. Yee, 2001, "Currency Fluctuations, Earnings Announcements, and Market Capitalization", Bank of America Risk Research Monograph, No. 162.

Derosa, D., 1996, *Managing Foreign Exchange Risk: Advanced Strategies for Global Investors, Corporations, and Financial Institutions*, (Chicago: Probus Publishing).

Espinosa, R., 2000, "Economic Exposures: An Overview", Bank of America Risk Research Monograph, No. 149.

Lidbark, J., 2002, "Exposure Identification and Hedging – Does Time Horizon Matter?", Bank of America Risk Research Monograph, No. 176.

Miller, M. H., and F. Modigliani, 1961, "Dividend Policy, Growth and the Valuation of Shares", *Journal of Business*, 34, pp. 411–433.

Miyamoto, A., 1997, "Why Hedge?" Bank of America Risk Research Monograph, No. 87.

Smith, C. W., and C. W. Smithson, 1998, *Managing Financial Risk: A Guide to Derivative Products, Financial Engineering, and Value Maximization*, (New York: McGraw-Hill)

Taleb, N., 1997, *Dynamic Hedging*, (New York: John Wiley & Sons).

22

The Use of Risk Management by Corporations

Rohan Williamson

Georgetown University

So far in this volume, we have investigated the theories of risk management along with the tools available for managing the firm's risk. The history of risk management has been explored and shows the long history of firms attempting to manage their risks. We have also examined the specific cases of firms managing risks and the success or failure of these firms' efforts. In this chapter, the author will examine the current use of risk management by corporations. The chapter will be focused on the empirical findings on what firms do to manage their risks and how risk management varies across firms.

INTRODUCTION

The use of risk management by non-financial corporations has grown over the years. Corporations take various approaches to how, why, and when to manage risks. The purpose of this chapter is to examine the use of risk management by corporations. Corporations face value changes that are driven by imperfections in the capital markets that deviate from the world that is assumed in Modigliani and Miller (1958), thus creating a need to manage risk. The decision to hedge varies with the type of exposure, the timeframe of the hedge, the type of instruments available to manage the risk, and the beliefs of management. The approach of this chapter will be to first discuss the general types of risk that firms face that are dependent on time, and which type of risk management approach is most useful in each case. The chapter will then examine the reasons behind the uses of risk management tools used by corporations. The rest of the chapter will focus on what researchers have found concerning the use of derivatives by corporations. To do this we examine the empirical literature on the use of risk management.

WHAT ARE THE APPROACHES TO RISK MANAGEMENT?

Most of the research on risk management is focused on the use of derivatives to manage a firm's exposures. As pointed out in Stulz and Williamson (2000), firms face three types of exposure; transactional, contractual, and economic/competitive. Transactional exposure is for a short time period, say within the next three to six months. The firm has a commitment to some cashflow stream with a firm position like a receivable or a payable. As we move further into the future, say over the next year, the firm has exposures to which it is committed, but there is some uncertainty in terms of the extent to which these are contractual exposures. As firms move further into the future, say beyond the next few years, the firm faces economic/competitive exposure in which the cashflows have much more uncertainty since there is likely uncertainty in sales volumes, costs and competitive interactions as well as the impact of the underlying risks to exchange rates, interest rates or commodity prices.

For short-term transactional and contractual exposures, firms are more likely to use derivative instruments to manage risks, while for economic/competitive exposure, firms are more likely to use operational hedges to manage risks, such as the switching of production locations for exchange rate exposure and the use of foreign debt. Consistent with this idea, Williamson (2001) finds that the building of production facilities in the United States and Europe has reduced the foreign exchange rate exposure of Japanese automotive firms.

WHAT IS THE EVIDENCE FOR THE USE OF RISK MANAGEMENT?

We have seen important reasons for firms to manage risk. Generally, a firm wants to manage the risk of losses that impose costs on the firm in addition to the loss itself – deadweight costs. We have also seen that risk management is more useful when there are imperfections in the capital markets, thus creating an opportunity for firms to increase value. The benefits and methods of managing risks vary across firms. We have discussed briefly the operational approaches to managing risks through changing production or financing. For transactional and contractual exposures, firms commonly make use of derivatives to manage these types of risks. We will now examine the use of derivative instruments, which has been the source of most empirical research on risk management.

There are two types of evidence for the use of risk management by firms. The first is survey evidence. The second is analysis of firm-specific data of derivatives usage and hedging. Research shows that firms that use derivatives have lower volatility and higher value. Stulz (2002) has a detailed review on the empirical studies on derivatives use.

Who uses risk management?

Using a survey of 244 of the Fortune 500 firms, Dolde (1993) reports that 85% of these firms use swaps, forwards, futures, or options in managing financial risks. Users of risk management tools were much larger firms than non-users. For instance, the average market value of equity for users is US$5.4 billion compared to the average market value of non-users of US$1.8 billion. Larger firms are less likely to hedge their foreign exchange and interest rate exposures intensively. Firms that hedge a greater fraction of their exposures than the median fraction of exposures hedged are about half the size of the firms that hedge less than the median fraction of exposures.

One important finding is that a firm's market views matter and have an impact on its hedging decision. A firm may finance its business issuing long-term debt and be concerned about long-term interest rates. It could decide to completely insulate itself from changes in long-term interest rates, whatever its views about future interest rates. Or, it could decide to hedge more when it expects rates to increase than when it expects them to decrease. The typical attitude of firms seems to be captured by the following quotation from a Fortune 500 manager: "Hedge 30% to 50% if we think the market will move our way, 100% if we think it will move against us" (Dolde, 1993, p. 40). When management holds a view, smaller firms hedge more than larger firms.

In another survey by Bodnar, Hayt, and Smithson (1995), the Wharton/Chase, which was sent to a random sample of 2,000 non-financial firms in November 1994, only 34.5% of the firms that responded use derivatives. When the authors split the firms according to size, they find that 65% of firms with market value above US$250 million use derivatives, but only 13% of firms with market value below US$50 million use them. Thus reinforcing the fact that large firms are more likely to hedge.

Firms use derivatives mostly to hedge firm commitments, such as transactional and contractual exposures (75.4% of the respond-ing firms use derivatives [for this reason]). The majority of these firms say they hedge risks frequently. The report shows that 44.8% of the firms frequently use derivatives to hedge transactions antici-pated within the next 12 months, but only 14.2% frequently hedge transactions anticipated beyond 12 months. About 66% state that they do not use derivatives to hedge economic or competitive exposures. Finally, 52.5% say that they never use them to reduce funding costs by taking a view.

In a second survey conducted by Bodnar, Hayt, and Marston (1996), the Wharton/CIBC was sent out in October 1995 to the same sample as the aforementioned survey, plus the Fortune 500 firms. For this study, 41% reported that they use derivatives. Interestingly, when only firms that responded to the first survey are considered, their use of derivatives had increased from 35% to 39% from the first to the second survey.

How do firms manage their risk?

The likely next issue is what types of instruments do firms use to manage risks and how do they go about it. In the second survey that was conducted by the Wharton School, it was reported that 76% of users use foreign currency derivative instruments and their most popular instrument is the forward contract. 73% of users use interest rate derivatives and their preferred instrument is the swap. Finally, 37% of the users use commodity derivative instruments, and their preferred instrument is futures contracts.

The goal of hedging varies somewhat across firms. Though firms agree that the goal of hedging is to minimise volatility, they are not in agreement as to the type of volatility that is of interest. The evidence shows that 49% of firms using derivatives identify the most important goal to be the management of cashflow volatility; 42% accounting earnings volatility; 8% the volatility of the market value of the firm; and 1% the balance sheet volatility. In the case of foreign exchange exposures, firms focus mostly on contractual commitments and anticipated transactions. They seem to pay little attention to exposures that mature in more than one year, what we refer to as economic/competitive exposures. For instance, 53% of firms that use derivatives hold only short-dated derivatives that mature within 180 days or before the end of the fiscal year.

WHY DO FIRMS' MANAGE THEIR RISKS?

To evaluate whether firms use risk management in a way consistent with academic theories, some studies rely on firm-specific information about risk management practices. These studies take two forms; one is the use of surveys of firms, while others attempt to relate the cross-sectional variation in firm exposure to infer firms' hedging practices and success.

Some of the imperfections that exist and motivate firms to hedge in order to increase firm value are the existence of taxes, the maintenance of high investment, and the avoidance of financial distress. Nance, Smith, and Smithson (1993) asked firms in the Fortune 500 and/or the S&P 400 whether they used derivatives and why. The authors document that firms with derivatives have significantly more investment tax credits than those without, and are more likely to have taxable income such that their tax rate increases with income. Firms with derivatives have significantly higher research and development (R&D) expenses as a fraction of firm value. Distress costs are likely to be more important for firms that have higher R&D expenditures because they face greater information asymmetries. Also, firms with more R&D expenditures are more likely to need substantial funds for investment.

Surprisingly perhaps, firms with derivatives and firms without derivatives do not significantly differ in leverage and interest coverage ratios. Everything else being equal, we would expect firms with higher leverage or a lower interest coverage ratio to be more subject to financial distress and hence to benefit more from risk management. In the Nance, Smith, and Smithson (1993) study, variables that measure the probability of financial distress do not seem to matter, however. It may be that firms with higher leverage or lower interest coverage have less cashflow volatility and lower costs of financial distress. In this case, it would be hard to make predictions about the use of derivatives by these firms because higher leverage would push them to use more derivatives while lower volatility and lower costs of financial distress would push them in the other direction. Firms with derivatives and those without do not differ in their market-to-book ratios in the Nance, Smith, and Smithson (1993) study. Finally, they use various regressions with different combinations of explanatory variables, they find that in general the probability that a firm uses derivatives increases with firm value, the ratio of R&D to firm value, and investment tax credits. Géczy, Minton, and Schrand (1997) study the publicly traded Fortune 500 firms for which data are available for the fiscal years 1990 and 1991 and find similar results along with financial distress as a key reason for firms to hedge risk through derivatives.

INDUSTRY LEVEL RISK MANAGEMENT USAGE

Risk management is more easily studied in some industries than others. Part of the problem with evaluating risk management by firms is determining the real exposures that are faced by a firm. There are a few studies that focus on industries that have clear exposures that can be examined.

Tufano (1996) explores the determinants of hedging in the gold mining industry. Because gold mining firms report very precisely how much they hedge, Tufano can compute the fraction of gold production over the next three years that is covered by risk management activities. There is wide variation in risk management practices within the industry. Few firms hedge nothing on average, but no firm hedges everything; the typical firm hedges 22.9% of its three-year production.

Why does hedging differ so much across firms? As the findings cover many industries, leverage does not seem to matter. Firms that explore more hedge less, which is rather surprising. Firms with more reserves also appear to hedge less. Finally, firms with more cash balances hedge less as well. Firms whose managers own more shares are firms that hedge more. The private benefits of hedging for management are that it bears less risk. Finally, management hedges less when it holds more options. This evidence shows that the hedging practices of firms depend crucially on the incentives of management. If managers own a lot of shares and these shares represent a large fraction of their wealth, it is not surprising that managers would want to reduce the riskiness of their shares.

Haushalter (2000) studies risk management in the oil and gas industry from 1992 to 1994. Like Tufano (1996), he tries to explain the hedge ratio of the industry. Derivatives in the oil and gas industry are more effective at hedging oil and gas extracted in some locations than others. Haushalter (2000) finds that firms that extract in locations where hedging can be undertaken more effectively tend to hedge more. Unlike other researchers, Haushalter (2000) finds strong results showing that firms hedge more as their leverage increases.

RISK MANAGEMENT, RISK, AND VALUE

The more direct question is whether the use of derivatives affects firm risk and value. Guay (1999) looks at firms that start using derivatives. He constructs a sample of 254 firms that start using derivatives from one year to the next. Firms are found to experience a significant decrease in volatility as they start using derivatives. Firms using interest-rate derivatives experience a decrease of 22% in the interest-rate exposure of their common stock; and firms using exchange-rate derivatives experience a decrease of 11% in the foreign exchange exposure of their common stock. When he investigates why firms start hedging programs, Guay finds that larger firms, firms with higher leverage, firms with lower interest coverage, firms with higher market-to-book ratios, and firms with greater operating income volatility are all more likely to start a hedging programme. He finds that the change in interest rate exposure over the previous three years plays a significant role in explaining why firms enter a hedging programme. In another study that looks at the impact of derivatives use on exposures, Tufano (1998) finds that hedging reduces the exposure of gold mining firms to gold prices.

Allayannis and Weston (2001) considers whether firms that use foreign exchange derivatives are worth more. They examine 720 large US non-financial firms between 1990 and 1995. They estimate for these firms a valuation measure called Tobin's q, which is roughly the market value of the firm over the book value of the firm's assets. If a firm has a higher Tobin's q, it creates more value out of the assets it purchases. The mean Tobin's q of firms with foreign sales that use derivatives is 1.27; the mean Tobin's q for firms with foreign sales that do not use derivatives is 1.10. The difference between the two means is highly significant. This evidence indicates that firms that use foreign exchange derivatives are worth more.

CONCLUSION

Corporations use risk management extensively, but the use and strategy varies across firms. Consistent with risk management theory, firms hedge for reasons such as taxes, financial distress and managerial incentives. The consensus evidence is that firms with more tax carry-forwards and more tax credits hedge more, presumably to preserve the value of these tax benefits. Significant results are that firms hedge less when they have greater interest coverage and hedge more when they have greater leverage. There is a strong relation between R&D expenses and hedging. Finally, the evidence seems fairly consistent that firms whose managers hold more equity hedge more.

Also, the evidence indicates that large firms are more likely to practice risk management with derivatives, firms tend to hedge cashflow and accounting earnings rather than market value, they focus on short-term instruments, and firms typically do not hedge systematically, but rather practice selective hedging taking their views into account when assuming derivatives positions. Most commonly, firms determine the approach to managing risk based on the time horizon of the exposure.

BIBLIOGRAPHY

Allayannis, G., and J. Weston, 2001, "The Use of Foreign Currency Derivatives and Firm Value", *Review of Financial Studies* 14, pp. 243–76.

Bodnar, G., G. Hayt, and R. Marston, 1996, "Wharton 1995 Survey of Derivatives Usage by U.S. Non-Financial Firms", *Financial Management*, 25 n.pp.

Bodnar, G., G. Hayt, R. Marston, and C. Smithson, 1995, "Wharton Survey of Derivatives Usage by U.S. Non-Financial Firms", *Financial Management*, 24 n.pp.

Chowdhry, B., and J. Howe, 1999, "Corporate Risk Management for Multinational Corporations: Financial and Operational Hedging Policies", *European Finance Review* 2, pp. 229–46.

Dolde, W., 1993, "The Trajectory of Corporate Financial Risk Management", *Journal of Applied Corporate Finance* 6, pp. 33–41.

Géczy, C., B. Minton, and C. Schrand, 1997, "Why Firms use Currency Derivatives", *Journal of Finance* 52, pp. 1323–55.

Guay, W., 1999, "The Impact of Derivatives on Firm Risk: An Empirical Examination of New Derivatives Users", *Journal of Accounting and Economics* 26, pp. 319–51.

Haushaulter, G. D., 2000, "Financing Policy, Basic Risk, and Corporate Hedging: Evidence from Oil and Gas Producers", *Journal of Finance* 55, pp. 107–52.

Modigliani, F., and M. Miller, 1958, "The Cost of Capital, Corporation Finance and the Theory of Investment", *American Economic Review* 48, pp. 261–97.

Nance, D. R., C. W. Smith, Jr., and C. W. Smithson, 1993, "On the Determinants of Corporate Hedging", *Journal of Finance* 48, pp. 267–84.

Stulz, R. M., 2002, *Risk Management and Derivatives* (Mason, OH: Southwestern College Publishing).

Stulz, R. M., and R. Williamson, 2000, "Identifying and Quantifying Exposures", in G. W. Brown and D. H. Chew (eds), *Corporate Risk: Strategies and Management* (London: Risk Books).

Tufano, P., 1996, "Who Manages Risk? An Empirical Investigation of Risk Management Practices in the Gold Mining Industry", *Journal of Finance* 51, pp. 1097–137.

Tufano, P., 1998, "The Determinants of Stock Price Exposure: Financial Engineering and the Gold Mining Industry", *Journal of Finance* 53, pp. 1015–52.

Williamson, R., 2001, "Exchange Rate Exposure and Competition: Evidence from the Automotive Industry", *Journal of Financial Economics* 59, pp. 441–75.

23

Risk in US Energy Markets

Edward N. Krapels

Energy Security Analysis, Inc

From the standpoint of risk management, energy markets might as well be divided into three different worlds. In the oil world, there are several deep, liquid, and trusted futures markets underlying a large and diverse array of over-the-counter providers. Deals are conducted globally and risk management has spread from the avocation of a few to a common part of professional practise.

In the natural gas world, there are three fundamentally different continents. In the United States, there is a vibrant gas market that has withstood the collapse of its biggest derivative provider, largely because the good health of the gas futures market made that provider less critical than many thought it was. In Europe, there is a nascent gas-on-gas market, but the bulk of gas prices are still determined by oil prices. Gas risk management, therefore, is conducted largely within the oil space, using Brent as a basis for many of the deals done. In Asia, most gas markets are liquefied natural gas (LNG)-based, and there is barely a market to speak of. Most deals are long-term, with take or pay provisions that look like refugees from the American market of the 1970s.

In electricity, there is chaos in virtually all markets except the east coast of the United States, where the PJM Interconnection is indicating that it has found the combination of regulatory structures that enable true power markets to evolve. PJM is well into its first decade of existence, and indeed it will be asserted in this chapter that it provides the framework within which risk management practitioners can develop their business for power sellers and buyers.

BACKGROUND

The past few years have vividly demonstrated the broad array of risks in US power markets, from the appalling destruction of a major load centre that occurred on September 11, 2001 to the complex array of market and regulatory phenomena that plagued the California power market, to the virtual collapse of power marketing companies that had positioned themselves as experts, not only in electricity trading, but masters of electricity risk management. It turns out that many of them did not understand their risks sufficiently well to avoid bankruptcy at worst, and an enormous loss of shareholder wealth at best.

The US power market is following a typical course for a deregulated market, with one significant exception. Because much regulation is still conducted at the state level, an assortment of deregulation models has been designed and allowed to evolve. Thus there are models in PJM, California, New England, New York, and Texas.

The models are quite different, as we shall briefly review below, and as a result it is impossible to review the state of risk management in the US power market as a whole. Risks manifest themselves differently in different power markets. In 2000, a combination of risks – weather, input fuels, and regulatory – led to a sustained increase in power prices in California that quickly produced a credit risk that has brought several California utilities to the brink of bankruptcy. That, in turn, led to actual and proposed changes in state and federal regulation. Given some states' disagreement with the federal intention to impose a "standard market design" (SMD) on all areas of the United States, there is now regulatory risk of a severity that may significantly impair investment in electricity in general and the California energy markets in particular.

Thus, electricity market risks manifest themselves quite differently across the various US wholesale power markets. The United States can be divided into areas where power market commodity forces are allowed to exist (to whatever degree) and where they are not, as follows.

1. *California* – short-and-medium term commodity price risk has been significantly reduced by the Federal Energy Regulatory Commission (FERC) regulation. California is now trying to launch a new market system. Opinion differs about the effects of this regulation on long-term risk in generation and transmission investment.

2. *New England, the mid-Atlantic, and New York* – electric commodity price risk determined by market forces with "independent system operator" (ISO) supervision leading to development of hub and spoke power price indexes in day-ahead and real-time markets, as well as transmission payments and hedging contracts that form the basis of "location marginal pricing" (LMP), on which more below. Significant levels of investment in generation have occurred in areas where siting restrictions are not prohibitive, and numerous proposals for merchant transmission investments have come forward.

3. *Remainder* – commodity price risk in wholesale power markets determined by bilateral market trades between wholesale market participants. Significant levels of investment in generation and transmission in most areas with important state-by-state differences created by comparative ease of siting.

In each of these markets, power buyers and sellers face different types of uncertainty about prices over time.

1. In California and the Western Systems Coordinating Council (WSCC), the primary risk is now regulatory, as market participants are uncertain as to the duration of FERC price controls and about how quickly SMD will follow them, if at all. The degree of regulatory risk is so high as to block development of normal market procedures and comprehensive hedging programs. Some limited hedging activities can take place in the most liquid hubs.

2. In the northeastern markets, there is a relatively strong consensus that energy market prices will be set by well-understood LMP rules. There is some uncertainty, however, about which specific protocols the SMD process will apply to the host of energy, capacity, ancillary services, and transmission market

transactions that constitute a functioning power market. Hedging activities have become more commonplace but there are still numerous significant obstacles to the development of a "best practises" commodity market.

3. In other pools, the absence of a strong ISO and the slow march towards acceptable multi-state and multi-utility regional transmission organisations (RTOs) has created an extremely Balkanised power market, with a few very strong hubs (eg, Into Cinergy) but generally poor conditions for the evolution of best practises hedging programs.

As each of these power markets evolve, they have to develop contracts transacting real-time, hourly, daily, weekly, monthly, quarterly, seasonal, annual and multi-year power flows. In principle, a survey of power market transactions across the United States and Canada should reveal a nation-wide array of thousands of transactions governing billions of dollars of sales and purchases with different timeframes. In practice, it reveals an patchwork quilt with a few strong markets where hedging is becoming routine while the majority of regions are still struggling to establish rules that work.

POLICY DEVELOPMENTS

In the absence of any federal legislation since the 1992 Energy Policy Act, FERC has been instrumental in providing a broad framework for electric market organisation through two pivotal orders – Order 888 in 1996 and Order 2000 – and their subsequent filings and hearings. Out of that process has emerged the variety of electric market models organised as ISOs, including PJM, NEISO (New England), NYISO (New York), ERCOT (most of Texas), and California. In addition, a number of utilities in the Midwest have organised into the Midwest ISO (MISO), which has agreed to a merger with the Southwest Power Pool (SPP).

With Order 2000, FERC emphasised the value to the economy of organising the US power market into a smaller number of regional transmission organisations (RTOs). This value was believed to emerge from a consolidation of the US electric system from one with "140 control areas, 10 regional reliability councils, 23 security coordinators, and 5 regional transmission groups" to one with a small number of RTOs.[1] In the course of subsequent discussion among market participants, a number of potential market combinations into potential RTOs have emerged. The number of RTOs that will ultimately exist is still unclear.

FERC noted that there would be a large number of operational and other benefits that would allow markets to emerge in electricity, and bring the benefits of competitive markets to this traditionally regulated sector, as it has to other sectors such as airlines and telecommunications.

GOVERNANCE

Electricity markets are regulated at both the federal and state levels, with the federal government focused largely on wholesale markets and interstate trade and the state governments focused largely on retail markets and siting issues. There has obviously been an array of governance issues pertaining to electric markets, ranging from the turmoil in the California power market to the allegations of improper trading activities by power marketing companies.

These market problems are among a variety of reasons why the regulation/deregulation dichotomy is inadequate to explain the governance of power markets, even under the proposed RTO regimes. A better characterisation is that there will be varied amounts of regulatory supervision among the many business activities involved in taking power from the source to the sink. Siting of power plants and transmission lines will continue to be heavily regulated. Operations of power plants within the RTO will be subject to a large array of RTO rules and procedures. Access to transmission lines within and between RTOs will be governed by an extensive set of constraints and privileges. Participation in RTO bidding – a crucial part of the deregulated market paradigm – will be subject to strict procedures and limits.

The sale of electric power to the residential sector will remain largely governed by state governments, whose preferred policies will range from extremely closely regulated to comprehensively deregulated. Figure 1 developed by the US Energy Information Administration, presents one characterisation of the restructuring policy process of all of the states. Within the footprint of the MISO-SPP market, there are some ten states where the restructuring policy is not active and four where it is. Within the PJM footprint, restructuring is actively being pursued by all of the states.[2]

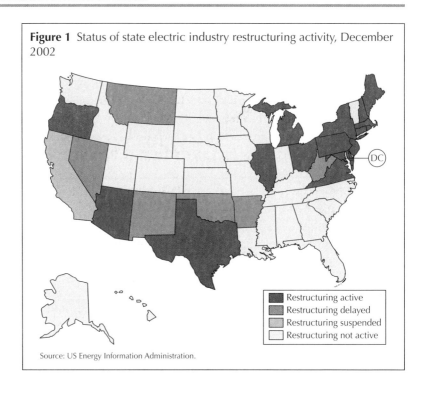

Figure 1 Status of state electric industry restructuring activity, December 2002

Source: US Energy Information Administration.

A COASIAN MODEL – BEST MARKETS ARE CLEARLY AND INTELLIGENTLY REGULATED

Even with this diversity of regulatory approaches, the events in the power markets over the last five years will inevitably produce a new commitment to effective regulation, *within which* market forces will be allowed to exert their powerful influence. To some, this may seem like a contradiction, but there has long been a tradition in economic theory for the coexistence of regulation and market forces.[3]

The Nobel Prize winning economist R. H. Coase is among those who has called attention to a paradox in the modern emergence of commodity and stock exchanges.

"These exchanges, often used by economists as examples of a perfect market and perfect competition, are markets in which transactions are highly regulated (and this is quite apart from any governmental regulation that there may be). It suggests, I think correctly, that for anything approaching perfect competition to exist, an intricate system of rules and regulations would normally be needed."[4]

The energy markets provide evidence to support Coase's argument: both the natural gas and the crude oil futures contracts traded on the New York Mercantile Exchange (NYMEX) are marvels of efficient markets whose price-setting dynamics have seldom been questioned.

Coase's argument also provides a framework for the development of RTOs power markets. Coase argues that any market develops to *facilitate* exchange, "to reduce the cost of carrying out exchange transactions". This will be one of the benchmarks whereby power markets will be judged.

The following pages will focus on the development of prices and practises in the PJM Interconnection, contrasted with those in the Midwest, where an ISO is in the process of being set up, and where power trading is still in a much more primitive stage.

THE LOCATION MARGINAL PRICING FRAMEWORK

The new FERC standard marker design relies on the development of location-based marginal prices. In the LMP paradigm, the electricity market consists of arrays of load and generation nodes connected by transmission lines of defined capacity. Generators are dispatched by an independent system operator in accordance with their bids subject to the availability of transmission capacity to carry their power to load areas. When a low-cost bidder's power cannot be transmitted to market, the power from the next highest bidder (again subject to transmission availability) is accepted instead.

Buyers and sellers can do business with each other directly – by executing so-called bilateral contracts – or they can buy and sell in the day-ahead and real time markets administered by the independent system operator (ISO) or regional transmission operator (RTO). The prices of the bilateral contracts are negotiated between buyer and seller. The prices emerging from the day ahead and real time operations administered by the ISO or RTO emerge from the bids.

In this bid-based market, prices in the pool-administered markets are determined through the bidding process by many factors, such as the fuel used to generate electricity, the capital cost of the power plant and how it was financed, the operations and maintenance costs of the facilities, and the financial plans and strategies of the bidding entities.

There is a similar bidding process involving consumers or their agents. They bid their demand levels into the daily auctions, determining the price of that part of their load that had not been procured via bilateral contracts with power sellers.

In the centre of this dynamic is the independent system operator or regional transmission organisation, responsible for maintaining the system's security and balance. Demand changes continuously, requiring continuous adjustment of dispatch in real time by the RTO.

It stands to reason in such a system that market-determined prices will constantly change, and as they change, the value of transmission between nodes will also change. If node A has a US$20 price and node B a US$30 price, the *ex ante* value of being able to sell from the cheap to the dear zone is US$10. It would be economically reasonable – all other things held constant – for the generator in node A to pay up to US$9.99 to the transmission owner to sell power in node B.

This intuitively reasonable description, however, may be misleading in the case of electricity, because in all practical respects the power generated by a particular seller does not flow directly to the buyer. Instead, in an AC system, power flows in an undifferentiated stream within the nodes, out of the nodes into neighbouring areas, within that area, and out of that area, with the inter-nodal or zonal or area flows determined in part by the capacity of transmission lines, and in part by the overall level of power flowing through adjacent areas.

So, obviously, transmission congestion and line losses are one determinant of the difference in the price of power between two interconnected nodes. The other determinants are the supply-demand situation within each node, and the differences in bidding behaviour by the respective generators in each area.

In practice, generators can sell their power via bilateral contracts with specific customers, or they can offer their power into day-ahead and real-time (balancing) markets. These are different transactions, each with its own transmission implications. Except in direct current (DC) systems, a *bilateral sale* in the RTO will not result in power flowing directly from seller to buyer. Instead, it entails the contracted injection of power on the part of the generator and the contracted withdrawal of power on the part of the buyer, at a price. The deal entails financial commitments between the parties, but not power flows directly between them. Those are handled by the RTO.

Within the RTO, transmission constraints will have enormous effects on the supply-demand-price balances in the constituent zones and sub-zones. The PJM platform provides a mechanism for hedging the price effects of the constraints via the market for financial transmission rights (FTR). The FTR is a hedging device by which parties can lock in the virtual cost of transmission, so that a seller in one zone can conduct business with a buyer in another zone without taking on the risk that unanticipated changes in supply, demand, or transmission capacity will change the expected spread of the transaction.

PJM MARKET STRUCTURE

In the PJM region, the demand for power in 2001 peaked at 54,030 megawatts (MW) at 3 pm on August 9th. It was one of the hottest and sultriest days of the year in the mid-Atlantic, and air conditioners were on full blast. The hourly peak price (the price for each hour from 8 am to 11 pm) averaged US$293/MW.

The lowest demand for power in the PJM grid was 18,549 MW, which occurred on April 15th at 5 am in the morning. Temperatures were mild, and people may have turned off all their lights and appliances to save money after sending in their tax payments! The hourly off-peak price averaged US$20 that morning, and at that price level only a distinct subset of PJM's generators could afford to operate.

The PJM power generation system – as Figure 2 illustrates – features about 13,000 MW of nuclear capacity, and about 20,000 MW

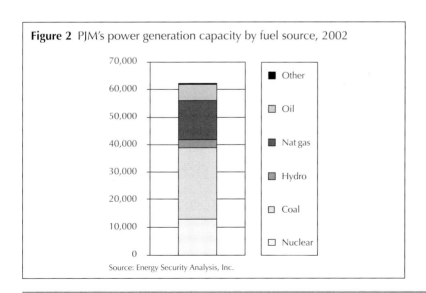

Figure 2 PJM's power generation capacity by fuel source, 2002

Source: Energy Security Analysis, Inc.

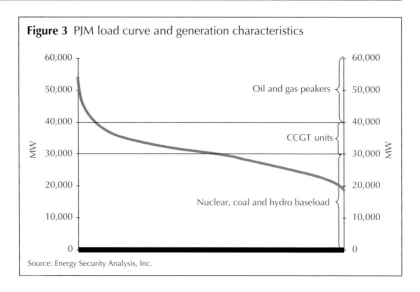

Figure 3 PJM load curve and generation characteristics

Source: Energy Security Analysis, Inc.

of coal capacity. These are the fuels of PJM's baseload plants, and they play a pivotal role in maintaining relatively low energy prices in PJM (and, as we shall see later, elsewhere in MISO as well).

During 2001, coal and nuclear power sources were capable of generating sufficient power to meet PJM's needs for 6,300 hours out of the total 8,760 hours of requirements. When PJM's load was less than 35,000 MW in 2001, the energy price averaged US$27/MW. When the load exceeded 35,000 MW, the price averaged US$58 per MWh.

As can be seen in Figure 3, PJM now has approximately 8,000 MW of modern combined cycle gas turbines (CCGTs). These gas-fired plants compete for various parts of this market. When gas prices are comparatively low (less than US$2.50 per MCF), PJM's new CCGTs can begin to compete when load is as low as 20,000 MW; when gas prices are high (more than US$4 per MCF), they may not be dispatched until load exceeds 40,000 MW. PJM's oldest peaking plants – oil and gas fired – meet the power requirements when load is in excess of 45,000 MW.

PJM INTERNAL MARKET DYNAMICS
The PJM market can be subdivided into a variety of different submarkets. PJM consists of a number of different utility service areas, whose boundaries have been determined by business history and

by recent merger activity. While this way of looking at the PJM zones is convenient, it does not accurately depict PJM's geography of electricity. Major electricity transmission lines have been built over the years in such a way that there are a variety of bulk power pathways that do not precisely coincide with these utility area designations.

Moreover, PJM's LMP system facilitates buying, selling, and pricing at hundreds of individual generation points, load buses, and interchanges within each zone, so that prices can reflect the best available information and expectations at all times. Given that essential feature of the LMP system, a zonal price is nothing more than the average of the prices at these hundreds of individual pricing stations.

While zonal pricing averages are therefore a gross simplification of the complex markets that exist within each of these designated PJM zones, it is natural nevertheless to examine PJM's internal pricing dynamics in terms of the zones. Certainly, state regulators and the retail customers of the utilities who continue to serve them under the variety of state regulatory systems that comprise PJM have a strong interest in the evolution of prices within each of the zones. And, any assessment of the effects of extending LMP pricing to broader areas outside of PJM is bound to include a similar zonal orientation.

Figures 4 and 5 present the generation capacity by type in four of PJM's transmission zones – PSEG (northern New Jersey), JCPL (northwest and southern New Jersey), PECO (Philadelphia area), and PenElec (western Pennsylvania). The PenElec area is dominated by coal, PECO has a mix in which nuclear is most prominent, while the JCPL and PSEG zones have a concentration of natural gas capacity.

Each of the zones also has a capacity to "import" power from other PJM zones and areas outside of PJM, and to "export" power to other PJM zones or areas outside of PJM. These import and export flows are determined both by economics – as manifest through participation of buyers and sellers in PJM's bilateral and ISO-administered markets – and by transmission capacities and interdependencies.

In 2001, the net effect of all of these differences and linkages yielded an average day-ahead market price of US$33.04/MWh in PSEG, US$31.38 in JCPL, US$32.03 in PECO, and US$30.46 in PenElec. This roughly US$2.50 *average* disparity between the highest

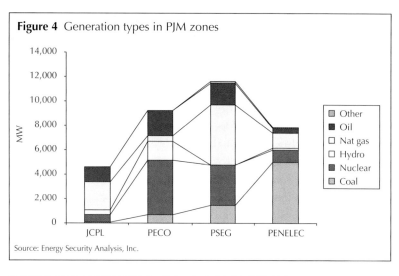

Figure 4 Generation types in PJM zones

Source: Energy Security Analysis, Inc.

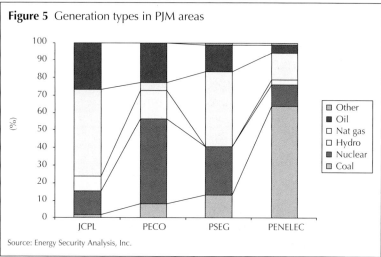

Figure 5 Generation types in PJM areas

Source: Energy Security Analysis, Inc.

and the lowest zonal prices in PJM masks higher *seasonal* differences in summer, when the limits on the transmission system's capacity to bring western power east are most binding. The western power would tend to flow to the east as long as the overall cost of generating power from coal sources is lower than generating power from natural gas and oil, which tend to be more prominent in the input fuel mix in the eastern zones.

The essence of this assessment of PJM's zonal prices is that they are explainable on fundamental grounds. That does not mean they are predictable – the price on any given hour in any given part of PJM depends on a complex mix of prices of the input fuels, on the exigencies of the weather, on outages of power plants and transmission lines, and on how buyers and sellers choose to bid in the auctions that constitute the market process. Taken together, these dynamics make PJM (and any other functioning power market's) prices as difficult to predict as, for example, the price of a particular stock in the New York Stock Exchange.

That unavoidable difficulty of prediction is, of course, the essence of market risk which, in a market society like that of the United States, can be mitigated by individuals and companies in a variety of ways, one of which will be discussed in the next section.

To conclude this section, while there has been much discussion about electricity pricing in other areas, in PJM the prices that have emerged from electric trading in the region as a whole, and in each of its constituent load zones, have transparent economic causes.

FIXED TRANSMISSION RIGHTS: PJM's TRANSMISSION CONSTRAINT HEDGING MECHANISM

If differences in zonal (and, be extension, nodal) energy prices are explainable but not easily predictable, anyone who would buy or sell power faces financial risk. In power, that risk can be confined to changes in the price within a given area. Thus, if it so desires, a generator located in PenElec zone may choose to sell power only within that zone. In that case, its power price risk can be largely defined as stemming from the dynamics of supply, demand, imports and exports within that zone.

In PJM, that same generator may, however, also choose to sell its power to a load serving entity or a trading company in the PSEG zone. By participating in the PJM interconnection, the generator has the right to make such a sale, subject to the condition that it does so according to PJM's protocols for such sales. In essence, that protocol was designed to maximise the value of the existing transmission lines by assigning the rights to capacity on those lines, and then establishing a market whereby those rights can be bought and sold. These "fixed transmission rights" (FTRs) are "financial contracts that entitle the holder to a stream of revenues (or charges) based on the (day ahead market) hourly energy price differences across the path".[5]

Table 1 Simplified example of hedging effect of FTRs

	Seller in PenElec zone (in US$)		Buyer in PSEG zone (in US$)
1. Bilateral deal	30		30
2. Assumed zonal clearing prices in PJM day-ahead market	28		35
3. Zonal price difference	7	←——→	7
	If neither side holds FTR		
	Seller		**Buyer**
4. Congestion cost	(7)		0
5. Net position	23		30
	Buyer buys FTR		
	Seller		**Buyer**
Price of FTR	(2)		
FTR credit	7		
Net position	28		30

Thus, any company that owns an FTR on a given path has a stake in the relative day-ahead market economics of the points on either side of the line. Assume that a generator in the PenElec zone contracts to sell energy to a load serving entity in PSEG via a one-year bilateral contract. Based on average 2001 price information, the PenElec price might be expected to be US$30.46, and the PSE&G price US$33.04. Neither party, of course, can be certain that this same US$2.58/MW price difference will prevail during the contract term of their new transaction. The FTR between the two points is financial contract, and thus the buyer or the seller in this transaction should be willing – if they believed the future prices would be exactly like the past – to pay up to US$2.58 for the FTR.

In the bilateral part of this transaction, assume the seller will make a commitment to the buyer at a stipulated price. As this particular transaction is executed in the PJM-administered market, the seller will obtain whatever the LMP price is in PenElec, the buyer pays whatever the LMP price is in PSEG, and whichever owns the FTR will get the payment (or pay the charge) equivalent to the price difference between the sink and the source. Table 1 presents one example in which a seller located in one zone buys an FTR in the secondary market as part of a strategy to sell to a buyer located in another zone.

The possibility of such a transaction should make the buyer and the seller aware of the world outside of each company's immediate utility zone. It draws attention to the transmission constraints that prevent them from dealing directly with one another. And, over time, the price differences between the zones should motivate investors to either build generation or transmission to capitalise on the differences.

BENEFITS OF PJM MARKET DESIGN AND EXPERIENCE

The array of rules and regulations that is today's PJM market has evolved over a decade of incremental implementation, adjustment, and reform. The PJM market has now weathered a sufficient variety of market conditions, increases and decreases in market participation by traders, regulatory scrutiny, information technology overhauls and other tests to create a widespread sense of confidence that it is a stable and flexible platform for the area which it serves.

As such, it is reasonable to examine how one might measure the benefits of its creation and perpetuation. To keep this important question within reasonable bounds, we will use R. H. Coase's trenchant formulation of the purpose of a market – "to reduce the cost of carrying out transactions" – subject to an electricity particular requirement that the supply be kept reliable. The transactions that are carried out in electricity are the same as in any other market – buying, selling, investing in new assets, and retiring assets from service.

The typical measures of a market's efficiency are volume (see Figure 6) and open interest. In these measures, bigger is typically better. In these terms, trading at PJM's western hub has surpassed by a significant amount trading in other power hubs. This measurement is complicated by the fact that, at PJM, volume includes transactions conducted with the ISO, as well as in the various bilateral trading platforms such as the Intercontinental Exchange. Most of PJM's day-ahead transactions are now made on the PJM platform itself, whereas the volume of other transactions – like Cinergy – is confined to what takes place in the various bilateral markets because there is at present no ISO-run Cinergy forward market.

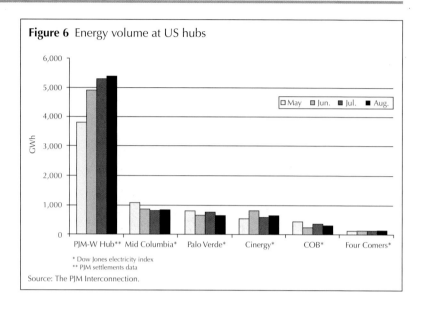

Figure 6 Energy volume at US hubs

* Dow Jones electricity index
** PJM settlements data

Source: The PJM Interconnection.

Market liquidity refers to the ability to trade on short notice, at low cost. Liquidity has both a price and a quantity dimension. The price dimension, known as the spread, refers to the cost of entering and liquidating a position (a "round-trip"), and is measured by the difference in the price at which traders are willing to sell (the ask), and the price at which they are willing to buy (the bid) in small volumes. The cost of buying or selling contracts is usually measured as half the spread, plus commission.

In the power over-the-counter markets (as in stock markets, and some options markets), firm bid and ask quotes are offered by market participants who have the capability to be market makers. The quantity dimension of liquidity, known as market depth, refers to the ease with which large buy or sell orders can be moved, and is measured by the relationship between the size of the buy (and respectively, sell) order and its effect on the ask (and respectively, bid) price. A market can be liquid along the dimension of low execution costs (ie, low bid-ask spread) for small orders, yet be too shallow to handle large orders (ie, large players cannot use the market without turning prices sharply against them).

Although we usually think of greater trading volume as indicating greater liquidity, this need not be the case. If volume rises because of increased participation by commercials for hedging

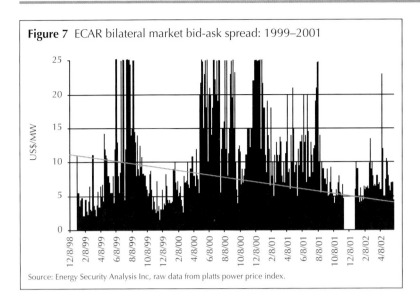

Figure 7 ECAR bilateral market bid-ask spread: 1999–2001

Source: Energy Security Analysis Inc, raw data from platts power price index.

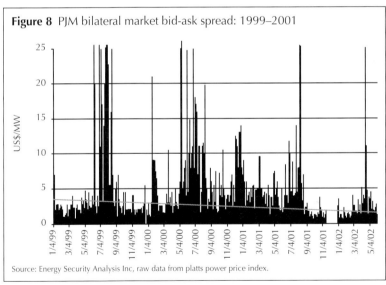

Figure 8 PJM bilateral market bid-ask spread: 1999–2001

Source: Energy Security Analysis Inc, raw data from platts power price index.

purposes, then market depth should increase, and bid-ask spreads should narrow. In contrast, if volume increases in times of market turmoil, then increased price volatility will usually cause traders to widen their spreads and decrease depth to reflect the heightened risk of large losses over very short time periods on their inventory of futures contracts.

We evaluated the PJM bilateral market's liquidity using the day-ahead bid-ask data from *Power Markets Week* for several bilateral markets. One such comparison is shown in Figures 7 and 8 that compare the 1999–2001 bid-ask spreads of the PJM bilateral market with that of ECAR, another widely traded power contract.

The mean bid-ask spread of the PJM bilateral market in the 1999–2001 period was US$3.21 and for the ECAR bilateral market was US$7.46/MWh. The standard deviation of the PJM spread was US$10.28/MWh and for ECAR was US$28.75. Applying the same test to the widely traded Cinergy market yields an average bid-ask spread of US$8.87 and a standard deviation of US$42.88.

This assessment of PJM bid-ask spreads could be extended further and fruitfully applied to PJM's internal auctions as well, via a careful analysis of its voluminous bid data. But in this case it would be difficult to compare PJM with the midwestern markets that are the focus of this study. We believe the comparatively good performance of the PJM bilateral market in these terms is due in large measure to the success of the PJM ISO-governed market. It gives market participants enough confidence to keep their bids and asks reasonably close (for electricity), and as is evident in Figure 8, the trend towards a narrowing of the bid-ask is pronounced, which is another positive sign.

While even the PJM bid-ask spreads are quite large, by normal commodity standards, they are due to the inevitable peculiarities of electricity as an unstorable item. Moreover, it is likely that the financial difficulties that the energy trading community experienced in late 2001–2002 will cause the spreads to widen again. Over a long period of time, however, once this credit crunch has been endured and given more efficient demand adjustment mechanisms, we can expect these spreads and the volatility to decline further, as long as market participants have confidence.

That leads us to a final point on the finances of the power market. In the financial turmoil that beset the power industry in 2001 and 2002, many of the single-company trading platforms that emerged in previous years experienced significant declines in volume. This occurred primarily because power buyers and sellers became increasingly concerned about the exposure to a single company's credit that accompanied trading on such platforms. This decline in trading volume on individual company platforms was accompanied by an increase in trading volume in exchanges with better credit standing. PJM as a trading platform for day ahead and real time power transactions continues to stand out as a safe harbour for all market participants that are eligible to participate in PJM activities.

INVESTING IN PJM

The other obvious form of expression of market confidence in PJM is the amount of new generation capacity built since the market opening in the 1990s. Table 2 presents the expansion in PJM states' generation capacity since 1990. Since 1990, more than 8,000 MW of new capacity has been added to the PJM states; from 2002 to 2005, another 9,000 MW will be completed.

To be certain, PJM is not unique in enjoying a surge of new generation investments. It participated in a national boom in that business. Now, in fact, it appears that PJM on the aggregate has more than enough capacity to meet reserve requirements. A significant period of time can elapse before the need for substantially more becomes urgent. We nevertheless believe that the scale of construction in PJM, when compared with certain other areas of the country, can be seen as a sign of confidence by investors in the effectiveness of the PJM market design.

Table 2 PJM generation capacity expansion

1990–2000	5,805
2001	2,251
2002	4,241
2003	3,383
2004	1,295
2005	788

Sources: 1990–2001, EIA; 2002–2005, ESAI.

MARKET EXPERIENCES

During the time that so much attention has been given to the difficulties experienced by the California power market, there have been several other power markets that have functioned without incident. As shown in Figure 9, the United States has evolved a number of liquid bilateral power trading hubs (marked with ⊗'s in

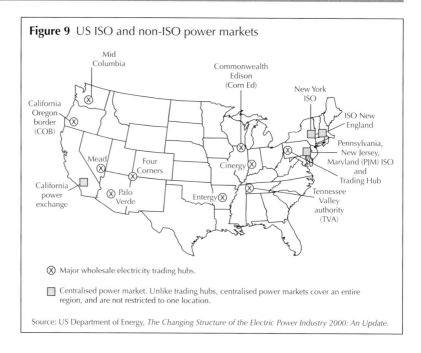

Figure 9 US ISO and non-ISO power markets

⊗ Major wholesale electricity trading hubs.

☐ Centralised power market. Unlike trading hubs, centralised power markets cover an entire region, and are not restricted to one location.

Source: US Department of Energy, *The Changing Structure of the Electric Power Industry 2000: An Update.*

Figure 9) as well as five power pools. While the California market design experiment failed, the New York and Nepool markets functioned sufficiently well to survive and PJM functioned so well that its market operations have become the standard that FERC has encouraged others to adopt PJM procedures. Thus, MISO-SPP are likely to embrace many of PJMs practises and procedures, while Nepool has committed to implement LMP pricing in coordination with either PJM and New York or with New York.

Whatever the details of the application of PJM rules to the proposed joint and common market with MISO-SPP, when that market does begin to function, there will be LMPs and FTRs in a market area spanning from Fargo to Newark (both New Jersey and Delaware!). While the specifics of the MISO-PJM-SPP market rules have not yet been spelled out, in principle the markets will be knit together by uniform transmission charges, hedging mechanisms, interconnection procedures, and trading rules.

As a result of this knitting together of these previously separate power markets, over time, the prices in each of the constituent markets – for energy, for capacity, and for ancillary services – will begin to influence one another. Just as in today's PJM market where the supply and demand for power in New Jersey is relevant to the price in Maryland, in tomorrow's joint and common MISO-PJM-SPP market the price of power in New Jersey will be relevant to the price in Illinois and in Oklahoma.

EVOLUTION OF POWER PRICES IN
THE MISO-PJM-SPP MARKET

PJM has had a fully functional locational pricing market yielding a rich array of information about energy prices since June 2000. Energy can be bought in PJM via bilateral transactions between principals, via the PJM-administered day-ahead market, or via the PJM real-time market. The prices in each of these markets have varied over time. Using monthly average energy prices as one benchmark, PJM prices have ranged between US$23 (in December) at a low and US$54/MWh (in August) as a high in 2001. In 2001, the price in the day-ahead market was US$0.37/MWh higher than the price in the real-time market.[6]

In general terms, PJM prices have been determined by nuclear and coal generation plants that provide more than half of the peak requirements, and by gas-fired plants in the so-called "mid-merit" dispatch range.

PJM energy prices also exhibit a tendency to increase as power moves from the relatively less densely populated West to the more densely populated East. Like virtually all other RTOs, PJM has some load pockets and some generation pockets where limits on transmission capacity influence the price at which power can be bought and sold. These zonal pricing differences should be seen as a natural texture, the warp and woof of a power market in an advanced industrial economy.

In the Midwest, prices have not had the opportunity to congeal into pool-wide or even zonal dynamics. The historic prices are best seen as a snapshot of the effects of atomistic, utility-level generation and transmission investment. Thus, a very low-price area may well abut a very high priced area for historically logical reasons. Utilities in the MISO-SPP area, as elsewhere, evolved from local to regional to multi-state service areas and built out their transmission accordingly.

The result of that evolution is a pattern of regulated energy prices that is suggestive – but only suggestive – of the flows of energy trade in the future. In the year 2001, MAPP prices averaged US$26/MWh, MAIN US$26/MWh, ECAR US$30/MWh, SPP US$27/MWh, and PJM US$31/MWh.

ENERGY PRICE DIFFERENCES WITHIN THE MAJOR ENERGY MARKETS

To a significant extent, energy price differences are a natural phenomenon. As in any other commodity, there are differences in the cost of production and transportation that make it inevitable (barring regulatory intervention) that prices in some places will be higher than in others.

To illustrate, consider an example in New York. In New York City, electricity prices are bound to be higher than in, say, rural New Jersey for similar reasons that other things are more expensive in the city than in the country. To build a power plant in the city, one would have to buy a suitable plot, which is likely to cost scores of millions of dollars. In the country, a power plant site will cost a few million dollars at most.

In New York, the cost of connecting the new plant to the dense network of transmission wires is likely to require excavation of city streets and extensive realignment of existing transmission connections. That is likely to cost tens of millions of dollars. In the country, assuming generation is not overbuilt, connecting to the transmission grid is likely to cost a few million dollars at most.

In New York City, providing a new gas pipeline for the power plant is likely to be an expensive proposition, one that the generator is likely to have to finance, which will raise its cost of gas compared to what a rural plant will have to pay.

These and other siting realities will render the cost of developing electricity generation in some areas higher than in others, and under the deregulated rules of electricity markets, such differences will no longer be socialised across all users. Instead, the differences will be allowed to manifest themselves in the marketplace, sending appropriate price signals both to consumers and to investors. If someone can provide electricity to New York City less expensively than by building a new generator there, under a free market they will be empowered to do so, if they can satisfy the various remaining regulatory requirements.

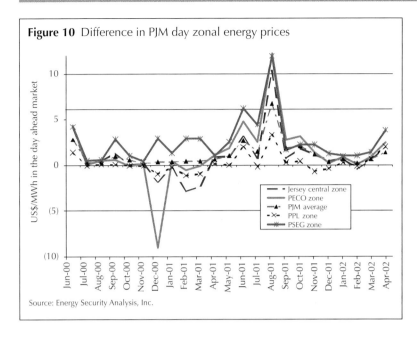

Figure 10 Difference in PJM day zonal energy prices

Source: Energy Security Analysis, Inc.

For these reasons, energy prices *within* the various MISO-PJM-SPP markets can be expected to continue to vary even if a joint and common power market is established. Put another way, a joint and common market will not eliminate local and zonal pricing differences, but it will allow those differences to become visible and effective so that both consumers and investors can take the appropriate actions in response to those prices.

This is clearly illustrated by the pricing history of PJM, which is arguably the most successful power pool in the United States (see Figure 10). In PJM, the highest zonal prices in 2001 were as much as US$4/MWh higher than the PJM average price.

These zonal pricing differences are the aggregates of the PJM market dynamics at each of the hundreds of constituent power infusion points and load buses. They reflect the economic decisions of thousands of market participants in hundreds of different market conditions – different weather patterns, economic cycles, outages, transmission line operations, and so forth.

PJM's accomplishment has been to create a centrally administered electric market whose very existence not only creates all of these locational prices, but also influences expectations about how the market will react to these price signals. At the end of the day,

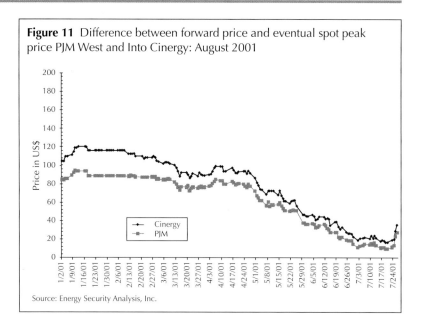

Figure 11 Difference between forward price and eventual spot peak price PJM West and Into Cinergy: August 2001

Source: Energy Security Analysis, Inc.

PJM is now sending day-ahead and real-time "spot" market prices that are the highest quality foundation yet in the power market for contracts settlements and derivatives pricing.

FORWARD-SPOT PRICE DIFFERENCES IN THE ENERGY MARKETS

Given that PJM's forte is in real-time and day-ahead market prices, longer-dated transactions are conducted via private, bilateral power contracts. One of the most important issues for the derivatives industry is the relationship between the signals sent by longer-dated bilateral prices and the ultimate spot price for the same period.

Figure 11 shows the relationship between the forward price of power for August 2001 and the ultimate average spot price in August during a trading period beginning in January 2001 and ending in July 2001. During this period, the August on-peak contract for PJM West and Into Cinergy were traded in sufficient volumes for its price to be quoted in *Power Markets Week*, the authoritative weekly power newsletter owned by McGraw-Hill.

Figure 11 indicates that both the PJM and Cinergy contracts traded at very large premiums in January. As August drew closer, and the information about market conditions in August improved, the premium declined substantially.

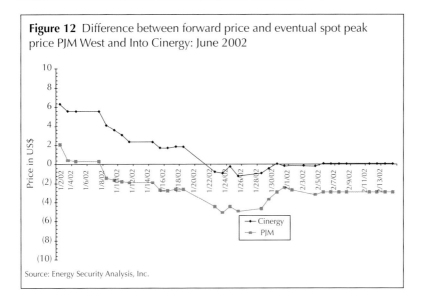

Figure 12 Difference between forward price and eventual spot peak price PJM West and Into Cinergy: June 2002

Source: Energy Security Analysis, Inc.

Such premiums between forward quotations and the ultimate spot price are not uncommon in markets, although these electricity market premiums are particularly large and reflect the immaturity and illiquidity of power markets in 2001.[7] What is interesting to observe, however, is the difference between the size of the premium between the relatively more liquid PJM West contract and the Cinergy contract. Since most electric consumers are in fact hedgers, this "forward contract liquidity advantage" may be the primary benefit of a PJM-style power market.

As power markets mature and become more efficient, a further change in the relationship between forward and spot prices can be anticipated. At times, the forward price should be lower than the ultimate spot price. In fact, over a long period of time, the periods when the forward price is higher and the periods when they are lower than the subsequent spot prices should even out. If they do not, the forward market by definition would have a bias that sellers would exploit (selling more and more of their supply in the forward markets) and buyers would shun (buying less and less in the forward markets). Both actions would tend to push forward prices down and spot prices up.[8]

In immature and inefficient power markets, the forward price will tend to carry a premium to the detriment of consumers.

Consumers in PJM will be heartened to see that in 2002, the forward spread for the June contract actually turned negative – it was cheaper to buy June power in January than in June, as shown in Figure 12; while in Cinergy it remained more expensive to buy power forward.

IMPLICATIONS FOR RISK MANAGEMENT IN THE ELECTRIC POWER SECTOR

The upshot of this analysis is that – in the midst of the turmoil afflicting particular companies in the power industry – a workable power market has developed in PJM. To the extent FERC is successful in pushing its SMD to other areas, we believe that other workable power markets will emerge in the United States. This should be good news for risk management providers.

There are caveats, however. First, the financial and operational health of the power markets will always be more regional than is the case for other energy markets. In electricity, transmission connections define the market. We believe the US market will ultimately house a northeastern market (New England and New York), a renamed "PJM" market that may extend as far south as South Carolina and as far west as Nebraska, a southern market, and a Texas market. In the west, it is difficult to be optimistic. Western states outside California should do all they can to avoid getting into a power market with that monstrously large energy consumer. California itself may not be able to muster the governance to create a set of rules that work.

In the eastern part of the country, however, there are reasons to be optimistic. The immediate challenge is to deal with the power financing problems. Too many plants were financed by people who did not understand how the markets would work, and those plants will have to be recapitalised to the chagrin of their current owners. Once that has been achieved, however, the eastern part of the United States will have assets valuations that make sense, and power market rules that work. That is fertile ground for good risk management practises.

---

1 FERC Order No. 2000 Notice of Proposed Rulemaking (NOPR), Docket No. RM99-2-000, p. 44.

2 See the web site of the US Energy Information Administration (www.eia.doe.gov) for a state-by-state review of electricity restructuring policies.

3   There is a renewed interest in the literature on what is now being called effective regulation. For the most recent addition to this literature, see John McMillan, *Reinventing the Bazaar, A Natural History of Markets*, W.W. Norton & Co., 2002.

4   R. H. Coase, *The Firm, The Market, and the Law*, (University of Chicago Press, 1988), p. 9.

5   From PJM, *PJM and LMP Refresher Course*, PJM Website.

6   Market Monitoring Unit, *PJM Interconnection State of the Market Report, 2001*, p. 42.

7   For an extensive discussion of this relationship in the oil market, see E. N. Krapels, *Crude Oil Hedging* (London: Risk Publications, 1998).

8   In the very long run, hedgers should expect to pay somewhat more in cash terms for their energy than non-hedgers: it should cost something to avoid the risks of spot price exposure.

BIBLIOGRAPHY

Coase, R. H., 1988, "The Firm, The Market, and the Law", p. 9 (University of Chicago Press).

Federal Energy Regulatory Commission, Order No. 2000 *Notice of Proposed Rulemaking (NOPR)*, (Washington, DC), Docket No. RM99-2-000.

Krapels, E. N., 2000, "Guide to Electricity Hedging" (London: Risk Publications).

Krapels, E. N., 2000, "Crude Oil Hedging" (London: Risk Publications).

Market Monitoring Unit, 2001, "State of the Market Report", PJM Interconnection.

McMillan, J., 2002, "Reinventing the Bazaar, A Natural History of Markets" (New York: W.W. Norton & Co).

US Energy Information Administration, 2002, "Derivatives and Risk Management in the Petroleum, Natural Gas, and Electricity Industries" (Washington, DC).

24

Risk Management in Asset Management

Gregory Connor and Robert A. Korajczyk

London School of Economics; Northwestern University

Investors are natural risk bearers, in part due to the vast array of risk management tools available to them. These tools allow a risk budgeting process that de-couples the asset allocation and active bets taken in the portfolio. The risk of non-traded assets in the portfolio can be reduced by selective hedging and insurance products. Non-traded assets and a dynamic risk-return trade-off lead to horizon specific asset allocation. Portfolios should be constructed to account for the systematic shifts in asset liquidity.

INTRODUCTION

The application of risk management techniques to portfolio management crucially depends upon modern portfolio theory, beginning with the seminal contributions of Markowitz (1952), Treynor (1961, 1999), Sharpe (1964), and Lintner (1965). These papers and their extensions are covered elsewhere in this book (see Chapters 4 and 5 in this volume) and that foundational material is not repeated here. In the next section we discuss risk budgeting and the decoupling of portfolio risk management into three separate components: strategic asset allocation, tactical asset allocation, and security selection. In the third section we consider risk-return dynamics and how these affect portfolio risk management. The fourth section deals with liquidity problems in portfolio risk management, and the last section contains a summary.

RISK BUDGETING THROUGH STRATEGIC AND TACTICAL ASSET ALLOCATION, AND ACTIVE DEVIATIONS FROM BENCHMARK PORTFOLIOS

The goal of risk management in portfolio management is not to eliminate risk, but to choose which risks to bear and to avoid unnecessary risks. What risks are appropriate for a particular portfolio will depend on the risk preferences of the investor and the role that particular portfolio plays in the investor's overall portfolio strategy. We will make the distinction between the investor's overall/total portfolio and sub-component portfolios. The total portfolio is the ultimate portfolio formed by combining sub-component portfolios. The goal of the investor is to construct a total portfolio from sub-component assets and portfolios that best suits the return requirements and risk aversion of the investor. What might constitute a good sub-component of the portfolio (eg, a hedge fund manager earning a high risk-adjusted return) may be totally inappropriate as the sole component of the total portfolio because of the high risk involved. Throughout, we treat the portfolio optimisation problem and risk budgeting as "flip-sides" to the same coin (also see Scherer, 2002).

The investor should begin by specifying the universe of investment styles, or benchmark portfolios, that make up the set of passive portfolios from which strategic asset allocation is chosen. Time variation in the risk premia or the level of risk of the benchmark portfolios leads to tactical shifts in asset allocation. Finally, the existence of superior or inferior investments (ie, mis-priced assets or active portfolio managers earning abnormal returns) leads to active shifts away from the passive benchmark portfolios. Each step entails managing the trade-off between extra return and extra risk.

To illustrate optimal portfolio construction, we will use a minor extension of Treynor and Black (1973) to the case of a k-style universe. In practice, the choice of the set of styles should be broad enough to encompass the set of risks that are compensated by risk premia, as discussed in Chapter 5 of this volume. These style portfolios make up the set of benchmarks against which portfolio managers and other investments are compared.

To simplify our example, we assume that there are two benchmark portfolios: an aggregate market portfolio and a portfolio of "value" stocks, whose rates of return from period $t - 1$ to period t are denoted $R_{m,t}$ and $R_{v,t}$, respectively (extensions to a greater selection of styles are straightforward but add unnecessary notation). Also let $R_{f,t}$ denote the return on an investment in a one-period risk-free asset. In addition to the benchmark style portfolios and the risk-free asset we have n other investments which might be individual assets/liabilities, mutual funds, hedge funds, derivative positions, and so on (with returns $R_{i,t}$ for $i = 1, 2, ..., n$). Returns in excess of the risk-free return are denoted $r_{m,t} = (R_{m,t} - R_{f,t})$, $r_{v,t} = (R_{v,t} - R_{f,t})$, and $r_{i,t} = (R_{i,t} - R_{f,t})$. Also let $\mu_{m,t}$, $\mu_{v,t}$, and $\mu_{i,t}$ denote the investor's expectations of $r_{m,t}$, $r_{v,t}$, and $r_{i,t}$ and let $\sigma_{m,t}$, $\sigma_{v,t}$, and $\sigma_{i,t}$ denote the investor's expectations of the standard deviations of $r_{m,t}$, $r_{v,t}$, and $r_{i,t}$. We can relate the value style portfolio to the market portfolio using the standard market model:

$$r_{v,t} = \alpha_{v,t} + \beta_{v,m} r_{m,t} + \varepsilon_{v,t} \tag{1}$$

In a capital asset pricing model (CAPM) world with no superior information, $\alpha_{v,t} = 0$. However, in a (non-CAPM) world where there are risk premia for additional sources of risk (see Chapter 5 in this volume) or a world in which our investor has superior insights into the mis-pricing of the value style, $\alpha_{v,t}$ need not be zero. It is either an additional risk premium or abnormal return to value stocks. Similarly, we can relate the additional n potential investments to the factor portfolios (the market and value portfolios in this example) using a multi-factor market model:

$$r_{i,t} = \alpha_{i,t} + \beta_{i,m} r_{m,t} + \beta_{i,v} r_{v,t} + \varepsilon_{i,t} \tag{2}$$

Since we assume that we have the correct style portfolios, $\alpha_{i,t}$ is the investor's forward looking expectation of the abnormal return on that asset or portfolio. It might be based on the investor's own information or the investor's expectation of the performance that will be obtained by the manager of portfolio i.

We will assume that the investor wishes to maximise the ratio of expected excess return to standard deviation, the Sharpe ratio (Sharpe, 1966), on the investor's total portfolio, p. Let X_m, X_v, X_i $(i = 1, 2, ..., n)$, and X_f, denote the fractions of the net portfolio value (assets less liabilities), or portfolio weights, invested in the market, the value index, asset or portfolio i, and the risk-free asset. Any wealth not invested in m, v, or assets/portfolios 1 through n will be invested in the risk-free asset. Positive (negative) values of X correspond to assets/long positions (liabilities/short positions). As in Treynor and Black (1973), for now we assume that there are no restrictions on the portfolio weights and we assume that the non-style returns to the n assets are uncorrelated (ie, corr($\varepsilon_{i,t}$, $\varepsilon_{j,t}$) = 0 if $i \neq j$).

The investor's portfolio has exposure to the second style portfolio, v, from two sources: the direct position in the style index and the indirect exposure through assets 1 to n. If we define X_v^* to be the total exposure to the value-style index, we have that:

$$X_v^* = X_v + \sum_{i=1}^{n} X_i \beta_{i,v} \tag{3}$$

Similarly, the investor's portfolio has exposure to the market factor portfolio from three sources: the direct position in the market, the exposure to the value-style index and the indirect exposure through assets 1 to n. If we define X_m^* to be the total exposure to the market, we have that:

$$X_m^* = X_m + X_v^* \beta_{v,m} + \sum_{i=1}^{n} X_i \beta_{i,m} \tag{4}$$

The portfolio weights that maximise the reward to risk (Sharpe) ratio are:

$$X_{m,t}^* = \lambda \left[\frac{\mu_{m,t}}{\sigma_{m,t}^2} \right] \tag{5}$$

$$X_{v,t}^* = \lambda \left[\frac{\alpha_{v,t}}{\sigma^2(\varepsilon_{v,t})} \right] \tag{6}$$

$$X_{i,t}^* = \lambda \left[\frac{\alpha_{i,t}}{\sigma^2(\varepsilon_{i,t})} \right] \tag{7}$$

The constant of proportionality, λ ($\lambda > 0$), reflects the investor's level of risk aversion. More risk-averse investors will have values of λ closer to zero. These portfolio weights embody the investor's strategic and tactical asset allocations as well as the investor's active bets.

The strategic asset allocation is determined by the investor's long run expectations of the returns on the style portfolios, μ_m and α_v, the risk of the market, σ_m, the tracking error of the v portfolio, $\sigma^2(\varepsilon_v)$, and the investor's risk aversion (reflected in λ). The tactical asset allocation is determined by the current deviation from the long run expectations of the returns and risks of the style portfolios: $\mu_{m,t} - \mu_m$, $\alpha_{v,t} - \alpha_v$, $\sigma_{m,t} - \sigma_m$, and $\sigma^2(\varepsilon_{v,t}) - \sigma^2(\varepsilon_v)$. Finally, the active positions are larger the higher the abnormal return, alpha, from the active positions, and smaller (in absolute value) the larger the tracking error of the active investment, $\sigma^2(\varepsilon_{v,t})$.

An important insight of the Treynor and Black (1973) analysis is that the tools of risk management allow us to completely decouple the asset allocation and active bets in the portfolio. This is quite different from the manner in which many portfolios are managed. For example, assume that our investor believes that $\alpha_{v,t} = 0$. This implies that the investor does not want any exposure to the value-style portfolio (beyond that inherent in the market index). In many traditional settings this would lead the investor to exclude value managers from the investor's active manager search. What if there exists a value manager that earns a large alpha relative to tracking error? The Treynor and Black analysis implies that the investor should hire that manager ($X_{i,t} > 0$ when $\alpha_{i,t} > 0$), but reverse the exposure to the value-style by taking a short position in the value index (for example, by shorting a futures contract). In essence, through this set of positions we can create a style-neutral portfolio (long the positive alpha style manager and short the style index). This allows us to have our cake and eat it too. We hire active managers on the basis of α relative to tracking error, not on the basis of our asset allocation decision. The risk is then managed by rebalancing the asset allocation to our desired position. Thus, decisions on active bets and decisions on asset allocation can be decoupled. The manager can go "over budget" on style risk with the asset allocation adjusted to stay within budget (ie, change X_v to get to the desired level X_v^*). This decoupling is referred to as "portable alpha" by Arnott (2002).

The above analysis also has important implications for active managers of sub-component portfolios. Active managers, whose clients are using risk management techniques effectively, should not worry about their Sharpe ratio. The Sharpe ratio rewards managers for superior alpha *and* for overall diversification. When the active manager's client is managing risk optimally, the manager does not need to worry about overall diversification, but needs to worry about providing the highest α per unit of tracking error. Thus, the total portfolio and the sub-component portfolios should be evaluated by different criteria. The analysis also provides a strong rationale for market- or style-neutral (long/short) portfolios. Not only can the managers specialise in information production, but they are in a better position to adjust the portfolio to remain style-neutral as the composition changes. Some institutions use this type of analysis to reverse engineer the implied α from a manager's position. That is, given the active position taken by the manager in asset i, X_i, we can determine the level of α_i consistent with the position from Equation (7), (Patel, 2002). The manager can then assess whether that level of abnormal return is reasonable.

The intuition of this analysis is clear and robust: α is good, tracking error is bad, and active positions and asset allocation need to be balanced effectively by the risk manager. Relaxing some of the assumptions will not change this intuition, but may change the optimal positions. The assumption that non-style returns are uncorrelated across assets (ie, $\text{corr}(\varepsilon_{i,t}, \varepsilon_{j,t}) = 0$ if $i \neq j$) can be approximately true, particularly when they include a large number of style benchmarks. However, active managers with the same style specialisation may have non-zero residual correlation. In practice, this is often handled by choosing only one manager per style, the manager with the highest α-to-tracking error ratio. This is generally sub-optimal, and can be improved upon by a simple mean variance optimisation across managers in the sub-style category.

We have placed no restrictions on the portfolio weights. In practice there may be such restrictions. Some portfolios are restricted from entering into short sales. Another common restriction is that the positions in certain assets and/or liabilities are not under the control of the portfolio manager. For example, for a typical investor one of the n assets is that investor's human capital. We cannot reduce the portfolio weight in human capital by selling that asset (which would amount to indentured servitude). A second example is a portfolio manager for an insurance company who may have liabilities that are dictated by the insurance policies written by the firm (and, hence, fixed from the portfolio manager's perspective). If the assets or liabilities are well diversified, in the sense of having very little tracking error (eg, the insurance company's liability portfolio might look like a long-term bond index fund), then we can use the style indices to return to our preferred asset allocation. If assets or liabilities have substantial tracking error, then the investor may choose to specifically hedge that risk by finding assets with negative correlation with $\varepsilon_{i,t}$ (eg, buying insurance in the human capital example).

The above analysis allows the investor's expectations to change over time, but the investor continues to act myopically, in the sense of solving a one-period mean/variance problem. We now turn to the problem of managing risk while taking into account the dynamics of the risk-return trade-off.

RISK-RETURN DYNAMICS AND THE PLANNING HORIZON

Some investors have very short planning horizons, such as one day for many floor traders and market makers, and other investors have very long planning horizons, such as a century or more for some university endowment funds. As Samuelson (1969) first noted, if asset prices follow a random walk and preferences are logarithmic, then the risk-return trade-off is unaffected by the planning horizon. Very short-term and very long-term investors measure the risk-return trade-off in the same way, without reference to their different planning horizons. If Samuelson's conditions do not hold – asset prices are not a random walk and/or preferences are not logarithmic – then the planning horizon can affect the measurement or cost-benefit valuation of risk. In addition, non-traded assets, such as human capital, can also lead to interactions between the planning horizon and optimal portfolio choice (Jagannathan and Kocherlakota, 1996).

It is the violation of the random walk assumption, more than the logarithmic preferences assumption, that tends to motivate extensions of the standard portfolio risk management model. It is abundantly clear that (log) prices do not follow a random walk. There are at least two categories of empirical violations: short-term risk dynamics and return predictability.

Short-term risk dynamics

Asset returns exhibit strong volatility clustering. High-risk days, for example, tend to be followed by high-risk days, and vice-versa for low-risk days. There are many methods for estimating the dynamics of volatility (see Chapter 13 in this volume). To illustrate some of the issues, we use a classic model of volatility clustering; the Garch (1,1) model. Let $\sigma^2_{t,t+1}$ denote the variance (conditional on information at time t) for the return of an asset at time $t + 1$. The Garch(1,1) model assumes that this conditional variance is a linear function of the previous period's conditional variance and the square of the current period's de-meaned return on the asset, z_t:

$$\sigma^2_{t,t+1} = \omega + az_t^2 + b\sigma^2_{t-1,t} \tag{8}$$

Note that the risk of the asset expressed in units of variance not only moves through time, but also depends upon the planning horizon of the investor. A one-period investor can use Equation (8) directly to measure risk. If the investor plans to hold the asset for k periods, then it is necessary to generate the conditional forecasts from Equation (8) for each future period, and temporally aggregate the forecasts across the holding period. Performing this calculation (see Bollerslev, Engle, and Nelson, 1994 for a general review of Garch-type models) gives:

$$\sigma^2_{t,t+k} = \omega \frac{1-(a+b)^k}{1-a-b} + \left((a+b)^k - \theta\right)\zeta^2_{t-k,t} + \theta\sigma^2_{t-k,t} \tag{9}$$

where $\sigma^2_{t,t+k}$ denotes the conditional variance of the k-period return (not to be confused with the k-step-ahead one-period conditional variance) and θ is a function of the parameters in Equation (8). As long as $a + b < 1$ (a necessary condition for covariance stationarity of the Garch model) the very long-term investor can approximately ignore Garch effects: the longer the holding period, the smaller the distinction between conditional and unconditional holding-period variance. This turns out to be an important practical consideration: empirically observed Garch effects are very strong at daily and higher frequency but die out fairly quickly. Correcting risk forecasts for Garch effects is much more important for short-term than long-term investors. As we will see, the opposite applies to mean-reversion effects, where short-term investors are not affected at all and long-term investors might be.

Return predictability and long-term mean reversion

A prominently discussed anomaly in empirical finance is the presence of "excess volatility" in returns (Shiller, 1991). However, such "excess volatility" is equivalent to time variation, or predictability in asset returns (Cochrane, 1991). Lo and MacKinlay (1988) note that excess volatility plus return stationarity necessarily implies that long-horizon returns have lower proportionate variance than short-horizon returns. This means that a long-term investor and a short-term investor face a different risk-return trade-off for the same multiple asset opportunity set. The difference in risk between high-risk equities and low-risk cash instruments is proportionately less for the long-term investor. Many analysts have used this finding to propose higher weightings on equities for longer-term holders. This advice has had considerable influence on investment practice in recent decades, particularly in North America.

Intuitively, the long-term investor experiences lower proportionate risk from equities since they can "ride out" the short-term price fluctuations due to excess volatility, holding long enough for prices to revert back toward fundamental values. Campbell and Viceira (2001) advocate a more aggressive policy for long-term investors. Excess volatility/mean reversion also implies some small degree of predictability in long-term returns. During "down markets" (defined by some statistical criteria such as yield ratios) the expected return to high-risk equities is higher than during "up markets." Long-term investors should tilt their asset allocation plan to account for this. This is not strictly speaking a risk management issue since it concerns expected returns rather than risk, but the effects of excess volatility/mean reversion are intimately connected.

Other dynamic features of returns and their implications for portfolio risk management

There are numerous other dynamic risk-return patterns observable empirically, but only a few will be mentioned here. Over annual horizons, returns seem to exhibit momentum rather than its opposite, mean reversion. This implies that over certain intermediate-length holding periods, variance increases proportionately with the holding period rather than decreasing. Another important empirical finding comes from Campbell, Lettau, Malkiel, and Xu (2001) who show that the proportion of asset-specific risk in total risk (for a typical individual asset) has experienced a secular increase over the last fifty years. This means that portfolio diversification, to a given tolerance level, requires more assets now than it did in earlier decades.

Another important dynamic feature in returns is the decline in kurtosis as the return interval gets longer. Daily and higher-frequency returns have very high positive excess kurtosis. Assuming reasonable limits on return interdependence over time, and the existence of finite higher moments, it follows from the central limit theorem that the excess kurtosis in multi-period returns will decline towards zero as the measurement interval grows. This strong decline in kurtosis is in fact observed empirically. If investors care about kurtosis and other higher moments of return, not just variance, in measuring risk, then their evaluation of risk of a given asset can change with the planning horizons due to this effect.

EXECUTION/LIQUIDITY RISK

A common finding is that "paper" (ie, simulated) portfolios always outperform real portfolios based on the same information. The reason is that the real portfolio incurs execution costs (commissions, price impact, partial executions, etc) that the "paper" portfolio does not (Treynor, 1983). There is a wide array of execution performance metrics. Many commonly used metrics, such as volume weighted average price (VWAP), can be easily gamed – especially if the order is large, necessitating working the order (Beebower, 1989). The extensive literature on "market microstructure" provides a set of models (see O'Hara, 1995 and Harris, 2002) and a growing empirical literature that can provide benchmarks against which trade execution can be evaluated (eg, Keim and Madhavan, 1995, 1997, 1998; Breen, Hodrick, and Korajczyk, 2002).

More importantly, there is evidence that there are systematic components to liquidity (Chordia, Roll, and Subrahmanyam, 2000;

Hasbrouck and Seppi, 2001; Pástor and Stambaugh, 2001; and Sadka, 2002). Thus, an investor might find that many of the assets in the portfolio are simultaneously difficult to trade. In fact, dramatic systematic shifts in liquidity appear to be an important factor in numerous financial crises (eg, Edwards, 1999). Sub-component portfolios that incorporate long/short strategies and leverage may have a higher chance of incurring margin calls during periods of low liquidity.

Portfolio construction should take into account the likelihood that assets will need to be traded in low liquidity environments. This is an area where extreme value theory (see Chapter 11 in this volume) or simulation and stress testing (see Chapter 10 in this volume) lead to useful insights.

CONCLUSION

There are many important aspects of risk management that, due to space constraints, we have not addressed. The inputs to the optimisation process often require the aggregation of information from historical data with prior beliefs about parameters. The risk management process must deal with the associated estimation risk. Some approaches are explicitly Bayesian (eg, Scherer, 2002, Chapter 4). Others impose constraints on holdings which can have a Bayesian interpretation (Jagannathan and Ma, 2002). Additionally, we have only tangentially addressed non-normality in asset returns, particularly for options held in the portfolio. This non-normality makes stress testing portfolios (see Chapter 10 in this volume) all the more important.

Portfolio optimisation and risk budgeting are flip sides of the same coin. The budget allocated to a particular source of risk depends on the investor's beliefs about the risk-reward trade-off for that source of risk. The budgeting process should allow opportunistic shifts in the risk budget across investments. The tools of risk management (eg, derivatives, insurance, leverage, exchange traded funds, etc) allow a risk budgeting process that de-couples the asset allocation and active bets taken in the port-folio. Non-traded assets and a dynamic risk-return trade-off lead to horizon specific asset allocation. Finally, portfolios need to be constructed to account for the systematic shifts in asset liquidity.

BIBLIOGRAPHY

Arnott, R. D., 2002, "Risk Budgeting and Portable Alpha", *Journal of Investing* 11(2), pp. 15–22.

Beebower, G., 1989, "Evaluating Transaction Cost", in W. H. Wagner, *The Complete Guide to Securities Transactions* (New York: John Wiley & Sons).

Bollerslev, T., R. F. Engle, and D. B. Nelson, 1994, "ARCH Models", in R. F. Engle and D. L. McFadden (eds), *Handbook of Econometrics,* Volume IV (Amsterdam: North Holland).

Breen, W. J., L. S. Hodrick, and R. A. Korajczyk, 2002, "Predicting Equity Liquidity", *Management Science* 48(4), pp. 470–83.

Campbell, J. Y., M. Lettau, B. G. Malkiel, and Y. Xu, 2001, "Have Individual Stocks Become More Volatile? An Empirical Exploration of Idiosyncratic Risk", *Journal of Finance* 61(1), pp. 1–43.

Campbell, J. Y. and L. M. Viceira, 2001, *Strategic Asset Allocation: Portfolio Choice for Long-term Investors* (Oxford University Press).

Chordia, T., R. Roll, and A. Subrahmanyam, 2000, "Commonality in Liquidity", *Journal of Financial Economics* 56(1), pp. 3–28.

Cochrane, J., 1991, "Volatility Tests and Efficient Markets", *Journal of Monetary Economics* 27(3), pp. 463–85.

Cochrane, J., and C. L. Culp, 2002, "Equilibrium Asset Pricing and Discount Factors: Overview and Implication for Derivatives Valuation and Risk Management", Chapter 5 of the present volume.

Connor, G., R. A. Korajczyk, and O. Linton, 2002, "The Common and Specific Components of Dynamic Volatility", Working paper #311, Northwestern University.

Duan, J.-C., 2002, "Modelling Volatility", Chapter 13 of the present volume.

Edwards, F. R., 1999, "Hedge Funds and the Collapse of Long Term Capital Management," *Journal of Economic Perspectives* 13(2), pp. 189–210.

Harris, L., 2002, *Trading & Exchanges* (Oxford University Press).

Jagannathan, R., and N. R. Kocherlakota, 1996, "Why Should Older People Invest Less in Stocks Than Younger People?" *Federal Reserve Bank of Minneapolis Quarterly Review* 26(2), pp. 11–23.

Jagannathan, R., and T. Ma, 2002, "Risk Reduction in Large Portfolios: Why Imposing the Wrong Constraints Helps", *Journal of Finance,* forthcoming.

Keim, D. B., and A. Madhavan, 1996, "The Upstairs Market for Large-Block Transactions: Analysis and Measurement of Price Effects", *Review of Financial Studies* 9(1), pp. 1–36.

Keim, D. B., and A. Madhavan, 1997, "Transactions Costs and Investment Style: An Inter-Exchange Analysis of Institutional Equity Trades", *Journal of Financial Economics* 46(3), pp. 265–92.

Keim, D. B., and A. Madhavan, 1998, "The Cost of Institutional Equity Trades", *Financial Analysts Journal* 54(4), pp. 50–69.

Lintner, J., 1965, "The Valuation of Risk Assets and the Selection of Risky Investments in Stock Portfolios and Capital Budgets", *Review of Economics and Statistics* 47(1), pp. 13–37.

Markowitz, H. M., 1952, "Portfolio Selection", *Journal of Finance* 7(1), pp. 77–91.

O'Hara, M., 1995, *Market Microstructure Theory* (Oxford: Blackwell).

Pástor, L., and R. F. Stambaugh, 2001, "Liquidity Risk and Expected Stock Returns", forthcoming *Journal of Political Economy*.

Patel, N., 2002, "Buying and Selling Risk", *Risk* 15(9), pp. S12–S14.

Samuelson, P. A., "Lifetime Portfolio Selection by Dynamic Stochastic Programming", *Review of Economics and Statistics* 51(3), pp. 239–46.

Sadka, R., 2002, "Momentum, Liquidity Risk, and Limits to Arbitrage", Working Paper, Northwestern University.

Scherer, B., 2002, *Portfolio Construction and Risk Budgeting* (London: Risk Books).

Sharpe, W. F., 1964, "Capital Asset Prices: A Theory of Market Equilibrium Under Conditions of Risk", *Journal of Finance* 19(3), pp. 425–42.

Sharpe, W. F., 1966, "Mutual Fund Performance", *Journal of Business* 39(1), pp. 119–38.

Shiller, R. J., 1991, *Market Volatility* (Cambridge, MA: MIT Press).

Treynor, J. L., 1961, "Toward a Theory of Market Value of Risky Assets", Unpublished manuscript, subsequently published as Treynor (1999).

Treynor, J. L., 1983, "Implementation of Strategy: Execution", in J. L. Maginn and D. L. Tuttle (eds), *Managing Investment Portfolios: A Dynamic Process*, pp. 537–72 (Boston: Warren, Gorham & Lamont).

Treynor, J. L., 1999, "Toward a Theory of Market Value of Risky Assets", in R. A. Korajczyk (ed), *Asset Pricing and Portfolio Performance: Models, Strategy and Performance Metrics* (London: Risk Books).

Treynor, J. L., and F. Black, 1973, "How to Use Security Analysis to Improve Portfolio Selection", *Journal of Business* 46(1), pp. 66–86.

25

Risk Management for Hedge Funds and Funds of Hedge Funds

Virginia Reynolds Parker

Parker Global Strategies

What exactly is risk? Risk, as it relates to investing, is "the potential for loss of control and/or value". The risks involved in hedge funds are quite similar to the risks involved in traditional investments. The risk management techniques, for those who do apply them to hedge funds, are perhaps more sophisticated and more disciplined than for traditional investment portfolios, but many of the potential exposures to risk are the same. This chapter will focus on the evolution of best practices for hedge funds, discuss some of the major portfolio and operational risks in hedge fund investing, suggest a method for effective risk management for funds of hedge funds investing, and review the recommendations of the Investor Risk Committee on transparency.

THE EVOLUTION OF BEST PRACTICES FOR HEDGE FUNDS

In July 1993, the Group of Thirty published "Recommendations for Dealers and End-users", a paper focused on risk management and measurement practices to help address the risks such institutions face.[1] The paper makes the suggestions that the risk management function should:

❏ determine the scope of activities and policies at the highest level of management;

❏ establish an *independent*, middle office reporting directly to senior management;

❏ empower professionals with appropriate skills to perform required duties;

❏ install systems capable of measuring, managing and reporting risks in a timely and accurate manner;

❏ perform stress tests and forecast funding needs; and

❏ value derivative positions at market.

Although these recommendations were primarily for banks, investment banks, and insurance companies active in dealing in derivatives and for end-users of derivatives, many of the suggestions may be applied to other types of investment pools, including hedge funds. Some of the large hedge funds started having an independent risk management function back in the mid-1990s. At the same time, there were smaller hedge funds whose principals came from banks and investment banks that also espoused the importance of risk management. Additionally, a few funds of hedge funds began trying to apply best practices risk oversight during the mid-1990s.

As one studies the development of risk management techniques for hedge funds, one finds that some of the earliest "best practices" originated from this study. Perhaps the most fundamental recommendation from this study is the importance of an *independent* middle office whose success is not tied to trading profits.

If one examines the major investment blowups over the years, a skilled independent middle office could have alerted senior management much earlier to the investment losses that were brewing. A middle office that follows skilled risk management practices cannot prevent losses, but it can mitigate losses in many instances. Quite often, the enormity of losses emanates from the period of successful cover-up, during which time the losses are allowed to continue to grow unchecked.

PORTFOLIO RISKS AND OPERATIONAL RISKS FOR HEDGE FUNDS

Risk management discussions often break risks into the categories of market and operational. In considering hedge fund risks, a more effective categorisation of risks is into portfolio and operational.

The major portfolio risks include market, liquidity, leverage, concentration, credit, hedge ratios, short volatility exposure, and style drift.

Portfolio risks

Market risk is the risk that losses are incurred due to market exposure. Most often, the portfolio loses value because one or more positions are on the wrong side of the market; shorts positions may be increasing in price and/or long security positions may be decreasing in price.

Over the past decade, important analytical tools have been developed to quantify market risk. Risk measurement for market risk must be tailored to the specific hedge fund strategy.

Analytics should include:

❏ value-at-risk (VAR): contribution to risk and incremental risk;
❏ gross and net analysis (Beta-adjusted): sector and country;
❏ stress testing: key drivers and factor analysis;
❏ scenario analysis: Monte Carlo and recursive models; and
❏ downside deviation: minimum acceptable returns and maximum acceptable loss.

Many of these analytics are available through software vendors and prime brokers. These are just one set of tools. One must understand the weakness of each of the analytics, and combine risk measurement with experience and keen judgement to practice effective risk management.

Liquidity risk is the risk that market liquidity dries up, and the manager is unable to liquidate the position. Liquidity risk is most severe during major, global market dislocations. But there can be liquidity risk in a single position. Some examples of severe liquidity risk were in October 1987, during the US equity market crash, trickling over into a global equity market crash. Perhaps the definition of liquidity risk was best seen during that time when the Hong Kong market closed for a number of days. In early 1994, liquidity risk emerged in the European government bond markets. Until some hedge funds and traditional investment portfolios tried to liquidate their holdings, few had understood just how small the European bond markets were, compared to the US government bond market. Imagine how shocked one would have been in

August of 2001, to know that a few weeks later the US equity markets would remain closed for days, following the tragedy of September 11.

Leverage risk is a risk most often associated with hedge fund investing. An important point to note, however, is that many hedge fund managers and strategies do not use leverage. The perils of hedge fund leverage became most famous following the collapse of Long Term Capital Management (LTCM). In considering the magnitude of LTCM's leverage when it collapsed, one should realise that LTCM had been trying, unsuccessfully, to liquidate its portfolio. As prices went against LTCM each day, the value of the equity in its portfolio was decreasing. There is an inverse relationship between equity and leverage. As equity decreases from portfolio losses, leverage increases.

Concentration risk is the risk that the portfolio lacks diversification. Some hedge fund managers may run portfolios of concentrated positions as their investment style. Others may suddenly create concentration risk when they feel very strongly about a position and make a large bet.

Credit risk comes in several varieties. There is the risk of changes in credit spreads, which presents a potential portfolio risk for certain hedge fund strategies. Another risk is that one or more positions experience a change in credit rating. Occasionally, a company or a country may have a major credit event take place before a change in its credit rating.

Hedge ratios are a risk most common to hedge funds, especially those that try to hedge. For arbitrage strategies, the hedge fund manager may make a mistake in the hedge ratio that it applies, or the manager may simply decide to take a directional bet, and therefore, intentionally over, or under, hedge.

Short volatility is a risk for some hedge funds. Short volatility strategies are arbitrage strategies, which purchase spreads, much like insurance. Or, a strategy may be short volatility by writing call options, where in theory, risk is unlimited.

Style drift is a risk to which investors in hedge fund strategies may be exposed. During the economic collapse of Russia in August 1998, there were numerous high yield bond managers, both hedge funds and traditional managers, with exposure to Russia. These managers were meant to have been US high yield managers.

Operational risk

Some of the major operational risks include counterparty, legal, regulatory, model, clearing, accounting, and human (which may include judgement, mistakes, or fraud).

An important operational risk on the counterparty side for hedge funds is exposure to the prime broker. Many people believe that the prime broker performs the function of custodian for hedge funds. The prime broker has custody of most hedge fund's securities; but the prime broker has custody of the assets for the benefit of the prime broker's interest, not for benefit of the hedge fund's interest.[2] A prime broker is in business to stay in business. The prime broker has a counterparty exposure to the hedge fund. If the prime broker is concerned about its exposure to losses from the hedge fund, should the hedge fund start to incur significant losses, the prime broker almost always has the right to start liquidating the portfolio. The prime broker is not after best execution; he is after liquidation to minimise his exposure to losses from the hedge fund. The prime broker's role is not a protection for the hedge fund or its investors.

The other operational risks mentioned above are also important risks faced by investors. On the legal and regulatory side, often the regulations of multiple domiciles may come into play when there is a problem. These risks are often complex and very expensive to litigate. Model risk includes the risk when one or more positions may be marked-to-model rather than marked-to-market, because the positions are thinly traded. There may be fundamental flaws in the model's methodology that are not recognised until after significant mistakes have been made marking positions. An example of clearing/settlement risk is when a buyer must send funds prior to receipt of the security, or vice versa where the seller must deliver the security prior to payment; this is rare, but does exist. If there is a failure, there may be little protection.

Accounting risk may come in several forms. One example, common to some famous corporate blowups over the years, is when positions are continually rolled forward and losses are not recognised. This happened in the case of Kidder Peabody. Accounting risks do not create the portfolio losses, but they may mis-state values. An example of an accounting error for hedge funds would be a material mistake in the mark-to-market of a position. When investors redeem and subscribe to a fund that has a material flaw in its valuation, there is a winner and loser.

Finally, human risk is one of the most concerning operational risks, especially the risk of fraud. Fraud is not nearly so prevalent in hedge funds as the headlines would make one believe. Nonetheless, the way that most hedge funds are structured makes them susceptible to fraud from a clever crook. Independent administrators and auditors are meant to help protect investors' interests, but the case of Manhattan illustrates that lax procedures may allow service providers to be duped. Another example is the Lipper convertible arbitrage fund where the positions were mis-marked.

RISK MANAGEMENT FOR FUNDS OF HEDGE FUNDS

Effective risk management for fund of hedge funds investors may be achieved through a three-pronged approach stressing diversification, transparency and independent oversight for investments. Such an approach is the proper institutional approach to hedge fund investing. The approach is similar to that followed by some of the banks providing hedge fund investments to their clients; this is especially true for some of the banks offering these investments via structured products. The benefits of this three-pronged approach may be appreciated and realised by individual investors as well, who may choose to rely on fund of funds or hedge fund consultants to assist them in gaining exposure to hedge funds along with independent risk monitoring.

Diversification

Thoughtful diversification, diversification that holds up from both a qualitative and a quantitative perspective, is the most rudimentary building block for portfolio construction and management. Many portfolio mistakes may be survived if one has achieved meaningful diversification. In the case of hedge funds, this means diversification across strategies, managers, markets, and risk factors. If one examines the performance of the Hedge Fund Research (HFR) indexes, representing the average performance of various hedge fund styles, one notes the cyclical nature of these styles. Economic events, market events, and political events create ebbs and flows of profit opportunity for the various styles. Carefully constructed portfolios may include directional strategies, spread dependent strategies, and managed futures strategies that, when combined, may withstand many market environments. Portfolio construction cannot necessarily prevent losses, but careful diversification may help lessen losses during market crises. In constructing the portfolio, one must recognise the various risks of each strategy. One must address the event risk that is often missing through a purely quantitative view of past performance. One must question the integrity of the portfolio's pricing, or marks-to-market. After all, portfolio net asset values (NAVs) are based upon a mark-to-market of each position, representing a moment in time, when the positions may have been sold at the "assigned" price. Or, the "assigned" price may have failed to recognise the large size of a position, the illiquidity of the market, the complexity of the derivative security, the flaw in the pricing model, or the circular reference of "independent" broker/dealer pricing. These pricing issues are but a few of the many pricing issues that an allocator to hedge funds should comprehend prior to selecting strategies and managers. As a rule of thumb, the more complicated the strategy and the less liquid the portfolio, the more knowledgeable and wary the allocator should be.

One also must be aware of potential concentration risk, concentration of allocation to managers, vs position concentration in the portfolio.

Transparency

Transparency is important for understanding past performance, and is also important for understanding current performance and portfolio risks. What is transparency? It is the willingness of the hedge fund manager to provide full disclosure of portfolio positions, along with pricing, and methodology of pricing, preferably directly from the prime broker who represents an independent source. Transparency also includes the investor's ability to examine all agreements to which the hedge fund company is a party. Such agreements include, but are not limited to, the prime brokerage and other counterparty agreements, the administration agreement, the engagement letter with the auditors, past audit reports, the registrar and transfer agreement, side letters for existing investors, and corporate registrations. Additionally, the hedge fund manager should be willing to disclose the monthly redemption and subscription history for the fund since its inception.

Portfolio transparency is the tool for getting *behind the numbers* in hedge fund investing. Neophytes will chase performance, taking reported numbers at face value. For those who have been allocating over a number of years, understanding how the numbers were generated, and in fact, *if* the numbers were generated, is imperative to successful hedge fund investing. Today we find many more hedge funds willing to offer some meaningful level of transparency when compared to what managers would provide back in the late 1980s. So many managers are willing to provide some meaningful level of portfolio transparency that one may build a strong multi-manager program without sacrificing returns.

Independent oversight

Completing the risk management paradigm for hedge fund investing requires regular, independent risk oversight. This regular monitoring of the portfolio requires sufficient transparency to assess the risk in the portfolio. There is much discussion today by those who believe risk exposures may be adequately monitored without the benefit of the underlying positions. With risk exposures, one may achieve a very general sense of the portfolio. But one may argue that if risk exposures without positions were truly able to capture detailed portfolio risk, one would likely see modification of "best practices" for dealers and end-users. If limiting transparency to risk exposures were really sufficient, why wouldn't prime brokers monitor their own risk to hedge funds in such a way? Risk exposures provide a high-level risk assessment, but the allocator and/or independent risk manager needs drill down capability to be able to probe portfolio issues.

Risks that should be evaluated regularly include market risk and various operational risks. Current "best practices" for assessing market risk include independent portfolio pricing; VAR by position, market, asset class, manager, and strategy; Monte Carlo simulations for portfolios containing optionality; and stress testing. One should examine concentrations of risk in the portfolio and key performance drivers. One must also evaluate liquidity risk. Although leverage is an ambiguous term across hedge fund strategies, one should measure the gross and net exposures, in aggregate and across industry sectors, for long short equity portfolios. For interest rate and fixed income positions, one must examine exposures across yield curve buckets and credit quality. For arbitrage strategies, one must dissect spread risk. In the late 1980s, risk measurement analytics were barely developed and required massive computing power along with a team of rocket scientists. Fortunately today, the risk manager may choose from off the shelf software, prime brokers, and even application service providers (ASPs) as a source of the risk measurement analytics. A risk manager must simply have the skill to understand the reports and the experience to know when to intervene.

Depending upon the particular circumstance, one may pursue independent oversight with, or without, some control. The best control for the allocator is investing via a managed account with the hedge fund. However, a managed account is not always possible or practical. Hedge fund managers often require very high minimum account sizes to run a managed account; some hedge fund managers are unwilling to run a managed account. Some investors, for regulatory or tax reasons are required to invest via a fund, and may be limited to the percentage ownership that they may represent to the total fund. Generally, with a managed account, the allocator may terminate the hedge fund manager immediately, and/or intervene in the portfolio. In a fund investment, the allocator's control is usually limited to redeeming on the next redemption date, provided the allocator has provided sufficient notice to the fund.

INVESTOR RISK COMMITTEE

Risk managers are hard pressed to measure, monitor, and manage risk without adequate information. The level of transparency that a hedge fund should provide has been a heated debate for many years. The debate continues, as more institutions are investing in, or considering investing in, these funds.

The Investor Risk Committee, (IRC), was launched by the International Association of Financial Engineers (IAFE) in January, 2000. The group includes hedge funds, institutional investors, regulators, software and technology vendors, consultants, prime brokers, custodians, academics, and others. The mission of the IRC is "to provide a forum for participants, teachers, and students of the field of investing to study risk and its surrounding issues."[3] The IRC has released two documents to date that attempt to answer the question, "what is the right level of disclosure by hedge funds?".

The IRC position is that investors have three primary objectives from disclosure: risk monitoring, risk aggregation across the entire portfolio, and strategy drift monitoring. The IRC states that full position level disclosure does not necessarily allow investors to achieve their objectives, and may compromise the hedge fund. The Committee suggests that a summary of risk, return, and position information can provide sufficient information for achieving the investor's ultimate objectives. According to the IRC, information from hedge funds may be evaluated on four dimensions: content, granularity, frequency, and delay.

Content focuses upon the quality and sufficiency of coverage of the hedge fund manager's activities including information about risks, returns, and positions on an actual and stress-tested basis. Among the suggested quantitative measures for assessing risk are: VAR, aggregate measures of a fund's exposure to different assets, aggregate measures of geographical exposures, NAV and stress measures of NAV, cash as a percent of equity, correlation to an appropriate benchmark, the various Greek measures, and key spread relationships.

Granularity focuses upon the level of portfolio detail provided. The IRC believes that larger hedge funds may be more impacted than smaller funds by providing too much disclosure. The IRC suggests that large funds must protect themselves from "predatory trading," and that top 10 positions may be useful so long as the information would not adversely impact the hedge fund. Alternatively, the IRC suggests, adequate disclosure may be by asset class and region.

Frequency is the third dimension of disclosure discussed by the IRC's document. The IRC suggests that monthly summary statistics are sufficient for most hedge funds, and quarterly may be sufficient for less liquid strategies or those with slow turnover. The IRC goes on to state that it can be useful to disclose performance attribution more frequently than risk attribution. Finally, the group suggests that daily profit and loss figures provided at month-end for funds marked-to-market daily may be valuable.

Delay is the fourth dimension of disclosure discussed in the IRC's paper. The IRC suggests that summary statistics should be disclosed as soon as possible following the reporting period, (preferably within 10 days). One method of determining the appropriate delay may be by applying the average holding period. Hedge funds may use "generic rather than specific names if the strategy is still active."

The IRC also recommends that reporting must be coupled with initial and ongoing due diligence reviews. Market, credit, liquidity, and operational risks are interrelated and should be included in discussions.

CONCLUSION

The Group of Thirty study's recommendation for an independent middle office is key for effective hedge fund risk management. The independent function may be served by an internal team, in the case of a hedge fund, or an external team, in the case of a fund of hedge fund manager or consultant. The study also stressed the importance of quantitative analytics and marking positions to market, practices that are central to risk measurement and monitoring for market risk. There are many portfolio risks and operational risks to which an investor in hedge funds is exposed. The prudent allocator and risk manager must judge the entire landscape of these risks initially and on an ongoing basis. The IRC has proposed some important recommendations for hedge fund transparency that can help investors and managers balance the need for information with the risks of disclosure. The suggested disclosure focuses on four dimensions: content, granularity, frequency and delay.

For the fund of hedge fund manager, this chapter suggests a three-pronged approach to risk management including diversification, transparency, and independent risk oversight. First and most importantly, one has a full set, or nearly full set, of information with which to make informed decisions much earlier than if one merely waited for the arrival of the monthly NAV to begin analysing facts and asking questions. Where such timely information cannot prevent losses, often losses may be slowed, because action may be taken sooner. Some examples of problems that may arise in a portfolio that can be recognised early on include excessive market risk relative to portfolio equity, inappropriate pricing of securities, increased volatility of performance, and style drift. Another advantage of risk monitoring is that the allocator may decide to hedge a portion of aggregate market exposure, using an overlay, during times of market trauma, or when there is an unanticipated concentration of risk in the aggregate portfolio. Finally, continuous monitoring of hedge fund portfolios and a deeper knowledge of hedge fund behaviour helps the investor to make better allocation decisions at the point of manager selection. Careful due diligence prior to investing, and ongoing qualitative and quantitative monitoring through transparency and risk measurement analytics after investing provide powerful weapons for successful hedge fund investing. These weapons can help stand the test of time through a vast range of market climates and global events.

1   The Group of Thirty (1993), *Derivatives: Practices and Principles.*
2   An exception would be bank loans.
3   IAFE Website.

BIBLIOGRAPHY

Group of Thirty, 1993, *Derivatives: Practices and Principles* July (Washington, DC).

International Association of Financial Engineers (IAFE), 2002, URL:http://www.iafe.org/committees/investor/risk_consensus.htm (1 October 2002).

Morgan, J. P., 1996, RiskMetrics Technical Document, Fourth Edition, Morgan Guaranty Trust Company, (New York) URL: http://www.riskmetrics.com/research.

26

Evolution of the Global Weather Derivatives Market

Jeffrey Porter*

Hess Energy Trading Company, LLC

INTRODUCTION

The weather derivatives market has enjoyed dramatic if not remarkable growth since its inception in the autumn of 1997.[1] According to the July 2002 survey conducted by PriceWaterhouseCoopers for the Weather Risk Management Association, the total notional amount of weather derivatives that have been traded is US$11.8 billion, and over US$4.3 billion of that had traded in the most recent twelve months leading up to the survey (WRMA, 2002). The weather derivative market has developed for a number of reasons, as follows.

❏ Plain vanilla weather derivative products based upon heating degree days and cooling degree days correlate very well with energy suppliers' sales of gas and power to residential customers. For example, when it is warm in the winter a local distribution energy supplier will deliver less energy to their customers.

*The author would like to express sincere gratitude to Ethan Kahn, Robert Dischel, and Tom Fletcher for discussions on the early history of the weather market and how trading strategies and trends have evolved over time. Also the author would like to thank Colt Heppe and Kendall Johnson for providing statistics and private conversations that greatly assisted the creation of this chapter. The author represents his own views based upon numerous discussions with numerous professionals involved in the weather market over several years, as well as his work as a founding board member of the Weather Risk Management Association.

The decrease in throughput will substantially negatively impact the local distribution energy suppliers' cashflow and earnings. The need for local distribution energy suppliers to hedge their energy delivery exposure through the use of weather derivatives was the main catalyst for the development of the weather derivatives market. In fact, in a survey of 200 US based utilities 80% of them listed weather risk as a major determinant of earnings (Cogen, 1998). In the United States the need for energy suppliers to hedge their delivery exposure has only been exacerbated by the recent extremely mild winters of 1997–98, 1998–99, 1999–00, and 2001–02. In fact four of the last five winters have been extremely mild or warm in the population centres of the United States (Dischel, 2002).

❏ Deregulation of energy markets has fostered competition in local markets. Competition has forced energy suppliers' management to focus on gaining competitive advantages over their competitors. The use of weather derivatives has played a prominent role for companies looking to control costs and strengthen balance sheets against competitors. Also, regulated utilities could pass on weather costs to customers in the form of increased rates. Passing on rate increases to customers due to adverse weather conditions is a luxury deregulated utilities do not possess.

❏ Energy companies, like Hess Energy Trading Company and Mirant, along with insurance companies, like Swiss Re and Element Re, have found that providing weather derivative products to customers and risk providers can provide profitable trading opportunities. The number of market participants in the July 2002 PriceWaterhouseCoopers Weather Market survey was 20 (WRMA, 2002). These 20 participants in the weather derivatives market would not offer products unless they believed that they could make a profit trading doing so.

The purpose of this chapter is to outline the evolution of the weather market. I will focus on the temperature market since temperature is the most actively traded weather index (see Figure 1).

I will examine how the weather market has evolved over time by analysing trends in the secondary traded market and then briefly touch on what I perceive the global weather market needs for future development.

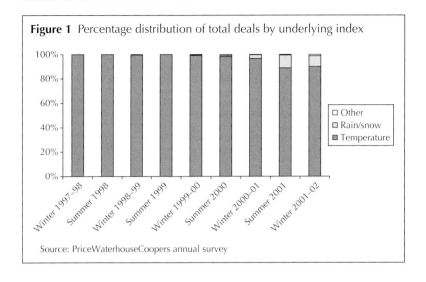

Figure 1 Percentage distribution of total deals by underlying index

Source: PriceWaterhouseCoopers annual survey

GLOBAL WEATHER MARKET TREND AND DEVELOPMENT OVER TIME

Winter is a bigger market than summer

The winter season for weather derivatives has always been larger than the summer season. Figure 2 breaks down the average notional amount that has traded during the winter and summer seasons. As can be seen, the winter market is approximately 2.4 times larger than the summer market.

There are a number of reasons for this. First, the market began trading in the winter and market participants seem to have more comfort trading in the winter period. Second, most of the dealers in this weather market are energy companies that have more winter risk than summer risk, so when they do deals to manage their own internal risk these deals tend to be larger in the winter than in the summer. Finally, winter temperatures tend to be more volatile than summer temperatures. Figure 3 shows the standard deviation of temperatures in New York City over time.

It is readily seen that the standard deviation of average temperature during the winter is larger than the summer. Although the example chosen is New York City, almost all North American and European cities would demonstrate the same finding.[2]

As the European market has developed and continues to grow, the winter market should always be larger than the summer

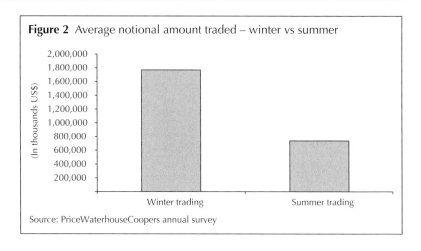

Figure 2 Average notional amount traded – winter vs summer

Source: PriceWaterhouseCoopers annual survey

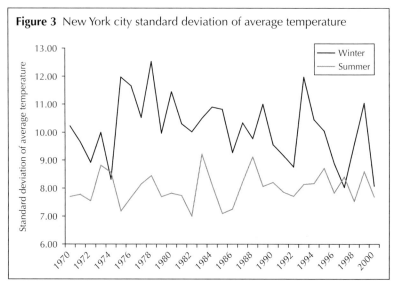

Figure 3 New York city standard deviation of average temperature

market because Europe doesn't have the same cooling demand needs as the United States.

Dealers involved in the weather derivatives market

The weather derivatives market started in the United States and in the first few traded seasons (winter 1997–98, summer 1998, winter 1998–99, and summer 1999) energy and insurance companies dominated the dealer network of weather derivatives in the US (Dischel, 2002). Insurance providers offered large bundles of one-way risk directly to customers and also to the energy players, which they used either to balance the risk in their own portfolios or to offer directly to their customers. Because energy companies were early users of US weather derivatives, the risk insurers primarily underwrote was risk of a warmer than normal winter and cooler than normal summer. This proved to be a risky proposition on a short timescale for the insurers, since the winters of 1997–98 and 1998–99 turned out to be two of the warmest winters on record (Dischel, 2002). The record warm winters caused losses, and in some case substantial losses, to be sustained by insurance companies. As a result, many insurance companies effectively ended large-scale participation as underwriters of weather risk for a number a seasons.

Recently, insurance companies have re-entered the weather market, but have decided to approach the business from a different angle. Rather than provide one-way capacity to the market ie, writing warm protection in the winter and cool protection in the summer, insurers have decided to take a more trading approach to the weather business. Swiss Re and XL Weather and Energy Trading are two examples of insurance companies that will buy and sell weather deals to customers and weather dealers, and that do not write one-way risks. Partner Re has recently announced that it will begin trading weather derivatives as well.

Other insurers teamed up with energy dealers on a quota share basis. Aquila had quota share agreements with a number of insurance companies. Aquila in this case was the entity entering into the weather deal, but any subsequent gains or losses were shared on a pro-rata basis between Aquila and the insurance companies. This arrangement allowed the insurance companies to do what they do best – provide risk capacity, and it allowed Aquila's weather desk to do what it does best – trade and structure weather products.

As the European weather market has grown in recent seasons banks have entered this market. Banks' strong customer relationships and distribution channels have proven to be beneficial to the development of the European market beyond the energy industry. European based banks like Deutsche Bank, Société Générale, ABN Amro and Hypovereinsbank have been successful in originating large transactions in the European weather market.

Trends in the data

The first few weather seasons in the US were dominated by a large number of transactions using a large number of weather stations. Weather stations as diverse as Stockton, Boise, Salt Lake City, Sault Saint Marie, Worcester, Seattle, Milwaukee, Charlotte, and Sioux Falls traded rather frequently. One of the more liquid weather stations in the first few seasons of weather trading was Tucson.

The tremendous amount of early trading activity in Tucson couldn't be justified by end-user business alone, something else had to be going on there. Looking at a graph of cooling degree-days at Tucson it starts to become apparent as to why the weather market traded this weather station so often in the first few seasons. As can be seen from Figure 4, there is a decided upward or warming trend to the time series of cooling degree-days.

In the early stages of the weather market, weather dealers had very divergent views on the nature of this trend and how it would continue into the future, if at all. As can be seen from Figure 4, a 10-year view of the trend, the 10-year historical average of Tucson cooling degree-days is 2,818, and a 20-year view of the trend, the 20-year historical average is 2,751, are very different. So if weather dealer A has an internal view that the 10-year trend is more appropriate for the future and weather dealer B has an internal view that the 20-year trend is more appropriate, it is readily seen that a trade between the two shops would be easily completed and that is

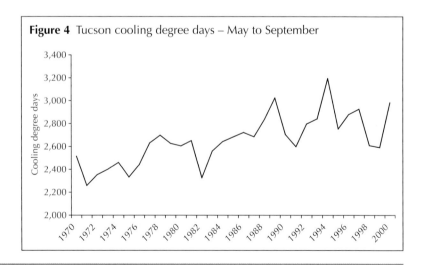

Figure 4 Tucson cooling degree days – May to September

exactly what happened. In essence, weather dealers and insurers were placing a "model" bet on the trend, and were putting trades on that reflected their internal view of the trend's future course. As the market has matured there has been a convergence on how to account for trends in weather data. Calculating trends is simple enough to do and can be learned from any basic statistics textbook. Trends can be easily calculated using parametric measures such as linear trends (Brix, Jewson and Ziehmann, 2002) or non-parametric measures such as moving averages (Cleveland and Devlin, 1988; Brix, Jewson and Ziehmann, 2002). As a result, trading at Tucson has fallen off considerably after the first few seasons, since it is probable that weather dealers calculate trends in a consistent manner.

Changes in instrumentation, instrumentation relocation, and calibration drift

Related to trends has been the treatment of weather data and the effect it has had on trading and liquidity at certain weather stations. As previously stated, there were many transactions using a large number of weather stations in the very early development of the weather market, but weather dealers quickly learned that data could not be taken at face value (Boissonnade, Heitkemper and Whitehead, 2002). Mark Gibbas of AIRWeather in a press release announcing AIR's new weather data products stated:

> "Evaluating a weather derivative contract using raw data can lead to devastating financial consequences as historical data can be inconsistent. If a station moved ... to a cooler location ... using the full [data] set will ... result in a flawed derivatives contract" (AIR, 2002).

In fact, climatologists have long recognised what weather dealers initially did not, in the very early seasons of the weather market, namely that climate data sets have certain problems associated with them. To quote a recent article by Risk Management Solutions:

> "Climatologists have long recognised that most climate datasets contain inhomogeneities or discontinuities introduced by non-climate factors, such as changes of instrumentation, changes of station physical location, changes in surroundings, changes in operation procedures, human errors and changes of operators ... occasional

malfunctions of instruments or "drifts" out of calibration ... can cause a slow warming/cooling trend or a "calibration drift" of the instrument" (Brix, Jewson and Ziehmann, 2002, p. 82).

If a station drifts out of calibration by a small amount, this fact might not be all that meaningful to the casual weather observer. A tourist planning her vacation to Charlotte, North Carolina (NC) doesn't care if the forecasted high for the day is 85° and it turns out to actually be 84°, but a weather dealer cares a lot. If a weather dealer has analysed the weather data set for Charlotte, entered into a weather contract, and then the actual temperature at Charlotte is consistently 1° cooler than the full data set would suggest at face value, that could mean a lot of money made or lost (depending upon which side of the trade she had in her book) on a trade with the typical tick size of US$5,000 per degree-day (Boissonnade, Heitkemper and Whitehead, 2002; AIR, 2002).

The Charlotte weather station is an interesting case study on how treatment of weather data has affected the way the weather market trades. Charlotte in the early trading seasons of the market was actually an actively traded weather station in the voice broker market, but since winter 2000–01 the number of trades in Charlotte has fallen off substantially. Table 1 is a summary of the number of brokered trades transacted with Charlotte as the weather station. One thing that needs to be kept in mind when looking at Table 1 is that early in the US weather market, on average only two or three trades were transacted per week, so the eight trades that TFS

Table 1 Number of trades at Charlotte Douglas international airport as reported in the secondary broker market

Trading season	TFS energy	United weather
Winter 1998–99	0	N/A
Summer 1999	1	0
Winter 1999–00	8	7
Summer 2000	1	3
Winter 2000–01	5	9
Summer 2001	0	0
Winter 2001–02	0	0
Summer 2002	1	0
Winter 2002–03	0	0

Energy reported in Winter 1999–00 represent about a month's worth of trading activity.

The story of Charlotte is very well documented (see Boissonnade, Heitkemper and Whitehead, 2002) In mid-1998 the weather station at Charlotte Douglas International Airport, NC was moved from an area near concrete and asphalt to a very grassy area at the end of a runway. This caused the Charlotte weather station to immediately start reading colder than it had in the past (Boissonnade, Heitkemper and Whitehead, 2002). A simple way to observe this change in Charlotte's weather station temperature readings is to compare it to a neighbouring station. Greensboro, NC is about 100 miles away and in terms of air temperature Greensboro and Charlotte have similar climates. Figure 5 shows very clearly a break in the relationship between Greensboro and Charlotte in terms of temperature readings in mid-1998.

It is very apparent from Figure 5 that something happened in the relationship between the two weather stations, and indeed it did: as stated above, Charlotte's station was moved. Profit opportunities resulted from weather dealers who understood this relationship better than less informed counterparties, and indeed there were a number of trades that occurred early in the weather market with

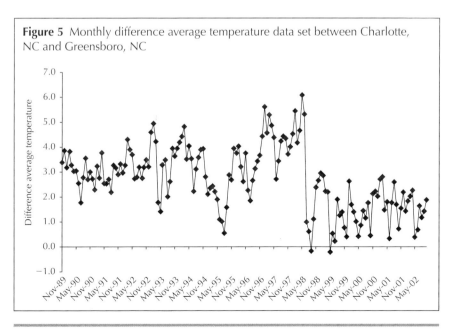

Figure 5 Monthly difference average temperature data set between Charlotte, NC and Greensboro, NC

Charlotte as the weather station as documented in Figure 1. Weather dealers were making station bias and calibration drift "bets".[3]

There are simple quantitative methods to deal with changes in temperature stations due to relocations, actual equipment changes, or calibration drift. But possibly the simplest solution is to stop trading on stations that have a clear bias (and even those with a not so clear bias) in their reporting and move most trading activity to stations that are known to be unbiased and largely free of any calibration drift. If a weather dealer discovers a calibration drift or data inconsistency in the temperature readings of a particular weather station and shows interest in doing a trade on this station in the secondary broker market, other weather dealers will simply quote an enormous bid offer spread on the new station until they have time to investigate the weather data and it is doubtful that a trade will ever be consummated. I would argue that this is one of the reasons that fewer weather stations trade in today's market vs the very early seasons of the weather market. Which leads to a related trend in the trading of weather derivatives – the convergence of trading on New York LaGuardia and Chicago O'Hare weather stations.

LaGuardia and O'Hare in the United States

As has already been stated, it is my opinion that the number of weather stations that traded in the early seasons of the US weather market was greater than the number of stations that trade in today's market. As an example, I will cite Hess Energy Trading Company's own recent trading experience. For the winter 2002–03 trading season, Hess Energy Trading Company had transacted weather trades at half as many locations as winter 2001–02. (Let me quickly point out that I am referring to trading in the secondary and not the primary end-user market.) The number of end-user deals transacted at various weather stations continues to increase season by season both in terms of the number of deals done and the locations for those deals, so this part of the market continues to grow. Also, the number of overall deals transacted in the secondary market continues to grow dramatically, however, the actual number of weather stations used as transaction points has decreased over time.[4] One of the reasons why I believe this is a result of observation of how weather trading has started to converge on basically

Table 2 Percentage of deals transacted each season at Chicago, O'hare (ORD) and New York, LaGuardia (LGA) weather stations as reported in the secondary broker market

| Trading season | TFS energy | | | United weather | | |
	LGA (%)	ORD (%)	Combined (%)	LGA (%)	ORD (%)	Combined (%)
Winter 1998–99	10	4	14	N/A	N/A	N/A
Summer 1999	2	10	12	N/A	N/A	N/A
Winter 1999–00	2	6	8	N/A	N/A	N/A
Summer 2000	5	6	11	5.2	2.4	7.6
Winter 2000–01	5	12	17	2.3	9.7	12
Summer 2001	8	13	21	6.8	7.8	14.6
Winter 2001–02	21	23	44	13.2	21	34.2
Summer 2002	22	27	49	19.9	21.2	41.1
Winter 2002–03	20	26	46	16.7	28.3	45

two weather stations – New York, LaGuardia (LGA) and Chicago, O'Hare (ORD). Table 2 shows the percentage of overall US based deals that have been done at LGA and ORD over time. Notice the dominance of LGA and ORD in recent trading seasons.

Why have LGA and ORD become such important weather stations in the US weather market? Why is the number of overall weather stations that are actively traded decreasing over time? Several factors are at work here, and I will only point out a few reasons; I am sure there are more.

Most East coast weather trading activity correlates well with LGA, so when a weather dealer does a trade with a customer located in the Northeast directly, she will want to hedge or lock in trading edge with the most liquid and highest correlated weather station she can find. Usually, based upon the tight bid offer spread and pricing, this turns out to be LGA. The same is true if the weather dealer does a direct deal with a customer in the Midwest. Chicago is the most liquid station in the Midwest and correlates very well with other Midwestern based stations such as Indianapolis, Milwaukee, Des Moines, and Detroit. So one factor explaining the dominance of these two weather stations is that they are actively used by weather dealers for hedging customer deals.

Another factor related to the increased liquidity of LGA and ORD is that the collective weather dealers in the US market are comfortable with the data at these two weather stations. ORD and LGA do not have the same type of calibration drift and station bias that other stations such as Charlotte have and don't require a lot of systematic analysis and data cleaning, therefore dealers are less concerned with "trend" risk or "data" bias in their models and are prepared to make tight bid offer spreads at these two stations. This is not to suggest that there is no trend at LGA or ORD, but unlike Tucson where there is a strong trend and very little end-user business in the Southwest, at these weather stations there exists a much smaller trend (that can be readily modelled) and much more end-user business close to these weather stations.

Focusing on fewer stations allows a weather dealer to better understand the risks inherent in her book and focus her efforts on more value added activities such as developing structured deals to help customers manage unique risks. Also, the dominance of these two weather stations should allow primary customers to get better pricing for their deals, as weather dealers can charge cheaper prices to their customers because they can hedge at these two liquid weather stations. Customers looking to do a weather deal should be aware of where the ORD and LGA markets are trading, since the market levels at these two stations will most likely have a tremendous impact upon the pricing of their deal.

The convergence of the secondary US weather market on fewer weather stations has taken out the "data" cleaning bet that one weather dealer could make against another weather dealer. The convergence of trading activity and liquidity to fewer weather stations overall and to LGA and ORD in particular has coincided with and is related to one of the latest trends in weather trading – monthly swaps.

Monthlies now dominate the weather derivative market

In the early season of the US weather market most of the deals transacted were seasonal options, relatively fewer swaps traded and almost no monthly or short-term deals traded. Early in the US weather market, weather dealers started trading options as early as April or May for the upcoming winter risk period which typically begins on November 1 and ends on March 31. Weather dealers typically bought or sold options and built up trading books throughout the first week or so of November. Then, after the first few weeks of November, very little trading activity occurred. Dealers sat on the risks they had and hoped that they had built a robust enough book to make money given the temperatures that came in. If the temperatures were favourable, great, but if not there wasn't a lot of liquidity and not very much a dealer could do to hedge unfavourable positions. Eventually, December–March deals, mostly options, would trade and weather dealers were able to hedge a bit, but there was no way to hedge December's position and keep the rest of the book untouched. For example, if a weather dealer had a warm bet on she could not hedge against a cold December and leave the remaining January to March warm bet on. Typically, her book contained a lot of options at many weather stations that were very illiquid and had wide bid offer spreads that made it difficult to transact at economically attractive levels. If she could find a deal to hedge VAR or risk limits moving against her warm winter bet she generally had to hedge by purchasing options for the remaining portion of the risk period and pricing on the options was generally very unfavourable. In today's market this is no longer the case.

A weather dealer can now hedge out a few weeks of weather that go against her in a very liquid short-term swap market, that is dominated by LGA and ORD. If a weather dealer sells a customer in Indianapolis a November–March weather put option at Indianapolis International Airport, she can now swap out her November portion of the risk early in the risk period most likely at ORD and keep the rest of her original position untouched. She would most likely only be willing to swap out of November if there is a very actively traded ORD monthly swap market, and if she believes that there is still a lot of value in the December–March portion of her trade.

Dynamically hedging and re-balancing trading portfolios during the risk period has been one factor in the development of a very robust short-term, monthly, usually swap, market. Table 3 demonstrates how the market has migrated from trading seasonal indices (which were typically options) to monthly indices (which are typically swaps). Concurrently, trading has migrated to fewer, more liquid weather stations and it is difficult to separate the dynamics of these two recent trends.

As seen above, in the US secondary weather market somewhere around 65% of all deals are monthly or even shorter-term deals. And this trend appears to be increasing. This is not to suggest that

Table 3 Percentage distribution of total deals between monthly and seasonal indices by season as reported in the US secondary broker market

	TFS Energy		United Weather	
Trading season	Monthly index (%)	Seasonal index (%)	Monthly index (%)	Seasonal index (%)
Winter 1998–99	12	88	N/A	N/A
Summer 1999	10	90	2.4	97.6
Winter 1999–00	15	85	2.6	97.4
Summer 2000	10	90	9.8	91.2
Winter 2000–01	15	85	9.7	91.3
Summer 2001	14	86	15.6	84.4
Winter 2001–02	15	85	19.8	81.2
Summer 2002	70	30	40.7	59.3
Winter 2002–03	75	25	60	40

the overall number of seasonal deals has decreased over time, quite the contrary. The overall number of seasonal indexed deals has been increasing each successive trading period, but the monthly index weather market has exploded in recent trading periods and dominates the overall trading activity in the secondary market as a percentage of all deals transacted.

It is my opinion that the number of monthly and short-term deals will continue to grow as a percentage of the number of over-all deals in the secondary weather market. There are a number of reasons for this.

First, weather dealers have been trading weather against gas or power or agricultural commodities since the weather market began trading in 1997. These "cross" commodity weather/energy/commodity trading books are receiving more risk capital allocated to them as liquidity improves and weather is "mis-priced" in other markets. Cross commodity trading improves liquidity in the short-term weather market because the price of natural gas or power over a five-month period is probably not highly correlated with weather, but the price of these commodities over a three or four-week period could be highly correlated with weather. Cross commodity traders need short-term liquid weather markets and are putting out more risk in the form of monthly weather swaps. LGA and ORD fit nicely into a cross commodity weather-trading book because they are large population groups and consumption of energy in these regions impacts the price of energy commodities.

Second, the monthly weather market provides weather dealers with the ability to quickly balance their portfolios, as new information becomes available. The newest information usually comes in the form of actual weather experience and forecast information. Short-term trades allow a weather dealer the opportunity to hedge risk that is going against her or take some profit on a strategy that has worked out nicely thus far.

Third, there are the benefits of price discovery and transparency resulting from the Chicago Mercantile Exchange's weather contracts. Although the volume of open interest on the CME's weather contracts is not large, the daily posting of markets has contributed to price discovery and stimulated monthly swap markets in the over-the-counter secondary market.

Finally, and probably most importantly, weather dealers can now trade the forecast. Weather dealers typically employ one or more meteorologists as a vital component of managing weather risk. Meteorologists are employed to provide weather information to help the traders develop the best trading book possible. As part of this role, many meteorologists develop a "view" where they believe that they have information or knowledge that is better than the prevailing market view. Since most of a meteorologist's confidence and skill in forecasting weather is over a short-term basis, typically less than a month, a short-term market is a natural place for meteorologists to put capital behind their view against the collective view of the market. As the market has migrated away from making bets based upon trends, data discontinuities and calibration drift, the market has moved to the last bastion of model bets – namely the forecast. Related to the development of the monthly market in terms of liquidity and timing has been the development of London Heathrow weather station as an actively traded market.

The importance of the London Heathrow weather station
The weather market began trading in the US in the autumn of 1997, but soon weather trading started to take place in other areas of the world as well. Weather deals have been transacted in Asia, Australia, and South America as well as in North America and

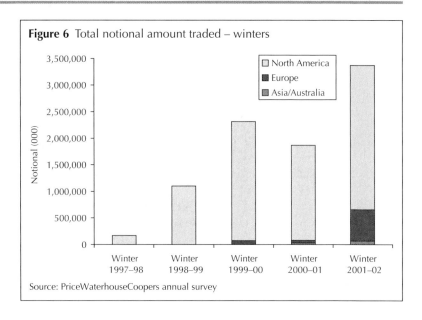

Figure 6 Total notional amount traded – winters

Source: PriceWaterhouseCoopers annual survey

Europe. But one of the most interesting recent trends has been the development of the European weather market, and more specifically of London Heathrow as the second or third most actively traded weather station in the global weather market. From the WRMA sponsored survey conducted by PriceWaterhouseCoopers, as shown in Figure 6, it is readily seen how the London market absolutely took off in the winter of 2001–02.

According to brokers in Europe, London Heathrow represents about 75% of all weather trading activity in the fast-growing European market.[5] London Heathrow typically trades with a smaller bid offer spread than any other weather station in the world.

POSSIBLE DEVELOPMENTS FOR CONTINUED FUTURE GROWTH
End-user customers are needed in the global weather market
The end-use customer has participated in the weather market since its inception, but the widespread use of weather risk management products across a wide variety of industry sectors has not yet occurred. There have been encouraging signs in the customer

market. For example, in the winter of 2001–02 over US$165,000,000 of notional seasonal weather exposure was hedged by US energy companies, which is more than has been hedged by the US energy sector than in any previous trading season.[6] Also, there was a very large multi-year Amsterdam deal brought to market by ABN Amro. These deals, along with transactions in Asia, Australia, and South America, are important developments in the weather market, but almost any dealer will tell you that the key to the future of the weather market is getting more customers and more risk capacity involved in the market.

In order for the weather market to gain traction the way other markets have, the task for weather dealers and originators is to figure out how to motivate customers to do deals. The Weather Risk Management Association (WRMA) recently unveiled a strategic plan designed to promote greater awareness amongst various industry groups about the benefits of managing weather exposure. It is hoped that the efforts of WRMA will greatly facilitate the development of the end-user market.

A very encouraging sign that the end-user market is growing, albeit slower than expected, is the growth of sophisticated, structured products and multi-year transactions. In the early seasons of the weather market degree-day options were considered sophisticated and very few average temperature or precipitation-based deals were transacted. Very quickly degree-day options and swaps have become "plan vanilla" products, and structured products like weather triggered gas daily options have been transacted quite frequently. Also, longer-term multi-year deals are being transacted with greater frequency in the primary end-user market (Star Gas, 2002). The development of more sophisticated products is a clear signal that primary end-users are becoming more comfortable with weather risk management products.

Securitisation could help boost the development of the global weather market

Given the relatively small number of global weather dealers and the large amount of weather risk embedded in national economies, there is a role for securitisation of weather risk to develop the market. To illustrate this, let's take an example of a very large Northeastern US-based entity hedging all of its weather exposure. Although not likely, it is possible that its hedging program would overwhelm the risk capacity in the weather market dedicated to the northeast. An alternative would be for the large entity to hedge its exposure in the much deeper capital markets. Weather could represent a very nice diversifying asset class for capital markets investors, since weather is not correlated with fixed income and equity markets. The problem with taking weather risk to the capital markets is that investors do not understand how weather risk is priced or even how it works, so investors would demand a "premium" over fair value to take on this risk. The question becomes how much premium would an investor need to be comfortable taking weather risk and would paying that premium still make it economical for a large entity to hedge its weather exposure? This is not easily answered, but I would put forward the argument that the premium a large entity would need to pay for its weather hedge could be lower than it would pay in the over-the-counter weather market as it currently exists. The risk capital dedicated to the collective weather market is simply miniscule compared to the vast capacity of the capital markets and a large deal can substantially move the weather market. A large entity might find the capacity in the capital markets would price the deal more attractively, even if a "we-don't-understand-weather-risk" premium needed to be paid in order to attract a broad base of investors. Also, one of the benefits of a large entity securitising its risk in the capital market is that the weather dealers would be eager purchasers of this risk, since they are already involved in the buying and selling of weather risk on a daily basis, but wouldn't have to be relied upon to be the only purchasers of this risk. The weather dealers could provide structuring and pricing guidance to the underwriting firm as well. Such a securitisation would benefit all participants. First, the large entity benefits by prudently hedging its weather exposure at an economically attractive price; second, the weather dealers could purchase the securitised risk, but not be relied upon exclusively to provide the large entity with the entire weather hedge; and third, investors would benefit because they would participate in an asset class that diversifies their portfolios because it is not correlated with their more typical asset classes like stocks and traditional bonds.

CONCLUSION

The weather market has evolved quickly in a relatively short period of time since the over-the-counter market developed in the autumn of 1997. The growth in this exciting market has been very impressive and the number of customers hedging their weather exposure has increased remarkably.

I have tried to show how winter is more actively traded than the summer market. As London Heathrow and the European weather market continues to grow this trend should continue in the future.

Energy and insurance companies in the US and banks and insurance companies in Europe and Asia dominate the types of dealers in the global weather market. As the weather market continues to grow, more banks and insurance companies will increase their participation and involvement in the market.

Weather dealers have migrated trading strategies across various quantitative "bets". Model "bets" have shifted from trends, data, and calibration drift to forecasts.

LaGuardia, O'Hare, and London Heathrow are now the most actively traded weather stations in the global weather market, as trading has migrated from many diverse weather stations to fewer more stable weather stations.

The advent, and now the domination, of monthly trading makes it possible for weather dealers to efficiently reposition and balance the risk in their weather portfolios and to bet on forecasts. Monthly weather markets also make it possible for weather dealers to effectively trade weather against other commodities. All of which has resulted in tighter bid offer spreads in the secondary and hence primary weather market.

I have also put forward the idea, although far from new or original, that in order for the weather market to have a more robust future more end-users will be needed; from those who have underlying weather exposure in their businesses and are motivated to hedge it. I have also argued that given the limited amount of risk capacity in the market, securitisation might be an effective way for very large companies to hedge their exposure while benefiting and not overwhelming the whole weather market.

It will be interesting to see how the weather market evolves over the next few trading seasons, especially given the turmoil that exists in the overall capital markets and the recent dislocations in the energy sector, but that is material for further work.

1   There might be some disagreement as to who carried out the first ever weather derivative, but there is clear consensus that the weather market started trading in earnest in autumn 1997.
2   Private conversations with Tony Hamilton, Hess Energy Trading Company Meteorologist.
3   Based on the author's experience and numerous conversations with market participants.
4   Based on the author's experience and numerous conversations with market participants.
5   Conversation with Olivia Goldsmith, GFI London.
6   The author's sources for this statement are SEC filings, request for pricing from brokers, and market intelligence based upon Hess Energy Trading's experience and participation in the market.

BIBLIOGRAPHY

AIR, 2002, *"AIRWeather Issues Updated Reconstructed Weather Data"*, Business Wire Press Release, URL: http://www.artemis.bm.

Boissonnade, A. C., L. J. Heitkemper and D. Whitehead, 2002, "Weather Data: Cleaning and Ehancement", in R. Dischel (ed), *Climate Risk and the Weather Market: Financial Risk Management with Weather Hedges* (London: Risk Books).

Brix, A., S. Jewson and C. Ziehmann, 2002, "Weather Derivative Modelling and Valuation: A Statistical Perspective", in R. Dischel (ed), *Climate Risk and the Weather Market: Financial Risk Management with Weather Hedges* (London: Risk Books).

Cleveland, W., and S. Devlin, 1988, "Locally-Weighted Regression: An Approach to Regression Analysis by Local Fitting", *Journal of the American Statistics Association*, 83, pp. 596–610.

Cogen, J., 1998, *"What is Weather Risk?"*, PMA Online Magazine, URL: http://www.retailenergy.com/articles/weather.htm.

Dischel, R., 2002, "Introduction to the Weather Market: Dawn to Mid-Morning", in R. Dischel (ed), *Climate Risk and the Weather Market: Financial Risk Management with Weather Hedges* (London: Risk Books).

Star Gas Partners, 2002, "Fitch Affirms 'BBB' Rating of Star Gas's Petro Subsidiary Debt; Star Minimizes Impact of Potential Weather Volatility With Long-Term Weather Insurance", Business Wire Press Release, URL: http://www.wrma.org/news.htm.

WRMA, 2002, "The Weather Risk Management Industry: Survey Findings for November 1997 to March 2001", Report prepared for Weather Risk Management Association by PriceWaterhouseCoopers, URL: http://www.wrma.org.

WRMA, 2002, Presentation made at Annual WRMA Weather Risk Management Conference, Miami, FL June 6, 2002, URL: http://www.wrma.org.

Part VII

Regulatory Issues and
Banking Supervision

27

Regulatory Origins of Risk Management

David Mengle

International Swaps and Derivatives Association

The risk management framework described in other chapters of this book did not arise as the result of regulatory fiat or under the influence of one regulatory agency. On the contrary, it evolved as part of a process of adaptation to changing market conditions across national boundaries and regulatory regimes. But even though risk management as we know it today was not a regulatory invention, its evolution did not occur in a vacuum and was certainly shaped by regulatory events along the way.

Perhaps the most important regulatory influence on risk management was not a government but a private, informal regulatory structure, described by one researcher as *private interbank discipline* (Oedel, 1993). In the present chapter, private market discipline consists of the network of voluntary, industry-wide agreements and market practices that underpin privately negotiated (or over-the-counter (OTC)) derivatives activity. This framework, characterised by interaction with diverse regulatory regimes, by striving for legal certainty, and by emphasising market discipline, created the medium in which risk management could grow.

This chapter has two objectives. The first is to describe the main characteristics of the swaps regulatory framework, and their relation to the risk management framework in use today. The second is to discuss those regulatory events that have been significant to the evolution of derivatives and risk management.

THE SWAPS REGULATORY FRAMEWORK[1]

Concern about "the largely unregulated OTC derivatives market" remains a staple of the financial press whenever financial problems of any size threaten. Journalistic hyperbole aside, "unregulated" appears to take on a narrow definition as "not governed by a single government agency". To understand the regulation of swaps activity, however, it is more useful to adopt the more basic definition of "regulate" as "to control, direct, or govern according to a rule, principle, or system" (Webster's New World Dictionary, 1988).

In the sense of the more basic definition, no activity will survive the disagreements and dislocations that arise in the working of financial markets if it is completely unregulated. Further, as Oedel has pointed out, private market disciplines, such as that found in swaps "nongovernmental" regulatory structures, have arisen to accomplish four tasks normally tended to by government regulators, namely:

> "...to ensure the integrity of the subject interbank operations; to check the monopolistic abuses that tend to arise in connection with large centralized ventures; to protect the interbank ventures from free riders and moral hazard; and to avoid negative externalities that might invite governmental regulation of the interbank disciplinarians." (Oedel 1993, pp. 330–1)

The swaps framework is an example of this basic form of regulation, and exhibits three main characteristics. First, there is no "market regulator" for OTC derivatives activity in the same sense as there is in the United States for securities (Securities and Exchange Commission), or futures (Commodity Futures Trading Commission). The majority of firms involved in derivatives are regulated by a government authority, most of them as banks or as securities firms across a large number of distinct jurisdictions. But at the same time, there are some firms (eg, finance companies) participating in the market that are not directly regulated by a government agency.

The Eurodollar market is arguably the template for the swaps regulatory framework in that it too evolved independently of a single regulator and encompasses participants in a variety of jurisdictions. A variety of factors contributed to the evolution of the market, but most agree that regulatory restrictions in the United States during the 1960s – for example, regulation Q limits on rates payable by banks, reserve requirements on deposits, and capital controls such as the interest equalisation tax – were a major factor that unintentionally encouraged the market's growth

(Stigum, 1990). Further, the cross-border nature of the market and the potential for activity to change jurisdictions discouraged efforts to impose a uniform regulatory regime on the Eurodollar market. Yet, as in the swaps market, most participants are regulated by at least one financial regulator, but the market has grown and market practices have evolved in response to the needs of participants, and not to the requirements set down by regulators.

A second characteristic of the swaps regulatory framework is its emphasis on the underlying legal infrastructure within which market participants conduct business rather on specific rules governing activity. The primary means of strengthening the legal infrastructure is to increase legal certainty across diverse jurisdictions. The International Swaps and Derivatives Association (ISDA), for example, has worked with a variety of jurisdictions to achieve enhancements to bankruptcy codes in order to facilitate the posting of collateral, to permit the early termination of swap contracts, and to recognise the enforceability of close-out netting of obligations. The implication for risk management has been to add certainty and transparency to risk measurement by reducing the scope for unpredictable decisions by a bankruptcy trustee or regulatory agency.

Finally, the swaps regulatory framework rests on a foundation of market discipline – in which firms are accountable for and will bear the losses that result from their decisions – as opposed to compliance with a detailed set of restrictions on conduct. The difference between a regime based on market discipline and one based on compliance shows up in the relative diversity of risk management and compliance structures. Compliance departments, on the one hand, are designed to respond to a specific set of requirements that are uniform across institutions, and the structure of such departments is likely to be dictated by the nature of the rules to be enforced; one would expect compliance structures to be somewhat uniform across firms. Risk management departments, on the other hand, serve a control and reporting function and will likely be structured to fit a particular corporate organisation and control culture; one would expect that, because firms differ, so too would risk management departments.

Privately negotiated, OTC derivatives appear to be highly suited to a market discipline regime. The reason is the central role of reputational considerations. Although a large number of swap transactions fall into a "plain vanilla" category along certain dimensions, swaps are by their nature customised and each transaction presents a unique situation for the parties to it. In a situation that is unique in many dimensions, participants choose their counterparties based on reputation because they are not able to determine quality before the transaction takes place. But in such an environment, reputations – which require a great deal of time and experience to develop – can be lost rapidly if clients' expectations are not met. Given the importance of reputation as an asset of a swap dealer, loss of reputation can be fatal to a firm. As Federal Reserve chairman Alan Greenspan pointed out in connection with the failure of Enron:

> "As the recent events surrounding Enron have highlighted, a firm is inherently fragile if its value added emanates more from conceptual as distinct from physical assets. A physical asset, whether an office building or an automotive assembly plant, has the capability of producing goods even if the reputation of the managers of such facilities falls under a cloud. The rapidity of Enron's decline is an effective illustration of the vulnerability of a firm whose market value largely rests on capitalized reputation. The physical assets of such a firm comprise a small proportion of its asset base. Trust and reputation can vanish overnight. A factory cannot." (US Federal Reserve System, 2002)

A firm operating in such an environment, even if it is subject to a stringent government regulatory regime, is likely to view its market reputation as its primary constraint. This is the type of environment in which risk managers operate today.

OTHER REGULATORY INFLUENCES ON RISK MANAGEMENT
Euro markets and capital market innovation
The first regulatory influence on risk management – the evolution of the Eurodollar market – has already been described. But its significance did not stop with serving as a template for private market regulation of swaps activity; it also showed the way for further capital market innovations and ultimately to markets for risk-shifting.

The success of the Eurodollar market was mirrored in that of the Eurobond market, which sprung from similar unintended regulatory consequences. The Eurobond market was notable for at least two features which later spread to swaps. First, the desire of market participants for uniform trading practices led to industry efforts by what is now the International Financial Markets Association. Second, the Eurobond markets proved to be a fertile medium for financial innovations, among them floating-rate notes and equity-linked bonds (Grabbe, 1996). As would later be the case with swaps, freedom from the inherent rigidity of a monolithic regulatory regime would facilitate the adaptation to changing market conditions.

In addition, the increased scope for innovation afforded by the Eurodollar and Eurobond markets led to growth in capital market alternatives to traditional forms of intermediation. The result was increased availability of substitutes for banking products and therefore more competitive financial markets. A by-product of this development of new forms of market for capital was the development of markets for risk shifting as well.

Finally, as capital and risk-shifting markets grew, the resulting innovation led to a blurring of distinctions between traditional forms of financial intermediation, in particular between bank credit and securities activity. As loan sales, syndications, and securitisations created a continuum between banking and securities, the regulatory structures built on these product distinctions became increasingly irrelevant to market participants.

Shift in regulatory attitudes

Financial markets were not the only institution undergoing innovation; regulation itself was undergoing innovation as well. The innovations occurred both in attitudes toward regulation and in the attitudes of regulators toward financial markets.

First, regulators and market participants, not to mention the informed public, became more knowledgeable about economic reasoning. And at the same time, economic reasoning had moved beyond its automatic advocacy of government regulation as a solution to "market failures" and acknowledged the possibility of "government failure" as well. As an alternative, economists generally moved to a "comparative institutions" approach, which compared the unregulated with the regulated outcome. The practical result for public policy has been recognition that regulation requires that:

1. a problem exists in an unregulated market; and
2. regulation will bring about an improvement over the unregulated situation.

A second change was on the part of the regulators themselves. As regulators grew in their economic sophistication, they also changed their approach to financial innovation from an adversary stance to one of attempting to understand the reasons for the innovation and its consequences for market stability. Such a change could well have resulted from the experience with the Euro markets as described above, in which markets evolved in an orderly manner even though they were not subject to a monolithic regulatory regime.

Finally, regulation during the 1980s changed in character from detailed restrictions on conduct to less intrusive forms that seek to influence behaviour instead of specify it in detail. The reason for the shift was the recognition that, as borders between markets became less of a barrier, prescriptive regulation was rapidly becoming less effective. As an alternative, regulators turned their attention to developing less intrusive forms of regulation, specifically capital regulation. These regulatory changes of the 1980s will be the subject of the following two sub-sections.

Regulatory reform in major jurisdictions

Financial regulation began in the 1980s as a highly restrictive set of rules. In the United Kingdom, for example, securities dealers were restricted to dealing in a "single capacity" as jobbers or brokers but not both, and commissions were fixed. This changed with the Big Bank in October 1986, in which all these restrictions were removed.

In the United States, deregulation went further. The three salient characteristics of US bank regulation in 1980 were price regulation, such as regulation Q restrictions on interest payments on deposits; geographical regulation, such as the McFadden Act restrictions on branching; and product regulation, such as the Glass–Steagall Act and the Bank Holding Company Act. By the early 1990s, all these restrictions were either gone or had become virtually irrelevant.

The first steps in deregulation in the United States took place against a background of rising interest rates following the inflation of the 1970s, which had encouraged consumers to move from bank deposits to uncontrolled alternatives. The Depository Institutions Deregulation and Monetary Control Act of 1980 and the Garn St. Germain Depository Institutions Act of 1982 sought to stem this disintermediation by freeing banks and thrifts from regulation Q restrictions on rates, and by permitting a wider range of product offerings to consumers. The result was increased competition among financial institutions, which by the end of the decade led to the disappearance of many thrift institutions that were exposed to a gap between long-term assets and short-term funding.

The experience of deregulation and the thrift crisis had at least two influences on risk management. First, it brought the problem of interest rate risk to the attention of a wide spectrum of institutions, and in the process led to increased efforts to quantify risks. As part of the emphasis on quantification, regulators added repricing gaps to the information reported by banks to their regulators. Second, regulators found themselves caught in a dilemma: on the one hand, they saw a need for strengthened regulation of insured institutions to counteract the moral hazard effects of the financial safety net; but on the other hand, they were aware of the limits of prescriptive regulation described above. The result was to turn their emphasis to risk-based capital regulation.

The Basel capital framework

In their effort to develop less intrusive but potentially more effective forms of regulation, financial supervisors sought to influence behaviour by basing capital requirements on the riskiness of a bank's assets. Further, the regulators found themselves facing two additional problems during the 1980s. One was the perception that banks were operating with too thin a capital base, largely because of the increased use of off-balance sheet instruments such as derivatives. The other was that banks in some countries, especially Japan, were subject to lax (or nonexistent) capital standards and were placing banks in other jurisdictions at a competitive disadvantage. The result, embodied in the 1988 Basel Accord, was to develop a set of capital standards that would be risk-based, would capture off-balance sheet activities, and would apply uniformly across jurisdictions. The 1988 standards applied only to credit risk, with the understanding that market risk in the trading book would be addressed at a later date.

The success of the 1988 Basel capital framework in achieving its objectives is open to debate, but it has unquestionably influenced the development of risk management since the standards came into effect. On the positive side, the standards have, by effectively assigning risk a price in the form of a capital charge, encouraged banks to identify, quantify, and monitor risks. But on the negative side, the Basel supervisors have shown reluctance to fully recognise the effectiveness of netting, and thereby created a disparity between the risk assessed by supervisors and that actually measured by a firm. In addition, as financial institutions develop models that are able to measure risks more accurately, there is an increasing divergence between regulatory capital requirements and internally measured economic capital.

These problems were to a large extent avoided in the 1996 Basel Committee Amendment to the Capital Accord to incorporate Market Risk, which extended capital standards to market risks in the trading book as well as currency and commodity price risks in the banking book. By allowing the use of banks' internal risk models, subject to regulators' specifications of parameters, the supervisors allowed a great deal more flexibility than did the original Basel Accord. Although it is reasonable to say that the 1996 Amendment encouraged those banks that had not already done so to move to rigorous risk measurement methodologies, it is more accurate to say that the risk management framework formed the basis of the 1996 Amendment, and not vice versa. Indeed, the 1996 Amendment might well be thought of as a regulatory vote of confidence in the risk management framework.

Looking to the future, the Basel Committee and the financial services industry are close to finishing the development of a New Accord, designed to achieve similar policy goals to the 1988 standards, but to avoid the unintended consequences. In particular, the New Accord seeks to avoid inconsistencies between regulatory capital and economic capital, and to a large extent strives for consistency with industry risk measurement and management practices. As with the 1996 Amendment, the New Accord will to a large extent provide a regulatory acknowledgement of the effectiveness of the current risk management framework. Once the New Accord is implemented in 2006, it is likely that capital regulation will embrace even more closely current risk management practices, most notably the use of internal models to measure credit risk and economic capital.

---

1   Mark Brickell, who served for nine years on the ISDA Board of Directors, including four years as its Chairman and two as Vice Chairman, originally articulated the ideas in this section.

BIBLIOGRAPHY

Basel Committee on Banking Supervision, 1996, "Amendment to the Capital Accord to Incorporate Market Risk" (Basel: Bank for International Settlements).

Board of Governors of the Federal Reserve System, 2002, Testimony of Chairman Alan Greenspan, Federal Reserve Board's semi-annual monetary policy report to the Congress, Committee on Financial Services, US House of Representatives, February 27.

Grabbe, J. O., 1996, *International Financial Markets*, Third Edition (New Jersey: Prentice Hall).

Oedel, D., 1993, "Private Interbank Discipline", *Harvard Journal of Law and Public Policy*, vol. 16 No. 3, Spring, 327–409.

Stigum, M., 1990, *The Money Market*, Third Edition (Ohio: Irwin).

Webster's New World Dictionary, 1988, Third Edition.

28

Regulatory Capital Treatment of Counterparty Credit Risk: the Need for a Reform

Emmanuelle Sebton

ISDA

Regulators have so far taken a piecemeal approach to charging capital against counterparty credit risk. The current regulatory framework discourages firms from diversifying their exposures across market risk factors, or across counterparties. A review is now in order, which should draw on positive steps taken by the Basel Committee in respect of securities financing, and reflect good counterparty credit risk management practice.

INTRODUCTION: A DEFINITION OF COUNTERPARTY CREDIT RISK

Counterparty credit risk is the risk arising for a party to a traded instrument contract of making a loss due to default by the other party. Instruments involving a delay between the transaction date and the date at which the contract matures or settles, such as over-the-counter (OTC) derivatives or stock lending and repurchase transactions, typically give rise to counterparty credit risk.

Regulators have long recognised the existence of this form of risk and sought to ensure that banks held enough capital to protect themselves against related losses (Basel Committee on Banking Supervision, 1995). Interestingly though, their approach has been instrument specific, rather than generic; different charges apply to different types of transaction regardless of the homogenous nature of the risk being capitalised.

This "siloing" of capital requirements by product has become a concern for the industry, where counterparty credit risk is increasingly managed and measured at counterparty, rather than transaction, level, ie, without distinguishing between the various trades constituting the underlying portfolio.

The first section of this chapter gives a brief description of the regulatory capital rules that apply to securities financing and OTC derivatives transactions, including an update on amendments to such rules currently envisaged by the Basel Committee.

The second section examines some of the flaws of the approach adopted by the Committee.

The third section discusses the use of expected positive exposure as a possible measure of future exposure for OTC derivatives.

We conclude by highlighting the need for regulatory recognition of portfolio credit risk models.

THE REGULATORY TREATMENT OF COUNTERPARTY RISK

Under both the current and proposed future Basel Capital Accord, the counterparty credit risk charge attempts to capture:

❏ the probability of the counterparty defaulting; and
❏ the size of the exposure.

On both counts, the 1988 Basel Capital Accord rules are a crude proxy for realistic measures of risk, as described below.

❏ The probability of default is, under the current Basel Capital Accord, captured by the product of a risk weight (0%, 10%, 20%, 50% or 100% depending on the type of counterparty), and the 8% solvency ratio. The Basel Committee on Banking Supervision has acknowledged the crudeness of this approach, and is currently reviewing it to include an assessment of the credit quality of the counterparty. The new ratings based capital charges will be implemented in 2006/7. The most risk sensitive approach available under the new Basel Capital Accord will be based on the banks' own internal ratings, and is known as the internal ratings based (IRB) approach.

❏ The size of the exposure is assessed differently depending on the type of instrument concerned. Where exposure on repurchase transactions in the trading book is generally deemed to be zero under the Capital Adequacy Directive, exposure on OTC derivatives' is systematically positive, equal to: max(MTM, 0) + an add-on for future exposure (calculated as a fixed percentage of the notional of the contract), where MTM is the replacement cost of the contract.[1,2] Netting of future exposure across OTC derivatives contracts entered into with a single counterparty is partially recognised, but the regulatory aggregation rule employed is an ad-hoc proxy for the real amount of diversification present in the portfolio.

The Basel Committee has undertaken a review of the measurement of exposure as part of the ongoing revision of the Basel Capital Accord. However, in keeping with past regulatory practice, this review has been instrument specific.

Stock lending and repurchase transactions in the trading book are expected to attract a capital charge based on a portfolio measure of future exposure, estimated at VAR 99th percentile, assuming a 5-day close-out and liquidation period for the collateral.

The treatment of OTC derivatives will however be left untouched.

INDUSTRY CONCERNS WITH THE REGULATORY APPROACH

The approach retained by the Basel Committee fails to accomplish a key objective of the Basel Capital Accord review, namely rendering the regulatory capital approach compatible with the way firms measure and manage risk internally.

This is particularly true of the estimation of exposure. Most financial institutions seek to estimate exposure at counterparty level across all types of contracts. Cross-product netting and cross-collateralisation agreements are being entered into in order to reduce the size of likely exposure to the counterparty in default.

By measuring future exposure on an inconsistent basis for securities financing and OTC derivatives transactions, the Basel Committee ignores industry practice, and may discourage the use of beneficial risk mitigating techniques.

From a risk management perspective, the question posed for repurchase transactions and OTC derivatives is the same, ie, how is the current value of a portfolio of trades modified during the time required to liquidate the collateral (typically between as little as 1 day and 10 days), or, for unsecured transactions, over the regulatory modelling horizon of one year?

The same market risk factors explain the variation in value of both OTC derivatives and securities financing trades; only the horizon changes.

In this light, the expected recognition by the Basel Committee of portfolio VAR measures of future exposure for securities financing transactions is a step in the right direction: diversification across market factors at last becomes part of the regulatory equation.

Firms would argue however that VAR is too onerous a measure of future exposure for the purpose of allocating capital internally, and hence of assigning regulatory capital. Where an exposure is used as part of the economic capital calculation, it tends to be expected positive exposure (EPE) or a related exposure.

EXPECTED POSITIVE EXPOSURE AS A MEASURE OF FUTURE EXPOSURE

EPE is the average exposure arising for a portfolio of trades over a specified horizon. Unlike VAR, no percentile is involved in the calculation.

Expressed mathematically:

The expected positive exposure is the average exposure over all paths $E_A(t) = \max(0, V_A(t))$, and over modelling horizon T:

$$\bar{E}_A = \mu(E_A) = \mu\left(\frac{1}{T}\int_{t=0}^{T} E_A(t)dt\right) = \frac{1}{T}\int_{t=0}^{T}\mu(E_A(t))dt$$

where μ denotes expectation over possible paths of the market.

Expressed graphically (as shown in Figure 1), assuming the future values of the portfolio are modelled using Monte Carlo simulation, EPE is the average taken over the modelling horizon of the average values of the portfolio at each node.

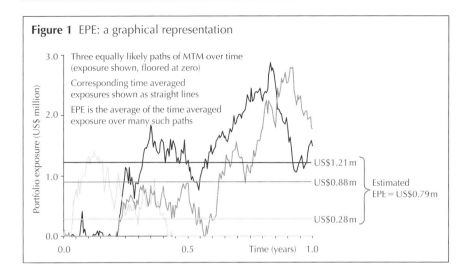

Figure 1 EPE: a graphical representation

It can be shown that using EPE produces an IRB capital require-ment consistent with that applied to loan exposures, subject to the following two restrictions.

❏ Counterparties' positions must be independent.
❏ There must be no positive correlation between the size of the exposure and the probability of default of the counterparty, ie, no wrong-way risk. Where these conditions do not hold, the adoption of a measure of future exposure more conservative than EPE is justified.

Worthy of note is the fact that EPE based capital requirements only cater for the systematic risk contribution of a counterparty. This is, however, consistent with the Basel Committee's approach, which ignores the unsystematic risk contribution in Pillar 1 of the new capital framework.

Members of the International Swaps and Derivatives Association (ISDA) are seeking to determine, based on industry practice as well as empirical testing, whether a single measure of future exposure can be proposed to the Basel Committee for both securities financing and OTC derivatives trades. ISDA is measuring empirically how, for hypothetical OTC derivatives portfolios, internal economic capital compares with IRB capital charges, and will aim to infer an average measure of future exposure from this comparison.

In addition, ISDA, jointly with The Bond Market Association and the London Investment Banking Association, is conducting a survey of counterparty credit risk management practices. This will describe industry practice, covering exposure measurement as well as management.

CONCLUSION: TOWARDS RECOGNITION OF PORTFOLIO CREDIT RISK MODELLING

The industry hopes that it will be possible to recommend the adoption by the Basel Committee of a unique measure of future exposure in respect of OTC derivatives and repurchase transactions, probably based on EPE.

For the Committee to adopt one such measure would however correct only one of the flaws inherent in their approach to counterparty credit risk; portfolio diversification effects continue to be ignored in the regulatory estimation of credit risk capital.

In support of its hostility towards credit portfolio modelling, the Committee raises doubts concerning the estimation of default correlation, and highlights simplifications made in public portfolio credit risk models.

Modelling methodologies evolve nevertheless. As firms collect more default data in order to qualify for treatment under the advanced credit risk approaches outlined in the new Basel Capital Accord, correlations, whether they be between probabilities of defaults (PDs) or between PDs and loss given default parameters, may become easier to validate. The growing trading of credit risk (credit derivatives, secondary loan markets, and securitisation) will further facilitate validation by providing market participants with publicly recognised values for an increasing number of credit risky instruments.

It is the industry's hope that the Basel Committee will soon re-establish the dialogue initiated in 1998 on the recognition of portfolio credit risk models, temporarily interrupted by the review of the Capital Accord.

---

1   Assuming the transaction is properly documented and daily margining applies.
2   By exception, OTC derivative contracts cleared by a clearing house acting as the legal counterparty and where all participants' margins on a daily basis are exempt from counterparty risk charge.

BIBLIOGRAPHY

Basel Committee on Banking Supervision, 2001, "The New Basel Capital Accord", January.

Basel Committee on Banking Supervision, 1995, "Treatment of Potential Exposure for Off – Balance Sheet Items", April, URL: http://www.bis.org.

ISDA, 2000, "A New Capital Adequacy Framework", February.

ISDA, 2001, "ISDA's Response to the Basel Committee on Banking Supervision's Consultation on the New Capital Accord", May.

Gordy, M., 2001, "A Risk Factor Model Foundation for Ratings-Based Bank Capital Rules", Working Paper, February.

Koyluoglu H. U. and A. Hickman, 1998, "Reconcilable differences", RISK, October.

29

Operational Risk –
The Empiricists Strike Back?

Richard Metcalfe

ISDA

Operational risk is not a new discipline, but its incorporation into the capital regime is a major challenge. Whereas credit and market risk readily lend themselves to quantitative analysis, the management of operational risk is proving somewhat harder to treat in such a systematic way. The regime to replace the Basel Accord of 1988 is still being finalised, while the industry's approach to the management of operational risk is still going through an evolutionary phase. The measurement and management of operational risk therefore represent crucial variables in the way firms think of risk and the regulatory environment in which they operate.

A number of techniques have been developed to deal with various facets of operational risk. Firms are tracking (and pooling) data as never before. Many are also working to optimise their overall framework for managing operational risk, taking into account cultural and structural factors as well as direct risk indicators. But, notwithstanding significant advances on all fronts, there is widespread consensus that the discipline may well evolve still further in the coming years.

INTRODUCTION

This chapter argues that, because the management of operational risk relies on cultural as well as quantitative techniques, its development and incorporation into the regulatory capital framework are proving challenging. The debate is many faceted. It concerns the definition of operational risk, its categorisation, its role within the capital regime, issues of quantification and correlation, and the means of assessing and possibly mitigating the risks involved. This chapter also notes that inclusion of operational risk in the regulatory regime raises special challenges for supervisors as well as firms.

RISK-X

At the time of writing few issues divide the risk management community so completely as operational risk. For one thing, it is a protean phenomenon, assuming different guises at different times, sometimes with obviously devastating effects. For another, it spreads into all parts of the entities it affects, with the consequence that there are as many perspectives on the phenomenon as there are stakeholders in a business. Most divisively of all, though, it is caught on a cusp, quantifiable in some respects but deeply resistant to anything but cultural measures in others. Now, in the past three years, onto this fragmented body has come the pressure of regulatory attention.

When G10 supervisors first confirmed in their June 1999 consultation paper on reforming the Basel Accord that they were, so to speak, "going to do something about operational risk", the definition issue loomed large. Rather too large for comfort, in fact, as it turned out that "OR" no longer stood for "operational risk" and had instead became "other" risk. This was meant to indicate that high-level "risks" – business risk, strategic risk, reputational risk even – were in scope and were liable to feed into the calculation of a capital charge; not just settlement fails and "fat-finger" trades.

Even for a relatively disunited discipline, this was too much and produced a concerted and resounding "no" from an industry that was in truth still deciding exactly what it thought (or wanted) operational risk to be. One thing it knew for certain though was that indirect, consequential problems such as reputational damage were so far from the spirit and letter of loss events as to be a distraction in an already complicated debate. Yes, they existed; no, they did not merit regulatory capital in the same way that a default by an obligor merits credit-risk capital. After thorough and lengthy testing of the industry's representations on this point, the Basel

Committee agreed, and took such risks out of "Pillar 1" of the proposed new Basel Accord.

The issue has not entirely gone away though. For one thing, the new Basel Accord will boast two other "Pillars": "2", for supervisory review; and "3", for disclosure (or "market discipline"). There will, therefore, be plenty of scope in the brave new regime for supervisors to quiz firms about "business risk" management and the rest of it; and, under Pillar 3, for firms to tell shareholders and market counterparties all about it in their public accounts. Now would appear to be a good time for firms to start thinking about those particular dialogues.

More fundamentally, three years down the line from that first consultation in 1999, the interaction between the risk manager and senior management (representing the ultimate risk owner, the shareholder) remains key. For if operational risk is partly a matter of day-to-day management of processes from the bottom up, and partly a matter of cultural leadership from the top down, then it is clear that the two processes – governance and hands-on, front-line actions – must mesh in an effective manner.

So much for the issue within operational risk. At the risk of stating the obvious, operational risk is not a "stand-alone" phenomenon. It can and does occur in an environment that is primarily one of market or credit risk. So the interaction between, say, market risk management and overall firm governance also matters. As does the interaction between the operational risk management function and the market risk management function. There's internal audit too – the "third line of defence" for many firms, which has to interact with all of the above and quite a lot of other involved parties too.

Get the feeling this could end up going round in circles? We could focus on one aspect of operational risk, only to find that it leads to another, and so on. On the other hand, maybe a (virtuous) circle is precisely what is needed. The industry suggested as much, through an ISDA paper, in September 2000 (ISDA, 2000). No rocket science in that particular piece of risk management.

There are those, meanwhile, who remain convinced that rocket science or anything approaching it has no legitimate place in any bit of the operational risk space. This might initially appear odd, given the well-known pedigree of advanced physics in other aspects of risk management. But the argument is not so perverse as one might think.

Such people would probably be more comfortable employing a behavioural psychologist than a quant, though to be absolutely accurate they would probably employ neither for operational risk management purposes. For there is an argument that there is nothing new under the sun, least of all operational risk, and that operational risk has by definition been around as long as financial services. The moral, this argument runs, is that managing operational risk is about "real" management, not risk management of the VAR-and-derivatives variety; and that the best hedge against it is experience and discipline. Theirs is a deterministic – not a stochastic – world.

To date, this argument has received pretty short shrift in the Basel Accord-reform debate. The final version of the proposed Basel Accord – which remains veiled in Delphic mist at the time of writing – might yet be more accommodating of more "qualitative" approaches to operational risk, with hints of such a framework appearing in the summer of 2002. Advocates of "scorecard" approaches continue to press their case for something that attempts to bridge the gap between the quantitative and qualitative, but validation is the critical and largely unresolved issue. The debate, though, is likely to run well beyond the finalisation of this round of the Basel Accord reform.

RISK AND REWARD

Meanwhile, the "quantistas" have pushed on, arguing that there are enough financial activities out there which generate neither market nor credit risk – but which do generate potentially volatile fee/service income – to allow one to talk about a risk-reward framework for operational risk. Naturally, these empiricists have targeted their loss modelling on those areas that are rich in data, most notably credit card losses and transaction processing.

Of course, even here the numbers can get rather unstable beyond confidence levels of 95%. Going beyond VAR and applying extreme value theory (EVT) depends on access to more data than most firms would even wish to have at their immediate disposal. (How many severe events would you want to have experienced?) Remember, too, that Basel has been talking (albeit ever less rigidly) about imposing the same modelling standard for operational risk as for credit: 99.9% with a one-year horizon.

"Modelling", by the way, is a contentious word in regulatory circles, because it implies more than Basel believes firms can do in relation to credit risk, let alone operational risk. Correlation in particular is given short shrift in the operational risk parts of Basel-II, which is disappointing given the wide range of operational risk species and their diverse – and diversifying – nature. In fact, this issue is likely to be a sore point for the industry as long as Basel-II is in force, if the Basel Accord assumes maximum correlation across asset classes as well as within the field of operational risk. Summing three 1-year/99.9% numbers for credit, market *and* operational risk gives you an overall capital number at considerably more than 99.9% – a point that has not received the acknowledgement it deserves in the debate.

Operational risk managers have adroitly used the pressure from Basel to galvanise industry-wide data-pooling exercises, which could go some way towards addressing the lack of data (and the relative scarcity of operational risk management IT applications). In fact, Basel may well expect firms to "use" external data, as well as internal data and scenario analysis, in order to qualify for the most advanced treatment.

Apart from determining what exactly is meant by the term "use" – for benchmarking? for scenario analysis? as a direct model input? for some combination of these things? – two big challenges remain. One is ensuring the relevance of any data taken from such a pool in technical terms: matching source and destination business lines and finding a means of scaling data, the latter task being treacherously difficult. The other is a subtler "environmental" match, to take account of any differences in control effectiveness. In principle, as a significant accommodation of "deterministic" science, Basel is also talking about permitting the "use" of qualitative adjustments to hard data, whether internal or external, to reflect special or particular circumstances, good or bad.

Data pooling comes up against issues of confidentiality and legal discoverability, but obviates one major problem with existing sources of external data, which tend to rely on public events (and which therefore are vulnerable to significant gaps in information about those events, for instance any subsequent recoveries). Insurance companies are a further potential source of external data, but that market is relatively green. Also, the structure of the insurance industry means that data sharing might raise monopoly issues.

However you do it, to be able to pool data you need to have a common format. This gets to the heart of what operational risk is and how you categorise it. One short of food manufacturers Heinz, the industry and regulators have cooked up 56 varieties, based on eight business lines times seven risk types (see the matrix in Table 1). In fact, there are more than 56 varieties, because there are sub-categories, which is helpful to those firms that specialise in any one of those eight business lines and wish, for management reasons, to employ the finer distinctions than encapsulated in "level 1" of the matrix; but a potential nightmare for those truly universal institutions that have diversified into all eight. Ultimately, the 56-cell matrix is the basis for data sharing because it offers some hope of recognising the diversity of risk types, at the same time as the prospect of a statistically meaningful amount of data in any one cell.

However, not everyone is fully comfortable with this categorisation. Some events might legitimately be categorised in more than one way at the same time. (For instance, in the view of some firms, "fraud" can overlap with "business practice".) More generally, as with any risk management process, firms would like to be able to use what works for them, which may be a different approach to categorisation (without being forced to allocate or "map" to regulatory buckets).

There is a further dimension to this categorisation problem. Any operational risk manager will tell you that events alone are not the whole story, and have gained prominence in part as the least bad basis for a capital charge. Events, though, have causes and, in practice, it is causes that you manage – not events. Most firms were, of course, doing precisely this, long before the Basel Committee raised the prospect of a capital charge.

Moreover, the relationship between cause and event may be complex. Multiple causes can combine in producing a single event, and equally, a single stimulus can result in many different symptoms. Causal modelling is the developing technique that attempts to systematically map these relationships, but seems destined to play second fiddle to loss distribution modelling. Bayesian belief networks go one stage further (see Alexander, 2000; King, 2001)

Table 1 Business line/event types classification

Business units	Level 1 Business lines	Internal fraud	External fraud	Employment practices & workplace safety	Clients, products & business practices	Damage to physical assets	Business disruption, system failures	Execution, delivery & process management
Investment banking	Corporate finance (including municipal/ government finance, merchant banking)							
	Trading and sales							
Banking	Retail banking							
	Commercial banking							
	Payment and settlement							
	Agency services & custody							
Others	Asset management							
	Retail brokerage							

but what that means in practice is attaching probabilities to the various stages of a given process, which is not a trivial task. To put this in some sort of perspective, data poolers have instead focused on the use of narrative supplements to data points.

The complete picture of operational risk management is even more complex than this brief summary suggests. There are other tools around, most notably "key risk indicators", and the last major industry survey on operational risk (BBA/ISDA/RMA, 1999) suggested that these tools were not only of predictive value to firms, but likely in future to be combined with other tools, such as self-assessment (see Figure 1 which shows that 71% of all firms surveyed in 1999 used or planned to use all five tools). That remains a valid goal for many.

One consensus point is that operational risk breaks down fairly neatly into two types of event: "high-frequency-low-impact" (HFLI) and "low-frequency-high-impact". How one appropriately combines these two very different sorts of event in a single loss distribution (which already tends to involve blending separate frequency and severity calculations) remains a point of debate, but that is precisely what the use of internal-plus-external data is designed to achieve. This means that, in operational risk, the exercises of scenario analysis and stress testing are doubly interesting.

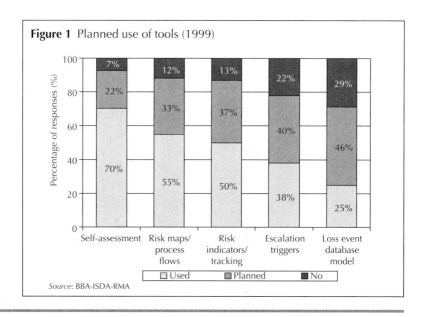

Figure 1 Planned use of tools (1999)

Source: BBA-ISDA-RMA

At the same time, where firms are able to demonstrate that they can and do price in or reserve for "expected" operational loss – which would include HFLI loss – they are likely to be able to reduce their regulatory capital requirement.

RISK MITIGATION

Another loose end concerns risk mitigation, including the use of insurance. Industry is getting comfortable with the idea of inter-changes with supervisors about firm's "tolerances" or "appetite" for operational risk, even though it insists that these may not always be quantified. It is certainly comfortable, for some sorts of risk at least, with insurance. This market may have some way to go, but it is conceptually acceptable to supervisors. The real question is can it develop beyond the existing blanket bond/physical damage/professional liability patch? A true market in multiline protection may be some way off.

And what about derivatives? After all, where there's a risk, there's a way. The wise comment would be "never say never", but the most enthusiasm seems to attach to something more like the catastrophe (cat) bond model, involving funded protection and the linking of investor returns to an index. Alternatively, there might be a simpler economic equivalent – equity.

There remains a well documented suspicion in some minds that the introduction of a capital charge for operational risk was largely the result of a desire to see overall capital levels pick up, rather than shoot down, as they might have been expected to under a genuinely risk-sensitive credit regime. Certainly, operational risk was getting more name checks in the press, Barings in 1995 being the most infamous; but was it actually ever going to be of legit-imate regulatory concern, to the extent of tipping an economy into recession? Unlikely, even when you do include some of the more outlandish "events", such as occasional rogue trading incidents. Undoubtedly, the "basic" and "standardised" approaches under Basel II, both of which key a capital charge off gross income (the one firm wide, the other by business lines), are perfectly suited to such a crude objective, namely keeping capital levels roughly where they are under the 1988 rules.

All that, however, is really water under the bridge, and refers exclusively to the way industry feels about the new charge.

The equally interesting (but largely unreported) implementation question is how supervisors are in practice going to police operational risk and its management in the new, three-pillar world. Even without the introduction of the operational risk charge, Basel II is a much more complicated regime for supervisors to operate. Add in the "advanced measurement approach" for operational risk (particularly its accommodation of qualitative adjustments) and you have two big challenges. You have a conceptual challenge as to how to incentivise good operational risk management on an internationally agreed and equivalent basis. And you have a resource issue, especially if you are in a jurisdiction that has always carried out its supervision at arm's length and in a relatively legalistic way and so has not traditionally employed armies of regulators.

If ever the allusion to Pandora's box was justified, it is here.

CONCLUSION

Operational risk is fundamental to financial institutions, yet currently far less tractable than other forms of risk. The debate about its nature and forms has led to some consensus about how it could and should be incorporated in the new capital framework, currently being finalised. But debate about how this should best be achieved continues, with the result that many firms argue that the discipline needs to be given the room to evolve, without particular techniques or models being prescribed.

BIBLIOGRAPHY

Alexander, C., 2000, "Bayesian Methods for Measuring Operational Risk", Discussion Papers in Finance, University of Reading. URL: http://papers.ssrn.com/sol3/papers.cfm?abstract_id=248148.

BBA/ISDA/RMA, 1999, Operational Risk – The Next Frontier.

ISDA, 2000, "Operational Risk Regulatory Approach Discussion Paper", URL: http://www.isda.org/speeches/index.html.

King, J. L., 2001, "Operational Risk: Measurement and Modelling", Disaster Center Bookstore. URL: http://www.disastercenter.com/Rothstein/cd554.htm.

Part VIII

Future Perspectives

30

Use of Price Derivatives in Commodity Producing Developing Countries

Panos Varangis, John Nash and Funke Oyewole

The World Bank

INTRODUCTION: BRIDGING THE GAP

While market-based tools (eg, futures and options) that insure against price volatility already exist and are widely used in high income countries, the vast majority of agricultural producers in developing countries are, in general, unable to access these markets for several reasons. First, the minimum size of contracts traded on organised exchanges far exceeds the annual quantity of production of individual small and medium-sized producers. Second, small producers, as well as many market intermediaries in developing countries, lack knowledge of such market-based price insurance instruments and an understanding of how to use them. Third, the sellers of such instruments, generally international banks and brokerage houses, are often unwilling to engage with a new and unfamiliar customer base of small-scale producers, characterised by high transaction costs, diminished access to credit, and perform-ance risk.

Even in the developed world, many agricultural producers do not access risk management markets directly. However, other entities involved in the physical business of the commodity may supply risk management products and services, for example, the physical commodity buyers or companies involved in storage or processing, such as grain elevators and oilseed crushing plants. These entities can supply risk management instruments by embedding them in

purchasing contracts. In these cases, the demands of individual producers for insurance are aggregated into a contract of a commercially viable size; thereby enabling even farmers that produce a
relatively small quantity of a commodity to indirectly purchase
insurance. Currently, entities able to provide this type of purchasing
arrangement rarely exist in the developing world.

For small farmers, reduction of this vulnerability to price
volatility can potentially provide a number of benefits, including
better access to credit, enhanced planning and asset management capability, and a reduction in uncertainty that will allow
them to adopt more productive but perhaps more risky production technology. Qualitative benefits alluded to by farmers
in interviews on the subject include greater certainty and peace
of mind.

One approach to mitigating the impact of price uncertainty on
these small developing country farmers is to give them access to
risk management instruments available mainly through international markets.[1] This approach has a number of advantages, but
it also has certain inherent limitations. The nature of these existing
instruments defines the parameters within which such a strategy
can operate. Thus, the focus must be on commodities with liquid
international markets for risk management, mainly coffee, cocoa,
rubber, cotton, grains, sugar and oilseeds – all highly significant
crops for developing countries – although there are commodities
for which liquid markets do not exist, as discussed below. For these
commodities there is a need to investigate other modes of managing price risks.

A further implication of the reliance on available products is that
the focus must be on managing short-term volatility, since existing
price risk management instruments cover price movements over
only relatively short time horizons, generally within a crop year.
For this reason, use of these instruments is not a solution to the secular, or even medium term cyclical, decline in prices of some commodities. Management of short-term price risks can be part of an
overall strategy to adjust to these depressed market conditions, but
the more fundamental solutions must be sought elsewhere,
through productivity growth, diversification, upgrading to
increased value added production, and improvements in marketing channels.

In 1999, the World Bank – with support from several donor governments, and in collaboration with other international organisations and private sector representatives – started a project to make price risk management instruments available to farmers (particularly the small ones) through cooperatives, producer organisations, banks and rural financial institutions, and traders.[2] The role of the World Bank is that of a facilitator, providing technical assistance and capacity building to farmers and intermediary institutions that link farmers to risk management markets. Hedging transactions are strictly commercially based and are only between the local intermediary and the provider (seller) of price risk management instruments. In 2002, the project entered into the implementation phase and several hedging transactions have now been concluded involving local producer organisations in Nicaragua, Tanzania and Uganda, and providers (mainly major international banks) in Europe and the US. These pilot transactions benefited 250 farmers in the case of Nicaragua, to about 450 farmers in the case of Uganda, and to a few thousand farmers in the case of Tanzania.

This chapter focuses on presenting some suggestions that would facilitate the adoption of commodity derivative instruments by agricultural producers and local intermediaries in commodity producing developing countries. The suggestions are primarily a result of the experiences of the World Bank in its 1999 project in this area.

LESSONS FROM IMPLEMENTING A PRICE RISK MANAGEMENT PROGRAMME FOR AGRICULTURAL COMMODITIES IN DEVELOPING COUNTRIES

Policy and domestic regulations matter

The policy environment, both domestic and international, has an impact on the incentives to manage price risks. This environment is conducive to the use of hedging instruments in countries where the markets are liberalised, with no direct government intervention in pricing, and where private marketing institutions are functioning well. On the other end of the policy spectrum, government interventions to artificially stabilise prices pre-empt the development of a market-based price risk management system.

Where the government has an interest in reforming a distorted policy environment, the alternative of a risk management instrument can serve as a catalyst for change. Some of the most costly interventions in many developing and transitional economies – including the operation of state-owned enterprises and other mechanisms to provide support prices – have as a key objective the insulation of the domestic market from the uncertainty that stems from fluctuations in world market prices of inputs or outputs. State involvement in rural financial markets is often justified by the argument that because of the inherently unpredictable nature of agricultural prices and yield, farmers are such high risks that commercial credit institutions will not lend to them. In countries where the governments recognise the shortcomings of the current policies, an alternative market based risk management instrument can provide a minimum price based on international prices for producers, while allowing the government to disengage from costly and counterproductive policies. The availability of such instruments may help persuade a government to adopt a reform programme or enhance its sustainability, thereby creating a more enabling business environment for the private sector.

International policies have also been found to impact on the feasibility of developing a system of price risk management. For example, several developing countries sell their sugar into quota markets at a fixed preferential price, and pay farmers a "blended price", which is essentially a weighted average of the preferential prices and the world price, with a very low weight on the latter. As a consequence, the farm gate price fluctuates relatively little, reducing the incentives for farmers to hedge their price risks using derivative markets. In such cases, where these policies suppress uncertainty, risk management is not a major issue for farmers.

In some countries, eg, India, current regulations prohibit the use of options by non-exporters, but the Government is currently analysing the implications of this, with a view to possibly granting an exemption. In other countries, it is difficult to transfer money abroad to purchase hedging instruments. Thus, it is important to investigate and analyse the domestic policy and regulatory environment when evaluating the feasibility of providing price hedging instruments in developing countries.

There is a need for focused technical assistance to facilitate hedging transactions by "bridging the gap" between buyers and sellers of risk management instruments

A central objective of technical assistance work is to prepare the local counterpart (intermediary) to conduct hedging transactions. This involves two main components:

❏ assistance with development of the risk management strategy, including training and help with the design of specific transactions; and

❏ assistance in implementation of the risk management strategy, which involves incorporating the transaction into existing business practices, and knowing how to manage it from start to finish.

In order to do business anywhere, commercial counterparties must exchange information about each other, and complete a process of due diligence – often called "know your client" – before entering into contractual agreements together. Providers must have comprehensive background information about new clients, and to date, the costs associated with gathering this information in developing countries outweigh the benefits of doing business there. At the same time, buyers are typically sceptical of providers and have little or no information about the big companies offering these products. There is therefore a need for some intermediary to help bridge this informational and confidence gap by directly providing information to both parties and by helping the prospective buyers collect necessary information and transmit it to the prospective providers of the instruments. Private sector providers have indicated that the technical assistance provided to these local intermediaries for hedging instruments to farmers is critical as it provides a level of comfort as to who this local intermediary is, and that it understands the mechanics and implications of hedging transactions. Without this technical assistance, private sector participants said that they would not have been willing and able to transact with these entities in developing countries.

Training local intermediaries and farmers requires very intensive upfront efforts

There is a great deal of training and capacity building required to prepare potential clients in developing countries to use hedging instruments. Even for relatively sophisticated users, such as managers and staff of producer organisations, the understanding of how hedging works and the capacity to manage the transactions is quite low, since this is a completely new area of business for these organisations. Training needs to focus on "introduction to price risk management" and "why to hedge", but also on "what to hedge" and "how to hedge". Risk management is a complicated business, even for sophisticated clients in developed countries, and seemingly small errors in timing or calculation can have large impacts on the financial outcome of a transaction. Therefore, producer organisations – both management and technical staff – need to have a very thorough understanding of risk management procedures and the importance of taking action with precision. Figure 1 shows an example of a training programme.

Technical assistance should cover important areas such as internal procedures, and include participatory training activities such as mock trade sessions and different market scenarios and outcomes. Technical assistance must also include assisting each producer organisation individually in making a comprehensive and coherent risk assessment. This analysis needs to compare/contrast risks

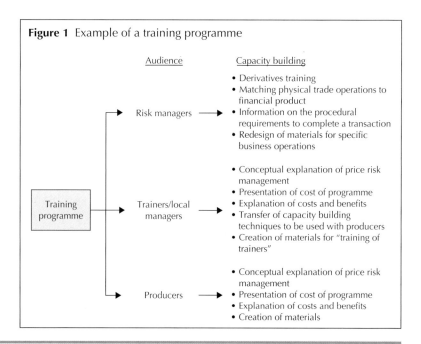

Figure 1 Example of a training programme

involved in their operations with and without hedging, and is a critical tool for their management who must have the capacity to make informed decisions about how to proceed with implementation and specific transactions. Finally, the above elements of technical assistance work (training and facilitating transactions) need to be collaborative efforts, with the management of the producer organisation committed to providing human resources, time, office space, and information. The efforts to focus on relatively sophisticated users run parallel with efforts to adapt training sessions for farmers to enable them to understand the basic mechanics of hedging and the costs and benefits of participation. Training instruments must be tailored to each target audience.

The type of institutions representing farmers has implications for implementing a risk management strategy

Given the small production volumes of most individual farmers, it is necessary to involve some kind of intermediary institution to aggregate the demands of individual farmers into an order for a risk management instrument of the minimum size traded on international markets. A number of types of institutions could in principle play this role.

Cooperatives are interested in combining risk management with the contract to purchase commodities from members. This improves their ability to compete and enables them to provide additional services as an advantage of cooperative membership. Cooperatives have different ways of operating. One model is a cooperative that has a centralised selling team with pre-authorisation to make marketing decisions. This same team can handle risk management as part of its pricing/selling operations. Another model is a cooperative that needs the authorisation from several primary cooperatives to market their crop. This requires consensus building before devising a selling strategy and entering into transactions. The levels of awareness needed and, therefore, the technical assistance requirements are simpler in the former case than in the latter.

Local financial institutions
Banks and other financial institutions are interested in linking loans to price risk management tools, thus protecting their own

risk profile. A reasonable hypothesis, not yet confirmed in practice, is that the banks will be able to expand their agricultural loan portfolios, and the farmers will have better access to credit and/or opportunity to borrow at better terms.

Local traders

In principle, local traders, including exporters and warehouse operators, could be intermediaries on behalf of farmers for hedging transactions. One drawback to having traders and exporters act as intermediaries for hedging is the problems associated with linking risk management instruments to the physical sales of the product. There is some indication that farmers do not want to be obligated to sell to a trader who provides the risk management product. They wish to maintain their ability to continue selling to their own cooperative or have the flexibility to sell to others. Additionally, traders themselves have shown reluctance to link risk management with the physical transactions. A trader who offers a purchase contract with an embedded risk management instrument has a higher default risk than he does when offering straightforward purchase contracts. If prices rise, the purchase contract with the embedded risk management instrument pays a lower net price to the producer than competing purchase offers without risk management. In this scenario, the producer's incentive to default is high since he can sell the product elsewhere and avoid having his price reduced to cover the cost of the premium.[3]

It should be noted as well that traders do not necessarily have an incentive to increase the capacity, sophistication and market knowledge of the producers. Many traders are enjoying high profit margins based on the very fact that the producers have little knowledge of the international market prices and hedging. Also, most traders hedge their price exposure already (back-to-back sales, use of forward and futures markets) and they may find little incentive to develop risk management instruments for farmers who have a different price exposure than they (traders) have. However there are some traders who do provide such services to producers because offering hedging instruments to farmers could be seen as providing additional services to them that enables these traders to capture more clients.

Finally, financial institutions and traders require more initial work than do cooperatives to convince them that this is a good line of business. However, these institutions may provide easier replication of this model and diffusion to more farmers. A financial institution could link its commodity loans to risk management and access the many farmers who receive formal credit. Here a possible limitation is the number of small farmers receiving formal credit. Microfinance institutions and credit unions may also prove feasible vehicles for replication, and are likely to have better access to smallholder farmers.

Relationships and cooperation with private sector providers requires significant upfront work

Most providers of price risk management instruments are not completely ready to transact with entities in developing countries, particularly with organisations of small producers. There are various reasons for this, including the following.

❑ Lack of familiarity with the developing countries, including lack of information about policy or regulatory issues involved in doing business with international partners, in particular commodity derivatives.

❑ Lack of familiarity with clients from developing countries. General "know-your-counterparty" rules require detailed due diligence on behalf of the provider, but gathering this information in developing countries requires resources that the providers are not currently willing to spend. The requirements are stringent and include among other things:

   a. financial statements for the last 3 years;
   b. description and proof of controlling interest and ownership;
   c. articles of incorporation; and
   d. authorisation of individuals to trade.

   Gathering the information about these requirements is an upfront, one-time, expense of the project. Once the procedures are in place the replication for future clients will likely be less expensive.

❑ Because of the events of September 11, 2001, regulatory authorities have put an increased emphasis on monitoring money flows, particularly from developing countries, in order to detect money laundering. This has led them to require that providers collect information above and beyond their previous due diligence requirements. Providers are now required to collect enough information to prove, if needed, that the clients (eg, producer organisations) are legitimate businesses and their funds come from legitimate sources.

❏ Regulatory authorities require that providers of risk management instruments have sufficient evidence that the client understands the transaction and the risk associated with buying these products. Classification of the counterpart is required to show the level of expertise of the client and accordingly, the level of service that the provider is obligated to supply. Most providers will not do business with inexperienced clients and need to show that new clients have experience in and understanding of commodity price risks.

❏ The volumes of transactions could be too small for providers to have adequate margins and sustain their interest in the long run. Identification of local intermediaries to aggregate smallholder demand is of obvious benefit to providers. Providers understand that all new business development starts small and they will be looking for replication to provide increases in both size and scope over time to lay the foundation for sustainability. This makes consolidation (ie, repeat business) essential for the longer-term sustainability and private sector take up of the programme.

In the early stages, options appear to be the most feasible risk management instrument

For providers, in addition to the administrative obstacles outlined above, the most important constraint to doing business with developing country commodity producers is credit risk. Structuring business so that products are simple put options with cash payment of the premium upfront removes credit risk from the provider's perspective and opens the door so that providers can do business with clients they otherwise would not be able to approach. Farmers, at least initially, also desire simple hedging products that they can understand. Thus, initial transactions could be based on the purchase of put options after the funds have been wired to the bank account of the provider.

In the cases where intermediaries are retailing the risk management product to farmers, the product offered by the intermediary may need to be based on an international price and currency. Specifically, in the case of coffee, if the local intermediary contracts with a provider for the option contract in New York (New York Board of Trade (NYBOT)) or London (London International Financial Futures Exchange (LIFFE)), but then offers a product to farmers in local price and local currency, the intermediary carries the basis risk and the currency risk. In some cases the intermediary may be willing to absorb these risks, but it is more likely that these could be unacceptable risks and would make offering the product an unsustainable business in the long run. One exporter acting as the local intermediary in a transaction indicated that he would be willing to continue to provide the risk management product, but could not carry the basis and currency risk for the transactions on an ongoing basis, as these risks could have damaging financial impact to his own operation. In general, therefore, it is expected that farmers will have to take the basis and currency risk. A similar situation exists for local banks and other non-risk takers (eg, traders, warehouse operators) acting as local intermediaries to retail hedging products to farmers. If protection is offered in international prices, the intermediary that retails the insurance product to farmers needs to provide access to international price information so farmers know what to expect in order to ensure a transparent process.

Since providers of the risk management products may not be willing to extend credit lines to local intermediaries, they often require payment of the premium via wire transfer prior to booking the transaction. They are recognising though, that they, in turn, need to require payment from farmers at the same time. Where farmers operate savings and loans societies or other informal, local credit systems that could facilitate the payment of the premium, the take up may be speedier. However, the upfront payment might, in some cases, become an issue if the transaction volumes increase and if commodity prices remain depressed. Experience has shown that local intermediaries understand the costs of the option contracts and maintain that 4–8% of the underlying commodity value may be a reasonable investment for a product that provides protection against future downward price movements.

As users in developing countries become more sophisticated in the use of hedging instruments and find an acceptable form of collateral for the provider, it is likely that other forms of hedging instruments can be used. For example, hedging structures based on collars (buying puts and selling calls), participating options, futures, etc, will likely be used.

EVALUATING THE BENEFITS OF HEDGING AND WILLINGNESS TO PAY FOR PRICE RISK MANAGEMENT
Willingness to pay

As part of the World Bank's price risk management project, a study was conducted to assess the demand assessment and willingness to pay for price insurance for Ghana. This study employs a model to derive the implicit demand for price insurance using the Ghana Living Standards Survey (GLSS) data. The results indicate that the overall benefit to households from minimum price insurance is higher than the insurance premium cost, because of the magnitude of the price uncertainty faced by Ghanaian cocoa farmers as well as their risk and consumption smoothing behaviours.

In addition to this, the project also undertook a survey to evaluate the willingness of coffee farmers in Nicaragua to pay for price insurance. The main results of the Nicaraguan willingness to pay survey are shown in Table 1. Table 2 indicates the market determined actual cost of insurance in September 2001 for put options expiring in January, March and May, 2002 with strike (minimum) price 50 cents per pound.

Table 1 indicates that only 16.7%, or approximately 1 in 6 producers were willing to pay US$5, or 10% of the value of the insured price level. This is likely to be the upper bound of a price insurance

Table 1 Percentage willing to pay to insure US$50/qq

Premium level	US$5.00	US$4.00	US$3.00	US$2.00	US$1.00	No interest
Premium as a % of the insured level	10%	8.0%	6.0%	4.0%	2.0%	
% willing to pay	16.7%	11.4%	22.0%	12.9%	12.9%	24.1%
Cumulative %	16.7%	28.1%	50.1%	63.0%	75.9%	100%

Table 2 Prices for put options strike price 50 cents per pound (US$50/qq)

	Options prices for different months in 2002, (in US$ and as % of strike price)					
	January		March		May	
Mon 9/17	2.95	5.9%	3.85	7.7%	3.95	7.9%
Tue 9/25	2.88	5.8%	4.20	8.4%	4.60	9.2%
Mon 10/1	3.30	6.6%	4.50	9.0%	5.00	10.0%

that would be offered to farmers. A total of 28.1% of the respondents (or less than one-third) reported that they would be willing to pay US$4.00 or 8% of the premium to insure a price level of US$50. If the premium were US$3 or 6%, about 50% of all respondents report that they would be willing to pay this amount to insure a price level of US$50. This corresponds to a short-term price insurance instrument (around four months: September–January) that could be used to protect the return on cash outlays that a producer makes in inputs shortly before harvest. Finally, almost a quarter of the respondents expressed no interest in price insurance. These results from the willingness to pay survey give only a very rough approximation of what the actual demand would be in the case of an actual transaction. The results do however give some support to the general hypothesis that the demand of a price insurance programme should try to target a range of premiums of around 4–8%.

Quantifying benefits of price insurance
One area of analytical work focuses on quantifying in different ways the costs and benefits of price insurance as perceived by clients. Potential users of risk management can be classified into two groups (with some overlap):

❏ individual purchasers who see the insurance product giving them improved predictability, with consequent added benefits such as improved creditworthiness, and ability to plan; and
❏ group users, such as cooperatives, who see the risk management product as a means to provide a wider service to members

in competition with other parts of the private sector (ie, traders and exporters).

General principles of arbitrage suggest that a farmer's long run average income should be roughly the same, whether he hedges or not, after adjusting for transaction costs. Although the data is skewed by the downtrend in commodity markets, back-testing a number of strategies for arabica and robusta coffee, copper and cocoa suggest that this condition does hold, and there is little long-run difference in the mean and standard deviation of income in any of these commodities from a decision to hedge, or not.

However, where there is a clear improvement is in the predictability of income. This can be measured by how far final output prices vary from the observed futures prices at the beginning of the season for agricultural products, ie, how hedging deals with intra-seasonal variation.

In the case of the commodities mentioned above, the use of options as hedge instruments achieves a reduction in variation of the final price from the initial price, as shown in Table 3.

The second group of potential users includes cooperatives who see risk management as a means of enabling them to compete better with the stronger private sector buyers, who have access to such instruments and use them as part of their purchasing and marketing strategies. Often, cooperatives will give farmers an advance payment on delivery of the produce, and make a second payment later if there are profits overall. In many cases, a high first advance has not been sustainable, as prices have fallen over a season leaving cooperatives and their bankers worse off. Risk management strategies put in place at the start of the season give the

Table 3 Standard deviations of intra seasonal price change with and without hedging

Commodity	Standard deviation of intra-seasonal price change without hedging	Standard deviation of intra-seasonal price change with hedging
Arabica coffee	0.41	0.35
Robusta coffee	0.45	0.41
Cocoa	0.24	0.16

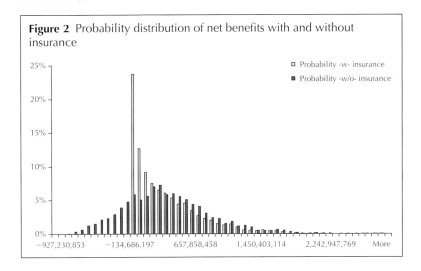

Figure 2 Probability distribution of net benefits with and without insurance

cooperative greater certainty in setting their advance payment, while preserving the possibility of making second payments. The cost is the premium payment, which means that if the price increases and the option is therefore not exercised, the average price net of the premium is slightly lower than it would have been had the insurance not been purchased.

An example of the interactions of the costs and benefits can be seen in Figure 2. The x-axis represents potential profit levels and the y-axis their probability. It can be seen that the use of risk management has removed the possibility of making a loss, but has also lowered the probability of the higher profit levels as a result of the risk management contract purchase price.

CONCLUSION

The fact that the World Bank project has been successful in facilitating transactions, some of which have been repeated, indicates the demand for risk management by small farmers in developing countries, and the technical feasibility of this approach to making it available to them. However, transactions so far have been on a relatively small scale (although growing in size) and have required intensive technical assistance and capacity building efforts. To have a significant impact on rural growth and poverty reduction, access to risk management must be expanded to many more farmers across the developing world. By expanding access, the possibility of repeat and

larger transactions increases, thereby enhancing the commercial viability for the private sector and presenting new business opportunities. The objective is for this project to have a demonstration effect,
which would result in the adoption of this model by local stakeholders (farmers, intermediary institutions, NGOs) and international
private sector providers, who will begin to realise the opportunities
for successful commercial involvement in these markets.

1 Some local hedging markets may also be good candidates for use of risk management,
   eg, Argentina, Brazil, Hungary, India, Malaysia, and South Africa.
2 Namely the European Union, and the governments of the Netherlands and Switzerland.
3 This is not an issue if traders require an upfront payment of the premium, but it may be
   difficult for them to do so. Farmers may also lack confidence that the trader will deliver the
   price insurance if prices decline.

Part IX

Derivatives Disasters – Case Studies

31

No Surprises

Yana O'Sullivan and Geoff Kates

Lepus

This chapter highlights the most noteworthy of rogue traders and investigates why they still succeed in today's risk-conscious environment. Although the lessons from previous rogue trader incidents seem to have been learnt, new loopholes in the system keep appearing all the time. This chapter outlines the top ten preventive measures that banks should consider implementing to protect themselves against fraudulent trade incidents in the future.

INTRODUCTION

Ever since the spring of 2001, when the "hi-tech boom" came to an end, the financial markets have demonstrated an alarming volatility. Losing money, it seems, keeps getting easier. It is no secret that nervous traders can make mistakes, and having incurred losses they sometimes take larger risks to try to recover these shortfalls – only to end up losing even more money. In this scenario, these traders then become fraudsters to cover their own tracks. You would be right in thinking that this sounds a little far-fetched and like a passage from a Hollywood script; except that some Hollywood films, such as "Rogue Trader" (1999), are actually based on real life.[1]

So, what do banks expect from their risk managers and front office supervisors during such times? The simple answer is: "*no surprises*". This, however, gains added sarcastic connotations in the light of the numerous rogue trader incidents that have occurred over the past ten years. Early in 2002, the whole of the banking community was shaken when it was revealed that John Rusnak defrauded AIB of US$750m by generating fictitious foreign exchange transactions. There have been only two other cases that have caused losses on such a grand scale. The most famous "rogue trader" to date is Nick Leeson who caused the collapse of Barings Bank under debts totalling US$1.3 billion in 1995. Even greater than this was the £1.8bn loss that the Japanese conglomerate Sumitomo incurred due to Yasuo Hamanaka's unauthorised trading over a 10-year period.

Unsurprisingly, "rogue traders" attract an amount of media attention that is almost directly in proportion to the amounts of money involved. This is why almost everyone is familiar with the three infamous incidents outlined above. However, not everybody understands the extent and frequency of similar frauds, most of which lack publicity only due to the smaller size of the incurred losses. In fact, if we look at the past decade, every year was marked by at least one or more "rogue trader" incidents.

Endless questions arise in conjunction with this sadly incessant chronology of trading frauds, such as "why does this still happen?", "why have lessons not been learnt?", and "what preventive measures should banks implement?". This chapter will attempt to answer these three questions that are at the top of the priority list for most banks today.

WHY DOES THIS STILL HAPPEN?

Understanding why rogue traders still succeed is the first step on the journey to preventing these fraudsters. The first of many reasons is the increased complexity of the current financial marketplace. This is mainly due to a recent wave of mergers and acquisitions as well as a general increase in the complexity of trading instruments. Another pressure that financial firms are currently experiencing is cost-efficiency. Greater competition and increased market volatility drive banks to cut their business costs. The discrepancies of this approach are particularly noticeable where smaller (and often overseas) branches are overseen with less degree of attention.

Apart from their insufficiency, internal controls often prove to be inefficient too. This may be due to the incompetence of individual supervisors. However, the whole process of controls may fail if there is not enough collaboration between the different parties involved in risk management and trade supervision. Besides, even the most efficient internal controls may be disabled by collusion between traders and supervisors. Senior managers are often reluctant to disclose to the authorities and/or regulators an incident of trading fraud. In order to evade the responsibility and also to save the reputation of their financial firm, they cover up the rogue trader. This can be viewed as a milder type of collusion, which nonetheless is just as dangerous, as this gives the rogue trader the time and resources to increase the damage to the institution.

All the deficiencies of the current system named above have the potential to be fixed in the future. Yet, there is a constant hazard imbedded in the investment banking model: investment bank traders do not have a concept of ownership. This takes away the edge of responsibility, which is present, for instance, in hedge funds that have clear shareholders and are more efficient in terms of operational risk.

WHY HAVE LESSONS NOT BEEN LEARNT?

Some lessons have been learnt. Larger top tier banks have allocated budgets, implemented more sophisticated risk management systems, and tightened controls after the Barings' collapse. There is, of course, slightly more uncertainty with smaller financial firms. A lack of resources has contributed to weaker operational risk controls in the mid and lower tier banks.

Regulators were also quick to react to Nick Leeson's incident. After the Barings collapse, teams of banking and compliance experts released detailed instructions about how to prevent another such rogue trader. The recommendations were acted upon and, in the UK, the Financial Services Authority (FSA), the Bank of England and clearing banks all collaborated in their attempts to raise the standards of internal controls and compliance. As a result, banks are generally better capitalised and have ensured that their front and back office operations are carried out independently from each other.

Although specific lessons have been learnt, new loopholes in the system seem to appear all the time. The sophistication of trader frauds increases together with the growing complexity of trading and risk controls. As a result, risk managers become victims of more loopholes and an upward spiral of surprise events, while rogue traders continue to flourish. Unfortunately, it is necessary to accept the incomplete nature of any particular risk management paradigm. Nobody has the power to completely eliminate rogue traders, but measures can be taken to reduce the ease and hence the frequency of trading frauds.

WHAT SHOULD BE DONE?

The ten preventive measures outlined in this chapter are not a universal cure, yet they can make the objectives of rogue traders very difficult to achieve. Our suggestions are as follows.

1. Reassign responsibilities

All banks should have a clear distribution of responsibilities for a potential trading fraud. This issue has already been addressed by the FSA in the UK. It issued a regulation under which all the senior managers should share responsibility for such incidents. The proactive attitude towards risk management and fraud control should be driven from the top of the organisation down to the bottom of the hierarchy, and all levels of employees should be empowered with the authority to prevent fraud.

2. Improve your basic risk management standards

Risk management standards still remain an unresolved issue in smaller (and commonly overseas) bank branches. Quite simply, it is vital that any risk management decisions are based on expert information. Management must understand the exposures that their institution faces at all levels and locations, the extent of these exposures and, most importantly, how these exposures are protected. In the last five years, most banks have started using value-at-risk (VAR) as their risk assessment model. Before this, risk managers used to rely on daily limits for every trader. VAR is undoubtedly a more advanced technique as it provides an absolute level of risk. The daily limits model revolves around profit and loss (P&L) and is less sophisticated than VAR – hence some banks have dropped it entirely and retained only VAR. However, VAR takes 24–48 hours to be calculated and consequently does not support intraday controls. Therefore, some risk managers still believe that in order to facilitate total control, both of the risk assessment models should be used.

3. Reassess your internal controls

In our view, the internal controls should include the following procedures.

Supervisory controls

All trading supervisors should have separate clearing and operational duties. Trading sheets should be checked and signed off daily.

Checks of trades against confirmations

Checks of individual trades against counterparty confirmations are also absolutely essential. Problems often arise as clients do not always respond to the confirmation calls. In this case traders should make a verbal contact with clients. If this fails too, risk managers should be notified. They can try to negotiate with clients and if they are still reluctant to confirm trades, risk managers should decide on whether their bank should trade with them at all.

Credit and trading limits controls

It is essential to consistently check whether traders keep within their credit and trading limits. Naturally, traders should not be discouraged to take risks, as this is how big profits can be made. However, if traders exceed their limits, this risk becomes unjustifiable and should be prevented. The standard check is the matching of P&L with the credit limits of every individual trader.

Cashflow control

Cash should be considered as one of the ultimate safeguards for banks. It is relatively easy for a trader to conceal a loss-making trade on paper. It is much harder to get the cash to pay the counterparty. Therefore, no matter what the paper records or the bank's trading books say, the bank's treasury should detect irregular trading activities from the cash outflow and unusual cash requests from traders. This method, however, is not perfectly efficient all the time, as some rogue traders might have a fairly steady level of trading and their cash calls would not necessarily stand out immediately. Yet, sooner or later the rogue trader will be unable to get sufficient cash and give themselves away.

Anti-collusion controls

Banks should have internal structures in place that help to avoid collusion. Traditional "whistleblowers" are one way of handling this problem and the introduction of scorecards for supervisors is another one. Independent supervisors can also be delegated from the bank's board of directors.

Counterparty controls

Counterparty controls can prove to be very efficient, as they are independent and are performed by traders, who have a very good knowledge of the marketplace. In some cases banks specifically request their counterparties to control their trading activities.

Checking cash trades offset with paper gains

As has become clear, many rogue traders were offsetting their losses in cash markets with paper gains on other holdings. Hence, banks should be more vigilant to such scenarios and pay special attention to similar cases within their own institutions.

Another issue to be considered is the required depth of internal controls. Indeed, even the most general monitoring of individual traders can prove to be fairly effective. Just by monitoring the irregularities of trading activities, and particularly those that look too good, it is possible to detect fraud. In fact, this approach is believed to be very efficient, as it allows supervisors to pass over many complexities and yet still detect potential problems. Detailed checks of balance sheets are just as important and should be undertaken by professional auditors who know the industry well and understand all the intricacies of the particular bank.

As for the frequency of internal checks, this should depend on the size and idiosyncrasies of individual financial firms. For second and third-tier banks with smaller volumes of trades, batch-based checks at the close of business might be sufficient. For larger banks intraday checks are probably necessary, as money losses can escalate dramatically within one trading day. The ideal scenario, of course, is constant supervision on a deal-by-deal basis. In the long term, a possible solution to preventing rogue traders would be a real-time settlement that allows for more efficient capital lines. If banks could achieve a $T + 0$ (settlement the same day) model with pure electronic cash and instant delivery, it would be very transparent who has capital, and supervisory functions would be significantly simplified.

Banks should also ensure that internal controls are carried out by multiple parties including supervisors, risk managers, traders, and counterparties, as well as by internal and external auditors. Indeed, the best supervisory tool is qualified staff with extensive experience and knowledge of the industry. However, in recent years, an increasing number of functions have been delegated to technology. Many banks are already relying on their systems to spot rogue traders. Some of them have also purchased operational risk management systems that have the capability of measuring operational risk and computing how much capital should be put aside for operational risk purposes.

4. Consider holistic risk management approach
The internal controls of a bank may fail if risk and finance managers do not communicate with each other. A possible solution to this problem is the *risk enterprise and accounting logic* (REAL) approach. This approach is based on accounting consistent with the economic evaluation of business. If the two parties come up with different sums, the discrepancies should be detected and investigated.

5. Escalation processes
Banks need to ensure that all the procedures in the front, middle and back office are managed efficiently. For instance, if trade contracts are not processed efficiently, it is easy to lose track of individual trades and this makes spotting problems virtually impossible. The escalation of processes is even more important when control weaknesses are found or a fraud is detected. Management must act decisively and quickly. Major reputation damage occurs where situations are not found out for a long period of time. Banks should be seen to take action and make any risk management statement clear, practical and public.

6. Reassess your remuneration policies
Traditionally, large bonuses have been the main incentive for traders to perform better but also an incentive to cheat. Banks should not pay the whole of the bonus upfront. That way, traders

would not be able to walk away with the money leaving a financial mess behind them. Another remuneration problem is the discrepancy of salaries between the front and the back office staff. This is believed to be damaging the collaboration between risk managers and traders. The salaries should be made more equal, that way risk managers would have a greater incentive and authority to police traders and increase the security of the bank's operations.

7. Listen to regulators

Indeed, banks must not ignore regulators. In the wake of major banking scandals, regulatory bodies around the world have come under criticism – some of it fair and some of it not so fair. The end result however, has been a toughening of attitudes and a determination to deliver a better product. Although the increased regulatory attention might seem too intrusive to some banks, regulators should not be perceived only as watchdogs but also as associates.

8. Protect yourself against insolvency

Despite the very best controls, audits and procedures, operational failures can and will still happen. Therefore, banks need to have sufficient financial support to offset these losses. Two main practices exist for these purposes. Firstly, the new Basel Accord recommends that all banks should allocate a certain amount of capital in order to offset losses in case of operational failures. While this document is still provisional, it is probably a good idea for financial firms to already comply with this requirement. Secondly, operational risk insurance is an external source of funds that can protect banks against the financial and reputational damage caused by rogue traders.

9. Consider outsourcing

For some investment banks it might be sensible to outsource their trading altogether. This is hardly an unexplored avenue, as some financial institutions have already started outsourcing their trading function. Salomon Brothers, after its merger with Citigroup, "outsourced" its proprietary trading to a hedge fund style operation. This was done in order to avoid the same operational incidents as the firm incurred prior to the merger.

10. Understand the psychology of your traders

This solution is not for everyone, yet it is useful to remember that rogue traders are primarily driven by their human weaknesses. Managers should understand the psychological inclinations of a rogue trader and foresee their actions. Three main factors that should be considered according to Emma Soane (see Soane, 1999) are dispositions, experiences, and the trading environment.

CONCLUSION

To conclude, it is important to restate that no banks should ever become complacent about their internal controls simply because it is impossible to test them against every possible fraud or other operational failure scenario. The best that banks can do is to establish a multi-tiered robust system of controls and hope that they will not all fail simultaneously, which always remains a possibility. Banks should also continuously reassess and improve their risk management systems. If the worst happens to an institution and a major fraud is perpetrated, then its reputation and that of its management can be defended.

This chapter has highlighted the most noteworthy of rogue traders and put forward several ways that may help banks to protect themselves against this type of fraud. If even some of these methods can be adopted across the industry, then the hope is that Hollywood may have to look further afield for its next "Wall Street drama" script.

1   "Rogue Trader" (1999), directed by James Dearden.

BIBLIOGRAPHY

Soane, E., 1999, "It could be you", Operational Risk supplement to *Risk* magazine, July.

32

Medium-Term Risk Management Lessons from Long-Term Capital Management

Philippe Jorion

University of California at Irvine

The 1998 failure of Long-Term Capital Management (LTCM) was one of the most spectacular failures in financial history, endangering the world financial system. The LTCM fiasco was particularly astonishing in view of the fact that the hedge fund seemed to combine the best trader team on Wall Street; that of John Meriwether with the best academic minds, including two Nobel Prize winners, Robert Merton and Myron Scholes. LTCM was viewed as the epitome of quantitative trading, employing scores of rocket scientists searching for inefficiencies in global financial markets. In 1994, Meriwether adorned Business Week's cover as "The Trader." In 1998 the cover read: "Failed Wizards of Wall Street".

This chapter discusses lessons from the LTCM story, drawing from the excellent books by Dunbar (2000), and Lowenstein (2000), and from the quantitative analysis in Jorion (2000). Each account brings a different perspective to LTCM. In "Inventing Money," Dunbar places the LTCM story in the context of the growth of financial derivatives. The book is best appreciated by readers already familiar with derivatives. Lowenstein places more emphasis on personal interactions at LTCM, based on interviews with key players.

It should be noted that neither of these accounts has been officially sanctioned by LTCM. Indeed, consistent with its tradition of secrecy, the hedge fund has been loath to reveal any information about its trading activities. Instead, LTCM has consistently denied responsibility for the US$4.4 billion loss. In his first public interview in 1999, Meriwether attributed LTCM's downfall to frontrunning by other banks: "It was the trades the market knew we had on that caused us trouble." This caused outrage among these banks, which had also lost mightily during the 1998 crisis and put up additional capital to save LTCM from sinking. Dunbar conveys a milder version of this argument, which is that a vicious circle of losses was created by risk managers forcing traders to cut their positions. Later that year, LTCM partners argued that the loss came from a sequence of once-in-a-lifetime events, or a "100-year flood" in financial markets. This argument was rebuffed in an article called "Welcome to this week's one-in-a-million event," by Finger and Malz (2001).

This chapter is structured as follows. The first section presents LTCM's trading strategies. In view of these, the crucial question for the hedge fund was the choice of its leverage and capital base, which is discussed in the second section. The third section then describes LTCM's fall. The fourth section draws on lessons for risk management. Finally, the last section provides some concluding comments.

HOW LONG-TERM CAPITAL MANAGEMENT CHOSE ITS TRADES

The seeds of LTCM can be traced to a highly profitable bond-arbitrage group at Salomon Brothers, which was run by John Meriwether. Meriwether left Salomon in 1994 and took with him a group of traders and academics to set up a hedge fund using similar principles to those they had been using at Salomon. The firm was charging lofty fees consisting of an annual charge of 2% of capital plus 25% of profits.

The core strategy of LTCM can be described as "relative-value", or "convergence-arbitrage" trades, attempting to take advantage of small differences in the prices closely-related securities. The typical example deals with on-the-run and off-the-run Treasury bonds. Thirty year T-bonds are issued every quarter. The most recently issued is called "on-the-run" and is the most liquid. As soon as a newer bond is issued, it becomes "off-the-run". These two bonds are nearly identical in terms of interest rate risk and credit risk. Yet the off-the-run trades at a positive yield spread, which reflects liquidity considerations. When this yield spread becomes too large, relative to the historical average, LTCM's strategy would be to buy the off-the-run and short the on-the-run. The trade would be unwound after the spread had reverted to its long-term value.

This strategy was used in a variety of markets, including:

❏ long swap-government spreads,
❏ long mortgage-backed securities vs short government,
❏ long high-yielding vs short low-yielding European government bonds,
❏ equity pairs (involving different share classes of the same stocks).

The firm also dabbled in non-arbitrage strategies, such as short positions in long-term equity options (dynamically hedged to be delta neutral), bets on takeover stocks, capital-structure trades (involving the corporate bond and the stock of the same company), emerging market debt, and even catastrophe bonds.

It is also worth noting that most of these positions were asymmetrical, like short positions in options. Obviously, swap spreads and volatilities cannot go below zero. They can increase, however, to several times their initial values.

The problem with convergence-arbitrage strategies is that they generate tiny profits. The yield spread between off- and on-the-run Treasury bonds for instance, typically varies between five and 15 basis points (bp) only. Even with a duration of 14 years, a 5 bp move translates into a return of 0.7% only. So, leverage has to be used to create attractive returns.

The crux of the issue for the hedge fund was the proper amount of leverage. Because of the nature of the trading strategies, leverage had to be high. By December 1997, LTCM had a total equity capital of US$5 billion, vs US$125 billion in assets, for a leverage ratio of 25-to-1.

Even more astonishing was the off-balance-sheet position, including swaps, options, and other derivatives, that added up to a notional principal amount of US$1.25 trillion. As of December 1997, total swap positions amounted to US$697 billion, futures to US$471 billion, with options and other over-the-counter (OTC) derivatives accounting for the rest. To give an idea of the size of these positions, the BIS reports a total swap market of US$29 trillion on the same date. Hence, LTCM's swap positions accounted for 2.4% of the global swap market. The futures positions accounted for 6% of the

US$7.8 trillion total. Only six banks had a notional derivatives amount of over US$1 trillion at the time.

Overall, the fund had 60,000 trades on its books. Many of these trades, however, were offsetting each other, so that these notional amounts are not very meaningful. What mattered was the total risk of the fund.

HOW LONG-TERM CAPITAL MANAGEMENT DETERMINED ITS LEVERAGE

LTCM managed its portfolio with a target risk no larger than the risk of an unleveraged position in the S&P 500. The fund started the year 1998 with US$4.7 billion in capital. Take an annual equity volatility of 15%. With independent and identically distributed returns, we can adjust the volatility by the square root of time, assuming 252 trading days in a year. This gives a daily dollar volatility of

$$US\$4,700 \text{ million} \times 0.15 / \sqrt{252} = US\$44 \text{ million}.$$

This number is consistent with LTCM's stated target daily volatility of US$45 million. Translating into a monthly number gives US$45 $\times \sqrt{21}$ = US$206 million. This limit constrained the amount of leverage as well as the size of trades. In practice, LTCM was maximising expected returns subject to a constraint in total volatility. The fund's risk profile was summarised by the "Risk Aggregator," which was discussed every Tuesday morning by LTCM principals.

Essentially, this was a value-at-risk (VAR) system, which predicts the worst loss over the horizon that will not be exceeded at some confidence level. Assuming a normal distribution, and a 21-trading day horizon with a 99% confidence level, the monthly VAR was

$$US\$45 \text{ million} \times 2.33 \times \sqrt{21} = US\$480 \text{ million}$$

where the 2.33 factor is the 99% deviate for a normal distribution. This risk profile seemed acceptable compared to an equity base of US$4.7 billion.

In hindsight, this application was fraught with problems. LTCM's strategy hinged on identifying trades between assets with high correlations over a recent history. Estimated correlations, however, are subject to sampling variability. If the period used to measure the

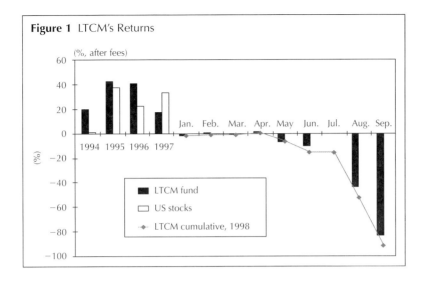

Figure 1 LTCM's Returns

correlation is too short or not representative, the sample correlation is likely to be biased upward, leading to an understatement of the true portfolio risk. A similar argument applies to volatilities. Jorion (2000) presents a stylised example of a portfolio optimisation with two highly correlated assets and shows that the true portfolio risk critically depends on the correlation coefficient.

Admittedly, blind reliance on models can be a danger of risk management. This has been called the "Man in White Coat" syndrome, ie, the mistaken impression of accuracy in models. In LTCM's case, however, the scientist's opinions were disregarded, as we shall see later.

Another issue is the choice of the horizon. For a hedge fund, the horizon should correspond to the period required to liquidate the portfolio or raise additional funds. This may be no easy matter, as additional capital will be needed precisely after the fund has suffered a large loss. After having lost US$2.5 billion, LTCM could not easily adjust its positions nor raise fresh funds.

HOW LONG-TERM CAPITAL MANAGEMENT LOST ITS CAPITAL

LTCM's strategy worked excellently in 1995 and 1996, with after-fees returns above 40%, as shown in Figure 1. By 1997, most spreads had narrowed sharply. This also meant that convergence

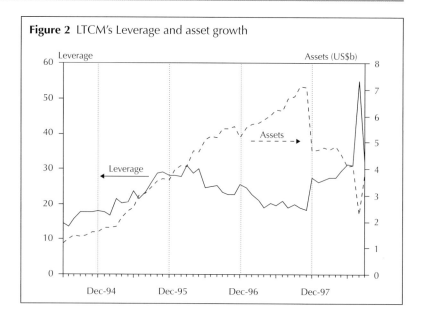

Figure 2 LTCM's Leverage and asset growth

trades had become less profitable, however. In 1997, the fund's return was down to 17%. While respectable, this was below the 33% return on US stocks.

In the meantime, capital had grown from US$1 billion to more than US$7 billion. Due to this asset growth, the leverage of the fund had decreased from 25 to 18, as shown in Figure 2. To achieve the 40% returns it had become accustomed to, the firm had to assume greater leverage. So, LTCM returned US$2.7 billion of capital to investors in December 1997, while keeping total assets at US$130 billion. LTCM explained that "investment opportunities were not large and attractive enough." By shrinking the capital base to US$4.7 billion, the leverage ratio went back up to 28, amplifying returns to investors that remained in the fund.

This decision, however, was controversial within LTCM. The hedge fund was becoming dominated by the two top traders, Hilibrand and Victor Haghani, who owned a large fraction of the fund. While the other partners, including Merton and Scholes, were uncomfortable with the increased risk, there was little they could do. The weekly risk meetings became "increasingly scripted," with results preordained – and Meriwether was unwilling to rein in his traders.

<table>
<tr><td colspan="2">Figure 3 Long-Term Capital Management timeline</td></tr>
<tr><td>February 1994:</td><td>LTCM starts operations with US$1 billion in capital</td></tr>
<tr><td>November 1997:</td><td>Capital at US$7 billion</td></tr>
<tr><td>December 1997:</td><td>Capital of US$2.7 billion returned to investors</td></tr>
<tr><td>May–June 1998:</td><td>LTCM loses US$700 million</td></tr>
<tr><td>August 1998:</td><td>Russian default; LTCM loses US$1,700 million</td></tr>
<tr><td>September 1998:</td><td>LTCM loses US$1,900 million</td></tr>
<tr><td>September 23, 1988:</td><td>LTCM bailout, new capital of US$3.6 billion</td></tr>
<tr><td>December 1999:</td><td>LTCM dissolves</td></tr>
</table>

In retrospect, the decision to return the funds was a fatal mistake. LTCM would most likely have survived the following year with an additional US$2.7 billion in capital.

Troubles began in May and June of 1998 (see Figure 3). A downturn in the mortgage-backed securities market led to a US$700 million loss, shrinking the capital from US$4.7 to US$4.0 billion. Scholes argued that LTCM should cut down all its positions equally, both liquid and illiquid. He was overruled. Instead, LTCM ended up selling off the liquid positions because they were less profitable. This decision turned out to have been another crucial error. This left the fund with illiquid trades and little room to manoeuvre.

Then came August 17. Russia announced that its was "restructuring" its bond payments – de facto defaulting on its debt. This bombshell led to a reassessment of credit and sovereign risks across all financial markets. LTCM lost US$550 million on August 21 alone. Swap spreads, which usually never moved by more than a couple of basis points every day, had moved by 21 basis points. True, it had happened in 1987 and again in 1992, but LTCM's models did not go back that far.

By August, the fund was down to US$2.3 billion. LTCM badly needed new capital but was unable to find takers right away. The next month, the portfolio's losses accelerated. On September 21, the fund lost another US$550 million, mostly due to increased volatility in equity markets.

As LTCM lost money, its cash position rapidly dwindled. Lending banks then started to fear that LTCM would not meet further margin calls. A liquidation of the fund would have forced dealers to sell off tens of billions of dollars of securities to cover their numerous derivatives trades with LTCM. Because lenders had required next-to-zero haircuts, there was a potential for losses, up to

US$5 billion, to accrue while the collateral was being liquidated. The New York Federal Reserve felt compelled to act. On September 23, it organised a bailout of LTCM, encouraging 14 banks to invest US$3.6 billion in return for a 90% stake in the firm. These fresh funds came just in time to avoid meltdown. By September 28, the fund's value had dropped to a mere US$400 million.

LTCM was then operated under the control of the 14-member consortium, formally known as Oversight Partners I LLC. Helped by recovering financial markets, the portfolio was unwound by December 1999. All the remaining money was paid back to investors.

LONG-TERM CAPITAL MANAGEMENT'S RISK MANAGEMENT LESSONS

As Dunbar states, the Risk Aggregator "either didn't work properly or was misused by the LTCM partners – none of whom will now accept responsibility." By August 31, the portfolio had lost US$1,710 million in one month only. Using the presumed US$206 million monthly standard deviation, this translates into an 8.3 standard deviation event. Assuming a normal distribution, such an event would occur once every 800 trillion years, or 40,000 times the age of the universe. The model must have been badly wrong.

Surely LTCM principals must not have believed a normal distribution was appropriate. But this was not even a once-in-a-hundred year event, as they stated later. A general rule of thumb is that every financial market experiences one or more daily price moves of four standard deviations or more each year. And in any year, there is usually at least one market that has a daily move that is greater than 10 standard deviations.

The Risk Aggregator understated risks because it relied on recent history and, in addition, optimised the portfolio to leverage these apparently high correlations. In addition, even with 60,000 trades, LTCM's positions were basically undiversified. The philosophy of the fund was to take exposures to illiquidity and volatility. As one observer said, "they had the same spread trade everywhere in the world." To illustrate this, Figure 4 plots the monthly returns against monthly changes in US credit spreads. The fit is remarkably good, indicating that a single risk factor would explain 90% of the variation up to the September bailout. So, diversification failed because the portfolio was not really diversified.

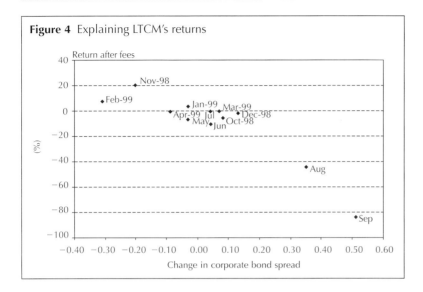

Figure 4 Explaining LTCM's returns

CONCLUSIONS

It seems clear that the LTCM failure was due to increasingly aggressive trading practices. The hedge fund took on more risk precisely at the wrong time in the economic cycle. Objections from academic partners were overruled for the sake of higher profits. In his book, "When Genius Failed," Lowenstein ascribes the failure first and foremost to greed and hubris.

Only lip service was paid to the risk control system. In addition, the Risk Aggregator underestimated the hedge fund's risks due to the focus on recent history and the reliance on artificially high correlations. Diversification failed because the portfolio was not fundamentally diversified. One can also argue that most of the convergence-arbitrage trades were akin to short option positions, which are designed to take a big loss once in a while.

The financial industry should have learned much from this episode. Traditional risk-management models ignore asset and funding liquidity. When positions are large and leveraged, it is important to account for the price impact of forced sales. The industry also needs to develop better stress tests, including potential instability in correlations, as in the work of Kim and Finger (2000).

Wall Street lenders now recognise the need to integrate market and credit risks. When viewed separately, these risks seem acceptable.

The problem arises when they compound each other. In addition, lending policies must account not only for current but also for potential exposure. The Counterparty Risk Management Policy Group (1999) and the Basel Committee (1999) make useful recommendations in that respect.

For all the tremors that shook financial markets in 1998, there has been remarkably little fallout from the LTCM fiasco. The report by the President's Working Group on Financial Markets has had little effect. Legislation to regulate hedge funds was proposed but never came to fruition. Perhaps this is for the best, as this hedge fund was not typical of the industry. Still, it would be in the best interests of the industry to disclose voluntarily aggregate exposures to lenders and investors.

John Meriwether has even started a new hedge fund, called JWM Partners LLC. As of mid-2001, the fund was reported to have capital of US$850 million. The fund operates with lower leverage, around 15-to-1, and under a strict regimen of stress tests. After losing US$4.4 billion, experience is an expensive school.

BIBLIOGRAPHY

Basel Committee on Banking Supervision, 1999, *Sound Practices for Banks' Interactions with Highly Leveraged Institutions*, Basel, Switzerland: BIS.

Counterparty Risk Management Policy Group, 1999, *Improving Counterparty Risk Management Practices* (New York).

Dunbar, N., 2000, *Inventing Money* (New York: Wiley).

Finger, C., and A. Malz, 2001, "Welcome to this week's one-in-a-million event", in *Mastering Risk*, J. Pickford (ed) (London: Pearson).

Jongwoo, K., and C. Finger, 2000, "A stress test to incorporate correlation breakdown", *Journal of Risk*, 2, Spring, 5–19.

Jorion, P., 2000, "Risk Management Lessons from Long-Term Capital Management", *European Financial Management*, 6, September, 277–300.

Jorion, P., 2001, *Value at Risk: The New Benchmark for Managing Financial Risk* (New York: McGraw Hill).

Lowenstein, R., 2000, *When Genius Failed: The Rise and Fall of Long-Term Capital Management* (New York: Random House).

President's Working Group on Financial Markets, 1999, *Hedge Funds, Leverage, and the Lessons of Long-Term Capital Management* (Washington, DC).

33

*Metallgesellschaft**

Christopher L. Culp

The University of Chicago and CP Risk Management LLC

In 1993, Metallgesellschaft AG's US marketing subsidiary, MG Refining and Marketing, booked a US$1.3 billion loss when it unwound a series of oil market hedge transactions and the underlying physical delivery contracts being hedged. Largely because the loss occurred as a part of the firm's hedging strategy, the MG case has been the subject of extensive analysis and debate. Three particular issues of the Metallgesellschaft controversy are worthy of careful consideration by risk managers. Did the programme that MG was trying to hedge make sense in the first place? Was MG's hedge implemented and constructed properly relative to the firm's risk management goals? Was the programme ended at the right time and in an appropriate manner?

INTRODUCTION

Practitioners, journalists, policy makers, and academics alike originally perceived the Metallgesellschaft AG (MG) fiasco as just another derivatives-related loss. Yet, unlike the other more recent derivatives disasters (eg, Barings with its rogue trader and Procter & Gamble with its leveraged interest rate bet), a feature of the MG episode that immediately distinguished it from the rest of the pack was that this firm had apparently lost over a billion US dollars *whilst hedging, not speculating.*

*Portions of this chapter are based heavily on Culp and Miller (1995b; 1999b,c).

The analysis and debate amongst various academics, practitioners, and policy makers over what happened at MG in 1993 is both instructive and confusing – instructive because the MG case does indeed contain many lessons for would-be hedgers and risk managers, and confusing because several *different* debates were actually occurring, all at the same time, all involving the same events at the same company, and all bearing on the current theory and practice of corporate hedging. This chapter makes no attempt to summarise all of those debates, but focuses instead on the three most interesting issues raised by MG for risk managers.

THE METALLGESELLSCHAFT REFINING AND MARKETING PROGRAMME

At the end of 1992, MG was a century-old industrial conglomerate with 251 subsidiaries involved in trade, engineering, and financial services activities. Owned largely by institutional investors, including Deutsche Bank, Dresdner Bank, Daimler-Benz, and the Kuwait Investment Authority, MG's subsidiary responsible for petroleum marketing in the United States was MG Refining and Marketing (MGRM).

In December 1991, MGRM recruited, from Louis Dreyfus Energy Corporation, Arthur Benson and his management team, whose key marketing strategy was to offer firm price guarantees to mostly retail customers for five to ten years on gasoline, heating oil, and diesel fuel purchased from MGRM. By September 1993, MGRM had sold forward the equivalent of over 160 million barrels of petroleum products in these contracts. The firm hedged its resulting exposure to spot oil price increases with futures contracts and futures-equivalent commodity swaps. The bulk of MGRM's futures positions were on the New York Mercantile Exchange in the most liquid contracts of between one and three months to maturity.

MGRM's hedging strategy was called a "one-for-one stack-and-roll hedge" – at any given time, an amount equivalent to the total remaining delivery obligation on the customer contracts was stacked in the short-dated futures. When the futures contracts matured each month, the total position (less current deliveries) was rolled forward into the next contract maturities. Because the term structure of oil futures prices – unlike other commodity markets – is normally downward sloping, the monthly rollovers were expected to generate steady backwardation gains.

But when futures prices fall unexpectedly, cash drains must be incurred to meet variation margin payments. After the Organization of the Petroleum Exporting Countries (OPEC) failed to reach production quota agreements in late 1993, oil prices did indeed plunge. Faced with rising margin calls, the supervisory board of MG AG in December ordered the liquidation of substantial portions of MGRM's futures hedge and subsequently cancelled up to 40 million barrels of its customer contracts. The early termination of the hedge and cancellation of the customer contracts resulted in an estimated net loss of about US$1.08 billion, earning MGRM its place as one of the largest "derivatives-related" disasters.

The unfortunate end of MGRM's programme has given rise to numerous questions about issues ranging from corporate governance to the valuation of long-dated commodity derivatives, many of which are surveyed in Culp and Miller (1999a). The questions most relevant to risk management discussed in the remainder of this chapter can be separated into three general categories.

❏ Given the obvious funding risks, did the programme make economic sense when it was first started?
❏ Did MGRM implement its hedge inappropriately – ie, did it get its "hedge ratios" wrong?
❏ Was the programme terminated at the right time and in an appropriate manner?

THE *EX ANTE* VALUE OF THE PROGRAMME

Many doubtless still believe that MGRM's programme was so fatally flawed that it was doomed to failure before it ever started, but the evidence in favour of that conclusion is far from compelling. Bollen and Whaley (1998) show, for example, that despite the funding risks of MGRM's programme, it would have resulted in substantial economic profits for the firm in almost any reasonable scenario. In addition, the position that the programme was flawed *from its inception* is hard to sustain if it can be shown that the programme had a positive initial discounted expected net present value, and Culp and Miller (1995a,d) attempted to demonstrate exactly that.

True, the funding risks of MGRM's programme were huge. Indeed, the inherent liquidity risk of using futures that are re-settled once or twice daily to hedge a long-dated forward exposure is itself a major "lesson" to be learned from the MGRM debacle. But despite this risk – a risk of which MGRM's managers were apparently keenly aware – MGRM undertook the programme anyway. Why?

It now seems that MGRM's management at the time believed that the firm had access to a "contingent capital" facility designed to provide up to US$1.3 billion in cash in the specific event of a liquidity crisis.[1] The "guarantee" from banks that were acting both as creditors to *and* major shareholders of MG AG was designed to provide an infusion of capital in exchange for revolving senior debt, the proceeds from which were to be used by MGRM to buy puts on oil futures. This would have converted MGRM's futures hedge into synthetic calls and completely terminated the huge margin outflows required to keep the hedge in place as oil prices fell.

The total cost of the puts that would have been required to halt the cash drain totally would have been about US$126 million – a far cry from the US$1.3 billion in the facility, and clearly worth it to preserve the US$800 million of value that Culp and Miller (1995a) estimate was locked up in the customer contracts when they were cancelled. Unfortunately, it seems that the only person authorised to draw on the facility was the chairman of the MG AG management board, Heinz Schimmelbusch, who was removed by the MG AG supervisory board before he had the chance to invoke the facility.

BASIS RISK, PRESENT VALUES, AND HEDGE RATIOS

Probably the most common criticism of MGRM's programme was that although the firm may have correctly calculated the *expected* value of its strategy, it failed to construct a hedging strategy appropriate to reduce the *risk* of its strategy. For most of MGRM's critics – eg, Brennan and Crew (1997), Edwards and Canter (1995), Hilliard (1999), Mello and Parsons (1995), Neuberger (1999), Pirrong (1997), and Ross (1997) – the firm's central failing was getting its hedge ratios wrong, either because it did not adopt a maturity matched hedge like a commodity swap, did not tail its hedge to account for differences in the present values of the cashflows on the underlying contracts relative to the futures, or did not choose a hedge ratio to minimise the variance of the changes in the value of the programme.[2,3]

Despite the prominent role of variance in any mechanical discussions of how firms hedge, surprisingly little work has been done to substantiate the role of variance at the theoretical level. Classic articles about why risk-averse *traders* hedge (eg, Johnson, 1960, Stein, 1961, Ederington, 1979) imply a variance minimisation objective, but articles on *corporate* hedging simply argue for the reduction in risk, usually with no specific attention to *variance* as a source of reduction in the value of the firm. Total variance is treated as a "bad" rather than a "good", as in the classic Markowitz investment paradigm, virtually *by assumption*.

The simplest example of the actual costs supposedly contributed by variance arise when increases in cashflow volatility force firms to turn to *external* financing sources, as in the models of Myers (1977) and Froot, Scharfstein, and Stein (1993) (hereinafter FSS). Myers (1977) argues that agency costs of external finance are most significant for firms with private information about intangible assets and investment opportunities. Those companies find it more difficult to convey the positive net present values (NPV) of their investments to external creditors and consequently face a higher cost of debt. FSS suggest that firms plagued with this problem would be well-advised to rely as little as possible on external finance and to eliminate their cashflow volatility by hedging.

Most of the variance in the cashflows of MGRM's programme, of course, was a result of the calendar basis risk associated with using short-dated futures to hedge a long-dated commitment. For a firm whose risk management objective was to reduce the costs of external finance or financial distress as in the models of Myers or FSS, the MGRM programme would have made little sense. Mello and Parsons (1995) and others thus argued that MGRM should have used maturity matched swaps. A properly calculated hedge ratio as presented by Pirrong (1997) and others is also broadly consistently with this risk management objective.

But the objective of reducing the costs of external finance through cashflow variance reduction is only a *presumptive* risk management goal. Evidence from MGRM's *Annual Reports* and elsewhere suggests that the firm's business mandate was essentially "basis trading". In this case, a risk management programme designed to minimise basis risk would have subverted the very reason that the firm was in business and thus would have made virtually no sense.[4]

The Myers and FSS analysis adopted by many of MGRM's critics, moreover, cannot have applied to MGRM for a variety of reasons. MGRM's hedged marketing programme was not an *intangible* asset at all. On the contrary, it had a significant positive NPV – easily verifiable by outside calculations – that would have served as ample collateral to prospective lenders. True, some *generic* firm following an MGRM-like strategy might have found it difficult to secure external financing *quickly* after a period of sharply declining oil prices. A company forced into the capital market for liquidity when prices fall could be forced to pay what some might consider "distress costs" for that liquidity, even if the long-run expected NPV of the programme was positive.

External financing costs are all almost totally irrelevant, however, as applied to MGRM. As noted earlier, this company's major shareholders *and* creditors were the two largest banks in Germany *and* members of the parent company's supervisory board. MGRM's financing thus was virtually all internal from "delegated monitors" who should have had no trouble seeing the positive NPV of MGRM's programme. Even in the models of Myers and FSS, *internal* financing does not impose any deadweight costs, and thus does not provide an *a priori* rationale for hedging designed to minimise cashflow volatility (see Culp, 2001, 2002a).

WAS THE METALLGESELLSCHAFT REFINING AND MARKETING PROGRAMME ENDED AT THE RIGHT TIME AND IN THE RIGHT MANNER?

If the positive NPV of MGRM's hedged marketing programme was so obvious, why, then, was it closed down at such great cost? The answer lies in one of the hardest problems in all of corporate finance – to wit, when is it rational to throw good money after bad? A simple example may help illustrate the poignancy of this dilemma. Suppose a multinational corporation has a subsidiary in France that is currently incurring net cashflow deficits at the rate of US$1 million per year. The multinational could shut the operation down, but severance pay and other termination expenses required under French law would run to about US$12 million cash, net after tax recoveries. Efforts to find a buyer for the subsidiary have not been successful. Suppose that consultants report one of the problems to be inadequate production capacity for some of the plant's products. Additional equipment can be purchased for a current expenditure of about US$4 million and will cut the net cash deficit to about US$500,000 per annum. Suppose the cost of capital is 10%, and the planning horizon is 25 years.

The multinational faces three alternatives: (i) continue operating at a loss of US$1 million per year; (ii) shut down the plant for a current expenditure of US$12 million; or (iii) invest US$4 million now to reduce losses to US$500,000 per annum. The NPV of each alternative can be calculated as follows:

$$NPV = \sum_{j=1}^{25} \frac{X(t+j)}{(1+r)^j} - I(t)$$

where r is the firm's cost of capital (ie, 10% by assumption), $X(t+j)$ is the net cashflow at time $t+j$, and $I(t)$ is the current investment cost (ie, expansion or shut-down). The NPV of the immediate shut-down alternative clearly is –US$12,000,000. To maintain the status quo yields a current NPV of –US$9,077,040. And to invest the additional US$4 million today and cut losses to US$500,000 per year thereafter yields a current NPV of –US$8,538,520. Counterintuitive as it may seem, the best alternative clearly is to invest the additional US$4 million today in plant improvements, even though the French subsidiary is a losing operation.[5]

When given in the classroom, less-experienced students faithfully compute the present values in the French subsidiary example and get the right answers. Experienced executives, however, often refuse to do the calculations at all. They say the solution is obvious: shut the plant down, and blame the previous management for the loss!

MGRM's situation may well have been no different from the example. MG AG officials argued that the course of action they took – winding down the programme by liquidating part of the futures/swaps hedge and cancelling some of the customer contracts *with no compensation required from customers* – was the only alternative, given the "untenable" situation into which MGRM's former management had put the firm. But as noted earlier, the firm might instead have purchased puts to abrogate the cash drains on its futures hedge, thereby allowing the programme to have been continued.

Even assuming that MG AG management was unwilling to continue the programme, the firm still had alternatives for *how* it ended the programme. The supervisory board might, for example, have directed that MGRM's hedged customer contracts be sold to another firm. Culp and Miller (1995a) estimated that if MGRM had been able to sell the combined programme for its year-end 1993 capital asset value, it would have received nearly US$800 million from the sale. MGRM's *net* 1993 loss would still have been about US$200 million – roughly the same as if the programme had been continued. But the sale would at least have halted the cash drains with which the supervisory board had become so obsessed.

Alternatively, the MG AG supervisory board could have instructed MGRM to buy back its customer contracts by unwinding them. As swap dealers know, when the market smells trouble, unwinding bilateral contracts rarely nets the unwinding firm a cashflow equal to the actual capital value of the contract. That MGRM might not have collected from its customers the same US$800 million it could have made by selling the programme to another firm is thus plausible. But between the time MGRM negotiated the fixed prices on its customer contracts and year-end 1993, the oil spot price had fallen by nearly US$5.75/bbl. Unless MGRM negotiated its contracts at a *massive initial loss*, customers should have been willing to pay *something* to get out of their contracts.[6]

So, contrary to its assertions, MG AG's supervisory board thus had several viable alternatives in December 1993. Instead, the supervisory board chose to liquidate much of the hedging programme and then let its customers off the hook, and then blamed former management for forcing it to pursue this financially catastrophic solution – *viz*, the French subsidiary example, redux.

CONCLUSION

Did the MGRM disaster occur because the MG AG supervisory board truly believed it was throwing good money after bad and had reached some kind of "optimal stopping rule"? Or did the disaster occur because the old MG AG management board *thought* the supervisory board was supporting the basis trading activities of MGRM when it actually was not? Or did the supervisory board support the programme initially and then subsequently abandon MGRM, perhaps in an effort to justify the ouster of the old management board that the supervisory board seemed to have been attempting for some time?

Unfortunately, even with the many separate lawsuits in which MG ultimately became involved, the settlements invariably had "shut-up" clauses that specified the closure of files to outside inspection. Thus alas, the answers to these questions and the full story of MGRM – who did what to whom, when, and why – will probably never come out.

1　For a discussion of contingent capital, see Culp (2002a,b,c).

2　Critics like Ross (1997) that concentrated on MGRM's failure to "tail" its hedge can generally be separated from critics like Edwards and Canter (1995) who were more concerned with reducing the basis risk of the combined programme. The issue of why MGRM may not have tailed its hedge – eg, the shortened *effective* maturity of the programme created by the presence of early termination options, as well as the need to be able to monitor and report a "fully hedged" position to customers – are explored in Culp and Miller (1995c,d).

3　Virtually all of the major academic articles analysing MGRM's hedging strategy – both for and against – are reprinted in Culp and Miller (1999a).

4　For more discussion of the relation between the strategy and tactics of risk management and the use of "selective hedging" methods, see Stulz (1996) and Culp (2001).

5　The unadjusted NPV criterion, of course, is not actually the best way even to answer this question. Following on the early work by Myers (1977) and Brennan and Schwartz (1985), the numerous recent developments in real options can help managers develop better and more systematic criteria than the NPV criterion alone.

6　A former MGRM employee explained in a critique of the special audit of MG that on December 22, 1993, one of MGRM's biggest customers paid MGRM US$2 million to unwind its fixed-price contracts. Two months later when many of MGRM's similar contracts had been cancelled with no compensation required from customers, MG *refunded* the US$2 million it had been paid earlier. Although there is no easy way to assess whether the US$2 million paid was a fair estimate of that customer's actual contract value, it is likely that if one of them was willing to pay, so were others.

BIBLIOGRAPHY

Bollen, N. P., and R. E. Whaley, 1998, "Simulating Supply", *Risk*, 11(9), pp. 143–7.

Brennan, M. J., and N. I. Crew, 1997, "Hedging Long Maturity Commodity Commitments with Short-Dated Futures Contracts", in M. A. H. Dempster and S. R. Pliska (eds), *Mathematics of Derivative Securities*, pp. 165–87 (Cambridge University Press).

Brennan, M. J., and E. S. Schwartz, 1985, "Evaluating Natural Resource Investments", *Journal of Business*, 58(2), pp. 135–57.

Culp, C. L., 2001, *The Risk Management Process: Business Strategy and Tactics* (New York: John Wiley & Sons).

Culp, C. L., 2002a, *The ART of Risk Management: Alternative Risk Transfer, Capital Structure, and the Convergence of Insurance and Capital Markets* (New York: John Wiley & Sons).

Culp, C. L., 2002b, "Contingent Capital and the ART of Corporate Finance", in M. Lane (ed), *Alternative Risk Strategies* (London: Risk Books).

Culp, C. L., 2002c, "Contingent Capital: Integrating Corporate Financing and Risk Management Decisions", *Journal of Applied Corporate Finance*, 15(1), pp. 9–18.

Culp, C. L., and M. H. Miller, 1995a, "Auditing the Auditors", *Risk*, 8(4), pp. 36–40.

Culp, C. L., and M. H. Miller, 1995b, "Blame Mismanagement, Not Speculation, for Metall's Woes", *The Wall Street Journal, Europe*, 25 April, p. 10.

Culp, C. L., and M. H. Miller, 1995c, "Hedging in the Theory of Corporate Finance: A Reply to Our Critics", *Journal of Applied Corporate Finance*, 8(1), pp. 121–7.

Culp, C. L., and M. H. Miller, 1995d, "Metallgesellschaft and the Economics of Synthetic Storage", *Journal of Applied Corporate Finance*, 7(4), pp. 62–76.

Culp, C. L., and M. H. Miller (eds), 1999a, *Corporate Hedging in Theory and Practice: Lessons from Metallgesellschaft* (London: Risk Books).

Culp, C. L., and M. H. Miller, 1999b, "Postscript: How the Story Turned Out", in C. L. Culp and M. H. Miller (eds), *Corporate Hedging in Theory and Practice: Lessons from Metallgesellschaft*, pp. 319–21 (London: Risk Books).

Culp, C. L., and M. H. Miller, 1999c, "Introduction: *Why* a Firm Hedges Affects *How* a Firm Hedges", in C. L. Culp and M. H. Miller (eds), *Corporate Hedging in Theory and Practice: Lessons from Metallgesellschaft*, pp. xix–xxiii (London: Risk Books).

Ederington, L. H., 1979, "The Hedging Performance of the New Futures Markets", *Journal of Finance*, 34(1), pp. 157–70.

Edwards, F. R., and M. S. Canter, 1995, "The Collapse of Metallgesellschaft: Unhedgeable Risks, Poor Hedging Strategy, or Just Bad Luck?" *Journal of Futures Markets*, 15(3), pp. 211–64.

Froot, K. A., D. S. Scharfstein, and J. C. Stein, 1993, "Risk Management: Coordinating Investment and Financing Policies", *Journal of Finance*, 48(5), pp. 1629–58.

Hilliard, J. E., 1999, "Analytics Underlying the Metallgesellschaft Hedge: Short Term Futures in a Multi-Period Environment", *Review of Quantitative Finance and Accounting*, 12(3), pp. 195–219.

Johnson, L. L., 1960, "The Theory of Hedging and Speculation in Commodity Futures", *Review of Economic Studies*, 27, pp. 139–51.

Mello, A. S., and J. E. Parsons, 1995, "Maturity Structure of a Hedge Matters: Lessons from the Metallgesellschaft Debacle", *Journal of Applied Corporate Finance*, 8(1), pp. 106–20.

Miller, M. H., 1997, *Merton Miller on Derivatives* (New York: John Wiley & Sons).

Myers, S. C., 1977, "Determinants of Corporate Borrowing", *Journal of Financial Economics*, 5, pp. 147–75.

Neuberger, A., 1999, "Hedging Long-Term Exposures with Multiple Short-Term Futures Contracts", *Review of Financial Studies*, 12(3), pp. 429–59.

Pirrong, S. C., 1997, "Metallgesellschaft: A Prudent Hedger Ruined, or a Wildcatter on NYMEX?" *Journal of Futures Markets*, 17(5), pp. 543–78.

Ross, S. A., 1997, "Hedging Long Run Commitments: Exercises in Incomplete Market Pricing", *Economic Notes*, n. pp.

Stein, J. L., "The Simultaneous Determination of Spot and Futures Prices", *American Economic Review*, 51(5), pp. 1012–25.

Stulz, R. M., 1996, "Rethinking Risk Management", *Journal of Applied Corporate Finance*, 9(3), pp. 8–24.

34

Analysis of the Orange County Disaster

Alan C. Shapiro

University of Southern California

On December 1, 1994, Orange County announced that its investment fund (known as the Orange County Investment Pool (OCIP)) had lost approximately US$1.5 billion. Several days later, as a result of these losses, Orange County filed for bankruptcy protection and began liquidating the assets held in the OCIP.[1] The total loss on the Pool was ultimately estimated to be about US$1.6 billion out of US$7.5 billion in invested funds. Although any investment loss – much less one of this magnitude (over 20%) – was shocking given the stated purpose of the County Pool and its investment guidelines, it should not have come as a surprise to anyone who actually examined the composition and management of the investment portfolio. The Pool's basic investment strategy was very simple and its risks were readily apparent: Robert Citron, the County Treasurer, used short-term funds to invest in higher yielding longer-term securities and he used financial leverage to increase the size of his investment portfolio. This strategy would work only if interest rates held steady or declined. A rise in interest rates, such as occurred in 1994, would and did lead to devastating losses.

THE COMPOSITION AND RISKS OF THE
ORANGE COUNTY INVESTMENT POOL IN 1994
How the Orange County Investment Pool was managed
The history of financial markets tells us that the only certain way to earn higher returns over time is to take on added risk. Mr Citron confronted this basic risk-return tradeoff head on. Rather than

stick to safe investments, which earned relatively low returns, he sought to increase the returns on the OCIP by "playing the yield curve". The yield curve relates the yield to maturity on bonds to their time to maturity. Entering 1994, the yield curve was (as is typical) upward sloping, indicating that longer-term interest rates exceeded shorter-term rates. For example, in January 1994, the 90-day Treasury bill yielded about 3%, whereas the five-year Treasury bond was yielding about 5%. By increasing the maturity of the OCIP's investments, Citron was able to earn the positive spread between short- and longer-term interest rates. In January 1994, this strategy would have increased the OCIP's annualised return by about 200 basis points (100 basis points equal one percentage point of interest). This strategy would also have increased the OCIP's risk since it is axiomatic that a rise in interest rates lowers the value of interest-bearing assets, with longer-term assets such as Treasury bonds being hit much harder by a rate increase than short-term assets such as Treasury bills, whose short maturity largely insulates it from price variations. It should be noted that the existence of interest rate risk is independent of credit risk, so even though Citron stuck to bonds issued by government entities – which bore essentially no credit risk – the OCIP was still exposed to the risk that these bonds would fall in value if interest rates rose prior to maturity.

Despite the ever-present interest rate risk, this strategy worked for Orange County for several years prior to 1994 as interest rates declined and Citron earned high returns for his investors. In fact, the OCIP earned returns that exceeded those of the comparable California state pool by about 2%. However, in a market where performance differences of 25 basis points attract attention, earning supposedly risk-free returns on the order of 200 basis points over the Treasury bill yield should by itself be a clear warning sign that something was terribly wrong.

Citron magnified the OCIP's interest rate risk by using borrowed short-term funds to acquire additional longer-term securities. By borrowing at the low interest rates associated with short-term securities and lending at the higher longer-term rates, he could add that spread to the returns already being earned on the OCIP's funds. He ratcheted up interest rate risk still further through the use of *structured notes*, which are securities whose interest rate is

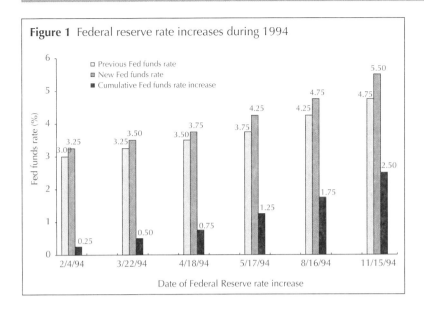

Figure 1 Federal reserve rate increases during 1994

not fixed but rather is reset periodically by reference to a formula tied to some pre-specified interest rate index. Many of these structured notes were *inverse floaters* whose yields rose as interest rates fell and vice versa. Overall, the Orange County investment portfolio was filled with securities whose returns varied inversely with interest rates and it was financed mainly with borrowed funds whose cost varied directly with the level of interest rates. The net result was that the OCIP was exposed to significant interest rate risk, with a big payoff if interest rates held steady or declined and huge losses if they rose. Simply put, Citron bet that interest rates would not rise and he used *financial leverage* (borrowing) to increase the size of his bet.

Up until early 1994, Mr Citron's bet on stable or declining interest rates had paid off handsomely, with the OCIP yielding investors returns that were several percentage points higher than other money market funds, such as the California state pool, were paying. However, beginning in February 1994, the Federal Reserve began a series of ultimately six interest rate increases that altogether boosted the Fed funds rate – a key short-term rate – by 250 basis points during the remainder of the year (see Figure 1). Longer-term interest rates rose by about the same amount during 1994.

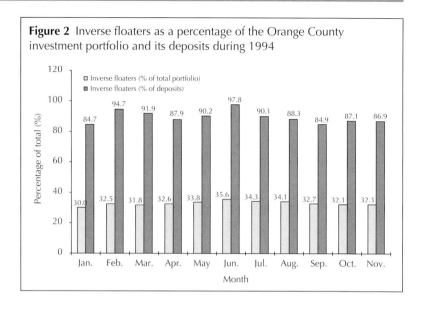

Figure 2 Inverse floaters as a percentage of the Orange County investment portfolio and its deposits during 1994

The effect of this rise in interest rates was to cause significant losses in the market value of the County Pool's portfolio. This loss translated into a much bigger percentage loss in the value of the Pool's invested funds because of the significant leverage being employed. We now examine some specifics of the County Pool's investments and their implications for risk.

Composition of the Orange County Pool's investment portfolio

As shown in Figure 2, from January 1994 to November 1994, the OCIP had between 30.0% and 35.6% of its assets in inverse floaters. As a percentage of deposits, inverse floaters were even more significant, ranging between 84.7% and 97.8% of depositors' funds. An *inverse floater* is a note that pays an interest rate that is calculated by subtracting a variable market interest rate (or a multiple thereof) from a fixed interest rate. Given their structure, inverse floaters pay above-market interest rates when interest rates fall or hold steady and below-market rates when interest rates rise. According to Figure 3, an additional 46.5%–53.9% of the pool's portfolio (125.0% to 145.0% of the pool's deposits) was invested in fixed-rate securities with maturities in excess of three years. All of these securities bore significant amounts of interest rate risk. Money

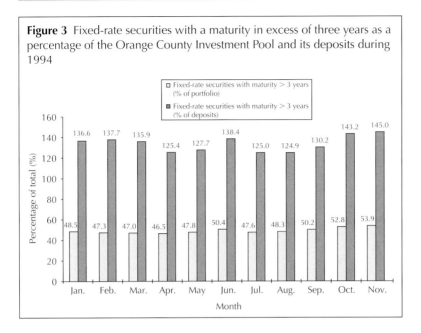

Figure 3 Fixed-rate securities with a maturity in excess of three years as a percentage of the Orange County Investment Pool and its deposits during 1994

market-type investments and floating-rate securities carrying little interest rate risk comprised less than 20% of the OCIP's portfolio.

Citron magnified the OCIP's exposure to interest rate risk by using *reverse repurchase* (or *repo*) agreements to leverage the initial investments in the pool with borrowed funds. In a reverse repo, the owner of government securities agrees to simultaneously sell these securities to a broker-dealer today and repurchase them at a later date at a pre-specified price. The difference between the sale and purchase prices is the interest charged on the reverse repo. In economic effect, a reverse repo is a loan collateralised by the securities being sold and repurchased. Figure 4 shows that during 1994, Citron used short-term (under 180 days) reverse repos to leverage the investors' deposits by a factor of 2.6 to 2.9 to 1, where *leverage* refers to the ratio of the Pool's book value of assets to its deposits.[2] In other words, for every dollar of depositors' funds, the Pool borrowed an additional US$1.60 to US$1.90 and used the proceeds to purchase longer-maturity (generally three- to five-year), interest-sensitive securities (which averaged over 80% of the portfolio's assets). This strategy would pay off only as long as interest rates did not rise.

The effect of this portfolio structure if interest rates were to rise is readily apparent to any finance professional. Most of the pool's

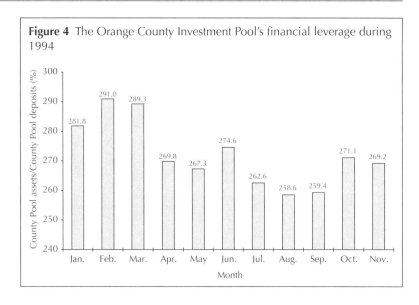

Figure 4 The Orange County Investment Pool's financial leverage during 1994

interest income would hold steady or decline as interest rates rose, whereas its repo interest expense would increase in line with the rise in interest rates. With a large enough move in interest rates, the interest spread that Citron was counting on would turn negative and the County Pool would start haemorrhaging cash. At the same time, the market value of the pool's investment portfolio would decline to reflect the below-market interest rates being earned on the large majority of its securities. If the pool had to liquidate its portfolio to meet collateral calls on its reverse repos (as the securities pledged as collateral fell sharply in value) or to meet redemptions by Pool participants seeing the strategy unwind, these losses in market value would be locked in.

The County Pool's strategy of borrowing short and lending long – which is similar to the strategy that bankrupted the US savings and loan industry – constituted a massive bet that interest rates would hold steady or decline. When interest rates instead rose during 1994, this speculative strategy led to a financial disaster for the OCIP and its participants. At the same time, many of the securities that the OCIP was investing in were highly illiquid, with few holders of the securities and little or no trading activity taking place. In fact, a number of the securities were custom designed for the OCIP and it held 100% of the issue outstanding. This lack of liquidity meant that if the pool had to sell these securities in a hurry to meet redemptions by its participants or for some other reason, there was a strong likelihood that the pool would have to take a large cut in price (relative to the price that it could expect to receive in an orderly liquidation).

ANALYSIS OF THE ORANGE COUNTY INVESTMENT POOL

To conduct a formal analysis of the riskiness of the OCIP, one would have required a listing of the securities being held in the pool along with term sheets giving the terms and conditions of these securities. One would also have needed the type of analytical models that all Wall Street firms have to value the OCIP's securities currently and to project the pool's range of values going forward.

A common valuation approach is to develop a Cox–Ingersoll–Ross (CIR) single-factor model of the interest rate process. The CIR model (or a proprietary variant) is widely used on Wall Street to value complex interest-bearing securities (since the value of any interest-bearing security is determined by the future course of interest rates, one can value any such security by specifying the process generating future interest rates). The term *interest rate process* refers to the fact that given the current interest rate along with various parameters relating to the nature of future interest rate changes (such as the shape of the yield curve; the volatility of interest rate changes; and the extent to which interest rates are mean reverting – that is, if the rate is high today, it is likely to revert to a lower value in the future and vice versa if it is relatively low today), one can determine the probability with which interest rates will move along various future paths. Such a model will also yield the term structure of interest rates, thereby providing the discount factors to calculate present values.

Duration analysis

Absent detailed information on the composition of the portfolio and its value and absent a formal valuation model, there was still enough other publicly available information that indicated serious risks in the portfolio. For example, according to an article that appeared in the *Wall Street Journal* on April 15, 1994, Mr Citron stated that the OCIP's duration was two years and one month. The significance of this statement lies in the fact that a bond's duration

503

provides an exact and widely used measure of interest rate sensitivity – the sensitivity of the bond's value to a change in the interest rate. A bond's *duration* is the weighted average term to maturity of the stream of cashflows, where the weights equal the fraction of total value represented by each cashflow. Specifically, a bond's duration is computed as

$$\text{Duration} = \frac{PV(X_1) \times 1 + PV(X_2) \times 2 + \cdots + PV(X_n) \times n}{V_0} \qquad (1)$$

where V_0 is the bond's current value, $PV(X_t)$ is the present value of the period t cashflow, X_t, provided by the bond, using the yield to maturity as the discount rate in these calculations, and n is the maturity of the bond. In effect, the duration of a bond equals the amount of time that elapses before the "average" dollar of present value from the bond's stream of payments is received. Thus, for example, the higher the coupon payments are, the shorter the duration of the bond will be, all other things being equal. Alternatively, a zero-coupon bond, with all its cashflows coming in the final year n, will have a duration of n, the highest one possible.

Consider, for example, two different five-year bonds. The first bond has a coupon of 12% and is priced at 104.50, and the second has a coupon of 8% and is priced at 89.30. Because bond prices are expressed as a percentage of their face value, and both bonds have face values of US$1,000, they sell for US$1,045 and US$893, respectively. Although the calculations are not shown, the yield to maturity (the internal rate of return) of the first bond is 10.79%, and the yield to maturity of the second bond is 10.89%.

Table 1 shows the calculations of duration for the two bonds. It can be seen that the cashflow in year 5 accounts for 64.2% of the price of the 12% bond but 72.1% of the 8% bond's value, because of the 12% bond's higher coupon payments. As expected, the duration of the 12% bond (4.06 years) is shorter than the duration of the 8% bond (4.27 years).

The bond's interest rate sensitivity or volatility, in turn, depends on its modified duration:

$$\text{Modified duration} = \frac{\text{Duration}}{(1 + \text{Yield})} \qquad (2)$$

Table 1 Duration calculations for 12% and 8% coupon bonds

		12% Coupon bond		
Year	Cashflow	Present value at 10.79%	Proportion of bond price	Proportion of bond price × time
1	120	108.31	0.104	0.104
2	120	97.76	0.094	0.187
3	120	88.24	0.084	0.253
4	120	79.65	0.076	0.305
5	1,120	670.99	0.642	3.211
		US$1,044.96	1.000	Duration = 4.06 years

		8% Coupon bond		
Year	Cashflow	Present value at 10.89%	Proportion of bond price	Proportion of bond price × time
1	80	72.14	0.081	0.081
2	80	65.06	0.073	0.146
3	80	58.67	0.066	0.197
4	80	52.91	0.059	0.237
5	1,080	644.11	0.721	3.607
		US$892.89	1.000	Duration = 4.27 years

Because the modified duration is inversely related to the coupon rate, Equation (2) implies that low-coupon bonds are more volatile than high-coupon bonds are.

For example, the volatilities of the 12% and 8% bonds are

$$\text{Volatility of 12\% bond} = \frac{4.06}{1.1079} = 3.66$$

$$\text{Volatility of 8\% bond} = \frac{4.27}{1.1089} = 3.85$$

The interpretation of these numbers is that a 1% increase (decrease) in the required yield will lead to an approximately 3.66% drop (rise) in the price of the 12% bond and a 3.85% drop (rise) in the price of the 8% bond. The higher volatility of the 8% bond is due to its lower coupon rate and, hence, its longer duration.

Both numbers are approximations because the measure of interest rate sensitivity reflects the effect of a *marginal* change in interest rates on bond prices. For finite (greater than zero) interest rate changes (such as a 1% change), the actual bond price movement will differ somewhat from that calculated using Equation (2).

Knowing the duration of a bond or bond portfolio allows one to compute the gains and losses on that bond or portfolio given a particular interest rate change as follows:

$$\text{Dollar gain (loss)} = \text{Modified duration} \\ \times \text{dollar value} \\ \times \text{interest rate decrease (increase)} \qquad (3)$$

In the case of the OCIP, the duration of two years and one month cited by Mr Citron translates into a modified duration of 1.97 given a 6% yield ((25/12)/1.06). In addition, by August 31, 1994, the three-year Treasury bond rate had climbed by about 1.94% since the beginning of the year. Applying these parameters along with Equation (3) to the County Pool's US$20.7 billion in par value as of August 31 leads to an estimated decline in market value since January 1 of US$790 million:

$$\text{Dollar loss on County Pool} \\ = 1.97 \times \text{US\$20.7 billion} \times 0.0194 = \text{US\$790 million}$$

To compute the potential for further losses in the future on the OCIP, it is necessary to specify the range of interest rate changes possible. The reason for focusing on interest rate changes is that given the low level of credit risk for the securities in the Orange County Pool's portfolio, the key factor driving changes in the portfolio's value are current and anticipated changes in interest rates. One approach to estimating the range of possible interest rate changes is to use historical data on actual changes. Using data from the 20-year period, January 1965–December 1994 for various interest rate series, we can construct probability distributions such as in Table 2 showing the relative frequency with which interest rate changes have occurred historically over particular periods of time. For example, the exhibit reveals that over a one-year period the three-year Treasury bond rate had a 10% chance of rising

Table 2 Histogram of change in three-year treasury note rate. Histogram analysis of changes in rate (basis-point change). (All interest rate changes, overlapping observations) 1/1965–12/1994*

Interval** (bp)	1-Year change			3-Year change			5-Year change		
	Freq	Percentage (%)	Cumul.# (%)	Freq	Percentage (%)	Cumul.# (%)	Freq	Percentage (%)	Cumul.# (%)
<=−500	1	0.3	0.3	4	1.2	1.2	20	6.7	6.7
(−500,−475]	2	0.6	0.9	2	0.6	1.9	1	0.3	7.0
(−475,−450]	0	0.0	0.9	5	1.5	3.4	4	1.3	8.3
(−450,−425]	2	0.6	1.4	6	1.9	5.2	7	2.3	10.7
(−425,−400]	4	1.1	2.6	7	2.2	7.4	5	1.7	12.3
(−400,−375]	3	0.9	3.4	8	2.5	9.9	3	1.0	13.3
(−375,−350]	1	0.3	3.7	7	2.2	12.0	2	0.7	14.0
(−350,−325]	1	0.3	4.0	5	1.5	13.6	3	1.0	15.0
(−325,−300]	4	1.1	5.2	7	2.2	15.7	3	1.0	16.0
(−300,−275]	2	0.6	5.7	9	2.8	18.5	7	2.3	18.3
(−275,−250]	6	1.7	7.5	8	2.5	21.0	5	1.7	20.0
(−250,−225]	6	1.7	9.2	6	1.9	22.8	6	2.0	22.0
(−225,−200]	8	2.3	11.5	7	2.2	25.0	8	2.7	24.7
(−200,−175]	9	2.6	14.1	8	2.5	27.5	6	2.0	26.7
(−175,−150]	9	2.6	16.7	9	2.8	30.2	6	2.0	28.7
(−150,−125]	15	4.3	21.0	3	0.9	31.2	4	1.3	30.0
(−125,−100]	8	2.3	23.3	18	5.6	36.7	11	3.7	33.7
(−100,−75]	15	4.3	27.6	13	4.0	40.7	5	1.7	35.3
(−75,−50]	26	7.5	35.1	12	3.7	44.4	4	1.3	36.7
(−50,−25]	19	5.5	40.5	11	3.4	47.8	7	2.3	39.0
(−25,0]	19	5.5	46.0	6	1.9	49.7	8	2.7	41.7
(0,25]	23	6.6	52.6	12	3.7	53.4	8	2.7	44.3
(25,50]	17	4.9	57.5	8	2.5	55.9	14	4.7	49.0
(50,75]	17	4.9	62.4	9	2.8	58.6	21	7.0	56.0
(75,100]	25	7.2	69.5	8	2.5	61.1	15	5.0	61.0
(100,125]	21	6.0	75.6	9	2.8	63.9	16	5.3	66.3
(125,150]	21	6.0	81.6	17	5.2	69.1	16	5.3	71.7
(150,175]	19	5.5	87.1	19	5.9	75.0	5	1.7	73.3
(175,200]	10	2.9	89.9	12	3.7	78.7	11	3.7	77.0
(200,225]	17	4.9	94.8	9	2.8	81.5	9	3.0	80.0
(225,250]	2	0.6	95.4	11	3.4	84.9	3	1.0	81.0
(250,275]	2	0.6	96.0	6	1.9	86.7	9	3.0	84.0
(275,300]	4	1.1	97.1	6	1.9	88.6	4	1.3	85.3
(300,325]	2	0.6	97.7	3	0.9	89.5	1	0.3	85.7
(325,350]	1	0.3	98.0	3	0.9	90.4	8	2.7	88.3
(350,375]	1	0.3	98.3	0	0.0	90.4	3	1.0	89.3
(375,400]	0	0.0	98.3	1	0.3	90.7	2	0.7	90.0
(400,425]	0	0.0	98.3	1	0.3	91.0	4	1.3	91.3
(425,450]	0	0.0	98.3	2	0.6	91.7	1	0.3	91.7
(450,475]	2	0.6	98.9	5	1.5	93.2	0	0.0	91.7
(475,500]	0	0.0	98.9	1	0.3	93.5	0	0.0	91.7
> 500	4	1.1	100.0	21	6.5	100.0	25	8.3	100.0
Total	348	324	300						

* Begins with first-month of data available from Citibase starting from 1965.
** The interval (0,25] means that the observation is greater than 0 and less than or equal to 25 basis points.
# Cumul. = Cumulative percentage.

by at least 196 basis points and a 5% chance of rising by at least 229 basis points. Corresponding 90th (95th) percentile figures for three-month and six-month LIBOR are 300 (393) and 288 (362) basis points. These data point to the potential for disaster in the OCIP. Moreover, these data are readily available to all finance professionals through any of the numerous online financial databases.

The modified duration model can be applied to the 90th and 95th percentile interest rate changes over the coming year to calculate projected one-year losses. Specifically, a further rise in the three-year Treasury bond interest rate of 196 basis points would lead to additional losses of US$800 million (1.97 × US$20.7 billion × 0.0196) and a rise of 229 basis points would raise these projected losses to US$930 million (1.97 × US$20.7 billion × 0.0229). Of course, these figures are just estimates and they don't take into account the "pull-to-par" effect or the fact that the duration formula is just an approximation for interest rate changes that are more than infinitesimal. Nonetheless, these back-of-the-envelope type calculations reveal that by August 31, 1994, the OCIP had already lost about US$790 million and had a 10% (5%) chance of losing an additional US$800 million (US$930 million) over the coming year, for combined losses of US$1.59 billion (US$1.72 billion). Even if these numbers are off by, say, 25%, they should still have raised big red flags, particularly given the steep rise in interest rates that had already occurred during 1994 and the strong likelihood of additional increases to come.

In fact, the duration numbers tend to provide a reasonably accurate picture of what happened in the case of the OCIP. The state auditor estimated that the OCIP's investment portfolio had a duration of about 7.4 years when it went bankrupt in December 1994.[3] Given a yield at the time of about 6%, the modified duration was about 7.0 (7.4/1.06). With a portfolio of US$7.6 billion, and a rise in the yield on three-year Treasury bonds of 2.83% by the end of November, Equation (3) predicts that the OCIP would have lost around US$1.5 billion (7.0 × US$7.6 billion × 0.0283). This amount closely approximates the portfolio's actual losses, particularly when account is taken of the various transaction costs associated with rapid liquidation of the portfolio's securities. For example, assuming liquidation costs of 1% of the US$20 billion portfolio, a forced liquidation would have led to a further US$200 million loss in portfolio value.

1   In reality, there were three Orange County Investment Pools, consisting of the Commingled Pool, the Bond Pool, and Specific Investments. References in this report to the Orange County Investment Pool are to the three Pools collectively.
2   For example, as of August 31, 1994, the Orange County Investment Pool's reverse repos had a weighted average maturity of 38.9 days, far less than the weighted average maturity of the pool's assets. The import of such a short maturity was that any rise in market interest rates would quickly feed through to a rise in the Orange County Investment Pool's cost of borrowing.
3   The duration was estimated for the pool's deposits and it took into account the degree of leverage applied to the pool through the use of reverse repos. The relation between portfolio duration and leverage is given as follows: effective portfolio duration = simple portfolio duration × leverage.

BIBLIOGRAPHY

Cox, J. C., J. E. Ingersoll, Jr., and S. A. Ross, 1985, "A Theory of the Term Structure of Interest Rates", *Econometrica*, 53, pp. 385–407.

Gottschalk Jr., E. C., 1994, "Derivatives Roil California Political Race", *Wall Street Journal*, April 15, pp. C1–C22.

Graham, J. D., 1994, "Regulation: A Risky Business", *Wall Street Journal*, May 18, p. A14.

Jorion, P., 1995, *Big Bets Gone Bad: The Largest Municipal Failure in U.S. History* (San Diego: Academic Press).

Jorion, P., 1997, "Lessons from the Orange County Bankruptcy", *The Journal of Derivatives*, Summer, pp. 61–6

Miller, M. H., and D. J. Ross, 1997, "The Orange County Bankruptcy and Its Aftermath: Some New Evidence", *The Journal of Derivatives*, Summer, pp. 51–60.

Vasicek, O. A., 1977, "An Equilibrium Characterization of the Term Structure", *Journal of Financial Economics*, 5, pp. 177–88.

Vogel, Jr., T. T., 1994, "Stocks and Bonds Tumble on Inflation Report: Producer-Price Rise May Augur Worse to Come", *Wall Street Journal*, September 12, p. C1.

35

*Allied Irish Bank**

Nikki Marmery

PORTRAIT OF A ROGUE TRADER

Foreign exchange (FX) traders are rarely shy and retiring types. The work-hard, play-hard ethos of the markets cultivates aggression in the dealing room and sometimes outrageous behaviour outside it. But John Rusnak did not fit that image. Indeed, many of the dealers who worked with him had trouble remembering him at all. "He just seemed to fade into the background," said one dealer who worked with Rusnak in the late 1980s at Harris Trust. And those who did remember Rusnak tended to describe him as a "regular guy", unlikely to have attracted much attention. "He didn't strike me as the sort who would cover up fraud. I would never have suspected him of breaking rules," said one dealer who worked with Rusnak at Chemical Bank in the early 1990s.

The story of how 37-year-old Rusnak ended up at Allfirst in Baltimore is the story of a survivor in the FX business rather than a star trader. In his early twenties he joined Harris Trust in Chicago in 1988. He worked on the bank's night desk and failed to make a lasting impression on his colleagues. One manager told of the astonishment at discovering Rusnak was at the centre of a US$691 million currency trading scam. "I even dragged his personnel file out to check it was the same John Rusnak," said the manager. Rusnak left Harris after a year and joined Chemical in New York in

*The material in this chapter first appeared in *FX Week* in February (Vol 13, No 7, p. 5) and March (Vol 13, No 11, p. 5), 2002.

October 1989. Chemical, then second only to Citibank among US banks in terms of forex trading revenues, is now part of the JP Morgan Chase banking group.

At Chemical, where he worked for around five years, Rusnak attracted a little more attention to himself. When Allfirst's losses were revealed, rumours circulated in New York that Rusnak had left Chemical under a cloud following an argument with managers. But a source who worked at the bank at the time insisted that Rusnak departed "of his own accord."

Whatever the true story, Rusnak's career was heading into the sidings. His next job was with First National Bank of Maryland and a two-man trading desk in Baltimore. First National changed its name to Allfirst Financial in 1999. And it was here in Baltimore, according to Allfirst's parent group, Allied Irish Banks in Dublin, that Rusnak falsified FX options trades throughout 2001 in an effort to cover up huge losses on spot and forward US dollar/yen trades.

The discovery of Rusnak's alleged fraud left the FX industry puzzled about two things above all. First, how could a trader at such a small bank be allowed by his managers to get into a position where he could lose so much money? Second, what prompted a seemingly honest and unremarkable dealer to commit the alleged frauds?

Whatever the answer to those questions, there were some clues that Rusnak's dealing activity was unusual for an operation that typically generated just US$10 million a year in forex revenues, according to some reports.

On behalf of Allfirst, Rusnak was a client of some of the largest banks in the world, and he was making huge bets that the US dollar would weaken dramatically against the yen.

Whatever his managers and colleagues thought about John Rusnak, they weren't looking closely enough.

RUSNAK'S TRADING STRATEGY REVEALED

The independent report commissioned by Allied Irish Banks, carried out by US banking specialist Eugene Ludwig, detailed how former Allfirst foreign exchange trader John Rusnak managed to hide his forex trading losses with the creation of bogus options transactions.

The report said that Rusnak lost the vast majority of his US$691 million losses from yen-US dollar currency forwards. In 1997, he began trading based upon the assumption that the value of the yen would strengthen against the dollar. When the yen's relative value continued to slide, so too did Rusnak's forwards positions.

To hide his trading losses, Rusnak created bogus options that capitalised on weaknesses in Allfirst's internal regulation and allowed the bogus options to be placed onto Allfirst's books. He simultaneously entered two false trades – one being the sale of a deep-in-the-money put option on yen and the other being the acquisition of a similar option. Both fake options involved the same currency and the same strike price, and appeared to leave Allfirst with no net cash exposure.

However, the option involving the receipt of a premium would expire on the day it was written, while the other option would expire at some point in the future, usually in one month. Despite the fact that the differences in the tenors should have led to a price difference in the premiums for these options, the trades were not found to be suspicious by Allfirst's regulators – nor did anybody notice that deep-in-the-money options were never exercised.

BACK-OFFICE FAILURE: HOW HE ESCAPED DETECTION

Eugene Ludwig's independent report on Allfirst's losses described over 14 pages how the "unusually clever and devious" rogue trader John Rusnak managed to escape detection for five years. The critical failure, found the report, was in the back office, which failed to confirm trades, spot Rusnak's bogus confirmations, or independently verify his positions.

The report showed that Rusnak convinced the back office it wasn't necessary to confirm trades that netted each other – even though some of the options trades he booked had different expiration dates.

In June 2000, when questioned about unconfirmed trades, Rusnak produced confirmations that did not match the trade in question. On at least one other occasion, Rusnak produced confirmations that showed the trade had taken place after it was queried, rather than the date stated when originally booked. He forged confirmations, using logos later found on his computer in a file labelled "fake docs".

Forex rates used to verify his positions were taken from rates supplied by Rusnak himself, which he manipulated to make it appear as though he was within his stop-loss limits, said the report. Rusnak suggested the system, which downloaded forex rates from a Reuters terminal, into his computer, then fed into a shared database used by the back office. He said he needed access to the rates to monitor his value-at-risk.

"This is a failed procedure," said an Allfirst risk analyst upon learning of the system. "Technically the trader/s could manipulate the rates." She was right. In Q1 2001, the analyst found the cells for yen and euro had links to Rusnak's machine, detouring outside of Reuters. When she asked why rates were not obtained independently, another risk official said Allfirst would not pay for a US$10,000 data feed from Reuters to the back-office.

36

Scenes from a Tragedy –
*Bankers Trust and Procter & Gamble**

William Falloon and Richard Irving

"Reputation, reputation, reputation. O! I have lost my reputation.
I have lost the immortal part of myself, and what remains is bestial!"
(Othello, Act 2, Scene 3)

According to Wall Street observers, the high profile dispute between Bankers Trust and Procter & Gamble remains the derivatives industry's darkest hour. It cost some of the brightest bankers on Wall Street their careers and laid low the reputation of one of the world's most innovative financial institutions. What follows is an epic tale of hubris and misfortune – a Shakespearean tragedy in three parts.

ACT 1: THE REGULATORS COME KNOCKING

Thursday, October 12, 1995. Behind the closed doors of a senior executive suite at Bankers Trust's Manhattan headquarters, a crisis meeting is in session. Eight of the bank's high command, including chairman Charles Sanford, president Eugene Shanks and derivatives co-head Brian Walsh, are poring over page proofs of the forthcoming edition of Business Week. They contain transcripts of telephone conversations in which Bankers' employees appear to glory in "ripping off" clients. The article is based on sealed court documents supplied in error by the bank's own lawyers. The papers

*This chapter is adapted from an article that originally appeared in *Risk* in December 1997.

relate to a bitter row with Procter & Gamble, a bastion of corporate America, which is suing the bank to recover swingeing trading losses. Finally, his face still deep in the papers, Walsh realises the sheer desperation of the situation. "These guys sure are playing hard ball," he mutters out loud.

Brian Walsh, now managing partner of Veritas Capital Management, a US$100 million relative value hedge fund based in Greenwich, Connecticut, remembers that moment as if it were yesterday. "I felt sick to my stomach," he recalls. "We thought we had come through the worst of the bad publicity when we settled with regulators some nine months earlier. Now the whole situation was getting opened up again." At issue was the controversial way the bank's senior management controlled its buccaneering derivatives group. "We had policies pre-1994 that were better than our competitors'. But were we as good at following those policies as we should have been? The answer is probably no," says Walsh. "I blame myself for not being prepared," he goes on. "We were product-focused, not client-focused, and while we were definitely trying to change that, it wasn't happening fast enough. For the most part, things worked well within the bank. But sitting on top of the pile is always dangerous – hubris is always lurking when you are on top. At the end of the day, I tried to instill the values I truly believed."

But it was the bank's values – rather than just Walsh's – that were dragged through the mire when P&G, the Cincinnati-based household products company, announced losses on two swaps it bought through Bankers Trust in late 1993 and early 1994. In both cases, P&G agreed to pay the bank a floating rate of interest pegged to complex formulae that made the swaps hypersensitive to rising rates. In return it received fixed payments, which effectively helped it achieve an all-in cost of funds substantially below the bellwether London interbank offered rate. Such was the risk embedded in one deal, in which the company's rate of interest was tied to the yields on five-year and 30-year US Treasuries, that the bank was forced to buy around US$3.4 billion worth of government long bonds to cover its own exposure to the trade. The second deal involved a smaller, but similarly risky, play on German interest rates.

When Federal Reserve Board chairman Alan Greenspan did indeed raise interest rates in February 1994, P&G's swaps plunged into loss – by almost US$200 million according to the company –

prompting chief executive Edwin Artzt, a man renowned for not ducking a legal challenge, to file a lawsuit in October alleging fraudulent misconduct. Ten days later, a second BT client, Gibson Greetings Cards, filed a similar suit seeking to recover US$23 million worth of losses.

Lawyers acting on behalf of both companies wasted no time in accusing the bank of "breach of fiduciary duty, negligence, deception and cheating". By December 1994, Bankers Trust had been publicly censured by the Securities and Exchange Commission and the Commodity Futures Trading Commission; it had been fined a staggering US$10 million – the largest civil fine ever to be levied against a commercial bank – and it had been forced to sign a "cease or desist" order, which effectively put the bank on notice to sort out its problems quickly or face the full penalty of the law. It had also agreed to an independent audit by leading New York attorneys Derrick Cephas and Benjamin Civiletti.

But it was the publication of those supposedly confidential telephone conversations that marked the bank's nadir. On one tape, employee Mark Schindler tells a colleague: "Funny business, you know? [You] lure people into that calm and then just totally f*** them." And on another, Gary Missner, a derivatives salesman, talks of "chipping away" at a whopping US$5 million differential between the theoretical loss the bank had put on a trade, and that which it had reportedly told a client. According to P&G, the transcripts, edited from more than 50,000 conversations over nearly 18 months, proved the existence of a "widespread pattern of racketeering ... and securities fraud spanning a number of years and involving multiple victims". Its lawyers went on to disclose details of a further seven clients, including Air Products and Chemicals, which, court documents alleged, lost US$105.8 million at the hands of Bankers' derivatives marketers, paper manufacturer Federal Paper Board, which allegedly lost US$47 million, and Swiss pharmaceuticals giant Sandoz, which P&G lawyers alleged lost US$78.5 million.

In May 1996, P&G and Bankers finally agreed to a settlement after a US district court judge ruled that banks selling over-the-counter derivatives had no fiduciary responsibility to their clients. And in June, attorneys Cephas and Civiletti finally cleared the bank of any "institutional effort to defraud" (although they uncovered conduct they found to "warrant severe criticism"), when they reported back to US regulators, some six months late and at a cost rumoured to be close to US$20 million. By then, of course, the damage had been done. Of all the senior managers slated in the investigator's report for "...failing to manage the derivatives business adequately", only Yves de Balmann, co-head of derivatives alongside Walsh, was still at the bank. Sanford, arguably one of Wall Street's biggest legends, had opted for early retirement; Shanks, once tipped as the next chairman, had resigned to set up a new risk management consultancy, NetRisk; and Walsh, himself once tipped to succeed Shanks, had taken up an offer from US money manager Taylor & Co.

Bankers Trust's bitter experience at the hands of disgruntled clients is today the reason why senior managers place as much emphasis on managing "reputational" risk as they do on market or credit risk. For those taped conversations not only stymied the bank's own defence, which largely rested on the well-reasoned principle of caveat emptor, or "buyer beware", they also deflected culpability away from clients who had willingly stood as principals to highly structured deals. According to one source close to the bank, who agreed to an interview only on condition of anonymity, the brawl with Gibson Greetings was particularly damaging. "From the moment Gibson filed its complaint, the scrutiny the bank got from the regulators was unbelievable. It got to the point where BT couldn't defend itself at all. Everybody seemed to be getting a free lunch out of them." "We didn't court power in Washington and that meant that the bank had few friends when it needed them most. We had a very hard time seeing the big picture from a political perspective," Walsh says.

The regulators countered that the bank had failed to exercise authority or control over its high-flying derivatives group. In an executive summary of their independent review of Bankers' operations, Cephas and Civiletti made no fewer than 47 separate criticisms, panning senior management for encouraging a culture in which customers' interests came second to the desire to maximise profit. "As is the case in many instances, your greatest strengths are also your greatest weaknesses," says Walsh. "Bankers Trust became an extremely creative institution with a strong product focus. It put rocket scientists in the trading room to keep on the leading edge. But by its very nature, when creativity is such a key part of the bank, management structure has to be flat, it has to be decentralised."

What makes Walsh sick to his stomach these days is the perception that events in 1994 and 1995 have somewhat overshadowed the bank's role as a prime mover in derivatives markets. "Bankers Trust," he says, "was the prime innovator in risk management." As early as 1987, the bank was marketing a forerunner to equity-linked notes, when it launched a series of so-called "securities participating in international equities" ("spies"). And in 1993 it won a raft of accolades when it developed a prepaid financing deal involving oil and interest rate swaps which subsequently enabled Shell Oil to raise US$700 million to fund a deep-water exploration project in the Gulf of Mexico.

It is just one aspect of the tragedy that befell Bankers that it lost the ambitious and creative Walsh to the leafy suburbs of Greenwich, some 60 miles away from the cut-and-thrust of Wall Street, from where he trades volatility and correlation. Almost alone among his contemporaries he stands ready to accept criticism for his part in the debacle. He is, one suspects, driven more by a desire to set the record straight than by a compunction to make his mark once more on the market he knows and loves. "Sure, we had some bad seeds, very bad seeds as it turned out, but it's very hard to assign blame to an entire institution. After the fact, I find it hard to be judgemental – to play God, if you like – when it comes to the particular individuals. On the other hand, it's not that we are all sinners."

ACT 2: "ACCOUNTABLE BUT NOT RESPONSIBLE"

November 1997: Charles Sanford, elder statesman of the trillion-dollar over-the-counter derivative markets, sits back in a chair at Bankers Trust's video conferencing centre, one leg resting nonchalantly on the knee of the other, a can of diet coke on the table. Senior bank spokesmen flank him – one at his side in New York, one here in London. Sanford is at ease. He talks lovingly of the bank he has taken from second-tier deposit-taker to premier capital markets powerhouse. He talks passionately of the future and the opportunities that await the ever-expanding group. He is the quintessential bank chairman, imposing, supremely confident and charming.

Yet this is late 1997, and Sanford is no longer chairman of Bankers Trust. In December 1995, at the height of the US$200 million dispute with P&G, and much to the surprise of close colleagues, Sanford opted for retirement – early, for a banker so obviously at the peak of his profession, earlier still, one might argue, for the man who dragged commercial banking into the twentieth century.

Sanford's 30-odd years in the industry are peppered with firsts. His bank was the first to sell commercial loans off its balance sheet; first, too, to base capital requirements on a risk management philosophy (later to become Raroc, or the risk adjusted return on capital), rather than off antiquated equity-to-asset ratios. Perhaps, most memorably, his bank, although not the creator of swaps or options, was the first to recognise the importance they would have in globalising the world's capital markets.

But while Sanford readily accepts the part Bankers Trust has played in developing the derivatives markets, he is near-impervious to the mark derivatives have left on his bank. "I am very proud of the systemic record of this institution and of my people," he says. "Of course, I am embarrassed at the boorish behaviour of a minority, but you have to put it in perspective – there were no more than 10 people out of a workforce of more than 13,000 that were disciplined as a result of their behaviour in the leveraged derivatives business. "I remember at the time, the director of another financial institution telling me: 'Go look at your competitors – everybody has problems', and he was right, some had truly systemic problems. We did not."

Bankers Trust, of course, attracted the censure of US regulators, and, specifically, a "cease or desist" order. "Any time you innovate," Sanford counters, "you run into problems. There was – and still is – nothing wrong with leveraged derivatives as a product class. They acted exactly how they were supposed to act. It's a bit like nuclear power – everyone whines about it, but it has served the world at large very well. When you are a market leader you run into a lot of flak." This much is certainly true. Sanford still values creativity, albeit in equal measure with success, above all else ("I don't care what my grandchildren do in life, so long as they do it well," he says). Three years into his retirement, he remains the most iconoclastic banker of his generation. Throughout his career, from his very early days as a commercial loan officer through to his time as chairman, much of his thinking bordered on heresy, at least to the establishment with which he did battle. "When I first started in the business, commercial banking operated almost as a utility. Profitability was very much a function of your cost of funds – how much you had to pay for term deposits. By the mid-seventies banks were desperately reaching out for loans. I realised then that we would have to do something radically different," he recalls. He had the idea of running the trading desk as a profit centre years before it became accepted industry practice. It was also his idea to use risk-adjusted returns to set capital adequacy levels. "He was always pushing back the envelope with the regulators," says a former close colleague. "He had a hard time hiding the fact that he believed many regulators to be empty blue suits."

But if Sanford is sensitive to Bankers' derivatives problems, he hides it well. In particular, he refutes any suggestion that the bank was a tragic victim of its own success: "I don't look at it that way at all. 1993 was our best year ever. We had one year that was a glitch, a hiccup – but really it was only one quarter – an isolated problem with a few people which we took care of."

Cephas and Civiletti put rather more emphasis on Sanford's role in the debacle. "There existed at Bankers Trust an entrepreneurial attitude and a decentralised management style that encouraged independence and the exercise of significant discretion at all professional levels," they concluded. "The goal was high profitability and public recognition of the bank as the market leader in risk management ... fostered by Charles Sanford. Concomitantly, there was a lack of hands-on involvement with, or detailed knowledge concerning, the derivatives business on the part of ... senior members of the bank's management."

If the bank's problems did indeed stem from the culture that Sanford and other senior managers fostered, it is a culture that the former chairman still vigorously defends: "I wanted people who could think broader than just around their own jobs, people who had the courage of their convictions. It wasn't just a question of shopping around Harvard and Wharton for the brightest intellectuals, I wanted to make sure the bank had innovators who wouldn't miss the big changes that were going on around us. I've seen too many companies lose their way because they miss the big picture. Look at the US railroad companies at the turn of the century, had they considered themselves transportation companies, rather than just railroads, they could have moved into motor transport, aircraft leasing, anything.

"We were a small bank relative to some of the players in the industry. To the extent that size generates turnover, we were never going to be able to compete with institutions two or three times bigger than us – we were never going to be the biggest bank in the business. So to stay up there, we had to be at the cutting edge. That's how we kept the upper hand." When the bank's competition was playing catch-up in interest rate and currency swaps, Bankers Trust was off working on tailored deals in new asset classes such as equities, commodities, and, when the bank's counterparty limits were full, groundbreaking credit structures. And when the competition caught up once again, the bank started to open up the exotic and leveraged markets, which it guarded with proprietary zeal. No client who approached the bank with a risk management problem left without a range of solutions, some plain vanilla, others highly structured.

The Sanford that took Wall Street by storm, rather like the Sanford that today advises a team of microbiologists at a hospital on Manhattan's Upper East Side, is something of an enigma. He claims not to miss Wall Street, but when referring to the bank always uses the royal "we", always in the present tense. He is intelligent yet obstinate, polite yet, on occasion, intensely combative. He continued to regard a negotiated truce with P&G chairman Artzt as a wimpish notion, and relations between the two adversaries remained strained – if not out-and-out hostile – right up until the day Sanford resigned.

So, with the benefit of hindsight, does Sanford regret digging in his heels rather than settling? "You should know better than to ask a question like that", he says, a wry smile flickering across his face. What then, is the low point in a career that boasts so many highs? "I don't know about the highs and lows," Sanford says, "but as far as the derivatives group is concerned, I was accountable, of course, but ultimate responsibility rests with those few people whose behaviour was a betrayal of their colleagues and our code of conduct."

ACT 3: DEATH OF A SALESMAN

March 1989: James Condon, treasurer of Hartmarx Corp, the world's largest maker of men's suits, is seeking insurance protection against further interest rate rises after borrowing costs on debts of up to US$375 million rise 325 basis points in less than a year. Condon experiments with interest rate caps but, as rates begin to turn down once more, he elects to set up a more complex interest rate collar strategy. It is, for the time, advanced corporate risk management of the highest order, negotiable only with a bank that can be trusted to the limit.

The salesman who helped introduce Condon to the wonderful world of interest rate swaps was none other than Gary Missner. The very same Missner who, it is alleged in documents lodged with the District Court of Ohio in 1995, fraudulently missold a brace of leveraged swaps to the Cincinnatti-based Gibson Greetings. Like P&G, the company revealed losses – of some US$27 million – when interest rates unexpectedly moved against it in early 1994.

It was the transcripts of telephone conversations in which Missner appeared to lie to his client, and then to laugh it off to colleagues, which did so much to undermine Bankers Trust's contention that Gibson was an arms-length counterparty rather than a trusting client. Perhaps more importantly, the transcripts transfixed regulators. While others at the bank might be construed to have engaged in more questionable sales practices, only Missner, a wiry graduate of Colorado University and Harvard Business School, could actually be hung by cold hard evidence. In one conversation, Missner told Gibson's assistant treasurer Kevin Rice: "…the total CMV [value] right now is about US$8.1 million." On the tape, Rice replies, "Okay," before Missner adds: "In any case, that was really the point of my phone call, to just make you aware of where things are right now … don't think it's time to panic and start pulling out." Later that day, according to lawyers, Missner made another call – this time to Bankers Trust sales associate Mitchell Vazquez – in which he stated: "[We] should call Kevin and maybe chip away at the differential a little more. I mean, we told him US$8.1 million when the real number is 14. So now that the real number is, you know, 16, we'll tell him it's 11. You know, just slowly chip away…" Bad enough, but not quite as damaging as a conversation in January 1994, in which Missner discussed another Gibson deal, this time a Libor-linked "wedding band" swap reportedly some US$5 million under water: "These … guys … have done some pretty wild stuff, and, you know, they probably don't understand it quite as well as they should. I think they have a pretty good understanding of it, but not perfect, and um, that's, like, perfect, for us."

But according to observers, some of whom have listened to these tapes extensively, the transcripts may have led to some conclusions about Missner that were far from the truth. States one observer who had listened to the tapes themselves: "I don't care what he said on that Gibson tape. He was not that cutthroat. When I look at Gary, he probably didn't have the courage to tell the client about a loss. He probably felt: the position has got to come back, and then we will get them out. I know him as a person, and what we are talking about is intent. A transcript will never tell you that." Missner's tone of voice on this tape and others, say those who heard it, was not that of a Wall Street shark. Of more than 3,500 recorded conversations passed to P&G lawyers, no more than a handful involving Missner, they say, caused any concerns at all. "In the court documents, what you don't have is Gary's tone. And I can tell you that if you don't care about a client, you don't have that tone. It was his personality to be upset in a situation like that, and he couldn't hide it," says one anonymous source familiar with the investigation. Condon is one who clearly believes that these sound bites do not capture the essence of the Gary Missner who sold derivatives to his company. "He was one of the brightest marketers that called on us and I have a lot of respect for him."Another defender of Missner's integrity as a derivative salesman is Ed Paules, a former BT marketer who worked at the bank in New York during the 1980s, now at the Federal Home Loan Bank of Boston. "I knew Gary up until 1990. [During that time,] I never heard him lie to customers and he had a lot of personal integrity while I was on the desk working with him." One corporate treasurer who also knew Missner personally and has read transcripts of the BT tapes defends him against those who judge him from two recorded conversations: "You can't reach any conclusion about Gary based on those tapes; you have to look at a person's character and put them within the context of the language of the Wall Street trading floor. Whenever there is a débâcle, someone is always very visible in the situation, and in this instance it was Gary. In order for an organisation to heal itself, sometimes you have to find a smoking gun and purge the system so that you can move on and say that things have been rectified. Maybe that's what happened to Gary – all the symptoms of the problems of the derivatives industry, real or perceived, became him. The regulators may have felt that he's symptomatic of that evil, and by taking care of him, they've taken care of the problem." Another marketer who worked with Missner in New York says that two others on the trading floor – one of whom now works at a European bank in London – employed more creative sales techniques. On more than one occasion, the former employee alleges, one marketer frequently smoothed over a customer's query about a leverage factor in a formula, often expressed in BT sales documents as a denominator, by identifying it as something else. This marketer alleges that a more senior executive also encouraged sales presentation documents to be skewed in a manner that made leveraged derivative trades more enticing to the client and understated the potential risk. As for Missner, he replies: "If Gary called me up to go on a ski trip, I'd be happy to go."

Such testimony raises the question of whether the regulatory reviews were as thorough and precise as they should have been. At no point, for example, did the independent counsel investigating BT's activities hold that Missner lied to clients over the value of existing positions, although they argue that BT marketers often quoted prices at which they were reluctant to exit a position. States the executive summary prepared in June 1996: "[The Independent Counsel] find no fault with BT for quoting different valuations for the same transaction if the different valuations were used for different purposes. Different valuations for the same transaction are not inherently improper and the Independent Counsel find no impropriety in BT's use of this practice."

Missner refuses to discuss his views about the consent decree entered into by Bankers Trust, or indeed the decree he personally signed, which resulted in him being banned from the derivatives industry for five years. When asked if he had second thoughts about anything he had said or done, Missner said that he stood by statements he had made in his defence in mid-1995. In those statements, he said: "I never lied to Gibson Greetings at any time about anything, including the extent of Gibson's losses on derivatives contracts entered into with Bankers Trust."

Do the sound bites on the tapes tell the whole story about Gary Missner? "I doubt it," says Condon. "When I read them, they didn't sound like the guy that I knew."

37

Singapore Sting – Barings*

Mark Nicholls

Derivatives disasters have not been the exclusive preserve of the loosely regulated over-the-counter markets. Despite the supposed safety provided by clearing houses and reporting requirements, exchange-traded derivatives can also be catastrophic in the wrong hands – such as those of Nick Leeson.

In February 1995, Leeson brought down Barings, the UK's oldest merchant bank. An egotistical hotshot, he "believed he could move the whole goddamn Japanese market", according to one Singaporean trader. Instead, he lost more than £800 million (US$1,300 million) and received a six-and-a-half year prison sentence.

Leeson was first posted to Singapore in 1992 and was soon running Barings Futures (Singapore). He began booking enormous, supposedly risk-free, profits, by claiming to arbitrage Nikkei 225 futures on the Singapore Monetary Exchange (Simex) and Osaka Stock Exchange (OSE). In 1994, Barings' structured products group reported profits of at least £28.5 million from these arbitrage plays (out of the group's total revenue of £52.9 million).

In fact, Leeson used an error account – numbered 88888 – to park losses from the trades and thus increase his profits. These losses totalled £2 million at the end of 1992 but had risen to £208 million by the end of 1994. He also used the account to put on and conceal increasingly large unauthorised trades.

*This chapter originally appeared as an article in *Risk* in December 1997.

Leeson's main rogue trading strategy from January 1994 was to sell straddles on the Nikkei, aggressively betting that volatility would remain range-bound. However, on January 17, 1995, an earthquake flattened the Japanese city of Kobe. The earthquake was scarcely kinder to Leeson's option position – the Nikkei 225 slumped by 8% in five days, and volatilities soared.

Leeson should have then sold futures to remain delta-neutral. Bizarrely, he began buying instead, apparently to try to force the market higher to support his straddle position. By January 20, he had built a long position of almost 11,000 March 1995 Nikkei futures – a huge position for a medium-size bank. Between then and February 23, he increased this to 55,000 March and 5,640 June futures – representing 49% and 24% of the open interest in the respective contracts on the OSE and Simex.

By January, both the Bank for International Settlements and Simex were questioning Barings' management in London on its trading activities and the funding of its positions. Senior Barings' staff ignored the warnings, convinced all was well. They were mesmerised by the profits Leeson had been claiming, ignorant about the nature of the Singapore operation and hamstrung by chronic failures in reporting and oversight.

Instead, they kept on posting the enormous margin payments Leeson required to sustain his positions. Eventually, the bubble had to burst. A senior settlements clerk was sent to Singapore to resolve a number of issues with Leeson, who left a meeting on February 23, never to return. He fled with his wife to Kuala Lumpur, and thence to Europe, where he was arrested at Frankfurt airport.

Over the weekend, Barings' management discovered the scale of the losses: by the close on February 27, these stood at £827 million. Uncertainty over the cost of closing out the losing positions made a rescue impossible. On the Sunday evening, the bank went into administration.

At this point, the bank's internal crisis threatened to turn into a systemic one. Barings' default cast doubts on the creditworthiness of the exchange clearing houses through which Leeson had been trading. Frantic intervention by international regulators, led by Mary Schapiro of the US Commodity Futures Trading Commission, obtained assurances that member firms' margin payments would not be used to cover Barings' liabilities.

In the aftermath of Barings, as many questions were asked about the behaviour of the exchanges involved as that of the bank's management. Regulators responded with the Windsor Declaration in May 1995, which, *inter alia*, set up arrangements to share large-exposure information between supervisors and exchanges.

38

A Question of Authority –
*Hammersmith and Fulham**

Mark Nicholls

In 1989 a nervous district auditor pulled the plug on the Hammersmith and Fulham Local Authority's massive swaps book in 1989. This was just the start of the notorious Hammersmith and Fulham debacle.

The subsequent default and legal battle, which ultimately involved more than 130 UK local authorities and 75 banks, cost the banks concerned an estimated £750 million, and focused derivatives providers' minds on legal risk.

The case drew out two issues. First, the question of capacity: whether local authorities had the power to enter into the deals. Second, the courts examined the extent to which counterparties can recover payments made under swap contracts later found to be void.

During the 1980s, a number of local authorities began to use interest rate swaps to help manage their portfolios. The size and risk profiles of some of their swaps books became considerable, particularly among opposition Labour-run councils, which were attempting to evade spending controls imposed by the then Conservative government.

By 1987, some councils were effectively taking leveraged bets on interest rate movements, betting against rate rises and using instruments such as deep discount swaps to obtain upfront funding in exchange for paying above market interest rates. Hammersmith and

*This chapter is adapted from an article that originally appeared in *Risk* in December 1997.

Fulham – which was responsible for around 40% of the outstanding business – was even acting as intermediary for other councils who could not enter into swaps because of government-imposed spending caps. At one point, the council had built up a £6 billion book of interest rate swaps and swaptions on a notional outstanding debt of only £390 million.

In July 1988, Hammersmith and Fulham's district auditor, Anthony Hazell, privately told the authority it had acted *ultra vires* (beyond its powers) in transacting the swaps and swaptions. The council, which was facing losses of more than £180 million as interest rates rose, then began to reduce its portfolio, which was down to £3.6 billion by February 1989. At this point, the auditor insisted the council should stop all swaps activity, including making payments on outstanding contracts.

Hammersmith and Fulham then asked government environment secretary Nicholas Ridley for permission to honour its swap contracts. The normally pro-free market minister refused; he saw the swaps as an attempt by both councils and banks to circumvent government controls on local authority spending. Hammersmith and Fulham's counterparties declared the council in default.

Later that year, the High Court declared the swaps illegal and thus void, offering Hammersmith and Fulham a way out of its loss-making positions. But the banks, facing enormous mark-to-market losses, took the case to the Appeal Court, which partly overturned the verdict. It held that swaps entered to hedge an underlying exposure were lawful. Speculative deals, however, were not.

However, the then head of the Audit Commission, Howard Davies, took the case to the House of Lords, the UK's highest judicial authority. In January 1991, their Lordships judged that all swaps entered into by Hammersmith and Fulham (and by implication all other UK local authorities) were illegal.

At this point, the two sides' lawyers settled down for a long haul. The ruling meant that the thousands of swap transactions entered into with local authorities were unenforceable. Not only were existing swaps to be unwound, but the banks also argued that payments made on deals that had matured before the ruling should also be returned.

These issues rumbled on in the courts, as the local authorities and their banks argued over the nuances of the restitution claims.

The balance of deals before 1988 had been largely to the councils' benefit. Thus, the banks sought to recoup an estimated £125 million paid to local authorities under swaps held to be void. Most cases were settled out of court, following the banks' success in winning lead cases in 1993.

39

Full Metal Racket – Sumitomo Corporation*

Mark Nicholls

If size is important in derivatives disasters, then forget Metallgesellschaft, Procter & Gamble and even Barings Bank. The unauthorised trader who made the biggest splash is Yasuo Hamanaka. As Sumitomo Corporation's star copper trader, he was known as "Mr Five Percent", after the amount of the world's copper market that he was said to control. Clearly unhappy with a mere 5%, he attempted to corner the market in a disastrous strategy that cost the Japanese trading giant US$2.6 billion.

Prosecutors alleged that Hamanaka and his former boss, Saburo Shimizu, began unauthorised trading in London Metal Exchange (LME) copper futures in 1985, to maintain the profitability of their division. When Shimizu left in 1987, Hamanaka took over, inheriting losses of US$57.5 million.

But the first sign that things were amiss came in November 1991 when Hamanaka sought confirmation of fictitious trades from a US-based trader. This was reported to the LME, which asked its regulator, the Securities and Investments Board (SIB), to investigate. SIB and LME officials met with Hamanaka, who claimed the request involved moving trades into different accounting periods for tax reasons.

In September 1993, the LME placed a US$5-a-tonne limit on daily backwardation (the premium paid for spot or nearby months)

---

*This chapter is adapted from an article that originally appeared in *Risk* in December 1997.

to ease a squeeze on the market. At the time, the squeeze was attributed by traders to Hamanaka's strategy, although the details remain unclear. However, from 1993, he began buying up physical stocks of copper to support the price at levels which bore no relation to the metal's fundamentals – with cash copper at around US$3,000 a tonne by the end of 1995. Later he was to sell huge quantities of out-of-the-money put options. The premiums earned were used to continue to support copper, so that the options would remain unexercised.

Following a request from a concerned International Wrought Copper Council, the LME investigated the market in November 1995. The exchange discovered that Sumitomo had large physical holdings of copper, as well as extensive credit on positions taken with LME member firms. UK regulators began an investigation. But it was the discovery of irregularities by an accounts clerk at Sumitomo that blew the whistle on Hamanaka. On May 17, 1996, he was "promoted" from his post as chief trader. Unsupported by Hamanaka, copper prices began their fall. Late on June 5, Sumitomo found the evidence of his unauthorised trading; by June 17, spot copper had dived to US$1,990.

On June 13, 1996, Sumitomo announced it had sacked Hamanaka, and reported losses of US$1.8 billion on unauthorised trades. In September that year, it revised the figure to US$2.6 billion as Hamanaka's loss-making long position was gradually unwound. Four months after Hamanaka was fired, he was arrested and charged with fraud and with forging documents authorising trades. On February 1, 1997, he pleaded guilty to both charges. The same month, Sumitomo's chairman, Tomiichi Akiyama, resigned over the lack of management oversight that led to the losses.

On June 19, 1997, despite the continued "orderly running" of the market, the LME asked the SIB to conduct a review of the metals markets. The regulator generally endorsed the way the LME is run. However, it recommended improvements to transparency on the exchange, and changes to the composition of the LME's board.

Appendix

Finance and Risk Thinkers

40

*Remembering Fischer Black (1938–1995)**

Emanuel Derman

One occasionally meets a person whose character forms a coherent whole even though its parts seem uncorrelated. You cannot easily guess their attitude to one question by knowing their opinion about another, and yet what they say makes sense. Fischer Black was one of those people, someone who liked to think through everything for himself. Not a rebel but always a bit of an outsider, his work had a vast impact on the world of insiders.

Fischer's most noticeable quality was his stubborn and meticulous devotion to clarity and simplicity in writing and speaking. When you spoke to him you had to be sure to understand the essence of your conjecture and then explain that understanding. He was not going to do your thinking for you. In writing, he stressed both content and style, revising manuscripts repeatedly until he was satisfied with both. Fischer was especially insistent about being clear and yet informal on technical subjects. I think he took an efficient-market attitude to the value of a manuscript he was working on – one new insight or piece of information was enough to make him re-evaluate the work in progress and discard everything, if necessary, and begin all over again.

Perhaps because he came to the field from outside it, Fischer's way of reasoning avoided the excessive formality of many trained economists. His approach to modelling seemed to consist of unafraid hard thinking, intuition and no great reliance on advanced mathematics. This was inspiring. He attacked problems

*This Biography first appeared in *Risk*, December 2002.

directly, with whatever skills he had at his command, and it often worked. He gave you the sense (perhaps misguided) that you too could discover deep things with whatever skills you had, if you were willing to think hard. Though his mathematical skills were fair, his insight and instinctive economic sense of what ought to happen in a theory was very strong, and he was tenacious in trying to attain insight before he resorted to mathematics. His office was dominated by a large Nike poster of a long road disappearing into the distance and the sentence "The race is not always to the swift, but to those who keep on running".

Fischer had a taste for the concrete in models: he liked to describe the financial world with variables that represented observable phenomena as opposed to hidden statistical factors. He was a rationalist, a determined believer in the value of equilibrium arguments. His initial derivation of the Black–Scholes equation was based on the contention that, in equilibrium, investors would value both a stock and its option so as to yield equal return per unit of risk – an approach I think he secretly preferred to the derivation by replication.

He had a strong pragmatic streak; he was as much or more a practitioner than an academic, willing to devote time and attention to software, trading systems and user interfaces. He thought these were just as important as the models themselves.

Fischer naturally had many unorthodox but well-thought-out ideas. He claimed he preferred applied research to pure. He thought university professors should be paid and hired for their teaching, not for their research. His sense of the important made him more interested in new content rather than new numerical methods. He wasn't overwhelmed by elegant analysis: he was quite happy that a model could be solved numerically, and didn't care if it had no analytic solution. He wrote a note suggesting that traders be paid for the rationale they articulated behind the strategy they used, rather than for the results they obtained, thus rewarding intelligence and thinking over the long run rather than the vagaries of markets over the short.

Fischer was free of artifice, though this sometimes made him difficult and awkward to deal with. I once heard him say that one of the things that limited his influence was the fact that he always told people the truth, even if they didn't want to hear it. And it was true – he didn't soft-pedal his opinion of work you had done or actions you had taken. In company politics, he had a strong sense of what was intrinsically rather than tactically important, and he always took the long and large view.

His objectivity extended to himself. Once, many years ago when I was going to give a talk at a conference where Bob Merton was the keynote speaker, I called Fischer (already ill but more than a year before his death) and left him a voicemail asking the appropriate way to refer to "his model" – should I call it "Black–Scholes" or "Black–Scholes–Merton?" Fischer responded by saying it was OK to call it the Black–Scholes–Merton model, and then, adding that Merton had come up with the replication argument for valuing an option, noted quite unperturbedly that "that's the part that many people think is the most important".

Fischer always seemed to me to be a consummate realist, someone who liked practice as much as theory. At his memorial service in Cambridge, I heard a moving speech by Jack Treynor, who concluded by saying that as regards death, "Fischer wasn't afraid at all". That's the way it seemed to me too. To the end, Fischer remained interested in work. From his home he communicated with anyone who wrote to him by e-mail. The last letter I got from him, in reply to the question of whether my occasional questions were bothering him, stressed that he enjoyed being involved.

41

*John Cox – Improving on Black–Scholes**

Navroz Patel

In his definitive introductory text on derivatives, *Options, futures and other derivatives* (Hull, 2002), John Hull describes risk-neutral valuation as "without doubt the single most important tool for the analysis of derivative securities". John Cox, currently the Nomura professor of finance at the Massachusetts Institute of Technology, firmly established the principle of risk-neutral valuation in a groundbreaking paper co-authored with Stephen Ross in 1976. "It was the first work I did in derivatives, and it remains the work I'm most proud of," Cox says.

The creation of the Black–Scholes–Merton model in 1973 kick-started the derivatives market's rapid development. Though their solution was correct, questions over exactly why it worked and which features were unique to it remained. Cox and Ross began to wonder about the foundations of option pricing.

The Black–Scholes derivation had envisaged that stock prices would evolve over time in a particular way. "We decided to investigate what option pricing would look like when the stock price follows an entirely different stochastic process and has a completely different probabilistic structure," Cox says.

Using a continuous time binomial model, Cox and Ross naturally arrived at an equation entirely different to that derived by Black and Scholes. "We worked on it for a while and even enlisted the help of some mathematicians – but we couldn't find a solution," Cox says. "The problem seemed intractable and we were

*This biography originally appeared in *Risk* in December 2002.

beginning to despair." But when the pair started to consider if any economic insights could help them they came to a simple, stunning and sudden realisation: in any situation where arbitrage pricing applies, risk-neutral pricing must apply. And with this, they wrote down the solution to the problem immediately.

The significance of their breakthrough was immense. It produced a powerful and convenient way to solve a variety of derivatives problems by providing a connection among all those problems that previously hadn't been apparent. Fischer Black had been aware of the arbitrage/risk-neutral connection within his model. But when the pair told Black of their discovery, even he had trouble believing the relationship was more general, so awesome were the implications. These days, risk-neutral pricing is thought of as the foundation of all derivatives pricing.

Cox did further work with Ross that gave rise to the binomial option pricing methodology and an early interest rate term structure model. Cox says that he owes a debt of gratitude to Bill Sharpe for the binomial model. Though its basis was in the earlier risk-neutral pricing work, it was Sharpe who suggested moving from continuous to discrete time.

Cox moved on to apply option pricing techniques to a classic problem of economics of tremendous academic importance – optimal portfolio consumption. Though he has acted as a consultant to a small number of clients over the past two decades, Cox says it's the pure intellectual stimulation of quantitative finance that most appeals. "It's still both fascinating and fun; I don't consider it work at all," he says.

BIBLIOGRAPHY

Hull, J.C., 2002, *Options, futures and other derivatives*, Fifth Edition (New Jersey: Prentice Hall).

42

The Worlds of Yesterday

Emanuel Derman

Columbia University

I never expected to be in the business world, not even a few years before I finally entered it. I got here by a series of languid apparently low-volatility Brownian diffusions within one little world interspersed with sudden jumps to another. The transitions were not truly unexpected; their probability built up inside me up like a bubble, slowly and predictably.

Growing up in Cape Town, where the college system required that you specialise immediately, I knew I wanted to be a scientist. Somewhat regretful to leave the more expansive world of other things, I nevertheless registered for a Bachelor of Science degree.

I began by studying physics, chemistry, pure and applied maths. I liked theory, was bad at lab work. In my second year I dropped chemistry and the next year I abandoned pure maths, steadily mean-reverting to theoretical physics and applied maths. Each course lasted a full academic year, and terminated in a massive final closed-book three-hour exam preceded by a several-week-long study period. You had to remember everything you might need in the large examining room filled with hundreds of people taking several different finals – Fourier and Mellin transforms, indefinite integrals, the works. We learned thoroughly and repetitively, so that after three or four years what little I knew I knew very well.

Physics was entrancing, precise and cosmic at the same time; it seemed a literally wonderful way to spend one's life. At the start of my Honours year in Cape Town I found myself applying for scholarships overseas, and ended up at Columbia University doing theoretical particle physics in the late 1960s. Though we didn't know it then, particle physics was nearing the end of its classification of the hordes of newly discovered particles and their symmetry-violating interactions. It was also the beginning of the era of unified quantum field theories. I wrote my 1973 thesis on how to test the Weinberg–Salam electro-weak model's prediction of small amounts of parity violation in electron-nucleon scattering, a signature discovered at SLAC a few years later in an experiment that set the final seal of approval on the model.

From 1973 to 1980 I continued to do research in particle physics at various universities around the world – many applicants, few jobs; exhilarating ups, and dispiriting downs. Post-doc jobs (if you found them) usually lasted no more than two years, and permanent jobs were hard to find, so you had to publish a quick paper and then start looking for your next musical chair. My wife was an academic too, and we lived peripatetically, each of us in different places half the time.

By 1980, I was an assistant professor in Boulder, Colorado with a wife and son in New York, so I committed treason: I left physics and took a job at Bell Laboratories in Murray Hill, New Jersey.

I worked for five years at Bell Labs in a Business Analysis Systems Center, where, despite its name, I learned mainly about computer science. What intrigued me most during that time was writing parsers and lexical analysers, because until then I had thought of computing mainly as a numerical activity. I divided my time at the Labs more or less equally between the pleasure of creating little UNIX worlds that users could control via the little modelling languages I wrote and between the displeasure of living in the little world of large bureaucratic organisations. Though I didn't learn much about finance during this time, UNIX and computer science turned out to be a near perfect background for a Wall Street where, when I arrived, quants still had to do all their own systems-building.

Headhunters came calling. Slowly I grew accustomed to the idea of leaving the Labs. Finally, in late 1985, I jumped to Goldman Sachs' fixed income research group, and I found I loved the realm of financial modelling. No one stood on ceremony, talent of any kind was almost always a virtue, work was informal and spontaneous, and it combined computing with the spirit of theoretical physics. Everything I had learned in those areas came together there.

Nowadays financial engineering is a discipline; in 1985 on Wall Street it was amateur heaven, a fluidly makeshift field filled with retreads from other fields who could learn quickly, solve equations and write their own programs. I liked it that way. There were only two textbooks I knew of – Jarrow and Rudd, and Cox and Rubinstein – and the only derivatives meeting I went to each year was the annual spring meeting of the Amex. Now there are tens of thousands of books, thousands of conferences and hundreds of degree programs.

I spent my first four years in the world of fixed-income derivatives, where the dominant issue of the 1980s was how to extend and calibrate the replication methodology of Black–Scholes and Merton to interest rates. Working with the fixed-income bond options traders was wonderful; it was a small world of motivated quants and traders, the latter eager to embrace whatever new model you could create.

I spent the next ten years in equity derivatives, where the dominant issue was the smile. The group I ran, called Quantitative Strategies, was full of hands-on people who were trying to understand risk at the front lines and then build systems to control it, not always in that order. What I liked most, when you could find it, was working closely with little worlds, small groups of quants, traders and salespeople interested in valuation and in doing something about it, without too much bureaucracy or too much rigor. We were lucky to be theorists living in the experimenters' laboratory, the first to hear about new irregularities. I liked the mix of business and theory. I enjoyed thinking about things slowly, figuring them out together with my colleagues, and then explaining them by talking or writing.

I spent my last two-and-a-half years in the bigger world of firmwide risk management, and then, in mid-2002, I left Goldman Sachs to take a break and write a book. I still like the world of financial research with its mix of theory and experiment, science and sociology, models and computer systems, doing and teaching, and expect to return to it.

WHAT DID I LEARN FROM ALL THIS?

I started out in 1985 thinking of quantitative finance as a branch of the natural sciences – I imagined you could search for an all-encompassing theory that would explain everything. Over the years, I've come to see less evidence for universal laws in prices, and progressively more evidence of the vagaries of human behaviour. I am still amazed and awed that anyone trades anything on the basis of a model. But I've learned that trading with a model is not the simple procedure academics imagine. Intelligent traders iterate between imagination and models in a way that belies easy categorisation. It's not a clockwork universe out there, and therefore, I learned to avoid needless rigor and axiomatisation.

I learned that it pays to build models as though you were working in the natural sciences, but you have to keep reminding yourself that you aren't. It's unbelievably hard to build a truly successful model. I learned what a once-in-a-lifetime thing a discovery like the Black–Scholes model is – not necessarily "right", but easily embraceable because it asks just enough of you, but not too much.

I learned that building trading systems that make it easy to use models is at least as hard as building the models themselves, and takes many more people. I learned to try to avoid middlemen: there's no substitute for communicating directly with traders and other model users.

Most importantly, I learned the value of colleagues. I've seen how easy it is to go down wrong paths when you work alone, and how just one remark from someone can set you straight.

Finally, I kept relearning that I like little worlds better than big ones, and that for me, the path to bigger issues is through the details of little ones.

I've been lucky to have been in this business at a time when it was still developing, when small contributions could exert disproportionate leverage. I wish, of course, that I'd been in this field even earlier.

43

Perspectives on Risk Management

John Hull

University of Toronto

I first became interested in the derivatives market in the early 1980s. At that time academic research was almost entirely concerned with pricing issues. The Black–Scholes model, the Cox–Ross–Rubinstein binomial tree, and finite difference methods had already been developed as key tools, and researchers were busy extending them to value the many non-standard deals that were beginning to trade in the over-the-counter market. At that time we gave very little thought to risk management except for investigating the performance of delta-hedging schemes.

It was the performance of delta hedging that led to my first major research projects with Alan White. In 1984 Alan and I gave a presentation to one of the large international banks on currency options. In advance of the presentation we developed some software to illustrate the performance of delta hedging. The software consisted of a Monte Carlo simulation of a trader who writes a foreign currency option and then delta hedges it. The exchange rate was assumed to follow geometric Brownian motion. During the presentation one of the participants quite rightly pointed out that in practice delta hedging does not work as well as our software indicated because of the constant volatility assumption underlying the software. After some discussion we agreed to adjust our software to incorporate a stochastic volatility. This dramatically reduced the effectiveness of delta hedging. Of course, this should not really have surprised us: a major source of uncertainty was being left unhedged.

Alan and I now realise that the 1984 presentation had a key impact on the development of our careers. It led to us spend the next three years developing stochastic volatility models and investigating the best ways of doing delta, gamma, and vega hedging in the foreign exchange market. In the course of this we taught ourselves a great deal about the theory underlying derivatives pricing. In a stochastic volatility model there are two uncertain variables: the stock price and its volatility. The first can be handled using Black–Scholes and Merton no-arbitrage arguments. The second is the value of something that is not the price of a traded security and requires a generalisation of those arguments.

I wrote the first edition of my book *Options, Futures and Other Derivatives* in 1987. There was one chapter on the Greek letters, but little else on risk management. Much has happened since then to make both derivatives practitioners and derivatives academics much more aware of the importance of risk management. We have seen a string of major derivatives disasters such as Orange County in 1994 and Barings in 1995. The G-30 policy recommendations were published in 1993 and regulators have become more proactive in the machinations of the derivatives industry. The 1988 BIS Accord forced banks to pay more attention to the credit risk in derivatives. The 1996 amendment pushed banks in the direction of developing internal models for calculating the value-at-risk (VAR) measure for assessing market risk. BIS II is pushing banks in the direction of devoting resources to developing internal models for the assessment of credit risk and operational risk.

During the second half of the 1990s risk management groups had to become more technically sophisticated and consequently, the salaries of people in risk management increased. There was a trend for quantitative analysts to move from front-office positions where they were concerned with pricing exotic deals to middle-office risk management positions – from poachers to gamekeepers! In their new positions they could apply their skills to managing large variance-covariance matrices, carrying out Monte Carlo simulations of credit ratings migrations, allocating capital, calculating RAROC, etc.

I have tried to move with the times. The amount of risk management in my books has increased with each new edition. The fifth edition of *Options, Futures, and Other Derivatives*, which came out in 2002, contains much more on risk management than the first edition. It includes material on how to calculate VAR, how to assess credit risk, hedging strategies, what risk management lessons we can learn from derivatives disasters, and so on. I am now working on a book concerned exclusively with risk management – having written articles on VAR, credit risk, and model risk. Currently I am heavily involved in both the theoretical and empirical work concerned with credit risk and the credit default swap market.

A particular interest of mine is model risk. Academics have tended to test idealised versions of the models that researchers have developed. I believe that we should spend more time testing models as they are actually used in the trading room. This will give us a better appreciation of the impact of the trader's practice of recalibrating a model daily to market data.

What does the future hold for risk management? One thing is certain. Regulators will continue to come up with new capital charges for banks and financial engineers will continue to engage in regulatory arbitrage by developing products that take advantage of weaknesses in the regulations. Technological innovations will allow risk managers to collect data more efficiently and distribute risk management information more effectively throughout their organisations. Market risk, credit risk, operational risk and liquidity risk will continue to be important. I do not believe that the much-talked-about idea of integrating market risk and credit risk will have its day. I do believe that model risk will get more attention from regulators, risk managers, and academics. I also believe that we will become better at managing the risks arising from the possibility of the extreme events that occur only once every five or ten years. Financial institutions will continue to devote more resources to assessing risks, both those that naturally lend themselves to quantification and those that do not. There can be little doubt that risk management will provide great careers in the decades to come for individuals with the appropriate blend of mathematical and interpersonal skills.

44

Jonathan Ingersoll –
*Driven to Simplicity**

Paul Lyon

Jonathan Ingersoll, Adrian C. Israel professor of international trade and finance at Yale University, received the financial engineer of the year award in February 2003 from the International Association of Financial Engineers' (IAFE). Ingersoll joined a prestigious list of recipients of the IAFE award: Emanuel Derman, John Hull, Robert Merton, Fischer Black and Mark Rubinstein are just a few of his peers to have won the honour.

Ingersoll is famous for the Cox–Ingersoll–Ross model, developed in collaboration with John Cox and Stephen Ross in the mid-1970s and published in 1985, which provided a consistent way to value interest rate derivatives, and is still widely used today. "Robert Merton had done some of the preliminary work on the area, but until the three of us devised the model there had been no attempt to explore interest rate term structures under a modern academic footing", Ingersoll says.

Leaving Chicago for Yale provided Ingersoll with an opportunity he had longed for: Myron Scholes had the monopoly on teaching derivatives courses at Chicago, so Ingersoll only taught his first derivatives class while at Yale. It was a fortunate opening. Indeed, Ingersoll has been known to come up with theories, later developed into papers, while teaching such classes.

Ingersoll says the paper he is probably most proud of was also one of the simplest. "'Digital contracts: simple tools for pricing complex derivatives' was one of my most enjoyable studies. Being able

*This is an adaptation of a biography that originally appeared in *Risk*, December 2002.

to explain complicated ideas in simple ways is what drives me", Ingersoll says. "Academics have a tendency to become far too complicated and the profession seems to go overboard on mathematical rigour".

Ingersoll still hopes his best work is yet to come. He is currently working on a paper entitled "The subjective and objective evaluation of incentive stock options", but believes that the heyday of derivatives research has past.

"Nothing coming out now is as fundamental as papers released in the 1970s or 1980s", Ingersoll says. "But one area I think we really need to address is the study of how information gets into and, consequently, drives derivatives prices. Nobody really understands the process of how information filters into pricing but a combination of disciplines (behavioural finance, derivatives and corporate finance) could come together to explore the issue."

45

Mathematics and Finance: A Fruitful Relationship

Robert Jarrow

Johnson Graduate School of Management, Cornell University

I graduated from Duke University in 1974 with a BA in mathematics and management science (operations research). My studies in finance began at Dartmouth College, where I earned an MBA in 1976. At the Amos Tuck School of Business, I was exposed to the Black–Scholes–Merton option-pricing model, which had just recently been published. This model, and the mathematics behind it, so fascinated me that I decided to continue my studies of option-pricing theory at the Massachusetts Institute of Technology. I received a PhD in financial economics from MIT in 1979 under the direction of Robert Merton, Stewart Myers, and Donald Lessard. During my studies, I also served as a teaching assistant for both Franco Modigliani and Fischer Black.

While studying finance at MIT, I felt that the mathematical underpinnings of the finance literature needed improvement. To better enable myself to pursue this line of research, I intensely studied more mathematics during my early years as a professor at the Johnson Graduate School of Management at Cornell University. David Heath taught one mathematics course that I took on stochastic calculus. Through continued discussions related to finance and stochastic calculus, David and I became research partners. This collaboration led to the joint publication of many papers, perhaps the most important being the Heath–Jarrow–Morton (HJM) term structure model for pricing interest rate options (Heath, Jarrow and Morton, 1992). Andy Morton, the third co-author, was a student of ours at Cornell.

As part of our collaboration, David and I trained many PhD students, and together we started Cornell's Financial Engineering program in 1995. This was an innovative joint program between Cornell's Engineering and Business Schools. Once started, it flourished and continues to this day.

David and I also held the first meeting in the field now called mathematical finance at Cornell University during the spring of 1989. We invited colleagues from other universities working in the interface between mathematics and finance to present papers and enjoy the Ithaca spring. During one of the conference lunches, Stan Pliska, Marc Davis and I hatched a plan for a new journal, called *Mathematical Finance*. The plan came to fruition with the three of us acting as editors, and Stan became the first managing editor. *Mathematical Finance* continues to this day, published by Basil Blackwell. Both Stan and Marc have since stepped down as editors, and I have taken over Stan's role as the managing editor.

I attempted an interesting entrepreneurial venture during the summer of 1992 with Andrew Rudd (chief executive officer of BARRA) and Stuart Turnbull. We approached Peter Field, editor of the fledging publication *Risk* magazine, with a business proposal. The proposal was to form a business partnership that would run for-profit educational conferences in the area of risk management. Andrew would provide business contacts, I would provide academic contacts, and Peter would provide the necessary marketing. It was a great idea, but for various reasons, the business partnership never materialised. Instead, Peter decided to pursue this business on his own. One of the first experimental conferences was on the Heath–Jarrow–Morton (HJM) model, given in London and New York City in 1996 by *Risk* with presentations by David Heath, Andrew Morton and me. It was a great success, and as they say, the rest is history.

Shortly after the HJM model was formulated, Stuart Turnbull invited me to visit him during the summer of 1990 at the Australian Graduate School of Management in New South Wales, Australia. Never having been to Australia, I accepted his invitation. During this visit, we developed the first reduced form credit-risk model, of which the essential details were published in *Risk*

(Jarrow and Turnbull, 1992). This model has since become known as the Jarrow–Turnbull model. This collaboration with Stuart also led to the writing of our textbook entitled *Derivative Securities*, currently in its second edition (Jarrow and Turnbull, 1996).

In 1995, David Shimko introduced me to Don van-Deventer, the chief executive officer of Kamakura, a small risk management software and consulting firm located in Japan (now based in the United States). Kamakura was one of the first software vendors to apply the HJM term structure models to asset and liability management. Don offered me a partnership in his firm and a position as director of research. Interested in applying my theories to practice, I accepted. Since that time, the company's goal has been to build integrated risk management software that addresses both market and credit risk. In the past two years, this goal has been realised with the inclusion of reduced form credit risk models into Kamakura's software.

In parallel to my study of term structure models, I became interested in market manipulation – the ability of "large traders" to manipulate markets to their financial advantage. This interest was fostered through my consulting as an expert witness in a court suit alleging market manipulation. As a result, I have studied this topic and published numerous papers related to my insights. My research shows that when a market is being manipulated, standard option-pricing techniques fail to apply. Although manipulation occurs, it is rare. A much more common and related market phenomenon is known as "liquidity risk". Liquidity risk relates to the impact that different trade sizes have on prices, under different market conditions. Because of liquidity risk's connection to market manipulation, I have also been seeking a model for option-pricing in its presence. During this past year, Phil Protter (a new addition to Cornell's faculty), Umut Cetin (a PhD student of ours) and I finished a paper accomplishing this goal (Cetin, Jarrow and Protter, 2002).

For the future, I see my research – and risk management research, in general – focusing more on firm-wide risk management issues, rather than the individual risks themselves (market, credit, liquidity). The foundational insights into these individual risks have been answered to my satisfaction. What remains in my mind are questions such as "why should firms hedge?"; "how should one allocate capital across different investment classes?"; and "what is the appropriate capital charge (if any) for a firm's investments?" Answering these questions is the task to which I now turn.

BIBLIOGRAPHY

Black, F., and M. Scholes, 1973, "The Pricing of Options and Corporate Liabilities", *Journal of Political Economy*, 81:3, pp. 637–54.

Heath, D., R. Jarrow, and A. Morton, 1992, "Bond Pricing and the Term Structure of Interest Rates: A New Methodology for Contingent Claims Valuation", *Econometrica*, 60(1).

Jarrow, R., and S. Turnbull, 1992, "Credit Risk: Drawing the Analogy", *Risk*, 5(9).

Jarrow, R., and S. Turnbull, 1996, *Derivative Securities*, Second Edition (Ohio: South-Western).

Cetin, U., R. Jarrow, and P. Protter, 2002, "Liquidity Risk and Arbitrage Pricing Theory", Working Paper, Cornell University.

46

*Adventures in Portfolio Theory**

Harry M. Markowitz

University of California, San Diego

I was born in Chicago in 1927, the only child of Morris and Mildred Markowitz who owned a small grocery store. We lived in a nice apartment, always had enough to eat, and I had my own room. I never was aware of the Great Depression.

Growing up, I enjoyed baseball and tag football in the nearby empty lot or the park a few blocks away, and playing the violin in the high school orchestra. I also enjoyed reading. At first, my reading material consisted of comic books and adventure magazines, such as *The Shadow*, in addition to school assignments. In late grammar school and throughout high school I enjoyed popular accounts of physics and astronomy. In high school I also began to read original works of serious philosophers. I was particularly struck by David Hume's argument that, though we release a ball a thousand times, and each time, it falls to the floor, we do not have a necessary proof that it will fall the thousand-and-first time. I also read *The Origin of Species* and was moved by Darwin's marshalling of facts and careful consideration of possible objections.

From high school, I entered the University of Chicago and took its two-year Bachelor's program, which emphasised the reading of original materials where possible. Everything in the program was interesting, but I was especially interested in the philosophers we read in a course called OII: Observation, Interpretation and Integration.

*Reprinted with permission of the Nobel Foundation © The Nobel Foundation 1990.

Becoming an economist was not a childhood dream of mine. When I finished the Bachelor's degree and had to choose an upper division, I considered the matter for a short while and decided on Economics. Micro and macro were all very fine, but eventually it was the "Economics of Uncertainty" which interested me – in particular, the Von Neumann and Morgenstern and the Marschak arguments concerning expected utility; the Friedman–Savage utility function; and L. J. Savage's defence of personal probability. I had the good fortune to have Friedman, Marschak and Savage among other great teachers at Chicago. Koopmans' course on activity analysis with its definition of efficiency and its analysis of efficient sets was also a crucial part of my education.

At Chicago I was invited to become one of the student members of the Cowles Commission for Research in Economics. If anyone knows the Cowles Commission only by its influence on Economic and Econometric thought, and by the number of Nobel laureates it has produced, they might imagine it to be some gigantic research centre. In fact it was a small but exciting group, then under the leadership of its director, T. Koopmans, and its former director, J. Marschak.

When it was time to choose a topic for my dissertation, a chance conversation suggested the possibility of applying mathematical methods to the stock market. I asked Professor Marschak what he thought. He thought it reasonable, and explained that Alfred Cowles himself had been interested in such applications. He sent me to Professor Marshall Ketchum who provided a reading list as a guide to the financial theory and practice of the day.

The basic concepts of portfolio theory came to me one afternoon in the library while reading John Burr Williams's *Theory of Investment Value*. Williams proposed that the value of a stock should equal the present value of its future dividends. Since future dividends are uncertain, I interpreted Williams's proposal to be to value a stock by its expected future dividends. But if the investor were only interested in expected values of securities, he or she would only be interested in the expected value of the portfolio; and to maximise the expected value of a portfolio one need invest only in a single security. This, I knew, was not the way investors did or should act. Investors diversify because they are concerned with risk as well as return. Variance came to mind as a measure of risk.

The fact that portfolio variance depended on security covariances added to the plausibility of the approach. Since there were two criteria, risk and return, it was natural to assume that investors selected from the set of Pareto optimal risk-return combinations.

I left the University of Chicago and joined the RAND Corporation in 1952. Shortly thereafter, George Dantzig joined RAND. While I did not work on portfolio theory at RAND, the optimisation techniques I learned from George (beyond his basic simplex algorithm which I had read on my own) are clearly reflected in my subsequent work on the fast computation of mean-variance frontiers (Markowitz, 1956, and Appendix A of Markowitz, 1959). My 1959 book was principally written at the Cowles Foundation at Yale during the academic year 1955–56, on leave from the RAND Corporation, at the invitation of James Tobin. It is not clear that Markowitz (1959) would ever have been written if it were not for Tobin's invitation.

My article on "Portfolio Selection" appeared in 1952. In the 38 years since then, I have worked with many people on many topics. The focus has always been on the application of mathematical or computer techniques to practical problems, particularly problems of business decisions under uncertainty. Sometimes we applied existing techniques; other times we developed new techniques. Some of these techniques have been more "successful" than others, success being measured here by acceptance in practice.

In 1989, I was awarded the Von Neumann Prize in Operations Research Theory by the Operations Research Society of America and The Institute of Management Sciences. They cited my works in the areas of portfolio theory, sparse matrix techniques and the SIMSCRIPT programming language. I have written above about portfolio theory. My work on sparse matrix techniques was an out-growth of work I did in collaboration with Alan S. Manne, Tibor Fabian, Thomas Marschak, Alan J. Rowe and others at the RAND Corporation in the 1950s on industry-wide and multi-industry activity analysis models of industrial capabilities. Our models strained the computer capabilities of the day. I observed that most of the coefficients in our matrices were zero; ie, the nonzeros were "sparse" in the matrix, and that typically the triangular matrices associated with the forward and back solution provided by Gaussian elimination would remain sparse if pivot elements were chosen with care. William Orchard-Hayes programmed the first sparse matrix code. Since then considerable work has been done on sparse matrix techniques, for example, on methods of selecting pivots and of storing the nonzero elements. Sparse matrix techniques are now standard in large linear programming codes.

During the 1950s I decided, as did many others, that many practical problems were beyond analytic solution, and that simulation techniques were required. At RAND I participated in the building of large logistics simulation models; at General Electric I helped build models of manufacturing plants. One problem with the use of simulation was the length of time required to program a detailed simulator. In the early 1960s, I returned to RAND for the purpose of developing a programming language, later called SIMSCRIPT, which reduced programming time by allowing the programmer to describe (in a certain stylised manner) the system to be simulated rather than describing the actions which the computer must take to accomplish this simulation. The original SIMSCRIPT compiler was written by B. Hausner; its manual by H. Karr who later co-founded a computer software company, CACI, with me. Currently SIMSCRIPT II.5 is supported by CACI and still has a fair number of users.

I am sorry I cannot acknowledge all the people I have worked with over the last 38 years and describe what it was we accomplished. As each of these people knows, I often considered work to be play, and derived great joy from our collaboration.

47

*Unexpected Roads, Happily Travelled**

Robert C. Merton

Harvard Business School

I was born in New York, on July 31, 1944, the middle child between two sisters, Stephanie and Vanessa, and I grew up in Hastings-on-Hudson. The local public school provided a fine education opportunity. I was a good student but not at the top of my class. I played varsity football and ran track, neither with great distinction. Schoolwork and intellectual interests such as music and the arts were not especially important to me while I was growing up, although mathematics, my favourite subject, was fun. Baseball was my first passion. Around age 11, that passion began to turn toward cars. I thought that I would become an automobile engineer when I grew up. Indeed, while in college, I spent two summers working for Ford in its headquarters in Dearborn, Michigan.

Both of my parents played important roles in my early life of learning. My father introduced me to baseball, poker, magic, and the stock market (only magic didn't take root). And books of every kind were everywhere. He said nothing directly about expected academic performance. There was no need to. Simply by self-exemplification, he set the standards for work effort and for clarity of thought and expression. My mother gave me much good,

*Revised version of Professor Merton's autobiography written for the Nobel Foundation, © The Nobel Foundation, 1997.

practical advice for getting through life. One such counsel in particular I have applied often and in varied arenas: "First show them that you can do it their way, so that you earn the right to do it your way."

My arrival at college marked the beginning of a serious focus on academic matters. Just one day after entering Columbia College I switched to the Engineering School. With its small and flexible program and fine faculty, it was a great place for an undergraduate to explore mathematics and its uses.

After Columbia, I went west to pursue a PhD in applied mathematics at the California Institute of Technology. My time at Cal Tech (1966–67), brief as it was, added significantly to my stock of mathematics. Even more valuable to me was its creed of placing students from the outset in a research framework, "playing" with their subject instead of merely passively learning the material. Sometime during the year, I decided to leave Cal Tech (and mathematics) to study economics. I applied to half a dozen good departments, but only one, the Massachusetts Institute of Technology (MIT), accepted me, and it gave me a full fellowship.

My decision to leave applied mathematics for economics was in part tied to the widely-held popular belief in the 1960s that macro-economics had made fundamental inroads into controlling business cycles and stopping dysfunctional unemployment and inflation. Thus, I felt that working in economics could "really matter" and that potentially one could affect millions of people. I also believed that my mathematics and engineering training might give me some advantage in analysing complex situations. Most important in my decision was the sense that I had a much better intuition and "feel" for economic matters than physical ones. Nowhere was that more apparent to me than in the stock market. At Cal Tech, many mornings I would get to a local brokerage house at 6:30 am (9:30 am in New York) for the opening of the stock market, spend a couple of hours watching the tape and trading, and then go to my classes. In addition to stocks, I traded warrants, convertible bonds, and over-the-counter options. Although I did apply mathematical skills, my valuation approaches were essentially *ad hoc*. Nevertheless, I learned much from those varied transactional experiences about markets and institutions, which proved useful in my later research.

When I arrived at MIT in the fall of 1967, I discovered why they had admitted me when no other institution had: Harold Freeman, statistician and member of the economics department from pre-Samuelson days. Harold had recognised some of the mathematicians who had written my letters of recommendation and convinced the department to take a flyer. Now in the role of first-year advisor, he saw my proposed, "traditional" course plan and told me "… you follow that and you'll leave here by the end of the term out of boredom … go take Paul Samuelson's mathematical economics course." I did. Not only did I get to interact with Paul Samuelson, but I met the then second-year students, Stanley Fischer and Michael Rothschild. I learned economics from Paul's *Foundations* and wrote a term paper on an optimal growth model with endogenous population changes, which was later published in 1969. As a result of our meeting in his course, Paul hired me as his research assistant that spring. Quite a yield from a single course!

Paul nominated me to be a Junior Fellow at Harvard. After being rejected I had no choice but to get a job. I spent the fall and winter of 1969 interviewing only with departments of economics, but I ended up taking an appointment to teach finance at MIT's Sloan School of Management. It was Franco Modigliani, with a foot in both the department and Sloan, who made the invitation, and who convinced me that I could teach there even though I had no formal training in finance. I had been a student of Franco's and my research on optimal lifetime consumption and portfolio selection supported his Life-Cycle Hypothesis. Our relationship, however, became even stronger in the years after I joined Sloan.

It was in the process of interviewing for the job at Sloan that I met Myron Scholes, a recent arrival to the faculty from the University of Chicago. It was here that I also met Fischer Black who was a regular visitor to Sloan. These meetings and consequent collaborations lead to our work on asset pricing and derivative pricing models. When I joined the finance group at MIT, the faculty consisted of assistant professors Myron Scholes, Stewart Myers, and Gerry Pogue and senior professors Daniel Holland and Franco Modigliani. Dan specialised in tax matters and Franco was involved in many things everywhere. As a consequence, *de facto*, the junior faculty "ran" everything in the group with respect to both teaching and research. It was a wonderful environment of benign neglect in which all of us could grow. I enjoyed teaching from the start.

Throughout the 18 years I spent at the Sloan School, it was a stimulating and happy place to do research. I shall always owe a great debt to my brilliant colleagues there: Myron Scholes and Fischer Black, Franco Modigliani, Stewart Myers, John Cox, Chi-fu Huang, Terry Marsh, Richard Ruback, Douglas Breeden (unfortunately, only as a visitor), and from the Economics Department, Stanley Fischer and Paul Samuelson.

I see my research interests as fitting into three regimes of roughly equal lengths across time: 1968–1977, 1977–1987, and 1988 to the present, with a reflective year 1987–1988. The first period was my most productive one for basic research, in terms of both the number of papers produced and the originality and significance of contribution. The central modelling theme was continuous-time stochastic processes with continuous-decision-making by agents. My first decade's research focus on developing dynamic models of optimal lifetime consumption and portfolio selection, equilibrium asset pricing, and contingent-claim pricing shifted in the 1978–1987 period to applications of those models. In 1987, I took my first-ever sabbatical year to write a book based on my work in continuous-time finance. It was a most enjoyable and productive time. Earlier writings were corrected and, in some cases, significantly expanded. Five new chapters were created incorporating my cumulative thoughts in the fields of optimal portfolio selection, option pricing, financial intermediation, and general equilibrium theory. This reflective year was a watershed, both for my research and for where it would take place. In effect, *Continuous-Time Finance* proved to be a synthesis of much of my earlier work. Its Chapter 14 on intermediation and institutions, however, represented a bridge to a new direction of my research. From that time until the present, I have focused on understanding the financial system with special emphasis on the dynamics of institutional change. There is, however, continuity of this line of inquiry with the past: Fischer's, Myron's and my derivative-security research provided much of the foundation for the contracting and security-design technology that is central to the extraordinary wave of real-world financial innovation of the past two decades.

My decision to move from MIT to the Harvard Business School in 1988 was significantly influenced by this turn in my research interests. Although it was a difficult decision to make, I have never since doubted that it was the right one. For nearly fifteen years, I have enjoyed developing the new work on the financial system: to begin with, on my own, but then quite soon after, in a delightful, productive and multi-faceted collaboration with Zvi Bodie, professor of finance at Boston University, whom I have known since the early 1970s when he was a student in the MIT department of economics.

Throughout the last 30 years of academic research, I have been involved in finance practice. The vast bulk of my research has been in mathematical finance theory, but I believe that my involvement in practice has shaped that research and in turn has been shaped by it, this interplay to the benefit of both. My first consulting experience was in 1969 for a southern California bank on the pricing of warrants. Myron Scholes and I began working together on consulting projects shortly after I joined the Sloan faculty. For the rest of the 1970s and much of the 1980s, I kept my hand in practice, serving on a few mutual fund boards and being elected a trustee of College Retirement Equities Fund. From 1988–1992, I served as a senior advisor to Office of the Chairman, Salomon Inc. In 1993, I co-founded Long-Term Capital Management and served as a principal until 1999. From 1999–2001, I was a senior advisor to JP Morgan & Co, Incorporated. My latest venture is a new financial-services firm, Integrated Finance Limited, of which I am co-founder.

In long retrospect, unexpected roads happily travelled.

Professor Merton received the Nobel Prize in Economic Science in 1997 for his work on derivatives with Myron Scholes and the late Fischer Black.

48

*Remembering Merton Miller (1923–2000)**

John Ferry

Merton Miller was a leading figure in the establishment of financial economics as a discipline. But he was also a great advocate of the derivatives contract as an effective and stabilising risk management tool when others saw it as little more than a gambling instrument. And he acted as a bridge between business, politics and academia, all of which had different views on derivatives.

Miller spent most of his career at the Graduate School of Business at the University of Chicago, which he joined in 1961 following a doctorate at Johns Hopkins and post-doctoral work at the London School of Economics and the Carnegie Institute of Technology (now Carnegie-Mellon University). At Carnegie he met Franco Modigliani, and in 1958 the two published the first of their ground-breaking papers on corporate finance.

Miller and Modigliani looked at the effect of leverage on a company, and showed that the greater the debt, the greater the return demanded by shareholders, because investors must be compensated for the additional risk. They also showed that dividend policies are irrelevant to the value of a company.

This revolutionary work showed that finance could be studied in a conceptual way like economics. Before, it had been taught in a more rigid fashion, devoid of theory. Bob Hamada, former dean of the University of Chicago's Graduate School of Business, was a colleague of Miller's for more than 30 years. "He legitimised the study of finance as a true branch of economics", Hamada says.

* This biography originally appeared in the "Hall of Fame" in *Risk*, December 2002.

Miller supervised a number of PhD students who would go on to lead the way in derivatives, among them Myron Scholes. He also worked with Fischer Black, and was influential in convincing the Chicago-based Journal of Political Economy to publish Black and Scholes' ground-breaking option pricing paper.

"Every major business school or finance faculty has someone who has been a student of his", Hamada says. "His students then became the mentors of the next generation and so on". Miller's contribution to financial economics was ultimately recognised in 1990 when he was awarded that year's Nobel prize in economics.

Miller served on the boards of the Chicago Board of Trade (CBOT) from 1983 to 1985 and the Chicago Mercantile Exchange from 1990 until his death in June 2000. This experience broadened his interests to economic and regulatory issues that affect derivatives exchanges, and he became a leading spokesman for the industry. "He spoke the academics' language, but he could also convey the issues and the problems of the futures industry to academics", says Hamada, who also served on the CBOT board. "For the last 15 years of his life he was really devoted to the role of derivatives".

After the stock market crash of 1987, some Wall Street bankers blamed the Chicago exchanges, arguing that the crisis was caused by futures market volatility. But Miller was quick to defend them, arguing that neither portfolio insurance nor index trading caused the crash. In the Chicago tradition, he advocated free-market solutions to economic problems.

49

*Inspired by America**

Franco Modigliani

Massachusetts Institute of Technology

I was born in Rome, Italy, the son of Enrico Modigliani and Olga Flaschel. My father was a leading paediatrician in the city and my mother was a volunteer social worker.

My school performance in the early years was good though not outstanding. Then, in 1932, a major trauma occurred. My father died as a consequence of an operation. I suddenly realised how deeply I loved and admired him and at 13 my whole world seemed to collapse. After this event my school performance for the next 3 years became spotty until I moved to Liceo Visconti, the best high school in Rome, and the challenge proved healthy and I seemed to blossom. Encouraged, I decided to skip the last year of the Liceo, passed the required difficult exams and entered the University of Rome at 17 (two years ahead of the norm).

My family hoped that I would follow in my father's steps, entering a career in medicine. I was torn for a while, but finally decided against it because of my low tolerance level for sufferings and blood. Instead I chose law, which in Italy opens the way to many career possibilities. In my second year I decided to enter a national competition sponsored by the student organisation I Littoriali della Coltura in the area of economics. To my surprise I won first prize and, although now I would hesitate to recommend that first essay as a significant contribution to economics, clearly, it served the

*Reprinted with permission of the Nobel Foundation © The Nobel Foundation 1985.

purpose of establishing my current interest in economics. Unfortunately, under fascism, teaching in this field was dismal, and only with the advice of the few good economists I knew personally, and especially of Riccardo Bachi, I began on my own to read the English and Italian classics.

The Littoriali had put me in contact with young antifascists, and my political opposition to the regime began then. My involvement with my future wife, Serena Calabi, and her remarkable father, Giulio, who was a long standing antifascist also contributed. In 1938 the Italian racial laws were promulgated and at the invitation of my future in-laws, I joined them in Paris where, in May 1939, Serena and I were married. I enrolled at the Sorbonne but found the teaching there uninspiring and a waste of time, so I spent my time studying on my own and writing my thesis at the Bibliotheque St Genevieve. In June 1939 I returned briefly to Rome to discuss my thesis and receive my degree of Doctor Juris from the University of Rome. Shortly after this, fearing that Europe was going to be soon engulfed in a bloody war, we applied for an immigration visa for the US and arrived in New York in August 1939, a few days before the beginning of World War II.

It became apparent that our stay in the US would be a long one and I immediately began thinking on how best to pursue my interest in economics. I had the great luck of being awarded a free tuition fellowship by the Graduate Faculty of Political and Social Science of the New School for Social Research, an institution freshly created to give haven to the European scholars who were victims of the three fascist dictatorships. Thus in fall 1939, I started on a routine that was to last three years, of studying at night from 6–10 pm, while working during the day selling European books to support my family which soon included our first son: Andre. I worked hard but, nonetheless, remember that period as an exciting one, as I was discovering my passion for economics, thanks also to excellent teachers, including Adolph Lowe and above all Jacob Marschak to whom I owe a debt of gratitude beyond words. He helped me develop solid foundations in economics and econometrics, some mathematical foundations, introduced me to the great issues of the day and gave me, together with his unforgettable kindness, constant encouragement. In particular I owe to him that blend of theory and empirical analysis, theories that can be tested and empirical work guided by theory – that has characterised a good deal of my later work. Marschak also provided me with an experience that contributed to my development, by inviting me to participate in an informal seminar, which met in New York around 1940–41, whose members included, among others, Abraham Wald, Tjalling Koopmans and Oscar Lange.

I consider that my formal training ended in 1941 when Marschak left the New School to join the University of Chicago, and I obtained my first teaching job as an instructor at New Jersey College for Women. My first published article in English, "Liquidity Preference and the Theory of Interest and Money", *Econometrica*, Vol 12, No 1, January 1944, which is also, substantially, my doctoral dissertation, and which I regard as one of my major contributions, appeared some two years later. The result of discussions in Marschak's seminar and of a running debate with Abba Lerner, it purports to integrate the Keynesian "revolution", then generally regarded as a total break with the past, with the mainstream of classical economics.

In 1942 I became an instructor in economics and statistics at Bard College, then a residential college of Columbia University, and came to appreciate the unique qualities of life in an American college campus, especially the intimate association with first rate students. In 1944 I returned to the New School as a Lecturer and a Research Associate at the Institute of World Affairs where together with Hans Neisser, I was responsible for a project whose results were eventually published in *National Income and International Trade*. During this period I also made my first contribution to the study of saving, which has since come to be known as the Duesenberry–Modigliani hypothesis.

In fall 1948 I left New York, having been awarded the prestigious Political Economy Fellowship of the University of Chicago as well as having been offered the opportunity of joining, as a Research Consultant, the Cowles Commission for Research in Economics, then the leading institution in its field. Shortly after my arrival I accepted an attractive position at the University of Illinois as director of a research project on "Expectations and Business Fluctuations". However, I remained in Chicago through the academic year 1949–50, greatly benefiting from my association with the Cowles Commission, staffed and visited by people like Marschak, Koopmans, Arrow,

Simon, at a time when the profession was absorbing two important revolutions, one centring on the theory of choice under uncertainty, initiated by von Neuman and Morgenstern, and the other on statistical inference from non-experimental observations, inspired by Haavelmo.

My association with the University of Illinois lasted only till 1952 because of internal strife. During that brief time, I befriended a brilliant young graduate student, Richard Brumberg. With his collaboration we laid the foundations for what was to become the "Life Cycle Hypothesis of Saving". It was elaborated in 1953 and 1954 in two papers; one dealing with individual behaviour and the other with aggregate saving. After we had both left the University of Illinois, Brumberg had gone to complete his PhD at the John Hopkins University and I joined Carnegie Institute of Technology, now Carnegie-Mellon University. The "aggregate" paper was only published in 1980 in my *Collected Papers* because the shock of Brumberg's untimely death in 1955 sapped my will to undertake the revisions and condensation that would have been required for publication in one of the standard professional journals.

My association with Carnegie, which lasted until 1960, was a very productive one. In addition to completing the two basic papers setting the foundations for the "Life Cycle Hypothesis", I collaborated on a book dealing with the problem of optimal production smoothing, and wrote the two essays with Miller on the effect of financial structure and dividend policy on the market value of a firm. I also published a paper with E. Grunberg on the predictability of social events when the agent reacts to prediction, which later was to provide one of the pillars for the "theory of rational expectations". All of these contributions represented, to some extent, the coming to fruition of seeds started during my research on "Expectations and Business Fluctuations".

In 1960 I was a visiting professor at the Massachusetts Institute of Technology, to which I returned after a year at Northwestern University, and where I have remained ever since. Supported by this unique institution and its unique colleagues, I have pursued the interests developed earlier in macroeconomics, including criticism of the monetarist positions, generalisations of the monetary mechanism and empirical tests of the "Life Cycle Hypothesis". I have also branched out into new areas and, in particular, international finance and the international payment system, the effects of and cures for inflation, stabilisation policies in extensively indexed open economies, and into various fields of finance such as credit rationing, the term structure of interest rates and the valuation of speculative assets.

In the late sixties I also had a major responsibility for designing a large-scale model of the US economy, the MPS, sponsored by the Federal Reserve Bank and still utilised by it. Finally, I have participated actively in the debate over economic policies both in Italy and the US, concentrating lately on the deleterious effects of the huge public deficits.

50

*Stephen Ross – Dedicated to the Real World**

Navroz Patel

Step on to any derivatives trading floor and the chances are some-one is using a binomial pricing methodology. Sophisticated money managers have used risk and allocation models based on arbitrage pricing theory (APT) for decades. And in graduate schools the world over, it would be hard to imagine a quantitative finance class where risk-neutral pricing isn't mentioned. Each technique is of such importance when taken individually that it's all the more remarkable that one man – Stephen Ross, Franco Modigliani professor of finance and economics at the Massachusetts Institute of Technology – had a hand in the creation of all of them.

But Ross is no ivory tower academic. He is a partner in IVC International – a London-based fund-of-hedge-funds manager founded in 2002 that has raised around US$500 million. IVC specialises in creating highly structured notes tailored to meet institutional investors' regulatory, tax and risk requirements. In addition, he co-founded Roll and Ross Asset Management with Richard Roll in 1985. The Pennsylvania-based equity fund follows an APT-based investment strategy.

Ross began his academic career proper as an undergraduate theoretical physicist at the California Institute of Technology. He came to realise that physics wasn't his calling: "I was tired of solving boundary value problems. I got tired of the mathematics", Ross says. Before graduating from CalTech in 1965, Ross took a course in game theory and linear programming. Intellectual curiosity roused,

*This biography originally appeared in the "Hall of Fame" in *Risk*, December 2002.

he went to graduate school at Harvard to pursue his new-found interest in economics. He specialised in international trade and, after receiving his economics PhD from Harvard, took an assistant professor post at the Wharton School at the University of Pennsylvania.

Ross remained unsettled though. "I soon became bored by international finance too – I was a fickle fellow!" he says. He began to attend a variety of seminars in the hope that he would stumble across an area that would capture his imagination. He didn't have to wait long; Fischer Black spoke about the Black–Scholes equation at a finance seminar. The following week, Richard Roll came along and gave a talk about the term structure of interest rates. Ross was hooked. "It was real science combined with a human, social element – it's what I'd been looking for", he says.

After doing research on the economic theory of agency, Ross turned his attention to the capital asset pricing model (CAPM). Ross appreciated the mathematics of the CAPM, but found it difficult to relate it to the concepts – such as diversification – that accompanied the model. Fundamental to the CAPM is the argument that investors require compensation – that is, excess returns – only for their portfolio's systematic risk. By moving away from making assumptions about investors' preferences or return distributions, Ross had developed a factor model – where factors can be viewed as macroeconomic variables such as inflation or interest rates, or simply statistical artefacts – and his APT paper was published in 1976.

During the same year – three years after Black and Scholes published their seminal options pricing paper – Ross made another groundbreaking discovery, this time in collaboration with John Cox. The APT model is based on a market that is in equilibrium and free from arbitrage. In his work with Cox, Ross began to look at option pricing theory more closely. Together they developed the concept of risk-neutral pricing that enabled the valuation of a whole host of securities. More than a quarter of a century on, risk-neutral pricing is the most important tool for the analysis of derivatives.

Binomial models are often used in science as teaching tools because of their simplicity. A stock price's rise or fall can be readily represented in such a model and, in 1976, Ross, Cox and Mark Rubinstein developed a binomial model for option pricing. Although the classic Black–Scholes–Merton model could be used to price European-style options, American-style options were beyond its scope. In addition to its simplicity, the main virtue of the Ross–Cox–Rubinstein binomial model was that it could handle early exercise. The binomial model and its modern-day descendants, the lattice tree models, are used by derivatives traders and quants the world over.

Conscious that most derivatives research had been concerned with equities, Ross's gaze turned to fixed income. In collaboration with Cox and Jon Ingersoll, Ross created the CIR model. One of the earliest models for consistently pricing interest rate derivatives, CIR won favour as it doesn't produce negative interest rates like the Vasicek model, for example, which was created independently at around the same time.

"What gives me enormous pleasure is seeing people using my work, or versions of it, on the trading floor", says Ross. "I've not done a lot of self-referential work – I'm interested in the real world", he adds. This is evidenced by Ross's latest work on executive salaries. He says that he first started to look at the problem because he is the board member responsible for compensation at a company. He says: "The topic is different, but the methodologies are similar – I haven't gone all touchy-feely".

51

All in All, it's been a Good Life

Mark Rubinstein

Haas School of Business

When the Black–Scholes 1973 paper was published, it shortly became clear, even to me, that it presaged a revolution in financial economics. I had just one uncomfortable problem (which I shared with many others): I really did not understand the economic intuition that underlay their model. So I found myself at a conference in Ein Bokek, Israel in 1975. At one of the breaks, I began talking with Bill Sharpe and was pleased to see that he shared my befuddlement. But Bill, always eager and often successful at seeing to the heart of things, wondered aloud whether the Black–Scholes model was in essence a two-state model. In that case, we knew that with three securities, the stock, cash and an option, the price of one of the securities could be derived in terms of the prices of the other two securities as long as there were no riskless arbitrage opportunities. This insight then led to my own later work with John Cox and Stephen Ross on binomial option pricing. At the same time, I had developed a more traditional approach to derive the Black–Scholes formula from discrete-time equilibrium (rather than arbitrage) theory. I became so besotted with the beauty of option pricing theory that for the next 20 years I turned away from my earlier research on equilibrium pricing models and worked largely on derivatives valuation and hedging problems.

But understanding options at a theoretical, or even empirical, level was not good enough. I wanted to have my own text,

Options Markets, which I eventually published with a more than equal intellectual contribution from my co-author John Cox. And I wanted to walk into the classroom and convince MBA students that I really knew what I was talking about. So in 1976, I briefly became a market maker in options on the new options floor of the Pacific Stock Exchange. About that time, my colleague Hayne Leland had the crazy idea that we could actually apply our understanding of options to revolutionise portfolio management by popularising the use of dynamic replication strategies. So, in 1981, with the help of John O'Brien, we launched our portfolio insurance firm Leland O'Brien Rubinstein Associates, and for a while we succeeded beyond my most optimistic imaginings. Unfortunately, we may have been too successful for our own good; our investment strategy was credited with causing the 1987 stock market crash. During the two weeks following October 19th, I became more depressed than at any time in my life, because I was worried: there was a distinct possibility that we may have indeed caused the crash, in turn the crash could create a serious recession in the US economy (remember what happened after the 1929 crash?), and in the modern world of 1987 that could trigger a challenge from the Soviet Union, and that could trigger a ... (I'll let you fill this in). I didn't really think this was likely; I just thought it was possible, and that was bad enough. Of course, my worst fears were not realised, thank God, since the economy and the stock market proved quite resilient.

In the end, I felt I had kind of overdone it on the experience side, so I turned back to research. For a year or so in 1991, I accepted a challenge from *Risk* magazine to write a regular column each issue that would entertain readers with a cute solution to an exotic options problem. In 1992 I was elected to the path that would make me President of the American Finance Association in 1994, when I had to give the Presidential Address. I almost didn't accept this honour because I was worried that I would not be able to come up with the high quality research the address called for. Steve Ross convinced me that that was silly, and I really should have more faith in myself. I worried even so, but by some miracle, I was able to work out the idea of implied binomial trees, a nifty generalisation of my earlier work (with John Cox and Steve Ross) on standard binomial trees to arbitrary expiration date risk-neutral probability distributions. So in the end, I was very pleased with myself and felt my 1994 paper would revolutionise option valuation, in the same way our earlier paper on binomial option pricing had. (It turned out I did not have the field all to myself since Bruno Dupire and Emanuel Derman with Iraj Kani developed a competing technique.)

Fast forwarding to 1999, because I couldn't let my colleague Jonathan Berk down, I foolishly agreed to debate the king of behavioural finance, Richard Thaler, publicly at a Berkeley Program in Finance conference about the empirical rationality of financial markets – foolish because he had written more papers than I could count on the subject which compared rather unfavourably with my record: one. Also, as our field had matured, it began to seem more and more quixotic to defend the affirmative position. To my surprise, I did not make a fool of myself and even ended up publishing a version of my argument in the *Financial Analysts Journal* in 2001, which took the "best paper of the year" award. All this caused me to rethink my preoccupation with derivatives. So I decided to return to my first love, the more general theory of investments with which I had begun my research career as a doctoral student. This has led to my current project, which is to write an academic history of the theory of investments from ancient times to the beginning of the 21st century. I have always enjoyed systematising knowledge, and seeing relations between apparently disparate lines of research. My first (unpublished) paper in finance as a doctoral student was actually a survey of 500 articles in investments and corporate finance. So in the twilight of my career, it seems only suitable that I should return full circle to where I started, but with whatever wisdom I have gleaned over the last 30 years.

Speaking generally about my vocation, I have never regretted that I became a professor. As a professor, I have had great personal freedom, including control over my time, where I live, what I wear and what I say; for the last 30 years, most days I wake up in the morning with no clear schedule or idea about what I will be doing that day; I get to do what I most like to do when I want to do it (the idea that someone would actually pay me to sit in a room and think, provided once in a while I come out and say what I have figured out, continues to amaze me). As a successful professor, I can choose to work in just about any city in the developed western world. I am frequently invited as an honoured guest to visit locations all around the world, all expenses paid, if only I agree to give a one-hour lecture (which is something I look forward to doing anyway). I don't really distinguish between weekdays and the weekend, or between work and play.

I regularly get to spend time with wonderful, very smart and interesting people (my fellow finance professors). When we are together, we talk not just about finance, but knowledgeably about just about everything – history, music, psychology, religion, philosophy, politics, economics, literature, mathematics, science, etc. Many have had considerable practical experience in business or government. I am always learning from them. Imagine meeting regularly throughout your working life with a group consisting of the top student from each high school in your city, and that is sort of what it is like. And imagine that the people you work with share essentially the same value system which places great emphasis on curiosity, reason and understanding, and working with people who are actually eager to have their mistakes politely corrected by others (so they won't make them again), and whose egos are subordinated to this process. The eradication of error and bias is a necessary condition for good research.

By good fortune, finance has also proven to be a great field to work in. It combines, as Keynes once stated about economics, the talents of the mathematician, the empiricist and the realist; its theoretical issues and puzzles are endlessly interesting; as a social science it concerns perhaps the most interesting subject, human behaviour; and among the social sciences, it has by far the richest and largest databases to test hypotheses; along with the broader subject of economics, it may be the most successful in explaining actual human behaviour; and academics have been able to contribute inventions that are often quickly applied by large numbers of people (I suspect that as I write, thousands of people all over the world are valuing options using binomial techniques, whether they know how their computers are programmed or not).

My research work is portable: with my laptop (and now cell phone), I can work with almost equal efficiency floating down the Nile as I can in my office at Berkeley. Teaching is not burdensome since, as an only child, I am addicted to being the centre of attention and am somewhat of a natural thespian; thanks to my father, I love trying to explain ideas to other people, and continually needing to provide these explanations hones my own understanding. In any event, teaching at a top university like Berkeley does not require a large commitment of time. While I was prepared to sacrifice income, that has really not been a problem since I can occasionally consult at an embarrassingly high per hour rate, have profited from my own business designed around commercially applying my own research, and finance professors have become among the highest paid university professors, with salaries that dwarf those in traditional fields such as English, history and physics.

All in all, it's been a good life.

52

Memoirs of an Early Finance Theorist

Paul A. Samuelson

Massachusetts Institute of Technology

When once asked to describe my specialisations in economics, I replied that perhaps I was the "last generalist" in economics – because pure theory, literary and mathematical economics, macro and micro, statistics and probability, foreign trade and managerial economics, were all principal research objects for me. This would imply, on a random basis, some preoccupation with finance and risk theory. But actually that would understate my degree of interest in and dedication to that area. Finance in general – personal and economy-wide – has been one of the most successful areas evolved in this last century, my century, and I've loved being a player.

Not everyone agrees. The record shows that Milton Friedman was cool toward Harry Markowitz's seminal 1952 Chicago PhD thesis, which to paraphrase, he thought *was hardly at all economics and not even interesting applied mathematics*. That this was not a temporary aberration was revealed when the press quoted his surprise years later that Stockholm would beatify the threesome of Markowitz, Sharpe and Miller, putting them ahead of a hundred other worthies. By contrast, I have found my extensive forays into finance rewarding. No other economic paradigms of elegance have equal intellectual and practical interest. Before I could vote, as a Chicago undergraduate, I began to follow the research efforts of Alfred Cowles III in testing forecasting methods and their batting averages. Before 1953 when Maurice Kendall documented the whiteness of noise in the speculative markets for shares, commodity spot and futures, and mutual fund markets, I pored over Holbrook Working's overlooked analyses of quasi-random grain prices. In 1935–37, newly at the Harvard Graduate School, I wrote my first paper on optimal life cycle consumption and saving. What led me to it was a notion, already in the air, that people's utility-of-wealth functions, subjective and introspective, could be measured non-introspectively from observing their stochastic choices. I even discovered then that knowledge of a Laplacian's smallest bets would pin down exactly how all his bets would behave. But I was so green as not to realise how extraordinary this finding was.

My family background, as interpreted to me by my risk-averse mother, involved World War prosperity and mid-1920s Florida real estate ventures that culminated in 1926 burst-bubble losses. My teacher of freshman high school math, with my juvenile help, became a victim of the 1929 Wall Street crash. I was not affluent in my early academic years, but being off to an early start, I was surrounded by good friends who could make do with less. So in the beginning, and later with my wife, I began to explore actual security selection. Avarice was not my guiding motive. Instead, it was an economist's curiosity. What was it like to sell short? What was it like to bet on a Packard–Studebaker merger? What was it like to dabble in puts and calls? My first interest in calls and warrants arose from a mistaken notion that their price patterns could tell me whether the public's expectational sentiments were "bullish" or "bearish". Only later, when I had perfected the arbitrage vector equivalences of puts and calls, did I come to realise that options were related to market volatility and not to expected levels or trends.

In the first half of the last century, practically nothing had been rigorously demonstrated in finance theory. "Don't put all your eggs in one basket" and anecdotes about "selling coal in winter and ice in summer" encoded the bare wisdom about the efficiency of diversification. That motivated my early publications to *prove* that the best meld of two independent but otherwise probabilistically identical stocks had to be a portfolio with *equal* weighting.

False aphorisms proliferated. At TIAA-CREF, a trustee destined for future ennoblement insisted that the Law of Large Numbers implied that an investor with an investment horizon ahead of 2N-periods must rationally be more equity-risk tolerant than a similar investor with only an N-period horizon. Evidently, he had not read my 1969 "Review of Economics and Statistics" paper, or those of a rash of others at the same time, which proved that constant-relative-risk aversion utility functions

$$\log(W) \quad \text{or} \quad W^{1-\gamma}/(1-\gamma), 0 < \gamma \neq 1$$

must myopically choose at all times in the future to aim for exactly the *same* optimised equity fraction.

Cleaning out Augean stables is not pleasant work, but someone has to do it. Again and again I have had to slay a new dragon who is tripping himself up on the notion that the geometric mean maximiser will achieve meaningful maximisation of a portfolio's "growth rate". If your one-period maximum is always the harmonic mean, because you are truly more risk-averse than Daniel Bernoulli's 1,738 U (W) = logW person, then following the GM maximising criterion will do you harm for all N however great, and the harm measured in your own risk-corrected dollars will soar with N!

When Savage asked economists: "who's this Bachelier guy?", I was able to locate that scholar's great 1900 Paris thesis. Converting its Gaussian–Brownian motion cum unlimited liability to Log-Gaussian motion, the astronomer Osborne and I independently were to provide Ito, Merton and Black–Scholes with a jumping-off place for instantaneous probabilities and rebalancings – a wonderland for elegant and virtually risk-free perfect hedgings. Separately, Eugene Fama and I could axiomatise efficient Martingale pricings, much like, but not identical to, Wiener random-walk noise.

Two-thirds of a century after my acne-age beginnings, I am still engaged in publishing basic critiques of Markowitz–Tobin–Sharpe quadratic-programming approximations involving means and variances. And side by side with Mark Machina, I have been developing the exact differential geometry that separates Laplacian expected {utility of outcomes} from more general functionals that do rank order any two or more probability distributions confronting the decision maker.

As the advertisements say, "we've come a long way, baby. And there's much more to come." As an adviser to non-profit agencies and as a theorist, I've certainly enjoyed the ride.

53

*Myron Scholes – From Theory to Practice**

Keith Brody

Myron Scholes, whose Nobel Prize-winning academic contributions have done much to shape the derivatives and risk management businesses, foreswore the ivory tower of academia and became one of the world's foremost theorist-practitioners.

His enduring legacy is, of course, co-authorship with Fischer Black of the Black–Scholes options pricing formula, published in the *Journal of Political Economy* in May 1973. Robert Merton also contributed importantly to the formula, which can be used to value a European option on a non-dividend-paying stock. The Black–Scholes paper has had more mentions in *Risk's* technical pages than any others in the last 15 years, and its dramatic and lasting effect on the development of the derivatives markets and the field of financial engineering were recognised when Scholes and Merton were awarded the Nobel Prize in 1997.

But Scholes' fame as an academic sits somewhat uneasily with his other claim to notoriety: his role as one of the principals of Long-Term Capital Management, the hedge fund which imploded in 1998 in a hailstorm of collateral calls after losing about US$4 billion from the simultaneous failure of several of its trading strategies. While its principals have often been vilified by regulators and in the press, the proper allocation of responsibility for LTCM's demise among them, their counterparties and their competitors remains a subject of some debate to this day.

---

*This biography originally appeared in the "Hall of Fame" in *Risk*, December 2002.

Scholes, who spent the better part of 30 years at the vanguard of financial engineering, was born in Canada in 1941, the son of a dentist and an entrepreneurial mother who founded a small chain of stores with an uncle. His interest in economics and finance was derived from his parents, particularly his mother, and from an early age he was involved as treasurer of various clubs to which he belonged, in the process gaining a rudimentary education in the areas and issues of probability and risk. He was also an enthusiastic investor, fascinated by the determinants of the level of stock prices.

Scholes attended McMaster University in Ontario as an undergraduate, where he majored in economics. After taking a computer programming position at the university, he became engaged with the challenge it presented, and has said that if computer science had been a discipline at the time, it is the direction he would probably have taken. At the same time, Scholes became increasingly enamoured with economics, and he entered the University of Chicago's PhD programme to study financial economics.

Scholes' particular interest was relative asset prices and the degree to which arbitrage prevented economic agents from earning abnormal profits in security markets. His PhD dissertation attempted to determine the shape of the demand curve for traded securities. He completed this in the autumn of 1968, and became an assistant professor of finance at the Sloan School of Management at MIT. It was here, in 1969, that he first worked with Merton.

Scholes, Merton and Fischer Black were mainly interested in asset pricing and derivatives pricing models, and their work led them to derive the Black–Scholes formula – a way to determine how much a European option on a non-dividend paying stock is worth. It is based on their observation that an investor can precisely replicate the payoff of a call option by buying the underlying stock and financing part of the stock purchase by borrowing. Even before the call option expires, they concluded that its future payoff could be matched by creating a replicating portfolio. The Black–Scholes formula calculates the fraction of stock and amount that must be borrowed to do this.

After publishing the Black–Scholes equation, Scholes returned to the Graduate School of Business at the University of Chicago, where he worked on the effects of taxation on asset prices and incentives and the interaction of incentives and taxes in executive compensation. He also became involved with the Center for Research in Security Prices at the University of Chicago. This led to the development of large research data files of daily security prices.

In 1981, Scholes became a permanent faculty member in the Business School at Stanford University, where he wrote several papers on pension planning and articles on investment banking and incentives. Along with Michael Wolfron, he developed a new theory of tax planning under uncertainty and information asymmetry.

In 1990 his interests shifted back to the role of derivatives in financial intermediation. John Meriwether hired him as a special consultant to Salomon Brothers and he subsequently became co-head of its fixed-income derivatives sales and trading group, while still conducting research and teaching at Stanford. However, Salomon's Treasury auction scandal in 1991 caused counterparties to abandon the investment bank in droves. Scholes stepped forward with a way to save the firm's derivatives business – he set up a triple-A rated derivatives product company called Salomon Swapco, with which counterparties were willing to trade.

In 1994 he joined John Meriwether in his new venture, Long-Term Capital Management. The fund thrived for several years before its crisis. But shrugging off an event that would have ended other careers, Scholes went back to research and a job advising the Bass family of Texas.

54

*William Sharpe – A Career-defining Risk**

Dwight Cass

William Sharpe is not standing still, despite already having had a long and very busy career in applied and theoretical finance. The Capital Asset Pricing Model, for which he shared the Nobel Prize in 1990, led to the notion of systematic risk, or beta, and its corollary, alpha. His Sharpe ratio, which divides a portfolio's return by its standard deviation, has become the standard measure of portfolio risk-adjusted return. Sharpe also originated the binomial asset-pricing model, a very useful variation on the Black–Scholes model, which after further development from other researchers gave a significant boost to the pricing of American options. Sharpe has also done important work on performance measurement for investment funds and asset allocation.

Sharpe's work, or what he calls "play-time", now concerns the field of behavioural finance. And though theoretical in nature, his efforts may have practical application. In 1996 Sharpe founded Financial Engines, an online financial advisory service geared to individual investors unable to afford individual advisors of their own. "It's trying to get the best out of finance theory and also behavioural theory and bring it to bear for people making real decisions", Sharpe explains. The service has hundreds of plan sponsor clients, dispensing advice to millions of individual investors.

Sharpe is now trying to determine how much the preferences of some individual investors vary from that of the "representative investor", on which historically most asset price models have been

*This biography originally appeared in the "Hall of Fame" in *Risk*, December 2002.

based. In practical terms, representative investors meet their retirement income goals with "constant mix" investment strategies, or portfolios of relatively stable portions of bonds and stocks. However, results from a recent study Sharpe performed on 60 individuals suggest that a substantial minority of investors are less risk averse than the representative investor. They might prefer non-linear payoff, or option-like, investment strategies. This suggestive finding, though requiring more complete studies, could mean a significant minority of retail investors find their true investment preferences unmet.

Sharpe thinks existing retail products offered by banks to this crowd, such as principal-protected notes, have shortcomings. "For all those products the vendor says they'll pay you such-and-so if they can and they're going to go off and do something with derivatives, which may entail counterparty and credit risk and you never know", he says.

The remedy could be simple, rules-based tradable funds that Sharpe calls "M-shares" ("M" stands for market). Unlike existing exchange-traded funds M-shares would consist of both stocks and bonds and have maturities. M-shares would be split into tranches, some of which would offer downside protection financed by other tranches bought by those willing to provide the protection.

The simplicity of the M-shares structure would be key. "It's very, very handy as a metaphor, because it makes it very clear that for everybody who gets downside protection, somebody somewhere is doubling up on their downside loss", Sharpe says.

55

*Reflections on a Revolution**

Oldrich Vasicek

The past 50 years or so have been a time of great bloom in the field of finance. This period has seen the birth of concepts such as: variance as a quantitative definition of risk; portfolio diversification as a means of controlling risk; portfolio optimisation in the mean/variance framework; expected utility maximisation as an investment; and consumption decision-making criterion. These notions were applied in the development of the capital asset pricing model (CAPM) to describe the market equilibrium, to the concepts of systematic and specific risks and the introduction of asset beta. We have witnessed the revolution brought about by the theory of options pricing. We have seen the appearance of the general principle of asset pricing as the present value of the cashflows expected under the risk-neutral probability measure, and we have seen the development of the theory of the term structure of interest rates and the pricing of interest rate derivatives.

These theoretical developments have been accompanied by equally exciting changes in investment practices and indeed in the nature of capital markets. Few of us can still envision investment decision-making without quantitative risk measurement, without hedging techniques, without deep and efficient markets for futures and options, without swaps and interest rate derivatives, and without computer models to price such instruments. And yet, these are all very recent developments. It was not much longer than some

*This autobiography originally appeared in the "Hall of Fame" in *Risk*, December 2002.

30 years ago that the very notion of an index fund was greeted with disbelief, if not outright ridicule.

I was lucky to be cast right into the middle of such developments when I joined the management science department of Wells Fargo Bank in 1969. The annual conferences organised by Wells Fargo in the early 1970s brought together people such as Franco Modigliani, Ross Miller, Jack Treynor, William Sharpe, Fischer Black, Myron Scholes, Robert Merton and many others. The second half of the twentieth century was in my eyes as exciting in the field of finance as the first half must have been in physics.

I have worked on various projects at Wells Fargo and later at the University of Rochester and the University of California at Berkeley, but one thing that bothered me for quite a while in the mid-1970s was the absence of solid results on the pricing of bonds. At that time, the CAPM was already in existence, and people had tried to apply it to bonds by measuring their betas to determine the yield, but that did not really lead anywhere. The options pricing theory had also been freshly developed by then, but it did not seem very feasible to apply a theory of pricing derivatives assets to assets as primary as government bonds. What would be the underlying?

And yet, it was obvious that there must be some conditions that govern interest rate behaviour in efficient markets. You cannot have, for instance, a fixed-income market in which the yield curves are always flat and move up and down in some random fashion through time, because then a barbell portfolio would always outperform a bullet portfolio of the same duration, so it would be possible to set up a profitable risk-free arbitrage. But what are these conditions?

The clue came from comparing the return to maturity on a term bond with that of a repeated investment in a shorter bond. The common denominator between bonds of any maturity would be a rollover of the very short bond, so it seemed natural to postulate that the pricing of a bond should be a function of the short rate over its term. And once the idea of describing the short rate by a Markov process came to me, it became obvious: the future behaviour of the short rate is determined by its current value, and therefore the price of the bond must be a function of the short rate. From then on, it's mathematics: to exclude risk-free arbitrage, this function must be such that the expected excess return on each bond is proportional to its risk, which gives rise to a partial differential equation.

The boundary condition of this equation is the maturity value, and the solution is the bond price. This was the basis of my 1977 paper, "An equilibrium characterisation of the term structure" (curiously, the thing that became known as the Vasicek model was just an example I put in that paper to illustrate the general theory on a specific case. Well, you never know).

After that, it was like opening Pandora's box. Many more papers followed, extending the model in various ways – multiple factors, non-Markov risk sources, development of various specific models for practical use. One paper I have great respect for is the Cox, Ingersoll and Ross article (for some reason, they did not publish the paper until 1985, although they did the work many years earlier), because it is about more than interest rates – it is about an equilibrium in the bond market.

A big shift came in 1986 with the publication of the Ho and Lee paper. This presented a simple interest rate model, which was just a special case of my theory. The shift was in the interpretation: Ho and Lee assumed the current bond prices were given (equal to the actual observed prices) and concerned themselves with pricing interest rate derivatives. This, of course, allows very useful applications for valuing various instruments from simple callable bonds to the most complex swaptions.

The Ho and Lee paper engendered a great development effort in that direction, including the 1992 paper by Heath, Jarrow and Morton, which formalised this approach. This direction was in fact taken further: there are models that assume as given not only the current bond prices, but also prices of caps and floors or even more. These models, used then to value other derivatives, have the great virtue of fitting the current market pricing of the more primary assets.

While I appreciate the usefulness of these models, I somewhat regret the direction away from the economics. To ask how derivatives are priced given the pricing of bonds seems to me to ignore the more interesting question: how are bonds priced? I hope to see a return to efforts to understand the economics, rather than just to aid trading.

A similar situation has arisen in default risk measurement and pricing, another subject dear to my heart. The so-called reduced-form models, which have been advocated for the purpose of credit risk analysis, assume that corporate debt prices are given and use these prices to value debt derivatives. Again, to me it seems that the more interesting question is how to price corporate debt. Fortunately, this is possible given the legacy of Merton, Black and Scholes, since corporate liabilities are derivatives of the firm's asset value, and a structural model of the firm can price its debt (and debt derivatives) from equity prices.

As appreciative as I am of the past in the field of finance, I am equally enthusiastic about its future. There will be no lack of problems to address, and there will be no lack of talent to solve them. Indeed, it is the professionals in this area of endeavour that are its greatest assets, and I am grateful to have worked with, and learned from, so many of them.

For 15 years, *Risk* magazine has been a major forum for bringing these developments to the investment practitioners, and for bringing the experience of the practitioners back to the people working on the theory. This mutual feedback is of essence in a field as dynamic, theoretically challenging and practically useful as modern finance, and I wish *Risk* equal success in the next 15 years and beyond.

Index